CompTIA Security+™

EXAM GUIDE

ALL ■ IN ■ ONE

CompTIA Security+™

EXAM GUIDE
Fourth Edition (Exam SY0-401)

Dr. Wm. Arthur Conklin
Dr. Gregory White
Chuck Cothren
Roger L. Davis
Dwayne Williams

Mc Graw Hill Education

New York   Chicago   San Francisco
Athens   London   Madrid   Mexico City
Milan   New Delhi   Singapore   Sydney   Toronto

Cataloging-in-Publication Data is on file with the Library of Congress

McGraw-Hill Education books are available at special quantity discounts to use as premiums and sales promotions, or for use in corporate training programs. To contact a representative, please visit the Contact Us pages at www.mhprofessional.com.

CompTIA Security+™ All-in-One Exam Guide, Fourth Edition (Exam SY0-401)

 5 6 7 8 9 10 DOC 19 18 17 16

ISBN: Book p/n 978-0-07-183737-8 and CD p/n 978-0-07-183736-1
of set 978-0-07-184124-5

MHID: Book p/n 0-07-183737-X and CD p/n 0-07-183736-1
of set 0-07-184124-5

Sponsoring Editor Meghan Riley Manfre	**Technical Editor** Chris Crayton	**Production Supervisor** George Anderson
Editorial Supervisor Janet Walden	**Copy Editor** William McManus	**Composition** Cenveo Publisher Services
Project Manager Anupriya Tyagi, Cenveo® Publisher Services	**Proofreader** Lisa McCoy	**Illustration** Cenveo Publisher Services
Acquisitions Coordinator Mary Demery	**Indexer** Jack Lewis	**Art Director, Cover** Jeff Weeks

ABOUT THE AUTHORS

Dr. Wm. Arthur Conklin, CompTIA Security+, CISSP, CSSLP, GISCP, CRISC, is an Associate Professor and Director of the Center for Information Security Research and Education in the College of Technology at the University of Houston. He holds two terminal degrees, a Ph.D. in business administration (specializing in information security), from The University of Texas at San Antonio (UTSA), and the degree Electrical Engineer (specializing in space systems engineering) from the Naval Postgraduate School in Monterey, CA. He is a fellow of ISSA, a senior member of ASQ, and a member of IEEE and ACM. His research interests include the use of systems theory to explore information security, specifically in cyber-physical systems. He has coauthored six security books and numerous academic articles associated with information security. He is active in the DHS-sponsored Industrial Control Systems Joint Working Group (ICSJWG) efforts associated with workforce development and cyber-security aspects of industrial control systems. He has an extensive background in secure coding and is a co-chair of the DHS/DoD Software Assurance Forum working group for workforce education, training, and development.

Dr. Gregory White has been involved in computer and network security since 1986. He spent 19 years on active duty with the United States Air Force and 11 years in the Air Force Reserves in a variety of computer and security positions. He obtained his Ph.D. in computer science from Texas A&M University in 1995. His dissertation topic was in the area of computer network intrusion detection, and he continues to conduct research in this area today. He is currently the Director for the Center for Infrastructure Assurance and Security (CIAS) and is a professor of computer science at the University of Texas at San Antonio (UTSA). Dr. White has written and presented numerous articles and conference papers on security. He is also the coauthor of five textbooks on computer and network security and has written chapters for two other security books. Dr. White continues to be active in security research. His current research initiatives include efforts in community incident response, intrusion detection, and secure information sharing.

Chuck Cothren, CISSP, is a Principal Solutions Specialist at Symantec Corporation applying a wide array of network security experience, including performing controlled penetration testing, incident response, and security management to assist a wide variety of clients in the protection of their critical data. He has also analyzed security methodologies for Voice over Internet Protocol (VoIP) systems and supervisory control and data acquisition (SCADA) systems. He is coauthor of the books *Voice and Data Security* and *Principles of Computer Security*.

Roger L. Davis, CISSP, CISM, CISA, is an Operations Manager at the Church of Jesus Christ of Latter-day Saints, managing several of the Church's information systems in over 140 countries. He has served as president of the Utah chapter of the Information Systems Security Association (ISSA) and various board positions for the Utah chapter of the Information Systems Audit and Control Association (ISACA). He is a retired Air Force lieutenant colonel with 30 years of military and information systems/security experience. Mr. Davis served on the faculty of Brigham Young University and the Air

Force Institute of Technology. He coauthored McGraw-Hill's *Principles of Computer Security* and *Voice and Data Security*. He holds a master's degree in computer science from George Washington University, a bachelor's degree in computer science from Brigham Young University, and performed post-graduate studies in electrical engineering and computer science at the University of Colorado.

Dwayne Williams, CISSP, is Associate Director, Technology and Research, for the Center for Infrastructure Assurance and Security at the University of Texas at San Antonio and is the Director of the National Collegiate Cyber Defense Competition. Mr. Williams has over 18 years of experience in information systems and network security. Mr. Williams's experience includes six years of commissioned military service as a Communications-Computer Information Systems Officer in the United States Air Force, specializing in network security, corporate information protection, intrusion detection systems, incident response, and VPN technology. Prior to joining the CIAS, he served as Director of Consulting for SecureLogix Corporation, where he directed and provided security assessment and integration services to Fortune 100, government, public utility, oil and gas, financial, and technology clients. Mr. Williams graduated in 1993 from Baylor University with a bachelor of arts in computer science. Mr. Williams is a coauthor of *Voice and Data Security* and *Principles of Computer Security*.

About the Technical Editor

Chris Crayton is an author, technical consultant, and trainer. He has worked as a computer technology and networking instructor, information security director, network administrator, network engineer, and PC specialist. Chris has authored several print and online books on PC repair, Microsoft Windows, CompTIA A+, and CompTIA Security+. He has also served as technical editor and content contributor on numerous technical titles for several of the leading publishing companies, including the *CompTIA A+ Certification All-in-One Exam Guide* and the *CompTIA A+ Certification Study Guide*. He holds multiple industry certifications, has been recognized with many professional teaching awards, and serves as a state-level SkillsUSA competition judge.

CompTIA Approved Quality Content

CompTIA.

It Pays to Get Certified

In a digital world, digital literacy is an essential survival skill. Certification demonstrates that you have the knowledge and skill to solve technical or business problems in virtually any business environment. CompTIA certifications are highly valued credentials that qualify you for jobs, increased compensation, and promotion.

LEARN	CERTIFY	WORK		
IT is Everywhere	**IT Knowledge and Skills Get Jobs**	**Job Retention**	**New Opportunities**	**High Pay-High Growth Jobs**
IT is mission critical to almost all organizations and its importance is increasing.	Certifications verify your knowledge and skills that qualifies you for:	Competence is noticed and valued in organizations.	Certifications qualify you for new opportunities in your current job or when you want to change careers.	Hiring managers demand the strongest skill set.
• 79% of U.S. businesses report IT is either important or very important to the success of their company	• Jobs in the high growth IT career field • Increased compensation • Challenging assignments and promotions • 60% report that being certified is an employer or job requirement	• Increased knowledge of new or complex technologies • Enhanced productivity • More insightful problem solving • Better project management and communication skills • 47% report being certified helped improve their problem solving skills	• 31% report certification improved their career advancement opportunities	• There is a widening IT skills gap with over 300,000 jobs open • 88% report being certified enhanced their resume

CompTIA Security+ Certification Helps Your Career

- **Security is one of the highest demand job categories** growing in importance as the frequency and severity of security threats continue to be a major concern for organizations around the world.
- **Jobs for security administrators are expected to increase by 18%**—the skill set required for these types of jobs maps to the CompTIA Security+ certification.
- **Network Security Administrators** can earn as much as $106,000 per year.
  - **CompTIA Security+ is the first step** in starting your career as a Network Security Administrator or Systems Security Administrator.
- **More than 250,000** individuals worldwide are CompTIA Security+ certified.
- **CompTIA Security+ is regularly used in organizations** such as Hitachi Systems, Fuji Xerox, HP, Dell, and a variety of major U.S. government contractors.
- **Approved by the U.S. Department of Defense (DoD)** as one of the required certification options in the DoD 8570.01-M directive, for Information Assurance Technical Level II and Management Level I job roles.

Steps to Getting Certified and Staying Certified

1. **Review the exam objectives.** Review the certification objectives to make sure you know what is covered in the exam: http://certification.comptia.org/examobjectives.aspx

2. **Practice for the exam.** After you have studied for the certification exam, review and answer sample questions to get an idea of what type of questions might be on the exam: http://certification.comptia.org/samplequestions.aspx

3. **Purchase an exam voucher.** You can purchase exam vouchers on the CompTIA Marketplace, www.comptiastore.com.

4. **Take the test!** Go to the Pearson VUE website, www.pearsonvue.com/comptia/, and schedule a time to take your exam.

5. **Stay certified!** Effective January 1, 2011, new CompTIA Security+ certifications are valid for three years from the date of certification. There are a number of ways the certification can be renewed. For more information go to http://certification.comptia.org/ce.

For More Information

- **Visit CompTIA online**   Go to http://certification.comptia.org/home.aspx to learn more about getting CompTIA certified.
- **Contact CompTIA**   Please call 866-835-8020 and choose Option 2, or e-mail questions@comptia.org.
- **Connect with CompTIA**   Find CompTIA on Facebook, LinkedIn, Twitter, and YouTube.

Content Seal of Quality

This courseware bears the seal of CompTIA Approved Quality Content. This seal signifies this content covers 100 percent of the exam objectives and implements important instructional design principles. CompTIA recommends multiple learning tools to help increase coverage of the learning objectives.

CAQC Disclaimer

The logo of the CompTIA Approved Quality Content (CAQC) program and the status of this or other training material as "Approved" under the CompTIA Approved Quality Content program signifies that, in CompTIA's opinion, such training material covers the content of CompTIA's related certification exam.

The contents of this training material were created for the CompTIA Security+ exam covering CompTIA certification objectives that were current as of the date of publication.

CompTIA has not reviewed or approved the accuracy of the contents of this training material and specifically disclaims any warranties of merchantability or fitness for a particular purpose. CompTIA makes no guarantee concerning the success of persons using any such "Approved" or other training material in order to prepare for any CompTIA certification exam.

This book is dedicated to the many information security professionals who quietly work to ensure the safety of our nation's critical infrastructures.
We want to recognize the thousands of dedicated individuals who strive to protect our national assets but who seldom receive praise and often are only noticed when an incident occurs.
To you, we say thank you for a job well done!

CONTENTS AT A GLANCE

CONTENTS

Part III Threats and Vulnerabilities

PREFACE

Information and computer security has moved from the confines of academia to mainstream America in the last decade. From the CodeRed, Nimda, and Slammer attacks to data disclosures to today's Advanced Persistent Threat (APT) that were heavily covered in the media and broadcast into the average American's home, information security has become a common topic. It has become increasingly obvious to everybody that something needs to be done in order to secure not only our nation's critical infrastructure, but also the businesses we deal with on a daily basis. The question is, "Where do we begin?" What can the average information technology professional do to secure the systems that he or she is hired to maintain? One immediate answer is education and training. If we want to secure our computer systems and networks, we need to know how to do this and what security entails.

Complacency is not an option in today's hostile network environment. While we once considered the insider to be the major threat to corporate networks, and the "script kiddie" to be the standard external threat (often thought of as only a nuisance), the highly interconnected networked world of today is a much different place. The U.S. government identified eight critical infrastructures a few years ago that were thought to be so crucial to the nation's daily operation that if one were to be lost, it would have a catastrophic impact on the nation. To this original set of eight sectors, more have been added, and they now total 17. Furthermore, analysis shows that in the United States, over 85 percent of this infrastructure is owned and operated by companies, not the government. A common thread throughout all of these critical infrastructures, however, is technology—especially technology related to computers and communication. Thus, if an individual, organization, or nation wanted to cause damage to this nation, it could attack not just with traditional weapons, but also with computers through the Internet. It is not surprising to hear that among the other information seized in raids on terrorist organizations, computers and Internet information are usually seized as well. While the insider can certainly still do tremendous damage to an organization, the external threat is again becoming the chief concern among many.

So, where do you, the IT professional seeking more knowledge on security, start your studies? The IT world is overflowing with certifications that can be obtained by those attempting to learn more about their chosen profession. The security sector is no different, and the CompTIA Security+ exam offers a basic level of certification for security. CompTIA Security+ is an ideal starting point for one interested in a career in security. In the pages of this exam guide, you will find not only material that can help you prepare for taking the CompTIA Security+ examination, but also the basic information that you will need in order to understand the issues involved in securing your computer systems and networks today. In no way is this exam guide the final source for learning all about protecting your organization's systems, but it serves as a point from which to launch your security studies and career.

One thing is certainly true about this field of study—it never gets boring. It constantly changes as technology itself advances. Something else you will find as you progress in your security studies is that no matter how much technology advances and no matter how many new security devices are developed, at its most basic level, the human is still the weak link in the security chain. If you are looking for an exciting area to delve into, then you have certainly chosen wisely. Security offers a challenging blend of technology and people issues. We, the authors of this exam guide, wish you luck as you embark on an exciting and challenging career path.

—*Wm. Arthur Conklin, Ph.D.*
—*Gregory B. White, Ph.D.*

ACKNOWLEDGMENTS

We, the authors of *CompTIA Security+ All-in-One Exam Guide, Fourth Edition*, have many individuals who we need to acknowledge—individuals without whom this effort would not have been successful.

The list needs to start with those folks at McGraw-Hill Education who worked tirelessly with the project's multiple authors and led us successfully through the minefield that is a book schedule and who took our rough chapters and drawings and turned them into a final, professional product we can be proud of. We thank the good people from the Acquisitions team, Meghan Manfre and Mary Demery; from the Editorial Services team, Janet Walden; and from the Production team, George Anderson. We also thank the technical editor, Chris Crayton; the project editor, Anupriya Tyagi of Cenveo Publisher Services; the copyeditor, William McManus; the proofreader, Lisa McCoy; and the indexer, Jack Lewis, for all their attention to detail that made this a finer work after they finished with it.

We also need to acknowledge our current employers who, to our great delight, have seen fit to pay us to work in a career field that we all find exciting and rewarding. There is never a dull moment in security because it is constantly changing.

We would like to thank Art Conklin for again herding the cats on this one.

Finally, we would each like to individually thank those people who—on a personal basis—have provided the core support for us individually. Without these special people in our lives, none of us could have put this work together.

To my loving wife Susan: You are my muse, my love, and my inspiration. And I apologize for all the time you suffered, waiting, as I work on books.

—*Art Conklin*

I would like to thank my wife, Charlan, for the tremendous support she has always given me.

—*Gregory B. White*

Josie, thank you for all the love and support. Macon, thank you for all the joy and laughs.

—*Chuck Cothren*

Geena, thanks for being my best friend and my greatest support. Anything I am is because of you. Love to my kids and grandkids!

—*Roger L. Davis*

To my wife and best friend Leah for your love, energy, and support—thank you for always being there. To my kids—this is what Daddy was typing on the computer!

—*Dwayne Williams*

INTRODUCTION

Computer security has become paramount as the number of security incidents steadily climbs. Many corporations now spend significant portions of their budget on security hardware, software, services, and personnel. They are spending this money not because it increases sales or enhances the product they provide, but because of the possible consequences should they not take protective actions.

Why Focus on Security?

Security is not something that we want to have to pay for; it would be nice if we didn't have to worry about protecting our data from disclosure, modification, or destruction from unauthorized individuals, but that is not the environment we find ourselves in today. Instead, we have seen the cost of recovering from security incidents steadily rise along with the number of incidents themselves. Cyber-attacks and information disclosures are occurring so often that one almost ignores them on the news. But the theft of over 40 million credit and debit card numbers from Target, with the subsequent resignation of the CIO and CEO, may indicate a new sense of urgency, a new sense of purpose with regard to securing data. The days of paper reports and corporate "lip-service" may be waning, and the time to meet the new challenges of even more sophisticated attackers has arrived. Then months later, Home Depot reports an even larger security breach. The battle will be long, with defenders adapting and protecting and attackers searching for weaknesses and vulnerabilities. Who will win? It depends on the vigilance of the defenders, for the attackers are here to stay.

A Growing Need for Security Specialists

In order to protect our computer systems and networks, we need a significant number of new security professionals trained in the many aspects of computer and network security. This is not an easy task as the systems connected to the Internet become increasingly complex with software whose lines of codes number in the millions. Understanding why this is such a difficult problem to solve is not hard if you consider just how many errors might be present in a piece of software that is several million lines long. When you add the factor of how fast software is being developed—from necessity as the market is constantly changing—understanding how errors occur is easy.

Not every "bug" in the software will result in a security hole, but it doesn't take many to have a drastic effect on the Internet community. We can't just blame the vendors for this situation, because they are reacting to the demands of government and industry. Most vendors are fairly adept at developing patches for flaws found in their software, and patches are constantly being issued to protect systems from bugs that may introduce security problems. This introduces a whole new problem for managers and administrators—patch management. How important this has become is easily illustrated by how many of the most recent security events have occurred as a result of a security bug that was discovered months prior to the security incident, and for which a patch has been available, but for which the community has not correctly installed the patch, thus making the incident possible. One of the reasons this happens is that many of the individuals responsible for installing the patches are not trained to understand the security implications surrounding the hole or the ramifications of not installing the patch. Many of these individuals simply lack the necessary training.

Because of the need for an increasing number of security professionals who are trained to some minimum level of understanding, certifications such as the CompTIA Security+ have been developed. Prospective employers want to know that the individual they are considering hiring knows what to do in terms of security. The prospective employee, in turn, wants to have a way to demonstrate his or her level of understanding, which can enhance the candidate's chances of being hired. The community as a whole simply wants more trained security professionals.

The goal of taking the CompTIA Security+ exam is to prove that you've mastered the worldwide standards for foundation-level security practitioners. The exam gives you a perfect opportunity to validate your knowledge and understanding of the computer security field, and it is an appropriate mechanism for many different individuals, including network and system administrators, analysts, programmers, web designers, application developers, and database specialists, to show proof of professional achievement in security. According to CompTIA, the exam is aimed at individuals who have

- A minimum of two years of experience in IT administration with a focus on security
- Day-to-day *technical* information security experience
- Broad knowledge of security concerns and implementation, including the topics that are found in the specific CompTIA Security+ domains

The exam objectives were developed with input and assistance from industry and government agencies, including such notable examples as the Federal Bureau of Investigation (FBI), the National Institute of Standards and Technology (NIST), the U.S. Secret Service, the Information Systems Security Association (ISSA), the Information Systems Audit and Control Association (ISACA), Microsoft Corporation, RSA Security, Motorola, Novell, Sun Microsystems, VeriSign, and Entrust.

The CompTIA Security+ exam is designed to cover a wide range of security topics—subjects about which a security practitioner would be expected to know. The test includes information from six knowledge domains:

Knowledge Domain	Percent of Exam
1.0 Network Security	20%
2.0 Compliance and Operational Security	18%
3.0 Threats and Vulnerabilities	20%
4.0 Application, Data and Host Security	15%
5.0 Access Control and Identity Management	15%
6.0 Cryptography	12%

The *Network Security* knowledge domain covers basic networking principles and devices. The domain is concerned with both wired and wireless networks and the security issues introduced when computers are connected to local networks as well as the Internet. The *Compliance and Operational Security* domain examines a number of operational security issues such as risk assessment and mitigation, incident response, disaster recovery and business continuity, training and awareness, and environmental controls. Since it is important to know what threats it is that you are protecting your systems and networks from, the third domain, *Threats and Vulnerabilities*, examines the many different types of attacks that can occur and the vulnerabilities that these attacks may exploit. The fourth domain, *Application, Data and Host Security*, covers those things that individuals can do to protect individual hosts. This may include items such as encryption, patching, antivirus measures, and hardware security. In the *Access Control and Identity Management* domain, fundamental concepts and best practices related to authentication, authorization, and access control are addressed. Account management and authentication services are also addressed in this domain. The last domain, *Cryptography*, has long been part of the basic security foundation of any organization, and an entire domain is devoted to details on its various aspects.

The exam consists of a series of questions, each designed to have a single best answer or response. The other available choices are designed to provide options that an individual might choose if he or she had an incomplete knowledge or understanding of the security topic represented by the question. The exam will have both multiple-choice and performance-based questions. Performance-based questions present the candidate with a task or a problem in a simulated IT environment. The candidate is given an opportunity to demonstrate his or her ability in performing skills. The exam questions are chosen from the more detailed objectives listed in the outline shown in Figure 1, an excerpt from the 2014 objectives document obtainable from the CompTIA website at http://certification.comptia.org/getCertified/certifications/security.aspx.

CompTIA recommends that individuals who want to take the CompTIA Security+ exam have the CompTIA Network+ certification and two years of technical networking experience, with an emphasis on security. Originally administered only in English, the exam is now offered in testing centers around the world in the English, Spanish, Japanese, Chinese, German, and other languages. Consult the CompTIA website at www.comptia.org to determine a location near you.

The exam consists of a maximum of 100 questions to be completed in 90 minutes. A minimum passing score is considered 750 out of a possible 900 points. Results are available immediately after you complete the exam. An individual who fails to pass the exam the first time will be required to pay the exam fee again to retake the exam, but no mandatory waiting period is required before retaking it the second time. If the individual again fails the exam, a minimum waiting period of 30 days is required for each subsequent retake. For more information on retaking exams, consult CompTIA's retake policy, which can be found on its website.

1.0 Network Security

1.1	Implement security configuration parameters on network devices and other technologies.
1.2	Given a scenario, use secure network administration principles.
1.3	Explain network design elements and components.
1.4	Given a scenario, implement common protocols and services.
1.5	Given a scenario, troubleshoot security issues related to wireless networking.

2.0 Compliance and Operational Security

2.1	Explain the importance of risk related concepts.
2.2	Summarize the security implications of integrating systems and data with third parties.
2.3	Given a scenario, implement appropriate risk mitigation strategies.
2.4	Given a scenario, implement basic forensic procedures.
2.5	Summarize common incident response procedures.
2.6	Explain the importance of security related awareness and training.
2.7	Compare and contrast physical security and environmental controls.
2.8	Summarize risk management best practices.
2.9	Given a scenario, select the appropriate control to meet the goals of security.

3.0 Threats and Vulnerabilities

3.1	Explain types of malware.
3.2	Summarize various types of attacks.
3.3	Summarize social engineering attacks and the associated effectiveness with each attack.
3.4	Explain types of wireless attacks.
3.5	Explain types of application attacks.
3.6	Analyze a scenario and select the appropriate type of mitigation and deterrent techniques.
3.7	Given a scenario, use appropriate tools and techniques to discover security threats and vulnerabilities.
3.8	Explain the proper use of penetration testing versus vulnerability scanning.

4.0 Application, Data and Host Security

4.1	Explain the importance of application security controls and techniques.
4.2	Summarize mobile security concepts and technologies.
4.3	Given a scenario, select the appropriate solution to establish host security.
4.4	Implement the appropriate controls to ensure data security.
4.5	Compare and contrast alternative methods to mitigate security risks in static environments.

5.0 Access Control and Identity Management

5.1	Compare and contrast the function and purpose of authentication services.
5.2	Given a scenario, select the appropriate authentication, authorization or access control.
5.3	Install and configure security controls when performing account management, based on best practices.

6.0 Cryptography

6.1	Given a scenario, utilize general cryptography concepts.
6.2	Given a scenario, use appropriate cryptographic methods.
6.3	Given a scenario, use appropriate PKI, certificate management and associated components.

Figure I   The CompTIA Security+ (SY0-401) exam objectives

Preparing Yourself for the CompTIA Security+ Exam

CompTIA Security+ All-in-One Exam Guide, Fourth Edition, is designed to help prepare you to take the CompTIA Security+ certification exam SY0-401.

How This Book Is Organized

The book is divided into sections and chapters to correspond with the objectives of the exam itself. Some of the chapters are more technical than others—reflecting the nature of the security environment, where you will be forced to deal with not only technical details, but also other issues such as security policies and procedures as well as training and education. Although many individuals involved in computer and network security have advanced degrees in math, computer science, information systems, or computer or electrical engineering, you do not need this technical background to address security effectively in your organization. You do not need to develop your own cryptographic algorithm, for example; you simply need to be able to understand how cryptography is used, along with its strengths and weaknesses. As you progress in your studies, you will learn that many security problems are caused by the human element. The best technology in the world still ends up being placed in an environment where humans have the opportunity to foul things up—and all too often do.

As you can see from the table of contents, the overall structure of the book is designed to mirror the objectives of the CompTIA Security+ exam. The majority of the chapters are designed to match the objectives order as posted by CompTIA. There are occasions where the order differs slightly, mainly to group terms by contextual use.

In addition, there are two appendixes in this book. Appendix A provides an additional in-depth explanation of the OSI Model and Internet protocols, should this information be new to you, and Appendix B explains how best to use the CD-ROM included with the book.

Located just before the Index, you will find a useful Glossary of security terminology, including many related acronyms and their meaning. We hope that you use the Glossary frequently and find it to be a useful study aid as you work your way through the various topics in this exam guide.

Special Features of the All-in-One Series

To make these exam guides more useful and a pleasure to read, the All-in-One series has been designed to include several features.

Objective Map

The objective map that follows this introduction has been constructed to allow you to cross-reference the official exam objectives with the objectives as they are presented and covered in this book. References have been provided for the objective exactly as CompTIA presents it, the section of the exam guide that covers that objective, and a chapter and page reference.

Icons

To alert you to an important bit of advice, a shortcut, or a pitfall, you'll occasionally see Notes, Tips, Cautions, and Exam Tips peppered throughout the text.

 NOTE   Notes offer nuggets of especially helpful stuff, background explanations, and information, and terms are defined occasionally.

 TIP   Tips provide suggestions and nuances to help you learn to finesse your job. Take a tip from us and read the Tips carefully.

 CAUTION   When you see a Caution, pay special attention. Cautions appear when you have to make a crucial choice or when you are about to undertake something that may have ramifications you might not immediately anticipate. Read them now so you don't have regrets later.

 EXAM TIP   Exam Tips give you special advice or may provide information specifically related to preparing for the exam itself.

End-of-Chapter Reviews and Questions

An important part of this book comes at the end of each chapter, where you will find a brief review of the high points along with a series of questions followed by the answers to those questions. Each question is in multiple-choice format. The answers provided also include a small discussion explaining why the correct answer actually is the correct answer.

The questions are provided as a study aid to you, the reader and prospective CompTIA Security+ exam taker. We obviously can't guarantee that if you answer all of our questions correctly you will absolutely pass the certification exam. Instead, what we can guarantee is that the questions will provide you with an idea about how ready you are for the exam.

The CD-ROM

CompTIA Security+ All-in-One Exam Guide, Fourth Edition, also provides you with a CD-ROM of even more practice exam questions and their answers to help you prepare for the certification exam. Read more about the companion CD-ROM in Appendix B.

Onward and Upward

At this point, we hope that you are now excited about the topic of security, even if you weren't in the first place. We wish you luck in your endeavors and welcome you to the exciting field of computer and network security.

Objective Map: Exam SY0-401

Official Exam Objective	All-in-One Coverage	Chapter No.	Page No.
1.0 Network Security			
1.1 Implement security configuration parameters on network devices and other technologies.	Network Device Configuration	1	3
1.2 Given a scenario, use secure network administration principles.	Secure Network Administration	2	25
1.3 Explain network design elements and components.	Secure Network Design	3	35
1.4 Given a scenario, implement common protocols and services.	Secure Network Design	3	45
1.5 Given a scenario, troubleshoot security issues related to wireless networking.	Secure Wireless Networking	4	63
2.0 Compliance and Operational Security			
2.1 Explain the importance of risk related concepts.	Risk Concepts	5	79
2.2 Summarize the security implications of integrating systems and data with third parties.	System Integration Processes	6	101
2.3 Given a scenario, implement appropriate risk mitigation strategies.	Risk Management	7	111
2.4 Given a scenario, implement basic forensic procedures.	Digital Forensics and Incident Response	8	132
2.5 Summarize common incident response procedures.	Digital Forensics and Incident Response	8	141
2.6 Explain the importance of security related awareness and training.	Security Awareness and Training	9	153
2.7 Compare and contrast physical security and environmental controls.	Physical Security and Environmental Controls	10	169
2.8 Summarize risk management best practices	Risk Management	7	114
2.9 Given a scenario, select the appropriate control to meet the goals of security.	Security Controls	11	193
3.0 Threats and Vulnerabilities			
3.1 Explain types of malware.	Attacks and Malware	12	205
3.2 Summarize various types of attacks.	Attacks and Malware	12	210
3.3 Summarize social engineering attacks and the associated effectiveness with each attack.	Social Engineering	13	235
3.4 Explain types of wireless attacks.	Application and Wireless Attacks	14	247
3.5 Explain types of application attacks.	Application and Wireless Attacks	14	253

PART I

Network Security

Network Device Configuration

In this chapter, you will

- Implement security configuration parameters on network devices
- Implement security configuration parameters on other technologies

Networks are composed of devices and are configured via software to perform the desired activities. The correct configuration of network devices is a key element of securing the network infrastructure. Proper configuration can greatly assist in the network security posture. Learning how to properly configure network devices is important for passing the CompTIA Security+ exam.

Network Devices

A complete network computer solution in today's business environment consists of more than just client computers and servers. Devices are used to connect the clients and servers and to regulate the traffic between them. Devices are also needed to expand this network beyond simple client computers and servers to include yet other devices, such as wireless and handheld systems. Devices come in many forms and with many functions, from hubs and switches, to routers, wireless access points, and special-purpose devices such as virtual private network (VPN) devices. Each device has a specific network function and plays a role in maintaining network infrastructure security.

 EXAM TIP Expect questions on how to implement security configuration parameters on network devices.

Firewalls

A firewall can be hardware, software, or a combination whose purpose is to enforce a set of network security policies across network connections. It is much like a wall with a window: the wall serves to keep things out, except those permitted through the window (see Figure 1-1). Network security policies act like the glass in the window; they permit

3

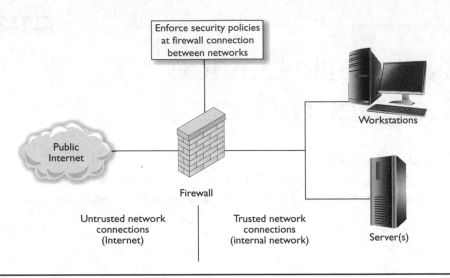

Figure 1-1 How a firewall works

some things to pass, such as light, while blocking others, such as air. The heart of a firewall is the set of security policies that it enforces. Management determines what is allowed in the form of network traffic between devices, and these policies are used to build rule sets for the firewall devices used to filter network traffic across the network.

Security policies are rules that define what traffic is permissible and what traffic is to be blocked or denied. These are not universal rules, and many different sets of rules are created for a single company with multiple connections. A web server connected to the Internet may be configured to allow traffic only on port 80 for HTTP and have all other ports blocked, for example. An e-mail server may have only necessary ports for e-mail open, with others blocked. The network firewall can be programmed to block all traffic to the web server except for port 80 traffic, and to block all traffic bound to the mail server except for port 25. In this fashion, the firewall acts as a security filter, enabling control over network traffic, by machine, by port, and in some cases based on application-level detail. A key to setting security policies for firewalls is the same as has been seen for other security policies—the principle of least access. Allow only the necessary access for a function; block or deny all unneeded functionality. How a firm deploys its firewalls determines what is needed for security policies for each firewall.

As will be discussed later, the security topology will determine what network devices are employed at what points in a network. At a minimum, the corporate connection to the Internet should pass through a firewall. This firewall should block all network traffic except that specifically authorized by the firm. Blocking communications on a port is simple—just tell the firewall to close the port. The issue comes in deciding what services are needed and by whom, and thus which ports should be open and which should be closed. This is what makes a security policy useful. The perfect set of network security policies for a firewall is one that the end user never sees and that never allows even a single unauthorized packet to enter the network. As with any other perfect item, it will be rare to find the perfect set of security policies for firewalls in an enterprise. When developing rules for a firewall, the principle of least access is best to use; you want the firewall to block as much traffic as possible, while allowing the authorized traffic through.

To develop a complete and comprehensive security policy, it is first necessary to have a complete and comprehensive understanding of your network resources and their uses. Once you know how the network will be used, you will have an idea of what to permit. In addition, once you understand what you need to protect, you will have an idea of what to block. Firewalls are designed to block attacks before they reach a target machine. Common targets are web servers, e-mail servers, DNS servers, FTP services, and databases. Each of these has separate functionality, and each has unique vulnerabilities. Once you have decided who should receive what type of traffic and what types should be blocked, you can administer this through the firewall.

How Do Firewalls Work?

Firewalls enforce the established security policies through a variety of mechanisms, including the following:

- Network Address Translation (NAT)
- Basic packet filtering
- Stateful packet filtering
- Access control lists (ACLs)
- Application layer proxies

One of the most basic security functions provided by a firewall is NAT, which allows you to mask significant amounts of information from outside of the network. This allows an outside entity to communicate with an entity inside the firewall without truly knowing its address. NAT is a technique used in IPv4 to link private IP addresses to public ones. Private IP addresses are sets of IP addresses that can be used by anyone and, by definition, are not routable across the Internet. NAT can assist in security by preventing direct access to devices from outside the firm, without first having the address changed at a NAT device. The benefit is that fewer public IP addresses are needed, and from a security point of view, the internal address structure is not known to the outside world. If a hacker attacks the source address, he is simply attacking the NAT device, not the actual sender of the packet. NAT is described in detail in Chapter 3.

NAT was conceived to resolve an address shortage associated with IPv4 and is considered by many to be unnecessary for IPv6. The added security features of enforcing traffic translation and hiding internal network details from direct outside connections will give NAT life well into the IPv6 timeframe.

Basic packet filtering, the next most common firewall technique, involves looking at packets, their ports, protocols, and source and destination addresses, and checking that information against the rules configured on the firewall. Telnet and FTP connections may be prohibited from being established to a mail or database server, but they may be allowed for the respective service servers. This is a fairly simple method of filtering based on information in each packet header, such as IP addresses and TCP/UDP ports. Packet filtering will not detect and catch all undesired packets, but it is fast and efficient.

To look at all packets and determine the need for each and its data requires *stateful* packet filtering. Stateful means that the firewall maintains, or knows, the context of a conversation. In many cases, rules depend on the context of a specific communication connection. For instance, traffic from an outside server to an inside server may be allowed if it is requested but blocked if it is not. A common example is a request for a web page. This request is actually a series of requests to multiple servers, each of which can be allowed or blocked. Advanced firewalls employ stateful packet filtering to prevent several types of undesired communications. Should a packet come from outside the network in an attempt to pretend that it is a response to a message from inside the network, the firewall will have no record of it being requested and can discard it, blocking the undesired external access attempt. As many communications will be transferred to high ports (above 1023), stateful monitoring will enable the system to determine which sets of high communications are permissible and which should be blocked. A disadvantage of stateful monitoring is that it takes significant resources and processing to perform this type of monitoring, and this reduces efficiency and requires more robust and expensive hardware.

 EXAM TIP   Firewalls operate by examining packets and selectively denying some based on a set of rules. Firewalls act as gatekeepers or sentries at select network points, segregating traffic and allowing some to pass and blocking others.

Some high-security firewalls also employ application layer proxies. Packets are not allowed to traverse the firewall, but data instead flows up to an application that in turn decides what to do with it. For example, a Simple Mail Transfer Protocol (SMTP) proxy may accept inbound mail from the Internet and forward it to the internal corporate mail server. While proxies provide a high level of security by making it very difficult for an attacker to manipulate the actual packets arriving at the destination, and while they provide the opportunity for an application to interpret the data prior to forwarding it to the destination, they generally are not capable of the same throughput as stateful packet inspection firewalls. The trade-off between performance and speed is a common one and must be evaluated with respect to security needs and performance requirements.

Firewalls can also act as network traffic regulators in that they can be configured to mitigate specific types of network-based attacks. In denial-of-service and distributed denial-of-service (DoS/DDoS) attacks, an attacker can attempt to flood a network with traffic. Firewalls can be tuned to detect these types of attacks and act as a flood guard, mitigating the effect on the network. Firewalls can be very effective in blocking a variety of flooding attacks, including port floods, SYN floods, and ping floods.

Routers

Routers are network traffic management devices used to connect different network segments together. Routers operate at the network layer of the Open Systems Interconnection (OSI) reference model (discussed in Chapter 3), routing traffic using the network address and utilizing routing protocols to determine optimal paths across a network. Routers form the backbone of the Internet, moving traffic from network to network, inspecting packets from every communication as they move traffic in optimal paths.

Routers operate by examining each packet, looking at the destination address, and using algorithms and tables to determine where to send the packet next. This process of examining the header to determine the next hop can be done in quick fashion.

Routers use ACLs as a method of deciding whether a packet is allowed to enter the network. With ACLs, it is also possible to examine the source address and determine whether or not to allow a packet to pass. This allows routers equipped with ACLs to drop packets according to rules built in the ACLs. This can be a cumbersome process to set up and maintain, and as the ACL grows in size, routing efficiency can be decreased. It is also possible to configure some routers to act as quasi-application gateways, performing stateful packet inspection and using contents as well as IP addresses to determine whether or not to permit a packet to pass. This can tremendously increase the time for a router to pass traffic and can significantly decrease router throughput. Configuring ACLs and other aspects of setting up routers for this type of use are beyond the scope of this book.

 EXAM TIP ACLs can be a significant effort to establish and maintain. Creating them is a straightforward task, but their judicious use will yield security benefits with a limited amount of maintenance. This can be very important in security zones such as a DMZ and at edge devices, blocking undesired outside contact while allowing known inside traffic.

One serious operational security issue with routers concerns the access to a router and control of its internal functions. Routers can be accessed using the Simple Network Management Protocol (SNMP) and Telnet and can be programmed remotely. Because of the geographic separation of routers, this can become a necessity, for many routers in the world of the Internet can be hundreds of miles apart in separate locked structures. Physical control over a router is absolutely necessary, for if any device, be it server, switch, or router, is physically accessed by a hacker, it should be considered compromised; thus, such access must be prevented. It is important to ensure that the administrative password is never passed in the clear, that only secure mechanisms are used to access the router, and that all of the default passwords are reset to strong passwords.

Just like switches, the most assured point of access for router management control is via the serial control interface port or specific router management Ethernet interface. This allows access to the control aspects of the router without having to deal with traffic-related issues. For internal company networks, where the geographic dispersion of routers may be limited, third-party solutions to allow out-of-band remote management exist. This allows complete control over the router in a secure fashion, even from a remote location, although additional hardware is required.

Figure 1-2   A small home office router for cable modem/DSL use

Routers are available from numerous vendors and come in sizes big and small. A typical small home office router for use with cable modem/DSL service is shown in Figure 1-2. Larger routers can handle traffic of up to tens of gigabytes per second per channel, using fiber-optic inputs and moving tens of thousands of concurrent Internet connections across the network. These routers, which can cost hundreds of thousands of dollars, form an essential part of the e-commerce infrastructure, enabling large enterprises such as Amazon and eBay to serve many customers concurrently.

Switches

Switches form the basis for connections in most Ethernet-based local area networks (LANs). Although hubs and bridges still exist, in today's high-performance network environment, switches have replaced both. A switch has separate collision domains for each port. This means that for each port, two collision domains exist: one from the port to the client on the downstream side and one from the switch to the network upstream. When *full duplex* is employed, collisions are virtually eliminated from the two nodes, host and client. This also acts as a security factor in that a sniffer can see only limited traffic, as opposed to a hub-based system, where a single sniffer can see all of the traffic to and from connected devices.

Switches operate at the data link layer of the OSI model, while routers act at the network layer. For intranets, switches have become what routers are on the Internet—the device of choice for connecting machines. As switches have become the primary network connectivity device, additional functionality has been added to them. A switch is usually a layer 2 device, but layer 3 switches incorporate routing functionality.

Switches can also perform a variety of security functions. Switches work by moving packets from inbound connections to outbound connections. While moving the packets, it is possible for switches to inspect the packet headers and enforce security policies. Port address security based on Media Access Control (MAC) addresses can determine whether a packet is allowed or blocked from a connection. This is the very function that a firewall uses for its determination, and this same functionality is what allows an 802.1x device to act as an "edge device."

One of the security concerns with switches is that, like routers, they are intelligent network devices and are therefore subject to hijacking by hackers. Should a hacker break into a switch and change its parameters, he might be able to eavesdrop on specific or all communications virtually undetected. Switches are commonly administered using the SNMP and Telnet protocol, both of which have a serious weakness in that they send passwords across the network in clear text.

EXAM TIP Simple Network Management Protocol (SNMP) provides management functions to many network devices. SNMPv1 and SNMPv2 authenticate using a cleartext password, allowing anyone monitoring packets to capture the password and have access to the network equipment. SNMPv3 adds cryptographic protections, making it a preferred solution.

A hacker armed with a sniffer that observes maintenance on a switch can capture the administrative password. This allows the hacker to come back to the switch later and configure it as an administrator. An additional problem is that switches are shipped with default passwords, and if these are not changed when the switch is set up, they offer an unlocked door to a hacker. Commercial-quality switches have a local serial console port or a management Ethernet interface for guaranteed access to the switch for purposes of control. Some products in the marketplace enable an out-of-band network, using these dedicated channels to enable remote, secure access to programmable network devices.

CAUTION To secure a switch, you should disable all access protocols other than a secure serial line or a secure protocol such as Secure Shell (SSH). Using only secure methods to access a switch will limit the exposure to hackers and malicious users. Maintaining secure network switches is even more important than securing individual boxes, for the span of control to intercept data is much wider on a switch, especially if it's reprogrammed by a hacker.

Load Balancers

Certain systems, such as servers, are more critical to business operations and should therefore be the object of fault-tolerance measures. A common technique that is used in fault tolerance is *load balancing*. This technique is designed to distribute the processing load over two or more systems. It is used to help improve resource utilization and throughput, but also has the added advantage of increasing the fault tolerance of the overall system since a critical process may be split across several systems. Should any one system fail, the others can pick up the processing it was handling. While there may be an impact to overall throughput, the operation does not go down entirely. Load balancing is often utilized for systems handling websites, high-bandwidth file transfers, and large Internet Relay Chat (IRC) networks. Load balancing works by a series of health checks that tell the load balancer which machines are operating, and by a scheduling mechanism to spread the work evenly. Load balancing is best for stateless systems, as subsequent requests can be handled by any server, not just the one that processed the previous request.

Proxies

Though not strictly a security tool, a *proxy server* can be used to filter out undesirable traffic and prevent employees from accessing potentially hostile websites. A proxy server takes requests from a client system and forwards them to the destination server on behalf of the client. Proxy servers can be completely transparent (these are usually called *gateways* or *tunneling proxies*), or they can modify the client request before sending it on or even serve the client's request without needing to contact the destination server. Several major categories of proxy servers are in use:

- **Anonymizing proxy** An anonymizing proxy is designed to hide information about the requesting system and make a user's web browsing experience "anonymous." This type of proxy service is often used by individuals concerned with the amount of personal information being transferred across the Internet and the use of tracking cookies and other mechanisms to track browsing activity.

- **Caching proxy** This type of proxy keeps local copies of popular client requests and is often used in large organizations to reduce bandwidth usage and increase performance. When a request is made, the proxy server first checks to see whether it has a current copy of the requested content in the cache; if it does, it services the client request immediately without having to contact the destination server. If the content is old or the caching proxy does not have a copy of the requested content, the request is forwarded to the destination server.

- **Content-filtering proxy** Content-filtering proxies examine each client request and compare it to an established acceptable use policy (AUP). Requests can usually be filtered in a variety of ways, including by the requested URL, the destination system, or the domain name or by keywords in the content itself. Content-filtering proxies typically support user-level authentication so access can be controlled and monitored and activity through the proxy can be logged and analyzed. This type of proxy is very popular in schools, corporate environments, and government networks.

- **Open proxy** An open proxy is essentially a proxy that is available to any Internet user and often has some anonymizing capabilities as well. This type of proxy has been the subject of some controversy, with advocates for Internet privacy and freedom on one side of the argument, and law enforcement, corporations, and government entities on the other side. As open proxies are often used to circumvent corporate proxies, many corporations attempt to block the use of open proxies by their employees.

- **Reverse proxy** A reverse proxy is typically installed on the server side of a network connection, often in front of a group of web servers. The reverse proxy intercepts all incoming web requests and can perform a number of functions, including traffic filtering, Secure Sockets Layer (SSL) decryption, serving of common static content such as graphics, and performing load balancing.

- **Web proxy** A web proxy is solely designed to handle web traffic and is sometimes called a *web cache*. Most web proxies are essentially specialized caching proxies.

Deploying a proxy solution within a network environment is usually done by either setting up the proxy and requiring all client systems to configure their browsers to use the proxy or by deploying an intercepting proxy that actively intercepts all requests without requiring client-side configuration.

From a security perspective, proxies are most useful in their ability to control and filter outbound requests. By limiting the types of content and websites employees can access from corporate systems, many administrators hope to avoid loss of corporate data, hijacked systems, and infections from malicious websites. Administrators also use proxies to enforce corporate acceptable use policies and track use of corporate resources.

Web Security Gateways

Some security vendors combine proxy functions with content-filtering functions to create a product called a *web security gateway*. Web security gateways are intended to address the security threats and pitfalls unique to web-based traffic. Web security gateways typically provide the following capabilities:

- **Real-time malware protection** (also known as malware inspection)   Some web security gateways have the ability to scan all outgoing and incoming web traffic to detect and block undesirable traffic such as malware, spyware, adware, malicious scripts, file-based attacks, and so on.

- **Content monitoring**   Some web security gateways provide the ability to monitor the content of web traffic being examined to ensure that it complies with organizational policies.

- **Productivity monitoring**   Some web security gateways measure how much web traffic is being generated by specific users, groups of users, or the entire organization as well as the types of traffic being generated.

- **Data protection and compliance**   Some web security gateways can scan web traffic for sensitive or proprietary information being sent outside of the organization as well as the use of social network sites or inappropriate sites.

VPN Concentrators

A virtual private network (VPN) is a construct used to provide a secure communication channel between users across public networks such as the Internet. As described later in the book, a variety of techniques can be employed to instantiate a VPN connection. The use of encryption technologies allows either the data in a packet to be encrypted or the entire packet to be encrypted. If the data is encrypted, the packet header can still be sniffed and observed between source and destination, but the encryption protects the contents of the packet from inspection. If the entire packet is encrypted, it is then placed into another packet and sent via tunnel across the public network. Tunneling can protect even the identity of the communicating parties.

The most common implementation of VPN is via IPsec, a protocol for IP security. IPsec is mandated in IPv6 and is optionally back-fitted into IPv4. IPsec can be implemented in hardware, software, or a combination of both. VPNs terminate at a specific point in the network, the VPN concentrator. VPN concentrators come in a variety of sizes, scaling to enable VPNs from small networks to large. A VPN concentrator allows multiple VPN connections to terminate at a single network point.

Intrusion Detection Systems

Intrusion detection systems (IDSs) are designed to detect, log, and respond to unauthorized network or host use, both in real time and after the fact. IDSs are available from a wide selection of vendors and are an essential part of network security. These systems are implemented in software, but in large systems, dedicated hardware is required as well. IDSs can be divided into two categories: network-based systems and host-based systems. Two primary methods of detection are used: signature-based and anomaly-based:

- **Host-based IDS (HIDS)** Examines activity on an individual system, such as a mail server, web server, or individual PC. It is concerned only with an individual system and usually has no visibility into the activity on the network or systems around it.

- **Network-based IDS (NIDS)** Examines activity on the network itself. It has visibility only into the traffic crossing the network link it is monitoring and typically has no idea of what is happening on individual systems.

 EXAM TIP Know the differences between host-based and network-based IDSs. A host-based IDS runs on a specific system (server or workstation) and looks at all the activity on that host. A network-based IDS sniffs traffic from the network and sees only activity that occurs on the network.

Whether or not it is network-based or host-based, an IDS will typically consist of several specialized components working together, as illustrated in Figure 1-3. These components are often logical and software-based rather than physical and will vary

Figure 1-3
Logical depiction of IDS components

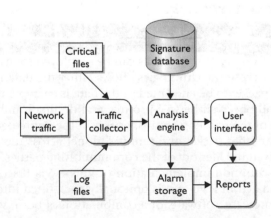

slightly from vendor to vendor and product to product. Typically, an IDS will have the following logical components:

- **Traffic collector (or sensor)**   This component collects activity/events for the IDS to examine. On a host-based IDS, this could be log files, audit logs, or traffic coming to or leaving a specific system. On a network-based IDS, this is typically a mechanism for copying traffic off the network link—basically functioning as a sniffer. This component is often referred to as a sensor.

- **Analysis engine**   This component examines the collected network traffic and compares it to known patterns of suspicious or malicious activity stored in the signature database. The analysis engine is the "brains" of the IDS.

- **Signature database**   The signature database is a collection of patterns and definitions of known suspicious or malicious activity.

- **User interface and reporting**   This component interfaces with the human element, providing alerts when appropriate and giving the user a means to interact with and operate the IDS.

Most IDSs can be tuned to fit a particular environment. Certain signatures can be turned off, telling the IDS not to look for certain types of traffic. For example, if you are operating in a pure UNIX environment, you may not wish to see Windows-based alarms, as they will not affect your systems. Additionally, the severity of the alarm levels can be adjusted depending on how concerned you are over certain types of traffic. Some IDSs will also allow the user to exclude certain patterns of activity from specific hosts. In other words, you can tell the IDS to ignore the fact that some systems generate traffic that looks like malicious activity because it really isn't.

Some analysts break down IDS models even further into four categories depending on how the IDS operates and detects malicious traffic (the same models can also be applied to intrusion prevention systems, discussed a bit later).

Behavior Based

This model relies on a collected set of "normal behavior"—what should happen on the network and is considered "normal" or "acceptable" traffic. Behavior that does not fit into the "normal" activity categories or patterns is considered suspicious or malicious. This model can potentially detect zero-day or unpublished attacks, but carries a high false-positive rate because any new traffic pattern can be labeled as "suspect."

Signature Based

This model relies on a predefined set of patterns (called *signatures*). The IDS has to know what behavior is considered "bad" ahead of time before it can identify and act upon suspicious or malicious traffic. Signature-based systems can be very fast and precise, but they rely on having accurate signature definitions beforehand.

Anomaly Based

This model is similar to behavior-based methods. The IDS is first taught what "normal" traffic looks like and then looks for deviations from those "normal" patterns. Anomalies can also be defined, such as Linux commands sent to Windows-based systems, and implemented via an artificial intelligence–based engine to expand the utility of specific definitions.

Heuristic

This model uses artificial intelligence to detect intrusions and malicious traffic. This is typically implemented through algorithms that help an IDS decide if a traffic pattern is malicious or not. For example, a URL containing a character repeated 10 times may be considered "bad" traffic as a single signature. With a heuristic model, the IDS will understand that if 10 repeating characters is bad, 11 is still bad, and 20 is even worse. This implementation of fuzzy logic allows this model to fall somewhere between signature-based and behavior-based models.

Intrusion Prevention Systems

An intrusion prevention system (IPS) has as its core an intrusion detection system. However, whereas an IDS can only alert when network traffic matches a defined set of rules, an IPS can take further actions. IPSs come in the same two forms as IDSs, host based (HIPS) and network based (NIPS). An IPS can take direct action to block an attack, with its actions governed by rules. By automating the response, an IPS significantly shortens the response time between detection and action.

 EXAM TIP Recognize that an IPS has all the same characteristics of an IDS but, unlike an IDS, can automatically respond to certain events, such as resetting a TCP connection, without operator intervention.

Protocol Analyzers

A *protocol analyzer* (also known as a *packet sniffer*, *network analyzer*, or *network sniffer*) is a piece of software or an integrated software/hardware system that can capture and decode network traffic. Protocol analyzers have been popular with system administrators and security professionals for decades because they are such versatile and useful tools for a network environment. From a security perspective, protocol analyzers can be used for a number of activities, such as the following:

- Detecting intrusions or undesirable traffic (IDS/IPS must have some type of capture and decode ability to be able to look for suspicious/malicious traffic)
- Capturing traffic during incident response or incident handling
- Looking for evidence of botnets, Trojans, and infected systems
- Looking for unusual traffic or traffic exceeding certain thresholds
- Testing encryption between systems or applications

From a network administration perspective, protocol analyzers can be used for activities such as these:

- Analyzing network problems
- Detecting misconfigured applications or misbehaving applications
- Gathering and reporting network usage and traffic statistics
- Debugging client/server communications

Regardless of the intended use, a protocol analyzer must be able to see network traffic in order to capture and decode it. A software-based protocol analyzer must be able to place the network interface card (NIC) it is going to use to monitor network traffic in *promiscuous mode* (sometimes called *promisc mode*). Promiscuous mode tells the NIC to process every network packet it sees regardless of the intended destination. Normally, a NIC will process only *broadcast* packets (that are going to everyone on that subnet) and packets with the NIC's MAC address as the destination address inside the packet. As a sniffer, the analyzer must process every packet crossing the wire, so the ability to place a NIC into promiscuous mode is critical.

With older networking technologies, such as hubs, it was easier to operate a protocol analyzer, as the hub broadcast every packet across every interface regardless of the destination. With switches becoming the standard for networking equipment, placing a protocol analyzer became more difficult because switches do not broadcast every packet across every port. While this may make it harder for administrators to sniff the traffic, it also makes it harder for eavesdroppers and potential attacks.

To accommodate protocol analyzers, IDS devices, and IPS devices, most switch manufacturers support *port mirroring* or a *Switched Port Analyzer (SPAN)* port. Depending on the manufacturer and the hardware, a mirrored port will see all the traffic passing through the switch or through a specific VLAN(s), or all the traffic passing through other specific switch ports. The network traffic is essentially copied (or mirrored) to a specific port, which can then support a protocol analyzer.

A popular open-source protocol analyzer is Wireshark (www.wireshark.org). Available for both UNIX/Linux and Windows operating systems, Wireshark is a GUI-based protocol analyzer that allows users to capture and decode network traffic on any available network interface in the system on which the software is running (including wireless interfaces). Wireshark has some interesting features, including the ability to "follow the TCP stream," which allows the user to select a single TCP packet and then see all the other packets involved in that TCP conversation.

 EXAM TIP Expect questions on how to implement security configuration parameters on IT technology components.

Spam Filter

The bane of users and system administrators everywhere, *spam* is essentially unsolicited or undesired bulk electronic messages. While typically applied to e-mail, spam can be transmitted via text message to phones and mobile devices, as postings to Internet forums, and by other means. If you've ever used an e-mail account, chances are you've received spam.

From a productivity and security standpoint, spam costs businesses and users billions of dollars each year, and it is such a widespread problem that the U.S. Congress passed the CAN-SPAM Act of 2003 to empower the Federal Trade Commission to enforce the act and the Department of Justice to enforce criminal sanctions against spammers. The act establishes requirements for those who send commercial e-mail, spells out penalties for spammers and companies whose products are advertised in spam if they violate the law, and gives consumers the right to ask e-mailers to stop spamming them. Despite all our best efforts, however, spam just keeps coming; as the technologies and techniques developed to stop the spam get more advanced and complex, so do the tools and techniques used to send out the unsolicited messages.

Here are a few of the more popular methods used to fight the spam epidemic; most of these techniques are used to filter e-mail, but could be applied to other mediums as well:

- **Blacklisting**   Blacklisting is essentially noting which domains and source addresses have a reputation for sending spam, and rejecting messages coming from those domains and source addresses. This is basically a permanent "ignore" or "call block" type capability. Several organizations and a few commercial companies provide lists of known spammers.

- **Content or keyword filtering**   Similar to Internet content filtering, this method filters e-mail messages for undesirable content or indications of spam. Much like content filtering of web content, filtering e-mail based on something like keywords can cause unexpected results, as certain terms can be used in both legitimate and spam e-mail. Most content-filtering techniques use regular expression matching for keyword filtering.

- **Trusted servers**   The opposite of blacklisting, a trusted server list includes SMTP servers that are being "trusted" not to forward spam.

- **Delay-based filtering**   Some Simple Mail Transfer Protocol (SMTP) servers are configured to insert a deliberate pause between the opening of a connection and the sending of the SMTP server's welcome banner. Some spam-generating programs do not wait for that greeting banner, and any system that immediately starts sending data as soon as the connection is opened is treated as a spam generator and dropped by the SMTP server.

- **PTR and reverse DNS checks**   Some e-mail filters check the origin domain of an e-mail sender. If the reverse checks show the mail is coming from a dial-up user, home-based broadband, or a dynamically assigned address, or has a generic or missing domain, then the filter rejects it, as these are common sources of spam messages.

- **Callback verification**   Because many spam messages use forged "from" addresses, some filters attempt to validate the "from" address of incoming e-mail. The receiving server can contact the sending server in an attempt to validate the sending address, but this is not always effective, as spoofed addresses are sometimes valid e-mail addresses that can be verified.

- **Statistical content filtering**   Statistical filtering is much like a document classification system. Users mark received messages as either spam or legitimate mail, and the filtering system learns from the user's input. The more messages that are seen and classified as spam, the better the filtering software should get at intercepting incoming spam. Spammers counteract many filtering technologies by inserting random words and characters into the messages, making it difficult for content filters to identify patterns common to spam.

- **Rule-based filtering**   Rule-based filtering is a simple technique that merely looks for matches in certain fields or keywords. For example, a rule-based filtering system may look for any message with the words "get rich" in the subject line of the incoming message. Many popular e-mail clients have the ability to implement rule-based filtering.

- **Egress filtering**   Some organizations perform spam filtering on e-mail leaving their organization as well, and this is called egress filtering. The same types of anti-spam techniques can be used to validate and filter outgoing e-mail in an effort to combat spam.

- **Hybrid filtering**   Most commercial anti-spam methods use hybrid filtering, or a combination of several different techniques to fight spam. For example, a filtering solution may take each incoming message and match it against known spammers, then against a rule-based filter, then a content filter, and finally against a statistical-based filter. If the message passes all filtering stages, it will be treated as a legitimate message; otherwise, it is rejected as spam.

Much spam filtering is done at the network or SMTP server level. It's more efficient to scan all incoming and outgoing messages with a centralized solution than it is to deploy individual solutions on user desktops throughout the organization. E-mail is essentially a proxied service by default: messages generally come into and go out of an organization's mail server. (Users don't typically connect to remote SMTP servers to send and receive messages, but they can.) Anti-spam solutions are available in the form of software that is loaded on the SMTP server itself or on a secondary server that processes messages either before they reach the SMTP server or after the messages are processed by the SMTP server. Anti-spam solutions are also available in appliance form, where the software and hardware are a single integrated solution. Many centralized anti-spam methods allow individual users to customize spam filtering for their specific inbox, specifying their own filter rules and criteria for evaluating inbound e-mail.

The central issue with spam is that, despite all the effort placed into building effective spam filtering programs, spammers continue to create new methods for flooding inboxes. Spam filtering solutions are good, but are far from perfect, and continue to fight the constant challenge of allowing in legitimate messages while keeping the spam out. The lack of central control over Internet traffic also makes anti-spam efforts more difficult. Different countries have different laws and regulations governing e-mail, which range from draconian to nonexistent. For the foreseeable future, spam will continue to be a burden to administrators and users alike.

UTM Security Appliances

Many security vendors offer "all-in-one security appliances," which are devices that combine multiple functions into the same hardware appliance. Most commonly, these functions are firewall, IDS/IPS, and antivirus, although all-in-one appliances can include VPN capabilities, anti-spam, malicious web traffic filtering, anti-spyware, content filtering, traffic shaping, and so on. All-in-one appliances are often sold as being cheaper, easier to manage, and more efficient than having separate solutions that accomplish each of the functions the all-in-one appliance is capable of performing. A common name for these all-in-one appliances is a Unified Threat Management (UTM). Using a UTM appliance simplifies the security activity as a single process, under a common software package for operations. This reduces the learning curve to a single tool rather than a collection of tools. A UTM appliance can have better integration and efficiencies in handling network traffic and incidents than a collection of tools connected together.

URL Filter

URL filters block connections to websites that are in a prohibited list. The use of an appliance, typically backed by a service to keep the list of prohibited websites updated, provides an automated means to block access to sites deemed dangerous or inappropriate. Because of the highly volatile nature of web content, automated enterprise-level protection is needed to ensure a reasonable chance of blocking sources of inappropriate content, malware, and other malicious content.

Content Inspection

Rather than just rely on a URL to determine the acceptability of content, appliances can also inspect the actual content being served. Content inspection is used to filter web requests that return content with specific components, such as names of body parts, music or video content, and other content that is inappropriate for the business environment.

Malware Inspection

Malware is another item that can be detected during network transmission, and appliances can be tuned to detect malware. Network-based malware detection has the advantage of having to update only a single system as opposed to all machines.

Web Application Firewall vs. Network Firewall

A network firewall is a device that enforces policies based on network address rules. Blocking of addresses and/or ports allows a network firewall to restrict network traffic. A web application firewall (WAF) is a device that performs restrictions based on rules associated with HTTP/HTTPS traffic. By definition, web application firewalls are content filters, and their programming capabilities allow significant capability and protections. The level of specificity in what can be allowed or blocked can go to granular levels, such as "Allow Facebook, but block Facebook games." WAFs can detect and block disclosure of critical data, such as account numbers, credit card numbers, and so forth. WAFs can also be used to protect websites from common attack vectors such as cross-site scripting, fuzzing, and buffer overflow attacks.

A web application firewall can be configured to examine inside an SSL session. This is important if an attacker is attempting to use an SSL-encrypted channel to mask their activity. Because legitimate SSL channels are instantiated by the system, the appropriate credentials can be passed internally to the WAF to enable SSL inspection.

Application-aware Devices

Network security was developed before application-level security was even a concern, so application-level attacks are not seen or blocked by traditional network security defenses. The security industry has responded to the application attack vector with the introduction of application-aware devices. Firewalls, IDSs/IPSs, proxies, and other devices are now capable of doing stateful inspection of traffic and detecting and blocking application-level attacks as well as network-level attacks.

Next-Generation Firewalls

Next-generation firewalls is a term used to describe firewalls that are capable of content-level filtering and hence are capable of application-level monitoring. Depending on the level of programming and sophistication, next-generation firewalls can perform many advanced security checks based on defined application rules.

IDS/IPS

Intrusion detection and prevention systems perform their security tasks by screening network traffic and then applying a set of rules. When the process is application aware, the specificity of rules can be even more exacting. Adding advanced rule-processing power that manages both stateful and content-aware rule processing allows these devices to detect malicious attacks to applications based on the application, not just based on an address. The engines used for IDS/IPS are being incorporated into firewalls, turning a simple network firewall into a next-generation firewall.

Application-Level Proxies

Proxies serve to manage connections between systems, acting as relays for the traffic. Proxies can function at the circuit level, where they support multiple traffic types, or they can be application-level proxies, which are designed to relay specific application traffic. An HTTP proxy can manage an HTTP conversation, as it understands the type and function of the content. Application-specific proxies can serve as security devices if they are programmed with specific rules designed to provide protection against undesired content.

Chapter Review

This chapter described network devices and their configurations. Firewalls, routers, switches, sniffers, load balancers, proxies, web security gateways, and VPN concentrators were covered. Security devices, including intrusion detection systems, protocol analyzers, spam filters, and all-in-one security appliances, were presented. The chapter concluded with an examination of application-aware devices, including next-generation firewalls and web application firewalls.

Questions

To help you prepare further for the CompTIA Security+ exam, and to test your level of preparedness, answer the following questions and then check your answers against the correct answers at the end of the chapter.

1. What do load balancers use to determine if a host is operational?

   A. Logixn

   B. Request count

   C. Health checking

   D. Time To Live (TTL)

2. What is meant by the word "stateful" with respect to firewalls?

   A. The firewall tracks what country requests are from.

   B. Only packets matching an active connection are allowed through.

   C. Only packets that are addressed to the internal server are allowed through.

   D. The firewall keeps a list of all addresses to prevent spoofing of an internal IP address.

3. What is the primary difference between a proxy and a firewall?

   A. A proxy allows access, while a firewall denies access.

   B. A firewall uses a hardened operating system, while a proxy does not.

   C. A proxy makes application-level requests on behalf of internal users, while a firewall typically just passes through authorized traffic.

   D. A firewall is capable of successfully performing Network Address Translation for internal clients, while a proxy is forced to reveal internal addressing schemes.

4. Why is it important for a web application firewall to perform SSL inspection?

   A. A lack of SSL inspection would allow a channel of threats past the firewall.

   B. SSL inspection is only used when you know you are under attack.

   C. Inspecting the SSL traffic assists with load balancing.

   D. None of the above.

5. An anomaly-based NIPS will alert in which case?

   A. When the network traffic matches a known attack pattern

   B. When the network traffic deviates from a predefined traffic profile

   C. When attack traffic alerts on a host-based intrusion detection system, forwarding a network cookie to allow the intrusion prevention system to block the traffic

   D. When the network traffic changes from a configured traffic baseline

6. What is the best policy to use when administrating a firewall?

   A. Quality of service (QoS)

   B. Least access

   C. First-in, first-out (FIFO)

   D. Comprehensive

7. Why does a network protocol analyzer need to be in promiscuous mode?

   A. To avoid network ACLs

   B. To tell the switch to forward all packets to a workstation

   C. To force the network card to process all packets

   D. Promiscuous mode is not required.

8. Which protocol can create a security vulnerability in switches, firewalls, and routers because it authenticates using a cleartext password?

   A. SNMP

   B. SSH

   C. SMTP

   D. NAT

9. Why should most organizations use a content-filtering proxy?

   A. To allow users to browse the Internet anonymously

   B. To provide a secure tunnel to the Internet

   C. To enforce a network acceptable use policy

   D. To reduce bandwidth usage with local copies of popular content

10. Why is delay-based filtering effective against spam?

    A. Spam generators will not send spam if they cannot do it immediately.

    B. Spam generators do not wait for the SMTP banner.

    C. Spam generators are poorly behaved and will quickly move on to the next server.

    D. Spam has a very short TTL value.

For questions 11–14, use the following scenario: Suspecting that a hacker has broken through your company's perimeter systems, the CISO has asked you to perform the incident response. After the team is assembled, you decide to tackle the network portion.

11. Which logs should be examined to determine if an intruder breached internal systems? (Choose all that apply).

    A. Router   E. IDS

    B. Firewall   F. Spam filter

    C. Caching proxy   G. VPN concentrator

    D. Switch

12. You find that the attack has come through the router and firewall to an unidentified desktop machine. You have the IP addresses but not the traffic content. What is likely your next step?

    A. Disconnect the router from the Internet to prevent further attack progress.

    B. Use ACLs to drop the IP address the attack came from.

    C. Use a protocol analyzer to see current attack traffic.

    D. Turn the findings over to management.

13. From analyzing the network traffic, you have determined that the attack has compromised a desktop in the sales department and is now sending outbound spam e-mails. Which devices can be used to eliminate this traffic? (Choose all that apply).

    A. Router   E. IDS

    B. Firewall   F. Spam filter

    C. Caching proxy   G. VPN concentrator

    D. Switch

14. How would an intrusion detection system help you respond to this incident?

    A. It would provide an earlier warning that the attack was happening.

    B. It would give more details about the attacker.

    C. It would provide more complete logs than the current equipment in place.

    D. It would not help because it is not an intrusion prevention system.

15. List four models that intrusion detection systems can use to detect suspect traffic.

Answers

1. C. A load-balancing device will send a request to each server in its list as a health check to ensure the application is responding.

2. B. A stateful firewall keeps track of all active connections and prevents spoofing by recognizing when a packet is not part of any current connections.

3. C. A proxy works at the application layer, while a firewall generally works at the transport and network layers.

4. **A.** Performing SSL inspection is important because otherwise an attacker could use the SSL channel to get threats past the firewall uninspected.

5. **D.** An anomaly-based NIPS will alert when network traffic deviates from a baseline of traffic established when the device is first installed.

6. **B.** The principle of least access is best to use when administering a firewall; you want the firewall to block as much traffic as possible, while allowing the authorized traffic through.

7. **C.** Promiscuous mode tells the network adapter to process all packets it receives, not just the packets for its MAC address and broadcast packets.

8. **A.** Simple Network Management Protocol (SNMP) provides management functions to many network devices, but SNMPv1 and SNMPv2 authenticate with a cleartext password, allowing anyone monitoring packets to capture the password and have access to the network equipment.

9. **C.** Content-filtering proxies are popular with corporations because they allow for the enforcement of an acceptable use policy by filtering any content the authenticated user is not allowed to see.

10. **B.** Spam generators do not wait for the SMTP banner and can be identified as a spammer by behaving poorly.

11. **A, B,** and **E.** Router, Firewall, and IDS are the primary logs that should be checked to determine what the attacker's path and target were.

12. **C.** Since you are not sure of the attack content or if it is still ongoing, it is best to use a protocol analyzer to examine the traffic in question and determine what the specifics of the attack are and if it is still ongoing.

13. **A, B,** and **F.** Routers and firewalls are both designed to effectively filter any unwanted traffic out, and can filter any e-mail connections going out from the desktop. A spam filter can filter e-mail not only in the inbound direction, but also in the outbound direction if it is part of your outbound e-mail stream, which can be helpful in the case of a malware infection.

14. **A.** IDS systems are designed to recognize an attack as soon as it happens, provide warning the attack is happening, and allow a quick response to mitigate the attack.

15. The four models are behavior based, signature based, anomaly based, and heuristic.

Secure Network Administration

2

In this chapter, you will

- Apply secure network administration principles
- Learn about rule-based management systems, including firewalls and switches
- Examine network protection mechanisms

This chapter examines network security mechanisms, including network devices such as routers, switches, firewalls, and security appliances. Discussion of security mechanisms such as access control lists, port security, 802.1x, flood guards, loop protection, and network separation is included as well because they form the foundational methods used in secure network administration.

Secure Network Administration Principles

Networks are composed of a combination of hardware and software, operated under policies and procedures that define desired operating conditions. The principles of secure network administration include properly configuring hardware and software and properly performing operations and maintenance. All of these elements need to be done with security in mind, from planning, to design, to operation.

Rule-based Management

Rule-based management is a common methodology for configuring systems. Desired operational states are defined in such manner that they can be represented as rules, and a control enforces the rules in operation. This methodology is used for firewalls, proxies, switches, routers, anti-malware, IDS/IPS, and more. As each packet is presented to the control device, the set of rules is applied and interpreted. This is an efficient manner of translating policy objectives into operational use.

Firewall Rules

Firewalls operate by enforcing a set of rules on the traffic attempting to pass. This set of rules, the firewall ruleset, is a mirror of the policy constraints at a particular point in the network. Thus, the ruleset will vary from firewall to firewall, as it is the operational implementation of the desired traffic constraints at each point. Firewall rules state whether the firewall should allow particular traffic to pass through or block it. The structure of a firewall rule can range from simple to very complex, depending upon the type of firewall and the type of traffic. A packet filter firewall can act on IP addresses and ports, either allowing or blocking based on this information. A stateful packet inspection firewall can act upon the state condition of a conversation—is this a new conversation or a continuation of a conversation, and did it originate inside or outside the firewall? Application layer firewalls can analyze traffic at an even deeper level, examining the application characteristics of traffic and blocking specific actions while allowing others, even inside web-connected applications.

 EXAM TIP Firewalls operate by examining packets and selectively denying some based on a set of rules. Firewalls act as traffic gatekeepers, or sentries, at select network points, allowing some packets to pass and blocking others.

All firewall rulesets should include an implicit deny rule that is in place to prevent any traffic from passing that is not specifically recognized as allowed. Firewalls execute their rules upon traffic in a top-down manner, with any allow or block rule whose conditions are met ending the processing. This means the order of rules is important. It also means that the last rule should be a deny all rule, for any traffic that gets to the last rule and has not met a rule allowing it to pass should be blocked.

VLAN Management

Another security feature that can be enabled in some switches is the concept of virtual local area networks (VLANs). Cisco defines a VLAN as a "broadcast domain within a switched network," meaning that information is carried in broadcast mode only to devices within a VLAN. Switches that allow multiple VLANs to be defined enable broadcast messages to be segregated into the specific VLANs. If each floor of an office, for example, were to have a single switch, with accounting functions on two floors, engineering functions on two floors, and sales functions on two floors, then separate VLANs for accounting, engineering, and sales would allow separate broadcast domains for each of these groups, even those that spanned floors. This configuration increases network segregation, increasing throughput and security.

Unused switch ports can be preconfigured into empty VLANs that do not connect to the rest of the network. This significantly increases security against unauthorized network connections. If, for example, a building is wired with network connections in all rooms, including multiple connections for convenience and future expansion, these unused ports become open to the network. One solution is to disconnect the connection at the switch, but this merely moves the network opening into the switch room. The better solution is to disconnect it and disable the port in the switch. This can be accomplished by connecting all unused ports into a VLAN that isolates them from the rest of the network.

VLANs can also be used to segregate traffic used to manage the network devices. A management VLAN is configured to allow remote access to the switch through Telnet, SSH, or a web interface built into the switch. It is important to note that VLANs are not as secure as VPNs, and thus you should not rely on a VLAN to protect sensitive data. For this reason, management VLANs are not always the best solution.

Secure Router Configuration

As discussed in Chapter 1, a serious operational security concern regarding routers is the access to and control of its internal functions. Like many network devices, a router can be accessed using SNMP and Telnet and can be programmed remotely. Because Telnet is plaintext, it is by nature not secure from eavesdropping. For secure access, a method such as Secure Shell (SSH) should be used. Because of the geographic separation of routers, remote access is a necessity, for many routers in the world of the Internet can be hundreds of miles apart in separate locked structures.

Physical control over a router is absolutely necessary, for if any device, be it server, switch, or router, is physically accessed by a hacker, it should be considered compromised; thus, such access must be prevented. As with all network devices, it is important to ensure that the administrative password is never passed in the clear, that only secure mechanisms are used to access the router, and that all of the default passwords are reset to strong passwords.

Just like switches, the most assured point of access for router management control is via the serial control interface port. This allows access to the control aspects of the router without having to deal with traffic-related issues. For internal company networks, where the geographic dispersion of routers may be limited, third-party solutions to allow out-of-band remote management exist. This allows complete control over the router in a secure fashion, even from a remote location, although additional hardware is required.

 EXAM TIP To connect to a router for the purpose of configuration, always employ a secure connection. Avoid plaintext connections such as Telnet, as they can expose credentials to eavesdroppers.

Access Control Lists

Access control lists (ACLs) are lists of users and their permitted actions. Users can be identified in a variety of ways, including by a user ID, a network address, or a token. The simple objective is to create a lookup system that allows a device to determine which actions are permitted and which are denied. A router can contain an ACL that lists permitted addresses or blocked addresses, or a combination of both. The most common implementation is for file systems, where named user IDs are used to determine which file system attributes are permitted to the user. This same general concept is reused across all types of devices and situations in networking.

Just as the implicit deny rule applies to firewall rulesets, discussed earlier in the chapter, the explicit deny principle can be applied to ACLs. When using this approach to ACL building, allowed traffic must be explicitly allowed by a **permit** statement. All of the specific **permit** commands are followed by a **deny all** statement in the ruleset. ACL entries are typically evaluated in a top-to-bottom fashion, so any traffic that does not match a "**permit**" entry will be dropped by a "**deny all**" statement placed as the last line in the ACL.

Port Security

Port security is a capability provided by switches that enables you to control which devices and how many of them are allowed to connect via each port on a switch. Port security operates through the use of MAC addresses. Although not perfect—MAC addresses can be spoofed—port security can provide useful network security functionality.

Port security has three variants:

- **Static learning**   A specific MAC address is assigned to a port. This is useful for fixed, dedicated hardware connections. The disadvantage is that the MAC addresses need to be known and programmed in advance, making this good for defined connections but not good for visiting connections.

- **Dynamic learning**   Allows the switch to learn MAC addresses when they connect. Dynamic learning is useful when you expect a small, limited number of machines to connect to a port.

- **Sticky learning**   Also allows multiple devices to a port, but also stores the information in memory that persists through reboots. This prevents the attacker from changing settings through power cycling the switch.

802.1x

IEEE 802.1x is an authentication standard that supports communications between a user and an authorization device, such as an edge router. IEEE 802.1x is used by all types of networks, including Ethernet, Token Ring, and wireless. This standard describes methods used to authenticate a user prior to granting access to an authentication server, such as a RADIUS server. 802.1x acts through an intermediate device, such as an edge switch, enabling ports to carry normal traffic if the connection is properly authenticated. This prevents unauthorized clients from accessing the publicly available ports on a switch, keeping unauthorized users out of a LAN. Until a client has successfully authenticated itself to the device, only Extensible Authentication Protocol over LAN (EAPOL) traffic is passed by the switch.

EAPOL is an encapsulated method of passing Extensible Authentication Protocol (EAP) messages over 802 frames. EAP is a general protocol that can support multiple methods of authentication, including one-time passwords, Kerberos, public keys, and security device methods such as smart cards. Once a client successfully authenticates itself to the 802.1x device, the switch opens ports for normal traffic. At this point, the client can communicate with the system's authentication, authorization, and accounting (AAA) method, such as a RADIUS server, and authenticate itself to the network.

Flood Guards

One form of attack is a flood. There are numerous types of flooding attacks: ping floods, SYN floods, Internet Control Message Protocol (ICMP) floods (Smurf attacks), and traffic flooding. Flooding attacks are used as a form of denial of service to a network or system. Detecting flooding attacks is relatively easy, but there is a difference between detecting the attack and mitigating the attack. Flooding can be actively managed through dropping connections or managing traffic. Flood guards act by managing traffic flows. By monitoring the traffic rate and percentage of bandwidth occupied by broadcast, multicast, and unicast traffic, a flood guard can detect when to block traffic to manage flooding.

 EXAM TIP   Flood guards are commonly implemented in firewalls and IDS/IPS systems to prevent DoS and DDoS attacks.

Loop Protection

Switches operate at layer 2 of the OSI model, and at this level there is no countdown mechanism to kill packets that get caught in loops or on paths that will never resolve. The layer 2 space acts as a mesh, where potentially the addition of a new device can create loops in the existing device interconnections. Open Shortest Path First (OSPF) is a link-state routing protocol that is commonly used between gateways in a single autonomous system. To prevent loops, a technology called spanning trees is employed by virtually all switches. The Spanning Tree Protocol (STP) allows for multiple redundant paths, while breaking loops to ensure a proper broadcast pattern. STP is a data link layer protocol, and is approved as IEEE standard 802.1D. It acts by trimming connections that are not part of the spanning tree connecting all of the nodes.

Implicit Deny

Implicit deny is a key security principle. If an action is not specifically permitted, then the action should be denied. This prevents unknown conditions from propagating through a system. Frequently used in rule-based systems, implicit deny is enacted by making the last rule be deny all. This means that if one of the previous permitted action rules has not been triggered, then the proposed action is clearly not one of the approved actions and thus should be blocked.

Network Separation

Separating network traffic into separate communication zones can enhance security. Traffic can be separated using bridges, switches, and VLANs. Traffic separation prevents sensitive traffic from being sniffed by limiting the range over which the traffic travels. Keeping highly sensitive traffic separated from areas of the network where less trusted traffic and access may occur prevents the inadvertent disclosure by traffic interception. Network separation can be used to keep development, testing, and production networks separated, preventing accidental cross-pollination of changes.

Log Analysis

Most managed network devices can log a variety of conditions. These log entries can provide significant information as to network operation, traffic conditions, and conditions such as attacks and compromise. This logged information is only useful if the logs are analyzed and examined for the hints that they contain. Logs seldom contain the exact information that is desired. What they do contain are hints and clues, data that needs to be analyzed and reconstructed into useful information.

Unified Threat Management

Unified threat management (UTM) is a marketing term used to describe all-in-one devices employed in network security. UTM devices typically provide a wide range of services, including switching, firewall, IDS/IPS, anti-malware, anti-spam, content filtering, and traffic shaping. These devices are designed to simplify security administration and are targeted for small and midsized networks. Because of the wide range of services they provide, they are typically located at the edge of the network, managing traffic in and out of the network.

Chapter Review

This chapter opened with an examination of secure network administration principles, including access control lists, port security, 802.1x, flood guards, loop protection, and network separation. The chapter then examined network security mechanisms, including network devices such as routers, switches, firewalls, and security appliances. Finally, security mechanisms, including log analysis, implicit deny, VLAN management, and rule-based security mechanisms, were presented to illustrate operational controls.

Questions

To help you prepare further for the CompTIA Security+ exam, and to test your level of preparedness, answer the following questions and then check your answers against the correct answers at the end of the chapter.

1. Flood guard functionality might protect against which of the following attacks?

    A. Smurf attack

    B. Address spoofing

    C. Brute force

    D. SQL injection

2. When building an access control list under an explicit deny approach, where would you place a "deny all" statement?

    A. At the beginning of the ACL entries

    B. Before any ACLs entries dealing with HTTP traffic

    C. At the end of the ACL entries

    D. On the ingress filter

3. Which of the following protocols is not used in loop protection efforts?

    A. Multiple Spanning Tree

    B. Rapid Spanning Tree

    C. Spanning Tree

    D. Open Shortest Path First

4. 802.1x defines the encapsulation of EAP. What is EAP?

    A. Extensible Autonomous Protocol

    B. Extensible Authentication Protocol

    C. Extended Authentication Protocol

    D. Encapsulation Authentication Protocol

5. A management VLAN allows administrators to do which of the following?

    A. Connect to the switch remotely

    B. Bundle VLANs based on traffic priority

    C. Copy all packets passing through the switch

    D. Automatically reorder VLANs based on time of day

6. In ACLs, an implicit deny will apply to network traffic that:

    A. Matches two or more rules in the ACL

    B. Does not match any entry in the ACL

    C. Originates from inside the DMZ

    D. Comes from a spoofed source address

7. Which of the following is not a best practice for secure router configuration?

    A. Disabling echo, CHARGEN, and other simple services

    B. Disabling IP source route

    C. Enabling Telnet access

    D. Enabling logging

8. When enabling port security on a switch interface, traffic is usually restricted based on:

    A. IP addresses

    B. Source port

    C. Protocol

    D. MAC addresses

9. Network separation is used primarily to:

   A. Maximize performance

   B. Limit the required number of SPAN ports

   C. Separate networks for security reasons

   D. Facilitate logging of suspicious traffic

10. A unified threat management appliance would most likely be placed:

   A. In a network operations center

   B. At the edge of the corporate network

   C. Inside the development network

   D. Between development and production networks

11. Your corporate firewall has the following rules applied to the incoming interface on the DMZ. If you need to block all web traffic from a malicious source IP address, where would you place an explicit deny statement for that malicious source IP address?

```
10   Permit SRC IP any DST IP 192.168.1.4 SRC PORT any DST PORT 80
20   Permit SRC IP any DST IP 192.168.1.5 SRC PORT any DST PORT 25
30   Permit SRC IP any DST IP 192.168.1.15 SRC PORT any DST PORT 443
40   Deny ANY ANY
```

   A. Between line 30 and 40

   B. Between line 20 and 30

   C. Between line 10 and 20

   D. Before line 10

12. You've been asked to help configure a router that is used to connect a remote branch office to your corporate headquarters. The router will need to be managed remotely from the corporate headquarters. Which of the following protocols would you recommend be used to manage the remote router?

   A. HTTP

   B. Telnet

   C. SSH

   D. SNMP

13. You are enabling port security on a switch that handles connections for your company's customer help desk. Company policy prohibits employees from connecting personal devices to the corporate network. To help ensure that only corporate computer systems are connected, what type of port security would you select?

   A. Static method

   B. Dynamic learning

C. Sticky method

D. LIFO method

14. Your company has a policy to not allow any connection from overseas addresses to its network. Which security mechanism is best to employ to accomplish this goal?

    A. VLAN management

    B. Access control lists

    C. Implicit deny

    D. Network separation

15. During your investigation of a security breach, you discover the corporate fileserver is connected to a VLAN that is accessible to systems in the development environment. This violates which security principle?

    A. VLAN management

    B. Least privilege

    C. Network separation

    D. Loop protection

Answers

1. **A.** Flood guard functionality is designed to protect against ping floods, port floods, and distributed denial-of-service attacks. A Smurf attack is a denial-of-service attack where an attacker sends ICMP packets with the victim's spoofed source IP address to a network broadcast address. The result is a flood of ICMP response packets targeted at the victim.

2. **C.** When using an "explicit deny" approach to ACL building, allowed traffic must be explicitly allowed by a permit statement. As ACL entries are typically evaluated in a top-to-bottom fashion, any traffic that does not match a "permit" entry will be dropped by a "deny all" statement placed as the last line in the ACL.

3. **D.** Open Shortest Path First (OSPF) is a link-state routing protocol that is commonly used between gateways in a single autonomous system.

4. **B.** In the context of 802.1x, EAP stands for the Extensible Authentication Protocol (EAP).

5. **A.** A management VLAN is configured to allow remote access to the switch through Telnet, SSH, or a web interface built into the switch.

6. **B.** In access control lists, an implicit deny is the "catch-all" rule at the end of the access list entries. All traffic will match the implicit deny rule, so any traffic that is not permitted by a previous line in the ACL will reach the end of the ACL and be denied. In certain firewalls and routers, the implicit deny rule is automatically enforced by the system at the end of every ACL.

7. **C.** Telnet is a cleartext protocol, meaning that anyone who can intercept the traffic can "see" inside the traffic. Telnet passes user IDs, passwords, and commands in cleartext and is inherently an insecure protocol. Telnet should be disabled on all routers, firewalls, and switches.

8. **D.** Port security allows you to restrict traffic based on MAC addresses.

9. **C.** Network separation is used primarily to separate networks for security purposes. For example, an organization may physically or logically separate the development environment from the production environment. Or a network passing sensitive traffic may be physically separated from a network used to provide public access to Internet-based services.

10. **B.** Unified threat management is the concept of combining multiple security services into a single device. For example, a UTM appliance might serve as a firewall, anti-virus solution, VPN gateway, load balancer, and content filter. Due to the functionality they provide, UTM appliances are most typically placed at the edge of the corporate network, where they can examine traffic entering and leaving the network.

11. **D.** Line 10 allows any source IP address to connect to a web server inside your DMZ on port 80. If you need to block *all* web traffic from a malicious source IP address, your explicit deny statement must come before line 10.

12. **C.** Of the protocols listed, SSH is the most secure choice for remote management of a router. SSH allows for remote command-line login, remote command execution, and other secure network services in an encrypted session.

13. **A.** The static method of port security would enable you to specifically define the MAC addresses that are allowed to connect to each port of the switch. This would enable you to ensure that only corporate assets with approved MAC addresses could connect to the network through that switch.

14. **B.** The use of an access control list at the edge device is a manner in which selected IP addresses can be blocked from access, either at a router or at a firewall.

15. **C.** Having production and development assets interconnected is a violation of the network separation principle. Physically or logically separating networks used for development and networks used for production is a security best practice.

Secure Network Design

In this chapter, you will

- Study network design elements
- Explore network components
- Discover how subnets are created
- Learn how to implement common protocols
- Learn how to implement common services

Secure network design is an objective that has component elements in hardware, software, and policies and procedures. Proper design begins with understanding the objectives of the network. The proper implementation and use of protocols are discussed with respect to achieving the design objectives.

Network Design Elements and Components

Unlike single servers, networks exist as connections of multiple devices. A key characteristic of a network is its layout, or *topology*. A proper network topology takes security into consideration and assists in "building security" into the network. Security-related topologies include separating portions of the network by use and function, strategically designing in points to monitor for IDS systems, building in redundancy, and adding fault-tolerant aspects.

 EXAM TIP This chapter is about designing networks with components. During the exam, it is expected that you will be familiar with basic network design elements and components.

DMZ Security Zones

The first aspect of security is a layered defense. Just as a castle has a moat, an outside wall, an inside wall, and even a keep, so, too, does a modern secure network have different layers of protection. Different zones are designed to provide layers of defense, with the outermost layers providing basic protection and the innermost layers providing the highest level of protection. A constant issue is that accessibility tends to be inversely related to level of protection, so it is more difficult to provide complete protection and unfettered access at the same time. Trade-offs between access and security are handled through zones, with successive zones guarded by firewalls enforcing ever-increasingly strict security policies.

The outermost zone is the Internet, a free area, beyond any specific controls. Between the inner, secure corporate network and the Internet is an area where machines are considered at risk. This zone has come to be called the *DMZ*, after its military counterpart, the demilitarized zone, where neither side has any specific controls. Within the inner, secure network, separate branches are frequently carved out to provide specific functional areas.

DMZ

The DMZ is a military term for ground separating two opposing forces, by agreement and for the purpose of acting as a buffer between the two sides. A DMZ in a computer network is used in the same way; it acts as a buffer zone between the Internet, where no controls exist, and the inner, secure network, where an organization has security policies in place (see Figure 3-1). To demarcate the zones and enforce separation, a firewall is used on each side of the DMZ. The area between these firewalls is accessible from either the inner, secure network or the Internet. Figure 3-1 illustrates these zones as caused by firewall placement. The firewalls are specifically designed to prevent access across the DMZ directly from the Internet to the inner, secure network.

Special attention should be paid to the security settings of network devices placed in the DMZ, and they should be considered at all times to be compromised by unauthorized use. A common industry term, *hardened operating system*, applies to machines whose functionality is locked down to preserve security. This approach needs to be applied to the machines in the DMZ, and although it means that their functionality is limited, such precautions ensure that the machines will work properly in a less secure environment.

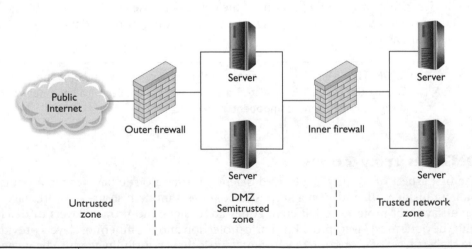

Figure 3-1 The DMZ and zones of trust

Many types of servers belong in this area, including web servers that are serving content to Internet users, as well as remote-access servers and external e-mail servers. In general, any server directly accessed from the outside, untrusted Internet zone needs to be in the DMZ. Other servers should not be placed in the DMZ. Domain name servers for your inner, trusted network and database servers that house corporate databases should not be accessible from the outside. Application servers, file servers, print servers—all of the standard servers used in the trusted network—should be behind both firewalls, plus routers and switches used to connect these machines.

The idea behind the use of the DMZ topology is to force an outside user to make at least one hop in the DMZ before he can access information inside the trusted network. If the outside user makes a request for a resource from the trusted network, such as a data element from a database via a web page, then this request needs to follow this scenario:

1. A user from the untrusted network (the Internet) requests data via a web page from a web server in the DMZ.

2. The web server in the DMZ requests the data from the application server, which can be in the DMZ or in the inner, trusted network.

3. The application server requests the data from the database server in the trusted network.

4. The database server returns the data to the requesting application server.

5. The application server returns the data to the requesting web server.

6. The web server returns the data to the requesting user from the untrusted network.

This separation accomplishes two specific, independent tasks. First, the user is separated from the request for data on a secure network. By having intermediaries do the requesting, this layered approach allows significant security levels to be enforced. Users do not have direct access or control over their requests, and this filtering process can put controls in place. Second, scalability is more easily realized. The multiple-server solution can be made to be very scalable, literally to millions of users, without slowing down any particular layer.

 EXAM TIP DMZs act as a buffer zone between unprotected areas of a network (the Internet) and protected areas (sensitive company data stores), allowing for the monitoring and regulation of traffic between these two zones.

Subnetting

An IP address (IPv4) consists of two parts, a network address and a host address, combined in a 32-bit number. The higher-order bits represent the network address, and the lower, or remaining bits, represent the host address. The point of separation is defined

Class	Addresses per Network	Number of Networks	Subnet Mask
Class A	16,777,214	128	255.0.0.0
Class B	65,534	16,384	255.255.0.0
Class C	254	2,097,152	255.255.255.0

Table 3-1 IPv4 Network Classes and Subnet Masks

as a subnet mask. Initially, the IPv4 address space was divided into a series of address ranges, based on some standard separations, as detailed in Table 3-1. Over time, this was deemed too restrictive and a new scheme called Classless Inter-Domain Routing (CIDR) was developed. CIDR allows the partitioning of the IPv4 address space into user-definable chunks, allowing greater flexibility.

CIDR allows address blocks to be broken into smaller networks referred to as subnets. Beginning with a Class C address, such as 192.168.x.x, CIDR can break it into a series of networks. If it is desired to break it into two networks, then the highest-order bit of the host space becomes a network address bit; this makes the new subnet mask 255.255.128.0. The effect is to use 17 bits for network addressing and 15 bits for hosts. CIDR uses a notation where the network address bits are marked with a "/" sign, so this example would be 192.168.x.x/17. This is the same as saying the subnet mask is 255.255.128.0. The resulting set of host addresses would be 192.168.0.1 through 192.168.127.254 on one network and 192.168.128.1 through 192.168.255.254 on the other. If you need three subnets, you will need to use 2 bits for four subnets, as the number of subnets will increase by powers of two. This may result in unused subnets, but it is unavoidable.

CIDR can either create a subnet, which is part of a class network, or a supernet, which is larger than a class network. Table 3-2 illustrates the relationships between a class network, a subnet, and a supernet. It might be confusing, but as the CIDR mask number increases, the number of networks goes down and the number of hosts goes up.

In Table 3-2 note that the number of usable hosts is two less than the mathematical number of hosts. This is because the addresses that end in all zeros or all ones are broadcast addresses—that is, addresses that target all hosts. So the .0 and .255 addresses in this example are not individual machines.

VLAN

A local area network (LAN) is a set of devices with similar functionality and similar communication needs, typically co-located and operated off a single switch. This is the lowest level of a network hierarchy and defines the domain for certain protocols at

CIDR Notation	Mask	Number of Usable Hosts	Size
X.X.X.X/25	255.255.255.128	126	Half of a Class C subnet
X.X.X.X/24	255.255.255.0	254	Class C subnet
X.X.X.X/23	255.255.254.0	510	Two Class C subnets

Table 3-2 CIDR Subnets and Supernets

the data link layer for communication. Virtual LANs (VLANs) use a single switch and divide it into multiple broadcast domains and/or multiple network segments, known as *trunking*. This very powerful technique allows significant network flexibility, scalability, and performance.

Trunking

Trunking is the process of spanning a single VLAN across multiple switches. A trunk-based connection between switches allows packets from a single VLAN to travel between switches, as shown in Figure 3-2. Two trunks are shown in the figure: VLAN 10 is implemented with one trunk, and VLAN 20 is implemented by the other. Hosts on different VLANs cannot communicate using trunks and are switched across the switch network. Trunks enable network administrators to set up VLANs across multiple switches with minimal effort. With a combination of trunks and VLANs, network administrators can subnet a network by user functionality without regard to host location on the network or the need to re-cable machines.

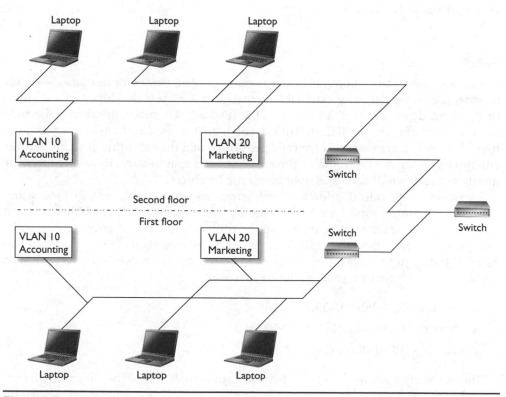

Figure 3-2 VLANs and trunks

Security Implications

VLANs are used to divide a single network into multiple subnets based on functionality. This permits engineering and accounting, for example, to share a switch because of proximity and yet have separate traffic domains. The physical placement of equipment and cables is logically and programmatically separated so adjacent ports on a switch can reference separate subnets. This prevents unauthorized use of physically close devices through separate subnets but the same equipment. VLANs also allow a network administrator to define a VLAN that has no users and map all of the unused ports to this VLAN. Then if an unauthorized user should gain access to the equipment, he will be unable to use unused ports, as those ports will be securely defined to nothing. Both a purpose and a security strength of VLANs is that systems on separate VLANs cannot directly communicate with each other.

CAUTION Trunks and VLANs have security implications that need to be heeded so that firewalls and other segmentation devices are not breached through their use. They also require understanding of their use to prevent an unauthorized user from reconfiguring them to gain undetected access to secure portions of a network.

NAT

Network Address Translation (NAT) uses two sets of IP addresses for resources—one for internal use and another for external (Internet) use. NAT was developed as a solution to the rapid depletion of IP addresses in the IPv4 address space; it has since become an Internet standard (see RFC 1631 for details). NAT is used to translate between the two addressing schemes and is typically performed at a firewall or router. This permits enterprises to use the nonroutable private IP address space internally and reduces the number of external IP addresses used across the Internet.

Three sets of private IP addresses are defined as nonroutable, which means that addresses will not be routed across the Internet. These addresses are routable internally, and routers can be set to route them, but the routers across the Internet are set to discard packets sent to these addresses. This approach enables a separation of internal and external traffic and allows these addresses to be reused by anyone and everyone who wishes to do so. The three private address spaces are

- **Class A**   10.0.0.0–10.255.255.255
- **Class B**   172.16.0.0–172.31.255.255
- **Class C**   192.168.0.0–192.168.255.255

The use of these addresses inside a network is unrestricted, and they function like any other IP addresses. When outside—that is, Internet-provided—resources are needed for one of these addresses, NAT is required to produce a valid external IP address for the resource. NAT operates by translating the address when traffic passes the NAT device, such as a firewall. The external addresses used are not externally mappable 1:1 to the internal addresses, for this would defeat the purpose of reuse and address-space conservation. Typically, a pool of external IP addresses is used by the NAT device, with the device keeping track of which internal address is using which external address at any given time. This provides a significant layer of security, as it makes it difficult to map the internal network structure behind a firewall and directly address it from the outside. NAT is one of the methods used for enforcing perimeter security by forcing users to access resources through defined pathways such as firewalls and gateway servers.

Several techniques are used to accomplish NAT. Basic NAT, also called *static NAT*, offers a 1:1 binding of external address to internal address; it is needed for services for which external sources reference internal sources, such as web servers or e-mail servers. For DMZ resources that reference outside resources, addresses can be shared through *dynamic* NAT, in which a table is constructed and used by the edge device to manage the translation. As the address translation can change over time, the table changes as well. Even finer-grained control can be obtained through Port Address Translation (PAT), where actual TCP/UDP ports are translated as well. This will enable a single external IP address to serve two internal IP addresses through the use of ports. Resources that need long-running NAT but only specific ports—such as a web server on port 80 or e-mail on port 25—can share a single external IP address, thereby conserving resources.

Remote Access

Remote access is the connection to a device from across the network. There are a variety of protocols that can be used to enable remote access. Remote Access Service (RAS) is a portion of the Windows OS that allows the connection between a client and a server via a dial-up telephone connection. Although slower than cable/DSL connections, this is still a common method for connecting to a remote network. When a user dials into the computer system, authentication and authorization are performed through a series of remote-access protocols. For even greater security, a callback system can be employed, where the server calls back to the client at a set telephone number for the data exchange. RAS can also mean Remote Access Server, a term for a server designed to permit remote users access to a network and to regulate their access. Today, remote access is commonly accomplished through the use of secure VPNs and remote desktop software.

Telephony

Data and voice communications have coexisted in enterprises for decades. Recent connections inside the enterprise of Voice over IP (VoIP) and traditional private branch exchange (PBX) solutions increase both functionality and security risks. Specific firewalls to protect against unauthorized traffic over telephony connections are available to counter the increased risk.

A PBX is an extension of the public telephone network into a business. Although typically considered a separate entity from data systems, PBXs are frequently interconnected and have security requirements as part of this interconnection as well as security requirements of their own. PBXs are computer-based switching equipment designed to connect telephones into the local phone system. Basically digital switching systems, they can be compromised from the outside and used by phone hackers (*phreakers*) to make phone calls at the business's expense. Although this type of hacking has decreased with the availability of lower-cost long distance, it has not gone away, and as several firms learn every year, voicemail boxes and PBXs can be compromised and the long-distance bills can get very high, very fast.

Another problem with PBXs arises when they are interconnected to the data systems, either by corporate connection or by rogue modems in the hands of users. In either case, a path exists for connections to outside data networks and the Internet. Just as a firewall is needed for security on data connections, one is needed for these connections as well. Telecommunications firewalls are a distinct type of firewall designed to protect both the PBX and the data connections. The functionality of a telecommunications firewall is the same as that of a data firewall: it is there to enforce security policies. Tele-communication security policies can be enforced even to cover hours of phone use to prevent unauthorized long-distance usage through the implementation of access codes and/or restricted service hours.

Network Access Control (NAC)

Networks comprise connected workstations and servers. Managing security on a net-work involves managing a wide range of issues, from various connected hardware and the software operating these devices. Assuming that the network is secure, each addi-tional connection involves risk. Managing the endpoints on a case-by-case basis as they connect is a security methodology known as network access control. Two main compet-ing methodologies exist: Network Access Protection (NAP) is a Microsoft technology for controlling network access of a computer host, and Network Admission Control (NAC) is Cisco's technology for controlling network admission.

Microsoft's NAP system is based on measuring the system health of the connecting machine, including patch levels of the OS, antivirus protection, and system policies. NAP was first utilized in Windows XP Service Pack 3, Windows Vista, and Windows Server 2008, and it requires additional infrastructure servers to implement the health checks. The system includes enforcement agents that interrogate clients and verify admission criteria. The client side is initiated whenever network connections are made. Response options include rejection of the connection request or restriction of admis-sion to a subnet.

Cisco's NAC system is built around an appliance that enforces policies chosen by the network administrator. A series of third-party solutions can interface with the appliance, allowing the verification of a whole host of options, including client policy settings, software updates, and client security posture. The use of third-party devices and soft-ware makes this an extensible system across a wide range of equipment.

Both Cisco NAC and Microsoft NAP are in their early stages of adoption. The client pieces are all in place, but enterprises have been slow to fully deploy the server side of this technology. The concept of automated admission checking based on client device characteristics is here to stay, as it provides timely control in the ever-changing network world of today's enterprises. With the rise of bring your own device (BYOD) in the enterprise, there is renewed interest in using NAC to assist in protecting the network from unsafe devices.

Virtualization

Virtualization is the creation of virtual systems rather than actual hardware and software. The separation of the hardware and software enables increased flexibility in the enterprise. On top of actual hardware, a virtualization layer enables the creation of complete systems, including computers and networking equipment as virtual machines. This separation of hardware and software enables security through a series of improvements. The ability to copy entire systems, back them up, or move them between hardware platforms can add to the security of a system.

One of the useful elements associated with virtualization is the concept of a *snapshot*. A snapshot is a point-in-time image of a system. Snapshots enable a host of useful functionality. Snapshots allow a system to return to a previous point in time. Snapshots enable faster backups, faster recoveries, and a means to make systems more stable.

Although vulnerabilities exist that can possibly allow processes in one virtual environment to breach the separation between virtual environments or the layer to the host, these are rare and exceptionally difficult to exploit. A new form of vulnerability—the ability to make copies of complete virtual systems—must be addressed, as this could lead to data and intellectual property loss. Protecting the storage of virtual systems must be on par with backups of regular systems to avoid wholesale loss.

Cloud Computing

Cloud computing is a common term used to describe computer services provided over a network. These computing services are computing, storage, applications, and services that are offered via the Internet Protocol. One of the characteristics of cloud computing is transparency to the end user. This improves usability of this form of service provisioning. Cloud computing offers much to the user: improvements in performance, scalability, flexibility, security, and reliability, among other items. These improvements are a direct result of the specific attributes associated with how cloud services are implemented.

Security is a particular challenge when data and computation are handled by a remote party, as in cloud computing. The specific challenge is how to allow data outside your enterprise and yet remain in control over the use of the data. The common answer is encryption. Through the proper use of encryption of data before it leaves the enterprise, external storage can still be performed securely by properly employing cryptographic elements.

Clouds can be created by many entities, internal and external to an organization. Commercial cloud services are already available, and are offered from a variety of firms as large as Google and Amazon, to smaller, local providers. Internal services in a firm can replicate the advantages of cloud computing while improving the utility of limited resources. The promise of cloud computing is improved utility and is marketed under the concepts of Platform as a Service, Software as a Service, and Infrastructure as a Service.

Use of cloud services is already becoming mainstream with ordinary users through such services as iCloud (Apple), OneDrive (formerly SkyDrive), and file services such as Dropbox. These are easy to use, easy to configure, and provide the basic services desired with minimal user difficulty.

Platform as a Service

Platform as a Service (PaaS) is a marketing term used to describe the offering of a computing platform in the cloud. Multiple sets of software working together to provide services, such as database services, can be delivered via the cloud as a platform. PaaS offerings generally focus on security and scalability, both of which are characteristics that fit with cloud and platform needs.

Software as a Service

Software as a Service (SaaS) is the offering of software to end users from within the cloud. Rather than installing software on client machines, SaaS acts as software on demand, where the software runs from the cloud. This has several advantages: updates can be seamless to end users, and integration between components can be enhanced. Common examples of SaaS are products that are offered via the Web by subscription services, such as Microsoft Office 365 and Adobe Creative Suite.

Infrastructure as a Service

Infrastructure as a Service (IaaS) is a term used to describe cloud-based systems that are delivered as a virtual platform for computing. Rather than building data centers, IaaS allows firms to contract for utility computing as needed. IaaS is specifically marketed on a pay-per-use basis, scalable directly with need.

 EXAM TIP   Be sure you understand the differences between cloud computing service models Platform as a Service, Software as a Service, and Infrastructure as a Service.

Private

If your organization is highly sensitive to sharing resources, you may wish to consider the use of a private cloud. Private clouds are essentially reserved resources used only for your organization—your own little cloud within the cloud. This service will be considerably more expensive, but it should also carry less exposure and should enable your organization to better define the security, processing, handling of data, and so on that occurs within your cloud.

Public

The term *public cloud* refers to when the cloud service is rendered over a system that is open for public use. In most cases, there is little operational difference between public and private cloud architectures, but the security ramifications can be substantial.

Although public cloud services will separate users with security restrictions, the depth and level of these restrictions, by definition, will be significantly less in a public cloud.

Hybrid

A hybrid cloud structure is one where elements are combined from private, public, and community cloud structures. When examining a hybrid structure, you need to remain cognizant that operationally these differing environments may not actually be joined, but rather used together. Sensitive information can be stored in the private cloud and issue-related information can be stored in the community cloud, all of which information is accessed by an application. This makes the overall system a hybrid cloud system.

Community

A community cloud system is one where several organizations with a common interest share a cloud environment for the specific purposes of the shared endeavor. For example, local public entities and key local firms may share a community cloud dedicated to serving the interests of community initiatives. This can be an attractive cost-sharing mechanism for specific data-sharing initiatives.

Layered Security/Defense in Depth

Secure network design relies upon many elements, a key one being defense in depth. Defense in depth is a security principle by which multiple, differing security elements are employed to increase the level of security. Should an attacker be able to bypass one security measure, one of the overlapping controls can still catch and block the intrusion. In networking, a series of defenses, including access control lists, firewalls, intrusion detection systems, and network segregation, can be employed in an overlapping fashion to achieve protection.

Protocols

Protocols act as a common language, allowing different components to talk using a common, known set of commands. Many different protocols exist, all of which are used to achieve specific communication goals.

EXAM TIP   During the exam, you should expect to be asked to implement common protocols and services when given a basic scenario.

IPsec

IPsec is a set of protocols developed by the IETF to securely exchange packets at the network layer (layer 3) of the OSI model (RFCs 2401–2412). Although these protocols work only in conjunction with IP networks, once an IPsec connection is established, it is possible to tunnel across other networks at lower levels of the OSI model. The set of security services provided by IPsec occurs at the network layer of the OSI model, so higher-layer protocols, such as TCP, UDP, Internet Control Message Protocol (ICMP), Border Gateway Protocol (BGP), and the like, are not functionally altered by the implementation of IPsec services.

The IPsec protocol series has a sweeping array of services it is designed to provide, including but not limited to access control, connectionless integrity, traffic-flow confidentiality, rejection of replayed packets, data security (encryption), and data-origin authentication. IPsec has two defined methods—transport and tunneling—that provide different levels of security. IPsec also has three modes of connection: host-to-server, server-to-server, and host-to-host.

The transport method encrypts only the data portion of a packet, thus enabling an outsider to see source and destination IP addresses. The transport method protects the higher-level protocols associated with a packet and protects the data being transmitted but allows knowledge of the transmission itself. Protection of the data portion of a packet is referred to as *content protection*.

Tunneling provides encryption of source and destination IP addresses, as well as of the data itself. This provides the greatest security, but it can be done only between IPsec servers (or routers) because the final destination needs to be known for delivery. Protection of the header information is known as *context protection*.

EXAM TIP In transport mode (end-to-end), security of packet traffic is provided by the endpoint computers. In tunnel mode (portal-to-portal), security of packet traffic is provided between endpoint node machines in each network and not at the terminal host machines.

It is possible to use both methods at the same time, such as using transport within one's own network to reach an IPsec server, which then tunnels to the target server's network, connecting to an IPsec server there, and then using the transport method from the target network's IPsec server to the target host. IPsec uses the term security association as a means of describing a unidirectional combination of specific algorithm and key selection to provide a protected channel. If the traffic is bidirectional, two security associations are needed and can in fact be different.

Basic Configurations

Four basic configurations can be applied to machine-to-machine connections using IPsec. The simplest is a host-to-host connection between two machines, as shown in Figure 3-3. In this case, the Internet is not a part of the security association (SA) between the machines. If bidirectional security is desired, two SAs are used. The SAs are effective from host to host.

The second case places two security devices in the stream, relieving the hosts of the calculation and encapsulation duties. These two gateways have an SA between them. The network is assumed to be secure from each machine to its gateway, and no IPsec is

Case 1:
Two SAs from host to host for bidirectional secure communications

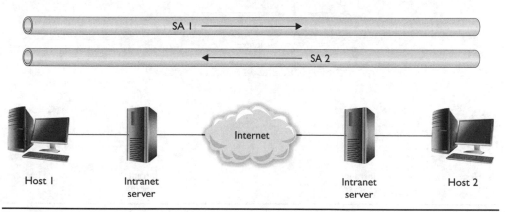

Figure 3-3 A host-to-host connection between two machines

performed across these hops. Figure 3-4 shows the two security gateways with a tunnel across the Internet, although either tunnel mode or transport mode could be used.

The third case combines the first two. A separate SA exists between the gateway devices, but an SA also exists between hosts. This could be considered a tunnel inside a tunnel, as shown in Figure 3-5.

Remote users commonly connect through the Internet to an organization's network. The network has a security gateway through which it secures traffic to and from its

Case 2:
IPsec between machines using gateway security devices

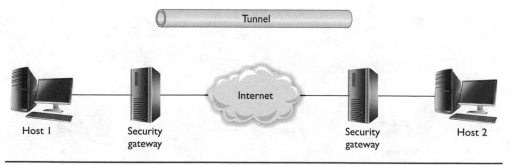

Figure 3-4 Two security gateways with a tunnel across the Internet

Case 3:
Separate IPsec tunnels, host to host and gateway to gateway

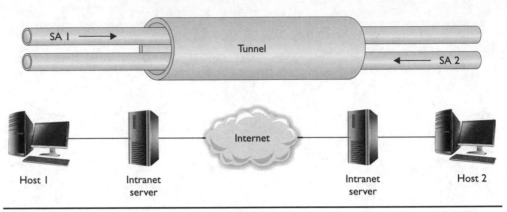

Figure 3-5 A tunnel inside a tunnel

servers and authorized users. In the last case, illustrated in Figure 3-6, the user establishes an SA with the security gateway and then a separate SA with the desired server, if required. This can be done using software on a remote laptop and hardware at the organization's network.

Windows can act as an IPsec server, as can routers and other servers. The primary issue is CPU usage and where the computing power should be implanted. This consideration has led to the rise of IPsec appliances, which are hardware devices that

Case 4:
Tunnel from host to gateway
Optional: Two SAs for bidirectional secure communications

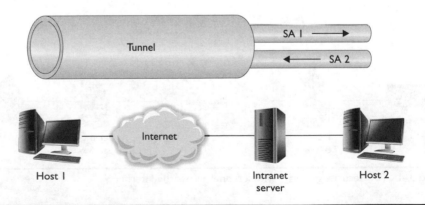

Figure 3-6 Tunnel from host to gateway

perform the IPsec function specifically for a series of communications. Depending on the number of connections, network bandwidth, and so on, these devices can be inexpensive for small office or home office use or quite expensive for large, enterprise-level implementations.

AH and ESP

IPsec uses two protocols to provide traffic security:

- Authentication Header (AH)
- Encapsulating Security Payload (ESP)

For key management and exchange, three protocols exist:

- Internet Security Association and Key Management Protocol (ISAKMP)
- Oakley
- Secure Key Exchange Mechanism for Internet (SKEMI)

These key management protocols can be collectively referred to as Internet Key Management Protocol (IKMP) or Internet Key Exchange (IKE).

IPsec does not define specific security algorithms, nor does it require specific methods of implementation. IPsec is an open framework that allows vendors to implement existing industry-standard algorithms suited for specific tasks. This flexibility is key in IPsec's ability to offer a wide range of security functions. IPsec allows several security technologies to be combined into a comprehensive solution for network-based confidentiality, integrity, and authentication. IPsec uses the following:

- Diffie-Hellman key exchange between peers on a public network
- Public key signing of Diffie-Hellman key exchanges to guarantee identity and avoid man-in-the-middle attacks
- Bulk encryption algorithms, such as IDEA and 3DES, for encrypting data
- Keyed hash algorithms, such as HMAC, and traditional hash algorithms, such as MD5 and SHA-1, for packet-level authentication
- Digital certificates to act as digital ID cards between parties

To provide traffic security, two header extensions have been defined for IP datagrams. The AH, when added to an IP datagram, ensures the integrity of the data and also the authenticity of the data's origin. By protecting the nonchanging elements in the IP header, the AH protects the IP address, which enables data-origin authentication. The ESP provides security services for the higher-level protocol portion of the packet only, not the IP header.

 EXAM TIP IPsec AH protects integrity, but it does not provide privacy. IPsec ESP provides confidentiality, but it does not protect integrity of the packet. To cover both privacy and integrity, both headers can be used at the same time.

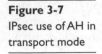

Figure 3-7
IPsec use of AH in
transport mode

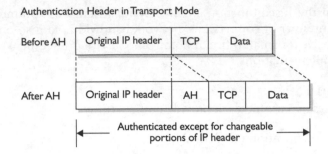

AH and ESP can be used separately or in combination, depending on the level and types of security desired. Both also work with the transport and tunnel modes of IPsec protocols. In transport mode, the two communication endpoints are providing security primarily for the upper-layer protocols. The cryptographic endpoints, where encryption and decryption occur, are located at the source and destination of the communication channel. For AH in transport mode, the original IP header is exposed, but its contents are protected via the AH block in the packet, as illustrated in Figure 3-7. For ESP in transport mode, the data contents are protected by encryption, as illustrated in Figure 3-8.

Tunneling is a means of encapsulating packets inside a protocol that is understood only at the entry and exit points of the tunnel. This provides security during transport in the tunnel, because outside observers cannot decipher packet contents or even the identities of the communicating parties. IPsec has a tunnel mode that can be used from server to server across a public network. Although the tunnel endpoints are referred to as *servers*, these devices can be routers, appliances, or servers. In tunnel mode, the tunnel endpoints merely encapsulate the entire packet with new IP headers to indicate the endpoints, and they encrypt the contents of this new packet. The true source and destination information is contained in the inner IP header, which is encrypted in the tunnel. The outer IP header contains the addresses of the endpoints of the tunnel.

As mentioned, AH and ESP can be employed in tunnel mode. When AH is employed in tunnel mode, portions of the outer IP header are given the same header protection that occurs in transport mode, with the entire inner packet receiving protection. This

Figure 3-8
IPsec use of ESP
in transport
mode

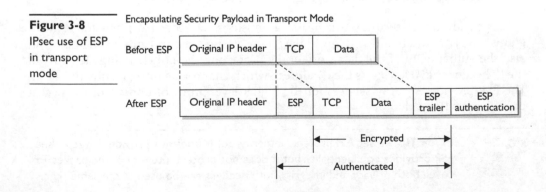

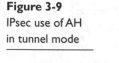

Figure 3-9
IPsec use of AH
in tunnel mode

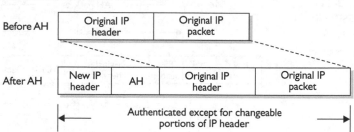

is illustrated in Figure 3-9. ESP affords the same encryption protection to the contents of the tunneled packet, which is the entire packet from the initial sender, as illustrated in Figure 3-10. Together, in tunnel mode, AH and ESP can provide complete protection across the packet, as shown in Figure 3-11. The specific combination of AH and ESP is referred to as a security association in IPsec.

In IPv4, IPsec is an add-on, and its acceptance is vendor driven. It is not a part of the original IP—one of the short-sighted design flaws of the original IP. In IPv6, IPsec is integrated into IP and is native on all packets. Its use is still optional, but its inclusion in the protocol suite will guarantee interoperability across vendor solutions when they are compliant with IPv6 standards.

IPsec uses cryptographic keys in its security process and has both manual and automatic distribution of keys as part of the protocol series. Manual key distribution is included, but it is practical only in small, static environments and does not scale to enterprise-level implementations. The default method of key management, IKE, is automated. IKE authenticates each peer involved in IPsec and negotiates the security policy, including the exchange of session keys. IKE creates a secure tunnel between peers and then negotiates the SA for IPsec across this channel. This is done in two phases: the first develops the channel, and the second the SA.

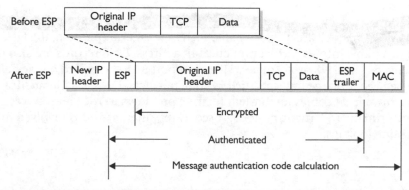

Figure 3-10 IPsec use of ESP in tunnel mode

Figure 3-11
IPsec ESP and
AH packet
construction in
tunnel mode

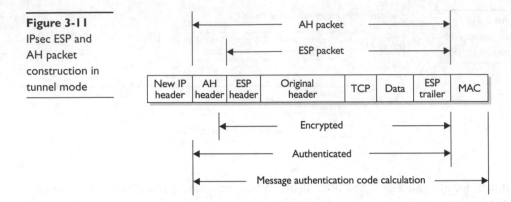

SNMP

The Simple Network Management Protocol (SNMP) is a standard for managing devices on IP-based networks. SNMP is an application layer protocol, part of the IP suite of protocols, and can be used to manage and monitor devices, including network devices, computers, and other devices connected to the IP network.

SSH

The Secure Shell (SSH) protocol is an encrypted remote terminal connection program used for remote connections to a server. SSH uses asymmetric encryption but generally requires an independent source of trust with a server, such as manually receiving a server key, to operate. SSH uses TCP port 22 as its default port.

 EXAM TIP   SSH uses public-key cryptography for secure remote terminal access and was designed as a secure replacement for Telnet.

DNS

The Domain Name Service (Server) (DNS) is a protocol for the translation of names into IP addresses. When users enter a name such as www.example.com, the DNS system converts this name into the actual numerical IP address. DNS records are also used for e-mail delivery. The DNS protocol uses UDP over port 53 for standard queries, although TCP can be used for large transfers such as zone transfers. DNS is a hierarchical system of servers, from local copies up through Internet providers to root-level servers. DNS is one of the primary underlying protocols used in the Internet and is involved in almost all addressing lookups.

TLS

Transport Layer Security (TLS) is an IETF standard for the employment of encryption technology and replaces SSL. Using the same basic principles, TLS updates the mechanisms employed by SSL. Although sometimes referred to as SSL, it is a separate standard.

SSL

Secure Sockets Layer (SSL) is an application of encryption technology developed for transport-layer protocols across the Web. This protocol uses public key encryption methods to exchange a symmetric key for use in confidentiality and integrity protection as well as authentication. The current version, V3, is outdated, having been replaced by the IETF standard TLS.

TCP/IP

The Transmission Control Protocol (TCP) is one of the most common protocols used in the Internet Protocol (IP) suite. TCP maintains a connection between the endpoints, enabling reliable communications. TCP connections are initiated with a three-way handshake consisting of a SYN, SYN-ACK, and an ACK.

 EXAM TIP TCP establishes a connection between endpoints, which enables elements such as transport-level security and reliable (guaranteed) delivery of packets. UDP is connectionless and depends on network reliability for error-free packet delivery.

FTP

The File Transfer Protocol (FTP) is an insecure, plaintext method of transferring files between machines. FTP uses TCP port 21 to negotiate the details of a transfer, which then occurs over a higher port address.

FTPS

FTPS is the implementation of FTP over an SSL/TLS secured channel. This supports complete FTP compatibility, yet provides the encryption protections enabled by SSL/TLS. FTPS uses TCP ports 989 and 990.

SFTP

SFTP is the use of FTP over an SSH channel. This leverages the encryption protections of SSH to secure FTP transfers. Because of its reliance on SSH, it uses TCP port 22.

TFTP

Trivial File Transfer Protocol (TFTP) is a file transfer protocol known for simplicity and lack of security mechanisms such as authentication. It uses UDP port 69, is designed only to read and write files, and typically is not used over the Internet.

HTTP

The Hypertext Transfer Protocol (HTTP) is the application protocol that forms the basis of the Web. It uses TCP port 80 and operates on a client/server model involving hyperlinks and browser-rendered content from collections of referenced content.

HTTPS

HTTPS is the use of SSL or TLS to encrypt a channel over which HTTP traffic is transmitted. This uses TCP port 443. HTTPS is the most widely used method to secure HTTP traffic.

SCP

File transfers between systems can be accomplished via Secure Copy Protocol (SCP), which is an SSH-enabled file transfer mechanism. Because of its reliance on SSH, it uses TCP port 22.

ICMP

Internet Control Message Protocol (ICMP) is the aspect of the Internet Protocol suite used for diagnostic, control, and error messaging. The most common ICMP traffic you are likely to encounter is ping, which is composed of an ICMP echo request and an ICMP echo reply. Optional in IPv4, ICMP is commonly blocked at the boundaries of a network because of a series of attack vectors that it enables, including ping floods and ping of death. In IPv6, ICMP is a must-carry component for the IP protocol to work end-to-end, meaning enterprises cannot block it at the network boundaries.

IPv4

Internet Protocol version 4 (IPv4) is the most common version of the IP protocol in use today. It is characterized by a 32-bit address notation expressed in dotted quad notation in the form of *X.X.X.X*, where *X* can range from 0 to 255. IPv4 is used to route packets across the Internet and provides a wide range of services through a suite of associated protocols including ICMP, TCP, and UDP.

IPv6

Internet Protocol version 6 (IPv6) is the replacement for IPv4. It uses a 128-bit address space, which represents approximately 3.4×10^{38} addresses. IPv6 addresses can be expressed in eight groups of four hexadecimal digits, using colons as separators. IPv6 offers many features in addition to increased address space, including autoconfiguration, enhanced security, IPsec support, and enhanced multicast support. IPv6 is not interoperable with IPv4 and presents several challenges to network and security personnel. IPv6 is designed for host-to-host connections, making older systems such as NAT obsolete. It also presents challenges to security vendors, as the tools and techniques used to secure IPv4 do not work in the same fashion for IPv6.

iSCSI

The Internet Small Computer System Interface (iSCSI) is a protocol for IP-based storage. iSCSI can be used to send data over existing network infrastructures, enabling storage area networks (SANs). Positioned as a low-cost alternative to Fibre Channel storage, the only real limitation is one of network bandwidth.

Fibre Channel

Fibre Channel (FC) is a high-speed network technology (with throughput up to 16 Gbps) used to connect storage to computer systems. The FC protocol is a transport protocol similar to the TCP protocol in IP networks. Carried via special cables, one of the drawbacks of FC-based storage is cost.

FCoE

The Fibre Channel over Ethernet (FCoE) protocol encapsulates the FC frames, enabling FC communication over 10-Gigabit Ethernet networks.

Telnet

Telnet is a plaintext method of instantiating a command-line console to a remote machine. Telnet uses TCP port 23 and sends all transmissions in unencrypted form, making the traffic subject to eavesdropping. Telnet is an old protocol that has been used for decades, but it has been replaced by SSH due to security concerns.

NetBIOS

NetBIOS is a separate naming scheme from DNS, used in older Windows systems. It uses TCP and UDP ports 137, 138, 139, and 445 over a local area network for things like file and printer sharing in Windows-based PCs. A frequent target for hackers, NetBIOS is largely obsolete and only found in older, smaller network environments.

Ports

Services are referenced by ports under both TCP and UDP protocol stacks. Table 3-3 lists common port assignments relevant to the CompTIA Security+ exam requirements.

EXAM TIP   It is important to know the port numbers for common protocols.

Port	TCP Port Assignment	UDP Port Assignment
21	FTP	
22	SSH	
25	SMTP	
53	DNS	DNS
80	HTTP	
110	POP3	
139	NetBIOS	
143	IMAP	
443	HTTPS	
3389	RDP	RDP

Table 3-3 Common TCP and UDP Port Assignments

OSI Relevance

To organize the vast array of protocols into usable layers, the abstraction layers of the Open Systems Interconnection (OSI) model are useful. This enables one to quickly determine what protocols can be used with or encapsulated over other protocols. Table 3-4 illustrates the separation of the protocols by the OSI abstraction layers.

OSI Layer	Protocols
7 – Application	DHCP, DNS, FTP, TFTP, SSH, LDAP, IMAP, POP3, Gopher, HTTP, NFS, NNTP, NTP, SIP, SSI, SMPP, SMTP, SNMP, Telnet
6 – Presentation	MIME, XDR, EBCDIC, RDP
5 – Session	Named Pipes, NetBIOS, PPTP, RTP, SAP, SOCKS, SPDY
4 – Transport	DCCP, SCTP, SPX, TCP, UDP
3 – Network	AppleTalk, IP (v4, v6), EGP, EIGRP, ICMP, IPsec, IGMP, IGRP, MPLS, IPX, X.25
2 – Data Link	ARP, ATM, Frame Relay, HDLC, IEEE 802.2, IEEE 802.3, LLC, L2TP, PPP, PPTP, LLDP, STP, SDLC, SLIP, X.25
1 – Physical	Bluetooth, DSL, ADSL, ISDN, IEEE 1394, IEEE 802.3, IEEE 802.11, IEEE 802.15, IEEE 802.16, RS-232, RS-485, SONET/SDH, USB

Table 3-4 Protocols by OSI Layer

Chapter Review

The chapter opened with an examination of how networks are segregated with design elements such as DMZs and subnets. The use of VLANs for traffic management and the security implications were examined, followed by Network Address Translation issues. The chapter continued through the concepts of remote access, network access control, telephony, and virtualization. Cloud computing was explored, both from the services provided, IaaS, SaaS, and PaaS, and from the cloud types, private, public, hybrid, and community. The chapter concluded with an examination of many of the common networking protocols and ports as well as the relevance of the OSI model.

Questions

To help you prepare further for the CompTIA Security+ exam, and to test your level of preparedness, answer the following questions and then check your answers against the correct answers at the end of the chapter.

1. Which of the following servers would you be least likely to place in a DMZ?

   A. Web server

   B. DNS server

   C. SMTP server

   D. File server

2. Which network mask corresponds to a /31 prefix?

   A. 255.255.255.0

   B. 255.255.255.192

   C. 255.255.255.248

   D. 255.255.255.254

3. Match the items (one-to-one) from the column on the left with corresponding items on the right:

   A. FTPS   1. Trunking

   B. SSH   2. PBX

   C. NAT   3. SSL/TLS

   D. VLAN   4. SaaS

                    5. TCP 22

                    6. PAT

4. If you need multiple internal hosts to share a single external IP address, you might use:

   A. Destination Network Address Translation

   B. Port Address Translation

   C. Source Network Address Translation

   D. Dynamic Network Address Translation

5. Which of the following is not a remote-access method?

   A. Remote desktop software

   B. Terminal emulation

   C. SaaS

   D. Secure Shell

6. Network access control (NAC) is implemented:

   A. When devices initially attempt to access the network

   B. When devices change MAC addresses

   C. When devices change protocols

   D. When zero-day attacks are detected

7. When discussing virtualization, a snapshot is:

   A. The amount of resources used by a virtual machine at a given point in time

   B. The state of a virtual machine at an exact point in time

   C. The state of the virtual disks associated with a specific virtual machine

   D. The use of hardware emulation in a given virtual machine

8. Application delivery-only Platform as a Service (PaaS) offerings generally focus on:

   A. Security and scalability

   B. Development capabilities

   C. Allowing developers to use any programming language

   D. Subscription-based services

9. A company adopting an Infrastructure as a Service (IaaS) model would typically:

   A. Own the infrastructure equipment

   B. Be responsible for housing and maintaining equipment

   C. Only support networking infrastructure

   D. Pay on a per-use basis

10. An organization wanting to create a restricted-access, Internet-accessible resource for processing sensitive data might consider using:

    A. Software as a Service

    B. A private cloud

    C. A public cloud

    D. A community cloud

11. Your organization is setting up three new buildings on a local campus, all connecting to the same core router. You have only one available address space, 10.10.10.0, to handle the routing between those three new buildings. What subnet mask will you need to use to create separate subnets for each of those three buildings?

    A. 255.255.255.128

    B. 255.255.255.192

    C. 255.255.255.240

    D. 255.255.255.252

12. Your organization is considering migrating from QuickBooks 2009 to QuickBooks Online (a web-based solution). QuickBooks Online is an example of:

    A. PaaS

    B. SaaS

    C. IaaS

    D. QaaS

13. You need to set up a DMZ but want to keep the servers inside the DMZ on a private address space. You have plenty of public IP address space and just want to map each server's private address to a unique public address. What type of NAT would be most appropriate?

    A. Static NAT

    B. Full-cone NAT

    C. Port Address Translation

    D. Dynamic NAT

14. Your organization is looking to redesign its network perimeter. Your boss wants to purchase a new "all in one" device and put everything behind that device on a flat network. Others in the meeting argue that it would be better to have a primary firewall, a DMZ for public services, a secondary firewall, and a firewall separating the server farm from the rest of the network. What security principle is your boss overlooking that the others in the meeting are not?

   A. Network separation

   B. Defense in depth

   C. Loop prevention

   D. Network access control

15. You are starting a sensitive application development project with another organization. Both organizations would like to share the same development platform, but neither organization wants to allow the other organization to access its internal networks. What is the most appropriate type of cloud service to use in this scenario?

   A. Private cloud

   B. Hybrid cloud

   C. Community cloud

   D. Public cloud

Answers

1. **D.** A DMZ is designed to allow your organization to expose public services to the Internet. Three of the most common types of servers you will find in a DMZ are web servers, DNS servers, and SMTP servers (e-mail). Of the servers listed, you are least likely to place a file server in a DMZ.

2. **D.** A network prefix size of /31 corresponds to a 255.255.255.254 network mask. With a /31 prefix you have 128 available subnets and 2 useable hosts per subnet.

3. **A.** 3. FTPS uses SSL/TLS to secure FTP.
   B. 5. SSH uses TCP port 22.
   C. 6. A form of NAT is PAT.
   D. 1. VLANs can involve trunking.

4. **B.** Port Address Translation allows multiple internal hosts to share a single external IP address.

5. **C.** Software as a Service is a cloud model, not a remote-access method.

6. **A.** Network access control (NAC) is a process for securing access to the network when a device initially attempts to access the network.

7. **B.** In virtualization, a snapshot is the state of a virtual machine at an exact point in time. The snapshot typically includes the state of a virtual machine's storage devices as well.

8. **A.** Application delivery–only Platform as a Service (PaaS) offerings generally focus on security and scalability.

9. **D.** A company adopting an Infrastructure as a Service (IaaS) model would typically pay on a per-use basis. IaaS is a provision model where an organization outsources the equipment used by its operations as well as the housing, maintenance, and operation of that equipment.

10. **B.** An organization wanting to create a restricted-access, Internet-accessible resource for processing sensitive data might consider using a private cloud.

11. **B.** To create at least three subnetworks from the 10.10.10.0 address space, you will need to use a 255.255.255.192 subnet mask. This will give you four separate networks with 62 host addresses each.

12. **B.** QuickBooks Online is an example of a Software as a Service (SaaS) model. The software is accessed via a web browser and can be used by any computer with an Internet connection and a compatible browser.

13. **A.** Static NAT, often called one-to-one NAT, maps a single private address to a single public address.

14. **B.** The others in your meeting are arguing for defense in depth (or layered defense), which uses multiple security layers to provide more resistance to potential attacks. Attackers must successfully penetrate multiple layers of defenses before they can penetrate the network.

15. **C.** A community cloud shares the resources between several different organizations, but still reserves those resources for use by those organizations (that is, they are not public resources).

Secure Wireless Networking

In this chapter, you will

- Given a scenario, troubleshoot security issues related to wireless networking
- Learn about the security implications of wireless networks
- Learn about the security built into different versions of wireless protocols
- Identify the different 802.11 versions and their security controls

Wireless is increasingly the way people access the Internet. Because wireless access is considered a consumer benefit, many businesses add wireless access points to lure customers into their shops. With the rollout of third-generation (3G) and fourth-generation (4G) cellular networks, people are also increasingly accessing the Internet from their mobile phones. The massive growth in popularity of nontraditional computers such as netbooks, e-readers, and tablets has also driven the popularity of wireless access.

As wireless use increases, the security of the wireless protocols has become a more important factor in the security of the entire network. As a security professional, you need to understand wireless network applications because of the risks inherent in broadcasting a network signal where anyone can intercept it. Sending unsecured information across public airwaves is tantamount to posting your company's passwords by the front door of the building.

This chapter looks at several current wireless protocols and their security features.

Wireless Networking

Wireless networking is the transmission of packetized data by means of a physical topology that does not use direct physical links. This definition can be narrowed to apply to networks that use radio waves to carry the signals over either public or private bands, instead of using standard network cabling.

The 802.11 protocol has been standardized by the IEEE for wireless local area networks (WLANs). Five versions are currently in production—802.11a, 802.11b, 802.11g, 802.11n, and 802.11ac. 802.11n is the latest standard, but provides backward compatibility with 802.11g hardware. It is difficult to keep this list updated, as there are even newer standards scheduled to be approved by IEEE in the 2014–15 timeframe.

SSID

The 802.11 protocol designers expected some security concerns and attempted to build provisions into the 802.11 protocol that would ensure adequate security. The 802.11 standard includes attempts at rudimentary authentication and confidentiality controls. Authentication is handled in its most basic form by the 802.11 access point (AP), forcing the clients to perform a handshake when attempting to "associate" to the AP. Association is the process required before the AP will allow the client to talk across the AP to the network.

The authentication function is known as the *service set identifier (SSID)*. This unique 32-character identifier is attached to the header of the packet. Association occurs only if the client has all the correct parameters needed in the handshake, among them the SSID. This SSID setting should limit access to only authorized users of the wireless network. The SSID is broadcast by default as a network name, but broadcasting this beacon frame can be disabled. Many APs also use a default SSID; for example, for many versions of Cisco APs, this default is *tsunami*, which can indicate an AP that has not been configured for any security. Renaming the SSID and disabling SSID broadcast are both good ideas; however, because the SSID is part of every frame, these measures should not be considered securing the network. As the SSID is, hopefully, a unique identifier, only people who know the identifier will be able to complete association to the AP.

While the SSID is a good idea in theory, it is sent in plaintext in the packets, so in practice, SSID offers little security significance—any sniffer can determine the SSID, and many operating systems—Windows XP and later, for instance—will display a list of SSIDs active in the area and prompt the user to choose which one to connect to. This weakness is magnified by most APs' default settings to transmit beacon frames. The beacon frame's purpose is to announce the wireless network's presence and capabilities so that WLAN cards can attempt to associate to it. This can be disabled in software for many APs, especially the more sophisticated ones. From a security perspective, the beacon frame is damaging because it contains the SSID, and this beacon frame is transmitted at a set interval (ten times per second by default). Since a default AP without any other traffic is sending out its SSID in plaintext ten times a second, you can see why the SSID does not provide true authentication. Scanning programs such as NetStumbler work by capturing the beacon frames, and thereby the SSIDs, of all APs.

 EXAM TIP   Although not considered the strongest security measures, renaming the SSID and disabling SSID broadcast are important concepts to know for the exam.

WEP

The designers of the 802.11 protocol also attempted to maintain confidentiality by introducing Wired Equivalent Privacy (WEP), which uses a cipher to encrypt the data as it is transmitted through the air. WEP has been shown to have an implementation problem that can be exploited to break security. WEP encrypts the data traveling across the network with an RC4 stream cipher, attempting to ensure confidentiality. (The details of the RC4 cipher are covered in Chapter 24.) This synchronous method of encryption ensures some method of authentication. The system depends on the client and the AP having a shared secret key, ensuring that only authorized people with the proper key have access to the wireless network. WEP supports two key lengths, 40 and 104 bits, though these are more typically referred to as 64 and 128 bits. In 802.11a and 802.11g, manufacturers extended this to 152-bit WEP keys. This is because in all cases, 24 bits of the overall key length are used for the initialization vector (IV).

The IV is the primary reason for the weaknesses in WEP. The IV is sent in the plaintext part of the message, and because the total keyspace is approximately 16 million keys, the same key will be reused. Once the key has been repeated, an attacker has two ciphertexts encrypted with the same key stream. This allows the attacker to examine the ciphertext and retrieve the key. This attack can be improved by examining only packets that have weak IVs, reducing the number of packets needed to crack the key. Using only weak IV packets, the number of required captured packets is reduced to around four or five million, which can take only a few hours on a fairly busy AP. For a point of reference, this means that equipment with an advertised WEP key of 128 bits can be cracked in less than a day, whereas to crack a normal 128-bit key would take roughly 2,000,000,000,000,000,000 years on a computer able to attempt one trillion keys a second. AirSnort is a modified sniffing program that can take advantage of this weakness to retrieve the WEP keys.

The biggest weakness of WEP is that the IV problem exists, regardless of key length, because the IV always remains at 24 bits. Most APs also have the ability to lock in access only to known MAC addresses, providing a limited authentication capability. Given sniffers' capacity to grab all active MAC addresses on the network, this capability is not very effective. An attacker simply configures his wireless cards to a known good MAC address.

 EXAM TIP WEP alone should not be trusted to provide confidentiality. If WEP is the only protocol supported by your AP, place it outside the corporate firewall and VPN to add more protection.

WPA

The first standard to be used in the market to replace WEP was Wi-Fi Protected Access (WPA). This standard uses the flawed WEP algorithm with the Temporal Key Integrity Protocol (TKIP). TKIP works by using a shared secret combined with the card's MAC address to generate a new key, which is mixed with the IV to make per-packet keys that encrypt a single packet using the same RC4 cipher used by traditional WEP. This overcomes the WEP key weakness, as a key is used on only one packet. The other advantage to this method is that it can be retrofitted to current hardware with only a software change, unlike Advanced Encryption Standard (AES) and 802.1x.

While WEP uses a 40-bit or 104-bit encryption key that must be manually entered on wireless access points and devices and does not change, TKIP employs a per-packet key, generating a new 128-bit key for each packet. This can generally be accomplished with only a firmware update, enabling a simple solution to the types of attacks that compromise WEP.

TKIP

Temporal Key Integrity Protocol (TKIP) was created as a stopgap security measure to replace the WEP protocol without requiring the replacement of legacy hardware. The breaking of WEP had left Wi-Fi networks without viable link-layer security, and a solution was required for already deployed hardware. TKIP works by mixing a secret root key with the IV before the RC4 encryption. WPA/TKIP uses the same underlying mechanism as WEP, and consequently is vulnerable to a number of similar attacks. TKIP is no longer considered secure and has been deprecated with the release of WPA2.

WPA2

IEEE 802.11i is the standard for security in wireless networks and is also known as Wi-Fi Protected Access 2 (WPA2). It uses 802.1x to provide authentication and uses the Advanced Encryption Standard (AES) as the encryption protocol. WPA2 uses the AES block cipher, a significant improvement over WEP's and WPA's use of the RC4 stream cipher. The 802.11i standard specifies the use of the Counter Mode with CBC-MAC Protocol (in full, the Counter Mode with Cipher Block Chaining–Message Authentication Codes Protocol, or simply CCMP).

WPS

Wi-Fi Protected Setup (WPS) is a network security standard that was created to provide users with an easy method of configuring wireless networks. Designed for home networks and small business networks, this standard involves the use of an eight-digit PIN to configure wireless devices. WPS consists of a series of Extensible Authentication Protocol (EAP) messages and has been shown to be susceptible to a brute-force attack. A successful attack can reveal the PIN and subsequently the WPA/WPA2 passphrase and allow unauthorized parties to gain access to the network. Currently, the only effective mitigation is to disable WPS.

Setting Up WPA2

If WPS is not safe for use, how does one set up WPA2? To set up WPA2, you need to have several parameters. Figure 4-1 shows the screens for a WPA2 setup in Windows 7.

The first element is to choose a security framework. When configuring an adapter to connect to an existing network, you need to match the choice of the network. When setting up your own network, you can choose whichever option you prefer. There are many selections, but for security purposes, you should choose WPA2-Personal or WPA2-Enterprise. Both of these require the choice of an encryption type, either TKIP or AES. TKIP has been deprecated, so choose AES. The last element is the choice of the network security key—the secret that is shared by all users. WPA2-Enterprise, which is designed to be used with an 802.1x authentication server that distributes different keys to each user, is typically used in business environments.

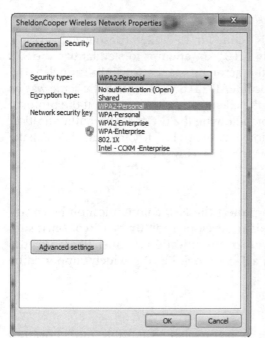

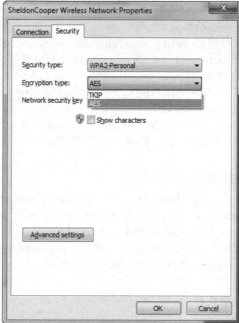

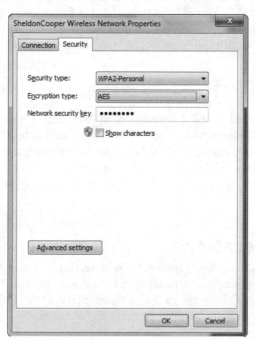

Figure 4-1   WPA2 setup options in Windows 7

EAP

Extensible Authentication Protocol (EAP) is defined in RFC 2284 (obsoleted by 3748). EAP-TLS relies on Transport Layer Security (TLS), an attempt to standardize the SSL structure to pass credentials. EAP-TTLS (the acronym stands for EAP–Tunneled TLS Protocol) is a variant of the EAP-TLS protocol. EAP-TTLS works much the same way as EAP-TLS, with the server authenticating to the client with a certificate, but the protocol tunnels the client side of the authentication, allowing the use of legacy authentication protocols such as Password Authentication Protocol (PAP), Challenge-Handshake Authentication Protocol (CHAP), MS-CHAP, or MS-CHAP-V2.

PEAP

PEAP, or Protected EAP, was developed to protect the EAP communication by encapsulating it with TLS. This is an open standard developed jointly by Cisco, Microsoft, and RSA. EAP was designed assuming a secure communication channel. PEAP provides that protection as part of the protocol via a TLS tunnel. PEAP is widely supported by vendors for use over wireless networks.

LEAP

Cisco designed a proprietary EAP known as Lightweight Extensible Authentication Protocol (LEAP); however, this is being phased out for newer protocols such as PEAP or EAP-TLS. Susceptible to offline password guessing, and with tools available that actively break LEAP security, this protocol has been deprecated in favor of stronger methods of EAP.

CCMP

As previously mentioned in the discussion of WPA2, CCMP stands for Counter Mode with Cipher Block Chaining–Message Authentication Codes Protocol (or Counter Mode with CBC-MAC Protocol). CCMP is a data encapsulation encryption mechanism designed for wireless use. CCMP is actually the mode in which the AES cipher is used to provide message integrity. Unlike WPA, CCMP requires new hardware to perform the AES encryption.

Wireless Operations

Wireless security is managed by protocols, discussed earlier, and operational characteristics. There are a variety of operational elements that can contribute to the security of a wireless network. MAC filtering, antenna types, placement, and power levels, as well as placement from site survey results can enhance security.

MAC Filter

MAC filtering is the selective admission of packets based on a list of approved Media Access Control (MAC) addresses. Employed on switches, this method is used to provide a means of machine authentication. In wired networks, this enjoys the protection afforded by the wires, making interception of signals to determine their MAC addresses difficult. In wireless networks, this same mechanism suffers from the fact that an attacker can see the MAC addresses of all traffic to and from the access point, and then can spoof the MAC addresses that are permitted to communicate via the access point.

 EXAM TIP   MAC filtering can be employed on wireless access points, but can be bypassed by attackers observing allowed MAC addresses and spoofing the allowed MAC address for the wireless card.

Antenna Placement

Wi-Fi is by nature a radio-based method of communication, and as such uses antennas to transmit and receive the signals. The actual design and placement of the antennas can have a significant effect on the usability of the radio frequency (RF) medium for carrying the traffic. Antennas come in a variety of types, each with its own transmission pattern and gain factor. High-gain antennas can deal with weaker signals, but also have more limited coverage. Wide-coverage, omnidirectional antennas can cover wider areas, but at lower levels of gain. The objective of antenna placement is to maximize the coverage over a physical area and reduce low-gain areas. This can be very complex in buildings with walls, electrical interference, and other sources of interference and frequently requires a site survey to determine proper placement.

 EXAM TIP   Because wireless antennas can transmit outside a facility, tuning and placement of antennas can be crucial for security. Adjusting radiated power through the power level controls will assist in keeping wireless signals from being broadcast outside areas under physical access control.

Power Level Controls

Wi-Fi power levels can be controlled by the hardware for a variety of reasons. The lower the power used, the less the opportunity for interference. But if the power levels are too low, then signal strength limits range. Access points can have the power level set either manually or via programmatic control. For most users, power level controls are not very useful, and leaving the unit in default mode is the best option. In complex enterprise setups, with site surveys and planned overlapping zones, this aspect of signal control can be used to increase capacity and control on the network.

Antenna Types

The standard access point is equipped with an omnidirectional antenna. Omnidirectional antennas operate in all directions, making the relative orientation between devices less important. Omnidirectional antennas cover the greatest area per antenna. The weakness occurs in corners and hard-to-reach areas, as well as boundaries of a facility where

Figure 4-2
Wireless access
point antennas

a   b   c

directional antennas are needed to complete coverage. Figure 4-2 shows a sampling of common Wi-Fi antennas: 4-2(a) is a common home wireless router, (b) is a commercial indoor wireless access point, and (c) is an outdoor directional antenna. Indoor WAPs can be visible, as shown, or hidden above ceiling tiles.

Wireless networking problems caused by weak signal strength can sometimes be solved by installing upgraded Wi-Fi radio antennas on the access points. On business networks, the complexity of multiple access points typically requires a comprehensive site survey to map the Wi-Fi signal strength in and around office buildings. Additional wireless access points can then be strategically placed where needed to resolve dead spots in coverage. For small businesses and homes, where a single access point may be all that is needed, an antenna upgrade may be a simpler and more cost-effective option to fix Wi-Fi signal problems.

Two common forms of upgraded antennas are the Yagi antenna and the panel antenna. An example of a Yagi antenna is shown in Figure 4-2(c). Both Yagi and panel antennas are directional in nature, spreading the RF energy in a more limited field, increasing effective range in one direction while limiting it in others. Panel antennas can provide solid room performance while preventing signal bleed behind the antennas. This works well on the edge of a site, limiting the stray emissions that could be captured offsite. Yagi antennas act more like a rifle, funneling the energy along a beam. This allows much longer communication distances using standard power. This also enables eavesdroppers to capture signals from much greater distances because of the gain provided by the antenna itself.

Captive Portals

Captive portal refers to a specific technique of using an HTTP client to handle authentication on a wireless network. Frequently employed in public hotspots, a captive portal opens a web browser to an authentication page. This occurs before the user is granted admission to the network. The access point uses this simple mechanism by intercepting all packets and returning the web page for login. The actual web server that serves up the authentication page can be in a walled-off section of the network, blocking access to the Internet until the user successfully authenticates.

Site Surveys

When developing a coverage map for a complex building site, you need to take into account a wide variety of factors, particularly walls, interfering sources, and floor plans. A site survey involves several steps: mapping the floor plan, testing for RF interference,

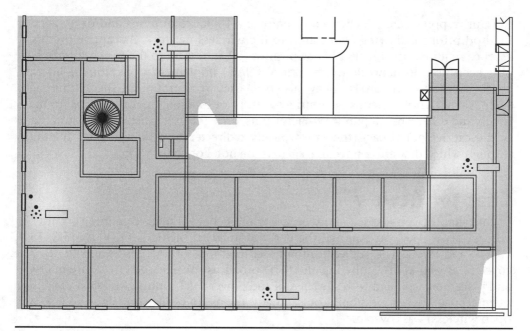

Figure 4-3 Example site survey

testing for RF coverage, and analysis of material via software. The software can suggest placement of access points. After deploying the APs, the site is surveyed again, mapping the results versus the predicted, watching signal strength and signal-to-noise ratios. Figure 4-3 illustrates what a site survey looks like. The different shades indicate signal strength, showing where reception is strong and where it is weak. Site surveys can be used to ensure availability of wireless, especially when it's critical for users to have connections.

 EXAM TIP   Functionality of wireless networks is dependent upon radio signals. Conducting a site survey and choosing the proper antenna type and placement are important steps to ensure proper coverage of a site, including areas blocked by walls, interfering signals, and echoes.

VPN (Over Open Wireless)

Wireless connections are often established in environments where the security of the communications should not be trusted, such as airports and public hotspots (coffee shops, libraries, and so on). Similarly, wireless networks are often used to connect to sites that are not protected via a secured channel such as SSL. In all of these instances, the wireless network connection should be considered suspect, and additional security measures should be taken to achieve the desired level of communications security.

Captive portals are widely used to enforce acceptance of terms and/or a payment method prior to allowing connection to the wireless network. As captive portals in essence require a specific user behavior prior to connection to the network, they have also been used in network access control (NAC) implementations, forcing an NAC check prior to connection. They have also been used to communicate specific messages, such as emergency bulletins or security alerts, prior to allowing connections. In many hotels and other types of public Wi-Fi hotspots, once the user satisfies the requirements of the captive portal page, they are typically redirected to a web page for the entity through which they are connecting, such as the hotel or coffee shop.

Chapter Review

In this chapter, you learned about secure wireless networking. Examining security issues with wireless, you explored the encryption-based methods of WEP, WPA, TKIP, CCMP, and WPA2. The authentication-based methods of EAP, LEAP, and PEAP were covered, as well as MAC filtering and SSID broadcast. You learned that antenna types and placement, coupled with site surveys and power level controls, assist in the design of enterprise-level wireless build-outs. Finally, the use of captive portals and VPN (over open wireless) was covered.

Questions

To help you prepare further for the CompTIA Security+ exam, and to test your level of preparedness, answer the following questions and then check your answers against the correct answers at the end of the chapter.

1. When would disabling SSID broadcasting make the most sense?

   A. When near an airport with a large, free Wi-Fi infrastructure

   B. When unable to encrypt the Wi-Fi signal due to noncompliant client machines

   C. When running a hotel network and you are concerned about access from the parking lot

   D. When providing guest wireless outside of the firewall that is not intended to be public

2. Why is a site survey important to wireless security?

   A. Higher-strength wireless increases the effectiveness of Wi-Fi encryption keys.

   B. Minimizing the strength of the signal sent outside of the physical walls of the building can reduce the risk of attacks.

   C. Configuring the fewest access points needed to provide adequate coverage offers the fewest possible targets for an attacker to compromise.

   D. The Wi-Fi signal can be restricted from external users when proper antennas are used.

3. What is the primary enhancement WPA2 has over WEP?

    A. WPA2 uses longer keys than WEP.

    B. AES and CCMP.

    C. Temporary WEP keys using TKIP.

    D. WPA2 supports the 802.1x protocol for secure client authentication.

4. Why is MAC address filtering rarely used?

    A. It is cumbersome to implement.

    B. Attackers can clone a working MAC address.

    C. The use of 802.1x for network authentication has replaced it.

    D. All of the above.

5. What does LEAP do?

    A. Modernizes Wi-Fi with a new encryption cipher

    B. Provides TLS support for Wi-Fi authentication under Windows

    C. Provides a lightweight mutual authentication protocol for clients and uses dynamic WEP keys

    D. Forces Cisco devices to use WPA2

6. When would you use a directional-type antenna?

    A. When you need to cover an entire warehouse floor.

    B. When you want to cover only the guest conference room.

    C. When you are allowed to transmit at a higher power.

    D. When you want to communicate with a single remote client.

7. How is TKIP a security benefit?

    A. It enforces security using a single WEP key for a short amount of time.

    B. It forces TLS authentication between the client and the access point.

    C. It provides a session key based upon a pre-shared key.

    D. All of the above.

8. When a wireless network allows you to connect but only allows access to a single website, it is called a(n) _____.

    A. guest wireless

    B. 802.1x

    C. VPN over open wireless

    D. captive portal

9. What is a threat to VPN over open wireless?

   A. Hackers can sniff all the VPN packets and decrypt them.

   B. The user must connect to the open wireless before starting VPN, allowing an attacker a potential window of time to compromise the machine.

   C. A certificate could be faked, allowing access into the corporate server.

   D. All of the above.

10. What two modes does WPA2 operate in, and what is the key difference between them?

   A. Public and Work; encryption

   B. Enterprise and Personal; authentication

   C. Enterprise and Guest; integrity

   D. AES and WEP; key length

For questions 11–14, use the following scenario: You have been hired to run the IT department of a small regional hotel chain, which plans to implement wireless access for all its guests and create a system that all the workers can use. The hotel chain needs the system to maximize security, but provide good usability to all the employees. Guests will use all manner of Wi-Fi devices, while employees will use a combination of desktops in the lobby and mobile tablets to automate room status updates.

11. Which security practice(s) will be best for the networks that are used for guests? (Choose all that apply.)

   A. MAC address filtering

   B. WPA2

   C. Captive portal

   D. LEAP

   E. Site survey

   F. Disable SSID broadcast

12. Which security practice(s) will be best for the networks that are used for employees? (Choose all that apply.)

   A. MAC address filtering

   B. WPA2

   C. Captive portal

   D. LEAP

   E. Site survey

   F. Disable SSID broadcast

13. Your boss asks you to reconfigure the network to also support a bring your own device (BYOD) initiative. Which security measure on the corporate network would not be compatible?

    A. WPA2

    B. Captive portal

    C. Site survey

    D. MAC address filter

14. Guests are able to connect to the wireless network but are unable to access any web pages. This is most likely a failure of the _____.

    A. access point power controls

    B. captive portal

    C. antenna placement

    D. capacity planning

15. Match the related terms, using a one-to-one mapping:

A. 802.11i	1. EAP
B. Captive portal	2. LEAP
C. TLS	3. CCMP
D. WPS	4. PEAP
	5. HTTP

Answers

1. **D.** Disabling SSID broadcasting is not an effective security measure, so it should only be utilized outside the firewall on guest systems.

2. **B.** Minimizing the signal transmitted to areas beyond the building can help prevent simplistic drive-by attacks on wireless systems.

3. **B.** AES and CCMP do away with the flawed WEP implementation of the RC4 cipher and provide temporary keys.

4. **D.** All of the above. A. MAC address filtering is cumbersome to implement because most MAC addresses have to be manually added to the access point system. B. By using a wireless card in promiscuous mode, an attacker can identify authorized MAC addresses and clone the address to their NIC. C. 802.1x can force a network user to authenticate before allowing any access to the network, reducing the need for MAC filtering.

5. **C.** LEAP is a Cisco proprietary protocol established to provide authentication and dynamic WEP keys.

6. **D.** Directional antennas are good for narrowly focusing a beam of signal to a single remote point.

7. **A.** TKIP enforces the short-term use of a WEP key before generating a new WEP key.

8. **D.** A captive portal will allow wireless connections but will not allow any traffic through until the user has authenticated to the portal website.

9. **B.** Once a user connects to open wireless, they are subject to any hostile traffic on the network until the VPN protection begins.

10. **B.** WPA2 can operate in either Enterprise mode or Personal mode, with Enterprise mode requiring an external 802.1x authentication and Personal mode utilizing a pre-shared key for authentication.

11. **C and D.** The captive portal will allow users who have never used the system before to successfully authenticate, and a site survey is always a good practice to ensure availability.

12. **B, E, and F.** WPA2 should be used to encrypt communications with the corporate network. A site survey will ensure good coverage for all the locations from which employees need access—a site survey provides availability assurance. Disabling SSID broadcast will not affect corporate-owned devices configured to only attach to a single wireless network, and eliminates guest confusion about which network to attach to.

13. **D.** With employees bringing in a variety of devices, filtering by MAC address would not work because you would not know the MAC addresses in advance of the devices being connected to the network. WPA2 should still be used to protect corporate confidentiality. Captive portals are rarely used on corporate networks, but would not have a problem supporting BYOD. Site surveys are always recommended.

14. **B.** This is most likely a failure of the captive portal.

15. **A. 3.** 802.11i can utilize CCMP.

    B. 5. Captive portals can be utilized over HTTP.

    C. 4. TLS can utilize PEAP.

    D. 1. WPS can utilize EAP.

PART II

Compliance and Operational Security

Risk Concepts

In this chapter, you will

- Learn important risk-related concepts
- Explore the use of policies to manage risk
- Learn the differences between qualitative and quantitative risk assessment
- Learn how to quantitatively calculate risk
- Examine risk associated with virtualization and cloud environments

Risk management can best be described as a decision-making process. In the simplest terms, when you manage risk, you determine what could happen to your business, you assess the impact if it were to happen, and you decide what you could do to control that impact as much as you or your management deems necessary. You then decide to act or not to act, and, finally, you evaluate the results of your decision. The process may be iterative, as industry best practices clearly indicate that an important aspect of effectively managing risk is to consider it an ongoing process.

An Overview of Risk Management

Risk management is an essential element of management from the enterprise level down to the individual project. Risk management encompasses all the actions taken to reduce complexity, increase objectivity, and identify important decision factors. There has been, and will continue to be, discussion about the complexity of risk management and whether or not it is worth the effort. Businesses must take risks to retain their competitive edge, however, and as a result, risk management must occur as part of managing any business, program, or project.

 NOTE   Risk management is about managing the future risks, not explaining the past risks.

Risk management is both a skill and a task that is performed by all managers, either deliberately or intuitively. It can be simple or complex, depending on the size of the project or business and the amount of risk inherent in an activity. Every manager, at all levels, must learn to manage risk. The required skills can be learned.

EXAM TIP This chapter contains several bulleted lists. These are designed for easy memorization in preparation for taking the CompTIA Security+ exam.

Key Terms for Understanding Risk Management

You need to understand a number of key terms to manage risk successfully. Some of these terms are defined here because they are used throughout the chapter. This list is somewhat ordered according to the organization of this chapter. More comprehensive definitions and other pertinent terms are listed alphabetically in the glossary at the end of this book.

 EXAM TIP These terms are important, and you should completely memorize their meanings before taking the CompTIA Security+ exam.

Risk The possibility of suffering harm or loss.

Risk Management The overall decision-making process of identifying threats and vulnerabilities and their potential impacts, determining the costs to mitigate such events, and deciding what actions are cost effective for controlling these risks.

Risk Assessment (or Risk Analysis) The process of analyzing an environment to identify the risks (threats and vulnerabilities), and mitigating actions to determine (either quantitatively or qualitatively) the impact of an event that would affect a project, program, or business.

Asset Resource or information an organization needs to conduct its business.

Mitigate Action taken to reduce the likelihood of a threat occurring.

Control Types

Security controls are the elements used to reduce the risk associated with security failures. A wide variety of tools can be employed; NIST SP 800-53 lists literally hundreds of controls that can be employed in systems to improve the security posture.

Technical

Technical controls are those that operate through a technological intervention in the system. Examples include elements such as user authentication (passwords), logical access controls, antivirus/malware software, firewalls, intrusion detection and prevention systems, and so forth.

Management

Management controls are those that operate on the management of an organization. They include controls such as policies, regulations, and laws. Management activities such as planning and risk assessment are common examples that are employed.

Types of Controls

Controls can be classified based on the types of actions they perform. Three classes of controls exist:

- Technical
- Management (or administrative)
- Operational (or physical)

For each of these classes, there are four types of controls:

- Preventive (deterrent)
- Detective
- Corrective (recovery)
- Compensating

Operational

Operational controls are those that are effective through the operations of an organization, typically through the actions taken by people. Examples include operational processes such as incident response, configuration management, personal security, and training and awareness.

False Positives

A test result that indicates a condition that does not actually exist is called a false positive. If a security system detects an incidence of attack when one does not actually exist, this is a false positive result. Another name for a false positive error is a false alarm. False positives can add to workload, forcing analysts to examine more data than necessary to find actual true events.

False Negatives

The failure of a system to detect a condition that is occurring is an example of a false negative. For instance, the failure of an IDS to detect an actual attack is a false negative. False negatives can be as damaging as false positives, and in some cases more damaging. A security system that fails to perform as expected can have significant consequences as the event goes undetected.

Importance of Policies in Reducing Risk

A security program (the total of all technology, processes, procedures, metrics, training, and personnel that are part of the organization's approach to addressing security) should be based on an organization's documented security policies, procedures, standards, and guidelines that specify what users and administrators should be doing to maintain the security of the systems and network. Collectively, these documents provide the guidance needed to determine how security will be implemented in the organization. Given this guidance, the specific technology and security mechanisms required can be planned for.

Policies are high-level, broad statements of what the organization wants to accomplish. *Standards* are mandatory elements regarding the implementation of a policy. Some standards can be externally driven. Government regulations for banking and financial institutions, for example, require that certain security measures be taken. Other standards may be set by the organization to meet its own security goals. *Guidelines* are recommendations relating to a policy. The key term in this case is *recommendations*—guidelines are not mandatory steps. *Procedures* are the step-by-step instructions on how to implement policies in the organization.

Just as the network itself constantly changes, the policies, standards, guidelines, and procedures should be included in living documents that are periodically evaluated and changed as necessary. The constant monitoring of the network and the periodic review of the relevant documents are part of the process that is the operational model. This operational process consists of four basic steps:

1. Plan (adjust) for security.
2. Implement the plans.
3. Monitor the implementation.
4. Evaluate the effectiveness.

In the first step, you develop the policies, procedures, and guidelines that will be implemented and design the security components that will protect your network. Once these are designed and developed, you can implement the plans. Next, you monitor to ensure that both the hardware and the software, as well as the policies, procedures, and guidelines, are working to secure your systems. Finally, you evaluate the effectiveness of the security measures you have in place. The evaluation step can include a *vulnerability assessment* (an attempt to identify and prioritize the list of vulnerabilities within a system or network) and a *penetration test* (a method to check the security of a system by simulating an attack by a malicious individual) of your system to ensure the security is adequate. After evaluating your security posture, you begin again with step one, this time adjusting the security mechanisms you have in place, and then continue with this cyclical process.

Privacy Policy

Customers place an enormous amount of trust in organizations to which they provide personal information. These customers expect their information to be kept secure so that unauthorized individuals will not gain access to it and so that authorized users will not use the information in unintended ways. Organizations should have a *privacy policy* that explains what their guiding principles will be in guarding personal data to which they are given access. In many locations, customers have a legal right to expect that their information is kept private, and organizations that violate this trust may find themselves involved in a lawsuit. In certain sectors, such as health care, federal regulations have been created that prescribe stringent security controls on private information.

It is a general practice in most organizations to have a policy that describes explicitly how information provided to the organization will be used (for example, it will not be sold to other organizations). Watchdog organizations monitor the use of individual information by organizations, and businesses can subscribe to services that will vouch for the organization to consumers, stating that the company has agreed to protect and keep private any information supplied to it. The organization is then granted permission to display a seal or certification on its website where customers can see it. Organizations that misuse the information they promised to protect will find themselves subject to penalties from the watchdog organization.

A special category of private information that is becoming increasingly important today is personally identifiable information (PII). This category of information includes any data that can be used to uniquely identify an individual. This would include an individual's name, address, driver's license number, and other details. With the proliferation of e-commerce on the Internet, this information is used extensively, and its protection has become increasingly important. You would not have to look far to find reports in the media of data compromises that have resulted in the loss of information that has led to issues such as identity theft. An organization that collects PII on its employees and customers must make sure that it takes all necessary measures to protect the data from compromise.

Acceptable Use

An acceptable use policy (AUP) outlines what the organization considers to be the appropriate use of its resources, such as computer systems, e-mail, Internet, and networks. Organizations should be concerned about any personal use of organizational assets that does not benefit the company.

The goal of the policy is to ensure employee productivity while limiting potential organizational liability resulting from inappropriate use of the organization's assets. The policy should clearly delineate what activities are not allowed. The AUP should address issues such as the use of resources to conduct personal business, installation of hardware or software, remote access to systems and networks, the copying of company-owned software, and the responsibility of users to protect company assets, including data, software, and hardware. Statements regarding possible penalties for ignoring any of the policies (such as termination) should also be included.

Related to appropriate use of the organization's computer systems and networks by employees is the appropriate use by the organization. The most important of such issues is whether the organization will consider it appropriate to monitor the employees' use of the systems and network. If monitoring is considered appropriate, the organization should include a statement to this effect in the banner that appears at login. This repeatedly warns employees, and possible intruders, that their actions are subject to monitoring and that any misuse of the system will not be tolerated. Should the organization need to use in either a civil or criminal case any information gathered during monitoring, the issue of whether the employee had an expectation of privacy, or whether it was even legal for the organization to be monitoring, is simplified if the organization can point to its repeatedly displayed statement that use of the system constitutes consent to monitoring. Before any monitoring is conducted, or the actual wording on the warning message is created, the organization's legal counsel should be consulted to determine the appropriate way to address this issue.

 EXAM TIP Make sure you understand that an acceptable use policy outlines what is considered acceptable behavior for a computer system's users. This policy often goes hand-in-hand with an organization's Internet usage policy.

Security Policy

In keeping with the high-level nature of policies, the *security policy* is a high-level statement produced by senior management that outlines what security means to the organization and what the organization's goals are for security. The main security policy can then be broken down into additional policies that cover specific topics. Statements such as "this organization will exercise the principle of least privilege in its handling of client information" would be an example of a security policy. The security policy can also describe how security is to be handled from an organizational point of view (such as describing which office and corporate officer or manager oversees the organization's security program).

In addition to policies related to access control, the organization's security policy should include the specific policies described in the next sections. All policies should be reviewed on a regular basis and updated as needed. Generally, policies should be updated less frequently than the procedures that implement them, since the high-level goals will not change as often as the environment in which they must be implemented. All policies should be reviewed by the organization's legal counsel, and a plan should be outlined describing how the organization will ensure that employees will be made aware of the policies. Policies can also be made stronger by including references to the authority who made the policy (whether this policy comes from the CEO or is a department-level policy) and also refer to any laws or regulations that are applicable to the specific policy and environment.

Mandatory Vacations

Organizations have been providing vacation time for their employees for many years. Until recently, however, few organizations forced employees to take this time if they didn't want to. Some employees are given the choice to either "use or lose" their vacation time, and if they do not take all of their time, they'll lose at least a portion of it. Many arguments can be made as to the benefit of taking time off, but more importantly, from a security standpoint, an employee who never takes time off is a potential indicator of nefarious activity. Employees who never take any vacation time could be involved in activity such as fraud or embezzlement and might be afraid that if they leave on vacation, the organization would discover their illicit activities. As a result, requiring employees to use their vacation time through a policy of mandatory vacations can be a security protection mechanism. Using mandatory vacations as a tool to detect fraud will require that somebody else also be trained in the functions of the employee who is on vacation. Having a second person familiar with security procedures is also a good policy in case something happens to the primary.

Job Rotation

Another policy that provides multiple benefits is *job rotation*. Rotating through jobs provides individuals with a better perspective of how the various parts of the organization can enhance (or hinder) the business. Since security is often of secondary concern to people in their jobs, rotating individuals through security positions can result in a much wider understanding of the organization's security problems. A secondary benefit is that it also eliminates the need to rely on one individual for security expertise. If all security tasks are the domain of one employee, security will suffer if that individual is lost from the organization. In addition, if only one individual understands the security domain, should that person become disgruntled and decide to harm the organization, recovering from their attack could be very difficult.

Separation of Duties

Separation of duties is a principle employed in many organizations to ensure that no single individual has the ability to conduct transactions alone. This means that the level of trust in any one individual is lessened, and the ability for any individual to cause catastrophic damage to the organization is also lessened. An example might be an organization in which one person has the ability to order equipment, but another individual makes the payment. An individual who wants to make an unauthorized purchase for his own personal gain would have to convince another person to go along with the transaction.

Separating duties as a security tool is a good practice, but it is possible to go overboard and break up transactions into too many pieces or require too much oversight. This results in inefficiency and can actually be less secure, since individuals may not scrutinize transactions as thoroughly because they know others will also be reviewing them. The temptation is to hurry something along and assume that somebody else will examine it or has examined it.

 EXAM TIP Another aspect of the separation of duties principle is that it spreads responsibilities out over an organization so no single individual becomes the indispensable individual with all of the "keys to the kingdom" or unique knowledge about how to make everything work. If enough tasks have been distributed, assigning a primary and a backup person for each task will ensure that the loss of any one individual will not have a disastrous impact on the organization.

Least Privilege

Two other common security principles are those of *need to know* and *least privilege*. The guiding factor here is that each individual in the organization is supplied with only the absolute minimum amount of information and privileges needed to perform the assigned work tasks. To obtain access to any piece of information, the individual must have a justified need to know. In addition, the employee will be granted only the bare minimum number of privileges that are needed to perform the job.

A policy spelling out these two principles as guiding philosophies for the organization should be created. The policy should also address who in the organization can grant access to information or may assign privileges to employees.

Qualitative Risk Assessment

Qualitative risk assessment is the process of subjectively determining the impact of an event that affects a project, program, or business. Qualitative risk assessment usually involves the use of expert judgment, experience, or group consensus to complete the assessment. To assess risk qualitatively, you compare the impact of the threat with the probability of occurrence. For example, if a threat has a high impact and a high probability of occurring, the risk exposure is high and probably requires some action to reduce this threat (see darkest box in Figure 5-1). Conversely, if the impact is low with a low probability, the risk exposure is low and no action may be required to reduce this threat (see white box in Figure 5-1). Figure 5-1 shows an example of a binary assessment, where only two outcomes are possible each for impact and probability. Either it will have an impact or it will not (or it will have a low or high impact), and it can occur or it will not (or it will have a high probability of occurring or a low probability of occurring).

In reality, a few threats can usually be identified as presenting high-risk exposure and a few threats present low-risk exposure. The threats that fall somewhere between (light gray boxes in Figure 5-1) will have to be evaluated by judgment and management experience.

If the analysis is more complex, requiring three levels of analysis, such as low-medium-high or red-green-yellow, nine combinations are possible, as shown in Figure 5-2. Again, the darkest boxes probably require action, the white boxes may or may not require action, and the gray boxes require judgment. (Note that for brevity, in Figures 5-2 and 5-3, the first term in each box refers to the magnitude of the impact, and the second term refers to the probability of the threat occurring.)

Other levels of complexity are possible. With five levels of analysis, 25 values of risk exposure are possible. In this case, the possible values of impact and probability could take on these values: very low, low, medium, high, or very high. Also, note that

Figure 5-1
Binary
assessment

Impact	High Impact/Low Probability	High Impact/High Probability
	Low Impact/Low Probability	Low Impact/High Probability

Probability

Figure 5-2
Three levels of
analysis

Impact

High Low	High Medium	High High
Medium Low	Medium Medium	Medium High
Low Low	Low Medium	Low High

Probability

the matrix does not have to be symmetrical. For example, if the probability is assessed with three values (low, medium, high) and the impact has five values (very low, low, medium, high, very high), the analysis would be as shown in Figure 5-3. (Again, note that the first term in each box refers to the impact, and the second term in each box refers to the probability of occurrence.)

So far, the examples have focused on assessing probability versus impact. Qualitative risk assessment can be adapted to a variety of attributes and situations in combination with each other. For example, Figure 5-4 shows the comparison of some specific risks that have been identified during a security assessment. The assessment identified the risk areas listed in the first column (weak intranet security, high number of modems, Internet attack vulnerabilities, and weak incident detection and response mechanisms). The assessment also identified various potential impacts listed across the top (business impact, probability of attack, cost to fix, and difficulty to fix). Each of the impacts has been assessed as low, moderate, or high—depicted using green (G), yellow (Y), and red (R), respectively. Each of the risk areas has been assessed with respect to each of the potential impacts, and an overall risk assessment has been determined in the last column.

Quantitative Risk Assessment

Quantitative risk assessment is the process of objectively determining the impact of an event that affects a project, program, or business. Quantitative risk assessment usually involves the use of metrics and models to complete the assessment. Whereas qualitative risk assessment relies on judgment and experience, quantitative risk assessment applies historical information and trends to attempt to predict future performance. This type of risk assessment is highly dependent on historical data, and gathering such data can be difficult. Quantitative risk assessment can also rely heavily on models that provide decision-making information in the form of quantitative metrics, which attempt to measure risk levels across a common scale.

Figure 5-3
A 3-by-5 level
analysis

Impact

Very High Low	Very High Medium	Very High High
High Low	High Medium	High High
Medium Low	Medium Medium	Medium High
Low Low	Low Medium	Low High
Very Low Low	Very Low Medium	Very Low High

Probability

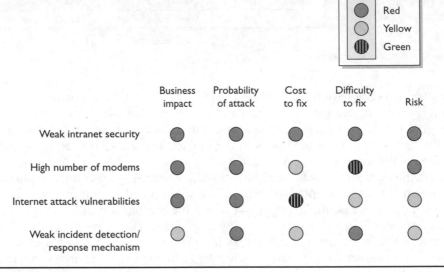

Figure 5-4 Example of a combination assessment

Adding Objectivity to a Qualitative Assessment

Making a qualitative assessment more objective can be as simple as assigning numeric values to one of the tables shown in Figures 5-1 through 5-4. For example, the impacts listed in Figure 5-4 can be prioritized from highest to lowest and then weighted, as shown in Table 5-1, with business impact weighted the most and difficulty to fix weighted least.

Next, values can be assigned to reflect how each risk was assessed. Figure 5-4 can thus be made more objective by assigning a value to each color that represents an assessment. For example, a red assessment indicates many critical, unresolved issues, and this will be given an assessment value of 3. Green means few issues are unresolved, so it is given a value of 1. Table 5-2 shows values that can be assigned for an assessment using red, yellow, and green.

Impact	Explanation	Weight
Business impact	If exploited, would this have a material business impact?	4
Probability of attack	How likely is a potential attacker to try this technique or attack?	3
Cost to fix	How much will it cost in dollars and resources to correct this vulnerability?	2
Difficulty to fix	How hard is this to fix from a technical standpoint?	1

Table 5-1 Adding Weights and Definitions to the Potential Impacts

Table 5-2	Assessment	Explanation	Value
Adding Values to Assessments	Red	Many critical, unresolved issues	3
	Yellow	Some critical, unresolved issues	2
	Green	Few unresolved issues	1

The last step is to calculate an overall risk value for each risk area (each row in Figure 5-4) by multiplying the weights depicted in Table 5-1 times the assessed values from Table 5-2 and summing the products:

$$\text{Risk} = W_1 \times V_1 + W_2 \times V_2 + \ldots W_4 \times V_4$$

The risk calculation and final risk value for each risk area listed in Figure 5-4 have been incorporated into Figure 5-5. The assessed areas can then be ordered from highest to lowest based on the calculated risk value to aid management in focusing on the risk areas with the greatest potential impact.

It is important to understand that key assumptions underlie any model, and different models will produce different results even when given the same input data. Although

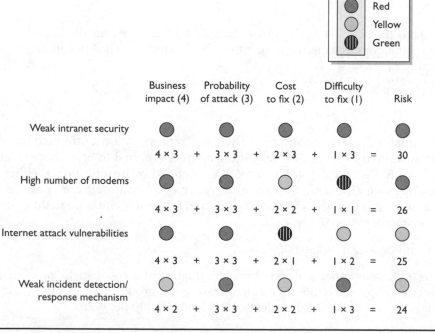

Figure 5-5   Final quantitative assessment of the findings

significant research and development have been invested in improving and refining the various risk analysis models, expert judgment and experience must still be considered an essential part of any risk-assessment process. Models can never replace judgment and experience, but they can significantly enhance the decision-making process.

Risk Calculation

More complex models permit a variety of analyses based on statistical and mathematical models. A common method is the calculation of the annualized loss expectancy (ALE). Calculating the ALE creates a monetary value of the impact. This calculation begins by calculating a single loss expectancy (SLE).

SLE

The single loss expectancy is calculated using the following formula:

SLE = asset value × exposure factor

Exposure factor is a measure of the magnitude of loss of an asset.

By example, to calculate the exposure factor, assume the asset value of a small office building and its contents is $2 million. Also assume that this building houses the call center for a business, and the complete loss of the center would take away about half of the capability of the company. Therefore, the exposure factor is 50 percent. The SLE is

$2 million × 0.5 = $1 million

ALE

The ALE is then calculated simply by multiplying the SLE by the likelihood or number of times the event is expected to occur in a year, which is called the annualized rate of occurrence (ARO):

ALE = SLE × ARO

ARO

The annualized rate of occurrence (ARO) is a representation of the frequency of the event, measured in a standard year. If the event is expected to occur once in 20 years, then the ARO is 1/20. Typically, the ARO is defined by historical data, either from a company's own experience or from industry surveys. Continuing our example, assume that a fire at this business's location is expected to occur about once in 20 years. Given this information, the ALE is

$1 million × 1/20 = $50,000

The ALE determines a threshold for evaluating the cost/benefit ratio of a given countermeasure. Therefore, a countermeasure to protect this business adequately should cost no more than the calculated ALE of $50,000 per year.

TIP Numerous resources are available to help in calculating ALE. There are databases that contain information to help businesses (member institutions) manage exposure to loss from natural disasters such as hurricanes, earthquakes, and so forth. There is information on property perils such as fire, lightning, vandalism, windstorm, hail, and so forth. It even includes information to help evaluate the effectiveness of your building's sprinkler systems.

Impact

The impact of an event is a measure of the actual loss when a threat exploits a vulnerability. Federal Information Processing Standards (FIPS) 199 defines three levels of impact using the terms high, moderate, and low. The impact needs to be defined in terms of the context of each organization, as what is high for some firms may be low for much larger firms. The common method is to define the impact levels in terms of important business criteria. Impacts can be in terms of cost (dollars), performance (service level agreement [SLA] or other requirements), schedule (deliverables), or any other important item. Impact can also be categorized in terms of the information security attribute that is relevant to the problem: confidentiality, integrity, and availability.

MTTR

Mean time to repair (MTTR) is a common measure of how long it takes to repair a given failure. This is the average time, and may or may not include the time needed to obtain parts.

MTBF

Mean time between failure (MTBF) is a common measure of reliability of a system and is an expression of the average time between system failures. The time between failures is measured from the time a system returns to service until the next failure. The MTBF is an arithmetic mean of a set of system failures:

$$MTBF = \Sigma \text{ (start of downtime – start of uptime) / number of failures}$$

MTTF

Mean time to failure (MTTF) is a variation of MTBF, one that is commonly used instead of MTBF when the system is replaced in lieu of being repaired. Other than the semantic difference, the calculations are the same, and the meaning is essentially the same.

Quantitative vs. Qualitative

It is recognized throughout industry that it is *impossible* to conduct risk management that is purely *quantitative*. Usually, risk management includes both qualitative and quantitative elements, requiring both analysis and judgment or experience. In contrast to quantitative assessment, it is *possible* to accomplish *purely qualitative* risk management. It is easy to see that it is impossible to define and quantitatively measure all

Measurement of Availability

Availability is a measure of the amount of time a system performs its intended function. Reliability is a measure of the frequency of system failures. Availability is related to, but different than reliability and is typically expressed as a percentage of time the system is in its operational state. To calculate availability, both the MTTF and the MTTR are needed:

Availability = MTTF / (MTTF + MTTR)

Assuming a system has an MTTF of 6 months and the repair takes 30 minutes, the availability would be

Availability = 6 months / (6 months + 30 minutes) = 99.9884%

factors that exist in a given risk assessment. It is also easy to see that a risk assessment that measures no factors quantitatively but measures them all qualitatively is possible.

The decision of whether to use qualitative versus quantitative risk management depends on the criticality of the project, the resources available, and the management style. The decision will be influenced by the degree to which the fundamental risk management metrics, such as asset value, exposure factor, and threat frequency, can be quantitatively defined.

 EXAM TIP Quantitative risk management involves assigning specific absolute values to risk, while qualitative risk management is accomplished with relative values.

Vulnerabilities

Vulnerabilities are characteristics of an asset that can be exploited by a threat to cause harm. Your system has a security vulnerability, for example, if you have not installed patches to fix a cross-site scripting (XSS) error on your website. Not all errors or bugs are vulnerabilities. For an error or bug to be classified as a vulnerability, it must be exploitable, meaning an attacker must be able to use the bug to cause a desired result. There are three elements needed for a vulnerability to occur:

- The system must have a flaw.
- The flaw must be accessible by an attacker.
- The attacker must possess the ability to exploit the flaw.

Vulnerabilities can exist in many levels and from many causes. From design errors, coding errors, or unintended (and untested) combinations in complex systems, there are numerous forms of vulnerabilities. Vulnerabilities can exist in software, hardware, and procedures. Whether in the underlying system, a security control designed to protect the system, or the procedures employed in the operational use of the system, the result is the same: a vulnerability represents an exploitable weakness that increases the level of risk associated with the system.

 EXAM TIP Vulnerabilities can be fixed, removed, and mitigated. They are part of any system and represent weaknesses that may be exploited.

Threat Vectors

A threat is any circumstance or event with the potential to cause harm to an asset. For example, a malicious hacker might choose to hack your system by using readily available hacking tools. Threats can be classified in groups, with the term *threat vector* describing the elements of these groups. A threat vector is the path or tool used by an attacker to attack a target. There are a wide range of threat vectors that a security professional needs to understand:

- The Web (fake sites, session hijacking, malware, watering hole attacks)
- Wireless unsecured hotspots
- Mobile devices (iOS/Android)
- USB (removable) media
- E-mail (links, attachments, malware)
- Social engineering (deceptions, hoaxes, scams, and fraud)

This listing is merely a sample of threat vectors. From a defensive point of view, it is important not to become fixated on specific threats, but rather to pay attention to the threat vectors. If a user visits a website that has malicious code, then the nature of the code, although important from a technical view in one respect, is not the primary concern. The primary issue is the malicious site, as this is the threat vector.

Probability/Threat Likelihood

The probability or likelihood of an event is a measure of how often it is expected to occur. From a qualitative assessment using terms such as frequent, occasionally, and rare, to the quantitative measure ARO, the purpose is to allow scaling based on frequency of an event. Determining the specific probabilities of security events with any accuracy is a nearly impossible feat. What is important in the use of probabilities and likelihoods is the relationship it has with respect to determining relative risk. Just as an insurance company cannot tell you when you will have an accident, no one can predict when a security event will occur. What can be determined is that over some course of time, say the next year, a significant number of users will click malicious links in e-mails. The threat likelihood of different types of attacks will change over time. Years ago, web defacements were all the rage. Today, spear phishing is more prevalent.

Risk Avoidance, Transference, Acceptance, Mitigation, Deterrence

Risks are absolutes—they cannot be removed or eliminated. Actions can be taken to change the effects that a risk poses to a system, but the risk itself doesn't really change, no matter what actions are taken to mitigate that risk. A high risk will always be a high risk. However, actions can be taken to reduce the impact of that risk if it occurs. A limited number of strategies can be used to manage risk. The risk can be avoided, transferred, mitigated, or accepted.

Avoiding the risk can be accomplished in many ways. Although threats cannot be removed from the environment, one's exposure can be altered. Not deploying a module that increases risk is one manner of risk avoidance.

Another possible action to manage risk is to transfer that risk. A common method of transferring risk is to purchase insurance. Insurance allows risk to be transferred to a third party that manages specific types of risk for multiple parties, thus reducing the individual cost. Another common example of risk transfer is the protection against fraud that consumers have on their credit cards. The risk is transferred to another party, so people can use the card in confidence.

Risk can also be mitigated through the application of controls that reduce the impact of an attack. Controls can alert operators so that the level of exposure is reduced through process intervention. When an action occurs that is outside the accepted risk profile, a second set of rules can be applied, such as calling the customer for verification before committing a transaction. Controls such as these can act to reduce the risk associated with potential high-risk operations.

In addition to mitigating risk or transferring risk, it may be acceptable for a manager to accept risk in that despite the potential cost of a given risk and its associated probability, the manager of the organization will accept responsibility for the risk if it does happen. For example, a manager may choose to allow a programmer to make "emergency" changes to a production system (in violation of good separation of duties) because the system cannot go down during a given period of time. The manager accepts that the risk that the programmer could possibly make unauthorized changes is outweighed by the high-availability requirement of that system. However, there should always be some additional controls, such as a management review or a standardized approval process, to ensure the assumed risk is adequately managed.

Understand that risk cannot be completely eliminated. A risk that remains after implementing controls is termed a *residual risk*. In this step, you further evaluate residual risks to identify where additional controls are required to reduce risk even more. This leads us to the earlier statement, in the chapter introduction, that the risk management process is iterative.

The Cloud

Cloud computing is a common term used to describe computer services provided over a network. These computing services are computing, storage, applications, and services that are offered via the Internet Protocol. One of the characteristics of cloud computing is transparency to the end user. This improves usability of this form of service provisioning. Cloud computing offers much to the user: improvements in performance, scalability, flexibility, security, and reliability, among other items. These improvements are a direct result of the specific attributes associated with how cloud services are implemented. The promise of cloud computing is improved utility and is marketed under the concepts of Platform as a Service, Software as a Service, and Infrastructure as a Service. The challenge in managing risk in the cloud is in the advance determination of who has what level of security responsibility—the cloud provider, the service provider, or the user?

Risks Associated with Cloud Computing and Virtualization

When examining a complex system such as a cloud or virtual computing environment from a risk perspective, several basic considerations always need to be observed. First, the fact that a system is either in the cloud or virtualized does not change how risk works. Risk is everywhere, and changing a system to a new environment does not change the fact that there are risks. Second, complexity can increase risk exposure. The addition of cloud and/or virtualization adds to the risk simply by adding complexity to the system.

There are specific risks associated with both virtualization and cloud environments. Having data and computing occur in environments that are not under the direct control of the data owner adds both a layer of complexity and a degree of risk. The potential for issues with confidentiality, integrity, and availability increases with the loss of direct control over the environment. The virtualization and cloud layers also present new avenues of attack into a system.

Security is a particular challenge when data and computation are handled by a remote party, as in cloud computing. The specific challenge is how to allow data outside your enterprise and yet remain in control over the use of the data. The common answer is encryption. Through the proper use of encryption of data before it leaves the enterprise, external storage can still be performed securely by properly employing cryptographic elements. The security requirements associated with confidentiality, integrity, and availability remain the responsibility of the data owner, and measures must be taken to ensure that these requirements are met, regardless of the location or usage associated with the data. Another level of protections is through the use of service level agreements (SLAs) with the cloud vendor, although these frequently cannot offer much remedy in the event of data loss.

Virtualization

Virtualization is the creation of virtual systems rather than actual hardware and software. The separation of the hardware and software enables increased flexibility in the enterprise. On top of actual hardware, a virtualization layer enables the creation of complete systems, including computers and networking equipment, as virtual machines. This separation of hardware and software enables security through a series of improvements. The ability to copy entire systems, back them up, or move them between hardware platforms can add to the security of a system.

Although vulnerabilities exist that can possibly allow processes in one virtual environment to breach the separation between virtual environments or the layer to the host, these are rare and exceptionally difficult to exploit. A new form of vulnerability—the ability to make copies of complete virtual systems—must be addressed, as this could lead to data and intellectual property loss. Protecting the storage of virtual systems must be on par with backups of regular systems to avoid wholesale loss. Virtualized systems should be updated/patched similar to nonvirtualized systems. Virtual systems still need security services to protect virtual machines from intrusions, malware, and the same threats that regular systems face.

Recovery Time Objective and Recovery Point Objective

The term *recovery time objective (RTO)* is used to describe the target time that is set for a resumption of operations after an incident. This is a period of time that is defined by the business, based on the needs of the enterprise. A shorter RTO results in higher costs because it requires greater coordination and resources. This term is commonly used in business continuity and disaster recovery operations.

Recovery point objective (RPO), a totally different concept from RTO, is the time period representing the maximum period of acceptable data loss. The RPO defines the frequency of backup operations necessary to prevent unacceptable levels of data loss. A simple example of establishing RPO is to answer the following questions: How much data can you afford to lose? How much rework is tolerable?

RTP and RPO are seemingly related but in actuality measure different things entirely. The RTO serves the purpose of defining the requirements for business continuity, while the RPO deals with backup frequency. It is possible to have an RTO of 1 day and an RPO of 1 hour, or an RTO of 1 hour and an RPO of 1 day. The determining factors are the needs of the business.

 EXAM TIP Although recovery time objective and recovery point objective seem to be the same or similar, they are very different. The RTO serves the purpose of defining the requirements for business continuity, while the RPO deals with backup frequency.

Chapter Review

In this chapter, you became acquainted with the principles of risk management. The chapter began by defining key terms associated with risk management. It then presented the three categories of security controls: management, technical, and operational. Next, it discussed the concepts of false positives and false negatives and how they relate to security systems.

You learned that security policies can have a direct impact on risk, and discovered the roles of policies, including the security policy, privacy policy, acceptable use policy,

HR-related policies such as job rotation and mandatory vacations, separation of duties, and least privilege policies. You then examined both qualitative and quantitative risk management methodologies, including a comparison of them. You learned how to calculate risk using ALE, SLE, and ARO, and were introduced to the concepts of MTTR, MTBF, and MTTF. Availability was presented as a function of MTTF and MTTR. The topic area concluded with a discussion of recovery time objective and recovery point objective and the distinction between them.

The chapter next presented the characteristics of vulnerabilities that enable exploitation, including the concept of probabilities and threat likelihood. The concept of threat vectors as a means by which attackers can attack a system was also presented. The chapter concluded with the four main strategies for management of risk (avoid, transfer, mitigate, and accept), and a discussion on the current trends of risk in the areas of virtualization and cloud computing.

Questions

To help you prepare further for the CompTIA Security+ exam, and to test your level of preparedness, answer the following questions and then check your answers against the correct answers at the end of the chapter.

1. Which of the following is a class of control?

    A. Preventive

    B. Management

    C. Mitigation

    D. Impact

2. Which of the following is a type of control?

    A. Operational

    B. Threat

    C. Risk

    D. Detective

3. Which of the following is an example of the principle of separation of duties?

    A. Software developers should not have access to production data and source code files.

    B. Software development, testing, quality assurance, and production can be assigned to some of the same individuals.

    C. The functions of creating, installing, and administering software programs can be assigned to some of the same individuals.

    D. Software developers and testers should have access to "live" production data.

4. Which of the following correctly defines the principle of least privilege?

   A. A control that prevents or detects errors and irregularities by assigning responsibilities to different individuals.

   B. The process of rotating individuals through various jobs in an organization.

   C. Providing a user with the minimum set of rights and privileges that he or she needs to perform required functions.

   D. Security controls that rely on protection mechanisms that are confusing and supposedly not generally known.

5. Which of the following correctly defines acceptable use policy?

   A. Outlines what the company will allow employees to send in terms of e-mail.

   B. Outlines what the organization considers to be the appropriate use of company resources.

   C. Addresses what sites employees are allowed to visit and what sites they are not allowed to visit.

   D. A high-level statement produced by senior management that outlines what security means to the organization.

6. Which of the following correctly identifies risk transference?

   A. The engagement of third-party organizations that manage specific types of risk for multiple parties.

   B. Action taken to reduce the likelihood of a threat occurring.

   C. Management accepts the risk and the associated impacts despite the potential costs.

   D. The possibility of suffering a loss.

7. What is the benefit of qualitative risk assessment over quantitative risk assessment?

   A. Quantitative risk assessment relies on expert judgment and experience.

   B. Qualitative risk assessment relies on the gathering of historical information and trends.

   C. It is impossible to conduct a purely qualitative risk assessment.

   D. Qualitative risk assessment does not require the gathering of historical information and trends.

8. Which of the following correctly defines exposure factor?

   A. On an annualized basis, the frequency with which an event is expected to occur.

   B. Monetary loss or impact of each occurrence of a threat.

   C. A measure of the magnitude of loss of an asset.

   D. The amount an event is expected to cost the business per year.

9. Fill in the blanks. Availability is calculated using the formula

    Availability = A / (B + C)

    A = _____
    B = _____
    C = _____

10. Annualized loss expectancy can best be defined by which of the following equations?

    A. Asset value × exposure factor

    B. SLE × exposure factor

    C. ARO × asset value

    D. SLE × ARO

11. The CFO has come to you seeking advice on important principles she should consider to prevent financial improprieties in the accounts payable department. Which of the following are elements that can help implement the principle of least privilege?

    A. Separation of duties

    B. Job rotation

    C. Implicit deny

    D. Layered security

    E. All of the above

    F. None of the above

12. Your boss is in a meeting and sends you an IM asking you to help him remember the four different types of controls. What do you send to him in your response?

    _____, _____, _____, _____

13. Following the scenario established in question 12, your boss is still in the same meeting and now asks you to give him for four examples of technical controls. What do you send to him in your response?

    _____, _____, _____, _____

For questions 14 and 15, use the following scenario: Your company provides telephone surveys under contract for other organizations. The asset value of a call center located on the East Coast is $10 million, and this call center performs the same functions as another equivalent call center located in the Mountain West. The complete destruction of the East Coast facility by a disaster would take away about half of the capability of the business. Assume that this sort of disaster is expected to occur about once every 100 years.

14. Which of the following is the calculated single loss expectancy?

   A. SLE = $100,000

   B. SLE = $5 million

   C. SLE = $50,000

   D. SLE = $10 million

15. Which of the following is the calculated annualized loss expectancy?

   A. ALE = $50,000

   B. ALE = $500,000

   C. ALE = $5 million

   D. ALE = $10 million

Answers

1. **B.** The classes of controls are management, technical, and operational.

2. **D.** The types of controls are preventive, detective, corrective, and compensating.

3. **A.** Software developers should not have access to production data and source code files. This prevents accidental changes to production systems by development teams.

4. **C.** Least privilege is a security principle in which a user is provided with the minimum set of rights and privileges that he or she needs to perform required functions.

5. **B.** An acceptable use policy defines proper use of company resources.

6. **A.** Transferring risk involves transferring the risk to a third party that manages specific types of risk for multiple parties.

7. **D.** Qualitative risk assessment relies primarily on expert judgment and experience.

8. **C.** Exposure factor measures the magnitude of a loss.

9. **A** = MTTF; **B** = MTTF; **C** = MTTR

10. **D.** Annualized loss expectancy is SLE × ARO.

11. **E.** All items listed help to implement the principle of least privilege.

12. The four types of controls are preventive, detective, corrective, and compensating.

13. Examples include elements such as user authentication (passwords), logical access controls, antivirus/malware software, firewalls, and intrusion detection and prevention systems.

14. **B.** SLE = asset value ($10 million) × exposure factor (1/2) = $5 million

15. **A.** ALE = SLE ($5 million) × annualized rate of occurrence (1/100) = $50,000

System Integration Processes

In this chapter, you will

- Learn the security implications of integrating systems and data with third parties
- Examine the different forms of interoperability agreements
- Examine risks associated with sharing data with third parties

Large systems are composed of a highly complex set of integrated components. These components can be integrated into a system designed to perform complex operations. System integration is the set of processes designed to produce synergy from the linkage of all of the components. In most business cases, third parties will be part of the value chain, necessitating the sharing of business information, processes, and data with them. This has security and risk implications that need to be understood before these relationships are established.

System-Level Processes

There are many processes that span across the enterprise, affecting more than a single business unit, and at times, the entire business. These processes can have security implications. These implications can at times manifest themselves in different areas than from where they are caused; hence, they are best dealt with from the enterprise level.

On-boarding/Off-boarding Business Partners

Just as it is important to manage the on- and off-boarding processes of company personnel, it is important to consider the same types of elements when making arrangements with third parties. Agreements with business partners tend to be fairly specific with respect to terms associated with mutual expectations associated with the process of the business. Considerations to the on-boarding and off-boarding processes are important, especially the off-boarding. When a contract arrangement with a third party comes to an end, issues as to data retention and destruction by the third party need to be addressed. These considerations need to be made prior to the establishment of the relationship, not added at the time that it is coming to an end.

EXAM TIP On-boarding and off-boarding business procedures should be well documented to ensure compliance with legal requirements.

Social Media Networks

The rise of social media networks has changed many aspects of business. Whether used for marketing, communications, customer relations, or some other purpose, social media networks can be considered a form of third party. One of the challenges in working with social media networks and/or applications is their terms of use. While a relationship with a typical third party involves a negotiated set of agreements with respect to requirements, there is no negotiation with social media networks. The only option is to adopt their terms of service, so it is important to understand the implications of these terms with respect to the business use of the social network.

Interoperability Agreements

Many business operations involve actions between many different parties—some within an organization, and some in different organizations. These actions require communication between the parties, defining the responsibilities and expectations of the parties, the business objectives, and the environment within which the objectives will be pursued. To ensure an agreement is understood between the parties, written agreements are used. Numerous forms of legal agreements and contracts are used in business, but with respect to security, some of the most common ones are the service level agreement, business partnership agreement, memorandum of understanding, and interconnection security agreement.

SLA A service level agreement (SLA) is a negotiated agreement between parties detailing the expectations between a customer and a service provider. SLAs essentially set the requisite level of performance of a given contractual service. SLAs are typically included as part of a service contract and set the level of technical expectations. An SLA can define specific services, the performance level associated with a service, issue management and resolution, and so on. SLAs are negotiated between customer and supplier and represent the agreed-upon terms. Once entered into, the SLA becomes a legally binding document.

Typically, a good SLA will satisfy two simple rules. First, it will describe the entire set of product or service functions in sufficient detail that their requirement will be unambiguous. Second, the SLA will provide a clear means of determining whether a specified function or service has been provided at the agreed-upon level of performance.

BPA A business partnership agreement (BPA) is a legal agreement between partners establishing the terms, conditions, and expectations of the relationship between the partners. These details can cover a wide range of issues, including typical items such as the sharing of profits and losses, the responsibilities of each partner, the addition or removal of partners, and any other issues. The Uniform Partnership Act (UPA), established by state law and convention, lays out a uniform set of rules associated with partnerships to resolve any partnership terms. The terms in a UPA are designed as "one size fits all" and are not typically in the best interest of any specific partnership. To avoid undesired outcomes that may result from UPA terms, it is best for partnerships to spell out specifics in a BPA.

MOU   A memorandum of understanding (MOU) is a legal document used to describe a bilateral agreement between parties. It is a written agreement expressing a set of intended actions between the parties with respect to some common pursuit or goal. It is more formal and detailed than a simple handshake, but it generally lacks the binding powers of a contract. It is also common to find MOUs between different units within an organization to detail expectations associated with the common business interest.

ISA   An interconnection security agreement (ISA) is a specialized agreement between organizations that have interconnected IT systems, the purpose of which is to document the security requirements associated with the interconnection. An ISA can be a part of an MOU detailing the specific technical security aspects of a data interconnection.

EXAM TIP   Be sure you understand the differences between the interoperability agreements SLA, BPA, MOU, and ISA for the CompTIA Security+ exam.

Privacy Considerations

Integration with third parties can result in privacy considerations. Privacy can be viewed as control over one's own data. When parties share data with a firm for business purposes, it is incumbent upon the firm to ensure that the appropriate safeguards and restrictions are put in place. It is important that personally identifiable information (PII) be properly handled both inside the firm and across third-party relationships.

The first step is to define the requirements for protection of PII. These requirements should be part of the organization's privacy policy. Privacy is the right to control information about you and what others can do with that information. With respect to personal data, the organization's privacy policy sets the terms and conditions that one should expect concerning protection of their personal data. By establishing and publishing the requirements associated with PII, an organization can ensure that the awareness of privacy requirements is spread throughout the organization and incorporated into plans, policies, and procedures.

The components of a privacy policy can vary by organization, but some common components include

- Clearly designate the elements of PII that are being collected and those that are stored.
- Clearly state what the PII will be used for, including any transfer to third parties.
- Designate security provisions and storage time for stored PII.

Risk Awareness

Having third parties play a role in business operations does not alleviate the responsibility to manage risk. All aspects of risk management need to be examined in light of third-party relationships. Consideration needs to be placed on risks associated with data flows and potential exposure of the data. The data security elements of confidentiality, integrity, and availability need to be considered as appropriately defined by data requirements. The requirements for data protection and subsequent risk exposures need to be updated to include the aspects associated with third-party handling.

Data Issues

System integration with third parties frequently involves the sharing of data. Data can be shared for the purpose of processing or storage. Control over data is a significant issue in third-party relationships. There are numerous questions that need to be addressed. The question of who owns the data, both the data shared with third parties and subsequent data developed as part of the relationship, is an issue that needs to be established.

Unauthorized Data Sharing

Unauthorized data sharing can be a significant issue, and in today's world, data has value and is frequently used for secondary purposes. Ensuring that all parties in the relationship understand the data-sharing requirements is an important prerequisite. Equally important is ensuring all parties understand the security requirements of shared data.

Data Ownership

Data requires a data owner. Data ownership roles for all data elements need to be defined in the business. Data ownership is a business function, where the requirements for security, privacy, retention, and other business functions are established. Not all data requires the same handling restrictions, but all data requires these characteristics to be defined. This is the responsibility of the data owner.

Data Backups

Data ownership requirements include backup responsibilities. Data backup requirements include determining the level of backup, restore objectives, and level of protection requirements. These can be defined by the data owner and then executed by operational IT personnel. Determining the backup responsibilities and developing the necessary operational procedures to ensure that adequate backups occur are important security elements.

Policies and Procedures

Policies and procedures govern the operation of the business and represent a set of requirements developed from both internal and external requirements. External requirements may come from laws and regulations, contractual terms such as incorporation of the Payment Card Industry Data Security Standard (PCI-DSS), or customer specifications. There are regulatory situations where specific business actions are required by law or regulation. In many cases, the laws or regulations specify that specific policies are in place to govern compliance. Understanding the specific requirements of the business environment may require assistance from supporting business functions, guidance from industry groups, or help from other sources. Determining the relevant security policies and procedures that apply to third-party relationships is a key element in ensuring that all elements of them are met during business operations. The bottom line is simple: in some business situations, policies and procedures may be mandated by outside regulation, and assistance may be required in ensuring compliance.

Agreements

Relationships with third parties are typically covered by a series of agreements of the types previously discussed in this chapter. It is important to have a process in place to assure that the agreements are properly reviewed to verify compliance and performance standards associated with the business.

Chapter Review

In this chapter, you became acquainted with the principles of integration with third parties. System integration with third parties expands the risk-associated business processes. The chapter opened with a discussion of the interoperability agreements, including service level agreements, business partnership agreements, memorandums of understanding, and interconnection security agreements. The chapter continued with an examination of the data issues and risk associated with sharing with third parties. It covered privacy considerations, including issues with PII, and then presented policies and procedures and how they are employed across third parties via agreements. The chapter closed with an examination of the challenges associated with sharing via social media networks.

 EXAM TIP It is important to understand the security implications of integrating systems and data with third parties.

Questions

To help you prepare further for the CompTIA Security+ exam, and to test your level of preparedness, answer the following questions and then check your answers against the correct answers at the end of the chapter.

1. Which of the following describes a memorandum of understanding (MOU)?

   A. Clearly defined statements of the service to be provided, including penalties if the agreed-upon service levels are not met

   B. A structured approach to identifying the gap between desired and actual privacy performance

   C. An application or tool used to assist in protecting privacy

   D. A non-contractual agreement that indicates an intended approach between parties

2. What is the definition of privacy?

   A. Business secrets protected through trade laws

   B. The right to control information about you and what others can do with that information

   C. Government information protected through laws concerning national security

   D. Information used to identify a specific individual

3. Which of the following represents two simple rules a good SLA should satisfy?

   A. Web standards and coding practices

   B. Technology and processes

   C. Services provided and level of performance

   D. Duration and protection

4. Which of the following describes system integration?

   A. The set of processes designed to produce synergy from the linkage of all the components

   B. Rules for documenting, handling, and safeguarding information

   C. The processes for performing and recording changes to the system

   D. The methods, techniques, and tools used to ensure a system is properly integrated

5. Which of the following describes the elements of interoperability agreements?

   A. Mandatory elements and accepted specifications providing specific details on how company decisions are to be enforced

   B. Responsibilities/expectations of the parties, business objectives, and environment

   C. What the organization considers to be appropriate use of third-party resources

   D. Step-by-step implementation instructions

6. Which of the following describes what a business partnership agreement typically includes?

   A. Profit sharing and the addition or removal of partners

   B. What the organizations consider appropriate use of e-mail, telephones, Internet access, etc.

   C. Clear statements on how to dispose of important company information

   D. The responsibilities of each partner when modifications are made to the IT infrastructure

7. Which of the following is a limitation of a memorandum of understanding?

   A. It helps control changes to a service level agreement.

   B. It is based on due care and due diligence.

   C. It only identifies assets that need to be managed.

   D. It is more formal than a handshake but lacks the binding powers of a contract.

8. Which of the following describes an interconnection security agreement?

   A. Defines rules for investigating security breaches

   B. Prevents hash collisions between systems

   C. Documents the security requirements associated with interconnected IT systems

   D. Physically connects systems shared by two parties

9. Which of the following is a challenge when using social networks for business purposes?

   A. Agreements are easily negotiated.

   B. They include resources and information.

   C. They identify what level of access is allowed.

   D. The terms of use typically can't be negotiated.

10. What is an important factor to remember regarding policies and procedures?

    A. They should always include step-by-step implementation instructions.

    B. They may be mandated by outside regulation.

    C. They enforce appropriate use of company resources.

    D. They describe how to dispose of important company information.

11. You have been asked to review a service level agreement (SLA) that has been provided to your company by a third-party service provider. List the three elements you should ensure are included in the SLA:

    _____, _____, _____, _____

12. List three issues that should be addressed when sharing personally identifiable information with a third party:

    _____, _____, _____

For questions 13–15, please select the appropriate term from the following list:

A. Compliance   E. On-boarding

B. Confidentiality   F. Secrecy

C. Control   G. Social media

D. Off-boarding   H. Terms of use

13. Regarding agreements between third-party organizations, _____ and _____ business procedures should be well documented to ensure _____ with legal requirements.

14. One of the challenges in working with _____ networks and/or applications is their _____.

15. Privacy can be viewed as _____ over one's own data.

Answers

1. **D.** An MOU is a non-contractual agreement that indicates an intended approach between parties.

2. **B.** Privacy is the right to control information about you and what others can do with that information.

3. **C.** The two simple rules a good SLA should satisfy are 1) they describe the services provided and 2) they detail the expected level of performance.

4. **A.** System integration is the set of processes designed to produce synergy from the linkage of all of the components.

5. **B.** Interoperability agreements define the responsibilities and expectations of the parties, the business objectives, and the environment within which the objectives will be pursued.

6. **A.** A business partnership agreement typically describes profit sharing, the responsibilities of each partner, and the addition or removal of partners.

7. **D.** An MOU is more formal and detailed than a simple handshake, but it generally lacks the binding powers of a contract.

8. **C.** An interconnection security agreement is a specialized agreement between organizations that have connected IT systems, the purpose of which is to document the security requirements associated with the interconnection.

9. **D.** A particular challenge with using social networks for business purposes is that the terms of use typically can't be negotiated.

10. **B.** It is important to understand that some policies and procedures may be mandated by outside regulations.

11. An SLA should contain these items (they typically are presented in this order): define specific services to be performed; specify the level of performance; and specify methods used to manage and resolve issues.

12. When sharing PII with third parties, you should clearly designate the elements that are being collected and stored; clearly state what the PII will be used for, including any transfer to third parties; and designate security provisions and storage time.

13. Regarding agreements between third-party organizations, **E.** on-boarding and **D.** off-boarding business procedures should be well documented to ensure **A.** compliance with legal requirements.

14. One of the challenges in working with **G.** social media networks and/or applications is their **H.** terms of use.

15. Privacy can be viewed as **C.** control over one's own data.

Risk Management

In this chapter, you will
- Learn how to implement appropriate risk mitigation strategies
- Study the use of policies for change and incident management
- Examine business continuity concepts
- Examine disaster recovery concepts

Risk management strategies provide management a method of handling the risk associated with change, incident management, business continuity, and disaster recovery. Understanding the elements and relationships of these interconnected activities is a key security element in the enterprise.

Risk Mitigation Strategies

Risk mitigation strategies are the action plans developed after a thorough evaluation of the possible threats, hazards, and risks associated with business operations. These strategies are employed to lessen the risks associated with operations. The focus of risk mitigation strategies is to reduce the effects of threats and hazards. Common mitigation strategies include change management, incident management, user rights and permission reviews, audits, and technology controls.

 EXAM TIP When taking the exam, be prepared to implement appropriate risk mitigation strategies when provided with scenarios.

Change Management

Change management has its roots in system engineering, where it is commonly referred to as configuration management. Most of today's software and hardware change management practices derive from long-standing system engineering configuration management practices. Computer hardware and software development have also evolved to the point that proper management structure and controls must exist to ensure the products operate as planned. It is normal for an enterprise to have a Change Control Board to approve all production changes and ensure the change management procedures are followed before changes are introduced to a system.

Configuration control is the process of controlling changes to items that have been baselined. Configuration control ensures that only approved changes to a baseline are allowed to be implemented. It is easy to understand why a software system, such as a web-based order-entry system, should not be changed without proper testing and control—otherwise, the system might stop functioning at a critical time. Configuration control is a key step that provides valuable insight to managers. If a system is being changed, and configuration control is being observed, managers and others concerned will be better informed. This ensures proper use of assets and avoids unnecessary downtime due to the installation of unapproved changes.

EXAM TIP Change management ensures proper procedures are followed when modifying the IT infrastructure.

Incident Management

When an incident occurs, having an incident response management methodology is a key risk mitigation strategy. One of the steps that should be taken to establish a plan to handle business interruptions as a result of a cyber event of some sort is the establishment of a Computer Incident Response Team (CIRT) or a Computer Emergency Response Team (CERT).

NOTE CERT is a trademark of Carnegie Mellon, and is frequently used in some situations, such as the US-CERT.

The organization's CIRT will conduct the investigation into the incident and make the recommendations on how to proceed. The CIRT should consist of not only permanent members, but also ad hoc members who may be called upon to address special needs depending on the nature of the incident. In addition to individuals with a technical background, the CIRT should include nontechnical personnel to provide guidance on ways to handle media attention, legal issues that may arise, and management issues regarding the continued operation of the organization. The CIRT should be created and team members should be identified before an incident occurs. Policies and procedures for conducting an investigation should also be worked out in advance of an incident occurring. It is also advisable to have the team periodically meet to review these procedures.

Incident response is the set of actions security personnel perform in response to a wide range of triggering events. These actions are vast and varied because they have to deal with a wide range of causes and consequences. Through the use of a structured framework, coupled with properly prepared processes, incident response becomes a manageable task. Without proper preparation, this task can quickly become impossible or intractably expensive.

User Rights and Permissions Reviews

User rights and permissions reviews are one of the more powerful security controls. But the strength of this control depends upon it being kept up-to-date and properly maintained. Ensuring that the list of users and associated rights is complete and up-to-date is a challenging task in anything bigger than the smallest enterprises. A compensating control that can assist in keeping user rights lists current is a set of periodic audits of the user base and associated permissions.

Perform Routine Audits

As part of any good security program, administrators must perform periodic audits to ensure things "are as they should be" with regard to users, systems, policies, and procedures. Installing and configuring security mechanisms is important, but they must be reviewed on a regularly scheduled basis to ensure they are effective, up-to-date, and serving their intended function. Here are some examples, but by no means a complete list, of items that should be audited on a regular basis:

- **User access** Administrators should review which users are accessing the systems, when they are doing so, what resources they are using, and so on. Administrators should look closely for users accessing resources improperly or accessing legitimate resources at unusual times.

- **User rights** When a user changes jobs or responsibilities, she will likely need to be assigned different access permissions; she may gain access to new resources and lose access to others. To ensure that users have access only to the resources and capabilities they need for their current positions, all user rights should be audited periodically.

- **Storage** Many organizations have policies governing what can be stored on "company" resources and how much space can be used by a given user or group. Periodic audits help to ensure that no undesirable or illegal materials exist on organizational resources.

- **Retention** In some organizations, how long a particular document or record is stored can be as important as what is being stored. A records retention policy helps to define what is stored, how it is stored, how long it is stored, and how it is disposed of when the time comes. Periodic audits help to ensure that records or documents are removed when they are no longer needed.

- **Firewall rules** Periodic audits of firewall rules are important to ensure the firewall is filtering traffic as desired and to help ensure that "temporary" rules do not end up as permanent additions to the ruleset.

Data Loss or Theft

Data is the primary target of most attackers. The value of the data can vary, making some data more valuable and hence more at risk of theft. Data can also be lost through a variety of mechanisms, with hardware failure, operator error, and system errors being common causes. Regardless of the cause of loss, an organization can take various actions to mitigate the effects of the loss. Backups lead the list of actions, for backups can provide the ultimate in protection against loss.

To prevent theft, a variety of controls can be employed. Some are risk mitigation steps, such as data minimization, which is the act of not storing what isn't needed. If it must be stored and has value, then technologies such as data loss prevention can be used to provide a means of protection. Simple security controls such as firewalls and network segmentation can also act to make data theft more difficult.

 EXAM TIP When taking the exam, understand the policies and procedures to prevent data loss or theft.

Technology Controls

Protecting data in the enterprise is a prime objective of security controls. Firewalls and network segregation can act as powerful barriers for the protection of critical data. The use of network segregation zones that correspond to the critical sensitivity of the data can provide significant protection for data. Restricting access at the network layer prevents the direct connection to the data from machines that are not in the proper network segment. Because the data is only useful if it can be used by those who are approved to access it, then the methods of access to the data can be architected to be protected from outside influence.

The use of tight access controls together with auditing can provide significant systemic protections against data loss, damage, and theft. These controls act as the core of network and data security and are the important primary elements of data protection.

Data Loss Prevention

Data loss prevention (DLP) refers to technology employed to detect and prevent transfers of data across an enterprise. Employed at key locations, DLP technology can scan packets for specific data patterns. This technology can be tuned to detect account numbers, secrets, specific markers, or files. When specific data elements are detected, the system can block the transfer. The primary challenge in employing DLP technologies is the placement of the sensor. The DLP sensor needs to be able observe the data, so if the channel is encrypted, DLP technology can be thwarted.

Risk Management Best Practices

Best practices are the best defenses that an organization can employ in any activity. One manner of examining best practices is to ensure that the business has the set of best practices to cover its operational responsibilities. At a deeper level, the details of these practices need to themselves be best practices if one is to get the best level of protection. At a minimum, risk mitigation best practices include business continuity, high availability, fault tolerance, and disaster recovery concepts.

None of these operate in isolation. In fact, they are all interconnected, sharing elements as they all work together to achieve a common purpose: the security of the data in the enterprise, which is measured in terms of risk exposure.

Business Continuity Concepts

Keeping an organization running when an event occurs that disrupts operations is not accomplished spontaneously, but requires advance planning and periodically exercising those plans to ensure they will work. A term that is often used when discussing the issue of continued organizational operations is *business continuity plan (BCP)*. You might wonder what the difference is between a disaster recovery plan (DRP) and a BCP. In reality, these two terms are sometimes used synonymously, and for many organizations, there may be no major difference in the two. There are, however, slight differences between a BCP and a DRP, one of which is the *focus*.

The focus of business continuity planning is the continued operation of the business or organization. The focus of a DRP is on the recovery and rebuilding of the organization after a disaster has occurred. The DRP is part of the larger BCP since business continuity is always an issue. In a DRP, the protection of human life should be addressed and is a major focus of the document. Evacuation plans and system shutdown procedures should be addressed. The safety of employees should be a theme throughout a DRP. In the rest of the BCP, on the other hand, you may not see the same level of emphasis placed on protection of employees. The focus of the BCP is the critical systems the organization needs in order to operate.

Another way to look at these two plans is that the BCP will be used to ensure that your operations continue in the face of whatever event has occurred that has caused a disruption in operations. If a disaster has occurred and has destroyed all or part of your facility, the DRP portion of the BCP will address the building or acquisition of a new facility. The DRP can also include details related to the long-term recovery of the organization.

However you view these two plans, an organization that is not able to restore business functions quickly after an operational interruption is an organization that will most likely suffer an unrecoverable loss and may cease to exist. The successful implementation of these plans is so critical to an organization in the event of a disaster that not only should the plans be developed, but they also need to be periodically tested to ensure that they are sufficient and will indeed accomplish what they were designed to do.

 EXAM TIP The terms DRP and BCP are often used synonymously, but there are subtle differences between them. Study this section carefully to ensure that you can discriminate between the two terms.

There are many risk management best practices associated with business continuity. The topics of business impact analysis, identification of critical systems and components, single points of failure, BCP, and more are detailed in the following sections.

Business Impact Analysis

The name often used to describe the document created by addressing the questions in the preceding section is a business impact analysis (BIA) (this may also be referred to as a business impact assessment). The BIA outlines what the loss of any of your critical functions will mean to the organization.

Identification of Critical Systems and Components

One of the most important risk mitigation strategies in an enterprise is to apply the proper level of security control to the proper system. A foundational element of a security plan is an understanding of the criticality of systems, the data, and the components. Identifying the critical systems and components is one of the first steps an organization needs to undertake in designing the set of security controls. As the systems evolve and change, the continued identification of the critical systems needs to occur, keeping the information up-to-date and current.

Removing Single Points of Failure

A key security methodology is to attempt to avoid a single point of failure in critical functions within an organization. When developing your BCP, you should be on the lookout for areas in which a critical function relies on a single item (such as switches, routers, firewalls, power supplies, software, or data) that, if lost, would stop this critical function. When these points are identified, think about how each of these possible single points of failure can be eliminated (or mitigated).

In addition to the internal resources you need to consider when evaluating your business functions, there are many resources external to your organization that can impact the operation of your business. You must look beyond hardware, software, and data to consider how the loss of various critical infrastructures can also impact business operations.

Business Continuity Planning and Testing

Business continuity plans require testing to ensure that they perform as desired. As the systems evolve over time, so must the plans. Plans are living documents and should be expected to be updated and changed as required. Regular testing of the plans should occur, and any deficiencies that are discovered should be viewed as opportunities for continuous refinement and improvement.

Risk Assessment

The principles of risk assessment (covered in Chapter 5) can be applied to BCP. Determining the sources and magnitudes of risks is necessary in all business operations, including business continuity planning.

Continuity of Operations

The continuity of operations is imperative, as it has been shown that businesses that cannot quickly recover from a disruption have a real chance of never recovering, and they may go out of business. The overall goal of business continuity planning is to determine which subset of normal operations needs to be continued during periods of disruption.

Disaster Recovery

It is important in a good DRP to include the processes and procedures needed to restore your organization so that it is functioning again and to ensure continued operation. What specific steps will be required to restore operations? These processes should be documented, and, where possible and feasible, they should be reviewed and *exercised* on a periodic basis. Having a plan with step-by-step procedures that nobody knows how to follow does nothing to ensure the continued operation of the organization. Exercising your disaster recovery plans and processes in a disaster recovery exercise before a disaster occurs provides you with the opportunity to discover flaws or weaknesses in the plan when there is still time to modify and correct them. It also provides an opportunity for key figures in the plan to practice what they will be expected to accomplish.

To begin creating your DRP, first identify all critical functions for your organization, and then answer the following questions for each of these critical functions:

- Who is responsible for the operation of this function?
- What do these individuals need to perform the function?
- When should this function be accomplished relative to other functions?
- Where will this function be performed?
- How is the function performed (what is the process)?
- Why is this function so important or critical to the organization?

By answering these questions, and addressing how you will recover from the loss of any of your critical functions, you can create an initial draft of your organization's DRP. The DRP created to address the loss of any critical function, of course, will need to be approved by management, and it is essential that they buy into the plan—otherwise, your efforts will more than likely fail. That old adage, "Those who fail to plan, plan to fail" certainly applies in this situation.

IT Contingency Planning

Important parts of any organization today are the information technology (IT) processes and assets. Without computers and networks, most organizations today could not operate. As a result, it is imperative that a BCP include IT contingency planning. Due to the nature of the Internet and the threats that exist on it, it is likely that the IT assets of an organization will face some level of disruption before the organization suffers from a disruption caused by a natural disaster. Events such as viruses, worms, computer intruders, and denial-of-service attacks could result in an organization losing part or all of its computing resources without any warning. Consequently, the IT contingency plans are more likely to be needed than the other aspects of a BCP. These plans should account for disruptions caused by any of the security threats discussed throughout this book as well as disasters or simple system failures.

Succession Planning

Business continuity planning is more than just ensuring that hardware is available and operational. The people who operate and maintain the system are also important, and in the event of a disruptive event, the availability of key personnel is as important as hardware for successful business continuity operations. The development of a succession plan that identifies key personnel and develops qualified personnel for key functions is a critical part of a successful BCP.

High Availability

One of the objectives of security is the availability of data and processing power when an authorized user desires it. *High availability* refers to the ability to maintain availability of data and operational processing (services) despite a disrupting event. Generally, this requires redundant systems, both in terms of power and processing, so that should one system fail, the other can take over operations without any break in service. High availability is more than data redundancy; it requires that both data and services be available.

Redundancy

RAID increases reliability through the use of *redundancy*. When developing plans for ensuring that an organization has what it needs to keep operating, even if hardware or software fails or if security is breached, you should consider other measures involving redundancy and spare parts. Some common applications of redundancy include the use of redundant servers, redundant connections, and redundant ISPs. The need for redundant servers and connections may be fairly obvious, but redundant ISPs may not be so, at least initially. Many ISPs already have multiple accesses to the Internet on their own, but by having additional ISP connections, an organization can reduce the chance that an interruption of one ISP will negatively impact the organization. Ensuring uninterrupted access to the Internet by employees or access to the organization's e-commerce site for customers is becoming increasingly important.

Many organizations don't see the need for maintaining a supply of spare parts. After all, with the price of storage dropping and the speed of processors increasing, why replace a broken part with older technology? However, a ready supply of spare parts can ease the process of bringing the system back online. Replacing hardware and software with newer versions can sometimes lead to problems with compatibility. An older version of some piece of critical software may not work with newer hardware, which may be more capable in a variety of ways. Having critical hardware (or software) spares for critical functions in the organization can greatly facilitate maintaining business continuity in the event of software or hardware failures.

 EXAM TIP   Redundancy is an important factor in both security and reliability. Make sure you understand the many different areas that can benefit from redundant components.

Tabletop Exercises

Exercising operational plans is an effort that can take on many different forms. For senior decision makers, the point of action is more typically a desk or a conference room, with their method being meetings and decisions. A common form of exercising operational plans for senior management is the tabletop exercise. The senior management team, or elements of it, are gathered together and presented with a scenario. They can walk through their decision-making steps, communicate with others, and go through the motions of the exercise in the pattern in which they would likely be involved. The scenario is presented at a level to test the responsiveness of their decisions and decision-making process. Because the event is frequently run in a conference room, around a table, the name tabletop exercise has come to define this form of exercise.

Fault Tolerance

Some other terms that are often used in discussions of continuity of operations in the face of a disruption of some sort are high availability and fault tolerance.

Fault tolerance basically has the same goal as high availability—the uninterrupted access to data and services. It can be accomplished by the mirroring of data and hardware systems. Should a "fault" occur, causing disruption in a device such as a disk controller, the mirrored system provides the requested data with no apparent interruption in service to the user. Certain systems, such as servers, are more critical to business operations and should therefore be the object of fault-tolerant measures.

EXAM TIP Fault tolerance and high availability are similar in their goals, yet they are separate in application. *High availability* refers to maintaining both data and services in an operational state even when a disrupting event occurs. *Fault tolerance* is a design objective to achieve high availability should a fault occur.

Hardware

Hardware forms the backbone of a system in a form of infrastructure. From network equipment to the servers, storage, and user machines, the hardware is all interconnected, providing a conduit across which the data is stored, processed, and used. This equipment forms the backbone of the operations and is the location where security activities will occur. Hardware components such as network control devices, firewalls, intrusion detection systems, and logging systems are essential to providing the required levels of security.

RAID

A common approach to increasing reliability in disk storage is Redundant Array of Inexpensive Disks, now known as *Redundant Array of Independent Disks (RAID)*. RAID takes data that is normally stored on a single disk and spreads it out among several others. If any single disk is lost, the data can be recovered from the other disks where the data also resides. With the price of disk storage decreasing, this approach has become increasingly popular to the point that many individual users even have RAID arrays for their home systems. RAID can also increase the speed of data recovery, as multiple drives can be busy retrieving requested data at the same time instead of relying on just one disk to do the work.

Several different RAID approaches can be considered:

- **RAID 0** (striped disks) simply spreads the data that would be kept on the one disk across several disks. This decreases the time it takes to retrieve data, because the data is read from multiple drives at the same time, but it does not improve reliability, because the loss of any single drive will result in the loss of all the data (since portions of files are spread out among the different disks). With RAID 0, the data is split across all the drives with no redundancy offered.

- **RAID 1** (mirrored disks) is the opposite of RAID 0. RAID 1 copies the data from one disk onto two or more disks. If any one disk is lost, the data is not lost since it is also copied onto the other disk(s). This method can be used to improve reliability and retrieval speed, but it is relatively expensive when compared to other RAID techniques.

- **RAID 2** (bit-level error-correcting code) is not typically used, as it stripes data across the drives at the bit level as opposed to the block level. It is designed to be able to recover the loss of any single disk through the use of error-correcting techniques.

- **RAID 3** (byte-striped with error check) spreads the data across multiple disks at the byte level with one disk dedicated to parity bits. This technique is not commonly implemented because input/output operations can't be overlapped due to the need for all to access the same disk (the disk with the parity bits).

- **RAID 4** (dedicated parity drive) stripes data across several disks but in larger stripes than in RAID 3, and it uses a single drive for parity-based error checking. RAID 4 has the disadvantage of not improving data retrieval speeds, since all retrievals still need to access the single parity drive.

- **RAID 5** (block-striped with error check) is a commonly used method that stripes the data at the block level and spreads the parity data across the drives. This provides both reliability and increased speed performance. This form requires a minimum of three drives.

RAID 0 through 5 are the original techniques, with RAID 5 being the most common method used, as it provides both the reliability and speed improvements. Additional methods have been implemented, such as duplicating the parity data across the disks (RAID 6) and a stripe of mirrors (RAID 10).

 EXAM TIP Knowledge of the basic RAID structures by number designation is a testable element and should be memorized for the exam.

Clustering

Another technique closely related to load balancing is *clustering*. This technique links a group of systems to have them work together, functioning as a single system. In many respects, a cluster of computers working together can be considered a single larger computer, with the advantage of costing less than a single comparably powerful computer. A cluster also has the fault-tolerant advantage of not being reliant on any single computer system for overall system performance.

Load Balancing

A common technique that is used in fault tolerance is load balancing. This technique is designed to distribute the processing load over two or more systems. It is used to help improve resource utilization and throughput, but also has the added advantage of increasing the fault tolerance of the overall system because a critical process may be split across several systems. Should any one system fail, the others can pick up the processing it was handling. While there may be an impact to overall throughput, the operation does not go down entirely. Load balancing is often utilized for systems that handle websites and high-bandwidth file transfers.

Servers

Servers act as focal points for the data at all stages: in storage, during access, and during processing. This makes servers a point of attack for those who wish to obtain the data. Taking the necessary security precautions on servers that handle critical data is a key element in risk mitigation. One should not have unnecessary services running on machines that handle critical data. All access to the machines should be controlled, both at the logical access control level and the logical network segmentation level.

Disaster Recovery Concepts

Many types of disasters, whether natural or caused by people, can stop your organization's operations for some length of time. Such disasters are unlike the threats to your computer systems and networks, because the events that cause the disruption are not specifically aimed at your organization. This is not to say that those other threats won't disrupt operations—they can, and industrial espionage, hacking, disgruntled employees, and insider threats all must be considered. The purpose of this section is to point out additional events that you may not have previously considered.

The amount of time your organization's operations are disrupted depends in part on how prepared it is for a disaster and what plans are in place to mitigate the effects of a disaster. Any of the events in Table 7-1 could cause a disruption in operations.

Fortunately, these types of events do not happen very often. It is more likely that business operations will be interrupted due to employee error (such as accidental corruption of a database, or unplugging a system to plug in a vacuum cleaner—an event that has occurred at more than one organization). A good disaster recovery plan will prepare your organization for any type of organizational disruption.

Table 7-1 Common Causes of Disasters				
	Fire	Flood	Tornado	Hurricane
	Electrical storm	Earthquake	Political unrest/riot	Blizzard
	Gas leak/explosion	Chemical spill	Terrorism	War

When disaster occurs, it is typically too late to begin the planning of a response. The following sections on backup plans and policies; backup execution and frequency; and cold sites, hot sites, and warm sites provide details needed to make appropriate preparations.

Backup Plans/Policies

Backups are important in any IT contingency plan and BCP, not only because of the possibility of a disaster, but also because hardware and storage media will periodically fail, resulting in loss or corruption of critical data. An organization might also find backups critical when security measures have failed and an individual has gained access to important information that may have become corrupted or at the very least can't be trusted. Data backup is thus a critical element in BCPs, as well as in normal operation. You must consider several factors in an organization's data backup strategy:

- How frequently should backups be conducted?
- How extensive do the backups need to be?
- What is the process for conducting backups?
- Who is responsible for ensuring backups are created?
- Where will the backups be stored?
- How long will backups be kept?
- How many copies will be maintained?

Keep in mind that the purpose of a backup is to provide valid, uncorrupted data in the event of corruption or loss of the original file or media where the data was stored. Depending on the type of organization, legal requirements for conducting backups can also affect how it is accomplished.

 NOTE The restoration process can be as simple as restoring a single critical system that may have experienced a hardware failure up to the restoration of all company functions in the event of a catastrophe such as a natural disaster. The DRP should take into account these different levels of recovery.

Backup Execution/Frequency

The amount of data that will be backed up and the time it takes to accomplish the backup have direct bearing on the type of backup that will be performed. Four basic types of backups, the amount of space required for each, and the ease of restoration using each strategy are outlined in Table 7-2.

The values for each of the strategies in Table 7-2 vary depending on your specific environment. The more files are changed between backups, the more these strategies will look alike. What each strategy entails bears further explanation.

Table 7-2		Full	Differential	Incremental	Delta
Characteristics of	Amount of space	Large	Medium	Medium	Small
Backup Types	Restoration	Simple	Simple	Involved	Complex

The easiest type of backup to understand is the *full backup*, in which all files and software are backed up onto the storage media and an archive bit is cleared. Restoration from a full backup is similarly straightforward—you must restore all the files onto the system. This process can take a considerable amount of time. Consider the size of even the average home PC today, for which storage is measured in tens and hundreds of gigabytes. Backing up this amount of data, or more, takes time.

In a *differential backup*, only files and software that have changed since the last full backup was completed are backed up. This also implies that periodically a full backup needs to be accomplished. The frequency of the full backup versus the interim differential backups depends on your organization and is part of your defined strategy. Restoration from a differential backup requires two steps: the last full backup first needs to be loaded, and then the differential backup can be applied to update the files that have been changed since the full backup was conducted. Although the differential backup process can take time, the amount of time required is much less than that of a full backup, and this is one of the advantages of this method. Obviously, if a lot of time has passed between differential backups, or if your environment results in most files changing frequently, then the differential backup does not differ much from a full backup. It should also be obvious that to accomplish the differential backup, the system has to have a method of determining which files have been changed since a given point in time. The archive bit is used for this purpose.

With *incremental backups*, even less information will be stored in each individual backup increment. The incremental backup is a variation on a differential backup, with the difference being that instead of backing up all files that have changed since the last full backup, as in the case of the differential, the incremental backup will back up only files that have changed since the last full or incremental backup occurred, thus requiring fewer files to be backed up. Just as in the case of the differential backup, the incremental backup relies on the occasional full backup. After that, you back up only files that have changed since the last backup of any sort was conducted. To restore a system using this type of backup method requires quite a bit more work. You first need to go back to the last full backup and reload the system with this data. Then you have to update the system with every incremental backup that occurred since then. The advantage of this type of backup is that it requires less storage and time to accomplish. The disadvantage is that the restoration process is more involved. Assuming that you don't frequently have to conduct a complete restoration of your system, however, the incremental backup is a valid technique.

Finally, the goal of the *delta backup* is to save as little information as possible each time you perform a backup. As with the other strategies, an occasional full backup is required. After that, when a delta backup is conducted at specific intervals, only the portions of the files that have been changed will be stored. The advantage of this is easy to illustrate. If your organization maintains a large database with thousands of records and several hundred megabytes of data, the entire database would be backed up in the previous backup types even if only one record is changed. For a delta backup, only the actual record that changed would be stored. The disadvantage of this method should also be readily apparent—restoration is a complex process since it requires more than just loading a file (or several files). It requires that application software be run to update the records in the files that have been changed. This process is also called a *transactional backup*.

Each type of backup has advantages and disadvantages. Which type is best for your organization depends on the amount of data you routinely process and store, how frequently it changes, how often you expect to have to restore from a backup, and a number of other factors. The type you select will greatly affect your overall backup strategy, plans, and processes.

 EXAM TIP Backup strategies are such a critical element of security that you need to make sure you understand the different types of backups and their advantages and disadvantages.

The type of backup strategy an organization employs is often affected by how frequently the organization conducts the backup activity. The usefulness of a backup is directly related to how many changes have occurred since the backup was created, and this is obviously affected by how often backups are created. The longer it has been since the backup was created, the more changes will likely have occurred. There is no easy answer, however, to how frequently an organization should perform backups. Every organization should consider how long it can survive without current data from which to operate. It can then determine how long it will take to restore from backups using various methods, and decide how frequently backups need to occur. This sounds simple, but it is a serious, complex decision to make.

Related to the frequency question is the issue of how long backups should be maintained. Is it sufficient to maintain a single backup from which to restore data? Security professionals will tell you no; multiple backups should be maintained, for a variety of reasons. If the reason for restoring from the backup is the discovery of an intruder in the system, it is important to restore the system to its pre-intrusion state. If the intruder has been in the system for several months before being discovered, and backups are taken weekly, it will not be possible to restore to a pre-intrusion state if only one backup is maintained. This would mean that all data and system files would be suspect and may not be reliable. If multiple backups were maintained at various intervals, it is easier to return to a point before the intrusion (or before the security or operational event that is necessitating the restoration) occurred.

Several strategies or approaches to backup retention include the common and easy-to-remember "rule of three," in which the three most recent backups are kept. When a new backup is created, the oldest backup is overwritten. Another strategy is to keep the most recent copy of backups for various time intervals. For example, you might keep the latest daily, weekly, monthly, quarterly, and yearly backups. Note that in certain environments, regulatory issues may prescribe a specific frequency and retention period, so it is important to know these requirements when determining how often you will create a backup and how long you will keep it.

If you are not in an environment for which regulatory issues dictate the frequency and retention for backups, your goal will be to optimize the frequency. In determining the optimal backup frequency, two major costs need to be considered: the cost of the backup strategy you choose and the cost of recovery if you do not implement this backup strategy (if no backups were created). You must also factor into the equation the probability that the backup will be needed on any given day.

When calculating the cost of the backup strategy, consider the following elements:

- The cost of the backup media required for a single backup
- The storage costs for the backup media and the retention policy
- The labor costs associated with performing a single backup
- The frequency with which backups are created

All these considerations can be used to arrive at an annual cost for implementing your chosen backup strategy, and this figure can then be used as previously described.

Related to the location of backup storage is where the restoration services will be located. If the organization has suffered physical damage to its facility, having offsite data storage is only part of the solution. This data will need to be processed somewhere, which means that computing facilities similar to those used in normal operations are required. This problem can be approached in a number of ways, including hot sites, warm sites, and cold sites.

Cold Site

A cold site will have the basic environmental controls necessary to operate but few of the computing components necessary for processing. Getting a cold site operational may take weeks.

Hot Site

A hot site is a fully configured environment, similar to the normal operating environment, that can be operational immediately or within a few hours depending on its configuration and the needs of the organization.

Warm Site

A warm site is partially configured, usually having the peripherals and software but perhaps not the more expensive main processing computer. It is designed to be operational within a few days.

EXAM TIP Alternate sites are highly tested on the CompTIA Security+ exam. It is also important to know whether the data is available or not at each location. For example, a hot site has duplicate data or a near-ready backup of the original site. A cold site has no current or backup copies of the original site data. A warm site has backups, but they are typically several days or weeks old.

Chapter Review

In this chapter, you became acquainted with the principles of risk mitigation strategies. The chapter first presented the concepts of change management, incident management, user rights and permissions, and routine audits. It then covered the use of security controls to prevent data loss or theft, including technical solutions such as DLP.

Next you were introduced to the topic of business continuity and the critical elements associated with accomplishing this activity. Fault tolerance and high availability concepts were covered, followed by the use of policies and procedures to enable disaster recovery, including backup strategies. The chapter closed with an examination of alternate sites and their capabilities.

Questions

To help you prepare further for the CompTIA Security+ exam, and to test your level of preparedness, answer the following questions and then check your answers against the correct answers at the end of the chapter.

1. Which of the following is *not* a type of backup?

    A. Incremental

    B. Partial

    C. Differential

    D. Delta

2. To achieve reliability and speed improvements through the use of RAID, which form would you use?

    A. RAID 0

    B. RAID 1

    C. RAID 5

    D. RAID 10

3. Which of the following defines differential backup?

    A. Only the files and software that have changed since the last full backup are backed up.

    B. All files and software are copied to storage media.

    C. Only the files and software that have changed since the last full or incremental backup are backed up.

    D. Only portions of files changed are backed up.

4. Which of the following describes a warm site?

    A. A fully configured environment that can be operational immediately or within a few hours

    B. A reciprocal site where similar organizations agree to assume processing for the other party should a disaster occur

    C. A site with basic environmental controls but few of the computing components necessary

    D. A partially configured site designed to be operational within a few days

5. What is the purpose of high availability?

    A. Distributing processing load over two or more systems

    B. Providing the ability to maintain availability of data and operational processing despite a disrupting event

    C. Mirroring of data and systems to avoid interruption in service to the user

    D. Linking a group of systems to work together and function as a single system

6. Which of the following can be a single point of failure?

    A. High availability

    B. Load balancing

    C. A cluster

    D. A process

7. Which of the following accurately describes IT contingency planning?

    A. One of the most important aspects of business continuity planning

    B. Details related to the long-term recovery of the organization

    C. Used to ensure that company operations continue in the face of whatever event has occurred

    D. Focused on recovery and rebuilding of the organization after a disaster has occurred

8. Which of the following defines RAID 1?

    A. Spreads data out to increase the speed of data access

    B. Spreads data across disks and adds parity

    C. Stripes data at the bit level

    D. An exact copy so that all data is mirrored on another drive

9. What is the correct description of a Computer Incident Response Team (CIRT)?

    A. Exercises that provide the opportunity for all parties to practice incident response procedures

    B. Personnel, processes, and plans to handle business interruptions

    C. A team test to identify planning flaws before an actual incident occurs

    D. A checklist walkthrough used to ensure all team members understand their role in a DRP

10. Which of the following correctly defines change management?

   A. Procedures followed when modifying software or IT infrastructure

   B. The process of identifying threats and vulnerabilities and their potential impacts

   C. The process of responding to, containing, analyzing, and recovering from a computer-related incident

   D. Mechanisms used to determine which access permissions subjects have for specific objects

11. You are a risk management consultant. You find yourself on the elevator with the VP of your client. She has asked you to give her the "elevator pitch" (two-minute summary) on developing a business impact analysis (BIA). List the six key questions that should be addressed during a BIA.

12. You are in the midst of presenting a proposal to your client on risk management. Just as you start your presentation, the CEO stops you and asks, "Tell me in two sentences the differences between business continuity planning and disaster recovery planning." Give a one-sentence description of business continuity planning and a one-sentence description of disaster recovery planning that distinguishes between the two terms.

For questions 13–15, use the following scenario: The probability of a backup being needed is 20%. The cost to restore with no backup is $100,000. The cost of implementing your backup strategy is $10,000. Assume these are annual costs.

13. What is the cost of not having backups?

   A. $100,000

   B. $120,000

   C. $8,000

   D. $20,000

14. Explain why you would choose to use backups or choose not to use backups.

15. List the following backup methods in order of size from smallest to largest: full, delta, incremental.

16. You have been tasked with implementing a risk management strategy to limit the risk associated with data loss or theft. Which of the following would you include in your implementation plan? (Choose all that apply.)

   A. Change management

   B. Perform routine audits

   C. Data Loss Prevention (DLP) controls

   D. Data minimization policies

Answers

1. **B.** Full, incremental, differential, and delta are types of backups.

2. **C.** RAID 5 offers both performance and reliability increases.

3. **A.** A differential backup copies all files and software that have changed since the last full backup.

4. **D.** A warm site is a partially configured site designed to be operational within a few days.

5. **B.** High availability refers to the ability to maintain availability of data and operational processing despite a disrupting event.

6. **D.** A single point of failure can be a special piece of hardware, a process, a specific piece of data, or an essential utility.

7. **A.** Because most organizations rely heavily on computing resources, IT contingency planning is one of the most important aspects of business continuity planning.

8. **D.** RAID 1 implements exact copies of disks so that all data is mirrored on another drive, providing complete redundancy.

9. **B.** A Computer Incident Response Team (CIRT) is personnel, processes, and plans to handle business interruptions.

10. **A.** Change management ensures proper procedures are followed when modifying the IT infrastructure.

11. First identify all critical functions, and then answer the following questions:

    - Who is responsible for the operation of this function?
    - What do these individuals need to perform that function?
    - When should this function be accomplished relative to other functions?
    - Where will this function be performed?
    - How is this function performed (what is the process)?
    - Why is this function so important or critical to the organization?

12. The focus of business continuity planning is on continued operation of a business, albeit at a reduced level or through different means during some period of time. Disaster recovery planning is focused specifically on recovering from a disaster.

13. **D.** The cost of not having backups is (probability the backup is needed) × (cost of restoring with no backup). 20% × $100,000 = $20,000.

14. The cost of backups, $10,000, is less than the annualized cost of restoring without a backup, so backups should be utilized.

15. Delta, incremental, and full.

16. **C** and **D**. DLP controls are security controls specifically designed to detect and limit data exfiltration from the enterprise by unauthorized parties. Data minimization policies are used to prevent the unnecessary storage of data that is not needed in the enterprise. This prevents release by not having the data to release.

Digital Forensics and Incident Response

In this chapter, you will

- Understand basic forensic procedures
- Understand common incident response procedures

Computer forensics is certainly a popular buzzword in computer security. This chapter addresses the key aspects of computer forensics in preparation for the CompTIA Security+ certification exam. It is not intended to be a legal tutorial regarding the presentation of evidence in a court of law. These principles are of value in conducting any investigative processes, including internal or external audit procedures, but many nuances of handling legal cases are far beyond the scope of this text.

The term *forensics* relates to the application of scientific knowledge to legal problems. Specifically, computer forensics involves the preservation, identification, documentation, and interpretation of computer data. In today's practice, computer forensics can be performed for three purposes:

- Investigating and analyzing computer systems as related to a violation of laws
- Investigating and analyzing computer systems for compliance with an organization's policies
- Investigating computer systems that have been remotely attacked

This last point is often referred to as *incident response* and can be a subset of the first two points. If an unauthorized person is remotely attacking a system, laws may indeed have been violated. However, a company employee performing similar acts may or may not violate laws and corporate policies. Any of these three purposes could ultimately result in legal actions and may require legal disclosure. Therefore, it is important to note that computer forensics actions may, at some point in time, deal with legal violations, and investigations could go to court proceedings. As a potential first responder, you should always seek legal counsel. Also, seek legal counsel ahead of time as you develop and implement corporate policies and procedures. It is extremely important to understand that even minor procedural missteps can have significant legal consequences.

Forensic Procedures

The following four-step process is associated with digital forensic investigations. These steps are broad categories with many individual elements:

1. **Collection**   The steps involved in searching for, recognizing, and collecting evidence.

2. **Examination**   The steps taken to facilitate the visibility of the evidence from all the materials collected. This involves revealing hidden and obscured information.

3. **Analysis**   The steps taken to structure the evidence in a manner that provides for its use in further proceedings. This includes explanations as to origin, significance, and veracity of specific elements and derived elements.

4. **Reporting**   The steps taken to create a written report containing the details of the examination and findings.

An important element of any forensics process is the definition of the *scope* of the investigation. Whether it is a single machine, a series of machines, or a specific set of activities across multiple machines, this information matters, as it defines the boundaries of all aspects of the forensics process. The larger the scope, the greater the resources that will be required for the investigation. If a scope is too big, the relevant material can be lost in all of the other materials that are deemed in scope. If the scope is defined too narrowly, relevant data may not be collected and then become unavailable for investigation.

Collection

Evidence consists of the documents, verbal statements, and material objects admissible in a court of law. Evidence is critical to convincing management, juries, judges, or other authorities that some kind of violation has occurred. It is vitally important to document all the steps taken in the collection of evidence, as these may be challenged in court, and the processes followed as evidenced by the documentation will be all that can be used to demonstrate the veracity of the processes.

The submission of evidence is challenging, but it is even more challenging when computers are used, because the people involved may not be technically educated and thus may not fully understand what's happened. Keep these points in mind as you collect evidence:

- Who collected the evidence?
- How was it collected?
- Where was it collected?
- Who has had possession of the evidence?
- How was it protected and stored?
- When was it removed from storage? Why? Who took possession?

Computer evidence presents yet more challenges, because the data itself cannot be sensed with the physical senses—that is, you can see printed characters, but you can't see the bits where that data is stored. Bits of data are merely magnetic pulses on a disk or some other storage technology. Therefore, data must always be evaluated through some kind of "filter" rather than sensed directly by human senses. This is often of concern to auditors, because good auditing techniques recommend accessing the original data or a version as close as possible to the original data.

Standards for Evidence

To be credible, especially if evidence will be used in court proceedings or in corporate disciplinary actions that could be challenged legally, evidence must meet three standards:

- **Sufficient evidence**   The evidence must be convincing or measure up without question.

- **Competent evidence**   The evidence must be legally qualified and reliable.

- **Relevant evidence**   The evidence must be material to the case or have a bearing on the matter at hand.

Types of Evidence

All evidence is not created equal. Some evidence is stronger and better than other, weaker evidence. Several types of evidence can be germane:

- **Direct evidence**   Oral testimony that proves a specific fact (such as an eyewitness's statement). The knowledge of the facts is obtained through the five senses of the witness, with no inferences or presumptions.

- **Real evidence**   Also known as associative or physical evidence, this includes tangible objects that prove or disprove a fact. Physical evidence links the suspect to the scene of a crime.

- **Documentary evidence**   Evidence in the form of business records, printouts, manuals, and the like. Much of the evidence relating to computer crimes is documentary evidence.

- **Demonstrative evidence**   Used to aid the jury and can be in the form of a model, experiment, chart, and so on, offered to prove that an event occurred.

Three Rules Regarding Evidence

An item can become evidence when it is admitted by a judge in a case. Three rules guide the use of evidence, especially if it could result in court proceedings:

- **Best evidence rule**   Courts prefer original evidence rather than a copy to ensure that no alteration of the evidence (whether intentional or unintentional) has occurred. In some instances, an evidence duplicate can be accepted, such as when the original is lost or destroyed by a natural disaster or in the normal course of business. A duplicate is also acceptable when a third party beyond the court's subpoena power possesses the original. Copies of digital records, where proof of integrity is provided, can in many cases be used in court.

NOTE Evidence rules exist at the federal and state levels and vary. Digital evidence is not always considered a "writing" and is not always subject to the best evidence rule.

- **Exclusionary rule** The Fourth Amendment to the U.S. Constitution precludes illegal search and seizure. Therefore, any evidence collected in violation of the Fourth Amendment is not admissible as evidence. Additionally, if evidence is collected in violation of the Electronic Communications Privacy Act (ECPA) or other related violations of the U.S. Code, or other statutes, it may not be admissible to a court. For example, if no policy exists regarding the company's intent to monitor network traffic or systems electronically, and the employee has not acknowledged this policy by signing an agreement, sniffing network traffic could be a violation of the ECPA.

- **Hearsay rule** Hearsay is second hand evidence—evidence offered by the witness that is not based on the personal knowledge of the witness but is being offered to prove the truth of the matter asserted. Typically, computer-generated evidence is considered hearsay evidence, as the maker of the evidence (the computer) cannot be interrogated. Exceptions are being made where items such as logs and headers (computer-generated materials) are being accepted in court.

NOTE The laws mentioned here are U.S. laws. Other countries and jurisdictions may have similar laws that would need to be considered in a similar manner.

Handling Evidence

When information or objects are presented to management or admitted to court to support a claim, that information or those objects can be considered as evidence or documentation supporting your investigative efforts. Senior management will always ask a lot of questions—second- and third-order questions that you need to be able to answer quickly. Likewise, in a court, credibility is critical. Therefore, evidence must be properly acquired, identified, protected against tampering, transported, and stored.

Capture System Image

Imaging or dumping the physical memory of a computer system can help identify evidence not available on a hard drive. This is especially appropriate for rootkits, where evidence on the hard drive is hard to find. Once the memory is imaged, you can use a hex editor to analyze the image offline on another system. (Memory-dumping tools and hex editors are available on the Internet.) Note that dumping memory is more applicable for investigative work where court proceedings will not be pursued. If a case is likely to end up in court, do not dump memory without first seeking legal advice to confirm that live analysis of the memory is acceptable; otherwise, the defendant will be able to dispute easily the claim that evidence was not tampered with.

The other system image is that of the internal storage devices. Making forensic duplicates of all partitions is a key step in preserving evidence. A forensic copy is a bit-by-bit copy and has supporting integrity checks in the form of hashes. The proper practice is to use a write blocker when making a forensic copy of a drive. This device allows a disk to be read, but prevents any writing actions to the drive, guaranteeing that the copy operation does not change the original media. Once a forensic copy is created, working copies from the master forensic copy can be created for analysis and sharing with other investigators. The use of hash values provides a means of demonstrating that all of the copies are true to each other and the original.

Hash Values

If files, logs, and other information are going to be captured and used for evidence, you need to ensure that the data isn't modified. In most cases, a tool that implements a hashing algorithm to create message digests is used.

A *hashing algorithm* performs a function similar to the familiar parity bits, checksum, or cyclic redundancy check (CRC). It applies mathematical operations to a data stream (or file) to calculate some number that is unique based on the information contained in the data stream (or file). If a subsequent hash created on the same data stream results in a different hash value, it usually means that the data stream was changed.

The mathematics behind hashing algorithms has been researched extensively, and although it is possible that two different data streams could produce the same message digest, it is very improbable. This is an area of cryptography that has been rigorously reviewed, and the mathematics behind Message Digest 5 (MD5) and Secure Hash Algorithm (SHA) is very sound. In 2005, weaknesses were discovered in the MD5 and SHA algorithms, leading the National Institute of Standards and Technology (NIST) to announce a competition to find a new cryptographic hashing algorithm named SHA-3. Although MD5 is still used, best practice would be to use SHA-2 series, and SHA-3 once it becomes integrated into tools.

The hash tool is applied to each file or log, and the message digest value is noted in the investigation documentation. It is a good practice to write the logs to a write-once media such as a CD-ROM. When the case actually goes to trial, the investigator may need to run the tool on the files or logs again to show that they have not been altered in any way.

 NOTE The number of files stored on today's hard drives can be very large, with literally hundreds of thousands of files. Obviously, this is far too many for the investigator to analyze. However, by matching the message digests for files installed by the most popular software products to the message digests of the files on the drive being analyzed, the investigator can avoid analyzing approximately 90 percent of the files because he can assume they are unmodified. The National Software Reference Library (NSRL) collects software from various sources and incorporates file profiles into a Reference Data Set (RDS) available for download as a service. See www.nsrl.nist.gov.

Record Time Offset

Files and events logged on a computer will have timestamp markings that are based on the clock time on the machine itself. It is a mistake to assume that this clock is accurate. To allow the correlation of timestamp data from records inside the computer with any external event, it is necessary to know any time offset between the machine clock and the actual time.

Network Traffic and Logs

An important source of information in an investigation can be the network activity associated with a device. There can be a lot of useful information in the network logs associated with network infrastructure. The level and breadth of this information is determined by the scope of the investigation. While the best data would be from that of a live network forensic collection process, in most cases, this type of data will not be available. There are many other sources of network forensic data, including firewall and IDS logs, network flow data, and event logs on key servers and services.

Capture Video

A convenient method of capturing significant information at the time of collection is video capture. Videos allow high-bandwidth data collection that can show what was connected to what, how things were laid out, desktops, and so forth. A picture can be worth a thousand words, so take the time to document everything with pictures. Pictures of serial numbers and network and USB connections can prove invaluable later in the forensics process. Complete documentation is a must in every forensics process, and photographs can assist greatly in capturing details that would otherwise take a long time and be prone to transcription error.

 EXAM TIP A digital camera is great for recording a scene and information. Screenshots of active monitor images may be obtained as well. Pictures can detail elements such as serial number plates, machines, drives, cable connections, and more. Photographs are truly worth a thousand words.

Screenshots

Particular attention should be paid to the state of what is on the screen at the time of evidence collection. The information on a video screen is lost once the system changes or power is removed. Taking screenshots, using a digital camera or video camera, can provide documentation as to what was on the screen at the time of collection. Because you cannot trust the system internals themselves to be free of tampering, do not use internal screenshot capture methods.

Witnesses

Remember that witness credibility is extremely important. It is easy to imagine how quickly credibility can be damaged if the witness is asked "Did you lock the file system?" and can't answer affirmatively. Or, when asked, "When you imaged this disk drive, did you use a new system?" the witness can't answer that the destination disk was new or had been completely formatted using a low-level format before data was copied to it.

Examination

When an incident occurs, you will need to collect data and information to facilitate your investigation. If someone is committing a crime or intentionally violating a company policy, that person will likely try to hide their tracks. Therefore, you should collect as much information as soon as you can. In today's highly networked world, evidence can be found not only on the workstation or mobile device, but also on company-owned file servers, security appliances, and servers located with the Internet service provider (ISP).

When an incident occurs and the computer being used is going to be secured, you must consider two questions: Should it be turned off? Should it be disconnected from the network? Forensics professionals debate the reasons for turning a computer on or turning it off. Some state that the plug should be pulled in order to freeze the current state of the computer. However, this results in the loss of any data associated with an attack in progress from the machine. Any data in RAM will also be lost. Further, it may corrupt the computer's file system and could call into question the validity of your findings.

On the other hand, it is possible for the computer criminal to leave behind a software bomb that you don't know about, and any commands you execute, including shutting down or restarting the system, could destroy or modify files, information, or evidence. The criminal may have anticipated such an investigation and altered some of the system's binary files.

Further, if the computer being analyzed is a server, it is unlikely management will support taking it offline and shutting it down for investigation. So, from an investigative perspective, either course may be correct or incorrect, depending on the circumstances surrounding the incident. What is most important is that you are deliberate in your work, you document your actions, and you can explain why you took the actions you performed.

Being methodical is extremely important while identifying evidence. Do not collect evidence by yourself—have a second person who can serve as a witness to your actions. Keep logs of your actions both during seizure and during analysis and storage. A sample log is shown here:

Item Description	Investigator	Case	Date	Time	Location	Reason
Dell Latitude laptop computer, 1530, Serial number: 6RKC1G0	Smith	C-25	30 Jan 2014	1325 MST	Room 312 safe	Safekeeping

Order of Volatility

There are many sources of data in a computer system, and if the machine is running, some of these sources can be volatile. Things such as the state of the CPU and its registers are always changing, as are memory and even storage. These elements tend to change at different rates, and you should pay attention to the order of volatility so that collection priority is devoted where it can matter.

The collection of electronic data can be a difficult task. In some cases, such as volatile data, there may only be one chance to collect it, after which it becomes lost forever. Volatile information locations such as the RAM change constantly, and data collection should occur in the order of volatility, or lifetime of the data.

Following is the order of volatility of digital information in a system:

1. CPU, cache, and register contents (collect first)

2. Routing tables, ARP cache, process tables, kernel statistics

3. Live network connections and data flows

4. Memory (RAM)

5. Temporary file system/swap space

6. Data on hard disk

7. Remotely logged data

8. Data stored on archival media/backups (collect last)

When collecting digital evidence, it is important to use proper techniques and tools. Some of the key elements are the use of write blockers when making forensic copies, hashing and verifying hash matches, documenting handling and storage, and protecting media from environmental change factors. Of particular note is that the data present on a system can be a function of both the file system and the hardware being employed. A physical hard disk drive will persist data longer than a solid state drive. And the newer file systems with journaling and shadow copies can have longer persistence of information than older systems such as File Allocation Table (FAT)–based systems. Raw disk blocks can be recovered in some file systems long after data has been rewritten or erased, due to the nature of how the file systems manage the data.

 EXAM TIP A common data element needed later in the forensics process is an accurate system time with respect to an accurate external time source. A record time offset is calculated by measuring system time with an external clock such as a Network Time Protocol (NTP) server. This can be lost if the system is powered down, so it is best collected while the system is still running.

Analysis

The process of analysis in a forensics sense is the building of a picture from separate elements. In many cases, the pieces of information collected present a partial picture. From these pieces, it is many times possible to analyze the material and determine various possibilities with respect to what happened. Then, additional information can be sought that supports or excludes the various possibilities presented from the initial data collection.

When the additional information is not available, is incomplete, or does not narrow down the possibilities, then the report will need to reflect that a singular conclusion cannot be supported.

Big Data Analysis

Big data refers to a new phenomenon where very large sets of data are used in a business process. Big data can be involved in forensics in two ways. First and foremost, many larger-scope investigations result in big data collections, at least in terms of sizes previously common for computer users. Terabyte drives can contain millions of records, and the process of discovering, recovering, sorting, and analyzing millions of things goes beyond a person's direct ability. Modern digital forensic tools provide the answer, as they can catalog and crunch through large amounts of data. The downside is time. With terabytes and large record sets, functions such as searching, cataloging, and hashing can take days of dedicated computer time to process.

Automated forensic tools also allow advanced operations such as timeline operations. Every file on the system has a set of metadata referred to as *MAC data*. This data records the modified, accessed, and creation times for the file. If the time of an incident is known, then a search of all file activity at that time can provide information as to the things that were occurring on the system. With a file structure having a hierarchy of folders and files and the MAC times not easily manipulated by the OS, coupled with potentially thousands of targets, it takes a specific tool to find and catalog activity by time.

The other aspect is the analysis of big data in response to digital forensic requests. If systems with petabytes and beyond of data are involved, then the simple searching of the thousands of devices that the data is stored across becomes a significant challenge. In these cases, the forensic examiner needs the cooperation of the data owners, as their tools that manage the data will be needed to navigate the complexity and sheer size of the data. Today, this problem exists in only a handful of firms, the large telcos, Internet companies, and some government agencies. But as more and more processes embrace big data, this will spread to greater numbers of investigations. Financial firms are using advanced algorithms to spot fraudulent financial transactions among millions of transactions in real time, a feat that is made possible by the big data repositories of account activity and typical uses.

Reporting

Reporting is an essential element of the forensics process, as this is how the results are communicated to those with a need to know. The report is not a simple collection of the facts discovered, for they seldom paint the picture that the requestor needs to understand. Many forensic investigations involve the collection and analysis of large amounts of data to paint a complete picture of what actually happened. The report is one of the key elements, as it lays out to the parties with a need to understand what the collected elements are and telling them what happened.

Track Man Hours and Expense

Demonstrating the efforts and tasks performed in the forensics process may become an issue in court and other proceedings. Having the ability to demonstrate who did what, when they did it, and how long it took can provide information to establish that the steps were taken per the processes employed. Having solid accounting data on man hours and other expenses can provide corroborating evidence as to the actions performed.

Chain of Custody

Evidence, once collected, must be properly controlled to prevent tampering. The chain of custody accounts for all persons who handled or had access to the evidence. The chain of custody shows who obtained the evidence, when and where it was obtained, where it was stored, and who had control or possession of the evidence for the entire time since the evidence was obtained.

The following shows the critical steps in a chain of custody:

1. Record each item collected as evidence.

2. Record who collected the evidence along with the date and time it was collected or recorded.

3. Write a description of the evidence in the documentation.

4. Put the evidence in containers and tag the containers with the case number, the name of the person who collected it, and the date and time it was collected or put in the container.

5. Record all message digest (hash) values in the documentation.

6. Securely transport the evidence to a protected storage facility.

7. Obtain a signature from the person who accepts the evidence at this storage facility.

8. Provide controls to prevent access to and compromise of the evidence while it is being stored.

9. Securely transport the evidence to court for proceedings.

 EXAM TIP Never analyze the seized evidence directly. The original evidence must be secured and protected with a chain of custody. It should never be subjected to a forensic examination because of the fragile nature of digital evidence. A forensic copy, however, can be examined and, if something goes wrong, can be discarded, and the copy process can be repeated. A good forensics process will prove that the forensic copy is identical to the original at the start and at the end of the examination. From a practical standpoint, investigators usually make multiple forensic copies and perform their analysis in parallel on the multiple copies.

Incident Response Procedures

Incident response is a term used to describe the steps an organization performs in response to any situation determined to be abnormal in the operation of a computer system. The causes of incidents are many, from the environment (storms), to errors on the part of users, to unauthorized actions by unauthorized users, to name a few. Although the causes may be many, the results can be classified into classes. A low-impact incident may not result in any significant risk exposure, so no action other than repairing the broken system is needed. A moderate-risk incident will require greater scrutiny and response efforts, and a high-level risk exposure incident will require the greatest scrutiny. To manage incidents when they occur, a table of guidelines for the incident response team needs to be created to assist in determining the level of response.

Two major elements play a role in determining the level of response. Information criticality is the primary determinant, and this comes from the data classification and the quantity of data involved. The loss of one administrator password is less serious than the loss of all of them. The second factor involves a business decision on how this incident plays into current business operations. A series of breaches, whether minor or not, indicates a pattern that can have public relations and regulatory issues.

The incident response cycle is a quick way to remember the key steps in computer forensics. Figure 8-1 graphically conveys the incident response cycle. There are five key steps:

1. **Discover and report** Organizations should administer an incident-reporting process to make sure that potential security breaches as well as routine application problems are reported and resolved as quickly as possible. Employees should be trained on how to report system problems.

2. **Confirm** Specialists or a response team member should review the incident report to confirm whether or not a security incident has occurred. Detailed notes should be taken and retained, as they could be critically valuable for later investigation.

3. **Investigate** A response team composed of network, system, and application specialists should investigate the incident in detail to determine the extent of the incident and to devise a recovery plan.

4. **Recover** The investigation is complete and documented at this point in time. Steps are taken to return the systems and applications to operational status.

5. **Lessons learned** A post-mortem session should collect lessons learned and assign action items to correct weaknesses and to suggest ways to improve.

Incident response activities at times are closely related to other IT activities involving IT operations. Incident response activities can be similar to disaster recovery and business continuity operations. Incident response activities are not performed in a vacuum, but rather are intimately connected to many operational procedures, and this connection is key to overall system efficiency.

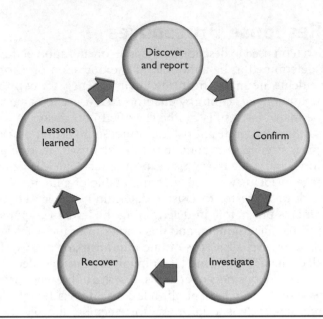

Figure 8-1 Incident response cycle

Preparation

Incident response is the set of actions security personnel perform in response to a wide range of triggering events. These actions are wide and varied, as they have to deal with a wide range of causes and consequences. Through the use of a structured framework coupled with properly prepared processes, incident response becomes a manageable task. Without proper preparation, this task can quickly become impossible or intractably expensive. Successful handling of an incident is a direct result of proper preparation.

First Responder

A first responder must do as much as possible to control damage or loss of evidence. Obviously, as time passes, evidence can be tampered with or destroyed. Look around on the desk, on the Rolodex, under the keyboard, in desktop storage areas, and on cubicle bulletin boards for any information that might be relevant. Secure floppy disks, optical discs, flash memory cards, USB drives, tapes, and other removable media. Request copies of logs as soon as possible. Most ISPs will protect logs that could be subpoenaed. Take photos (some localities require use of Polaroid photos, as they are more difficult to modify without obvious tampering) or video tapes. Include photos of operating computer screens and hardware components from multiple angles. Be sure to photograph internal components before removing them for analysis.

Incident Response Teams

Although the initial response to an incident may be handled by an individual, such as a system administrator, the complete handling of an incident typically takes an entire team. An incident response team is a group of people who prepares for and responds to any emergency incident, such as a natural disaster or an interruption of business operations. A computer security incident response team is typically formed in an organization of key skilled members who bring a wide range of skills to bear in the response effort. Incident response teams are common in corporations as well as in public service organizations.

Incident response team members ideally are trained and prepared to fulfill the roles required by the specific situation (for example, to serve as incident commander in the event of a large-scale public emergency). Incident response teams are frequently dynamically sized to the scale and nature of an incident, and as the size of an incident grows and as more resources are drawn into the event, the command of the situation may shift through several phases.

In a small-scale event, or in the case of a small firm, usually only a volunteer or ad hoc team may exist to respond. In cases where the incident spreads beyond the local control of the incident response team, higher-level resources through industry groups and government groups exist to assist in the incident.

To function in a timely and efficient manner, ideally, a team has already defined a protocol or set of actions to perform to mitigate the negative effects of most common forms of an incident.

Incident Identification

An *incident* is defined as a situation that departs from normal, routine operations. Whether an incident is important or not is the first point of decision as part of an incident response process. A single failed login is technically an incident, but if it is followed by a correct login, then it is not of any consequence. In fact, this could even be considered normal. But 10,000 failed attempts on a system, or failures across a large number of accounts, are distinctly different and may be worthy of further investigation.

A key first step is in the processing of information and the determination of whether or not to invoke incident response processes. Incident information can come from a wide range of sources, including logs, employees, help desk calls, system monitoring, security devices, and more. The challenge is to detect that something other than simple common errors that are routine is occurring. When evidence accumulates, or in some cases specific items such as security device logs indicate a potential incident, the next step is to escalate the situation to the incident response team.

Escalation and Notification

When a threshold of information becomes known to an operator and the operator decides to escalate the situation, the incident response process moves to a notification and escalation phase. Not all incidents are of the same risk profile, and incident response efforts should map to the actual risk level associated with the incident. When the incident response team is notified of a potential incident, its first steps are to confirm the existence, scope, and magnitude of the event and respond accordingly. This is typically done through a two-step escalation process, where a minimal quick-response team begins and then adds members as necessitated by the issue.

Making an assessment of the risk associated with an incident is an important first step. If the characteristics of an incident include a large number of packets destined for different services on a machine (an attack commonly referred to as a *port scan*), then the actions needed are different from those needed to respond to a large number of packets destined for a single machine service. Port scans are common, and to a degree relatively harmless, while port flooding can result in denial of service. Making a determination of the specific downstream risks is important in prioritizing response actions.

Mitigation Steps

All data that is stored is subject to breach or compromise. Given this assumption, the question becomes, what is the best mitigation strategy to reduce the risk associated with breach or compromise? Data requires protection in each of the three states of the data lifecycle: in storage, in transit, and during processing. The level of risk in each state differs due to several factors:

- **Time** Data tends to spend more time in storage, and hence is subject to breach or compromise over longer time periods. Data spends less time in transit and processing.

- **Quantity** Data in storage tends to offer a greater quantity to breach or compromise than data in transit, and data in processing offers even less. If records are being compromised while being processed, then only records being processed are subjected to risk.

- **Access** Different protection mechanisms exist in each of the domains, and this has a direct effect on the risk associated with breach or compromise. Operating systems tend to have very tight controls to prevent cross-process data issues such as error and contamination.

The next aspect of processing risk is within process access, and a variety of attack techniques address this channel specifically. Data in transit is subject to breach or compromise from a variety of network-level attacks and vulnerabilities. Some of these are under the control of the enterprise, and some are not.

One primary mitigation step is data minimization. Data minimization efforts can play a key role in both operational efficiency and security. One of the first rules associated with data is this: Don't keep what you don't need. A simple example of this is the case of spam remediation. If spam is separated from e-mail before it hits a mailbox, one can assert that it is not mail and not subject to storage, backup, or data retention issues. Because spam can comprise greater than 50 percent of incoming mail, this can dramatically improve operational efficiency in terms of both speed and cost.

This same principle holds true for other forms of information. When processing credit card transactions, certain data elements are required for the actual transaction, but once the transaction is approved, they have no further business value. Storing of this information provides no business value, yet it does represent a risk in the case of a data breach. For credit card information, the rules and regulations associated with data elements are governed by contract and managed by the Payment Card Industry Data Security Standard (PCI DSS). Data storage should be governed not by what you can store, but by the business need to store. What is not stored is not subject to breach, and minimizing storage to only what is supported by business need reduces risk and cost to the enterprise.

Minimization efforts begin before data even hits a system, let alone a breach. During system design, the appropriate security controls are determined and deployed, with periodic audits to ensure compliance. These controls are based on the sensitivity of the information being protected. One tool that can be used to assist in the selection of controls is a data classification scheme. Not all data is equally important, nor is it equally damaging in the event of loss. Developing and deploying a data classification scheme can assist in preventative planning efforts when designing security for data elements.

 EXAM TIP Data breaches may not be preventable, but they can be mitigated through minimization and encryption efforts.

Lessons Learned

In the reporting process, a critical assessment of what went right, what went wrong, what can be improved, and what should be continued is prepared as a form of lessons learned. This is a critical part of self-improvement, and is not meant to place blame, but rather to assist in future prevention. Having things go wrong in a complex environment is part of normal operations; having repeat failures that are preventable is not. The key to the lessons learned section of the report is to make the necessary changes so that a repeat event will not occur. Because many incidents are a result of attackers using known methods, once the attack patterns are known in an enterprise and methods exist to mitigate them, then it is the task of the entire enterprise to take the necessary actions to mitigate future events.

Reporting

After the system has been restored, the incident response team creates a report of the incident. Detailing what was discovered, how it was discovered, what was done, and the results, this report acts as a corporate memory and can be used for future incidents. Having a knowledge base of previous incidents and the actions used is a valuable resource because it is in the context of the particular enterprise. These reports also allow a mechanism to close the loop with management over the incident and, most importantly, provide a roadmap of the actions that can be used in the future to prevent events of identical or similar nature.

Part of the report will be recommendations, if appropriate, to change existing policies and procedures, including disaster recovery and business continuity. The similarity in objectives makes a natural overlap, and the cross-pollination between these operations is important to make all processes as efficient as possible.

Recovery/Reconstitution Procedures

Recovery efforts from an incident involve several specific elements. First, the cause of the incident needs to be determined and resolved. This is done through an incident response mechanism. Attempting to recover before the cause is known and corrected will commonly result in a continuation of the problem. Secondly, the data, if sensitive and subject to misuse, needs to be examined in the context of how it was lost, who would have access, and what business measures need to be taken to mitigate specific business damage as a result of the release. This may involve the changing of business plans if the release makes them suspect or subject to adverse impacts.

A key aspect in many incidents is that of external communications. Having a communications expert who is familiar with dealing with the press, with the language nuances necessary to convey the correct information and not inflame the situation is essential to the success of any communication plan. Many firms attempt to use their legal counsel for this, but generally speaking, the legally precise language used by an attorney is not useful from a PR standpoint, and a more nuanced communicator may provide a better image. In many cases of crisis management, it is not the crisis that determines the final costs, but the reaction to and communication of details after the initial crisis.

Recovery can be a two-step process. First, the essential business functions can be recovered, enabling business operations. The second step is the complete restoration of all services and operations. Staging the recovery operations in a prioritized fashion allows a graceful return to an operating condition.

Incident Isolation

Once an incident is discovered and characterized, the most important step in the incident response process involves the isolation of the problem. Many incidents can spread to other machines and expand the damage surface if not contained by the incident response team. Determining the steps to isolate specific machines and services can be a complex endeavor, and is one best accomplished before an incident, through the preparation phase. When a particular machine or service becomes compromised, the team can invoke the preplanned steps to isolate the infected unit from others. This may have an impact on performance, but it will still be less than if the compromise is allowed to spread and more machines become compromised.

Quarantine

One method of isolating a machine is through a quarantine process. The machine may be allowed to run, but its connection to other machines is broken in a manner to prevent the spread of infection. Quarantine can be accomplished through a variety of mechanisms, including the erection of firewalls restricting communication between machines. This can be a fairly complex process, but if properly configured in advance, the limitations of the quarantine operation can allow the machine to continue to run for diagnostic purposes, even if it no longer processes workload.

Device Removal

A more extreme response is device removal. In the event that a machine becomes compromised, it is simply removed from production and replaced. When device removal is the physical change of hardware, this is a resource-intensive operation. The reimaging of a machine can be a time-consuming and difficult endeavor. The advent of virtual machines changes this entirely, as the provisioning of virtual images on hardware can be accomplished in a much quicker fashion.

Data Breach

A *data breach* is the release of information to an environment that is not trusted. Any loss of control over data can be considered a breach until it is determined that the data cannot be obtained by an unauthorized party. Data breaches can be the result of an accident or an intentional act. Any time sensitive or protected information is copied, transmitted, viewed, stolen, or accessed by an unauthorized party, a data breach has occurred.

Damage and Loss Control

The gold standard to prevent data loss from breach or compromise is encryption. When properly employed, encryption can protect data during storage, in transit, and in some cases even during processing. Data that is encrypted no longer has direct value to an unauthorized party, for without the appropriate key, the data can't be accessed; all that is accessible is a stream of apparently random values. The purpose of encryption is not to make it impossible to obtain the data, but rather to increase the work factor to a level that makes it not viable in either economic or time-based terms. Any sensitive information being sent over a network should be encrypted, as the network cannot guarantee that no unauthorized parties have access to data being transmitted across the network. For wireless networks, this is obvious, but the same issues can exist within a wired network with respect to unauthorized parties. Although HTTPS is far from perfect security, it does provide a reasonable level of protection for many Internet-based data transfers. The use of virtual private networking (VPN) technology expands this level of protection from web-associated data transfers into the more general case of network transfer of data.

Chapter Review

In this chapter, you became acquainted with the principles of forensics and incident response. The chapter presented the digital forensics process, including elements of data collection and administrative issues such as chain of custody. It also covered technical issues such as recording the time offset, if any, photographing and videoing scenes, taking screenshots, and hashing of all information.

The chapter next covered the incident response process, step by step, presenting details on each of the steps. Among the topics presented were preparation, incident identification, escalation, isolation, damage and loss controls, mitigation, reporting, and lessons learned.

Questions

To help you prepare further for the CompTIA Security+ exam, and to test your level of preparedness, answer the following questions and then check your answers against the correct answers at the end of the chapter.

1. When collecting evidence for a computer forensics investigation, which of the following is last in the order of volatility?

   A. File system information

   B. Memory contents

   C. Swap files

   D. Raw disk blocks

2. In which of the following areas is evidence *most* likely to be lost if a compromised system is shut down before evidence collection is complete?

   A. Raw disk blocks

   B. Memory contents

   C. File system information

   D. USB drives

3. When capturing a system image from a computer system, what type of device should you use when connecting to the evidence drive?

   A. Track pro

   B. iSCSI HBA

   C. Write blocker

   D. Memory imager

4. While examining your network logs, you notice a large amount of TCP traffic coming from an external IP address directed at the web server in your DMZ. The destination TCP port seems to be different for each packet you examine. What type of traffic are you likely seeing in your logs?

   A. Smurf attack

   B. Port scan

   C. Ping sweep

   D. DNS transfer

5. Your organization experienced a physical break-in that was captured by a security camera system. When handing the drive containing the video of the break-in over to the police, you're asked to fill out a form that documents the description of the drive, serial number, condition, and so on. Why would you be asked to fill out that kind of form?

   A. To ensure the drive is not a copy

   B. To verify the drive is functional

C. To maintain a chain of custody for evidence

D. To ensure you get the same drive back after the investigation is complete

6. What does MAC stand for when discussing MAC times in file analysis?

A. Modified, available, and closed

B. Modified, accessed, and created

C. Modified, accessed, and copied

D. Modified, appended, and created

7. Which of the following is not a commonly used file-hashing algorithm?

A. MD5

B. SHA-1

C. SHA-2

D. TLS

8. A web server in your DMZ is being overwhelmed with ICMP packets from a large number of source addresses. Which of the following might be an appropriate mitigation step?

A. Turn off the web server

B. Block all ICMP packets at the firewall

C. Move the web service to a different port

D. Reboot the web server

9. Which of the following techniques is most likely to be employed by a credit card company looking for fraudulent transactions?

A. Big data analysis

B. Network forensics

C. Script mining

D. Drive imaging

10. Your organization has experienced a widescale, network-based compromise and customer records have been stolen. You've been asked to assemble an incident response team at your organization. Which of the following individuals are you least likely to put on your response team?

A. Rajesh from Public Relations

B. Tina from Human Resources

C. Jose from Network Operations

D. Carl from Legal

11. Place the following collection items in order of volatility: ARP cache, USB drives, memory (RAM), temporary file system/swap space, CPU register contents, live network connections, data on hard disk.

12. You suspect a user's workstation is infected with malware and are about to begin an investigation. If you want to reduce the likelihood that this workstation will infect other systems on your network, but you still want to preserve as much evidence as possible, which of the following should you do?

    A. Shut down the workstation

    B. Remove the power cord from the workstation

    C. Remove the network cable from the workstation

    D. Remove all USB devices and peripherals from the system

13. Your organization has just recovered from a large system failure and the members of the incident response team are about to go back to their normal duties. What should you do with the entire group before the response team is officially disbanded?

    A. Format any drives used during the response process

    B. Document any lessons learned during the recovery process

    C. Review the organization's continuity of operations plan

    D. Head out for happy hour

14. While working on an investigation, a colleague hands you a list of file creation and access times taken from a compromised workstation. In order to match the times with file access and creation times from other systems, what do you need to account for?

    A. Record time offsets

    B. Network Time Protocol

    C. Created, modified, and accessed times

    D. Operating system offsets

15. Place the following elements in order of volatility, from most to least volatile with respect to data during a forensic collection: network connections, swap space, ARP cache, data stored on archival media/backups (USB stick), memory (RAM).

Answers

1. **D.** Raw disk blocks are last in the order of volatility. Evidence in raw disk blocks will survive much longer than evidence contained in other areas such as memory, swap files, running processes, and so on.

2. **B.** Memory contents are the most volatile for digital evidence. When a system is shut down, digital evidence that may be in a computer system's memory is lost.

3. **C.** Using a write blocker when connecting to an evidence drive ensures that no data is written to the evidence drive. This helps to ensure that no changes are made to the evidence as it is collected.

4. **B.** When you see a large amount of traffic coming from one source IP address where the destination port (either UDP or TCP) changes with almost every

packet, this is most likely a port scan. The attacker probes a large number of ports looking for open services on the destination system.

5. **C.** Evidence collected from the scene of a crime should be documented on a chain of custody form to show the evidence was properly collected, transported, stored, and controlled from the time it was initially gathered until it is presented in court.

6. **B.** When discussing "MAC times" in a digital forensics investigation, one is usually referring to modified, accessed, and created dates and times.

7. **D.** TLS stands for "Transport Layer Security" and is a protocol used in the encryption of web traffic. TLS is not used as a file-hashing algorithm.

8. **B.** Mitigation steps reduce or eliminate the impact or risk of something. If a web server in your DMZ is being overwhelmed with ICMP packets, blocking those ICMP packets at the firewall and preventing them from ever reaching the web server would be an appropriate mitigation step. If you stop the ICMP packets from reaching the web server, they can't overwhelm the server.

9. **A.** In order for a credit card company to identify fraudulent transactions, it must be able to comb through millions and millions of records looking for patterns and indicators of fraudulent activity. That process of examining tremendous amounts of data in an effort to uncover hidden patterns and unknown correlations is called big data analysis (or big data analytics).

10. **B.** Of the groups listed, Human Resources is the least critical to your incident response process. Because customer records were stolen, you'll need to know what the legal implications of the breach are, and you'll likely need to send some sort of notification to the affected customers. And because this was a network-based attack, someone from Network Operations would also be critical to your team composition.

11. CPU register contents, ARP cache, live network connections, memory (RAM), temporary file system/swap space, data on hard disk, USB drives.

12. **C.** Although removing the network cable could potentially lose evidence, such as ongoing network connections, it is the only step that will help prevent malware propagation while still protecting highly volatile evidence such as memory contents.

13. **B.** A critical step in any incident response process is to document any lessons learned during the entire process. These lessons can be used to update incident response plans and disaster recovery plans, improve future incident responses, prevent future incidents, and so on.

14. **A.** When attempting to match file creation and access times between different systems, you need to account for record time offsets. Without knowing the frame of reference for each set of time stamps, it will be impossible for you to identify patterns and trends or conduct your investigation properly.

15. ARP cache, network connections, memory (RAM), swap space, data stored on archival media/backups (USB stick).

Security Awareness and Training

In this chapter, you will

- Consider the importance of security-related awareness and training
- Study the use of information classification
- Learn about the importance of data labeling
- Explore the role of user habits with respect to security
- Examine new threat vectors

People play an important role in the securing of information within the enterprise. To engage in the security effort, they require training and education. Policies may form the cornerstone of an organization's information security program, but unless they are communicated to the employees in a manner to facilitate their use, the policies will have little if any effect. A solid security awareness and training effort is key to ensuring that all employees are engaged in a supportive manner.

Security Awareness and Training

Security awareness and training programs can enhance an organization's security posture in two direct ways. First, they teach personnel how to follow the correct set of actions to perform their duties in a secure manner. Second, they make personnel aware of the indicators and effects of social engineering attacks.

There are many tasks that employees perform that can have information security ramifications. Properly trained employees are able to perform their duties in a more effective manner, including their duties associated with information security. The extent of information security training will vary depending on the organization's environment and the level of threat, but initial employee security training at the time of being hired is important, as is periodic refresher training.

A strong security education and awareness training program can go a long way toward reducing the chance that a social engineering attack will be successful. Security awareness programs and campaigns, which might include seminars, videos, posters, newsletters, and similar materials, are also fairly easy to implement and are not very costly. There is no reason for an organization to not have a security awareness program in place. Many government organizations have created security awareness posters to constantly remind individuals of the risk that occurs from complacency. Security newsletters, often in the form of e-mail, have also been used to remind employees of their security responsibilities.

Security Policy Training and Procedures

Personnel cannot be expected to perform complex tasks without training with respect to the tasks and expectations. This applies both to the security policy and to operational security details. If employees are going to be expected to comply with the organization's security policy, they must be properly trained in its purpose, meaning, and objectives. Training with respect to the information security policy, individual responsibilities, and expectations is something that requires periodic reinforcement through refresher training.

Because the security policy is a high-level directive that sets the overall support and executive direction with respect to security, it is important that the meaning of this message be translated and supported. Second-level policies such as password, access, information handling, and acceptable use policies also need to be covered. The collection of policies should paint a picture describing the desired security culture of the organization. The training should be designed to ensure that people see and understand the whole picture, not just the elements.

Role-based Training

For training to be effective, it needs to be targeted to the user with regard to their role in the subject of the training. While all employees may need general security awareness training, they also need specific training in areas where they have individual responsibilities. Role-based training with regard to information security responsibilities is an important part of information security training.

If a person has job responsibilities that may impact information security, then role-specific training is needed to ensure that the individual understands the responsibilities as they relate to information security. Some roles, such as system administrator or developer, have clearly defined information security responsibilities. The roles of others, such as project manager or purchasing manager, have information security impacts that are less obvious, but these roles require training as well. In fact, the less obvious but wider-impact roles of middle management can have a large effect on the information security culture, and thus if a specific outcome is desired, it requires training.

As in all personnel-related training, two elements need attention. First, retraining over time is necessary to ensure that personnel keep proper levels of knowledge. Second, as people change jobs, a reassessment of the required training basis is needed, and additional training may be required. Maintaining accurate training records of personnel is the only way this can be managed in any significant enterprise.

Personally Identifiable Information

When information can be used to identify an individual person, failure to protect it can have specific consequences. Business secrets are protected through trade secret laws, government information is protected through laws concerning national security, and privacy laws protect information associated with people. A set of elements that can lead to the specific identity of a person is referred to as *personally identifiable information (PII)*. By definition, PII can be used to identify a specific individual, even if an entire set is not disclosed.

PII is an essential element of many online transactions, but it can also be misused if disclosed to unauthorized parties. For this reason, it should be protected at all times, by all parties that possess it. TRUSTe (www.truste.com), an independent trust authority, defines personally identifiable information as

> *any information... (i) that identifies or can be used to identify, contact, or locate the person to whom such information pertains, or (ii) from which identification or contact information of an individual person can be derived. Personally Identifiable Information includes, but is not limited to: name, address, phone number, fax number, e-mail address, financial profiles, medical profile, social security number, and credit card information.*

The concept of PII is used to identify which data elements require a specific level of protection. When records are used individually (not in aggregate form), then PII is the concept of connecting a set of data elements to a specific purpose. If this can be accomplished, then the information is PII and needs specific protections. The U.S. Federal Trade Commission (FTC) has repeatedly ruled that if a firm collects PII, it is responsible for it through the entire lifecycle, from initial collection, through use, retirement, and destruction. Only after the PII is destroyed in all forms and locations is the company's liability for its compromise eliminated.

Notice, Choice, and Consent

Privacy is defined as the power to control what others know about you and what they can do with this information, and PII represents the core items that should be controlled; communication with the end user concerning privacy is paramount. Privacy policies are presented later in the chapter, but with respect to PII, three words can govern good citizenry when collecting PII. *Notice* refers to informing the customer that PII will be collected and used and/or stored. *Choice* refers to the opportunity for the end user to consent to the data collection or to opt out. *Consent* refers to the positive affirmation by a customer that she read the notice, understands her choices, and agrees to release her PII for the purposes explained to her.

Safe Harbor

There are significant differences between the United States and the European Union when it comes to data privacy. The differences in approach with respect to data protection led to the European Union issuing expressions of concern about the adequacy of data protection in the United States, a move that could have paved the way to the blocking of data transfers. After negotiation, it was determined that U.S. organizations that voluntarily joined an arrangement known as Safe Harbor would be considered adequate in terms of data protection. Safe Harbor is a mechanism for self-regulation that can be enforced through trade practice law via the FTC. A business joining the Safe

Harbor Consortium must make commitments to abide by specific guidelines concerning privacy. Safe Harbor members also agree to be governed by certain self-enforced regulatory mechanisms, backed ultimately by FTC action.

Safe Harbor is built upon seven principles:

- **Notice** A firm must give notice of what is being collected, how it will be used, and with whom it will be shared.

- **Choice** A firm must allow the option to opt out of transfer of PII to third parties.

- **Onward Transfer** All disclosures of PII must be consistent with the previous principles of Notice and Choice.

- **Security** PII must be secured at all times.

- **Data Integrity** PII must be maintained accurately and, if incorrect, the customer has the right to correct it.

- **Access** Individuals must have appropriate and reasonable access to PII for the purposes of verification and correction.

- **Enforcement** Issues with privacy and PII must have appropriate enforcement provisions to remain effective.

Information Classification

A key component of IT security is the protection of the information processed and stored on the computer systems and network. Organizations deal with many different types of information, and they need to recognize that not all information is of equal importance or sensitivity. This prompts a classification of information into various categories, each with its own requirements for its handling. Factors that affect the classification of specific information include its value to the organization (what will be the impact to the organization if it loses this information?), its age, and laws or regulations that govern its protection.

The most widely known classification of information is that implemented by the U.S. government and military, which classifies information into categories such as unclassified, sensitive but unclassified, confidential, secret, and top secret. Businesses have similar desires to protect information but often use categories such as publicly releasable, proprietary, company confidential, or for internal use only. Each policy for a classification of information should describe how it should be protected, who may have access to it, who has the authority to release it, and how it should be destroyed.

All employees of the organization should be trained in the procedures for handling the information that they are authorized to access. It doesn't matter what the different levels of classification are—whether high, medium, and low, or private, public, and confidential, or any other set of descriptors. The important element is a clear definition of the criteria used to differentiate the classification. Employees need to be able to understand the information classification scheme if they are to implement it in practice.

EXAM TIP   Information classification categories you should be aware of for the CompTIA Security+ exam include high, medium, low, confidential, private, and public.

Data Labeling, Handling, and Disposal

Effective data classification programs include data labeling, which enables personnel working with the data to know when it is sensitive and to understand the levels of protection required. When the data is inside an information-processing system, the protections should be designed into the system. But when the data leaves this cocoon of protection, whether by printing, downloading, or copying, it becomes necessary to ensure continued protection by other means. This is where data labeling assists users in fulfilling their responsibilities. Training to ensure that labeling occurs and that it is used and followed is important for users whose roles can be impacted by this material.

Many potential intruders have learned the value of dumpster diving. An organization must be concerned about how it handles not only paper trash and discarded objects, but also the information stored on discarded devices such as computers. Several government organizations have been embarrassed upon disclosure that their old computers sold to salvagers proved to contain sensitive documents on their hard drives. It is critical for every organization to have a strong disposal and destruction policy and related procedures, and to include these in the training program to ensure that users follow them.

Important papers should be shredded, and "important" in this case means anything that might be useful to a potential intruder. It is amazing what intruders can do with what appear to be innocent pieces of information.

Before magnetic storage media (such as disks or tapes) is discarded in the trash or sold for salvage, it should have all files deleted, and should be overwritten at least three times with all 1s, all 0s, and then random characters. Commercial products are available to destroy files using this process. It is not sufficient simply to delete all files and leave it at that, since the deletion process affects only the pointers to where the files are stored and doesn't actually get rid of all the bits in the file. This is why it is possible to "undelete" files and recover them after they have been deleted.

Training plays an important role in ensuring proper data handling and disposal. Personnel are intimately involved in several specific tasks associated with data handling and data destruction/disposal and, if properly trained, can act as a security control. Untrained or inadequately trained personnel will not be a productive security control and, in fact, can be a source of potential compromise.

Compliance with Laws, Best Practices, and Standards

There is a wide array of laws, regulations, contractual requirements, standards, and best practices associated with information security. Each places its own set of requirements upon an organization and its personnel. The only effective way for an organization to address these requirements is to build them into their own policies and procedures. Training to one's own policies and procedures would then translate into coverage of these external requirements.

It is important to note that many of these external requirements impart a specific training and awareness component upon the organization. Organizations subject to the requirements of Payment Card Industry Data Security Standard (PCI DSS), Gramm Leach Bliley Act (GLBA), or Health Insurance Portability Accountability Act (HIPAA) are among the many that must maintain a specific information security training program. Other organizations should do so as a matter of best practice.

User Habits

Individual user responsibilities vary between organizations and the type of business each organization is involved in, but there are certain very basic responsibilities that all users should be instructed to adopt:

- Lock the door to your office or workspace.
- Do not leave sensitive information inside your car unprotected.
- Secure storage media containing sensitive information in a secure storage device.
- Shred paper containing organizational information before discarding it.
- Do not divulge sensitive information to individuals (including other employees) who do not have an authorized need to know it.
- Do not discuss sensitive information with family members. (The most common violation of this rule occurs in regard to HR information, as employees, especially supervisors, may complain to their spouse or friends about other employees or about problems that are occurring at work.)
- Protect laptops and other mobile devices that contain sensitive or important organization information wherever the device may be stored or left. (It's a good idea to ensure that sensitive information is encrypted on the laptop or mobile device so that, should the equipment be lost or stolen, the information remains safe.)
- Be aware of who is around you when discussing sensitive corporate information. Does everybody within earshot have the need to hear this information?
- Enforce corporate access control procedures. Be alert to, and do not allow, piggybacking, shoulder surfing, or access without the proper credentials.
- Be aware of the correct procedures to report suspected or actual violations of security policies.
- Follow procedures established to enforce good password security practices. Passwords are such a critical element that they are frequently the ultimate target of a social engineering attack. Though such password procedures may seem too oppressive or strict, they are often the best line of defense.

EXAM TIP User responsibilities are easy training topics about which to ask questions on the exam, so commit to memory your knowledge of the points listed here.

Acceptable Use

An acceptable use policy (AUP) outlines what the organization considers to be the appropriate use of its resources, such as computer systems, e-mail, Internet, and networks. Organizations should be concerned about any personal use of organizational assets that does not benefit the company.

The goal of the policy is to ensure employee productivity while limiting potential organizational liability resulting from inappropriate use of the organization's assets. Training associated with the policy should clearly delineate what activities are not allowed. The AUP should address issues such as the use of resources to conduct personal business, installation of hardware or software, remote access to systems and networks, the copying of company-owned software, and the responsibility of users to protect company assets, including data, software, and hardware. Statements regarding possible penalties for ignoring any of the policies (such as termination) should also be included.

Related to appropriate use of the organization's computer systems and networks by employees is the appropriate use by the organization. The most important of such issues is whether the organization will consider it appropriate to monitor the employees' use of the systems and network. If monitoring is considered appropriate, the organization should include a statement to this effect in access banners and in training so that employees are reminded. This repeatedly warns employees, and possible intruders, that their actions are subject to monitoring and that any misuse of the system will not be tolerated. Should the organization need to use any information gathered during monitoring in either a civil or criminal case, the issue of whether the employee had an expectation of privacy, or whether it was even legal for the organization to be monitoring, is simplified if the organization can point to its repeatedly displayed statement that use of the system constitutes consent to monitoring.

 EXAM TIP Make sure you understand that an acceptable use policy outlines what is considered acceptable behavior for a computer system's users. This policy often goes hand-in-hand with an organization's Internet usage policy.

Password Behaviors

Poor password selection is one of the most common poor security practices, and one of the most dangerous. Numerous studies that have been conducted on password selection have found that while overall, more users are learning to select good passwords, a significant percentage of users still make poor choices. The problem with this, of course, is that a poor password choice can enable an attacker to compromise a computer system or network more easily. Even when users have good passwords, they often resort to another poor security practice—writing the password down in an easily located place, which can also lead to system compromise if an attacker gains physical access to the area.

 EXAM TIP Know the rules for good password selection. Generally, these are to use eight or more characters in your password; to include a combination of upper- and lowercase letters; to include at least one number and one special character; to not use a common word, phrase, or name; and to choose a password that you can remember so that you do not need to write it down.

A password policy is one of the most basic policies that an organization can have. Make sure you understand not only the basics of what constitutes a good password, but also the other issues that surround password creation, expiration, sharing, and use.

Data Handling

Understanding the responsibilities of proper data handling associated with one's job is an important training topic. Information can be deceptive in that it is not directly tangible, and people tend to develop bad habits around other job measures...at the expense of security. Employees require training in how to recognize the data classification and handling requirements of the data they are using, and they need to learn how to follow the proper handling processes. If certain data elements require special handling because of contracts, laws, or regulations, there is typically a training clause associated with this requirement. The spirit of the training clause is you get what you train, and if security over specific data types is a requirement, then it should be trained. This same principle holds for corporate data-handling responsibilities; you get the behaviors you train and reward.

Clean Desk Policies

Preventing access to information is also important in the work area. Firms with sensitive information should have a "clean desk policy" specifying that sensitive information must not be left unsecured in the work area when the worker is not present to act as custodian. Even leaving the desk area and going to the bathroom can leave information exposed and subject to compromise. The clean desk policy should identify and prohibit things that are not obvious upon first glance, such as passwords on sticky notes under keyboards and mouse pads or in unsecured desk drawers.

Shoulder Surfing

Shoulder surfing does not involve direct contact with the user, but instead involves the attacker directly observing the target entering sensitive information on a form, keypad, or keyboard. The attacker may simply look over the shoulder of the user at work, watching as a coworker enters their password. An attacker can attempt to obtain information such as a PIN at an automated teller machine, an access control entry code at a secure gate or door, or a calling card or credit card number. It is important for users to be aware of when they are entering sensitive information and adopt a user habit of hiding their activity.

Although defensive methods can help make shoulder surfing more difficult, the best defense is for a user to be aware of their surroundings and to not allow individuals to get into a position from which they can observe what the user is entering. A related security comment can be made at this point: a person should not use the same PIN for all of their different accounts, gate codes, and so on, since an attacker who learns the PIN for one could then use it for all the others.

Prevent Tailgating

A technique closely related to shoulder surfing is piggybacking (which may also be called tailgating). In this case, the attacker will attempt to gain unauthorized access to a facility by following closely behind an authorized employee. When the employee uses an access code, card, or key to gain access, the intruder follows closely behind before the door or gate can close. Most companies that have an access control system that utilizes cards or codes will also have a policy that forbids employees to allow anyone to follow so closely that they do not have to use their own access device, but human nature is such that this is very common. Employees don't want to challenge other individuals or force them to use their own device. Attackers can increase the odds of an employee allowing them in by simply making sure that their arms are full carrying something. Often, the employee not only won't challenge the individual, but will in fact offer to hold the door open for them.

Personally Owned Devices

Bring your own device (BYOD) is a current trend that has security implications. Employees require training in the security implications of BYOD. Seemingly innocent acts, such as charging a cell phone from a USB port on a computer, can result in the inadvertent opening of an attack surface. Using a personal device to read company e-mail can expand the information perimeter, and controls should be in place to prevent certain levels of information from going to these devices. But the ultimate security endpoint protection device is the user, and the user should be trained as to the potential risks, the company policy, and the correct actions to take with regard to BYOD usage.

New Threats and Security Trends/Alerts

At the end of the day, information security practices are about managing risk, and it is well known that the risk environment is one marked by constant change. The ever-evolving threat environment is one marked by new threats, new security issues, and new forms of defense. Training people to recognize the new threats necessitates continual awareness and training refresher events.

New Viruses

New forms of viruses, or malware, are being created every day. Some of these new forms can be highly destructive and costly, and it is incumbent upon all users to be on the lookout for and take actions to avoid exposure. Poor user practices are counted on by malware authors to assist in the spread of their attacks. One way of explaining proper actions to users is to use an analogy to cleanliness. Training users to practice good hygiene in their actions can go a long way toward assisting the enterprise in defending against these attack vectors.

Phishing Attacks

Phishing attacks are a form of social engineering attacks. As such, they specifically target users in an attempt to get users to perform specific actions that can be used as an attack vector. Phishing attacks take on a wide range of forms, including highly targeted phishing attacks against specific high-value targets, a technique referred to as *spear phishing*. A newer form of spear phishing, known as *whaling*, targets specific senior executives or others who have extremely high influence.

The best defense against phishing and other social engineering attacks is an educated and aware body of employees. Continuous refresher training about the topic of social engineering and specifics about current attack trends are needed to keep employees aware of and prepared for new trends in social engineering attacks. Attackers rely upon an uneducated, complacent, or distracted workforce to enable their attack vector. Social engineering has become the gateway for many of the most damaging attacks in play today. The Advanced Persistent Threat (APT) that has been in the news for the past couple of years depends upon social engineering as one of its infection vectors. Phishing and other social engineering attacks are used because they are successful. An aware and informed workforce is much less likely to fall prey to these attack vectors, and an active training and awareness program is the best method of preparing employees for this threat.

Zero-day Exploits

Zero-day exploits are, by their nature, unknown attack mechanisms for which a specific defense is not yet devised, hence the term zero-day. This means that an IT department has zero days to counter an attack. There are an unknown number of potential zero-day attack vectors, and a reasonably small number of actively detected zero-day exploits where vendors are working on defenses. It is incumbent upon an organization to have specific personnel trained to coordinate the active remediation of systems with active zero-day attacks.

When a zero-day exploit is being exploited and this becomes a known exploit, the vendor whose product has the issue must pursue defenses immediately. An organization that depends on this product must quickly assess the potential security breach and the risk to the enterprise. Should it be a critical system, some form of compensating control may be necessary until the vulnerability is patched.

Active participation in this defense aspect requires a trained and aware group of specialists who have the knowledge and abilities to maintain an adequate defensive posture. Maintaining an awareness of current zero-day issues is not an annual or quarterly event, but one that requires literally a daily check with a variety of security information sources to maintain an active, current knowledge base.

Social Networking and P2P

With the rise in popularity of peer-to-peer (P2P) communications and social networking sites—notably Facebook, Twitter, and LinkedIn—many people have gotten into a habit of sharing too much information. Using a status of "Returning from sales call to XYZ company" reveals information to people who have no need to know this information. Confusing sharing with friends and sharing business information with those who don't need to know is a line people are crossing on a regular basis. Don't be the employee who mixes business and personal information and releases information to parties who should not have it, regardless of how innocuous it may seem.

Users need to understand the importance of not using common programs such as torrents and other file sharing in the workplace, as these programs can result in infection mechanisms and data-loss channels. The information security training and awareness program should cover these issues. If the issues are properly explained to employees, their motivation to comply won't simply be to avoid adverse personnel action for violating a policy; they will want to assist in the security of the organization and its mission.

Training Metrics and Compliance

Training and awareness programs can yield much in the way of an educated and knowledgeable workforce. Many laws, regulations, and best practices have requirements for maintaining a trained workforce. Having a record-keeping system to measure compliance with attendance and to measure the effectiveness of the training is a normal requirement. Simply conducting training is not sufficient. Following up and gathering training metrics to validate compliance and security posture is an important aspect of security training management.

A number of factors deserve attention when managing security training. Because of the diverse nature of role-based requirements, maintaining an active, up-to-date listing of individual training and retraining requirements is one challenge. Monitoring the effectiveness of the training is yet another challenge. Creating an effective training and awareness program when measured by actual impact on employee behavior is a challenging endeavor. Training needs to be current, relevant, and interesting to engage employee attention. Simple repetition of the same training material has not proven to be effective, so regularly updating the program is a requirement if it is to remain effective over time.

 EXAM TIP   Requirements for both periodic training and retraining drive the need for good training records. Maintaining proper information security training records is a requirement of several laws and regulations and should be considered a best practice.

Chapter Review

In this chapter, you became acquainted with the elements required to establish an effective security training and awareness program. The chapter opened with a description of the basis of requirements for an information security training program. From there, it detailed requirements in areas such as information classification, labeling, and handling. User education with respect to roles, habits, and activities was covered, followed by an examination of the role of training to be compliant with the various rules, regulations, laws, and contractual requirements in the information security arena. The chapter next examined the training ramifications of new attack vectors such as new forms of malware, phishing, and zero-day exploits, and then explored the implications of P2P and social media. The chapter closed with a discussion of the need to follow up and gather training metrics to validate compliance and security posture.

Questions

To help you prepare further for the CompTIA Security+ exam, and to test your level of preparedness, answer the following questions and then check your answers against the correct answers at the end of the chapter.

1. Which of the following is a security label used by the U.S. government to implement mandatory access control (MAC)?

   A. Top secret

   B. Secret

   C. Confidential

   D. Unclassified

   E. All of the above

   F. None of the above

2. Which of the following most accurately describes an acceptable use policy?

   A. A policy that helps ensure maximum employee productivity and limits potential liability to the organization from inappropriate use of the Internet in the workplace.

   B. A policy that describes what the company will allow employees to send in, or as attachments to, e-mail messages.

   C. A policy that describes how to dispose of company assets and destroy documents without exposing sensitive information.

   D. A policy that communicates to users what specific uses of computer resources are permitted.

3. Which of the following defines security policy?

   A. Step-by-step instructions that prescribe exactly how employees are expected to act in a given situation or to accomplish a specific task.

   B. High-level statements created by management that lay out the organization's positions on particular issues.

C. General terms and definitions that are applicable to all organizations.

D. Procedures followed when modifications to the IT infrastructure are made.

4. Which of the following correctly describes data that can be used to identify a specific individual or from which contact information of an individual can be derived?

   A. Health insurance portability and accountability

   B. Protected health information

   C. Personally identifiable information

   D. Notice of privacy practices

5. What is a zero-day exploit?

   A. A piece of malicious code that attaches itself to another piece of code in order to replicate.

   B. An attack that exploits a previously unknown vulnerability.

   C. A piece of software that appears to provide one service but that also hides another purpose.

   D. Malware specifically designed to modify the operation of the operating system.

6. List five typical data classification categories.

7. Which of the following correctly defines phishing?

   A. The use of social engineering to trick a user into responding to an e-mail to initiate a malware-based attack.

   B. The use of social engineering to talk someone into revealing credentials.

   C. The hacking of computer systems and networks associated with the phone company.

   D. Looking over the shoulder or using a camera to view a user entering sensitive data.

8. Which of the following best defines social engineering?

   A. An attempt by an attacker to discover unprotected wireless networks.

   B. The targeting of high-value individuals.

   C. The art of deceiving another person to reveal confidential information.

   D. An attempt by an attacker to gain unauthorized access through the telephone system.

9. Which of the following can mandate information security training?

   A. PCI DSS

   B. HIPAA

   C. Best practices

   D. All of the above

10. Which of the following correctly defines the Safe Harbor principle of Notice?

    A. A firm must identify what information is being collected, how it will be used, and with whom it will be shared.

    B. A firm must allow the option to opt out of transfer of personally identifiable information to third parties.

    C. Personally identifiable information must be secured at all times.

    D. Personally identifiable information must be maintained accurately and, if incorrect, the customer has the right to correct it.

11. The CISO has come to you seeking advice on fostering good user habits. Outline at least seven important principles that could be incorporated into an annual employee training program.

12. You've been working in the security business for a few years now. You've just hired a new intern. You have about 15 minutes before your next meeting and would like to share some of your security experience with your new intern. List five aspects of Safe Harbor principles that you could discuss with your employee.

13. Your boss calls you into his office and asks you to outline a plan to implement security policies. Discuss the first two policies you'd implement, and justify why you would implement them.

14. Your boss calls you into his office and asks you to outline a plan to implement a security awareness program. Outline a training program with at least two areas of training you think all personnel should receive.

15. Describe why a data classification system is important to an enterprise.

Answers

1. **E.** All of these are security labels used by the U.S. government to implement MAC. The level of information sensitivity is independent of the mechanism used to enforce access rights.

2. **D.** An acceptable use policy communicates to users which specific uses of computer resources are permitted.

3. **B.** Policies are high-level statements created by management that lay out the organization's positions on particular issues.

4. **C.** Personally identifiable information is any information (i) that identifies or can be used to identify, contact, or locate the person to whom such information pertains, or (ii) from which identification or contact information of an individual person can be derived.

5. **B.** A zero-day exploit is an attack that exploits a previously unknown vulnerability.

6. High, medium, low, sensitive, unclassified, confidential, secret, top secret, public.

7. **A.** Phishing is the use of social engineering to trick a user into responding to an e-mail to initiate a malware-based attack.

8. **C.** Social engineering is the art of deceiving another person to reveal confidential information.

9. **D.** Information security training requirements are part of PCI DSS, HIPAA, and also many best practices.

10. **A.** The Safe Harbor principle of Notice states that a firm must identify what information is being collected, how it will be used, and with whom it will be shared.

11. Good training about user habits should include the following rules: lock the door to your office or workspace (keep a clean desk); do not leave sensitive information inside your car unprotected; secure storage media containing sensitive information in a secure storage device; shred paper containing organizational information; do not divulge sensitive information to individuals who do not have an authorized need to know; do not discuss sensitive information with family members; protect laptops and other mobile devices that contain sensitive organizational information; be aware of who is around you when discussing sensitive information; enforce corporate access control procedures (to avoid piggybacking, shoulder surfing, and so on); be aware of correct procedures to report violations of security policies; follow procedures to enforce good password security practices.

12. The Safe Harbor principles are Notice, Choice, Onward Transfer, Security, Data Integrity, Access, and Enforcement.

13. An acceptable use policy, an Internet usage policy, and an e-mail usage policy should be among the first policies implemented.

14. The training program should include the topics to be trained (a list of policies), based on the policies established, and should include a plan to initially train all employees, tracking completion, and define the period of recurring training.

15. A data classification system ensures that company information is properly protected. It provides the foundation for a company disposal and destruction policy. It also is fundamental for defining access controls and role-based access controls.

Physical Security and Environmental Controls

In this chapter, you will

- Explore environmental controls
- Explore physical security controls
- Compare and contrast physical security and environmental controls
- Examine control types in physical security

Physical security is an important topic for businesses dealing with the security of networks and information systems. Businesses are responsible for securing their profitability, which requires securing a combination of assets: employees, product inventory, trade secrets, and strategy information. These and other important assets affect the profitability of a company and its future survival. Companies therefore perform many activities to attempt to provide physical security—locking doors, installing alarm systems, using safes, posting security guards, setting access controls, and more.

Environmental controls play an important role in the protection of the systems used to process information. Most companies today have invested a large amount of time, money, and effort in both network security and information systems security. In this chapter, you will learn about how the strategies for securing the network and for securing information systems are linked, and you'll learn several methods by which companies can minimize their exposure to physical security events that can diminish their network security.

Environmental Controls

While the confidentiality of information is important, so is its availability. Sophisticated environmental controls are needed for current data centers. Heating and cooling are important for computer systems as well as users. Fire suppression is an important consideration when dealing with information systems. Electromagnetic interference, or EMI, is also an environmental issue.

HVAC

Controlling a data center's temperature and humidity is important to keeping servers running. Heating ventilating and air conditioning (HVAC) systems are critical for keeping data centers cool, because typical servers put out between 1000 and 2000 BTUs of heat (1 BTU equals the amount of energy required to raise the temperature of one pound of liquid water one degree Fahrenheit).

Multiple servers in a confined area can create conditions too hot for the machines to continue to operate. This problem is made worse with the advent of blade-style computing systems and with many other devices shrinking in size. While physically smaller, they tend to still expel the same amount of heat.

Fire Suppression

According to the Fire Suppression Systems Association (www.fssa.net), 43 percent of businesses that close as a result of a significant fire never reopen. An additional 29 percent fail within three years of the event. The ability to respond to a fire quickly and effectively is thus critical to the long-term success of any organization. Addressing potential fire hazards and vulnerabilities has long been a concern of organizations in their risk analysis process. The goal obviously should be never to have a fire, but in the event that one does occur, it is important that mechanisms are in place to limit the damage the fire can cause.

Water-Based Fire Suppression Systems

Water-based fire suppression systems have long been, and still are today, the primary tool to address and control structural fires. Considering the amount of electrical equipment found in today's office environment and the fact that, for obvious reasons, this equipment does not react well to large applications of water, it is important to know what to do with equipment if it does become subjected to a water-based sprinkler system. The 2013 *NFPA 75: Standard for the Protection of Information Technology Equipment* outlines measures that can be taken to minimize the damage to electronic equipment exposed to water. This guidance includes these suggestions:

- Open cabinet doors, remove side panels and covers, and pull out chassis drawers to allow water to run out of equipment.
- Set up fans to move room-temperature air through the equipment for general drying. Move portable equipment to dry, air-conditioned areas.
- Use compressed air at no higher than 50 psi to blow out trapped water.
- Use handheld dryers on the lowest setting to dry connectors, backplane wirewraps, and printed circuit cards.
- Use cotton-tipped swabs for hard-to-reach places. Lightly dab the surfaces to remove residual moisture. Do not use cotton-tipped swabs on wirewrap terminals.
- Use water-displacement aerosol sprays containing Freon-alcohol mixtures as an effective first step in drying critical components. Follow up with professional restoration as soon as possible.

Even if these guidelines are followed, damage to the systems may have already occurred. Since water is so destructive to electronic equipment, not only because of the immediate problems of electronic shorts to the system but also because of longer-term corrosive damage water can cause, alternative fire suppression methods have been sought. One of the more common alternative methods used was halon-based systems.

Halon-Based Fire Suppression Systems

A fire needs fuel, oxygen, and high temperatures for the chemical combustion to occur. If you remove any of these, the fire will not continue. Halon interferes with the chemical combustion present in a fire. Even though halon production was banned in 1994, a number of these systems still exist today. They were originally popular because halon will mix quickly with the air in a room and will not cause harm to computer systems. Halon is also dangerous to humans, especially when subjected to extremely hot temperatures (such as might be found during a fire), when it can degrade into other toxic chemicals. As a result of these dangers, and also because halon has been linked with the issue of ozone depletion, halon is banned in new fire suppression systems. It is important to note that under the Environmental Protection Agency (EPA) rules that mandated no further production of halon, existing systems were not required to be destroyed. Replacing the halon in a discharged system, however, will be a problem, since only existing stockpiles of halon may be used and the cost is becoming prohibitive. For this reason, many organizations are switching to alternative solutions. These alternatives are known as *clean-agent fire suppression systems*, since they not only provide fire suppression capabilities but also protect the contents of the room, including people, documents, and electronic equipment. Examples of clean agents include carbon dioxide, argon, Inergen, and FM-200 (heptafluoropropane).

Clean-Agent Fire Suppression Systems

Carbon dioxide (CO_2) has been used as a fire suppression agent for a long time. The Bell Telephone Company used portable CO_2 extinguishers in the early part of the 20th century. Carbon dioxide extinguishers attack all three necessary elements for a fire to occur. CO_2 displaces oxygen so that the amount of oxygen remaining is insufficient to sustain the fire. It also provides some cooling in the fire zone and reduces the concentration of "gasified" fuel. Argon extinguishes fire by lowering the oxygen concentration below the 15 percent level required for combustible items to burn. Argon systems are designed to reduce the oxygen content to about 12.5 percent, which is below the 15 percent needed for the fire but is still above the 10 percent required by the EPA for human safety. Inergen, a product of Ansul Corporation, is composed of three gases: 52 percent nitrogen, 40 percent argon, and 8 percent carbon dioxide. In a manner similar to pure argon systems, Inergen systems reduce the level of oxygen to about 12.5 percent, which is sufficient for human safety but not sufficient to sustain a fire. Another chemical used to phase out halon is FE-13, or trifluoromethane. This chemical was originally developed as a chemical refrigerant and works to suppress fires by inhibiting the combustion chain reaction. FE-13 is gaseous, leaves behind no residue that would harm equipment, and is considered safe to use in occupied areas. Other halocarbons are also approved for use in replacing halon systems, including FM-200 (heptafluoropropane), a chemical used as a propellant for asthma medication dispensers.

Handheld Fire Extinguishers

Computer security professionals typically do not have much influence over the type of fire suppression system that their office includes. It is, however, important that they are aware of what type has been installed, what they should do in case of an emergency, and what needs to be done to recover after the release of the system. One area that they can influence, however, is the type of handheld fire extinguisher that is located in their area.

Automatic fire suppression systems designed to discharge when a fire is detected are not the only systems you should be aware of. If a fire can be caught and contained before the automatic systems discharge, it can mean significant savings to the organization in terms of both time and equipment costs (including the recharging of the automatic system). Handheld extinguishers are common in offices, but the correct use of them must be understood or disaster can occur.

There are four different classes of fire, as shown in Table 10-1. Each class of fire has its own fuel source and method for extinguishing it. Class A systems, for example, are designed to extinguish fires with normal combustible material as the fire's source. Water can be used in an extinguisher of this sort, since it is effective against fires of this type. Water, as we've discussed, is not appropriate for fires involving wiring or electrical equipment. Using a class A extinguisher against an electrical fire will not only be ineffective but can result in additional damage. Some extinguishers are designed to be effective against more than one class of fire, such as the common ABC fire extinguishers. This is probably the best type of system to have in a data processing facility. All fire extinguishers should be easily accessible and should be clearly marked. Before anybody uses an extinguisher, they should know what type of extinguisher it is and what the source of the fire is. When in doubt, evacuate and let the fire department handle the situation.

 EXAM TIP The type of fire distinguishes the type of extinguisher that should be used to suppress it. Remember that the most common type is the ABC fire extinguisher, which is designed to handle all types of fires except flammable-metal fires, which are rare.

Class of Fire	Type of Fire	Examples of Combustible	Materials Example Suppression Method
A	Common combustibles	Wood, paper, cloth, plastics	Water or dry chemical
B	Combustible liquids	Petroleum products, organic solvents	CO_2 or dry chemical
C	Electrical	Electrical wiring and equipment, power tools	CO_2 or dry chemical
D	Flammable metals	Magnesium, titanium	Copper metal or sodium chloride

Table 10-1 Types of Fire and Suppression Methods

Fire Detection Devices

An essential complement to fire suppression systems and devices are fire detection devices (fire detectors). Detectors may be able to detect a fire in its very early stages, before a fire suppression system is activated, and sound a warning that potentially enables employees to address the fire before it becomes serious enough for the fire suppression equipment to kick in.

There are several different types of fire detectors. One type, of which there are two varieties, is activated by smoke. The two varieties of smoke detector are ionization and photoelectric. A photoelectric detector is good for potentially providing advance warning of a smoldering fire. This type of device monitors an internal beam of light. If something degrades the light, for example, by obstructing it, the detector assumes it is something like smoke and the alarm sounds. An ionization style of detector uses an ionization chamber and a small radioactive source to detect fast-burning fires. Shown in Figure 10-1, the chamber consists of two plates, one with a positive charge and one with a negative charge. Oxygen and nitrogen particles in the air become "ionized" (an ion is freed from the molecule). The freed ion, which has a negative charge, is attracted to the positive plate, and the remaining part of the molecule, now with a positive charge, is attracted to the negative plate. This movement of particles creates a very small electric current that the device measures. Smoke inhibits this process, and the detector will detect the resulting drop in current and sound an alarm.

Both of these devices are often referred to generically as smoke detectors, and combinations of both varieties are possible. For more information on smoke detectors, see http://home.howstuffworks.com/home-improvement/household-safety/fire/smoke2.htm. Because both of these devices are triggered by the interruption of a signal, without regard to why, they can give false alarms. They are unable to distinguish the difference between the smoke from a kitchen fire and burned toast.

Another type of fire detector is activated by heat. These devices also come in two varieties. Fixed-temperature or fixed-point devices activate if the temperature in the area ever exceeds some predefined level. Rate-of-rise or rate-of-increase temperature devices activate when there is a sudden increase in local temperature that may indicate the beginning stages of a fire. Rate-of-rise sensors can provide an earlier warning but are also responsible for more false warnings.

A third type of detector is flame activated. This type of device relies on the flames from the fire to provide a change in the infrared energy that can be detected. Flame-activated

---

Figure 10-1

An ionization chamber for an ionization type of smoke detector

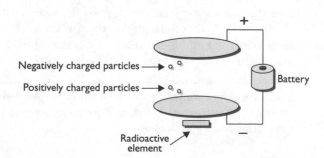

devices are generally more expensive than the other two types, but can frequently detect a fire sooner.

EMI Shielding

Electromagnetic interference, or EMI, can plague any type of electronics, but the density of circuitry in the typical data center can make it a haven for EMI. EMI is defined as the disturbance of an electrical circuit caused by that circuit's reception of electromagnetic radiation. Magnetic radiation enters the circuit by induction, where magnetic waves create a charge on the circuit. The amount of sensitivity to this magnetic field depends on a number of factors, including the length of the circuit, which can act like an antenna. EMI is grouped into two general types: narrowband and broadband. Narrowband is, by its nature, electromagnetic energy with a small frequency band and, therefore, typically sourced from a device that is purposefully transmitting in the specified band. Broadband covers a wider array of frequencies and is typically caused by some type of general electrical power use such as power lines or electric motors.

In the United States, the Federal Communications Commission has responsibility for regulating products that produce EMI and has developed a program for equipment manufacturers to adhere to standards for EMI immunity. Modern circuitry is designed to resist EMI. Cabling is a good example; the twist in unshielded twisted pair (UTP), or Category 5 or 6, cable is there to prevent EMI. EMI is also controlled by metal computer cases that are grounded; by providing an easy path to ground, the case acts as an EMI shield. Shielding can be important for network cabling. It is important not to run lengths of network cabling in parallel with power cables. Twisted pair offers some degree of protection, but in electrically noisy environments such as industrial facilities, shielded twisted pair (STP) may be necessary.

A bigger example of shielding would be a Faraday cage or Faraday shield, which is an enclosure of conductive material that is grounded. These can be room-sized or built into a building's construction; the critical element is that there is no significant gap in the enclosure material. These measures can help shield EMI, especially in high radio frequency environments.

While we have talked about the shielding necessary to keep EMI radiation out of your circuitry, there is also technology to try and help keep it in. Known by some as TEMPEST, it is also known as Van Eck emissions. A computer's monitor or LCD display produces electromagnetic radiation that can be remotely observed with the correct equipment. TEMPEST was the code word for a National Security Agency (NSA) program to secure equipment from this type of eavesdropping. While some of the information about TEMPEST is still classified, there are guides on the Internet that describe protective measures, such as shielding and electromagnetic-resistant enclosures. A company has even developed a commercial paint that offers radio frequency shielding.

 EXAM TIP   Be sure you understand the principles behind environmental control systems such as HVAC and fire suppression, as well as environmental monitoring and EMI shielding.

Hot and Cold Aisles

The trend toward smaller, more dense servers means more servers and devices per rack, putting a greater load on the cooling systems. This encourages the use of a hot aisle/cold aisle layout. A data center that is arranged into hot and cold aisles dictates that all the intake fans on all equipment face the cold aisle, and the exhaust fans all face the opposite aisle. The HVAC system is then designed to push cool air underneath the raised floor and up through perforated tiles on the cold aisle. Hot air from the hot aisle is captured by return air ducts for the HVAC system. The use of this layout is designed to control airflow, with the purpose being never to mix the hot and cold air. This requires the use of blocking plates and side plates to close open rack slots. The benefits of this arrangement are that cooling is more efficient and can handle higher density.

Environmental Monitoring

Environmental monitoring, when it pertains to information technology, is the electronic tracking of temperature and humidity in the data center. The use of thermometers to measure temperature dates back to the 17th century. Everyone is familiar with the classic analog temperature reading provided by the mercury in glass tube type of thermometer, but increasingly, measurements of temperature are electronic. Consumer-grade models are inexpensive and can receive readings from remote wireless transmitters, allowing measurements from indoor and outdoor locations. More advanced units can track data on temperature, pressure, humidity, wind speed, rainfall, and a host of other data. Since data centers commonly have a lot of network infrastructure and are increasingly remotely controlled, it makes the most sense to add these environmental sensors to the network. Modern monitoring applications use an array of sensors to measure air flow, temperature, humidity, and pressure. Coupled with database software, the environmental conditions of the data center can be mapped over time to allow for expansion planning and to provide alerts when there is a problem.

Temperature and Humidity Controls

Server temperatures are a common concern, but the level of humidity is just as important. Too high of a humidity level can lead to condensation in cold areas, and too low of a humidity level can lead to static electricity.

Physical Security

Physical security is an important topic for businesses dealing with the security of networks and information systems. Physical access to the hardware, networks, servers, client machines, and components can be used to compromise security controls. Companies therefore perform many activities to attempt to provide physical security—locking doors, installing alarm systems, using safes, posting security guards, setting access controls, and more.

Physical access is the most common way of obtaining an image of a hard drive, and the biggest benefit for the attacker is that drive imaging leaves absolutely no trace of the crime. Besides physically securing access to your computers, you can do very little to prevent drive imaging, but you can minimize its impact. The use of encryption even for a few important files provides protection. Full encryption of the drive protects all files stored on it. Alternatively, placing files on a centralized file server keeps them from being imaged from an individual machine, but if an attacker is able to image the file server, the data will be copied.

Centralized storage management moves the physical security problem to the server room, but this simplifies the problem. Rather than worrying about numerous places to secure, centralized storage of high-value material allows centralized security enhancements. This allows the economical use of a combination of physical security mechanisms, including locks, alarms, cameras, and other mechanisms.

 EXAM TIP Drive imaging is a threat because all existing access controls to data can be bypassed and all the data stored on the drive can be read from the image.

Hardware Locks

Locks are a common security measure that are used with near ubiquity. Everyone is familiar with using a lock to secure something. Just as locks can keep your car from being stolen, they can secure computers as well. Laptops are popular targets for thieves and should be locked inside a desk when not in use, or secured with special computer lockdown cables. Laptop thefts from cars can occur in seconds, and thieves have been caught taking them from security screening areas at airports while the owner was distracted in screening. If desktop towers are used, use computer desks that provide a space in which to lock the computer. In some cases, valuable media are stored in a safe designed for that purpose. All of these measures can improve the physical security of the computers themselves, but most of them can be defeated by attackers if users are not knowledgeable about the security program and do not follow it.

Although locks have been used for hundreds of years, their design has not changed much: a metal "token" is used to align pins in a mechanical device. Because all mechanical devices have tolerances, it is possible to sneak through these tolerances by "picking" the lock. Most locks can be easily picked with simple tools, some of which are shown in Figure 10-2.

Figure 10-2
Lock-picking
tools

Figure 10-3
A high-security
lock and its key

Because we humans are always trying to build a better mousetrap, high-security locks have been designed to defeat attacks, such as the one shown in Figure 10-3; these locks are more sophisticated than a standard home deadbolt system. Typically found in commercial applications that require high security, these locks are made to resist picking and drilling, as well as other common attacks such as simply pounding the lock through the door. Another common feature of high-security locks is *key control*, which refers to the restrictions placed on making a copy of the key. For most residential locks, a trip to the hardware store will allow you to make a copy of the key. Key control locks use patented keyways that can only be copied at a locksmith, who will keep records on authorized users of a particular key.

High-end lock security is more important now that attacks such as "bump keys" are well known and widely available. A bump key is a key cut with all notches to the maximum depth, also known as "all nines." This key uses a technique that has been around a long time, but has recently gained a lot of popularity. The key is inserted into the lock and then sharply struck, bouncing the lock pins up above the shear line and allowing the lock to open. High-security locks attempt to prevent this type of attack through various mechanical means such as nontraditional pin layout, sidebars, and even magnetic keys.

Mantraps

The implementation of a mantrap is one way to combat tailgating. A mantrap comprises two doors closely spaced that require the user to card through one and then the other sequentially. Mantraps make it nearly impossible to trail through a doorway undetected—if you happen to catch the first door, you will be trapped in by the second door.

EXAM TIP A mantrap door arrangement can prevent unauthorized people from following authorized users through an access-controlled door, which is also known as *tailgating*.

Video Surveillance

Video surveillance is typically done through closed-circuit television (CCTV). The use of CCTV cameras for surveillance purposes dates back to at least 1961, when cameras were installed in the London Transport train station. The development of smaller camera components and lower costs has caused a boon in the CCTV industry since then.

CCTV cameras are used to monitor a workplace for security purposes. These systems are commonplace in banks and jewelry stores, places with high-value merchandise that is attractive to thieves. As the expense of these systems dropped, they became practical for many more industry segments.

Traditional cameras are analog based and require a video multiplexer to combine all the signals and make multiple views appear on a monitor. IP-based cameras are changing that, as most of them are stand-alone units that are viewable through a web browser, such as the camera shown in Figure 10-4.

These IP-based systems add useful functionality, such as the ability to check on the building from the Internet. This network functionality, however, makes the cameras subject to normal IP-based network attacks. A DoS attack launched at the CCTV system just as a break-in is occurring is the last thing that anyone would want (other than the criminals). For this reason, IP-based CCTV cameras should be placed on their own separate network that can be accessed only by security personnel. The same physical separation applies to any IP-based camera infrastructure. Older time-lapse tape recorders are slowly being replaced with digital video recorders. While the advance in technology is significant, be careful if and when these devices become IP-enabled, since they will become a security issue, just like everything else that touches the network.

If you depend on the CCTV system to protect your organization's assets, carefully consider camera placement and the type of cameras used. Different iris types, focal lengths, and color or infrared capabilities are all options that make one camera superior over another in a specific location.

Figure 10-4
IP-based cameras leverage existing IP networks instead of needing a proprietary CCTV cable.

Fencing

Fences serve as a physical barrier around property. They can serve to keep people out and in, preventing the free movement across unauthorized areas. Fencing can be an important part of a physical security plan. Properly employed, it can help secure areas from unauthorized visitors. Outside of the building's walls, many organizations prefer to have a perimeter fence as a physical first layer of defense. Chain-link-type fencing is most commonly used, and it can be enhanced with barbed wire. Anti-scale fencing, which looks like very tall vertical poles placed close together to form a fence, is used for high-security implementations that require additional scale and tamper resistance.

Proximity Readers

One method of electronic door control is through the use of contactless access cards (such as the example shown in Figure 10-5). A keypad, a combination of the card, and a separate PIN code would be required to open the door to the server room.

Many organizations use electronic access control systems to control the opening of doors. The use of proximity readers and contactless access cards provides user information to the control panel. Doorways are electronically controlled via electronic door strikes and magnetic locks. These devices rely on an electronic signal from the control panel to release the mechanism that keeps the door closed. These devices are integrated into an access control system that controls and logs entry into all the doors connected to it, typically through the use of access tokens. Security is improved by

Figure 10-5
Contactless access cards act as modern keys to a building.

having a centralized system that can instantly grant or refuse access based upon access lists and the reading of a token that is given to the user. This kind of system also logs user access, providing nonrepudiation of a specific user's presence in a controlled environment. The system will allow logging of personnel entry, auditing of personnel movements, and real-time monitoring of the access controls.

Access List

Access lists work in the physical world in the same way they work in the electronic world. Access lists define the group of individuals who are authorized to utilize a resource. Entry into a server room, access to equipment rooms, and keys for locks protecting sensitive areas are all examples of elements that require access control.

Many organizations use electronic access control systems to control the opening of doors. The use of proximity readers and contactless access cards provides user information to the control panel. Doorways are electronically controlled via electronic door strikes and magnetic locks. These devices rely on an electronic signal from the control panel to release the mechanism that keeps the door closed. These devices are integrated into an access control system that controls and logs entry into all the doors connected to it, typically through the use of access tokens. Security is improved by having a centralized system that can instantly grant or refuse access based upon access lists and the reading of a token that is given to the user. This kind of system also logs user access, providing nonrepudiation of a specific user's presence in a controlled environment. The system will allow logging of personnel entry, auditing of personnel movements, and real-time monitoring of the access controls.

Proper Lighting

Proper lighting is essential for physical security. Unlit or dimly lit areas allow intruders to lurk and conduct unauthorized activities without a significant risk of observation by guards or other personnel. External building lighting is important to ensure that unauthorized activities cannot occur without being observed and responded to. Internal lighting is equally important, for it enables more people to observe activities and see conditions that are not correct. As described later, in the "Barricades" section, windows can play an important role in assisting the observation of the premises. Having sensitive areas well lit and open to observation through windows prevents activities that would otherwise take place in secret. Unauthorized parties in server rooms are more likely to be detected if the servers are centrally located, surrounded in windows, and well lit.

Signs

Signs act as informational devices and can be used in a variety of ways to assist in physical security. Signs can provide information as to areas that are restricted, or indicate where specific precautions, such as keeping doors locked, are required. A common use of signs in high-security facilities is to delineate where visitors are allowed versus secured areas where escorts are required. Visual security clues can assist in alerting users to the need for specific security precautions. Visual clues as to the types of protection required can take the form of different-color name badges that dictate the level of access, visual lanyards that indicate visitors, colored folders, and so forth.

Guards

Guards provide an excellent security measure, because guards are a visible presence with direct responsibility for security. Other employees expect security guards to behave a certain way with regard to securing the facility. Guards typically monitor entrances and exits and can maintain access logs of who has entered and departed the building. In many organizations, everyone who passes through security as a visitor must sign the log, which can be useful in tracing who was at what location and why.

Security personnel are helpful in physically securing the machines on which information assets reside, but to get the most benefit from their presence, they must be trained to take a holistic approach to security. The value of data typically can be many times that of the machines on which the data is stored. Security guards typically are not computer security experts, so they need to be educated about the value of the data and be trained in network security as well as physical security involving users. They are the company's eyes and ears for suspicious activity, so the network security department needs to train them to notice suspicious network activity as well. Multiple extensions ringing in sequence during the night, computers rebooting all at once, or strange people parked in the parking lot with laptop computers or other mobile computing devices are all indicators of a network attack that might be missed without proper training.

Barricades

The primary defense against a majority of physical attacks are the barriers between the assets and a potential attacker—walls, fences, gates, and doors. Some organizations also employ full- or part-time private security staff to attempt to protect their assets. These barriers provide the foundation upon which all other security initiatives are based, but the security must be designed carefully, as an attacker has to find only a single gap to gain access. Barricades can also be used to control vehicular access to and near a building or structure.

 EXAM TIP All entry points to server rooms and wiring closets should be closely controlled, and, if possible, access should be logged through an access control system.

Walls may have been one of the first inventions of humans. Once they learned to use natural obstacles such as mountains to separate them from their enemy, they next learned to build their *own* mountain for the same purpose. Hadrian's Wall in England, the Great Wall of China, and the Berlin Wall are all famous examples of such basic physical defenses. The walls of any building serve the same purpose, but on a smaller scale: they provide barriers to physical access to company assets. In the case of information assets, as a general rule, the most valuable assets are contained on company servers. To protect the physical servers, you must look in all directions. Doors and windows should be safeguarded, and a minimum number of each should be used in a server room when they are all that separate the servers from the personnel allowed to access them. Less obvious entry points should also be considered: Is a drop ceiling used in the server room? Do the interior walls extend to the actual roof, raised floors, or crawlspaces? Access to the server room should be limited to the people who need access, not to all employees of the organization. If you are going to use a wall to protect an asset, make sure no obvious holes appear in that wall.

NOTE Windows or no windows? Windows provide visibility allowing people to observe activities in the server room. This can provide security if those doing the observing have authority to see the activity in the server room. If those outside do not have this authority, then windows should be avoided.

Another method of preventing surreptitious access is through the use of windows. Many high-security areas have a significant number of windows so that people's activities within the area can't be hidden. A closed server room with no windows makes for a quiet place for someone to achieve physical access to a device without worry of being seen. Windows remove this privacy element that many criminals depend upon to achieve their entry and illicit activities.

Biometrics

Biometrics use the measurements of certain biological factors to identify one specific person from others. These factors are based on parts of the human body that are unique. The most well known of these unique biological factors is the fingerprint. Fingerprint readers have been available for several years in laptops and other mobile devices, such as shown in Figure 10-6, and as stand-alone USB devices.

However, many other biological factors can be used, such as the retina or iris of the eye, the geometry of the hand, and the geometry of the face. When these are used for authentication, there is a two-part process: enrollment and then authentication. During enrollment, a computer takes the image of the biological factor and reduces it to a

Figure 10-6
Newer laptop computers often include a finger-print reader.

numeric value. When the user attempts to authenticate, their feature is scanned by the reader, and the computer compares the numeric value being read to the one stored in the database. If they match, access is allowed. Since these physical factors are unique, theoretically, only the actual authorized person would be allowed access.

In the real world, however, the theory behind biometrics breaks down. Tokens that have a digital code work very well because everything remains in the digital realm. A computer checks your code, such as 123, against the database; if the computer finds 123 and that number has access, the computer opens the door. Biometrics, however, take an analog signal, such as a fingerprint or a face, and attempt to digitize it, and it is then matched against the digits in the database. The problem with an analog signal is that it might not encode the exact same way twice. For example, if you came to work with a bandage on your chin, would the face-based biometrics grant you access or deny it?

Engineers who designed these systems understood that if a system was set to exact checking, an encoded biometric might never grant access since it might never scan the biometric exactly the same way twice. Therefore, most systems have tried to allow a certain amount of error in the scan, while not allowing too much. This leads to the concepts of false positives and false negatives. A *false positive* occurs when a biometric is scanned and allows access to someone who is not authorized—for example, two people who have very similar fingerprints might be recognized as the same person by the computer, which grants access to the wrong person. A *false negative* occurs when the system denies access to someone who is actually authorized—for example, a user at the hand geometry scanner forgot to wear a ring he usually wears and the computer doesn't recognize his hand and denies him access. For biometric authentication to work properly, and also be trusted, it must minimize the existence of both false positives and false negatives. To do that, a balance between exacting and error must be created so that the machines allow a little physical variance—but not too much.

False Positives and False Negatives

When a decision is made on information and an associated range of probabilities, the conditions exist for a false decision. Figure 10-7 illustrates two overlapping probabilities; an item belongs to either the curve on the left, or right, but not both. The problem in deciding which curve an item belongs to occurs when the curves overlap.

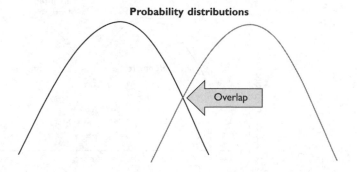

Figure 10-7
Overlapping probabilities

Probability distributions

Overlap

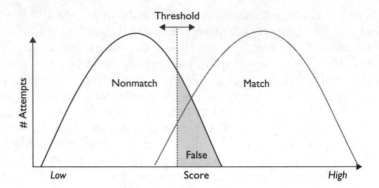

When there is an overlapping area, it is typically referred to as the *false positive and false negative rate*. Note that in the accompanying figures, the size of overlap is greatly exaggerated to make it easy to see. Figure 10-8 illustrates a false positive detection. If the value observed is the dotted line, then it could be considered either a match or a nonmatch. If in fact it should not match, and the system tags it as a match, it is a false positive. In biometrics, a false positive would allow access to an unauthorized party.

Figure 10-9 illustrates a false negative detection. If the value observed is the dotted line, then it could be considered either a match or a nonmatch. If in fact it should match, and the system tags it as a nonmatch, it is a false negative. A false negative would prevent an authorized user from obtaining access.

To solve the false positive and false negative issue, the probabilistic engine must produce two sets of curves that do not overlap. This is equivalent to very low, <0.001%, false positive and false negative rates. Because the curves technically have tails that go forever, there will always be some false rates, but the numbers have to be exceedingly small to assure security. Figure 10-10 illustrates the desired, but typically impractical, separation of the curves. Another concern with biometrics is that if someone is able to steal the uniqueness factor that the machine scans—your fingerprint from a glass, for example—and is able to reproduce that factor in a substance that fools the scanner, that

Figure 10-9
False negative

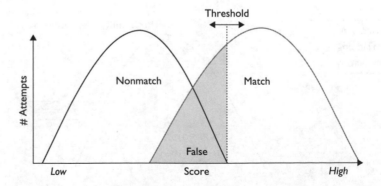

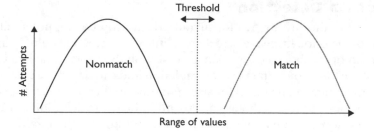

Figure 10-10
Desired situation

person now has your access privileges. This idea is compounded by the fact that it is impossible for you to change your fingerprint if it gets stolen. It is easy to replace a lost or stolen token and delete the missing one from the system, but it is far more difficult to replace a human hand. Another problem with biometrics is that parts of the human body can change. A human face can change, through scarring, weight loss or gain, or surgery. A fingerprint can be changed through damage to the fingers. Eye retinas can be affected by some types of diabetes or by pregnancy. All of these changes force the biometric system to allow a higher tolerance for variance in the biometric being read. This has led the way for high-security installations to move toward multiple-factor authentication.

Protected Distribution (Cabling)

Interception of network traffic should always be a concern to the security team. Securing the actual network wiring from physical tapping is not a topic most security people think of, but in high-security networks, this can be an important consideration. Just as switches and routers should be in locked rooms to prevent unauthorized access, network cabling requires physical protection as well. In places where the network traffic requires significant security measures, protecting the traffic by physically securing the cabling can be important.

Alarms

Alarms serve to alert operators to abnormal conditions. Physical security can involve numerous sensors, intrusion alarms, motion detectors, switches that alert to doors being opened, video and audio surveillance, and more. Each of these systems can gather useful information, but it is only truly useful if it is acted upon. When one of these systems has information that can be of use to operational personnel, an alarm is the easiest method of alerting personnel to the condition. Alarms are not simple; if one has too many alarm conditions, especially false alarms, then the operators will not react to the condition as desired. Tuning alarms so that they provide useful, accurate, and actionable information is important if you want them to be effective.

Motion Detection

When monitoring an area for unauthorized activity, one potentially useful tool is a motion detector. In areas where there is little or no expected traffic, a motion detector can alert an operator to activity in an area. Motion detectors come in a variety of types, but most are based on infrared (heat) radiation and can detect the changes of a warm body moving. They can be tuned for size, ignoring smaller movement such as small animals in outdoor settings. Although not useful in busy office buildings during normal daily use, motion detectors can be useful during off-hours, when traffic is minimal. Motion detectors can be used to trigger video systems so they do not record large amounts of "empty" activity. Video monitoring of the loading dock area in the back of the building can be triggered in this fashion, using the motion detector to turn on cameras whenever activity is occurring.

Control Types

Just as security controls play a role in information security, the proper application of controls can assist in the risk management associated with physical security. Controls can be of a variety of types, as described next.

 EXAM TIP The types of physical security controls are commonly tested on the exam—memorization is recommended.

- **Deterrent**   A deterrent control acts to influence the attacker by reducing the likelihood of success. An example would be laws and regulations that increase punishment.

- **Preventive**   A preventative control is one that prevents specific actions from occurring, such as a mantrap prevents tailgating. Preventative controls act before an event, preventing it from advancing.

- **Detective**   A detective control is one that facilitates the detection of a physical security breach. Detective controls act during an event, alerting operators to specific conditions. Alarms are common examples of detective controls.

- **Corrective**   Corrective controls are used post event in an effort to minimize the extent of damage. Backups are a prime example of a corrective control, as they can facilitate rapid resumption of operations.

- **Compensating**   A compensating control is one that is used to meet a requirement when the requirement cannot be directly met. Fire suppression systems do not stop fire damage, but if properly employed, they can mitigate or limit the level of damage from fire.

- **Technical**   A technical control is the use of some form of technology to address a physical security issue. Biometrics are technical controls.

- **Administrative**   An administrative control is a policy or procedure used to limit physical security risk. Instructions to guards act as administrative controls.

NIST provides a catalog of controls in its *NIST SP 800-53* document. The current revision, revision 4, lists over 600 controls grouped into 18 functional categories. The 18 functional categories are grouped under three major categories, Management, Technical, and Operational. Although the vast majority of these controls are associated with the electronic security of information, many of them extend into the physical world. Elements such as Awareness and Training, Access Control, Media Protection, and Physical and Environmental Protection are directly connected to physical security activities.

Chapter Review

In this chapter, you became acquainted with the principles of physical security. Environmental controls, fire suppression, EMI shielding, hot and cold aisles, environmental monitoring, and temperature and humidity controls were detailed with respect to how they protect systems. The chapter covered physical security controls designed to assist the enterprise in controlling access to the information systems network and its components. It also looked at controls used to ensure that the systems have both reliability and resilience, including environmental controls and fire suppression methods. The chapter also examined elements such as shielding to protect signals from inadvertent loss or interception by unauthorized parties.

The chapter closed with an examination of the types of controls, and how they are employed. These controls operate in the physical realm as opposed to the pure electronic realm where most security controls reside. These controls are useful in ensuring the system is protected from physical vectors that can interfere with desired operations.

Questions

To help you prepare further for the CompTIA Security+ exam, and to test your level of preparedness, answer the following questions and then check your answers against the correct answers at the end of the chapter.

1. The twist in Category 5 or 6 network cabling is designed to prevent _____.

    A. cable separation

    B. false negatives

    C. TCP retransmissions

    D. electromagnetic interference

2. What are the two primary types of CCTV cameras?

    A. Indoor, outdoor

    B. Pan-tilt-zoom, fixed

    C. Analog, IP

    D. Ethernet, Wi-Fi

3. Contactless cards are most often used where?

   A. To log in to your workstation

   B. Door access control systems

   C. Time clocks

   D. Emergency exits

4. Why can't smoke detectors tell the difference between cooking smoke and furnishings being on fire?

   A. They only detect heat.

   B. They measure air particulates, and all smoke contains particulates.

   C. They measure ions in the air, and any smoke inhibits the ions.

   D. None of the above is correct.

5. What is the primary benefit of hot and cold aisles?

   A. Higher server density in the data center

   B. Easier server installation

   C. No need for complicated rack systems

   D. Lower power consumption

6. Why is halon no longer used in fire suppression systems?

   A. Halon has poor fire suppression characteristics.

   B. They used argon, which is very expensive to isolate.

   C. Halon systems are easily triggered accidentally.

   D. EPA regulations have banned halon systems.

7. What are the advantages of non-water-based fire suppression?

   A. Lower cost

   B. Less damage to electrical systems

   C. No need for a fire department response

   D. All of the above

8. What is a false positive in terms of biometrics?

   A. The system does not allow an authorized user to gain access.

   B. The system does not positively encode the user's biometric, forcing a rescan.

   C. The system allows access to an unauthorized user.

   D. The system authenticates the user, but does not open the door strike.

9. What is the cause of false positives in biometric systems?

   A. Poorly designed sensors

   B. Conversion from an analog value to a digital encoding

   C. Too many users on the system

   D. The use of a non-globally unique biometric criteria

10. If you are trying to extinguish an electrical fire, what class of handheld fire extinguisher should you use?

   A. Class A

   B. Class B

   C. Class C

   D. Class E

For questions 11–13, use the following scenario: You are the IT director for a medium-sized grocery store chain. The company has outgrown the data center that was part of its primary distribution warehouse and is going to be implementing a brand-new data center in a newly leased building. The data center build-out has not yet been done, and the CEO has asked you to make recommendations on the proposal with a focus on security.

11. What fire suppression system(s) would you recommend? (Choose all that apply.)

   A. Standard water sprinklers

   B. Type ABC handheld extinguishers

   C. Halon flood system

   D. Type A handheld extinguishers

   E. Inergen-based system

   F. Type D handheld extinguishers

12. For the interior doors that provide access to the server room, what access control systems do you select?

   A. Biometrics

   B. Proximity access cards

   C. Both A and B

   D. Neither A nor B

13. For the exterior building doors, what access control systems do you select?

   A. Biometrics

   B. Proximity access cards

   C. Both A and B

   D. Neither A nor B

14. When electronic equipment is exposed to water, even if all the recommended cleanup procedures are followed, what can cause long-term damage?

    A. Voltage spikes due to wet capacitors

    B. Decreased magnetic potential of spinning hard drives

    C. Corrosion of the metal components

    D. Chemical etching

15. Complete the following table listing types of controls for three problems:

Problem	Preventative Control	Detective Control	_____ Control
Unauthorized entry into server room			Machines locked with passwords
Unauthorized persons entering workplace			Clean desk policy
	Keep server room clean of trash	Fire detector	

Answers

1. **D.** The twist in the cable is design to prevent electromagnetic interference (EMI) by causing the inductive forces to cancel themselves out.

2. **C.** Analog and IP are the two primary types, with analog being the traditional cameras and IP cameras being network based and usually run over Ethernet.

3. **B.** Contactless cards are most often used with proximity readers on door access control systems.

4. **C.** Smoke detectors measure ions in the air, and the smoke interferes with the ions, creating a measurable difference in air movement.

5. **A.** Hot and cold aisles better manage airflow in the data center, enabling higher server density.

6. **D.** Because halon systems have been linked to ozone depletion and halon gas poses a danger of being converted to toxic compounds, the EPA has banned halon systems.

7. **B.** Clean-agent fire suppression causes less damage to electrical systems and electronics than other fire suppression systems.

8. **C.** A false positive is when the system accepts an unauthorized user as an authorized one and allows access.

9. **B.** Biometrics are analog signals that must be encoded into digital values. Since the sensor may read the biometric value slightly differently every time, the encoded value must have some tolerance for imperfection.

10. **C.** Electrical fires are listed under the Type C of handheld fire extinguishers.

11. **B and E.** The best answers are Type ABC fire extinguishers and Inergen-based clean agent systems.

12. **C.** Highly secure areas such as server rooms are best protected by multifactor access control systems. Combining proximity cards with a biometric sensor pairs something you have with something you are for two factors of authentication. This also reduces the likelihood of false negatives and false positives.

13. **B.** While biometrics provide good security, the delays requiring each person entering to be biometrically scanned and verified would be too cumbersome. Therefore, contactless access cards can quickly authorize user access to the building without delay.

14. **C.** Water can cause corrosion of many of the components that make electronic devices, particularly copper electrical traces; this corrosion can cause equipment to malfunction in unexpected ways.

15.

Problem	Preventative Control	Detective Control	Corrective Control
Unauthorized entry into server room	Locked door	Door sensor/motion sensor	Machines locked with passwords
Unauthorized persons entering workplace	Guards and restricted entry	Visible name badges	Clean desk policy
Fire in server room	Keep server room clean of trash	Fire detector	Backups

Similar items may also be correct.

Security Controls

In this chapter, you will

- Determine the appropriate control to meet the goals of security
- Examine the controls used to ensure confidentiality
- Examine the controls used to ensure integrity
- Examine the controls used to ensure availability
- Examine the controls used to ensure safety

Security controls are the mechanisms employed to minimize exposure to risk and mitigate the effects of loss. Using the security attributes of confidentiality, integrity, and availability associated with data, it is incumbent upon the security team to determine the appropriate set of controls to achieve the security objectives. The elements confidentiality, integrity, and availability are commonly referred to as the CIA of security.

Confidentiality

Confidentiality typically comes to mind when the term *security* is brought up. Confidentiality is the ability to keep some piece of data a secret. In the digital world, encryption excels at providing confidentiality. Confidentiality is used on stored data and on transmitted data. In both cases, symmetric encryption is favored because of its speed and because some asymmetric algorithms can significantly increase the size of the object being encrypted. In the case of a stored item, symmetric methods are favored, both for speed and because there really isn't a key exchange problem. In the case of transmitted data, public key cryptography is typically used to exchange the secret key, and then symmetric cryptography is used to ensure the confidentiality of the data being sent.

Asymmetric cryptography does protect confidentiality, but its size and speed make it more efficient at protecting the confidentiality of small units for tasks such as electronic key exchange. In all cases, the strength of the algorithms and the length of the keys ensure the secrecy of the data in question.

Another method of protecting confidentiality is through the use of access controls. Access controls can restrict access to an object based on user IDs and access control lists (ACLs). This is a common method used in file systems because it provides relative protection that is efficient, although not as strong as encryption.

EXAM TIP Confidentiality can be achieved through encryption, access control lists, or data hiding. Encryption is the strongest form, access control scales well, and data hiding is the least secure.

A last method of providing confidentiality is through a process such as steganography, a form of data hiding. This is not the preferred method, as it has been known for a long time that security via obscurity is not a strong method of protection.

Integrity

Integrity is better known as *message integrity*, and it is a crucial component of message security. When a message is sent, both the sender and recipient need to know that the message was not altered in transmission. This is especially important for legal contracts—recipients need to know that the contracts have not been altered. Signers also need a way to validate that a contract they sign will not be altered in the future.

Integrity is provided with one-way hash functions and digital signatures. The hash functions compute the message digests, and this guarantees the integrity of the message by allowing easy testing to determine whether any part of the message has been changed. The message now has a computed function (the hash value) to tell the users to resend the message if it was intercepted and interfered with.

This hash value is combined with asymmetric cryptography by taking the message's hash value and encrypting it with the user's private key. This enables anyone with the user's public key to decrypt the hash and compare it to the locally computed hash, which not only ensures the integrity of the message, but also positively identifies the sender.

EXAM TIP Integrity can be verified through hashing. The employment of hash functions in operations such as digital signatures enables verification of integrity and non-repudiation.

Using hash values to verify integrity is commonly done behind the scenes. When a user needs to use an asymmetric key, they use a certificate that holds the key and supporting information. Using hash values on the certificate, the validity of the information can be verified. Using the signing keys on the certificate, the veracity of the key can be determined, acting as a form of non-repudiation.

Availability

Availability is the third leg of the CIA triad, and refers to the property of system access being available to authorized users when they are authorized to have access. For some systems, availability can be a significant operational concern. This has led to the development of fault-tolerant and redundant systems to ensure the continuous availability of critical systems. A key operational process to ensure availability of systems is the change configuration board. A properly functioning change configuration board can ensure that systems have maximum availability, even when they need to be taken down for patching. In a system of multiple identical servers, only a portion is changed at any given time, allowing the efficacy of the change to be fully tested in production before committing all machines. Provided that the changes are permitted only during slack user periods, there should be sufficient slack space to allow rolling changes while maintaining availability.

 EXAM TIP Availability can be achieved through fault-tolerant and redundant systems.

The use of standby systems can also improve availability in the event of disasters and the implementation of business continuity plans. Having a hot site as a standby system is the best solution, as warm and cold sites will add a period of downtime to continuous operations. In the case of extreme failover needs, as in no lost time or data, then an active-active architecture is needed. When the data centers are active-active and applications are also active-active, the result is continuous availability. An active-active system will process data on both the primary and backup systems, allowing instant failover, but with the drawback of needing bidirectional replication–capable software.

Data availability can also become an issue, especially when a significant amount of data is stored on individual machines and mobile devices. Daily data, viewed as critical by many workers, may not be backed up at the same frequency as enterprise data. If workers' daily work has value, then the data should also receive appropriate attention in the form of backup protections.

Safety

Safety and security are related in several ways. A secure system performs the tasks it is supposed to do and only those tasks, and these qualities are needed for safety. Safety systems come in a wide range and in various forms, but many are related to physical security issues.

Fencing

Fencing can be used for physical isolation and protection. Fencing can be used to separate security zones, provide safe areas, and maintain traffic separation. From simple chain-link fencing to high-security fencing, each can provide a level of protection. Chain-link fences can provide for simple crowd control, but offer little in terms of blocking a determined adversary. High-security fencing, such as palisade fencing, offers significant levels of anti-climb protection, and delay factors for intrusions.

Lighting

Lighting is essential for several reasons. It can provide illumination necessary for surveillance systems, such as CCTV systems. It can also provide needed guidance for people during evacuation drills. Appropriate levels of lighting in work areas is common, but it is equally important to provide adequate lighting in other areas such as egress venues and stairwells.

Locks

Locks provide a means of controlling access, acting as physical manifestations of an access control list. Because locks are physical devices that can be vulnerable to tampering, for high-security locks, measures need to be taken to prevent bypassing them. Many high-security lock manufacturers will patent and tightly control key blanks. This will make blanks unavailable to unauthorized persons and eliminate bump keys. Physical keyways can also be of more complex designs than ordinary key locks, making physical manipulation (lock picking) extremely difficult.

CCTV

Closed-circuit TV systems can provide surveillance and monitoring over large areas and allow monitoring from a central or remote location. These systems can provide the ability to coordinate many efforts in emergency conditions. CCTV can be combined with facial recognition technology with the potential to track individuals as they pass cameras connected to the system.

Escape Routes

Escape routes are methods of egress planned into buildings. Typically required by building codes, escape routes can be used to navigate egress to a safe place in the event of a hazardous condition. Egress may require transiting secured doors, and in the event of emergencies, a fail-safe condition can be employed to open doors for people evacuating.

Escape Plans

Escape plans can be devised to enable employees to safely evacuate buildings, structures, and complex systems such as industrial plants. Preparation for emergencies that includes the development, posting, and training of escape plans can result in saving lives if the plans are ever needed in a real emergency. Escape routes, plans, and drills can work together to achieve a prepared workforce for the task of emergency egress.

Drills

Drills are used to practice specific behaviors so that when an emergency occurs, people will know how to act without additional training or instruction. In the case of a situation where increased physical security measures are needed, doors and windows, with their locks, can be employed. A lockdown drill can engage numerous people to achieve this behavior.

Testing Controls

Controls are not foolproof. The proper employment of them is generally a complex event and one that requires extensive planning. Once they are deployed, security controls require periodic testing as to their effectiveness and coverage. Systems change over time, as do threats. Ensuring appropriate mitigation of risk through security controls requires regular reevaluation of their employment and efficacy. This is done through scheduled testing of controls in both singular and all-hazard environments.

Chapter Review

In this chapter, you became acquainted with the principal security control attributes of confidentiality, integrity, and availability. The chapter also covered usage of specific types of controls for safety purposes and emphasized the need for testing security control structures.

Questions

To help you prepare further for the CompTIA Security+ exam, and to test your level of preparedness, answer the following questions and then check your answers against the correct answers at the end of the chapter.

1. What is a key advantage of palisade steel fencing?

    A. It cannot be knocked over.

    B. Its gates are tightly integrated.

    C. It is easily constructed.

    D. It is nearly impossible to climb.

2. How do many types of high-security locks accomplish bump resistance?

    A. They use higher-strength pins.

    B. They use patented keyways and control blank distribution.

    C. They have more tightly controlled mechanical tolerances.

    D. They don't; no lock can effectively resist bumping techniques.

3. What is the primary benefit of steganography over encryption?

    A. Can hold more data securely

    B. Harder to brute force the key

    C. Difficulty in detecting it

    D. Ease of implementation

4. What redundancy scheme could provide instantaneous failover?

    A. Hot standby

    B. Cold standby

    C. Active-active

    D. Warm-standby

5. A message digest provides integrity by:

   A. Providing encryption that cannot be unlocked

   B. Providing a value that can be independently verified to show if the message changed

   C. Providing message confidentiality so other users cannot see the message

   D. Applying a signature to the message

6. A lockdown drill dictates:

   A. All occupants should follow the evacuation route to the designated safe area.

   B. All occupants are to line up against an interior wall and cover their heads.

   C. All occupants are to move silently to their designated station.

   D. All occupants are to stay inside and lock all doors and windows.

7. What does *fail-safe* mean when it is used to describe electronic access control systems?

   A. All door strikes lock securely to ensure the people are safely inside.

   B. All door strikes open so people may safely exit.

   C. All door strikes assume their default locked/unlocked status.

   D. None of the above.

8. Advances in technology allow a CCTV system to be paired with _____ for tracking individuals.

   A. facial recognition

   B. GPS sensors

   C. cellular triangulation

   D. computerized body movement analysis

9. Which is an example of fault tolerance in a computer system?

   A. Dual power supplies

   B. RAID 5 configured disks

   C. Multiple network interface controllers

   D. All of the above

10. A building escape route is usually required by:

    A. The building's architecture

    B. Building owners

    C. Local building codes

    D. Tenants

For questions 11–15, assume the following scenario: After a break-in at your company, the board decides to transition your role from Director of Information Security to Chief Security Officer. They have asked you to assume all physical security responsibilities and bolster security so that another incident does not happen.

11. To improve physical security against intrusions, what security controls should you immediately review for effectiveness? (Choose all that apply.)

    A. Fencing

    B. Control testing

    C. Non-repudiation

    D. Lighting

    E. Escape plans

    F. Certificates

12. What software controls should you review to make sure no data was compromised during the break-in? (Choose all that apply.)

    A. Access controls

    B. CCTV

    C. Encryption

    D. Hashing

    E. Locks

    F. Fault tolerance

13. Your newly instated control testing policy has identified a problem with escape routes, as shown by confused personnel during a drill. What is the best remediation?

    A. Clearer signage and a modified escape plan

    B. Better fencing

    C. Office redesign to funnel people only to the larger stairs at the south end

    D. Better emergency lighting

14. Regular evacuation drills have shown that employees are taking too much time getting out of the building because they are bringing their laptops with them. When questioned, they state that critical data only exists on their machines. What is the security control to correct the issue?

    A. More drills

    B. Better escape plans

    C. More data redundancy

    D. Faster escape routes

15. The company has used the same locks for several years. What are the justifications you would use to request a card-based access control system?

    A. It provides time-based access controls.

    B. It makes it easier to remove access to parties that are no longer authorized.

    C. It is fail-safe in an emergency situation, improving evacuation.

    D. All of the above.

Answers

1. **D.** A steel palisade fence consisting of multiple vertical bars offers excellent climb resistance and is often referred to as an anti-climb fence.

2. **B.** Many high-security lock manufacturers will patent and tightly control keyways. This will make blanks unavailable to unauthorized persons, and if blanks are found, they will only work on locks in a small physical area.

3. **C.** Steganography has a key advantage of being difficult to detect, as its encoding can resemble visual noise present in images or video frames.

4. **C.** An active-active system processes data on both the primary and backup systems, which allows instant failover but has the drawback of needing bidirectional replication–capable software.

5. **B.** A message digest produced by a hashing function provides a value that can be independently computed to verify that the message has not been changed.

6. **D.** A lockdown drill is a response to a criminal threat, so the proper action is to stay inside and lock all doors and windows tightly to resist access by the potential threat.

7. **B.** *Fail-safe* means the doors will unlock to safely allow users to exit the building in the case of a fire or other emergency.

8. **A.** CCTV can be combined with facial recognition technology with the potential to track individuals as they pass cameras connected to the system.

9. **D.** All are examples of fault-tolerant designs: one for a power cord or supply failing, one for the loss of a single hard drive, and one for the loss of network connectivity.

10. **C.** Local building codes will specify the need for building emergency escape routes, almost always with one at either side of the building and clearly marked with lighted signs.

11. **A, B,** and **D.** The best answers are fencing, control testing, and lighting. Fencing and lighting are self-explanatory; regularly testing security controls is vital to ensuring their effectiveness.

12. **A, C, and D.** Access controls, encryption, and hashing are the best answers. Access control permissions should be checked for any change and to determine if they are configured too loosely. Encryption is a primary protection for data confidentiality, and you must ensure that access to the keys was not compromised. Finally, you must check hashes for message integrity to make sure files have not been altered to change the existing data or that critical system files have not been altered to include malware.

13. **A.** Clearer signage allows employees at a glance to know the escape path from anywhere in the building. A modified escape plan to better control traffic flows and to make sure everyone is familiar with their escape route and plan will better avoid confusion.

14. **C.** While A, B, and D are all good things to do, this issue is best resolved through data redundancy. Critical data should always be stored in multiple, redundant locations.

15. **D.** All are correct answers.

PART III

Threats and Vulnerabilities

Attacks and Malware

In this chapter, you will

- Examine the types of malware
- Learn about various types of computer and network attacks, including denial-of-service, spoofing, hijacking, and password guessing
- Understand the different types of malicious software that exist, including viruses, worms, Trojan horses, logic bombs, and time bombs
- Understand the various types of attacks

Attacks can be made against virtually any layer or level of software, from network protocols to applications. When an attacker finds a vulnerability in a system, he exploits the weakness to attack the system. The effect of an attack depends on the attacker's intent and can result in a wide range of effects, from minor to severe. An attack on a system might not be visible on that system because the attack is actually occurring on a different system, and the data the attacker will manipulate on the second system is obtained by attacking the first system.

Malware

Malware refers to software that has been designed for some nefarious purpose. Such software can be designed to cause damage to a system, such as by deleting all files, or it can be designed to create a backdoor in the system to grant access to unauthorized individuals. Generally, the installation of malware is done so that it is not obvious to the authorized users. Several different types of malicious software can be used, such as viruses, Trojan horses, logic bombs, spyware, and worms, and they differ in the ways they are installed and their purposes.

Adware

The business of software distribution requires a form of revenue stream to support the cost of development and distribution. One form of revenue stream is advertising. Software that is supported by advertising is called *adware*. Adware comes in many different forms. With legitimate adware, the user is aware of the advertising and agrees to the arrangement in return for free use of the software. This type of adware often offers an alternative, ad-free version for a fee. Adware can also refer to a form of malware, which is characterized by software that presents unwanted ads. These ads are sometimes an irritant, and at other times represent an actual security threat. Frequently, these ads are in the form of pop-up browser windows, and in some cases, they cascade upon any user action.

Virus

The best-known type of malicious code is the virus. Much has been written about viruses because several high-profile security events have involved them. A *virus* is a piece of malicious code that replicates by attaching itself to another piece of executable code. When the other executable code is run, the virus also executes and has the opportunity to infect other files and perform any other nefarious actions it was designed to do. The specific way that a virus infects other files, and the type of files it infects, depends on the type of virus. The first viruses created were of two types—boot sector viruses and program viruses.

Worms

It was once easy to distinguish between a worm and a virus. Recently, with the introduction of new breeds of sophisticated malicious code, the distinction has blurred. *Worms* are pieces of code that attempt to penetrate networks and computer systems. Once a penetration occurs, the worm will create a new copy of itself on the penetrated system. Reproduction of a worm thus does not rely on the attachment of the virus to another piece of code or to a file, which is the definition of a virus.

Viruses were generally thought of as a system-based problem, and worms were network-based. If the malicious code is sent throughout a network, it may subsequently be called a worm. The important distinction, however, is whether the code has to attach itself to something else (a virus) or if it can "survive" on its own (a worm).

Some recent examples of worms that have had high profiles include the Sobig worm of 2003, the SQL Slammer worm of 2003, the 2001 attacks of Code Red and Nimba, and the 2005 Zotob worm that took down CNN Live. Nimba was particularly impressive in that it used five different methods to spread: via e-mail, via open network shares, from browsing infected websites, using the directory traversal vulnerability of Microsoft IIS 4.0/5.0, and most impressively through the use of backdoors left by Code Red II and sadmind worms.

 EXAM TIP Worms act like a virus but also have the ability to travel without human action.

Spyware

Spyware is software that "spies" on users, recording and reporting on their activities. Typically installed without user knowledge, spyware can perform a wide range of activities. It can record keystrokes (commonly called *keylogging*) when the user logs onto specific websites. It can monitor how a user applies a specific piece of software, such as to monitor attempts to cheat at games. Many uses of spyware seem innocuous at first, but the unauthorized monitoring of a system can be abused very easily. In other cases, the spyware is specifically designed to steal information. Many states have passed legislation banning the unapproved installation of software, but spyware can circumvent this issue through complex and confusing end-user license agreements.

Trojan

A Trojan horse, or simply *Trojan*, is a piece of software that appears to do one thing (and may, in fact, actually do that thing) but hides some other functionality. The analogy to the famous story of antiquity is very accurate. In the original case, the object appeared to be a large wooden horse, and in fact it was. At the same time, it hid something much more sinister and dangerous to the occupants of the city of Troy. As long as the horse was left outside the city walls, it could cause no damage to the inhabitants. It had to be taken in by the inhabitants, and it was inside that the hidden purpose was activated. A computer Trojan works in much the same way. Unlike a virus, which reproduces by attaching itself to other files or programs, a Trojan is a stand-alone program that must be copied and installed by the user—it must be "brought inside" the system by an authorized user. The challenge for the attacker is enticing the user to copy and run the program. This generally means that the program must be disguised as something that the user would want to run—a special utility or game, for example. Once it has been copied and is inside the system, the Trojan will perform its hidden purpose with the user often still unaware of its true nature.

A good example of a Trojan is Back Orifice (BO), originally created in 1999 and now offered in several versions. BO can be attached to a number of types of programs. Once it is attached, and once an infected file is run, BO will create a way for unauthorized individuals to take over the system remotely, as if they were sitting at the console. BO is designed to work with Windows-based systems. Many Trojans communicate to the outside through a port that the Trojan opens, and this is one of the ways Trojans can be detected.

 EXAM TIP Ensure you understand the differences between viruses, worms, Trojans, and various other types of threats for the exam.

Rootkits

Rootkits are a form of malware that is specifically designed to modify the operation of the operating system in some fashion to facilitate nonstandard functionality. The history of rootkits goes back to the beginning of the UNIX operating system, where rootkits were sets of modified administrative tools. Originally designed to allow a program to take greater control over operating system function when it fails or becomes unresponsive, the technique has evolved and is used in a variety of ways. One high-profile case occurred at Sony BMG Corporation, when rootkit technology was used to provide copy protection technology on some of the company's CDs. Two major issues led to this being a complete debacle for Sony: first, the software modified systems without the users' approval; and second, the software opened a security hole on Windows-based systems, creating an exploitable vulnerability at the rootkit level. This led the Sony case to be labeled as malware, which is the most common use of rootkits.

A rootkit can do many things—in fact, it can do virtually anything that the operating system does. Rootkits modify the operating system kernel and supporting functions, changing the nature of the system's operation. Rootkits are designed to avoid, either by subversion or evasion, the security functions of the operating system to avoid detection. Rootkits act as a form of malware that can change thread priorities to boost an application's performance, perform keylogging, act as a sniffer, hide other files from other applications, or create backdoors in the authentication system. The use of rootkit functionality to hide other processes and files enables an attacker to use a portion of a computer without the user or other applications knowing what is happening. This hides exploit code from antivirus and anti-spyware programs, acting as a cloak of invisibility.

Rootkits can load before the operating system loads, acting as a virtualization layer, as in SubVirt and Blue Pill. Rootkits can exist in firmware, and these have been demonstrated in both video cards and expansion cards. Rootkits can exist as loadable library modules, effectively changing portions of the operating system outside the kernel. Further information on specific rootkits in the wild can be found at www .antirootkit.com.

 EXAM TIP   Five types of rootkits exist: firmware, virtual, kernel, library, and application level.

Once a rootkit is detected, it needs to be removed and cleaned up. Because of rootkits' invasive nature, and the fact that many aspects of rootkits are not easily detectable, most system administrators don't even attempt to clean up or remove a rootkit. It is far easier to use a previously captured clean system image and reimage the machine than to attempt to determine the depth and breadth of the damage and attempt to fix individual files.

Backdoors

Backdoors were originally (and sometimes still are) nothing more than methods used by software developers to ensure that they could gain access to an application even if something were to happen in the future to prevent normal access methods. An example would be a hard-coded password that could be used to gain access to the program in the event that administrators forgot their own system password. The obvious problem with this sort of backdoor (also sometimes referred to as a *trapdoor*) is that, since it is hard-coded, it cannot be removed. Should an attacker learn of the backdoor, all systems running that software would be vulnerable to attack.

The term *backdoor* is also, and more commonly, used to refer to programs that attackers install after gaining unauthorized access to a system to ensure that they can continue to have unrestricted access to the system, even if their initial access method is discovered and blocked. Backdoors can also be installed by authorized individuals inadvertently, should they run software that contains a Trojan horse (introduced earlier). Common backdoors include NetBus and Back Orifice. Both of these, if running on your system, can allow an attacker remote access to your system—access that allows them to perform any function on your system. A variation on the backdoor is the rootkit, discussed in the previous section, which is established not to gain root access, but rather to ensure continued root access.

Logic Bomb

Logic bombs, unlike viruses and Trojans, are a type of malicious software that is deliberately installed, generally by an authorized user. A *logic bomb* is a piece of code that sits dormant for a period of time until some event or date invokes its malicious payload. An example of a logic bomb might be a program that is set to load and run automatically, and that periodically checks an organization's payroll or personnel database for a specific employee. If the employee is not found, the malicious payload executes, deleting vital corporate files.

If the event is a specific date or time, the program will often be referred to as a *time bomb*. In one famous example of a time bomb, a disgruntled employee left a time bomb in place just prior to being fired from his job. Two weeks later, thousands of client records were deleted. Police were eventually able to track the malicious code to the disgruntled ex-employee, who was prosecuted for his actions. He had hoped that the two weeks that had passed since his dismissal would have caused investigators to assume he could not have been the individual who had caused the deletion of the records.

Logic bombs are difficult to detect because they are often installed by authorized users and, in particular, have been installed by administrators who are also often responsible for security. This demonstrates the need for a separation of duties and a periodic review of all programs and services that are running on a system. It also illustrates the need to maintain an active backup program so that if your organization loses critical files to this sort of malicious code, it loses only transactions that occurred since the most recent backup, resulting in no permanent loss of data.

Botnets

A botnet is a term that combines the terms bot and network into a functioning entity. A bot is a functioning piece of software that performs some task, under the control of another program. A series of bots is controlled across the network in a group, and the entire assembly is called a botnet. Some botnets are legal and perform desired actions in a distributed fashion. Illegal botnets work in the same fashion, with bots distributed and controlled from a central set of servers. Bots can do a wide array of things, from spam to fraud to spyware and more.

Botnets continue to advance malware threats. Some of the latest botnets are designed to mine bitcoins, using distributed processing power for gain. Some of the more famous botnets include Zeus, a botnet that performs keystroke logging and is used primarily for the purpose of stealing banking information. Zeus has been linked to the delivery of cryptlocker ransomware. Another famous botnet is conficker, which has infected millions of machines worldwide. The conficker botnet is one of the most studied pieces of malware, with a joint industry–government working group convened to battle it.

Ransomware

Ransomware is a form of malware that performs some action and extracts ransom from a user. A current ransomware threat, appearing in 2013, is cryptolocker. Cryptolocker is a Trojan horse that will encrypt certain files using RSA public key encryption. When the user attempts to get the files, they are provided with a message instructing them how to purchase the decryption key. Because the system is using 2048-bit RSA encryption, brute-force decryption is out of the realm of recovery options. The system is highly automated, and users have a short time window to get the private key. Failure to get the key will result in the loss of the data.

Polymorphic Malware

The detection of malware by anti-malware programs is primarily done through the use of a signature. Files are scanned for sections of code in the executable that act as markers, unique patterns of code that enable detection. Just as the human body creates antigens that match marker proteins, anti-malware programs detect malware through unique markers present in the code of the malware.

Malware writers are aware of this functionality and have adapted methods to defeat it. One of the primary means of avoiding detection by sensors is the use of *polymorphic code*, which is code that changes on a regular basis. These changes or mutations are designed not to affect the functionality of the code, but rather to mask any signature from detection. Polymorphic programs can change their coding after each use, making each replicant different from a detection point of view.

Armored Virus

When a new form of malware/virus is discovered, anti-virus companies and security researchers will decompile the program in an attempt to reverse engineer its functionality. Much can be determined from reverse engineering, such as where the malware came from, how it works, how it communicates, how it spreads, and so forth. Armoring malware can make the process of determining this information much more difficult, if not impossible. Some malware, such as Zeus, comes encrypted in ways to prevent criminals from stealing the intellectual property of the very malware that they use.

Attack Methods

Although hackers and viruses receive the most attention in the news, they are not the only methods used to attack computer systems and networks. This section addresses many different ways computers and networks are attacked on a daily basis. Each type of attack threatens at least one of the three security requirements: confidentiality, integrity, and availability (the CIA of security).

From a high-level standpoint, attacks on computer systems and networks can be grouped into two broad categories: attacks on specific software (such as an application or the operating system) and attacks on a specific protocol or service. Attacks on a specific application or operating system are generally possible because of an oversight in the code (and possibly in the testing of that code) or because of a flaw, or bug, in the code (again indicating a lack of thorough testing). Attacks on specific protocols or services are attempts either to take advantage of a specific feature of the protocol or service or to use the protocol or service in a manner for which it was not intended. This section discusses various forms of attacks of which security professionals need to be aware.

Man-in-the-Middle

A *man-in-the-middle attack*, as the name implies, generally occurs when an attacker is able to place himself in the middle of two other hosts that are communicating. Ideally (from the attacker's perspective), this is done by ensuring that all communication going to or from the target host is routed through the attacker's host (which can be accomplished if the attacker can compromise the router for the target host). The attacker can then observe all traffic before relaying it, and can actually modify or block traffic. To the target host, it appears that communication is occurring normally, since all expected replies are received. Figure 12-1 illustrates this type of attack.

There are numerous methods of instantiating a man-in-the-middle attack. One of the common methods is via *session hijacking*, which can occur when information such as a cookie is stolen, allowing the attacker to impersonate the legitimate session. This attack can be a result of a cross-site scripting attack, which tricks a user into executing code resulting in cookie theft. The amount of information that can be obtained in a man-in-the-middle attack will be limited if the communication is encrypted. Even in this case, however, sensitive information can still be obtained, since knowing what communication is being conducted, and between which individuals may in fact provide information that is valuable in certain circumstances.

Man-in-the-Middle Attacks on Encrypted Traffic

The term "man-in-the-middle attack" is sometimes used to refer to a more specific type of attack—one in which the encrypted traffic issue is addressed. Public-key encryption, discussed in detail in Chapter 23, requires the use of two keys: your public key, which

Figure 12-1
A man-in-the-middle attack

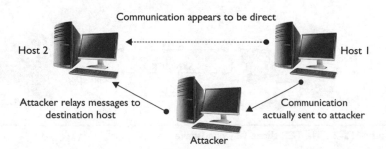

Communication appears to be direct

Host 2   Host 1

Attacker relays messages to destination host

Communication actually sent to attacker

Attacker

anybody can use to encrypt or "lock" your message, and your private key, which only you know and which is used to "unlock" or decrypt a message locked with your public key.

If you wanted to communicate securely with your friend Bob, you might ask him for his public key so you could encrypt your messages to him. You, in turn, would supply Bob with your public key. An attacker can conduct a man-in-the-middle attack by intercepting your request for Bob's public key and the sending of your public key to him. The attacker would replace your public key with her public key, and she would send this on to Bob. The attacker's public key would also be sent to you by the attacker instead of Bob's public key. Now when either you or Bob encrypt a message, it will be encrypted using the attacker's public key. The attacker can now intercept it, decrypt it, and then send it on by re-encrypting it with the appropriate key for either you or Bob. Each of you thinks you are transmitting messages securely, but in reality, your communication has been compromised. Well-designed cryptographic products use techniques such as mutual authentication to avoid this problem.

Denial-of-Service

Denial-of-service (DoS) attacks can exploit a known vulnerability in a specific application or operating system, or they can attack features (or weaknesses) in specific protocols or services. In a DoS attack, the attacker attempts to deny authorized users access either to specific information or to the computer system or network itself. This can be accomplished by crashing the system—taking it offline—or by sending so many requests that the machine is overwhelmed.

The purpose of a DoS attack can be simply to prevent access to the target system, or the attack can be used in conjunction with other actions to gain unauthorized access to a computer or network. For example, a *SYN flooding* attack can be used to prevent service to a system temporarily in order to take advantage of a trusted relationship that exists between that system and another.

SYN flooding is an example of a DoS attack that takes advantage of the way TCP/IP networks were designed to function, and it can be used to illustrate the basic principles of any DoS attack. SYN flooding uses the TCP three-way handshake that establishes a connection between two systems. Under normal circumstances, the first system sends a SYN packet to the system with which it wants to communicate. The second system responds with a SYN/ACK if it is able to accept the request. When the initial system receives the SYN/ACK from the second system, it responds with an ACK packet, and communication can then proceed. This process is shown in Figure 12-2.

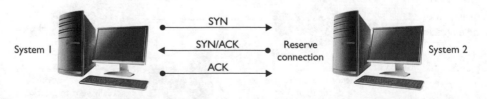

Figure 12-2 The TCP three-way handshake

In a SYN flooding attack, the attacker sends fake communication requests to the targeted system. Each of these requests will be answered by the target system, which then waits for the third part of the handshake. Since the requests are fake (a nonexistent IP address is used in the requests, so the target system is responding to a system that doesn't exist), the target will wait for responses that never come, as shown in Figure 12-3. The target system will drop these connections after a specific time-out period, but if the attacker sends requests faster than the time-out period eliminates them, the system will quickly be filled with requests. The number of connections a system can support is finite, so when more requests come in than can be processed, the system will soon be reserving all its connections for fake requests. At this point, any further requests are simply dropped (ignored), and legitimate users who want to connect to the target system will not be able to do so because use of the system has been denied to them.

Another simple DoS attack is the infamous ping of death (POD), and it illustrates the other type of attack—one targeted at a specific application or operating system, as opposed to SYN flooding, which targets a protocol. In the POD attack, the attacker sends an Internet Control Message Protocol (ICMP) ping packet equal to, or exceeding, 64KB (which is to say, greater than $64 \times 1024 = 65,536$ bytes). This type of packet should not occur naturally (there is no reason for a ping packet to be larger than 64KB). Certain systems are not able to handle this size of packet, and the system will hang or crash.

Distributed Denial-of-Service

DoS attacks are conducted using a single attacking system. A DoS attack employing multiple attacking systems is known as a distributed denial-of-service (DDoS) attack. The goal of a DDoS attack is also to deny the use of or access to a specific service or system. DDoS attacks were made famous in 2000 with the highly publicized attacks on eBay, CNN, Amazon, and Yahoo!.

In a DDoS attack, service is denied by overwhelming the target with traffic from many different systems. A network of attack agents (sometimes called *zombies*) is created by the attacker, and upon receiving the attack command from the attacker, the attack agents commence sending a specific type of traffic against the target. If the attack

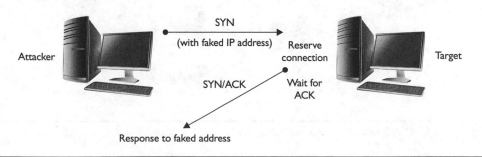

Figure 12-3 A SYN flooding DoS attack

network is large enough, even ordinary web traffic can quickly overwhelm the largest of sites, such as the 400-Gbps CloudFlare attack in early 2014.

Creating a DDoS network is no simple task. The attack agents are not willing agents—they are systems that have been compromised and on which the DDoS attack software has been installed. To compromise these agents, the attacker has to have gained unauthorized access to the system or tricked authorized users to run a program that installed the attack software. The creation of the attack network may in fact be a multistep process in which the attacker first compromises a few systems that are then used as *handlers* or *masters*, which in turn compromise other systems. Once the network has been created, the agents wait for an attack message that will include data on the specific target before launching the attack. One important aspect of a DDoS attack is that with just a few messages to the agents, the attacker can have a flood of messages sent against the targeted system. Figure 12-4 illustrates a DDoS network with agents and handlers.

How can you stop or mitigate the effects of a DoS or DDoS attack? One important precaution is to ensure that you have applied the latest patches and upgrades to your systems and the applications running on them. Once a specific vulnerability is discovered, it does not take long before multiple exploits are written to take advantage of it. Generally, you will have a small window of opportunity in which to patch your system between the time the vulnerability is discovered and the time exploits become widely available. A vulnerability can also be discovered by hackers, and exploits provide the first clues that a system has been compromised. Attackers can also reverse engineer patches to learn what vulnerabilities have been patched, allowing them to attack unpatched systems.

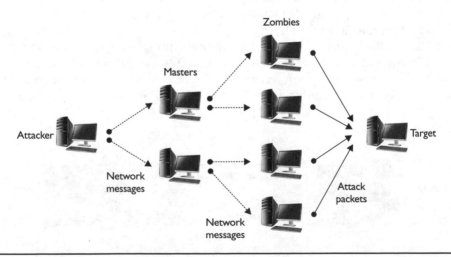

Figure 12-4   DDoS attacks

Another approach involves changing the time-out option for TCP connections so that attacks such as the SYN flooding attack are more difficult to perform because unused connections are dropped more quickly.

For DDoS attacks, much has been written about distributing your own workload across several systems so that any attack against your system would have to target several hosts to be completely successful. While this is true, if large enough DDoS networks are created (with tens of thousands of zombies, for example), any network, no matter how much the load is distributed, can be successfully attacked. Such an approach also involves additional costs to your organization to establish this distributed environment. Addressing the problem in this manner is actually an attempt to mitigate the effect of the attack, rather than preventing or stopping an attack.

To prevent a DDoS attack, you must either be able to intercept or block the attack messages or keep the DDoS network from being established in the first place. Tools have been developed that will scan your systems, searching for sleeping zombies waiting for an attack signal. Many of the current antivirus/spyware security suite tools will detect known zombie-type infections. The problem with this type of prevention approach, however, is that it is not something you can do to prevent an attack on your network—it is something you can do to keep your network from being used to attack other networks or systems. You have to rely on the community of network administrators to test their own systems to prevent attacks on yours.

A final option you should consider that will address several forms of DoS and DDoS attacks is to block ICMP packets at your border, since many attacks rely on ICMP. Carefully consider this approach before implementing it, however, because it will also prevent the use of some possibly useful troubleshooting tools.

Replay

A *replay attack* occurs when the attacker captures a portion of a communication between two parties and retransmits it at a later time. For example, an attacker might replay a series of commands and codes used in a financial transaction to cause the transaction to be conducted multiple times. Generally, replay attacks are associated with attempts to circumvent authentication mechanisms, such as the capturing and reuse of a certificate or ticket.

The best way to prevent replay attacks is with encryption, cryptographic authentication, and time stamps. If a portion of the certificate or ticket includes a date/time stamp or an expiration date/time, and this portion is also encrypted as part of the ticket or certificate, replaying it at a later time will prove useless, since it will be rejected as having expired.

 EXAM TIP The best method for defending against replay attacks is through the use of encryption and short time frames for legal transactions. Encryption can protect the contents from being understood, and a short time frame for a transaction prevents subsequent use.

PART III

Spoofing

Spoofing is nothing more than making data look like it has come from a different source. This is possible in TCP/IP because of the friendly assumptions behind the protocols. When the protocols were developed, it was assumed that individuals who had access to the network layer would be privileged users who could be trusted.

When a packet is sent from one system to another, it includes not only the destination IP address and port, but the source IP address as well. You are supposed to fill in the source with your own address, but nothing stops you from filling in another system's address. This is one of the several forms of spoofing.

Spoofing E-Mail

In e-mail spoofing, a message is sent with a From address that differs from that of the sending system. This can be easily accomplished in several different ways using several programs. To demonstrate how simple it is to spoof an e-mail address, you can Telnet to port 25 (the port associated with e-mail) on a mail server. From there, you can fill in any address for the From and To sections of the message, whether or not the addresses are yours and whether they actually exist or not.

You can use several methods to determine whether an e-mail message was probably not sent by the source it claims to have been sent from, but most users do not question their e-mail and will accept where it appears to have originated. A variation on e-mail spoofing, though it is not technically spoofing, is for the attacker to acquire a URL similar to the URL they want to spoof so that e-mail sent from their system appears to have come from the official site—until you read the address carefully. For example, if attackers want to spoof XYZ Corporation, which owns XYZ.com, the attackers might gain access to the URL XYZ.Corp.com. An individual receiving a message from the spoofed corporation site would not normally suspect it to be a spoof but would take it to be official. This same method can be, and has been, used to spoof websites. The most famous example of this is probably www.whitehouse.com. The www.whitehouse.gov site is the official site for the White House. The www.whitehouse.com URL takes you to a pornographic site. In this case, nobody is likely to take the pornographic site to be the official government site, and it was not intended to be taken that way. If, however, the attackers made their spoofed site appear similar to the official one, they could easily convince many potential viewers that they were at the official site.

IP Address Spoofing

IP is designed to work so that the originators of any IP packet include their own IP address in the From portion of the packet. While this is the intent, nothing prevents a system from inserting a different address in the From portion of the packet. This is known as *IP address spoofing*. An IP address can be spoofed for several reasons.

Smurf Attack

In a specific DoS attack known as a *Smurf* attack, the attacker sends a spoofed packet to the broadcast address for a network, which distributes the packet to all systems on that network. In the Smurf attack, the packet sent by the attacker to the broadcast address is an echo request with the From address forged so that it appears that another system (the target system) has made the echo request. The normal response of a system to an echo request is an echo reply, and it is used in the ping utility to let a user know whether a remote system is reachable and is responding. In the Smurf attack, the request is sent to all systems on the network, so all will respond with an echo reply to the target system, as shown in Figure 12-5. The attacker has sent one packet and has been able to generate as many as 254 responses aimed at the target. Should the attacker send several of these spoofed requests, or send them to several different networks, the target can quickly become overwhelmed with the volume of echo replies it receives.

EXAM TIP A Smurf attack allows an attacker to use a network structure to send large volumes of packets to a victim. By sending ICMP requests to a broadcast IP address with the victim as the source address, the multitudes of replies will flood the victim system.

Spoofing and Trusted Relationships

Spoofing can also take advantage of a *trusted relationship* between two systems. If two systems are configured to accept the authentication accomplished by each other, an individual logged on to one system might not be forced to go through an authentication process again to access the other system. An attacker can take advantage of this arrangement by sending a packet to one system that appears to have come from a trusted system. Since the trusted relationship is in place, the targeted system may perform the requested task without authentication.

Since a reply will often be sent once a packet is received, the system that is being impersonated could interfere with the attack, since it would receive an acknowledgement

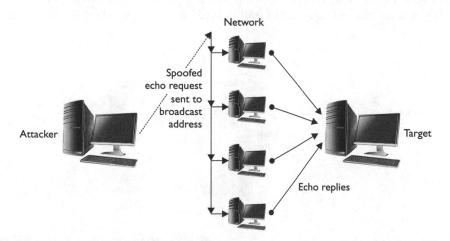

Figure 12-5 Spoofing used in a Smurf DoS attack

for a request it never made. The attacker will often initially launch a DoS attack (such as a SYN flooding attack) to temporarily take out the spoofed system for the period of time that the attacker is exploiting the trusted relationship. Once the attack is completed, the DoS attack on the spoofed system would be terminated and the administrators, apart from having a temporarily nonresponsive system, possibly may never notice that the attack occurred. Figure 12-6 illustrates a spoofing attack that includes a SYN flooding attack.

Because of this type of attack, administrators are encouraged to strictly limit any trusted relationships between hosts. Firewalls should also be configured to discard any packets from outside of the firewall that have From addresses indicating they originated from inside the network (a situation that should not occur normally and that indicates spoofing is being attempted).

Spoofing and Sequence Numbers

How complicated the spoofing is depends heavily on several factors, including whether the traffic is encrypted and where the attacker is located relative to the target. Spoofing attacks from inside a network, for example, are much easier to perform than attacks from outside of the network, because the inside attacker can observe the traffic to and from the target and can do a better job of formulating the necessary packets.

Formulating the packets is more complicated for external attackers because a sequence number is associated with TCP packets. A sequence number is a 32-bit number established by the host that is incremented for each packet sent. Packets are not guaranteed to be received in order, and the sequence number can be used to help reorder packets as they are received and to refer to packets that may have been lost in transmission.

In the TCP three-way handshake, two sets of sequence numbers are created, as shown in Figure 12-7. The first system chooses a sequence number to send with the original SYN packet. The system receiving this SYN packet acknowledges with a SYN/ACK. It sends an acknowledgement number back, which is based on the first sequence

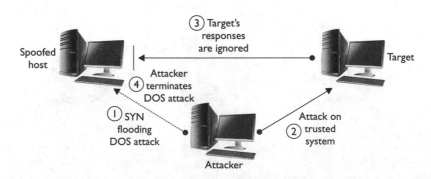

Figure 12-6 Spoofing to take advantage of a trusted relationship

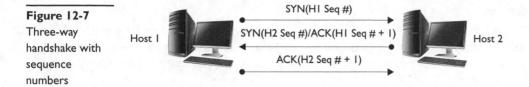

Figure 12-7
Three-way
handshake with
sequence
numbers

number plus one (that is, it increments the sequence number sent to it by one). It then also creates its own sequence number and sends that along with it. The original system receives the SYN/ACK with the new sequence number. It increments the sequence number by one and uses it as the acknowledgement number in the ACK packet with which it responds.

The difference in the difficulty of attempting a spoofing attack from inside a network and from outside involves determining the sequence number. If the attacker is inside of the network and can observe the traffic with which the target host responds, the attacker can easily see the sequence number the system creates and can respond with the correct sequence number. If the attacker is external to the network and the sequence number the target system generates is not observed, it is next to impossible for the attacker to provide the final ACK with the correct sequence number. So the attacker has to guess what the sequence number might be.

Sequence numbers are somewhat predictable. Sequence numbers for each session are not started from the same number, so that different packets from different concurrent connections will not have the same sequence numbers. Instead, the sequence number for each new connection is incremented by some large number to keep the numbers from being the same. The sequence number may also be incremented by some large number every second (or some other time period). An external attacker has to determine what values are used for these increments. The attacker can do this by attempting connections at various time intervals to observe how the sequence numbers are incremented. Once the pattern is determined, the attacker can attempt a legitimate connection to determine the current value, and then immediately attempt the spoofed connection. The spoofed connection sequence number should be the legitimate connection incremented by the determined value or values.

Sequence numbers are also important in session hijacking, which is discussed in the "TCP/IP Hijacking" section of this chapter.

Spam

Though not generally considered a social engineering issue, nor a security issue for that matter, spam can, however, be a security concern. *Spam*, as just about everybody knows, is bulk unsolicited e-mail. It can be legitimate in the sense that it has been sent by a company advertising a product or service, but it can also be malicious and could include an attachment that contains malicious software designed to harm your system, or a link to a malicious website that may attempt to obtain personal information from you.

Spim

Though not as well known, a variation on spam is *spim*, which is basically spam delivered via an instant messaging application such as Yahoo! Messenger or AOL Instant Messenger (AIM). The purpose of hostile spim is the same as that of spam—the delivery of malicious content or links.

Phishing

Phishing (pronounced "fishing") is a type of social engineering in which an attacker attempts to obtain sensitive information from users by masquerading as a trusted entity in an e-mail or instant message sent to a large group of often random users. The attacker attempts to obtain information such as usernames, passwords, credit card numbers, and details about the users' bank accounts. The message that is sent often encourages the user to go to a website that appears to be for a reputable entity such as PayPal or eBay, both of which have frequently been used in phishing attempts. The website the user actually visits is not owned by the reputable organization, however, and asks the user to supply information that can be used in a later attack. Often, the message sent to the user states that the user's account has been compromised and requests, for security purposes, the user to enter their account information to verify the details.

In another very common example of phishing, the attacker sends a bulk e-mail, supposedly from a bank, telling the recipients that a security breach has occurred and instructing them to click a link to verify that their account has not been tampered with. If the individual actually clicks the link, they are taken to a site that appears to be owned by the bank but is actually controlled by the attacker. When they supply their account and password for "verification" purposes, they are actually giving it to the attacker.

Spear Phishing

Spear phishing is the term that has been created to refer to a phishing attack that targets a specific group with something in common. By targeting a specific group, the ratio of successful attacks (that is, the number of responses received) to the total number of e-mails or messages sent usually increases because a targeted attack will seem more plausible than a message sent to users randomly.

Vishing

Vishing is a variation of phishing that uses voice communication technology to obtain the information the attacker is seeking. Vishing takes advantage of the trust that some people place in the telephone network. Users are unaware that attackers can spoof (simulate) calls from legitimate entities using Voice over IP (VoIP) technology. Voice messaging can also be compromised and used in these attempts. Generally, the attackers are hoping to obtain credit card numbers or other information that can be used in identity theft. The user may receive an e-mail asking him or her to call a number that is answered by a potentially compromised voice message system. Users may also receive a recorded message that appears to come from a legitimate entity. In both cases, the user will be encouraged to respond quickly and provide the sensitive information so that access to their account is not blocked. If a user ever receives a message that claims to be from a reputable entity and asks for sensitive information, the user should not provide it, but instead should use the Internet or examine a legitimate account statement to find a phone number that can be used to contact the entity. The user can then verify that the message received was legitimate or report the vishing attempt.

Xmas Attack

The *Xmas attack* or Christmas attack comes from a specific set of protocol options. A Christmas tree packet is a packet that has all of its options turned on. The name comes from the phrase that these packets are lit up like a Christmas tree. When sent as a scan, a Christmas tree packet has the FIN, URG, and PSH options set. Many OSs implement their compliance with the RFC governing IP packets, RFC 791, in slightly different manners. Their response to the packet can tell the scanner what type of OS is present. Another option is in the case of a DoS attack, where Christmas packets can take up significantly greater processing on a router, consuming resources.

Simple stateless firewalls check for the SYN flag set to prevent SYN floods, and Christmas packets are designed not to have SYN set, so they pass right past these devices. Newer security devices such as advanced firewalls can detect these packets, alerting people to the scanning activities.

Pharming

Pharming consists of misdirecting users to fake websites that have been made to look official. Using phishing, individuals are targeted one by one by e-mails. To become a victim, the recipient must take an action (for example, respond by providing personal information). In pharming, the user will be directed to the fake website as a result of activity such as DNS poisoning (an attack that changes URLs in a server's domain name table) or modification of local host files, which are used to convert URLs to the appropriate IP addresses. Once at the fake website, the user may supply personal information, believing that they are connected to the legitimate site.

Privilege Escalation

Cyber-attacks are multistep processes. Most attacks begin at a privilege level associated with an ordinary user. From this level, the attacker exploits vulnerabilities that enable them to achieve root- or admin-level access. This step in the attack chain is called *privilege escalation* and is essential for many attack efforts.

There are a couple of ways to achieve privilege escalation. One pathway is to use existing privilege and do an act that allows you to steal a better set of credentials. The use of sniffers to grab credentials, getting the SAM or *etc/passwd* file, is one method of obtaining "better" credentials. Another method is through vulnerabilities or weaknesses in processes that are running with escalated privilege. Injecting malicious code into these processes can also achieve escalated privilege.

EXAM TIP Blocking privilege escalation is an important defensive step in a system. This is the rationale behind Microsoft's recent reduction in processes and services that run in elevated mode. This greatly reduces the attack surface available for an attacker to perform this essential task.

Malicious Insider Threat

All activity on a system takes place under an account. Accounts define the levels of privilege assigned to a user. Users have this access because trust is required for them to perform their duties, and this trust is reflected in the permissions given to their account. When an insider is acting maliciously, they are abusing this trust. But they also have a significant leg up on an outside attacker because they have basic privileges on a system. In the attack chain, one of the early steps, and sometimes a difficult step, is establishing basic user access on a system. The malicious insider threat, in essence, begins with this step being complete.

If the malicious insider is one with elevated privileges, such as a system administrator, then this form of attack can be especially harmful. A malicious insider with root-level access and skills can bypass many security measures and perform many damaging tasks while avoiding detection. The recent case of the NSA insider Edward Snowden shows how devastating this form of attack vector can be to an organization.

The best defense against insiders lies in a layered defense consisting of two parts. The first is through HR screening of new hires and monitoring of employee activity and morale. The other tool is separation of duties. Ensuring that system admins do not have the ability to manipulate the logs on the systems they administer can be managed with multiple log servers and multiple sets of administrative controls.

 EXAM TIP Managing the malicious insider problem is a combination of people management through HR and separation of duties on the technical side.

Cache Poisoning

Many network activities rely upon various addressing schemes to function properly. When you point your web browser at your bank, by typing the bank's URL, your browser consults the system's DNS system to turn the words into a numerical address. When a packet is being switched to your machine by the network, a series of address caches is involved. Whether the cache is for the DNS system or the ARP system, it exists for the same reason: efficiency. These cashes prevent repeated redundant lookups, saving time for the system. But they can also be poisoned, sending incorrect information to the end user's application, redirecting traffic, and changing system behaviors.

DNS Poisoning

The DNS system is used to convert a name into an IP address. There is not a single DNS system, but rather a hierarchy of DNS servers, from root servers on the backbone of the Internet, to copies at your ISP, your home router, and your local machine, each in the form of a DNS cache. To examine a DNS query for a specific address, you can use the **nslookup** command. Figure 12-8 shows a series of DNS queries executed on a Windows machine. In the first request, the DNS server was with an ISP, while on the second request, the DNS server was from a VPN connection. Between the two requests, the network connections were changed, resulting in different DNS lookups. This is a form of DNS poisoning attack.

At times, nslookup will return a nonauthoritative answer, as shown in Figure 12-9. This typically means the result is from a cache as opposed to server that has an authoritative (that is, known to be current) answer.

There are other commands you can use to examine and manipulate the DNS cache on a system. In Windows, the ipconfig /displaydns command will show the current DNS cache on a machine. Figure 12-10 shows a small DNS cache. This cache was recently emptied using the ipconfig /flushdns command to make it fit on the screen.

Looking at DNS as a complete system shows that there are hierarchical levels from the top (root server) down to the cache in an individual machine. DNS poisoning can occur at any of these levels, with the effect of the poisoning growing wider the higher up it occurs. In 2010, a DNS poisoning event resulted in the "Great Firewall of China" censoring Internet traffic in the United States until caches were resolved.

DNS poisoning is a variant of a larger attack class referred to as *DNS spoofing*. In DNS spoofing, an attacker changes a DNS record through any of a multitude of means. There are many ways to perform DNS spoofing, a few of which include compromising a DNS server, the use of the Kaminsky attack, and the use of a false network node advertising a false DNS address. An attacker can even use DNS cache poisoning to result in DNS

Figure 12-8   nslookup of a DNS query

Figure 12-9   Cache response to a DNS query

spoofing. By poisoning an upstream DNS cache, all of the downstream users will get spoofed DNS records.

Because of the importance of integrity on DNS requests and responses, a project has begun to secure the DNS infrastructure using digital signing of DNS records. This project, initiated by the U.S. government and called Domain Name System Security Extensions (DNSSEC), works by digitally signing records. This is done by adding

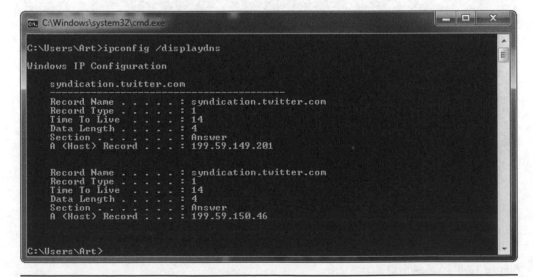

Figure 12-10   Cache response to a DNS table query

records to the DNS system, a key and a signature attesting to the validity of the key. With this information, requestors can be assured that the information they receive is correct. It will take a substantial amount of time (years) for this new system to propagate through the entire DNS infrastructure, but in the end, the system will have much greater assurance.

ARP Poisoning

In moving packets between machines, a device sometimes needs to know where to send a packet using the MAC or layer 2 address. Address Resolution Protocol (ARP) handles this problem through four basic message types:

- **ARP request**   "Who has this IP address?"
- **ARP reply**   "I have that IP address; my MAC address is…"
- **Reverse ARP request (RARP)**   "Who has this MAC address?"
- **RARP reply**   "I have that MAC address; my IP address is…"

These messages are used in conjunction with a device's ARP table, where a form of short-term memory associated with these data elements resides. The commands are used as a simple form of lookup. When a machine sends an ARP request to the network, the reply is received and entered into all devices that hear the reply. This facilitates efficient address lookups, but also makes the system subject to attack.

When the ARP table gets a reply, it automatically trusts the reply and updates the table. Some operating systems will even accept ARP reply data if they never heard the original request. There is no mechanism to verify the veracity of the data received. An attacker can send messages, corrupt the ARP table, and cause packets to be misrouted. This form of attack is called ARP poisoning and results in malicious address redirection. This can allow a mechanism whereby an attacker can inject themselves into the middle of a conversation between two machines, a man-in-the-middle attack.

TCP/IP Hijacking

TCP/IP hijacking and *session hijacking* are terms used to refer to the process of taking control of an already existing session between a client and a server. The advantage to an attacker of hijacking over attempting to penetrate a computer system or network is that the attacker doesn't have to circumvent any authentication mechanisms, since the user has already authenticated and established the session. Once the user has completed the authentication sequence, the attacker can then usurp the session and carry on as if the attacker, and not the user, had authenticated with the system. To prevent the user from noticing anything unusual, the attacker can decide to attack the user's system and perform a DoS attack on it, taking it down so that the user, and the system, will not notice the extra traffic that is taking place.

Hijack attacks generally are used against web and Telnet sessions. Sequence numbers as they apply to spoofing also apply to session hijacking, since the hijacker will need to provide the correct sequence numbers to continue the appropriate sessions.

Transitive Access

Transitive access is a means of attacking a system by violating the trust relationship between machines. A simple example is when servers are well protected and clients are not, and the servers trust the clients. In this case, attacking a client can provide transitive access to the servers.

 EXAM TIP Understanding how hijacking attacks are performed through poisoning the addressing mechanisms is important for the exam.

Client-side Attacks

The web browser has become the major application for users to engage resources across the Web. The popularity and the utility of this interface have made it a prime target for attackers to gain access and control over a system. A wide variety of attacks can occur via a browser, typically resulting from a failure to properly validate input before use. Unvalidated input can result in a series of injection attacks, header manipulation, and other forms of attack.

Injection Attacks

When user input is used without input validation, this results in an opportunity for an attacker to craft input to create specific events to occur when the input is parsed and used by an application. *SQL injection attacks* involve the manipulation of input, resulting in a SQL statement that is different than intended by the designer. XML and LDAP injections are done in the same fashion. As SQL, XML, and LDAP are used to store data, this can give an attacker access to data against business rules. Command injection attacks can occur when input is used in a fashion that allows command-line manipulation. This can give an attacker command-line access at the privilege level of the application.

Header Manipulations

When HTTP is being dynamically generated through the use of user inputs, unvalidated inputs can give attackers an opportunity to change HTTP elements. When user-supplied information is used in a header, it is possible to create a variety of attacks, including cache-poisoning, cross-site scripting, cross-user defacement, page hijacking, cookie manipulation, or open redirect.

Password Attacks

The most common form of authentication is the user ID and password combination. While it is not inherently a poor mechanism for authentication, the combination can be attacked in several ways. All too often, these attacks yield favorable results for the attacker, not as a result of a weakness in the scheme, but usually due to the user not following good password procedures.

Poor Password Choices

The least technical of the various password-attack techniques consists of the attacker simply attempting to guess the password of an authorized user of the system or network. It is surprising how often this simple method works, and the reason it does is because people are notorious for picking poor passwords. Users need to select a password that they can remember, so they create simple passwords, such as their birthday, their mother's maiden name, the name of their spouse or one of their children, or even simply their user ID itself. All it takes is for the attacker to obtain a valid user ID (often a simple matter, because organizations tend to use an individual's names in some combination—first letter of their first name combined with their last name, for example) and a little bit of information about the user before guessing can begin. Organizations sometimes make it even easier for attackers to obtain this sort of information by posting the names of their "management team" and other individuals, sometimes with short biographies, on their websites.

Even if a person doesn't use some personal detail as their password, the attacker may still get lucky, since many people use a common word for their password. Attackers can obtain lists of common passwords—a number of such lists exist on the Internet. Words such as "password" and "secret" have often been used as passwords. Names of favorite sports teams also often find their way onto lists of commonly used passwords.

Dictionary Attack

Another method of determining passwords is to use a password-cracking program that uses a list of dictionary words to try to guess the password, hence the name *dictionary attack*. The words can be used by themselves, or two or more smaller words can be combined to form a single possible password. A number of commercial and public-domain password-cracking programs employ a variety of methods to crack passwords, including using variations on the user ID.

These programs often permit the attacker to create various rules that tell the program how to combine words to form new possible passwords. Users commonly substitute certain numbers for specific letters. If the user wanted to use the word *secret* for a password, for example, the letter *e* could be replaced with the number 3, yielding *s3cr3t*. This password will not be found in the dictionary, so a pure dictionary attack would not crack it, but the password is still easy for the user to remember. If a rule were created that tried all words in the dictionary and then tried the same words substituting the number 3 for the letter *e*, however, the password would be cracked.

Rules can also be defined so that the cracking program will substitute special characters for other characters or combine words. The ability of the attacker to crack passwords is directly related to the method the user employs to create the password in the first place, as well as the dictionary and rules used.

Brute-Force Attack

If the user has selected a password that is not found in a dictionary, even if various numbers or special characters are substituted for letters, the only way the password can be cracked is for an attacker to attempt a *brute-force attack*, in which the password-cracking program attempts all possible password combinations.

The length of the password and the size of the set of possible characters in the password will greatly affect the time a brute-force attack will take. A few years ago, this method of attack was very time consuming, since it took considerable time to generate all possible combinations. With the increase in computer speed, however, generating password combinations is much faster, making it more feasible to launch brute-force attacks against certain computer systems and networks.

A brute-force attack on a password can take place at two levels: It can attack a system where the attacker is attempting to guess the password at a login prompt, or it can attack against the list of password hashes contained in a password file. The first attack can be made more difficult if the account locks after a few failed login attempts. The second attack can be thwarted if the password file is securely maintained so that others cannot obtain a copy of it.

Hybrid Attack

A *hybrid* password attack is a system that combines the preceding methods. Most cracking tools have this option built in, first attempting a dictionary attack, and then moving to brute-force methods.

Birthday Attack

The *birthday attack* is a special type of brute-force attack that gets its name from something known as the birthday paradox, which states that in a group of at least 23 people, the chance that two individuals will have the same birthday is greater than 50 percent. Mathematically, we can use the equation $1.25k^{1/2}$ (with k equaling the size of the set of possible values), and in the birthday paradox, k would be equal to 365 (the number of possible birthdays). This same phenomenon applies to passwords, with k (number of passwords) being quite a bit larger.

Rainbow Tables

Rainbow tables are precomputed tables or hash values associated with passwords. This can change the search for a password from a computational problem to a lookup problem. This can tremendously reduce the level of work when passwords are being attacked. The best defense against rainbow tables is salted hashes, as the addition of a salt value increases the complexity of the problem by making the precomputing process not replicable between systems.

Typo Squatting/URL Hijacking

Typo squatting is an attack form that involves capitalizing upon common typo errors. If a user mistypes a URL, then the result should be a 404 error, or "resource not found." But if an attacker has registered the mistyped URL, then you would land on the attacker's page. This attack pattern is also referred to as *URL hijacking*, *fake URL*, or *brandjacking* if the objective is to deceive based on branding.

There are several reasons that an attacker will pursue this avenue of attack. The most obvious is one of a phishing attack. The fake site collects credentials, passing them on to the real site, and then steps out of the conversation to avoid detection once the credentials are obtained. It can also be used to plant drive-by malware on the victim machine. It can move the packets through an affiliate network, earning click-through revenue based on the typos. There are numerous other forms of attacks that can be perpetrated using a fake URL as a starting point.

Watering Hole Attack

The most commonly recognized attack vectors are those that are direct to a target. Because of their incoming and direct nature, defenses are crafted to detect and defend against them. But what if the user "asked" for the attack by visiting a website? Just as a hunter waits near a watering hole for animals to come drink, attackers can plant malware at sites where users are likely to frequent. First identified by RSA, watering hole attacks involve the infecting of a target website with malware. In some of the cases detected, the infection was constrained to a specific geographical area. These are not simple attacks, yet they can be very effective at delivering malware to specific groups of end users. Watering hole attacks are complex to achieve and appear to be backed by nation-states and other high-resource attackers. In light of the stakes, the typical attack vector will be a zero-day attack to further avoid detection.

Chapter Review

In this chapter, you became acquainted with the principles of attacks and malware. The chapter opened with an examination of malware in its various forms. Each of these forms fits either a purpose of an attack or a type of vulnerability. The forms covered include worms, viruses, Trojan horses, backdoors, and logic bombs as common attack vector agents. Adware, spyware, and ransomware characterize malware aimed for a particular purpose. The more advanced and complex forms of rootkits, botnets, polymorphic, and armored malware were also covered.

Turning to types of attacks, the chapter presented a wide array of current attack patterns. From denial-of-service and distributed denial-of-service, to spoofing, pharming, and privilege escalation, these forms of attack are technical means to an end. Man-in-the-middle, phishing, spear phishing, vishing, spam, and spim are other avenues to achieve the delivery of malware.

Questions

To help you prepare further for the exam, and to test your level of preparedness, answer the following questions and then check your answers against the correct answers at the end of the chapter.

1. Your friend recommended a free software package that helps organize your playlists. You've tried it and it is great—except for the fact that you have to wait 30 seconds every time it starts for a product video to finish before you can use it. This type of software is known as:

   A. DNS redirector

   B. Adware

   C. Bloatware

   D. Browser hijacker

2. When examining a packet capture from your network, you notice a large number of packets with the URG, PUSH, and FIN flags set. What type of traffic are you seeing in that packet capture?

A. Botnet control channel

B. Smurf attack

C. Xmas attack

D. Replay attack

3. If an attacker is able to insert himself into an encrypted conversation between you and a secure web server, he has successfully executed what type of attack?

A. Smurf attack

B. Replay attack

C. Clickjacking attack

D. Man-in-the-middle attack

4. Your entire office is passing around a PowerPoint presentation of dancing and singing hamsters. Everyone thinks it's great until the next morning when everyone's hard drives appear to have been erased. The dancing hamster file is an example of a:

A. Virus

B. Trojan

C. Rootkit

D. Exploit

5. Your friend's computer is showing a pop-up that reads "WARNING! Your computer has been used in illegal activities and has been locked by the authorities. To access your computer you must pay a fine to…" Nothing your friend does will get rid of the pop-up and they can't use their computer. What has your friend's computer been infected with?

A. Ransomware

B. Rootkit

C. Botnet

D. Bloatware

6. You boot your computer on April 1st and a large pop-up appears that reads "Ha Ha Ha" with the Joker's face underneath it. When the pop-up disappears, all the icons are missing from your desktop. What type of malware was your computer infected with?

A. Rootkit

B. Armored virus

C. Adware

D. Logic bomb

7. The Smurf attack is an example of what kind of attack?

   A. DDoS

   B. DoS

   C. SQL injection

   D. Clickjacking

8. Your organization is infected with a piece of malware that you just can't seem to get rid of. It seems like every time a system is cleaned and you update all the antivirus definitions within your organization, another system shows signs of the infection. What type of malware might you be facing in this example?

   A. Polymorphic malware

   B. Trojan horse

   C. Botnet

   D. Cookie monster

9. What type of network attack uses repetition or delay of valid data transmissions?

   A. Botnet

   B. Cross-site scripting

   C. Token hijacking

   D. Replay attack

10. www.whitehouse.com is a famous example of:

   A. Logic bomb

   B. Typo squatting

   C. Phishing

   D. Pharming

11. Everyone in your organization's sales department received an e-mail stating they were going to receive an award as the salesperson of the year. At the end of the e-mail was a link that would allow them to enter the name they wanted to be placed on the award they would receive. The e-mail turned out to be a fake, and clicking the link infected the user's computer with malware. What type of activity is this?

   A. Spear phishing

   B. Spoofing

   C. Vishing

   D. Client-side attack

12. You've noticed some strange behavior today on your organization's system. This morning things were working fine, but now when you enter the URL for your company's main web page, you get a web page written in a foreign language. Which of the following attacks is occurring at your organization?

    A. Man-in-the-middle

    B. Watering hole attack

    C. DNS poisoning

    D. Spam

13. Your antivirus solution has detected malware on one of your computers. The AV program tells you the malware is located in a certain directory, but when you go to remove the malware, you discover that the directory does not exist. This is most likely an example of:

    A. A Trojan horse

    B. An armored virus

    C. A transient virus

    D. A mobile malware infection

14. You want to install some new software on a system for which you have only a regular user account, and the system won't allow you to load new software. Your friend gives you a USB key with a program called "runme.bat" on it. After you run the program, the screen flashes and all the programs you had open close, but you are now able to install the new software. What did that program on the USB key do?

    A. Removed disk quotas

    B. Deleted unnecessary file structures

    C. Executed a privilege escalation

    D. Poisoned the ARP cache

15. While performing a port scan of your organization, you discover an Ubuntu-based system with TCP port 65123 open on it. When you connect to the port using Telnet, all you see is a prompt that looks like ##. You try typing a few commands and notice that you are able to do almost anything on the system, including displaying the contents of /etc/shadow. What did you just discover on this Ubuntu-based system?

    A. Spyware

    B. Backdoor

    C. Fileware

    D. Remote-access software

Answers

1. **B.** Adware is the term used to describe software that typically is free of charge but contains embedded advertisements or the ability to display advertisements while the software is being used. Often, the advertising function can be removed by purchasing the software.

2. **C.** The Xmas attack uses packets with the URG, PUSH, and FIN flags set. Different devices will respond differently to Xmas attacks. Some systems will slow down, some will reboot or crash, and some will drop the packets completely.

3. **D.** If an attacker is able to insert himself into the middle of an encrypted conversation and have each victim believe they are still talking to their original parties in the conversation, then the attacker has successfully executed a man-in-the-middle attack. A man-in-the-middle attack can only succeed if the attacker can impersonate both endpoints in the conversation successfully.

4. **B.** Trojans are malicious programs that often appear to be or do one thing while performing undesirable actions without user approval. Trojan software is named after the Trojan horse from the Trojan War.

5. **A.** Your friend's computer has been infected with ransomware, software designed to block access to a system until a "ransom" is paid.

6. **D.** If a malicious action takes place at a certain time or date or when specific conditions occur, it is most likely the work of a logic bomb. Logic bombs are malware designed to run undetected until certain conditions are met—a specific time, a specific date, a certain number of mouse clicks, and so on. When those conditions are met, the logic bomb executes its "payload," which is often something designed to damage, disrupt, or destroy the infected system.

7. **A.** The Smurf attack is one of the very first examples of a DDoS (distributed denial-of-service) attack. In a Smurf attack, the attacker spoofs an ICMP echo request packet from the target's address and sends it to one or more network addresses. Each host that receives the packet will respond to the target address with an echo reply packet. The attacker is able to distribute the attack among multiple sources and overwhelm the target with traffic.

8. **A.** If you have a piece of malware that is extremely difficult to eradicate no matter how many times you update antivirus signatures, you are most likely facing polymorphic malware. Polymorphic malware is designed to constantly change and make itself increasingly more difficult to detect or remove. The malware "evolves" through techniques like filename changes, compression techniques, variable key encryption, and so on.

9. **D.** A replay attack is a network attack that repeats or delays valid data transmissions. In most replay attack scenarios, an attacker captures a valid traffic stream (such as the submission of login credentials) and "replays" the traffic at a later date.

PART III

10. **B.** www.whitehouse.com is a famous example of typo squatting. Typo squatting involves setting up a website using common misspellings, typos, or errors that occur when users are attempting to reach legitimate sites. For example, users wishing to reach www.whitehouse.gov might mistakenly type ".com" instead of ".gov" and be directed to a completely different website than they intended to visit.

11. **A.** This is an example of a spear phishing attack. Spear phishing uses fraudulent e-mails targeted at a specific organization or group within an organization. The attack is much more selective and targeted than a phishing attack.

12. **C.** Your organization is most likely under a DNS poisoning attack. In a DNS poisoning attack, the attacker attempts to corrupt DNS servers or DNS caches in a way that returns an incorrect IP address when DNS resolution takes place. This type of attack is commonly used to divert traffic to one of the attacker's systems.

13. **B.** Tricking AV software into believing the malware is located in one location when it's actually located in another is a common technique used by an armored virus. Armored viruses are designed to be more resistant to detection, reverse engineering, and removal.

14. **C.** If you are allowed to do something you were previously not allowed to do before running a program (like install software), then the program most likely performed a privilege escalation attack. A privilege escalation attack exploits a bug, flaw, or misconfiguration that allows elevated access to resources and actions that are normally not available to the average user.

15. **B.** If you are able to access a system on an uncommon port and bypass normal authentication mechanisms, you have most likely discovered a backdoor.

CHAPTER 13

Social Engineering

In this chapter, you will

- Define basic terminology associated with social engineering
- Identify common user actions that may put an organization's information at risk
- Recognize methods attackers may use to gain information about an organization
- Examine risks associated with virtualization and cloud environments

Social engineering is the process of convincing an authorized individual to provide confidential information or access to an unauthorized individual. It is a technique in which the attacker uses various deceptive practices to convince the targeted person to divulge information they normally would not divulge or to convince the target of the attack to do something they normally wouldn't do.

Social Engineering Methods

Social engineering is an attack against a user, and typically involves some form of social interaction. The weakness that is being exploited in the attack is not necessarily one of technical knowledge, or even security awareness. Social engineering at its heart involves manipulating the very social nature of interpersonal relationships. It in essence preys on several characteristics that we tend to desire. The willingness to help, for instance, is a characteristic one would like to see in a team environment. We want employees who help each other, and we tend to reward those who are helpful and punish those who are not.

If our work culture is built around collaboration and teamwork, then how can this be exploited? It is not simple, but it can be accomplished through a series of subtle ruses. One is built around the concept of developing a sense of familiarity—making it seem as if you belong to the group. For example, by injecting yourself into a conversation or encounter, armed with the right words and the correct information, you can make it seem as if you belong. Through careful name dropping and aligning your story with current events and expectations, you can just slip in unnoticed. Another example is by arriving at a door at the same time as a person with an ID card, carrying something in both your hands, you probably can get them to open and hold the door for you. An even more successful technique is to have a conversation on the way to the door over something that makes you fit in. People want to help, and this tactic empowers the person to help you.

A second method involves creating a hostile situation. People tend to want to avoid hostility, so if you are engaged in a heated argument with someone as you enter the group you wish to join—making sure not only that you are losing the argument, but that it also seems totally unfair—you instantly can build a connection to anyone who has been similarly mistreated. Play on sympathy, their desire for compassion, and use that moment to bypass the connection moment.

A good social engineer understands how to use body language to influence others— how to smile at the right time, how to mirror movements, how to influence others not through words but through body language cues. Any woman that has used body language to get a man to do something without directly asking him to do it understands this game. Men understand as well, and they play because they are attempting to get something as well. When someone has the key information you need for a project, a proposal, or any other important thing, trading a quid quo pro is an unspoken ritual. And if you do this with someone who has malicious intent, then remember the saying, "Beware of Greeks bearing gifts."

The best defense against social engineering attacks is a comprehensive training and awareness program that includes social engineering, but this does not mean that employees should be trained to be stubborn and unhelpful. Rather, training should emphasize the value of being helpful and working as a team, but doing so in an environment where trust is verified and is a ritual without social stigma. No one will get past TSA employees with social engineering techniques when checking in at an airport, because they dispassionately enforce and follow set procedures, but they frequently do so with kindness, politeness, and helpfulness while also ensuring that the screening procedures are always completed.

 EXAM TIP　For the exam, be familiar with all of the various social engineering attacks and the associated effectiveness of each attack.

Shoulder Surfing

Shoulder surfing does not necessarily involve direct contact with the target, but instead involves the attacker directly observing the individual entering sensitive information on a form, keypad, or keyboard. The attacker may simply look over the shoulder of the user at work, for example, or may set up a camera or use binoculars to view the user entering sensitive data. The attacker can attempt to obtain information such as a personal identification number (PIN) at an automated teller machine (ATM), an access control entry code at a secure gate or door, or a calling card or credit card number. Many locations now use a small shield to surround a keypad so that it is difficult to observe somebody as they enter information. More sophisticated systems can actually scramble the location of the numbers so that the top row at one time includes the numbers 1, 2, and 3 and the next time includes 4, 8, and 0. While this makes it a bit slower for the user to enter information, it thwarts an attacker's attempt to observe what numbers are pressed and then enter the same buttons/pattern, since the location of the numbers constantly changes.

Dumpster Diving

The process of going through a target's trash in hopes of finding valuable information that might be used in a penetration attempt is known in the security community as *dumpster diving*. One common place to find information, if the attacker is in the vicinity of the target, is in the target's trash. The attacker might find little bits of information that could be useful for an attack. The tactic is not, however, unique to the computer community; it has been used for many years by others, such as identity thieves, private investigators, and law enforcement personnel, to obtain information about an individual or organization. If the attackers are very lucky, and the target's security procedures are very poor, they may actually find user IDs and passwords.

An attacker may gather a variety of information that can be useful in a social engineering attack. In most locations, trash is no longer considered private property after it has been discarded (and even where dumpster diving is illegal, little enforcement occurs). An organization should have policies about discarding materials. Sensitive information should be shredded, and the organization should consider securing the trash receptacle so that individuals can't forage through it. People should also consider shredding personal or sensitive information that they wish to discard in their own trash. A reasonable quality shredder is inexpensive and well worth the price when compared with the potential loss that could occur as a result of identity theft.

Tailgating

As discussed in Chapter 9, tailgating (or piggybacking) is the simple tactic of following closely behind a person who has just used their own access card or PIN to gain physical access to a room or building. People are often in a hurry and will frequently not follow good physical security practices and procedures. Attackers know this and may attempt to exploit this characteristic in human behavior. An attacker can thus gain access to the facility without having to know the access code or having to acquire an access card. It is similar to shoulder surfing in that it relies on the attacker taking advantage of an authorized user who is not following security procedures. Frequently, the attacker may even start a conversation with the target before reaching the door so that the user may be more comfortable with allowing the individual in without challenging them. In this sense piggybacking is related to social engineering attacks.

Both the piggybacking and shoulder surfing attack techniques can be easily countered by using simple procedures to ensure nobody follows you too closely or is in a position to observe your actions. Both of these rely on the poor security practices of an authorized user in order to be successful. A more sophisticated countermeasure to piggybacking is a *man trap*, which utilizes two doors to gain access to the facility. The second door does not open until the first one is closed, and the doors are closely spaced so that an enclosure is formed that only allows one individual through at a time.

Impersonation

Impersonation is a common social engineering technique and can be employed in many ways. It can occur in person, over a phone, or online. In the case of an impersonation attack, the attacker assumes a role that is recognized by the person being attacked, and in assuming that role, the attacker uses the potential victim's biases against their better judgment to follow procedures.

Third-Party Authorization

Using previously obtained information about a project, deadlines, bosses, and so on, the attacker arrives with 1) something the victim is quasi-expecting or would see as normal, 2) uses the guise of a project in trouble or some other situation where the attacker will be viewed as helpful or as one not to upset, and 3) they name-drop "Mr. Big," who happens to be out of the office and unreachable at the moment, avoiding the reference check. And the attacker seldom asks for anything that on the face of it seems unreasonable, or is unlikely to be shared based on the circumstances. These actions can create the appearance of a third-party authorization, when in fact there is none.

Help Desk/Tech Support

Calls to or from help desk and tech support units can be used to elicit information. Posing as an employee, you can get a password reset, information about some system, or other useful information. The call can go the other direction as well, where the social engineer is posing as the help desk or tech support. Then, by calling employees, the attacker can get information on system status and other interesting elements that they can use later.

Contractors/Outside Parties

It is common in many organizations to have outside contractors clean the building, water the plants, and do other routine chores. In many of these situations, without proper safeguards, an attacker can simply put on clothing that matches a contractor's uniform, show up to do the job at a slightly different time than it's usually done, and, if challenged, play on the sympathy of the workers by saying they are filling in for X or covering for Y. The attacker then roams the halls unnoticed because they blend in, all the while photographing desks and papers and looking for information.

Online Attacks

Impersonation can be employed in online attacks as well. In these cases, technology plays an intermediary role in the communication chain. Some older forms, such as pop-up windows, tend to be less effective today, because users are wary of them. Yet phishing attempts via e-mail and social media scams abound.

Defenses

In all of the cases of impersonation, the best defense is simple—have processes in place that require employees to ask to see a person's ID before engaging with them if the employees do not personally know them. That includes challenging people such as delivery drivers and contract workers. Don't let people in through the door, piggybacking, without checking their ID. If this is standard process, then no one becomes offended, and if someone fakes offense, it becomes even more suspicious. Training and awareness do work, as proven by trends such as the diminished effectiveness of pop-up windows. But the key to this defense is to make the training periodic and to tailor it to what is currently being experienced, rather than a generic recitation of best practices.

 EXAM TIP A training and awareness program is still the best defense against social engineering attacks.

Hoaxes

At first glance, it might seem that a hoax related to security would be considered a nuisance and not a real security issue. This might be the case for some hoaxes, especially those of the urban legend type, but the reality of the situation is that a hoax can be very damaging if it causes users to take some sort of action that weakens security. One real hoax, for example, described a new, highly destructive piece of malicious software. It instructed users to check for the existence of a certain file and to delete it if the file was found. In reality, the file mentioned was an important file used by the operating system, and deleting it caused problems the next time the system was booted. The damage caused by users modifying security settings can be serious. As with other forms of social engineering, training and awareness are the best and first line of defense for both users and administrators. Users should be trained to be suspicious of unusual e-mails and stories and should know who to contact in the organization to verify their validity if they are received. A hoax often also advises the user to send it to their friends so that they know about the issue as well—and by doing so, they help spread the hoax. Users need to be suspicious of any e-mail telling them to "spread the word."

Whaling

High-value targets are referred to as *whales*. A whaling attack is thus one where the target is a high-value person, such as a CEO or CFO. Whaling attacks are not performed by attacking multiple targets and hoping for a reply, but rather are custom-built to increase the odds of success. Spear phishing is a common method used against whales, as it is designed to appear to be ordinary business for the target, being crafted to imitate a non-suspicious communication. Whales can be deceived in the same manner as any other person; the difference is that the target group is limited, hence an attacker cannot rely upon random returns from a wide population of targets.

Vishing

As introduced in Chapter 12, vishing is an attack method using Voice over IP technology. Vishing relies upon trust, a falsely placed belief that a phone call is coming from a specific party solely based on a number on the phone screen. In VoIP attacks, it is possible to spoof the number the call is coming from. This is used to establish a form of trust that is then exploited by the attacker over the phone.

Social Engineering Principles

Social engineering is very successful for two general reasons. The first is the basic desire of most people to be helpful. When somebody asks a question for which we know the answer, our normal response is not to be suspicious, but rather to answer the question. The problem with this is that seemingly innocuous information can be used either directly in an attack or indirectly to build a bigger picture that an attacker can use to create an aura of authenticity during an attack—the more information an individual has about an organization, the easier it will be to convince others that he is part of the organization and has a right to even sensitive information.

The second reason that social engineering is successful is that individuals normally seek to avoid confrontation and trouble. If the attacker attempts to intimidate the target, threatening to call the target's supervisor because of a lack of help, the target may give in and provide the information to avoid confrontation.

Tools

The tools in a social engineer's toolbox are based on a knowledge of psychology and don't necessarily require a sophisticated knowledge of software or hardware. The social engineer will employ strategies aimed to exploit people's own biases and beliefs in a manner to momentarily deny them the service of good judgment and the use of standard procedures. The following list of "techniques" that can be employed are common in many social engineering attacks:

- **Authority**   If an attacker can convince others that he has authority in a particular situation, he can entice them to act in a particular manner. Act like a boss is requesting something, and people are less likely to withhold it.

- **Intimidation**   Intimidation can be either subtle, through perceived power, or more direct, through the use of communications that build an expectation of superiority.

- **Consensus/social proof**   Consensus is a group-wide decision. It frequently comes not from a champion, but rather through rounds of group negotiation. These rounds can be manipulated to achieve desired outcomes.

- **Scarcity**   If something is in short supply and is valued, then arriving with what is needed can bring rewards—and acceptance. "Only X left at this price" is an example of this technique.

- **Urgency**   Time can be manipulated to drive a sense of urgency and prompt shortcuts that can lead to opportunities for interjection into processes. Limited-time offers should always be viewed as suspect.

- **Familiarity/liking**   People do things for people they like or feel connected to. Building this sense of familiarity and appeal can lead to misplaced trust.

- **Trust**   Trust is defined as having an understanding of how something will act under specific conditions. Social engineers can shape the perceptions of a worker to where they will apply judgments to the trust equation and come to false conclusions.

Employing these tools is second nature to a social engineer, and with skill, they can switch these tools in and out in any particular circumstance, just as a plumber uses various hand tools and a system administrator uses OS commands to achieve complex tasks. When watching any of these professionals work, we may marvel at how they wield their tools, and the same is true for social engineers—except their tools are more subtle, and the target is people and trust.

Chapter Review

In this chapter, you became acquainted with the principles of social engineering attacks. You examined the methods of social engineering, along with specific attack vectors such as shoulder surfing, dumpster diving, tailgating, impersonation, hoaxes, whaling, and vishing. These social engineering–based attacks, are presented so that they can be recognized. For all of them, the common defense mechanism is training and awareness. The chapter concluded with an examination of the principal tools used by social engineers and why they are effective.

Questions

To help you prepare further for the CompTIA Security+ exam, and to test your level of preparedness, answer the following questions and then check your answers against the correct answers at the end of the chapter.

1. At the main door of your office building you see a man standing by the card swipe talking on his phone. He waits until someone swipes their card and walks through the door. Then, just before the door closes, he grabs the door, opens it, and walks through without swiping. This man just gained access to your building by:

   A. Shoulder surfing

   B. Bypassing

   C. Tailgating

   D. Hijacking

2. On the bus one morning you notice a woman peering over the seat in front of her at the screen of the laptop being used by the man sitting in that seat. The woman appears to be taking notes as well. What is this woman possibly doing?

   A. Tailgating

   B. Shoulder surfing

   C. Snarfing

   D. Watering hole attack

3. The CEO of your organization calls you in to his office to ask you about an e-mail he's received. The e-mail instructs him to click a link and verify his user ID, password, date of birth, and Social Security number. As far as you know, he is the only person in your organization who has received that e-mail. What type of attack is this?

   A. Impersonation

   B. Replay attack

   C. Clickjacking attack

   D. Whaling

4. Your office phone rings and the person on the other end tells you she is from Human Resources and is conducting a random audit of employee records. She requests your full name, e-mail address, date of birth, Social Security number, and bank account number to validate the information stored in HR's records. The caller ID shows a number inside your organization. This could be what type of attack?

   A. Vishing

   B. Hoaxing

   C. Twinning

   D. Infojacking

5. A colleague asks you to look at his computer screen. He has received an e-mail from his bank asking him to log in and verify a recent withdrawal. The colleague did click the link but hasn't done anything else because the website looks a bit "off" to him. The page layout looks like that of his bank, but there are several misspellings on the page and it's an unencrypted HTTP session. What attack technique might be in use in this case?

   A. Bluejacking

   B. Snarfing

   C. Impersonation

   D. Whaling

6. You see several people digging in the trash bins behind your office building. When they see you, they run away holding several large bags. What might these people have been doing?

   A. Vishing

   B. Rooting

   C. Dumpster diving

   D. Bluejacking

7. A man is standing outside your building in a dark-blue windbreaker with the letters "FBI" on the back. He is asking everyone entering your building to show him their driver's license and employee ID. He then asks each person a series of questions about where they work, what they do, how long they've been with the company, and so on. When one person asks to see the person's badge, the man in the windbreaker threatens to throw them in jail for failing to cooperate with a federal investigation. What type of social engineering principle might be in use here?

   A. Scarcity

   B. Intimidation

   C. Social proof

   D. Trust

8. Your entire group receives an e-mail from your boss that instructs you to take the rest of the day off but to leave all your work papers where they are and your terminals unlocked as you leave. The e-mail says the Audit department needs to check everyone's system for illegal software. You notice the e-mail address has an extra letter in the spelling of the company name. What type of social engineering principle might be in use here?

   A. Social proof

   B. Urgency

   C. Consensus

   D. Authority

9. Which of the following is not a social engineering principle?

   A. Scarcity

   B. Intimidation

   C. Condolence

   D. Trust

10. An e-mail is circulating around your organization warning people of a new virus. The e-mail instructs you to search your system for files named "mmsystem.dll" and delete them if you find any. What type of social engineering attack might this be?

   A. Logic bomb

   B. Typosquatting

   C. Hoax

   D. Pharming

11. Your coworker has just run to the printer to retrieve a piece of paper and is now getting ready to run out the door. When you ask where she is going, she says, "I have to go now—there's only a few left." You look at the piece of paper in her hand and it appears to be an advertisement for a 65-inch LCD TV sale. The ad lists an address for "Bob's TV Warehouse" that is way across town. What type of social engineering principle is in use in this example?

    A. Tailgating

    B. Scarcity

    C. Whaling

    D. Client-side attack

12. A very attractive woman is standing at the door of your building asking for someone to let her into the building because she has forgotten her ID. A young man stops and chats with the woman for a few minutes and then finally lets her into the building. What social engineering principle is the woman using to gain access to the building?

    A. Urgency

    B. Familiarity/liking

    C. Social proof

    D. Trust

13. You are about to enter your PIN at an ATM when you notice a flash behind you. There's only one person behind you and they have their phone out. They are frantically tapping buttons on the screen and are avoiding any eye contact with you. What type of attack might this person be attempting?

    A. Tailgating

    B. Impersonation

    C. Shoulder surfing

    D. Vishing

14. You receive a Facebook "friend" request from someone you don't recognize personally, but you seem to have a lot of friends in common. You accept the request. A few weeks later you receive a request from the same person asking you to click a link and take a survey. You notice quite a few of your coworkers have already taken the same quiz. When you click the link, your antivirus program warns you that the site you are connecting to is attempting to load malware on your system. What social engineering principle did you fall victim to?

    A. Urgency

    B. Trust

    C. Consensus/social proof

    D. Scarcity

15. An e-mail appears in your inbox. When you open it, it asks you to click the link for a special offer. When you click the link, it takes you to a web page that describes a "fantastic offer" on a new car. All you have to do is click the link, complete a 15-minute survey, and print out a coupon worth $10,000 off a new car. There's also a big red timer at the top of the page counting down from 30 to 0. The web page states that you have only 30 seconds to begin the survey before the offer expires. What type of social engineering principle is at work in this case?

   A. Scarcity

   B. Intimidation

   C. Urgency

   D. Trust

Answers

1. **C.** This man is tailgating—following someone into a secured or restricted area without their consent and permission. This is also known as piggybacking.

2. **B.** This woman may be shoulder surfing. Shoulder surfing is spying on the user of a computer, mobile device, laptop, ATM, or other device in order to steal information such as logins, passwords, personal information, and so on.

3. **D.** Phishing attacks that target senior executives are known as whaling attacks. They are essentially the same as other phishing attacks except their targets are only the "big ones" in your organization.

4. **A.** A social engineering attack over the phone is known as vishing. Attackers call victims and attempt to coax information from the victims or convince the victims to perform actions on behalf of the attacker.

5. **C.** When a hostile computer system attempts to masquerade as a trusted computer, this is known as impersonation.

6. **C.** Dumpster diving is the act of searching through an organization's trash looking for useful, valuable, or sensitive information that may have been discarded. Attackers are looking for anything that might help them conduct additional attacks, such as employee rosters, password lists, company policies, used CDs, old hard drives, and so on.

7. **B.** The man in the dark windbreaker is using intimidation on his victims. He is pretending to be someone of authority and threatening to throw people in jail if they question what he is doing or do not comply with his requests. He is trying to scare people into doing what he asks.

8. **D.** The social engineering principle in use is authority. The attacker is spoofing an e-mail from your boss and hoping that people will comply without questioning it because it appears to be coming from the boss.

9. **C.** Condolence is not a social engineering principle.

10. **C.** This is most likely a hoax. Mmsystem.dll is a valid Windows system file and will most likely be found on Windows-based workstations. This e-mail looks real and has some valid information in it—the recipient will most likely find the file mentioned in the e-mail on their system. But because the file is a part of the Windows operating system and not a threat, this is a hoax.

11. **B.** When a social engineering attack uses the idea of a limited number of something, the principle in use is scarcity. The attacker is attempting to convince their victim to act quickly as there are a limited number of items or opportunities available.

12. **B.** The woman is using the principle of familiarity/liking. People are more likely to be influenced by something they like or something that feels familiar to them.

13. **C.** This could be a shoulder surfing attempt. Mobile phones make it possible to discreetly take photos or videos of keystrokes, such as entering a PIN number, typing a user ID/password, and so on.

14. **C.** This is an example of consensus/social proof. In this case you accepted both the initial request and the survey request based on the fact that many of your coworkers and peers had already done so. You trusted in the judgment of the group rather than your own.

15. **C.** The limited time/must act now nature of the offer is using the urgency principle to trick you into clicking that next link. This web page is attempting to pressure you into clicking the link before you've had time to examine it and consider whether or not the link is legitimate.

Application and Wireless Attacks

In this chapter, you will

- Explain types of wireless attacks
- Explain types of application attacks

Attacks exploit vulnerabilities in systems to enable an attacker to obtain access to the system. Two common modes of attacks are via the wireless network, using the ability to connect without a physical connection to stealthily launch attacks, and via the applications being run in the system. Applications represent an avenue to attack because they typically have more vulnerabilities than a modern patched operating system.

Wireless Attacks

As wireless use increases, the security of the wireless protocols has become a more important factor in the security of the entire network. As a security professional, you need to understand wireless network applications because of the risks inherent in broadcasting a network signal where anyone can intercept it. Sending unsecured information across public airwaves is tantamount to posting your company's passwords by the front door of the building.

This chapter looks at the types of wireless attacks and the defenses to manage risk associated with the use of wireless technology.

Rogue Access Points

If an unauthorized wireless access point is set up, it is known as a *rogue access point*. These may be set up by well-meaning employees or may be hidden by an attacker with physical access. An attacker might set up a rogue access point if they can gain limited physical access to an organization, perhaps by sneaking into the building briefly. The attacker can then set up an AP on the network and, by placing it behind the external firewall or network IDS (NIDS) type of security measures, can attach to the wireless network at a later date at their leisure. This approach reduces the risk of getting caught by physical security staff, and if the AP is found, it does not point directly back to any kind of traceable address.

Jamming/Interference

Wireless networking requires a connection over a radio link. Radio signals are prone to jamming and interference, which would act as a denial-of-service type of attack on a wireless network. Not all jamming and interference is intentional. The layout of wireless network access points relative to other RF devices can result in areas of poor signal or interference, resulting in network connectivity issues.

Evil Twin

An *evil twin* attack is the use of an access point owned by an attacker that usually has been enhanced with higher-power and higher-gain antennas to look like a better connection to the users and computers attaching to it. By getting users to connect through the evil access point, attackers can more easily analyze traffic and perform man-in-the-middle–type attacks. For simple denial-of-service, an attacker could use interference to jam the wireless signal, not allowing any computer to connect to the access point successfully.

War Dialing and War Driving

War dialing is the term used to describe an attacker's attempt to discover unprotected modem connections to computer systems and networks. The term's origin is the 1983 movie *WarGames*, in which the star has his machine systematically call a sequence of phone numbers in an attempt to find a computer connected to a modem. In the case of the movie, the intent was to find a machine with games the attacker could play, though obviously an attacker could have other purposes once access is obtained.

War dialing is surprisingly successful, mostly because of rogue modems—unauthorized modems attached to computers on a network by authorized users. Generally, the reason for attaching the modem is not malicious—an individual may simply want to be able to go home and then connect to the organization's network to continue working. The problem, however, is that if a user can connect, so can an attacker. If the authorized user has not implemented any security protection, this means of access could be totally open. This is often the case.

Another avenue of attack on computer systems and networks has seen a tremendous increase over the last few years because of the increase in the use of wireless networks. Wireless networks have some obvious advantages—they free employees from the cable connection to a port on their wall, allowing them to move throughout the building with their laptops and still be connected. And wireless is almost always on, hence available 24/7. An employee could, for example, leave her desk with her laptop and move to a conference room where she could then make a presentation, all without ever having to disconnect her machine from the wall or find a connection in the conference room.

The problem with wireless networks is that it is difficult to limit access to them. Since no physical connection exists, the distance that a user can go and still remain connected is a function of the wireless network itself and where the various components of the network are placed. To ensure access throughout a facility, stations are often placed at numerous locations, some of which may actually provide access to areas outside of the organization to ensure that the farthest offices in the organization can be reached. Frequently, access extends into adjacent offices or into the parking lot or street. Attackers can locate these access areas that fall outside of the organization and attempt to gain unauthorized access.

The term *war driving* has been used to refer to the activity in which attackers wander throughout an area (often in a car) with a computer with wireless capability, searching for wireless networks they can access. Some security measures can limit an attacker's ability to succeed at this activity, but, just as in war dialing, the individuals who set up the wireless networks don't always activate these security mechanisms. And in most cases, the individuals running wireless networks would not even notice someone using their network. This can lead to issues when the unauthorized party performs actions that are against the terms of service the network owner has with their ISP, such as the illegal sharing of music, videos, and software. In these cases, the ISP and the content owners will point the finger at the network owner, not the person who drove by and borrowed the bandwidth.

When wireless was still "rare," in some areas symbols began appearing on curbs and other places indicating the presence of an open or unprotected Wi-Fi network. Much like the hobo markings of a previous century, these chalk marks were meant to guide others to safe areas and steer them away from danger. These marks became known as *war chalking*, and they can still be found all over the globe, in inner cities, and neighborhoods of all types. As Wi-Fi has become more ubiquitous, the need and usage of war chalking are fading, just like the hobo symbols of the past.

 EXAM TIP Understand the terms war driving (driving and looking for Wi-Fi hotspots) and war chalking (marking locations for others) for the exam.

Bluetooth Attacks

As Bluetooth became popular, people started trying to find holes in it. Bluetooth features easy configuration of devices to allow communication, with no need for network addresses or ports. Bluetooth uses pairing to establish a trust relationship between devices. To establish that trust, the devices advertise capabilities and require a passkey. To help maintain security, most devices require the passkey to be entered into both devices; this prevents a default passkey–type attack. The Bluetooth's protocol advertisement of services and pairing properties is where some of the security issues start.

Bluejacking

Bluejacking is a term used for the sending of unauthorized messages to another Bluetooth device. This involves sending a message as a phonebook contact:

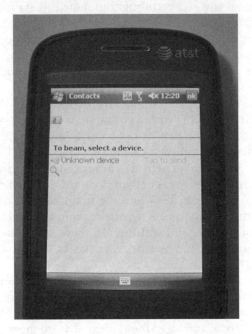

Then the attacker sends the message to the possible recipient via Bluetooth. Originally, this involved sending text messages, but more recent phones can send images or audio as well. A popular variant of this is the transmission of "shock" images, featuring disturbing or crude photos. Because Bluetooth is a short-range protocol, the attacker and victim must be within roughly 10 yards of each other. The victim's phone must also have Bluetooth enabled and must be in discoverable mode. On some early phones, this was the default configuration, and while it makes connecting external devices easier, it also allows attacks against the phone. If Bluetooth is turned off, or if the device is set to nondiscoverable, bluejacking can be avoided.

Bluesnarfing

Bluesnarfing is similar to bluejacking in that it uses the same contact transmission protocol. The difference is that instead of sending an unsolicited message to the victim's phone, the attacker copies off the victim's information, which can include e-mails, contact lists, calendar, and anything else that exists on that device. More recent phones with media capabilities can be snarfed for private photos and videos. Bluesnarfing used to require a laptop with a Bluetooth adapter, making it relatively easy to identify a possible attacker, but bluesnarfing applications are now available for mobile devices. Bloover, a portmanteau of Bluetooth and Hoover, is one such application that runs as a Java applet. The majority of Bluetooth phones need to be discoverable for the bluesnarf attack to work, but it does not necessarily need to be paired. In theory, an attacker can also brute force the device's unique 48-bit name. A program called RedFang attempts to perform this brute-force attack by sending all possible names and seeing what gets a response. This approach was addressed in Bluetooth 1.2 with an anonymity mode.

Bluebugging

Bluebugging is a far more serious attack than either bluejacking or bluesnarfing. In blue-bugging, the attacker uses Bluetooth to establish a serial connection to the device. This allows access to the full AT command set—GSM phones use AT commands similar to Hayes-compatible modems. This connection allows full control over the phone, including the placing of calls to any number without the phone owner's knowledge. Fortunately, this attack requires pairing of the devices to complete, and phones that were initially vulnerable to the attack have updated firmware to correct the problem. To accomplish the attack now, the phone owner would need to surrender her phone and allow an attacker to physically establish the connection. This attack is a reminder of how technology can have significant hidden risk.

 EXAM TIP Bluetooth should always have discoverable mode turned off unless you're deliberately pairing a device.

Packet Sniffing

Wireless networks are characterized by connectivity via radio waves. The RF signal can be intercepted by all receivers in range of the transmitter, and this is referred to as *packet sniffing*. Whether a coffee shop, airport, or work environment, any machine in range can intercept a wide array of conversations between devices and an access point. The solution is remarkably simple, yet frequently not employed—encryption. Employing WPA2, as discussed in Chapter 4, will prevent other devices from being able to intercept communications.

Near Field Communication

Near field communication (NFC) is a contactless communication method used with low power over short distances, less than one foot. NFC uses magnetic induction to trigger a communication between NFC devices. One of the devices can be a passive tag, such as an RFID tag. NFC has several potential security issues, from eavesdropping to data corruption, interception, and device theft. The range of the NFC channel itself makes most interception and eavesdropping attacks difficult to enact. For sensitive data, a secure channel mode involving encryption can be employed, making practical interception meaningless.

Secure channel mode communications can also reduce the ability of an attacker to manipulate the data transfer. It is still possible to create a disruption or denial-of-service, but the integrity of a successful transfer can be assured when using secure mode.

Because NFC is frequently associated with mobile devices, one security threat is the loss of the device itself. If the device does not have basic security, such as being password enabled, then information, such as credit card information, that is commonly transferred by NFC can be gained by whomever has the device. The basic mobile security practice of locking the device mitigates this risk.

Replay Attacks

A *replay attack* occurs when the attacker captures a portion of a communication between two parties and retransmits it at a later time. For example, an attacker might replay a series of commands and codes used in a financial transaction to cause the transaction to be conducted multiple times. Generally, replay attacks are associated with attempts to circumvent authentication mechanisms, such as the capturing and reuse of a certificate or ticket. In wireless systems, replay is easier, as other signals can be copied over the air.

The best way to prevent replay attacks is with encryption, cryptographic authentication, and time stamps. If a portion of the certificate or ticket includes a date/time stamp or an expiration date/time, and this portion is also encrypted as part of the ticket or certificate, replaying it at a later time will prove useless, since it will be rejected as having expired.

 EXAM TIP Wireless connections are especially prone to replay attacks. The best method for defending against replay attacks is through the use of encryption and short time frames for legal transactions.

IV Attack

WEP and WPA both rely upon an initialization vector (IV) to form the encryption key, as described in Chapter 4. In WEP, a short, 24-bit IV is used, resulting in reused IVs with the same encryption key. This opens the door to attacks against the key, resulting in WEP being easily cracked. WPA uses a longer, but still insufficient IV mechanism.

WEP/WPA Attacks

WEP relies on an RC4 implementation that is now known to be improperly implemented and to have severe flaws in various aspects of its protocol. These problems make breaking WEP a near-trivial exercise. One attack involves sending special de-auth packets, which cause legitimate clients to reauthenticate to the AP. The attacker then captures the initialization vectors from these reauthentication packets and uses them to crack the WEP key in minutes. Another attack is the chopchop attack, whereby a weakness in the use of a checksum allows an attacker to manipulate a packet, return it to the WAP, and based on the results, determine over many iterations the contents of the encrypted packet.

WPA replaces the weak IV implementation with a Temporal Key Integrity Protocol (TKIP) implementation that addresses all of the known attacks against WEP. But other weaknesses were discovered in WPA, as it was designed to have a level of compatibility with WEP systems. Using short packets with known structure, such as local DNS requests, it is possible to brute force the packet stream without triggering certain protection issues such as message integrity code (MIC). This does not reveal the key, but does allow for manipulation of packets that were supposed to be protected by the encryption methodology. Today, WPA2 with AES is most often used to overcome the issues with WPA/TKIP.

WPS Attacks

Wi-Fi Protected Setup (WPS) is a simplified method of streamlining the installation and setup of wireless networks. The idea in developing the standard was to create a method that enables users without specific training in wireless security principles to easily set up WPA and add new devices to the network. WPS provides for a method of easily connecting a new device to the network, either by pressing a button on the access point and the new device or by using a PIN. The PIN can be used either on the new device or on the access point.

In 2011, it was discovered that the PIN method could be brute forced in as little as a few hours. Once the PIN is discovered, it is possible to discover the WPA/WPA2 preshared key. Because WPS is shipped by default on a wide range of equipment, during setup, it is important to disable this feature.

Application Attacks

Attacks against a system can occur at the network level, at the operating system level, at the application level, or at the user level (social engineering). Early attack patterns were against the network, but most of today's attacks are aimed at the applications, primarily because that is where the objective of most attacks resides; in the infamous words of bank robber Willie Sutton, "because that's where the money is." In fact, many of today's attacks on systems use combinations of vulnerabilities in networks, operating systems, and applications, all means to an end to obtain the desired objective of an attack, which is usually some form of data.

Application-level attacks take advantage of several facts associated with computer applications. First, most applications are large programs written by groups of programmers, and by their nature have errors in design and coding that create vulnerabilities. For a list of typical vulnerabilities, see the Common Vulnerabilities and Exposures (CVE) list maintained by MITRE, http://cve.mitre.org. Second, even when vulnerabilities are discovered and patched by software vendors, end users are slow to apply patches, as evidenced by the SQL Slammer incident in January 2003. The vulnerability exploited was a buffer overflow, and the vendor supplied a patch six months prior to the outbreak, yet the worm still spread quickly due to the multitude of unpatched systems.

Cross-site Scripting

Cross-site scripting is abbreviated XSS to distinguish it from Cascading Style Sheets (CSS). A cross-site scripting attack is a code injection attack in which an attacker sends code in response to an input request. This code is then rendered by the web server, resulting in the execution of the code by the web server. Cross-site scripting attacks take advantage of a few common elements in web-based systems. First is the common failure to perform complete input validation. XSS sends script in response to an input request, even when script is not the expected or authorized input type. Second is the nature of web-based systems to dynamically self-create output. Web-based systems are frequently collections of images, content, text, scripts, and more, which are presented by a web server to a browser that interprets and renders the material into displayable form. XSS attacks can exploit the dynamically self-created output by executing a script in the client browser that receives the altered output.

Injections

Use of input to a function without validation has already been shown to be risky behavior. Another issue with unvalidated input is the case of *code injection*. Rather than the input being appropriate for the function, code injection changes the function in an unintended way. Whenever input-supplied material is used without validation, one should realize that this can give total control to an attacker.

SQL Injection

A SQL injection attack is a form of code injection aimed at any Structured Query Language (SQL)–based database, regardless of vendor. An example of this type of attack is where the function takes the user-provided inputs for username and password and substitutes them into a *where* clause of a SQL statement with the express purpose of changing the *where* clause into one that gives a false answer to the query.

Assume the desired SQL statement is

```
select count(*) from users_table where username = 'JDoe' and
password = 'newpass'
```

The values JDoe and newpass are provided from the user and are simply inserted into the string sequence. Though seemingly safe functionally, this can be easily corrupted by using the sequence

```
' or 1=1 —
```

since this changes the *where* clause to one that returns all records:

```
select count(*) from users_table where username = 'JDoe' and
password = '' or 1=1 —'
```

The addition of the *or* clause, with an always true statement and the beginning of a comment line to block the trailing single quote, alters the SQL statement to one in which the *where* clause is rendered inoperable.

LDAP Injection

LDAP-based systems are also subject to injection attacks. When an application constructs an LDAP request based on user input, a failure to validate the input can lead to bad LDAP requests. Just as the SQL injection can be used to execute arbitrary commands in a database, the LDAP injection can do the same in a directory system. Something as simple as a wildcard character (*) in a search box can return results that would normally be beyond the scope of a query. Proper input validation is important before passing the request to an LDAP engine.

XML Injection

XML can be tampered with via injection as well. XML injections can be used to manipulate an XML-based system. Because XML is nearly ubiquitous in the web application world, this form of attack has a wide range of targets.

The primary method of defense against injection attacks is similar to that for buffer overflows: validate all inputs. But rather than validating toward just length, you need to validate inputs for content. Imagine a web page that asks for user input, and then uses that input in the building of a subsequent page. Also imagine that the user puts the text for a JavaScript function in the middle of their input sequence, along with a call to the script. Now, the generated web page has an added JavaScript function that is called when displayed. Passing the user input through an **HtmlEncode** function before use can prevent such attacks.

 EXAM TIP For the exam, you should understand injection-type attacks and how they manipulate the systems they are injecting, SQL, LDAP, and XML.

Directory Traversal/Command Injection

A directory traversal attack is when an attacker uses special inputs to circumvent the directory tree structure of the file system. Adding encoded symbols for "../.." in an unvalidated input box can result in the parser resolving the encoding to the traversal code, bypassing many detection elements, and passing the input to the file system, resulting in the program executing commands in a different location than designed. When combined with a command injection, the input can result in execution of code in an unauthorized manner. Classified as an input validation error, these can be difficult to detect without doing code walkthroughs and specifically looking for them. This illustrates the usefulness of the top 25 programming errors checklist at code reviews, as it would alert developers to this issue during development.

Directory traversals can be masked by using encoding of input streams. If the security check is done before the string is decoded by the system parser, then recognition of the attack form may be impaired. There are many ways to represent a particular input form, the simplest is called the *canonical form*. Parsers are used to render the canonical form for the OS, but these embedded parsers may act after input validation, making it more difficult to detect certain attacks from just matching a string.

Buffer Overflow

A common weakness that attackers have often exploited is a buffer overflow. A *buffer overflow* occurs when a program is provided more data for input than it was designed to handle. For example, what would happen if a program that asks for a 7- to 10-character phone number instead receives a string of 150 characters? Many programs will provide some error checking to ensure that this will not cause a problem. Some programs, however, cannot handle this error, and the extra characters continue to fill memory, overwriting other portions of the program. This can result in a number of problems, including causing the program to abort or the system to crash. Under certain circumstances, the program can execute a command supplied by the attacker. Buffer overflows typically inherit the level of privilege enjoyed by the program being exploited. This is why programs that use root-level access are so dangerous when exploited with a buffer overflow, as the code that will execute does so at root-level access.

Buffer overflows have been shown to be exploitable in a wide range of programs, from UNIX, to Windows, to applications such as Internet Explorer, Firefox (Mozilla), and many more. Historically, more than 50 percent of the security incidents by type are due to buffer-overflow exploits. It is one of the most common hacks used, and the primary defense users have is to keep their machines up-to-date with patches from software manufacturers. Unfortunately, patching has not proven to be a very effective method of protection. Many people don't keep up-to-date with the patches, as demonstrated by the Slammer worm attack, which took place almost six months after Microsoft had released a patch specifically for the vulnerability. Even with the patch widely available, both in a hotfix and in a service pack, many SQL servers had not received the patch and were affected by this worm, which used a buffer overflow to propagate.

 EXAM TIP Buffer overflows can occur in any code, and code that runs with privilege has an even greater risk profile. In 2014, a buffer overflow in the OpenSSL library, called Heartbleed, left hundreds of thousands of systems vulnerable and exposed critical data for tens to hundreds of million users worldwide.

Buffer overflows are input validation attacks designed to take advantage of input routines that do not validate the length of inputs. Surprisingly simple to resolve, all that is required is the validation of all input lengths prior to writing to memory. This can be done in a variety of manners, including the use of safe library functions for inputs. This is one of the vulnerabilities that has been shown to be solvable, and in fact, the prevalence is declining substantially among major security-conscious software firms.

Integer Overflow

An *integer overflow* is a programming error condition that occurs when a program attempts to store a numeric value, an integer, in a variable that is too small to hold it. The results vary by language and numeric type. In some cases, the value saturates the variable, assuming the maximum value for the defined type and no more. In other cases, especially with signed integers, it can roll over into a negative value, as the most significant bit is usually reserved for the sign of the number. This can create significant logic errors in a program.

Integer overflows are easily tested for, and static code analyzers can point out where they are likely to occur. Given this, there are not any good excuses for having these errors end up in production code.

Zero-day

Zero-day is a term used to define vulnerabilities that are newly discovered and not yet addressed by a patch. Most vulnerabilities exist in an unknown state until discovered by a researcher or the developer. If a researcher or developer discovers a vulnerability but does not share the information, then this vulnerability can be exploited without a host's ability to fix it, because for all practical knowledge, the issue is unknown, except to the person who found it. From the time of discovery until a fix or patch is made available, the vulnerability goes by the name zero-day, indicating that it has not been addressed yet. The most frightening thing about zero-days is the unknown factor—their capability and effect on risk are unknown because they are unknown.

Cookies and Attachments

Cookies are small chunks of ASCII text passed within an HTTP stream to store data temporarily in a web browser instance. Invented by Netscape, cookies pass back and forth between web server and browser and act as a mechanism to maintain state in a stateless world. *State* is a term that describes the dependence on previous actions. By definition, HTTP traffic served by a web server is *stateless*—each request is completely independent of all previous requests, and the server has no memory of previous requests. This dramatically simplifies the function of a web server, but it also significantly complicates the task of providing anything but the most basic functionality in a site. Cookies were developed to bridge this gap. Cookies are passed along with HTTP data through a Set-Cookie message in the header portion of an HTTP message.

A cookie is actually a series of name-value pairs that is stored in memory during a browser instance. The specification for cookies established several specific name-value pairs for defined purposes. Additional name-value pairs may be defined at will by a developer. The specified set of name-value pairs include the following:

- **Expires** This field specifies when the cookie expires. If no value exists, the cookie is good only during the current browser session and will not be persisted to the user's hard drive. Should a value be given, the cookie will be written to the user's machine and persisted until this date-time value occurs.

- **Domain** This name-value pair specifies the domain where the cookie is used. Cookies were designed as memory-resident objects, but as the user or data can cause a browser to move between domains, say from comedy.net to jokes.org, some mechanism needs to tell the browser which cookies belong to which domains.

- **Path** This name-value pair further resolves the applicability of the cookie into a specific path within a domain. If path = /directory, the cookie will be sent only for requests within /directory on the given domain. This allows a level of granular control over the information being passed between the browser and server, and it limits unnecessary data exchanges.

- **Secure** The presence of the keyword [secure] in a cookie indicates that it is to be used only when connected in an SSL/TLS session. This does not indicate any other form of security, as cookies are stored in plaintext on the client machine. In fact, one browser-based security issue was the ability to read another site's cookies from the browser cache and determine the values by using a script.

Cookie management on a browser is normally an invisible process, but most browsers have methods for users to examine and manipulate cookies on the client side. Chrome users can examine, delete, and block individual cookies through the interface shown in Figure 14-1.

Internet Explorer has a similar interface, with just a Delete option in the browser under Browsing History (see Figure 14-2). Additional cookie manipulation can be done through the file processing system because cookies are stored as individual files, as shown in Figure 14-3. This combination allows easier bulk manipulation, which is a useful option, as cookies can become quite numerous in short order.

So what good are cookies? Disable cookies in your browser and go to some common sites that you visit, and you'll quickly learn the usefulness of cookies. Cookies store a variety of information, from customer IDs to data about previously visited websites. Because cookies are stored on a user's machine in a form that will allow simple

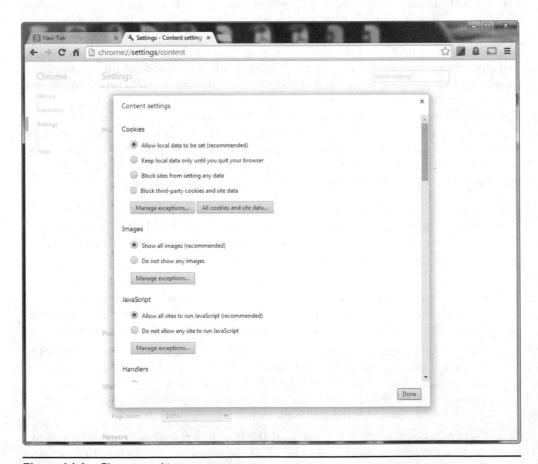

Figure 14-1   Chrome cookie management

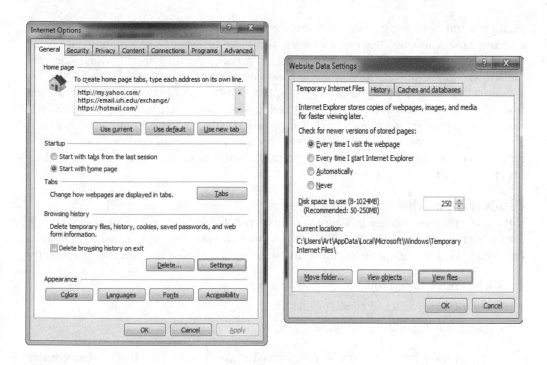

Figure 14-2   Internet Explorer 11 cookie management

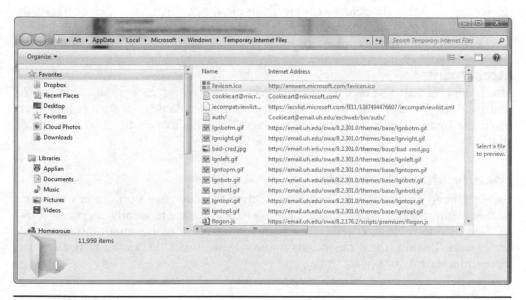

Figure 14-3   Internet Explorer 11 cookie store

PART III

manipulation, they must always be considered suspect and are not suitable for use as a security mechanism. They can, however, allow the browser to provide crucial pieces of information to a web server. Advertisers can use them to control which ads you are shown, based on previous ads you have viewed and regardless of ad location by site. Specific sites can use cookies to pass state information between pages, enabling functionality at the user's desired levels. Cookies can also remember your ZIP code for a weather site, your ID for a stock tracker site, the items in your shopping cart—these are all typical cookie uses. In the end analysis, cookies are a part of daily web experience, here to stay and useful if not used improperly (such as to store security data and to provide ID and authentication).

Disabling Cookies

If the user disables cookies in a browser, this type of information will not be available for the web server to use. IETF RFC 2109 describes the HTTP state-management system (cookies) and specifies several cookie functions to be enabled in browsers, specifically

- The ability to turn on and off cookie usage
- An indicator as to whether cookies are in use
- A means of specifying cookie domain values and lifetimes

Several of these functions have already been discussed, but to surf cookie-free requires more than a simple step. Telling a browser to stop accepting cookies is a setup option available through an Options menu, but this has no effect on cookies already received and stored on the system. To prevent the browser from sending cookies already received, the user must delete the cookies from the system. This bulk operation is easily performed, and then the browser can run cookie-free. Several third-party tools enable even a finer granularity of cookie control.

Attachments

Attachments can also be used as an attack vector. If a user inputs a graphics file, for instance, a JPEG file, and that file is altered to contain executable code such as Java, then when the image is rendered, the code is executed. This can enable a wide range of attacks.

Locally Shared Objects

Locally shared objects (LSOs) are pieces of data that are stored on a user's machine to save information from an application, such as a game. Frequently, these are cookies used by Adobe Flash, called Flash Cookies, and can store information such as user preferences. Because these can be manipulated outside of the application, they can represent a security or privacy threat.

Malicious Add-ons

Add-ons are pieces of code that are distributed to allow additional functionality to be added to an existing program. An example of these are browser helper objects (BHOs), which provide a means of creating a plug-in module that is loaded with Internet Explorer and provide a means of adding capability to the browser. The functionality can be significant, as in the case of the Adobe Acrobat BHO that allows PDFs to be rendered in the browser. A BHO has unrestricted access to the Internet Explorer event model and can do things such as capture keystrokes.

Other programs can have add-ons that utilize the permissions given the master program. You should only use add-ons from trusted sources, and you need to understand the level of interaction risk they pose. ActiveX is a technology implemented by Microsoft to enhance web-enabled systems through significant additions to user controls. Unless signed by a trusted authority using Authenticode, ActiveX content should not be allowed in browsers, as the nature of the code changes can present significant risk.

Session Hijacking

When communicating across the Web, it is common to create a session to control communication flows. Sessions can be established and controlled using a variety of methods including SSL/TLS and cookies. It is important to securely implement the set-up and teardown of a session, for if one party ends the communication without properly tearing down the communication session, an interloper can take over the session, continue after one of the parties has left, and impersonate that party. If you log in to your bank to conduct transactions, but allow a session hijacker in, then the hijacker can continue banking after you leave using your account. This is one of the reasons it is so important to log off of banking and financial sites, rather than just closing the browser.

There are numerous methods of session hijacking, from man-in-the-middle attacks, to sidejacking and browser takeovers. Sidejacking is the use of packet sniffing to steal a session cookie. Securing only the logon process and then switching back to standard HTTP can enable this attack methodology.

The best defenses are to use encryption correctly (no SSL 2.0 or before) and to log out of and close applications when done. When using multitabbed browsers, it is best to close the entire browser instance, not just the tab.

Client-Side Attacks

The web browser has become the major application for users to engage resources across the Web. The popularity and the utility of this interface have made the web browser a prime target for attackers to gain access and control over a system. A wide variety of attacks can occur via a browser, typically resulting from a failure to properly validate input before use. Unvalidated input can result in a series of injection attacks, header manipulation, and other forms of attack.

Injection Attacks

When user input is used without input validation, this results in an opportunity for an attacker to craft input to create specific events to occur when the input is parsed and used by an application. SQL injection attacks involve the manipulation of input, resulting in a SQL statement that is different than intended by the designer. XML and LDAP injections are done in the same fashion. Because SQL, XML, and LDAP are used to store data, this can give an attacker access to data against business rules. Command injection attacks can occur when input is used in a fashion that allows command-line manipulation. This can give an attacker command-line access at the privilege level of the application.

Header Manipulations

When HTTP is being dynamically generated through the use of user inputs, unvalidated inputs can give attackers an opportunity to change HTTP elements. When user-supplied information is used in a header, it is possible to create a variety of attacks, including cache poisoning, cross-site scripting, cross-user defacement, page hijacking, cookie manipulation, or open redirect.

 EXAM TIP A wide variety of attack vectors can be used against a client machine, including cache poisoning, cross-site scripting, cross-user defacement, page hijacking, cookie manipulation, and open redirect. All attacks should be known for the exam.

Arbitrary/Remote Code Execution

One of the risks involved in taking user input and using it to create a command to be executed on a system is arbitrary or remote code execution. This attack involves an attacker preparing an input statement that changes the form or function of a prepared statement. A form of command injection, this attack can allow a user to insert arbitrary code and then remotely execute it on a system. This is a form of an input validation failure, as users should not have the ability to change the way a program interacts with the host OS outside of a set of defined and approved methods.

Chapter Review

In this chapter, you explored application and wireless attacks. The chapter opened with a discussion of wireless attacks, including rogue access points, jamming and interference, evil twin, Bluetooth attacks (bluejacking, bluesnarfing, and bluebugging), and war chalking and war driving. It then covered attacks against encryption, including IV attacks, WEP/WPA attacks, and WPS attacks. For the exam, you will be expected to be able to explain these types of attacks.

The second half of the chapter presented application attacks, beginning with cross-site scripting. Injection attacks followed, including SQL, LDAP, XML, and directory traversal/command injections. Overflow attacks, including buffer and integer, were presented. The category of zero-day attacks was defined. The chapter continued with cookies, malicious add-ons, session hijacking, and header manipulation. Arbitrary code execution and remote code execution completed the material in the chapter. The exam expects you to be able to explain these types of application attacks.

Questions

To help you prepare further for the CompTIA Security+ exam, and to test your level of preparedness, answer the following questions and then check your answers against the correct answers at the end of the chapter.

1. What is being compromised during an IV attack?

   A. A weak SSID

   B. The user's authentication credentials

   C. Wi-Fi

   D. Encryption

2. What makes a website vulnerable to SQL injection?

   A. Poorly filtered input fields

   B. A website that has a Microsoft SQL database powering it

   C. Overly long text input boxes

   D. Low password strength requirements

3. A list of Wi-Fi access points in an area is most likely generated by?

   A. WEP cracking attacks

   B. Rouge access points

   C. War driving

   D. War chalking

4. Why is the buffer overflow such a popular attack?

   A. It is easy to accomplish over the Internet.

   B. Attackers can use it to break any encryption.

   C. The same code will work on any system.

   D. It can provide arbitrary code execution.

5. How can you prevent bluesnarfing?

   A. Use WPA2.

   B. Turn off pairing when not actively adding a device.

   C. Do not use a headset with the phone.

   D. Change your phone's MAC address.

6. Why is cross-site scripting successful?

    A. It uses a different memory register every time.

    B. Its code runs in an encrypted state.

    C. It uses zero-day vulnerabilities.

    D. It folds malicious code in with verified content from a compromised site.

7. How is near field communication like Ethernet?

    A. It does not enforce security itself, but relies on higher-level protocols such as SSL.

    B. It forces each endpoint to communicate through a switch.

    C. It provides collision avoidance.

    D. All of the above.

8. Why is free Wi-Fi, such as in coffee shops, a popular target for session hijacking?

    A. The unsecured Wi-Fi allows an attacker to place malicious files on the user's machine.

    B. The site uses a captive portal.

    C. Unsecured Wi-Fi allows the attacker to sniff the wireless session for a user's session cookie.

    D. The user does not engage VPN over wireless.

9. What makes rouge access points a threat?

    A. They are loaded with malware.

    B. They potentially allow any person access to the corporate network.

    C. They only support WEP, which is easily broken.

    D. Wireless signals are short range, so extra access points are not a threat.

10. Why would an integer overflow be a security issue?

    A. It can crash applications.

    B. It can cause applications to corrupt data.

    C. It can create buffer overflow opportunities.

    D. All of the above.

For questions 11–15, assume the following: You are administering your corporate website, which includes an e-commerce capability, and have been given responsibility for security on the website.

11. What threats will you attempt to eliminate through input sanitization? (Choose the best two answers for the web server.)

    A. Buffer overflows

    B. SQL injection

    C. Cross-site scripting

    D. LDAP injection

    E. Header manipulation

    F. War driving

12. What change should you make to prevent session hijacking?

    A. Encrypt cookie files.

    B. Sanitize all the input fields.

    C. Outsource your site to the cloud.

    D. Apply SSL to the entire site, instead of just the login page.

13. You have seen several users attempting to perform directory traversal attacks on your site. What action will you take?

    A. Add firewall rules to block those users.

    B. Check web access control lists and validate all directory permissions.

    C. Update your web server software to the most current version.

    D. Use SSL on all session traffic, not just the login traffic.

14. Due to your good work on the website, the CISO has asked for your help with random behavior occurring on the Wi-Fi system. In some parts of the building the wireless signal is available but does not allow any traffic through. What measures could help with this issue? (Choose all that apply.)

    A. Conduct a site survey.

    B. Enable WPA2.

    C. Find rouge access points.

    D. Search for sources of interference.

    E. Perform capacity planning.

15. Your site survey has discovered hidden in the ceiling a rouge access point resembling one of the fire detectors. What type of device is this likely to be?

    A. An AP bought at the office supply store to boost the Wi-Fi signal near the sales department cubes

    B. Part of the normal corporate wireless LAN that is simply designed to blend in with the office

    C. A custom wireless evil twin that is attempting to gather user information

    D. A bluesnarfer

Answers

1. **D.** An initialization vector (IV) attack seeks to attack the implementation of encryption around the way the cipher initializes. This is a known weakness in the WEP encryption standard for Wi-Fi networks.

2. **A.** SQL injection is accomplished by using a delimiter or other SQL command structures inside an input field that has poor input filtering. The web page then passes the field on to the database, which then executes the injected command.

3. **C.** War driving involves driving around with a wireless scanner and GPS and logging the location of Wi-Fi access points.

4. **D.** The buffer overflow is a popular attack because it can provide arbitrary code execution by inserting the code directly into memory.

5. **B.** Bluesnarfing depends on pairing to the mobile device, so turning off pairing stops the bluesnarfing attack.

6. **D.** Cross-site scripting folds malicious content, typically from a third-party website, into a portion of the verified content delivered correctly from the web server.

7. **A.** Near field communication does not have an integrated encryption functionality and relies on higher-level protocols to provide security.

8. **C.** Frequently, SSL is only used for a website's login page, so an attacker sniffing the Wi-Fi could capture the user's session cookie and use it to impersonate the user.

9. **B.** A rouge access point established outside of IT's control will typically let anyone who can detect the access point connect to the internal corporate network.

10. **D.** All of the answers are correct. An integer overflow can occur when two large numbers are added and go beyond the specified number of integers, resulting in a very small number. This can lead to unexpected application behavior.

11. **B** and **D** (SQL injection and LDAP injection) are the best answers. Sanitizing input helps ensure that no raw commands are passed directly to supporting applications.

12. **D.** Session hijacking can be prevented by using encryption for the entire site, preventing an attacker from stealing an already established user session.

13. **B.** Directory traversal attacks center on executing items that should not be accessible to external users. Proper permissions and removal of all unnecessary execute rights will assist in mitigating the attack.

14. **A, C,** and **D.** These measures would help determine the possible causes of poor wireless signals localized to a specific area. Interference can be caused by devices emitting 2.4-GHz signals, such as cordless phones or microwave ovens. Rouge access points are often configured on the default channel, which can interfere with the properly configured corporate wireless system. Site surveys can identify dead spots and possible bad equipment.

15. **C.** A wireless evil twin is likely to be disguised to avoid detection while it attempts to capture user accounts from unsuspecting wireless users.

Mitigation Techniques

In this chapter, you will

- Learn how to select the appropriate type of mitigation and deterrent technique
- Learn how monitoring of system logs can mitigate risk
- Learn how system hardening can mitigate risk
- Learn how employing network security techniques can mitigate risk

A part of any security strategy is the mitigation of the effect of risk. There are some standard methods used as common mitigation techniques. Different situations call for different mitigation techniques. This chapter explores the common standard mitigation techniques.

Monitoring System Logs

Log files are records of activity: what happened, when it happened, who did it, where it came from, and so on. Although many administrators dread the auditing and analysis of log files, the simple truth is that effective logging and analysis of log files can be excellent tools for maintaining and securing a network. The first and most critical step is to enable logging on systems and network devices and ensure that the correct activities are logged. Logging failed logins is good, but logging each time a common file is successfully accessed by a legitimate user may be overkill. Determining what to log, how to log it, and how long to maintain audit logs are topics of lengthy discussions among system administrators.

One of the key determinants for deciding what should be logged is an examination of what information needs to be kept as part of a forensic record. Logging events as they happen allows investigators to examine activity after the fact by consulting the log. Logs by themselves are not a panacea, for they need to be examined and interpreted to be useful, and this requires an ongoing effort and resources to examine the logs. This is the second key determinant of what should be logged—logging items that are never reviewed is a common problem.

Common Logs

Many events in a computer system can be logged. Events from different levels of the OSI model can all be logged in a common logging scheme. Maintaining logs on a remote server offers security and simplicity in maintaining a centralized log monitoring solution. Following are examples of some areas where logging is effective and necessary:

- **Security applications**   Generically, a "security application" can be anything that helps assess or secure the network. Any security application that has the ability to generate a log file should be configured to do so, and the resulting logs should be analyzed on a regular basis.

- **DNS**   A DNS server can be configured to log transactions—resolution requests, updates made or attempted, requests forwarded for resolution, and so on. DNS log files should be audited to help identify attempted intrusions, attacks, fraudulent updates, poisoning attempts, and so on.

- **System**   System logs track events on the system—failures, program crashes, system shutdowns and restarts, process start and stop times, and so on. System logs can be valuable tools in identifying suspicious, undesirable, or malicious activity.

- **Performance**   Performance logs track items such as memory usage, CPU usage, disk usage, network traffic, and so on. Performance logs can be another good indicator of malicious activity, as the system may be either unusually "busy" or unusually "quiet" when compared to normal levels.

- **Event**   Event logs are a form of application log that tracks what is occurring on a system.

- **Access**   Tracking which user accessed a certain resource, how they used it, what they did to or with that resource, and when the access occurred is a crucial logging activity. Auditing access logs can be an excellent method of detecting malicious activity, lapses in proper user management, and other activities.

- **Firewall**   Firewall activity logs track attempted connections, network volume, source addresses, destination addresses, ports used, and so on. Firewall logs should be audited periodically to ensure that the firewall is functioning as intended, to help identify common sources of attack traffic, to identify commonly targeted systems and services, and so on.

- **Antivirus**   Antivirus logs often track infected e-mails or files, the sources of offending e-mails or files, update status, scanning activity, and so on. Periodic auditing is required to ensure the antivirus program is providing the desired level of protection and is effectively scanning e-mail traffic and systems.

- **IDS/IPS**   Intrusion detection system and intrusion prevention system logs are also excellent sources of tracking suspicious, undesirable, or malicious activities. These logs can identify attack traffic, sources of attack traffic, targeted resources, possible and actual compromises, data loss, and other information.

Periodic Audits of Security Settings

As part of any good security program, administrators must perform periodic audits to ensure things "are as they should be" with regard to users, systems, policies, and procedures. Installing and configuring security mechanisms is important, but they must be reviewed on a regularly scheduled basis to ensure they are effective, up-to-date, and serving their intended function. Here are some examples, but by no means a complete list, of items that should be audited on a regular basis:

- **User access**   Administrators should review which users are accessing the systems, when they are doing so, what resources they are using, and so on. Administrators should look closely for users accessing resources improperly or accessing legitimate resources at unusual times.

- **User rights**   When a user changes jobs or responsibilities, she will likely need to be assigned different access permissions; she may gain access to new resources and lose access to others. To ensure that users have access only to the resources and capabilities they need for their current positions, all user rights should be audited periodically.

- **Storage**   Many organizations have policies governing what can be stored on "company" resources and how much space can be used by a given user or group. Periodic audits help to ensure that no undesirable or illegal materials exist on organizational resources.

- **Retention**   How long a particular document or record is stored can be as important as what is being stored in some organizations. A records retention policy helps to define what is stored, how it is stored, how long it is stored, and how it is disposed of when the time comes. Periodic audits help to ensure that records or documents are removed when they are no longer needed.

- **Firewall rules**   Periodic audits of firewall rules are important to ensure the firewall is filtering traffic as desired and to help ensure that "temporary" rules do not end up as permanent additions to the rule set.

EXAM TIP   Logging, reviewing logs, and performing audits are standard security tasks, and you should be familiar with the standard log types for the exam.

System Hardening

A key element in maintaining security in an enterprise is the security posture of the hardware and software employed in the infrastructure of the enterprise. Ensuring that systems are properly configured and all systems are patched and up-to-date is a key component of a secure enterprise. The many uses for systems and operating systems require flexible components that allow users to design, configure, and implement the systems they need. Yet it is this very flexibility that causes some of the biggest weaknesses in computer systems. Computer and operating system developers often build and deliver systems in "default" modes that do little to secure the system from external attacks. From the view of the developer, this is the most efficient mode of delivery, as there is no way they could anticipate what every user in every situation will need. From the user's view, however, this means a good deal of effort must be put into protecting and securing the system before it is ever placed into service. The process of securing and preparing a system for the production environment is called *hardening*. Unfortunately, many users don't understand the steps necessary to secure their systems effectively, resulting in hundreds of compromised systems every day.

 EXAM TIP System hardening is the process of preparing and securing a system and involves the removal of all unnecessary software and network services.

Disabling Unused Interfaces and Unused Application Service Ports

The key management issue for running a secure system setup is to identify the specific needs of a system for its proper operation and to enable only items necessary for those functions. Keeping all other services and users off the system improves system throughput and increases security. Reducing the attack surface area associated with a server reduces the vulnerabilities now and in the future as updates are required.

 EXAM TIP Specific security needs vary depending on the server's specific use, but as a minimum, the following precautions are beneficial:

- Remove unnecessary protocols such as Telnet, NetBIOS, Internetwork Packet Exchange (IPX), and File Transfer Protocol (FTP).

- Remove all shares that are not necessary.

- Disable all services and ports that are not needed; simple TCP services such as ECHO, CHARGEN, and so on should typically be disabled as part of any system hardening process.

- Rename the administrator account, securing it with a strong password.

- Remove unnecessary user accounts.

- Keep the OS patched and up to date.

- Control physical access to servers.

Once a server has been built and is ready to place into operation, the recording of hash values on all of its crucial files will provide valuable information later in case of a question concerning possible system integrity after a detected intrusion. The use of hash values to detect changes was first developed by Gene Kim and Eugene Spafford at Purdue University in 1992. The concept became the product Tripwire, which is now available in commercial and open source forms. The same basic concept is used by many security packages to detect file-level changes.

Protecting Management Interfaces and Applications

Some machines have "management interfaces" that allow for remote management of the devices themselves. A management interface allows connections to the device's management application, an SSH service, or even a web-based configuration GUI that are not allowed on any other interface. Due to this high level of access, management interfaces and management applications must be secured against unauthorized access. They should not be connected to public network connections (that is, the Internet) or to DMZ connections. Where possible, access to management interfaces and applications should be restricted within an organization so that employees without the proper access rights and privileges cannot even connect to those interfaces and applications.

Password Protection

Password protection is one of those critical activities that is often neglected as part of a good security baseline. The heart of the problem is that most systems today are protected only by a simple user ID and password. If an attacker discovers the right user ID and password combination—either by hand or by using any of the numerous, freely available brute-force attack tools—they are in, and they have completely bypassed all the normal steps taken to secure the system. Worse still, on a server system supporting multiple users, the attacker only has to guess one correct user ID and password combination to gain access.

This basic security challenge exists for every topic we examine in this chapter, from operating systems to applications. Selecting a good password for all user accounts is critical to protecting information systems. What makes a good password? One that is still relatively easy to remember but still difficult to guess? Unfortunately, no magic answer covers all situations, but if you follow some basic guidelines and principles in choosing passwords, you can ensure that the passwords used on your system will protect your assets.

Password Policy Guidelines

Requiring a username and password for authentication is arguably the most popular security mechanism in use today. Unfortunately, it's also the most poorly configured, neglected, and easily circumvented system. The first step in addressing the password issue is to create an effective and manageable *password policy* that system administrators and users alike can work with. In creating a policy, you should examine your business and security needs carefully. What level of risk is acceptable? How secure does the system need to be? How often should users change their passwords? Should you ever lock accounts? What guidelines should users use when selecting passwords? Your list of questions will vary greatly, but the key is to spend time identifying your concerns and addressing them specifically in your password policy.

PART III

Once you have created your password policy, spread the word. Make sure every user gets a copy. Post it on your company intranet. Have new users read a copy of the policy before you create an account for them. Periodically send out e-mail reminders highlighting items in the password policy. Make announcements at company gatherings. The method is less important than the goal, which is simply to ensure that every single user understands the policy—and follows it.

Once you have taught everyone about the policy, you must enforce it to make it effective. Set a minimum number of characters to use for passwords, and never accept a shorter password. Implement password aging (discussed a bit later) and prompt users to change passwords on a regular basis. Do not accept passwords based on dictionary words. Do not allow users to use the same password over and over. Many operating systems have built-in utilities or add-ons that allow administrators to enforce good password selection, force password aging, and prevent password reuse.

Take the time to audit your own password files by running some of the popular password cracking utilities against them. In a large organization with many user accounts (more than a thousand), this will take some time and computing power, but it is well worth the effort. Perform these audits as often as you can—monthly, every other month, or every quarter. If you find accounts with easily cracked passwords, have the users review the password policy and change their passwords immediately.

Most password auditing/cracking tools can examine a password file using any or all of the following techniques:

- **Dictionary attack**   Uses a list of words as potential passwords. The tool reads each word from the list, encrypts it, and then attempts to match the encrypted result against the passwords in the password file. If the encrypted result matches a password from the password file, the tool records the user ID and the matching password. This attack method is named after the practice of using entire dictionaries as the input list; many dictionary and specialized dictionary files are available for use in cracking/auditing efforts.

- **Hybrid attack**   Uses a word list and performs character substitutions or character additions on those words. For example, the tool might add numbers to the beginning or end of a word or substitute the number 3 for the letter *e*. This method takes longer than a straight dictionary attack using the same word list, because multiple modifications are made to each word in the list.

- **Brute force**   The user defines the character set to use (A–Z, a–z, 0–9, and so on) and the minimum and maximum length of the password string. Then the tool proceeds to guess every possible combination of characters using the defined character set and password length (*a*, then *aa*, then *aaa*, and so on). This method takes a substantial amount of time and processing power.

Another password auditing/cracking method that has gained popularity is the use of rainbow tables. A *rainbow table* is a lookup table of precomputed password strings (usually called *hashes*). Using a lookup table of precomputed hashes can reduce the time and processing power required to audit/crack some password files, as the attacker does not need to compute the hash on-the-fly—he can simply read the already encrypted hash from the rainbow table and match it against the password file. Not all auditing/ cracking tools can make use of rainbow tables.

Selecting a Password

The many different methods of selecting a password range from random generation to one-time use. Each method has its own advantages and weaknesses, but typically when security increases, usability tends to decrease. For example, random generation tends to produce secure passwords composed of random letters (no dictionary words, and a mix of uppercase and lowercase letters with usually one or two numbers) that are very difficult to guess and will defeat most password-cracking utilities. Unfortunately, randomly generated passwords tend to be difficult to remember, and users often write down these passwords, usually in a location close to the machine, thus defeating the purpose of the password. The best compromise between security and usability lies in teaching users how to select their own secure password based on an easy-to-remember passphrase.

A password based on a passphrase can be formed in many ways: using the first letter of each word in a sentence; using the first letter from the first word, second letter from the second word, and so on; combining words; or replacing letters with other characters. Here are some passphrase examples and the resulting passwords:

- Use the first letter of each word in the following sentence:
  Sentence   I love to drive my 1969 Mustang!
  Password   Iltdm69M!

- Combining words and replacing letters with characters:
  Sentence   Bad to the Bone
  Password   Bad2theB1

Passphrases can be almost anything—lines from your favorite movie, lyrics from your favorite song, or something you make up on the spot. Use any method you choose, but the end result should be a difficult-to-guess, easy-to-remember password.

Components of a Good Password

By using the passphrase method, users should be able to create their own easy-to-remember passwords. However, since a password is meant to protect access and resources from intruders, it should not be easy for someone else to guess or obtain using password-cracking utilities, such as John the Ripper or Crack. To make a password more difficult to guess or obtain, it should meet the following guidelines:

- Should be at least eight characters long (some operating systems require longer passwords by default)

- Should have at least three of the following four elements:
  - One or more uppercase letters (A–Z)
  - One or more lowercase letters (a–z)

- One or more numerals (0–9)
- One or more special characters or punctuation marks (!@#$%^&*,.:;?)
- Should not consist of dictionary words
- Should never be the same as the user's login name or contain the login name
- Should not consist of the user's first or last name, family member's name, birth date, pet name, or any other item that is easily identified with the user

Password Aging

Given enough time and computing power, virtually any password can be cracked by simply testing all possible passwords using the brute-force method. If the same password is used forever, an attacker will, in most cases, eventually be able to get the password and access the user's account. Changing passwords on a regular basis helps protect against brute-force attacks because when the password is changed, the attacker must restart the attack from the beginning. If the password is changed often enough, an attacker will never be able to cycle through all the possible combinations before the password is changed again.

Because almost any password can be cracked eventually, it is also important to prevent users from "recycling" passwords (using the same password over and over). Changing passwords frequently can also reduce the potential damage to the system and access an attacker has should a password be compromised. If an attacker gains access to a user account and the password is changed, the attacker may lose access to that account and have to start all over in an attempt to crack the new password. Many operating systems have options allowing system administrators to enforce password aging and prevent password reuse. Consider using the following guidelines:

- Have users change their passwords every 60 to 90 days (very secure facilities may want to change passwords every 30 to 45 days).
- Have the system "remember" each user's last five to ten passwords, and do not allow the user to use those passwords again.

While ensuring that every account has a decent password is essential, it is also a very good idea to simply disable or delete unnecessary accounts. If your system does not need to support guest or anonymous accounts, then disable them. When user or administrator accounts are no longer needed, remove or disable them. As a best practice, all user accounts should be audited periodically to ensure that there are no unnecessary, outdated, or unneeded accounts on your systems.

Disabling Unused Accounts

Adding new user accounts is a necessary task when new users are added to a system. Maintaining a good list of which users still require access at later times is a more challenging task. User account maintenance is an important hardening task. All new accounts being added or privileges being increased should be logged and monitored. Whenever an employee leaves a firm, all associated accounts should be disabled to prevent further access. Disabling is preferable to removal, as removal may result in permission and ownership problems. Periodic audits of user accounts to ensure they still need access is also a good security measure.

Network Security

While considering the baseline security of systems, you must consider the role the network connection plays in the overall security profile. The tremendous growth of the Internet and the affordability of multiple PCs and Ethernet networking have resulted in almost every computer being attached to some kind of network, and once computers are attached to a network, they are open to access from any other user on that network. Proper controls over network access must be established on computers by controlling the services that are running and the ports that are opened for network access. In addition to servers and workstations, however, network devices must also be examined: routers, switches, and modems, as well as other various components.

Today's network infrastructure components are similar to other computing devices on the network—they have dedicated hardware that runs an OS, typically with one or more open ports for direct connection to the OS, as well as ports supporting various network services. Any flaws in the coding of the OS can be exploited to gain access, as with any "regular" computer. These network devices should be configured with very strict parameters to maintain network security. Like normal computer OSs that need to be patched and updated, the software that runs network infrastructure components needs to be updated regularly. Finally, an outer layer of security should be added by implementing appropriate firewall rules and router ACLs.

Network Software Updates

Maintaining current vendor patch levels for your software is one of the most important things you can do to maintain security. This is also true for the infrastructure that runs the network. While some equipment is unmanaged and typically has no network presence and few security risks, any managed equipment that is responding on network ports will have some software or firmware controlling it. This software or firmware needs to be updated on a regular basis.

The most common device that connects people to the Internet is the network router. Dozens of brands of routers are available on the market, but Cisco Systems products dominate. The popular Internetwork Operating System (IOS) runs on more than 70 of Cisco's devices and is installed countless times at countless locations. Its popularity has fueled research into vulnerabilities in the code, and over the past few years, quite a few vulnerabilities have been reported. These vulnerabilities can take many forms, as routers send and receive several different kinds of traffic, from the standard Telnet remote terminal, to routing information in the form of Routing Information Protocol (RIP) or Open Shortest Path First (OSPF) packets, to Simple Network Management Protocol (SNMP) packets. This highlights the need to update the IOS software on a regular basis.

Cisco IOS also runs on many of Cisco's Ethernet switching products. Like routers, these have capabilities for receiving and processing protocols such as Telnet and SNMP. Smaller network components do not usually run large software suites and typically have smaller software loaded on internal nonvolatile RAM (NVRAM). While the update process for this kind of software is typically called a *firmware update*, this does not change the security implications of keeping it up to date. In the case of a corporate network with several devices, someone must take ownership of updating the devices, and updates must be performed regularly according to security and administration policies.

Network Device Configuration

As important as it is to keep software up to date, properly configuring network devices is equally, if not more, important. Many network devices, such as routers and switches, now have advanced remote management capabilities with multiple open ports accepting network connections. Proper configuration is necessary to keep these devices secure. Choosing a good password is very important in maintaining external and internal security, and closing or limiting access to any open ports is also a good step for securing the devices. On the more advanced devices, you must carefully consider what services the device is running, just as with a computer.

 EXAM TIP Remember that while a router is essentially just a device that forwards packets between networks, it can also be used to help secure the network by controlling traffic flowing into and leaving your network.

In many cases, a network device's primary protection method is a password. Good passwords are one of the most effective security tools, because a good password can be resistant to several forms of attack. This resistance makes an attacker use simple brute-force methods, taking tremendous amounts of time and generating a large amount of network traffic, both increasing the likelihood of the attacker's efforts being detected. Unfortunately, good passwords are often hard to remember, so weaker passwords are usually used.

To recognize the impact on security that a bad password can have, consider the fact that a typical brute-force program can try every word in the unabridged English dictionary in less than a day, but it would take several thousand years to attempt to brute force an eight-character password. This is based upon using not only the standard 26-character alphabet, but also adding capitalization for 26 more characters, numeric digits for 10 more, and special characters, adding another 32 different characters. This totals 94 different characters that can be used, giving 6,704,780,954,517,120, or 6 quadrillion, different possibilities for a one- to eight-character password. This is in stark contrast to the estimated 2 million words in the English language, or the 217 billion possibilities provided by simple lowercase alphabetic characters.

The best kinds of passwords bear no resemblance to actual words, such as "AvhB42^&nFh." However, although such passwords provide greater security, they are difficult to remember, leading users to choose passwords that are based on regular dictionary words. While this is a concern for any password on any system, it is of greater concern on network infrastructure equipment, because many pieces of network equipment require only password authentication for access—typically, no username is required.

One of the password-related issues that many administrators overlook is SNMP, which was developed in 1988 and has been implemented on a huge variety of network devices. Its wide implementation is directly related to its simplicity and extensibility. Since every manufacturer can add objects to the Management Information Base (MIB), one manufacturer can add functionality without interfering with any other manufacturer's portion of the MIB tree. This feature of the protocol lets manufacturers make SNMP very powerful for configuration and monitoring purposes. The downside is that many devices have SNMP turned on by default. Network administrators not using SNMP will often forget to disable SNMP or will forget to change the well-known default passwords—typically "public" for read-only access and "private" for read/write access. With the SNMP service active and using a default password, an attacker can retrieve a great deal of interesting information from a network device, as well as altering any SNMP-capable settings. If SNMP is employed, well-thought-out passwords should be used, as well as a schedule for password updates.

 EXAM TIP   The use of the word "public" as a public SNMP community string is an extremely well-known vulnerability. Any system using an SNMP community string of "public" should be changed immediately.

Keep in mind that SNMP passwords are often passed in the clear, so it should never be treated as a trusted protocol. The SNMP service should also be limited only to connections from the management station's IP address. If SNMP is not used, the service should be disabled, if possible. Otherwise, the ports for SNMP should not be accessible from anywhere on the external or internal network.

Another best practice for network devices is to eliminate the use of cleartext protocols such as Telnet and implement more secure alternatives such as *SSH*. SSH (Secure Shell) is an encrypted protocol that can be used to create a command-line–based connection to remote network devices and servers. Unlike Telnet, SSH is encrypted from end to end, so anything that is typed within an SSH session cannot be easily intercepted and viewed by potential attackers.

As with any system, security is largely dependent on proper configuration of the system itself. A router can be secured with proper configuration just as easily as it can be left unsecured through poor configuration. Good passwords and knowledge of what services the devices are running are important to maintaining the security of those devices.

802.1x

As described in Chapter 2, 802.1x acts a method of limiting access to a network to only authorized users. Also known as *port-based network access control*, 802.1x is an IEEE standard and part of the IEEE 802.1 network protocol set. Employing edge-based access control for all systems increases the security posture. 802.1x is port-based security that ensures that authentication occurs before allowing a device to connect to a port.

EXAM TIP 802.1x is an authentication method that controls access to a port on a device and is also called port-based network access control or port-based authentication.

MAC Limiting and Filtering

The use of MAC addresses to perform port-level security on switches adds a layer of security to the system. This layer of security ensures that the hardware associated with the network is approved for use and connected as designed. This prevents the insertion of unauthorized communication channels into the network layer. MAC filtering can be very useful to ensure that the network connections are not rerouted to other machines, or that unauthorized connections to existing network jacks do not occur.

MAC limiting is the use of setting a limit to the number of MAC addresses a switch or port can learn. This prevents a wide variety of attacks including flooding attacks, as it ignores large numbers of "new" MAC addresses. Ports can also be constrained to specific MACs or groups of MACs to limit the ability of outside connections to a network.

Disabling Unused Interfaces and Unused Application Service Ports

Just as in servers, an important management issue for running a secure system is to identify the specific needs of a system for its proper operation and to enable only items necessary for those functions. Keeping all other services and users off the system improves system throughput and increases security. Networks have ports and connections that need to be disabled if not in use. If a switch is prewired to outlets in rooms that are not used, these ports should be disabled until needed, preventing an attacker from using unused ports. Similarly, management interfaces and other options should be restricted and disabled if not actively used to prevent unauthorized use of these network functions. An attacker that gains access to a network device can reconfigure the device if open management interfaces are discoverable and used. Reducing the attack surface area associated with the network configuration reduces the vulnerabilities now and in the future as updates are required.

EXAM TIP When designing and building out a network, any ports or functions that are not actively used should be disabled until needed, and only then enabled for use. This minimalist setup is similar to the implicit deny philosophy and can significantly reduce an attack surface.

Rogue Machine Detection

One method of infiltrating a network is through the installation of rogue devices. Another case is where a user adds a device for some unauthorized purpose, such as a local wireless access point. These devices and network changes pose a variety of security issues, and thus it is important to detect rogue or unauthorized devices. The concept of bring your own device (BYOD) has raised the level of rogue device risks, and having mechanisms in place to detect and isolate them is important in critical sections of an enterprise network.

Security Posture

The security posture of a system is a function of its configuration and settings, and the set of users that have the ability to modify these settings. Properly setting up a system and then ensuring that only authorized users can change these settings is an important step in setting up a secure system.

Initial Baseline Configuration

To secure systems effectively and consistently, you must take a structured and logical approach. This starts with an examination of the system's intended functions and capabilities to determine what processes and applications will be housed on the system. As a best practice, anything that is not required for operations should be removed or disabled on the system; then all the appropriate patches, hotfixes, and settings are applied to protect and secure it.

This process of establishing a system's security state is called *baselining*, and the resulting product is a security *baseline* that allows the system to run safely and securely. Once the process has been completed for a particular hardware and software combination, any similar systems can be configured with the same baseline and achieve the same level and depth of security and protection. Uniform baselines are critical in large-scale operations, as maintaining separate configurations and security levels for hundreds or thousands of systems is far too costly.

After administrators have finished patching, securing, and preparing a system, they often create an initial baseline configuration. This represents a secure state for the system or network device and a reference point that can be used to help keep the system secure. If this initial baseline can be replicated, it can also be used as a template when deploying similar systems and network devices.

Updates (aka Hotfixes, Service Packs, and Patches)

Operating systems are large and complex mixes of interrelated software modules written by dozens or even thousands of separate individuals. With the push toward GUI-based functionality and enhanced capabilities that has occurred over the past several years, OSs have continued to grow and expand. As OSs continue to grow and introduce new functions, the potential for problems with the code grows as well. It is almost impossible for an OS vendor to test its product on every possible platform under every possible circumstance, so functionality and security issues do arise after an OS has been released. To the average user or system administrator, this means a fairly constant stream of updates designed to correct problems, replace sections of code, or even add new features to an installed OS.

Vendors typically follow a hierarchy for software updates:

- **Hotfix**   This term refers to a (usually) small software update designed to address a specific problem, such as a buffer overflow in an application that exposes the system to attacks. Hotfixes are typically developed in reaction to a discovered problem and are produced and released rather quickly.

- **Patch**   This term refers to a more formal, larger software update that can address several or many software problems. Patches often contain enhancements or additional capabilities as well as fixes for known bugs. Patches are usually developed over a longer period of time.

- **Service pack**   This refers to a large collection of patches and hotfixes rolled into a single, rather large package. Service packs are designed to bring a system up to the latest known good level all at once, rather than requiring the user or system administrator to download dozens or hundreds of updates separately.

Every OS, from Linux to Solaris to Windows, requires software updates, and each has different methods of assisting users in keeping their systems up to date. Microsoft, for example, typically makes updates available for download from its website. While most administrators or technically proficient users may prefer to identify and download updates individually, Microsoft recognizes that nontechnical users prefer a simpler approach, which Microsoft incorporated in a browser-like console interface for updates. Windows 7 can be updated either via the Control Panel or Start button. By selecting Windows Update from the Start menu in Windows, users will be taken to the Microsoft update site. By selecting Scan For Updates, users can allow their systems to be examined for needed or required updates. The website will identify which updates the user's system needs and provide the user with the option to download and install the required updates. While this typically requires admin or power-user level access, it does simplify the update process for most users.

Windows can be set to automatically identify, download, and install updates. Figure 15-1 shows the options for Windows Update available when one accesses the Control Panel option for Windows Update.

Continuous Security Monitoring

While patching single systems is possible, in an enterprise, keeping all systems updated takes more work. Automation is a key strategy in managing large numbers of systems. Setting up a system that continuously monitors the state of all systems and provides guidance on when updates are needed is an essential tool in today's rapidly changing environment.

Continuous monitoring solutions allow multiple systems to be maintained with fewer resources. They also improve compliance with policies that require up-to-date and patched systems. The MITRE Corporation has developed an entire automation environment, called Making Security Measurable, that has the tools and necessary environments to automate system security updating (see http://makingsecuritymeasurable.mitre.org for details).

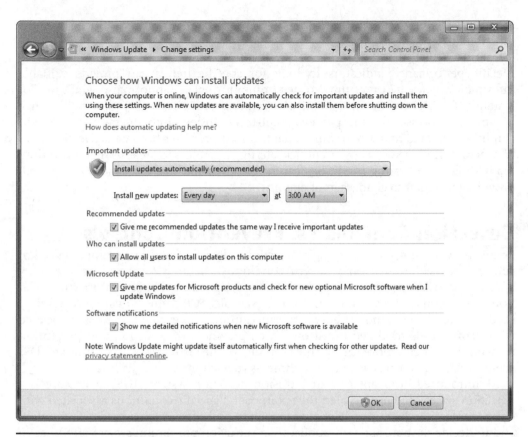

Figure 15-1 Setting Windows to automatically update

Remediation

The remediation of vulnerabilities can be achieved through a variety of methods. If possible, patching or updating software is usually an effective method. Other methods can include configuration changes, architecture changes, and system redesign. Although patches may offer simplicity compared to these other methods, better long-term vulnerability reduction and risk mitigation may come from these more intensive methods.

Reporting

A wide variety of mechanisms are used to operationally measure security activity. *Alerts* can be issued by a wide range of security appliances, alerting the operator to a specific condition being present. Alerts act as a signal that specific situations may be present. *Alarm* is another term used to denote an alerting of an operator to a specific condition. Alerts and alarms still require intervention on the part of the security team. The first step may be an investigation to confirm whether the alert or alarm is a true or false positive. As most alerts and alarms are based on specific deterministic conditions, automatically acting without investigating for false alarms may result in reduced business functionality and in system stability issues.

Another activity that the operational security team can employ is *trending*. Measuring specific performance indicators to look for specific trends can provide valuable information when it comes time to determine normal vs. abnormal operations. For instance, for a given server, a trend of operating processes will indicate the range of normal processes for the processor and even insight into operating levels and conditions. Should malware or other unauthorized processes become active, the trend of processes running will show an uptick, alerting operators to an abnormal condition. Many different operating conditions can be trended, and this too can be automated, providing insight into changes in operations.

Detection Controls vs. Prevention Controls

There are two distinct sets of mitigating actions, detection and prevention. Detection controls enable the detection of adverse conditions, enabling the enterprise to employ appropriate reactions. Prevention controls are designed to change a connection relationship by employing specific actions. For example, TCP connections can be reset by sending a reset command. Although threats cannot be prevented, the risk associated with them can be modified based on the employment of detection and prevention principles in the enterprise. Two prime examples of the distinct sets of controls are IDSs (detection) vs. IPSs (prevention), and cameras (detection) vs. guards (prevention).

As introduced in Chapter 1, an intrusion detection system (IDS) at its core is a detection system designed to alert the enterprise to specific conditions associated with defined rules. It is then up to an analyst to make a decision as to the veracity of the alert, and to decide the appropriate responses. An intrusion prevention system (IPS) has in its core an IDS that makes the detection step. Rather than just giving alerts, the IPS has the ability to take specific predefined actions based on specific detection conditions. This closing of the loop offers a faster response than using an analyst, but it also has no direct method of dealing with false positives.

Video-based surveillance, typically through closed-circuit TV (CCTV) cameras, provides a useful tool for monitoring large areas for physical security violations. Cameras can act as detection devices, but the response time is based on the monitoring time and subsequent response from a physical intervention, either guards or police. If the camera system is not actively monitored, then detection may be delayed until the recordings are reviewed. The use of a security guard service for physical security can close the monitoring delay, offering faster response to conditions. Just as in the IDS/IPS situation, if the response is fast enough, it can interrupt the attack prior to serious damage, thus acting to prevent loss.

Chapter Review

In this chapter, you became acquainted with how to select appropriate types of mitigation and deterrent techniques for a wide range of attacks. The chapter opened with a discussion of monitoring system logs, with common logs including security, DNS, system, performance, event, access, firewall, antivirus, and IDS/IPS logs. The chapter continued with periodic audits of security settings. System hardening and the protection of management interfaces is presented with sections on disabling unnecessary services, protecting management interfaces and applications, password protection, and disabling unnecessary accounts.

It then reviewed password selection criteria, password policy guidelines, the components of a good password, and password aging. The chapter continued with network security, covering the topics of MAC limiting and filtering, 802.1x, disabling unused interfaces and unused application service ports, and rogue machine detection. The next topic was security posture, where system baseline initialization and updates, continuous security monitoring, and remediation were presented.

The chapter closed with a review of the differences between detection controls and prevention controls.

Questions

To help you prepare further for the CompTIA Security+ exam, and to test your level of preparedness, answer the following questions and then check your answers against the correct answers at the end of the chapter.

1. A user is having issues with her domain account locking multiple times throughout the day. She suspects someone is trying to brute force her account or lock her out on purpose. Which of the following logs would most likely show the source of the other login attempts?

   A. Event logs

   B. Syslogs

   C. Security logs

   D. Access logs

2. Your boss wants you to come up with a "set starting point" for all the Windows 8 workstations in your organization. He wants you to build a golden image that's secure and can be used to load all the other desktops before any department-specific software is loaded. What has your boss asked you to create?

   A. Gold image point

   B. Initial snapshot

   C. Initial baseline configuration

   D. Security baseline

3. Your organization has a computer in an open lobby at the front of the building. The system is secured in a locked cabinet at night, but someone has been unplugging the PC from the wall and using the network jack behind the desk to surf the Internet with another computer. What type of mitigation technique could you use to stop unauthorized use of that network jack?

   A. MAC filtering

   B. Replay prevention

   C. Auditing

   D. Process tracking

4. Your colleague tells you that he has prepared a server for the production environment. He says that he has patched it, made sure all the accounts have strong passwords, and removed all the development code that was on it. When you scan the server, a large number of open ports respond. What did your colleague forget to do when securing this server?

A. Install antivirus software

B. Disable unnecessary services

C. Enable auditing

D. Disable MAC filtering

5. Your boss is trying to find more information about port-based network access control. Which of the following IEEE standards should she be looking at?

A. 802.1x

B. 802.11x

C. 802.x

D. 801.2x

6. Your organization is having a serious problem with people bringing in laptops and tablets from home and connecting them to the corporate network. The organization already has a policy against this, but it doesn't seem to help. Which of the following mitigation techniques might help with this situation?

A. Disabling unnecessary services

B. Rogue machine detection

C. Syslog auditing

D. Password protection

7. Your boss wants a network device that will detect malicious network traffic as it happens and stop it from reaching systems inside your network. She has asked you to come up with several different options and present them to her in the morning. You should start researching which of the following?

A. Intrusion detection systems

B. Intrusion prevention systems

C. Firewalls

D. Continuous auditing systems

8. Which of the following is not a step you'd perform when hardening a production system?

A. Disable unnecessary services

B. Disable unnecessary accounts

C. Enable simple TCP services

D. Configure auditing

9. A buffer overflow attack was launched against one of your Windows-based web servers. You'd like to know what process was affected on the server itself. Where might you look for clues as to what process was affected?

   A. Access log

   B. Application log

   C. Security log

   D. Setup log

10. An intrusion detection system is most like which of the following physical security measures?

   A. Locked door

   B. Electrified fence

   C. Security camera

   D. Mantrap entry

11. Which of the following can be used to assist in hardening a network? (Choose all that apply.)

   A. MAC limiting

   B. 802.11

   C. Rogue user detection

   D. Disable unused ports

12. Your boss is considering outsourcing the network security tasks for your organization. There are several proposals to look at, many of which claim to "collect information from security controls and perform analysis based on pre-established metrics." What capability are these vendors referring to?

   A. Global monitoring service

   B. Continuous security monitoring

   C. Intrusion prevention system

   D. Metrics-based security analysis

13. Which of the following types of log entries will you not find in Windows Security logs?

   A. Account logon events

   B. Object access events

   C. Policy change events

   D. System shutdown events

14. Which of the following are common logs associated with a system? (Choose all that apply.)

    A. Security

    B. Failure

    C. System

    D. Data integrity

15. A password policy should address the following questions: _____, _____, and _____.

Answers

1. **C.** The best source of information for this situation is going to be the security logs. Because this is a domain account and most likely on a Windows system, you will want to look at all failed logins associated with this account. Those are stored in the security logs.

2. **C.** Your boss just asked you to create an initial baseline configuration. The configuration you develop will become the starting point for all Windows 8 desktops. While the desktops may look different as department-specific software packages are loaded, they will all start off with the same attributes and security configuration from that initial baseline.

3. **A.** MAC filtering techniques can control which MAC addresses are allowed to send or receive traffic across specific switch ports. If you were to lock down that network jack to the MAC address of the PC in the locked cabinet, that would help stop anyone else from using the network jack without permission.

4. **B.** If a server has a large number of active ports, it is likely running a large number of services. Disabling unnecessary services should be part of the system build process for all production (and development) systems. Disabling or removing unnecessary services can reduce the attack surface of the system.

5. **A.** If your boss is researching port-based network access control, then she should be looking at IEEE 802.1x.

6. **B.** Rogue machine detection is a mitigation technique to find unwanted, unauthorized devices and systems on your network. Once you've discovered the rogue machines, you can track them down and discipline those responsible for connecting them to the network.

7. **B.** Your boss is looking for an intrusion prevention system (IPS). An IPS is very similar to an intrusion detection system (IDS), with one marked difference: an IPS is designed to interact with and stop malicious traffic.

8. **C.** When hardening a system, one of the objectives is to remove or disable unnecessary services. The simple TCP services such as ECHO, CHARGEN, and so on should typically be disabled as part of any system hardening process.

9. **B.** On a Windows-based server, the best place to look for information about what processes were affected by a buffer overflow attack would be the application logs.

10. **C.** An intrusion detection system is most like a security camera. An IDS has the ability to monitor for suspicious activity and can record what it has "seen."

11. **A and D.** MAC limiting and disabling unused ports are valuable security functions in setting up a network. 802.11 is the designation for Ethernet, and is not a direct issue (802.1x is, not 802.11). Rogue user detection is beyond the network function.

12. **B.** Continuous security monitoring is an attempt to answer that age-old question, "Are we secure?" By collecting data from implemented security controls such as firewalls, IDS/IPS, policies, and so forth and analyzing the data against established metrics, organizations hope to gain a better picture of the security state of their networks. For example, if the perimeter firewall records a sharp rise in outbound traffic on UDP port 33456, this could be an early indication of some type of botnet infection.

13. **D.** System shutdown events would be noted in the System event log, not the Security log.

14. **A and C.** Security and System logs are examples of common system logs.

15. A password policy should address: What is an acceptable level of risk? How secure does the system need to be? How often should users change their passwords? What account lockout policy should be used? What password composition rules should be enforced?

PART III

Threat and Vulnerability Discovery

In this chapter, you will

- Explore threat and vulnerability discovery methods
- Learn how to interpret results of security assessment tools
- Understand the use of appropriate tools and techniques to discover security threats and vulnerabilities
- Learn the differences between penetration testing and vulnerability scanning

A wide range of security tools and techniques can be employed to examine what is happening on a network and the servers connected by it. Learning how to use the appropriate tools and techniques to discover security threats and vulnerabilities is an important part of a security professional's job.

Interpret Results of Security Assessment Tools

Learning how to use security assessment tools in a manner that they provide useful, actionable information is an important foundational element of a security program. Many different tools are employed in the enterprise, and many have multiple uses. An important element in monitoring security is proper planning of the use of tools so that they provide the needed information. The key is in choosing the right tool that can provide the desired information and then correctly obtaining the information and analyzing what it means with respect to system security.

Tools

Tools are a vital part of any security professional's skill set. You may not be an "assessment professional" who spends most of his or her career examining networks looking for vulnerabilities, but you can use many of the same tools for internal assessment activities, tracking down infected systems, spotting inappropriate behavior, and so on. Knowing the right tool for the job can be critical to performing effectively.

Protocol Analyzer

As introduced in Chapter 1, a *protocol analyzer* is simply a tool (either hardware or software) that can be used to capture and analyze traffic passing over a communications channel, such as a network. Although protocol analyzers exist for many types of communication channels, such as telecommunications traffic and system buses, the most common use of a protocol analyzer is for the capture and examination of network traffic. In the networking world, this is most commonly referred to by a variety of names such as *packet sniffer*, *network analyzer*, or *network sniffer*. Sniffers can be used to capture and analyze wired or wireless traffic and can be software based (most common) or a dedicated hardware/software platform. An effective sniffer must have the ability to place a network interface in promiscuous mode, which tells the interface to accept and process every packet it sees—not just packets destined for this specific system or sent to a broadcast, multicast, or unicast address. On a switched network, sniffers are typically plugged into a SPAN (discussed in the next section) or monitor ports that are configured to receive copies of packets passing through one or more interfaces on the same switch. Capabilities of packet analyzers vary greatly—some do nothing more than simple packet capture, whereas others attempt to reconstruct entire TCP/IP sessions with decoded packets and color-coded traffic streams.

From a security perspective, protocol analyzers are very useful and effective tools. Want to see if any system on your network is transmitting traffic on a specific port? Want to see if any packets are being sent to an address at a rival company? Want to see which employees spend all day surfing eBay? Want to find the system that's flooding the local network with broadcast traffic? A protocol analyzer can help you address all these issues and more—if you have the analyzer plugged into the right location of your network and can "see" the traffic you are concerned about. Most organizations will have multiple points in the network where traffic can be sniffed—in the core switch, between the user base and the server farm, between remote users and the core network, between the organization and any link to the Internet, and so on. Knowing how to ensure the sniffer can "see" the traffic you want to analyze, knowing where to place the analyzer, and knowing how to use the analyzer are all keys to getting the best results from a protocol analyzer.

Switched Port Analyzer

The term *Switched Port Analyzer (SPAN)* is usually associated with Cisco switches—other vendors refer to the same capability as *port mirroring* or *port monitoring*. A SPAN has the ability to copy network traffic passing through one or more ports on a switch or one or more VLANs on a switch and forward that copied traffic to a port designated for traffic capture and analysis (as shown in Figure 16-1). A SPAN port or mirror port creates the collection point for traffic that will be fed into a protocol analyzer or IDS/IPS. SPAN or mirror ports can usually be configured to monitor traffic passing into interfaces, passing out of interfaces, or passing in both directions. When configuring port mirroring, you need to be aware of the capabilities of the switch you are working with. Can it handle the volume of traffic? Can it successfully mirror all the traffic, or will it end up dropping packets to the SPAN if traffic volume gets too high?

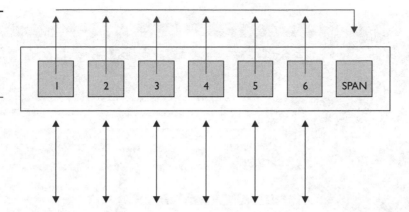

Figure 16-1
A SPAN port collects traffic from other ports on a switch.

Vulnerability Scanner

A vulnerability scanner is a program designed to probe hosts for weaknesses, misconfigurations, old versions of software, and so on. There are essentially three main categories of vulnerability scanners: network, host, and application.

A *network vulnerability scanner* probes a host or hosts for issues across their network connections. Typically, a network scanner will either contain or use a port scanner to perform an initial assessment of the network to determine which hosts are alive and which services are open on those hosts. Each system and service is then probed. Network scanners are very broad tools that can run potentially thousands of checks, depending on the OS and services being examined. This makes them a very good "broad sweep" for network-visible vulnerabilities. Due to the number of checks they can perform, network scanners can generate a great deal of traffic and a large number of connections to the systems being examined, so care should be taken to minimize the impact on production systems and production networks. Network scanners are essentially the equivalent of a Swiss army knife for assessments. They do lots of tasks and are extremely useful to have around—they may not be as good as a tool dedicated to examining one specific type of service, but if you can only run a single tool to examine your network for vulnerabilities, you'll want that tool to be a network vulnerability scanner. Figure 16-2 shows a screenshot of Nessus from Tenable Network Security, a very popular network vulnerability scanner.

Bottom line: If you need to perform a broad sweep for vulnerabilities on one or more hosts across the network, a network vulnerability scanner is the right tool for the job.

Host vulnerability scanners are designed to run on a specific host and look for vulnerabilities and misconfigurations on that host. Host scanners tend to be more specialized because they're looking for issues associated with a specific operating system or set of operating systems. A good example of a host scanner is the Microsoft Baseline Security Analyzer (MBSA), shown in Figure 16-3. MBSA is designed to examine the security state of a Windows host and offer guidance to address any vulnerabilities,

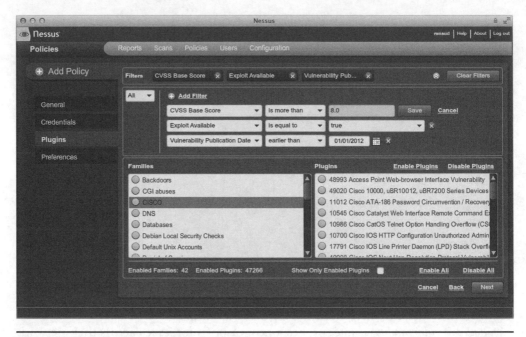

Figure 16-2 Nessus—a network vulnerability scanner

misconfigurations, or missing patches. Although MBSA can be run against remote systems across the network, it is typically run on the host being examined and requires you to have access to that local host (at the Administrator level). The primary thing to remember about host scanners is that they are typically looking for vulnerabilities on the system they are running on.

 EXAM TIP If you want to scan a specific host for vulnerabilities, weak password policies, or unchanged passwords and you have direct access to the host, a host vulnerability scanner might be just the tool to use.

It's worth noting that some tools (such as Nessus) really cross the line between network-based and host-based scanners. If you supply Nessus with host/login/domain credentials, it can perform many checks that would be considered "host based."

Selecting the right type of vulnerability scanner isn't that difficult. Just focus on what types of vulnerabilities you need to scan for and how you will be accessing the host/services/applications being scanned. It's also worth noting that to do a thorough job, you will likely need both network-based and host-based scanners—particularly for critical assets. Host- and network-based scanners perform different tests and provide visibility into different types of vulnerabilities. If you want to ensure the best coverage, you'll need to run both.

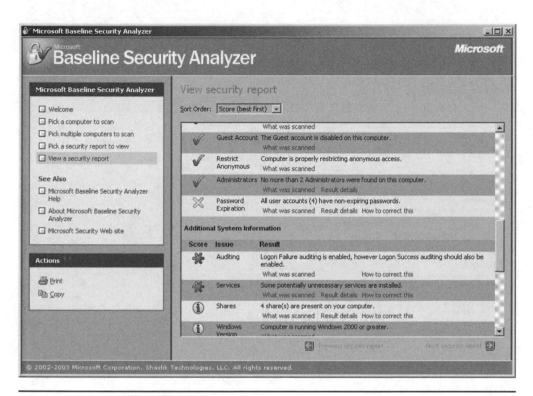

Figure 16-3   Microsoft Baseline Security Analyzer

Application vulnerability scanners are designed to look for vulnerabilities in applications or certain types of applications. Application scanners are some of the most specialized scanners—even though they contain hundreds or even thousands of checks, they only look for misconfigurations or vulnerabilities in a specific type of application. Arguably the most popular type of application scanners are designed to test for weaknesses and vulnerabilities in web-based applications. Web applications are designed to be visible, interact with users, and accept and process user input—all things that make them attractive targets for attackers. As such, a relatively large number of web application scanners are available, ranging from open source to subscription fee basis. To be an effective web application scanner, the tool must be able to perform thousands of checks for vulnerabilities, misconfigurations, default content, settings, issues, and so on, with a variety of web technologies from IIS to Apache to PHP to ASP and everything else in between. Application scanners are usually capable of performing advanced checks, such as SQL injection or JavaScript injection, that require interacting with the web application being examined and modifying requests and responses based on feedback from the application. Figure 16-4 shows a screenshot of Acunetix WVS (Web Vulnerability Scanner), an application scanner specifically for web technologies.

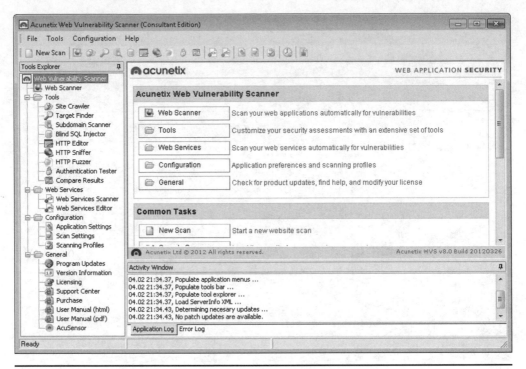

Figure 16-4 Acunetix WVS

 EXAM TIP If you want to examine a specific application or multiple instances of the same type of application (such as a website), an application scanner is the tool of choice.

Honeypots

A *honeypot* is a server that is designed to act like the real server on a corporate network, but rather than having the real data, the data it possesses is fake. Honeypots serve as attractive targets to attackers. A honeypot acts as a trap for attackers, as traffic in the honeypots can be assumed to be malicious.

Honeynets

A *honeynet* is a network designed to look like a corporate network, but is made attractive to attackers. A honeynet is a collection of honeypots. It looks like the corporate network, but because it is known to be a false copy, all of the traffic is assumed to be illegitimate. This makes it easy to characterize the attacker's traffic and also to understand where attacks are coming from.

Port Scanner

A *port scanner* is a tool designed to probe a system or systems for open ports. Its job is to probe for open (or listening) ports and report back to the user which ports are closed, which are filtered, and which are open. Port scanners are available for virtually every operating system and almost every popular mobile computing platform—from tablets to smartphones. Having a good port-scanning tool in your toolset and knowing how to use it can be very beneficial. The good news/bad news about port scanners is that the "bad guys" use them for basically the same reasons the good guys use them. Port scanners can be used to do the following:

- *Search for "live" hosts on a network.* Most port scanners enable you to perform a quick scan using ICMP, TCP, or UDP packets to search for active hosts on a given network or network segment. ICMP is still very popular for this task, but with the default blocking of ICMPv4 in many modern operating systems, such as Windows 7 and beyond, users are increasingly turning to TCP or UDP scans for these tasks.

- *Search for any open ports on the network.* Port scanners are most often used to identify any open ports on a host, group of hosts, or network. By scanning a large number of ports over a large number of hosts, a port scanner can provide you (or an attacker) with a very good picture of what services are running on which hosts on your network. Scans can be done for the "default" set of popular ports, a large range of ports, or every possible port (from 1 to 65535).

- *Search for specific ports.* Only looking for web servers? Mail servers? Port scanners can also be configured to just look for specific services.

- *Identify services on ports.* Some port scanners can help identify the services running on open ports based on information returned by the service or the port/service assigned (if standards have been followed). For example, a service running on port 80 is likely to be a web server.

- *Look for TCP/UDP services.* Most port scanners can perform scans for both TCP and UDP services, although some tools do not allow you to scan for both protocols at the same time.

As a security professional, you'll use port scanners in much the same way an attacker would: to probe the systems in your network for open services. When you find open services, you'll need to determine if those services should be running at all, if they should be running on the system(s) you found them on, and if you can do anything to limit what connections are allowed to those services. For example, you may want to scan your network for any system accepting connections on TCP port 1433 (Microsoft SQL Server). If you find a system accepting connections on TCP port 1433 in your Sales group, chances are someone has installed something they shouldn't have (or someone installed something for them).

So how does a port scanner actually work? Much will depend on the options you select when configuring your scan, but for the sake of this example, assume you're running a standard TCP connect scan against 192.168.1.20 for ports 1–10000. The scanner will attempt to create a TCP connection to each port in the range 1–10000 on 192.168.1.20. When the scanner sends out that SYN packet, it waits for the responding SYN/ACK. If a SYN/ACK is received, the scanner will attempt to complete the three-way handshake and mark the port as "open." If the sent packet times out or an RST packet is received, the scanner will likely mark that port as "closed." If an "administratively prohibited" message or something similar comes back, the scanner may mark that port as "filtered." When the scan is complete, the scanner will present the results in a summary format— listing the ports that are open, closed, filtered, and so on. By examining the responses from each port, you can typically deduce a bit more information about the system(s) you are scanning, as detailed here:

- **Open**   Open ports accept connections. If you can connect to these with a port scanner, the ports are not being filtered at the network level. However, there are instances where you may find a port that is marked as "open" by a port scanner that will immediately drop your connections if you attempt to connect to it in some other manner. For example, port 22 for SSH may appear "open" to a port scanner but will immediately drop your SSH connections. In such a case, the service is likely being filtered by a host-based firewall or a firewall capability within the service itself.

- **Closed**   You will typically see this response when the scanned target returns an RST packet.

- **Filtered**   You will typically see this response when an ICMP unreachable error is returned. This usually indicates that port is being filtered by a firewall or other device.

- **Additional types**   Some port scanners will attempt to further classify responses, such as dropped, blocked, denied, timeout, and so on. These are fairly tool specific, and you should refer to any documentation or help file that accompanies that port scanner for additional information.

In general, you will want to run your scanning efforts multiple times using different options to ensure you get a better picture. A SYN scan may return different results than a NULL scan or FIN scan. You'll want to run both TCP and UDP scans as well. You may need to alter your scanning approach to use multiple techniques at different times of the day/night to ensure complete coverage. The bad guys are doing this against your network right now, so you might as well use the same tools they do to see what they see. Port scanners can also be very useful for testing firewall configurations because the results of the port scans can show you exactly which ports are open, which ones you allow through, which ports are carrying services, and so on.

So how do you defend against port scans? Well, it's tough. Port scans are pretty much a part of the Internet traffic landscape now. Although you can block IP addresses that scan you, most organizations don't because you run the risk of an attacker spoofing source addresses as decoys for other scanning activity. The best defense is to carefully control what traffic you let in and out of your network using firewalls, network filters, and host filters. Then carefully monitor any traffic that you do allow in.

Passive vs. Active Tools

Tools can be classified as active or passive. *Active tools* interact with a target system in a fashion where their use can be detected. Scanning a network with Nmap (Network Mapper) is an active act that can be detected. In the case of Nmap, the tool may not be specifically detectable, but its use, the sending of packets, can be detected. When you need to map out your network or look for open services on one or more hosts, a port scanner is probably the most efficient tool for the job. Figure 16-5 shows a screen shot of Zenmap, a cross-platform version of the very popular Nmap port scanner available from insecure.org.

Passive tools are those that do not interact with the system in a manner that would permit detection, as in sending packets or altering traffic. An example of a passive tool

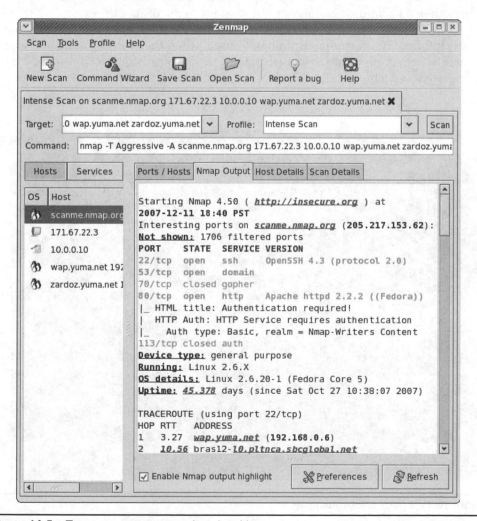

Figure 16-5 Zenmap—a port scanner based on Nmap

is Tripwire, which can detect changes to a file based on hash values. Another passive example is the OS mapping by analyzing TCP/IP traces with a tool such as wireshark. Passive sensors can use existing traffic to provide data for analysis.

 EXAM TIP Passive tools receive traffic only and do nothing to the traffic flow that would permit others to know they are interacting with the network. Active tools modify or send traffic and are thus discoverable by their traffic patterns.

Banner Grabbing

Banner grabbing is a technique used to gather information from a service that publicizes information via a banner. Banners can be used for many things; for example, they can be used to identify services by type, version, and so forth, and they enable administrators to post information, including warnings, to users when they log in. Attackers can use banners to determine what services are running, and typically do for common banner-issuing services such as HTTP, FTP, SMTP, and Telnet. Figure 16-6 shows a couple of

```
Telnet localhost

<!DOCTYPE HTML PUBLIC "-//IETF//DTD HTML 2.0//EN">
                                        <html><head>
                                                <title>501 Method
Not Implemented</title>
                        </head><body>
                                <h1>Method Not Implemented</h1>
                                                <p>♥ to /inde
x.html.en not supported.<br />
                        </p>
                        <hr>
                                <address>Apache/2.0.65 (Win32) Server at s
targazer.example.com Port 8080</address>
                                        </body></html>

TTP/1.1 400 Bad Request
Content-Type: text/html; charset=us-ascii
Server: Microsoft-HTTPAPI/2.0
Date: Sun, 23 Feb 2014 23:33:21 GMT
Connection: close
Content-Length: 326

<!DOCTYPE HTML PUBLIC "-//W3C//DTD HTML 4.01//EN""http://www.w3.org/TR/html4/str
ict.dtd">
<HTML><HEAD><TITLE>Bad Request</TITLE>
<META HTTP-EQUIV="Content-Type" Content="text/html; charset=us-ascii"></HEAD>
<BODY><h2>Bad Request - Invalid Verb</h2>
<hr><p>HTTP Error 400. The request verb is invalid.</p>
</BODY></HTML>

Connection to host lost.

Press any key to continue...
```

Figure 16-6 Banner grabbing using Telnet

banner grabs being performed from a Telnet client against a web server. In this example, Telnet sends information to two different web servers and displays the responses (the banners). The top response is from an Apache instance (Apache/2.0.65) and the bottom is from Microsoft IIS (Microsoft-HTTPAPI/2.0).

Risk Calculations

One element of assessing a system's security posture is to determine the risks that face the system. Although there are numerous potential threats and vulnerabilities, it is important to prioritize the actions and defenses against the attack vectors that represent the greatest risk. Risk is measured by the chance of occurrence and the severity of the threat. These two measures characterize the risk and can be used to make appropriate decisions based on impact to the system.

As illustrated in detail in Chapter 5, a common method used in risk calculations is

$$Risk = Threat \times Vulnerability\ (Impact) \times Asset\ Value$$

You must determine appropriate values for the threat, impact, and asset value to calculate risk.

Threat vs. Likelihood

The severity of the threat to a system is an important measure. If an attack is successful but the result is of no significant consequence, then this attack may not pose much of a true risk. A different attack may be so damaging as to render the system unusable, and this clearly needs mitigation. A separate measure is the likelihood of the attack being successful. Should the likelihood be low, then the risk is diminished. If the likelihood is high, then the risk is higher. The true measure is the combination of the severity and likelihood, which are typically multiplied together. A high likelihood and high severity combination is especially dangerous and deserves significantly more attention than lower levels of combinations.

Attackers use the same measures, as they will spend more time on methods that have higher chances of success. This provides a method of prioritizing defensive measures if all other aspects are equal.

Assessment Types

There are several types of assessments that can be performed. An *assessment* is an examination of a system with respect to a specific set of conditions. Assessments can be geared toward threats, vulnerabilities, and risk. Each of these assessments has an output that is focused on providing information with respect to what is actually being assessed. So, while the various types of assessment may all be used interchangeably, they do have different results.

Risk

The terms *risk analysis* and *vulnerability assessment* are sometimes used interchangeably, but that's not accurate. The terms analysis and assessment may be interchanged without issue, but risk is different from vulnerability. Vulnerability is covered later in this chapter.

Risk analysis is typically done from a quantitative perspective or a qualitative perspective. Quantitative risk analysis attempts to put a number to the probability of something bad occurring and the resulting loss from that event (typically in dollars). Qualitative risk analysis relies more on estimated and potential losses with associated risk levels. Know the difference between risk analysis and vulnerability assessment.

EXAM TIP Quantitative risk analysis attempts to put a number to the probability of something bad occurring and the resulting loss from that event, while qualitative risk analysis relies on relative levels for occurrence and impact. See Chapter 5 for more detail.

Threat

A *threat assessment* is a structured analysis of the threats that confront an enterprise. Threats are important to understand, for you generally cannot change the threat—you can only change how it affects you. A threat assessment begins with an enumeration of the threats that exist, followed by an estimate of the likelihood of success for each threat. Analyzing each threat as to the potential impact to the enterprise provides a prioritized list of threats requiring attention.

Vulnerability

A *vulnerability assessment* is good for evaluating the security posture of your network and its critical systems. All systems have vulnerabilities, so understanding what specific vulnerabilities exist in your systems is a key to securing the system. Being able to identify the vulnerabilities that are present and quantifying their impact can help you determine what mitigation/protection strategies to pursue. Vulnerability assessments can help to determine where to spend security budgets and where to devote manpower, and can even be used to help obtain additional resources. Often the first step in securing your network or systems is finding out how badly they are broken.

Assessment Technique

A variety of techniques can be employed to perform an assessment of a system. Each technique has its own advantages and is designed to detail some specific aspect of a system. Baseline reporting can measure the security posture of a system in its baseline configuration. Code reviews are useful as an assessment tool for examining applications where the code base is reviewable. Examining the attack surface and reviewing the architecture are yet other ways of determining the security posture.

Baseline Reporting

Baseline reporting on a system can provide information as to the state of the system's security aspects. As discussed earlier in the chapter, tools such as the Microsoft Baseline Security Analyzer (illustrated in Figure 16-3) exist to measure the baseline security configuration of a system. While the previous example focused on the security posture of the operating system, separate tools exist to perform the same analysis on the installed application base. Figure 16-7 shows the results of a Secunia Personal Software Inspector (PSI) scan of a system. Secunia PSI is a program designed to monitor application updates and assist users in keeping their applications updated.

Code Review

Code review is essentially proofreading of source code. Code reviews are intended to find programming errors and poor coding practices that can lead to vulnerabilities such as buffer overflows, memory leaks, unhandled exceptions, and so on. Code reviews can be done in various ways, ranging from the informal (one programmer looks over the shoulder of a fellow developer) to the extremely formal (such as a team walkthrough of an entire codebase). Code reviews can be performed manually, but tools exist that

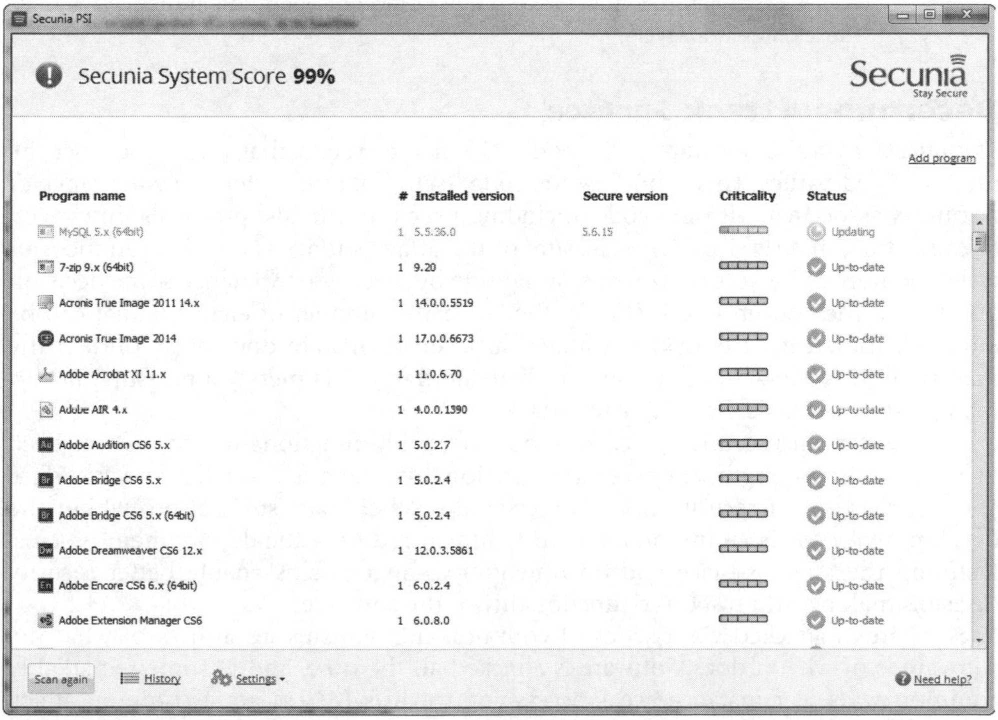

PART III

Figure 16-7 Application monitoring

provide automated code review capabilities. These automated review tools can be used to scan large codebases and identify potential issues or areas where issues may exist. Developers can then focus in on those areas without having to scan the entire codebase manually. Automated scanning followed by manual review is a widely accepted common practice that provides good coverage for far less "cost" than a manual review of the entire codebase.

The key benefit to code reviews is to find and address bugs and vulnerabilities as soon as possible—preferably before the software even enters formal testing. The earlier in the development process a bug can be caught and addressed, the cheaper it is to fix. Consider Microsoft Word—if a bug is caught in development, it is far, far cheaper to correct it there than it is to correct the bug in a released product. Addressing the bug in development may involve a few developers and a few lines of code with comments. Addressing that same bug in a released product involves code revisions, configuration management, regression testing, patch development, patch note development, and so on. As you can see, the sheer amount of effort required to address bugs post-production encourages many organizations to perform code reviews early and often during the development cycle.

 EXAM TIP Code reviews are a powerful security tool in the development process. Code reviews involve the inspection of code for vulnerabilities or weaknesses before advancing to the next level of operation in the development lifecycle.

Determine Attack Surface

The *attack surface* of software is the code within the system that can be accessed by unauthorized parties. This is not just the code itself, but also includes a wide range of resources associated with the code, including user input fields, protocols, interfaces, resource files, and services. One measure of the attack surface is the sheer number or weighted number of accessible items. Weighting by severity may change some decision points, but the bottom line is simple: the larger the number of elements that can be attacked, the greater the risk. The attack surface of software does not represent the quality of the code—it does not mean there are flaws; it is merely a measure of how many features/items are available for attack.

A long-standing security practice is not to enable functionality that is not used or needed. By turning off unnecessary functionality, there is a smaller attack surface and there are fewer security risks. Understanding the attack surface throughout the development cycle is an important security function during the development process. Defining the attack surface and documenting changes helps enable better security decision making with respect to functionality of the software.

Software is attacked via a series of common mechanisms, regardless of what the software is or what it does. Software is attacked all the time, and in some remarkably common ways. For instance, weak access control lists (ACLs) are a common attack point, and these can be exploited regardless of the operating system. Attacks against the operating system can be used against many applications, including software that is otherwise secure. Attack surface evaluation is a means of measuring and determining the risks associated with the implications of design and development.

To understand a product's attack surface, you need to measure the number of ways it can be "accessed." Each software product may be different, but they will also share elements. Like many other security items, the first time a team builds an attack surface elements list, it is more difficult. But, over time, the incremental examination will detail more items, making future lists easier to develop. In this light, here is a published list from Microsoft on attack surface elements associated with Windows. Although this list may not be totally applicable, it does provide a starting point and acts as a guide of the types of elements associated with an attack surface.

- Open sockets
- Open remote procedure call (RPC) endpoints
- Open named pipes
- Services
- Services running by default
- Services running as SYSTEM
- Active web handlers (ASP files, HTR files, and so on)
- Active Internet Server Application Programming Interface (ISAPI) filters
- Dynamic web pages (ASP and such)
- Executable virtual directories
- Enabled accounts
- Enabled accounts in admin group
- Null sessions to pipes and shares
- Guest account enabled
- Weak ACLs in the file system
- Weak ACLs in the registry
- Weak ACLs on shares

Another source of information is in the history of known vulnerabilities associated with previous developments. Determining the root cause of old vulnerabilities is good for fixing them and preventing future occurrences, and it is also valuable information that can be used in determining the attack surface.

The list of features that form the attack surface is the same list that attackers use to attack a specific piece of software. The items on the list are not necessarily vulnerabilities, but they are items that attackers will attempt to compromise. These elements are at the base of all vulnerabilities, so while a particular vulnerability may or may not exist for a given attack surface element, there will be one under each vulnerability that is uncovered. This makes measuring the attack surface a solid estimation of the potential vulnerability surface.

PART III

Review Architecture

A review of the architecture of a system can provide significant clues as to system weaknesses and vulnerabilities. Architecture reviews should cover the components, how the data is transferred between the components, access control lists for components, data transfers, and user connections. There are a number of security architecture frameworks that can be used to assist in the proper design of a system. A common one for web applications is the Open Web Application Security Project (OWASP), a community-driven, open-source activity that is focused on web application security. Other architecture guides can be found in Control Objectives for Information and Related Technology (COBIT) and the Information Technology Infrastructure Library (ITIL).

Review Designs

Designs need to be reviewed against security requirements, including access control requirements, data security, and system configuration requirements. Using the results of the documentation from the attack surface area and the threat model enables the security team to properly evaluate the security functionality in the application. Code walkthroughs, design reviews, examination of the attack surface area, and threat modeling documentation with an eye toward completeness are key elements of these reviews.

Penetration Testing

A *penetration test* (or *pentest*) simulates an attack from a malicious outsider—probing your network and systems for a way in (often any way in). Pentests are often the most aggressive form of security testing and can take on many forms, depending on what is considered "in" or "out" of scope. For example, some pentests simply seek to find a way into the network—any way in. This can range from an attack across network links, to social engineering, to having a tester physically break into the building. Other pentests are limited—only attacks across network links are allowed, with no physical attacks.

Regardless of the scope and allowed methods, the goal of a pentest is the same: to determine if an attacker can bypass your security and access your systems. Unlike a vulnerability assessment, which typically just catalogs vulnerabilities, a pentest attempts to exploit vulnerabilities to see how much access that vulnerability allows. Penetration tests are very useful in that they

- Can show relationships between a series of "low-risk" items that can be sequentially exploited to gain access (making them a "high-risk" item in the aggregate).

- Can be used to test the training of employees, the effectiveness of your security measures, and the ability of your staff to detect and respond to potential attackers.

- Can often identify and test vulnerabilities that are difficult or even impossible to detect with traditional scanning tools.

EXAM TIP Penetration tests are focused efforts to determine the effectiveness of the security controls used to protect a system.

Verify a Threat Exists

One aspect of a penetration test is the demonstration of the threat vectors that can be experienced in real-world situations. Because a pentest is designed to provide information that can be used to strengthen the security of a system, mimicking real-world threats is important. The scope of potential attack vectors is derived from the environment of attacks used in the wild.

Bypass Security Controls

One of the key tests that a penetration tester will perform is an attempt to bypass security controls. If a security control is missing, ineffective, or not properly configured, it is the job of the penetration tester to find this situation. When a gap in the security defenses is discovered, then the next step is the exploitation of the security hole.

Actively Test Security Controls

Security controls exist to mitigate the risk presented by threats against a system. Penetration testing can actively attack these controls in an attempt to characterize their ability to perform under real-world operational conditions.

Exploiting Vulnerabilities

A key element of a penetration test is the actual exploitation of a vulnerability. Exploiting the vulnerabilities encountered serves two purposes. First, it demonstrates the level of risk that is actually present. Second, it demonstrates the viability of the mechanism of the attack vector. During a penetration test, the exploitation activity stops short of destructive activity.

Vulnerability Scanning

One very valuable method that can help administrators secure their systems is vulnerability scanning. *Vulnerability scanning* is the process of examining your systems and network devices for holes, weaknesses, and issues and finding them before a potential attacker does. Specialized tools called *vulnerability scanners* are designed to help administrators discover and address vulnerabilities. But there is much more to vulnerability scanning than simply running tools and examining the results—administrators must be able to analyze any discovered vulnerabilities and determine their severity, how to address them if needed, and whether any business processes will be affected by potential fixes. Vulnerability scanning can also help administrators identify common misconfigurations in account setup, patch level, applications, and operating systems. Most organizations look at vulnerability scanning as an ongoing process, as it is not enough to scan systems once and assume they will be secure from that point on.

Passively Testing Security Controls

When an automated vulnerability scanner is used to examine a system for vulnerabilities, one of the side effects is the passive testing of the security controls. This is referred to as *passive testing* because the target of the vulnerability scanner is the system, not the controls. If the security controls are effective, then the vulnerability scan may not properly identify the vulnerability. If the security control prevents a vulnerability from being attacked, then it may not be exploitable.

Identify Vulnerability

Vulnerabilities are known entities; otherwise, the scanners would not have the ability to scan for them. When a scanner finds a vulnerability present in a system, it makes a log of the fact. In the end, an enumeration of the vulnerabilities that were discovered is part of the vulnerability analysis report.

Identify Lack of Security Controls

If a vulnerability is exposed to the vulnerability scanner, then a security control is needed to prevent the vulnerability from being exploited. As vulnerabilities are discovered, the specific environment of each vulnerability is documented. Because the security vulnerabilities are all known in advance, the system should have controls in place to protect against exploitation. Part of the function of the vulnerability scan is to learn where controls are missing or are ineffective.

Identify Common Misconfigurations

One source of failure with respect to vulnerabilities is in the misconfiguration of a system. Common misconfigurations include access control failures and failure to protect configuration parameters. Vulnerability scanners can be programmed to test for these specific conditions and report on them.

Intrusive vs. Non-intrusive

Vulnerability scanners need a method of detecting whether or not a vulnerability is present and exploitable. One method is to perform a test that changes the system state, an intrusive test. The other method is to perform the test in a manner that does not directly interact with the specific vulnerability. This non-intrusive method can be significantly less accurate in the actual determination of a vulnerability. If a vulnerability scan is going to involve a lot of checks, the non-intrusive method can be advantageous, as the servers may not have to be rebooted all the time.

Credentialed vs. Non-credentialed

A vulnerability scanner can be programmed with the credentials of a system, giving it the same access as an authorized user. This is assumed to be easier than running the same tests without credentials, widely considered to be a more real-world attempt. It is important to run both, for if an attacker is able to compromise an account, they may well have insider credentials. Credentialed scans will be more accurate in determining whether the vulnerabilities exist, as they are not encumbered by access controls.

False Positive

Tools are not perfect. Sometimes they will erroneously report things as an issue when they really are not a problem—and other times they won't report an issue at all. A *false positive* is an incorrect finding—something that is incorrectly reported as a vulnerability. The scanner tells you there is a problem when in reality nothing is wrong. A *false negative* is when the scanner fails to report a vulnerability that actually does exist—the scanner simply missed the problem or didn't report it as a problem.

Testing

Testing methodologies can be employed when describing the environment for vulnerability and penetration testing. Just as in the test environment, the terms black box, white box, and gray box testing are employed to identify the system knowledge level associated with testing.

Black Box

Black-box testing is a software-testing technique that consists of finding implementation bugs using malformed/semi-malformed data injection in an automated fashion. Black-box techniques test the functionality of the software, usually from an external or user perspective. Testers using black-box techniques typically have no knowledge of the internal workings of the software they are testing. They treat the entire software package as a "black box"—they put input in and look at the output. They have no visibility into how the data is processed inside the application, only the output that comes back to them. Tests cases for black-box testing are typically constructed around intended functionality (what the software is supposed to do) and focus on providing both valid and invalid inputs.

Black-box software testing techniques are very useful for examining any web-based application. Web-based applications are typically subjected to a barrage of valid, invalid, malformed, and malicious input from the moment they are exposed to public traffic. By performing black-box testing before an application is released, developers can potentially find and correct errors in the development or testing stages.

Black-box testing can also be applied to networks or systems. Pentests and vulnerability assessments are often performed from a purely external perspective, where the testers have no inside knowledge of the network or systems they are examining.

PART III

White Box

White-box testing is almost the polar opposite of black-box testing. Sometimes called clear-box testing, white-box techniques test the internal structures and processing within an application for bugs, vulnerabilities, and so on. A white-box tester will have detailed knowledge of the application they are examining—they'll develop test cases designed to exercise each path, decision tree, input field, and processing routine of the application.

White-box testing is often used to test paths within an application (if X, then go do this; if Y, then go do that), data flows, decision trees, and so on. Sometimes the term *white-box testing* is applied to network assessments where the tester will have detailed knowledge of the network, including but not limited to IP addresses, network routes, valid user credentials, and so on. In those cases, the tester is typically referred to as a "white hat."

Gray Box

So what happens when you mix a bit of black-box testing and a bit of white-box testing? You get gray-box testing. In a gray-box test, the testers typically have some knowledge of the software, network, or systems they are testing. For this reason, gray-box testing can be very efficient and effective because testers can often quickly eliminate entire testing paths, test cases, and toolsets and can rule out things that simply won't work and are not worth trying.

 EXAM TIP The key difference between black-box testing and white-box testing is the perspective and knowledge of the tester. Black-box testers have no knowledge of the inner workings and perform their tests from an external perspective. White-box testers have detailed knowledge of the inner workings and perform their tests from an internal perspective.

Chapter Review

In this chapter, you became acquainted with threat and vulnerability discovery. The chapter opened with an examination of various security tools and how to interpret their results. The tools covered include protocol analyzers, vulnerability scanners, honeypots and honeynets, port scanners, and banner grabbing. These tools provide a mechanism for assessing the security level of a system.

The chapter continued by examining risk calculation. The use of risk calculations and design of assessments—including risk, threat, and vulnerability assessments—can provide information that allows for the prioritization of security actions. The next section, on assessment techniques, covered baseline reporting, code review, determining the attack surface, architecture reviews, and design reviews as methods of performing assessments.

The chapter next discussed penetration testing and vulnerability scanning. It covered the steps of penetration testing, the process of vulnerability scanning, false-positive and false-negative conditions, and, finally, white-box, black-box, and gray-box testing.

Questions

To help you prepare further for the CompTIA Security+ exam, and to test your level of preparedness, answer the following questions and then check your answers against the correct answers at the end of the chapter.

1. Your boss promised to help out the Audit department and has enlisted you. They're looking for a list of every system in the server farm and what services are responding on each of those systems. What kind of tool might you use to create this type of list?

   A. Vulnerability scanner

   B. Port scanner

   C. Proxy tool

   D. Protocol analyzer

2. You want to hire someone to test an application your company just developed. The app handles sensitive data, so you want to limit the amount of information you release about the application to people outside your company. Which of the following testing types are you looking for?

   A. White-box testing

   B. Gray-box testing

   C. Closed-box testing

   D. Black-box testing

3. What is the process used to identify potential hazards and evaluate their impact called?

   A. Risk assessment

   B. Business continuity planning

   C. Architecture review

   D. Process tracking

4. Your boss just read an article about how companies are setting up fake websites to trick attackers into focusing on the fake websites instead of the actual production systems. Now he wants you to build something similar for your DMZ. He tells you to "make it inviting" to the attackers. What is your boss really asking you to set up?

   A. Intrusion detection system

   B. Vulnerability assessment

   C. Honeypot

   D. Gray box

5. An application is being delayed after one of the testers discovered a major bug. Now developers are being tasked to examine each other's code line by line and find any remaining bugs. What are these developers doing?

A. Quality assurance

B. Code review

C. Risk assessment

D. Code analysis

6. List three items that are important for determining risk: _____, _____, _____.

7. You need something that will help you more effectively analyze the traffic on your network, something that will record traffic at the packet level so you can look for problems like ARP storms, duplicate MAC addresses, and so on. What type of tool should you be shopping for?

A. White-box analyzer

B. Network scanner

C. Passive scanner

D. Protocol analyzer

8. Your organization wants someone to examine your intranet portal to assess the threat from a malicious insider. What kind of testing is the most appropriate for this situation?

A. Credentialed testing

B. Code review

C. Active testing

D. Risk assessment

9. Which of the following tools or methods is most likely to show you which servers in your server farm allow anonymous access to shares, have TCP port 80 open, and are running an old version of PHP?

A. Protocol analyzer

B. Port scanner

C. Vulnerability scanner

D. Baseline review

10. You've found a printout with a bunch of IP addresses and descriptions next to them such as "220 Microsoft ESMTP MAIL Service ready" and "220 Microsoft FTP Service." What type of activity might have generated this type of list?

A. Risk assessment

B. Banner grabbing

    C. Telnet mapping

    D. Black-box testing

11. Your vulnerability scanning tool reports that your website is vulnerable to a SQL injection attack that manipulates the values of a hidden parameter. You've tested this thoroughly by hand but cannot validate the finding. Each time you try, you get a nonstandard error message indicating the query has been terminated. Your vulnerability scanner is most likely reporting:

    A. An invalid redirect

    B. A user error

    C. A false negative

    D. A security control bypass

12. You've been asked to perform some testing on a new web application your organization has developed. The CEO wants you to perform gray-box testing. What will you need in order to perform this type of testing?

    A. Just the URL of the application

    B. The URL of the application and documentation of the data structures and algorithms used

    C. All knowledge of the application, including URL, documentation of the data structures and algorithms used, and a list of all functionality paths through the application

    D. No knowledge of the application

13. Which of the following best describes the attack surface of an application?

    A. All logins and user inputs

    B. All logins, user inputs, and data fields

    C. All logins, user inputs, data fields, and certificates in use

    D. All logins, user inputs, data fields, paths for data in/out of the application, and code that protects data paths

14. You want to place a tool on the network that will continuously look for vulnerabilities on your network. Your network admin refuses to allow anything that might interfere with network traffic. What type of tool could you use that would be a compromise between the two positions?

    A. Active network vulnerability scanner

    B. Passive network vulnerability scanner

    C. Intrusion prevention system

    D. Passive firewall

15. You are working on a penetration test and discover a web server that appears to be vulnerable to SQL injection attacks in the login field. Your team lead clears you to see if you can get into the system using the SQL injection attack. It works. What penetration testing step have you just performed?

    A. Passive testing of security controls

    B. White-box testing

    C. Vulnerability identification

    D. Vulnerability exploitation

Answers

1. **B.** If all the audit department needs is a list of the systems and the open services on each of those systems, a port scanner is all you need. Any decent port scanner, such as Nmap, will be able to detect the systems and probe any active ports on those systems.

2. **D.** If you want someone to test your application without any knowledge of how the software works internally or how the software was built, then you are looking for a black-box testing service. Black-box testing examines the functionality of the software with no knowledge of the data structures in use or internal workings of the software.

3. **A.** A risk assessment is the process used to identify potential hazards and analyze the impact should those hazards actually occur.

4. **C.** Your boss is really looking for a honeypot—a system that is intentionally set up with vulnerabilities and misconfigurations to make it attractive to potential attackers. Honeypots are often used to study the methods and tools attackers use.

5. **B.** The developers are performing a code review—a systematic examination of source code to find and eliminate bugs, mistakes, typos, and so on.

6. Three items that are important for determining risk are likelihood of threat, discoverability of vulnerability, and value of impact to asset. You must account for the threat, impact, and asset value to calculate risk.

7. **D.** If you are looking for a tool to help you analyze network traffic, you should be shopping for a protocol analyzer. Protocol analyzers are tools used to capture and examine signals and data across a communication channel. Protocol analyzers exist for almost every kind of communication channel.

8. **A.** If you want to assess the threat from a malicious insider, you will most likely use credentialed testing. Credentialed testing uses a set of valid user credentials when tests are conducted. This allows the tester to examine the application from the same viewpoint and with the same permissions as a valid user would have.

9. **C.** A vulnerability scanner is the only tool or method listed that will supply all three pieces of information. A port scanner could tell you whether or not port 80 is open, but would not test for share access or vulnerable versions of PHP. Most vulnerability scanners, such as Nessus, will perform basic TCP port scanning as well as scanning for misconfigurations, insecure versions of software, and so on.

10. **B.** A list showing service "banners" such as "220 Microsoft FTP Service" is usually created by banner grabbing. There are a number of tools that specialize in banner grabbing, but you can accomplish the same thing by simply using a Telnet client to connect to a service. In most cases, the service will return a banner telling you various details about the service.

11. **B.** There must be a user error in testing. When any scanning tool reports a "finding" that isn't really there and doesn't really exist, this is known as a false positive.

12. **B.** Gray-box testing is a combination of white- and black-box testing. The tester has some knowledge of the system or application being examined, such as the data structures and algorithms, but doesn't know everything about the application, as they would during white-box testing.

13. **D.** The attack surface of an application is really a description of all the different places where an attacker could penetrate or disrupt the application. This would include all data paths into and out of the application, all data used by the application, and the code that protects and processes the data and data paths.

14. **B.** If you want a tool that will look for vulnerabilities but won't interfere with network traffic, your best compromise will be some type of passive network vulnerability scanner. A "passive" scanner waits for data to come to it—it doesn't perform any scans or probes on its own and doesn't interact with the traffic it observes.

15. **D.** Any time you find a vulnerability and then use tools or techniques that exercise that vulnerability to gain access or manipulate data, you have performed vulnerability exploitation. Identifying vulnerabilities stops short of doing something with the discovered vulnerabilities. Using a SQL injection attack to gain access to a system would definitely qualify as exploiting a vulnerability.

PART III

PART IV

Application, Data, and Host Security

Application Security Controls

In this chapter, you will

- Discover the importance of secure coding concepts
- Understand the importance of application security controls and techniques
- Discover the importance of input handling
- Learn about the tools and techniques used in secure coding
- Learn about application hardening techniques

Application security controls and techniques are important in ensuring that the applications deployed are as secure as possible. Beginning with secure coding techniques, and then providing defense in depth by adding security controls, the security of an application is established. Using application hardening techniques and proper configuration and change controls provides a process-driven method to ensure continued security per a defined risk profile.

Secure Coding Concepts

Application security begins with code that is secure and free of vulnerabilities. Unfortunately, all code has weaknesses and vulnerabilities, so instantiating the code in a manner that has effective defenses preventing the exploitation of vulnerabilities can maintain a desired level of security. Proper handling of configurations, errors and exceptions, and inputs can assist in the creation of a secure application. Testing of the application throughout the system lifecycle can be used to determine the actual security risk profile of a system.

There are numerous individual elements in the Software Development Lifecycle (SDL) that can assist a team in developing secure code. Correct SDL processes, such as input validation, proper error and exception handling, and cross-site scripting and cross-site request forgery mitigations, can improve the security of code. Process elements such as security testing, fuzzing, and patch management also help to ensure applications meet a desired risk profile.

317

There are two main enumerations of common software errors: the Top 25 list maintained by MITRE, and the OWASP Top Ten list for web applications. Depending on the type of application being evaluated, these lists provide a solid starting point for security analysis of known error types. MITRE is the repository of the industry standard list for standard programs, and OWASP for web applications. Because the causes of common errors do not change quickly, these lists are not updated every year.

Error and Exception Handling

Every application will encounter errors and exceptions, and these need to be handled in a secure manner. One attack methodology includes forcing errors to move an application from normal operation to exception handling. During an exception, it is common practice to record/report the condition, including supporting information such as the data that resulted in the error. This information can be invaluable in diagnosing the cause of the error condition. The challenge is in where this information is captured. The best method is to capture it in a log file, where it can be secured by an ACL. The worst case is when it is echoed to the user. Echoing error condition details to users can provide valuable information to attackers when they cause errors on purpose.

 EXAM TIP   All errors/exceptions should be trapped and handled in the generating routine.

Improper exception handling can lead to a wide range of disclosures. Errors associated with SQL statements can disclose data structures and data elements. Remote procedure call (RPC) errors can give up sensitive information such as filenames, paths, and server names. Programmatic errors can give up line numbers that an exception occurred on, the method that was invoked, and information such as stack elements.

Input Validation

With the move to web-based applications, the errors have shifted from buffer overflows to input-handling issues. Users have the ability to manipulate input, so it is up to the developer to handle the input appropriately to prevent malicious entries from having an effect. Buffer overflows could be considered a class of improper input, but newer attacks include canonicalization attacks and arithmetic attacks. Probably the most important defensive mechanism that can be employed is input validation. Considering all inputs to be hostile until properly validated can mitigate many attacks based on common vulnerabilities. This is a challenge, as the validation efforts need to occur after all parsers have completed manipulating input streams, a common function in web-based applications using Unicode and other international character sets.

Input validation is especially well suited for the following vulnerabilities: buffer overflow, reliance on untrusted inputs in a security decision, cross-site scripting (XSS), cross-site request forgery (XSRF), path traversal, and incorrect calculation of buffer size. Input validation may seem suitable for various injection attacks, but given the complexity of the input and the ramifications from legal but improper input streams, this method falls short for most injection attacks. What can work is a form of recognition and whitelisting approach, where the input is validated and then parsed into a standard structure that is then executed. This restricts the attack surface to not only legal inputs, but also expected inputs.

 EXAM TIP Consider all input to be hostile. Input validation is one of the most important secure coding techniques employed, mitigating a wide array of potential vulnerabilities.

Output validation is just as important in many cases as input validation. If querying a database for a username and password match, the expected forms of the output of the match function should be either one match or none. If using record count to indicate the level of match, which is a common practice, then a value other than 0 or 1 would be an error. Defensive coding using output validation would not act on values >1, as these are clearly an error and should be treated as a failure.

Fuzzing

One of the most powerful tools that can be used in testing is *fuzzing* (aka fuzz testing), which is the systematic application of a series of malformed inputs to test how the program responds. Fuzzing has been used by hackers for years to find potentially exploitable buffer overflows, without any specific knowledge of the coding. Fuzz testing works perfectly fine regardless of the type of testing, white box or black box. Fuzzing serves as a best practice for finding unexpected input validation errors.

A tester can use a fuzzing framework to automate numerous input sequences. In examining whether a function can fall prey to a buffer overflow, a tester can run numerous inputs, testing lengths and ultimate payload-delivery options. If a particular input string results in a crash that can be exploited, the tester would then examine this input in detail. Fuzzing is still relatively new to the development scene, but is rapidly maturing and will soon be on nearly equal footing with other automated code-checking tools.

Cross-site Scripting Prevention

Cross-site scripting (XSS) is one of the most common web attack methodologies. The cause of the vulnerability is weak user input validation. If input is not validated properly, an attacker can include a script in their input and have it rendered as part of the web process. There are several different types of XSS attacks, which are distinguished by the effect of the script:

- **Non-persistent XSS attack** The injected script is not persisted or stored, but rather is immediately executed and passed back via the web server.

- **Persistent XSS attack** The script is permanently stored on the web server or some back-end storage. This allows the script to be used against others who log in to the system.

- **DOM-based XSS attack** The script is executed in the browser via the Document Object Model (DOM) process as opposed to the web server.

PART IV

Cross-site scripting attacks can result in a wide range of consequences, and in some cases, the list can be anything that a clever scripter can devise. Common uses that have been seen in the wild include

- Theft of authentication information from a web application
- Session hijacking
- Deploying hostile content
- Changing user settings, including future users
- Impersonating a user
- Phishing or stealing sensitive information

Controls to defend against XSS attacks include the use of anti-XSS libraries to strip scripts from the input sequences. Various other ways to mitigate XSS attacks include limiting types of uploads and screening the size of uploads, whitelisting inputs, and so on, but attempting to remove scripts from inputs can be a tricky task. Well-designed anti-XSS input library functions have proven to be the best defense. Cross-site scripting vulnerabilities are easily tested for and should be a part of the test plan for every application. Testing a variety of encoded and unencoded inputs for scripting vulnerability is an essential test element.

Cross-site Request Forgery

Cross-site request forgery (XSRF) attacks utilize unintended behaviors that are proper in defined use but are performed under circumstances outside the authorized use. This is an example of a "confused deputy" problem, a class of problems where one entity mistakenly performs an action on behalf of another. An XSRF attack relies upon several conditions to be effective. It is performed against sites that have an authenticated user and exploits the site's trust in a previous authentication event. Then, by tricking a user's browser to send an HTTP request to the target site, the trust is exploited. Assume your bank allows you to log in and perform financial transactions, but does not validate the authentication for each subsequent transaction. If a user is logged in and has not closed their browser, then an action in another browser tab could send a hidden request to the bank, resulting in a transaction that appears to be authorized but in fact was not done by the user.

There are many different mitigation techniques that can be employed, from limiting authentication times, to cookie expiration, to managing some specific elements of a web page like header checking. The strongest method is the use of random XSRF tokens in form submissions. Subsequent requests cannot work, as the token was not set in advance. Testing for XSRF takes a bit more planning than for other injection-type attacks, but this, too, can be accomplished as part of the design process.

Application Hardening

Application hardening works in the same fashion as system hardening (discussed in Chapter 15). The first step is the removal of unnecessary components or options. The second step is the proper configuration of the system as it is implemented. Every update or patch can lead to changes to these conditions, and they should be confirmed after every update.

The primary tools used to ensure a hardened system are a secure application configuration baseline and a patch management process. When properly employed, these tools can lead to the most secure system.

Application Configuration Baseline

A *baseline* is the set of proper settings for a computer system. An *application configuration baseline* outlines the proper settings and configurations for an application or set of applications. These settings include many elements, from application settings to security settings. Protection of the settings is crucial, and the most common mechanisms used to protect them include access control lists and protected directories. The documentation of the desired settings is an important security document, assisting administrators in ensuring that proper configurations are maintained across updates.

Application Patch Management

Application patch management is a fundamental component of application and system hardening. The objective is to be running the most secure version of an application, and, with very few exceptions, that would be the most current version of software, including patches. Most updates and patches include fixing security issues and closing vulnerabilities. Current patching is a requirement of many compliance schemes as well.

Patching does not always go as planned, and some patches may result in problems in production systems. A formal system of patch management is needed to test and implement patches in a change-controlled manner.

 EXAM TIP Patch management might be referred to as *update management, configuration management,* or *change management.* Although these terms are not strictly synonyms, they might be used interchangeably on the exam.

NoSQL Databases vs. SQL Databases

Current programming trends include topics such as whether to use SQL databases or NoSQL databases. SQL databases are those that use Structured Query Language to manipulate items that are referenced in a relational manner in the form of tables. *NoSQL* refers to data stores that employ neither SQL nor relational table structures. Each system has its strengths and weaknesses, and both can be used for a wide range of data storage needs.

SQL databases are by far the most common, with implementations by IBM, Microsoft, and Oracle being the major players. NoSQL databases tend to be custom built using low-level languages and lack many of the standards of existing databases. This has not stopped the growth of NoSQL databases in large-scale, well-resourced environments.

The important factor in accessing data in a secure fashion is in the correct employment of programming structures and frameworks to abstract the access process. Methods such as inline SQL generation coupled with input validation errors is a recipe for disaster in the form of SQL injection attacks.

Server-side vs. Client-side Validation

In a modern client-server environment, data can be checked for compliance with input/output requirements either on the server or on the client. There are advantages to verifying data elements on a client before sending to the server, namely efficiency. Doing checks on the client saves a round-trip, and its delays, before a user can be alerted to a problem. This can improve usability of software interfaces.

The client is not a suitable place to perform any critical value checks or security checks. The reasons for this are twofold. First, the client can change anything after the check. And second, the data can be altered while in transit or at an intermediary proxy. For all checks that are essential, either for business reasons or security, the verification steps should be performed on the server side, where the data is free from unauthorized alterations. Input validation checks can only be safely performed on the server side.

 EXAM TIP All input validation should be performed on the server side of the client-server relationship, where it is free from outside influence and change.

Chapter Review

In this chapter, you became acquainted with the principles of application security controls. Among the testable controls are fuzzing, cross-site scripting prevention, cross-site request forgery prevention, and the secure coding concepts of error and exception handling and input validation. The application hardening processes of patch management and baseline configuration settings were presented. The chapter closed with an examination of NoSQL vs. SQL databases and the role of client-side vs. server-side validation efforts.

Questions

To help you prepare further for the CompTIA Security+ exam, and to test your level of preparedness, answer the following questions and then check your answers against the correct answers at the end of the chapter.

1. Which of the following describes fuzzing?

   A. Iterative development

   B. Removing and not using old code

   C. Systematic application of malformed inputs

   D. Buffer overflows

2. Which of the following correctly defines SQL injection?

   A. Modifying a database query statement through false input to a function

   B. The process by which application programs manipulate strings to a base form

   C. Inputs to web applications that are processed by different parsers

   D. Character code sets that allow multilanguage capability

3. Which of the following is one of the most common web attack methodologies?

   A. Cross-site scripting (XSS)

   B. Cross-site request forgery (XSRF)

   C. Buffer overflows

   D. RPC errors

4. Which of the following is not a common use of cross-site scripting attacks?

   A. Information theft

   B. Deploying malware

   C. Website defacement

   D. Session hijacking

5. Which of the following is the least favorable location for security checks?

   A. Server-side code

   B. Client-side code

   C. Server-side input validation

   D. Server-side output validation

6. Which of the following is a way to defend against buffer overflow errors?

   A. Write fast code

   B. Use pointers

   C. Use unbounded string manipulation

   D. Treat all input from outside a function as hostile

7. Which of the following correctly describes cross-site scripting (XSS)?

   A. Overflowing the allocated storage area to corrupt a running program

   B. Attempting to break a cryptographic system

   C. Exploiting the trust a site has in the user's browser

   D. Exploiting the trust a user has for the site

8. Which of the following correctly describes cross-site request forgery (XSRF)?

   A. Attacking a system by sending malicious input and relying upon the parsers and execution elements to perform the requested actions

   B. An enhanced data cryptographic encapsulation method

   C. Attacking a system by sending script commands and relying upon the parsers and execution elements to perform the requested actions

   D. Attempting to break a cryptographic system

9. Error and exception handling should be performed in what fashion?

   A. All errors/exceptions should be trapped and handled in the main program.

   B. All errors/exceptions should be trapped and handled in the generating routine.

   C. Errors and exceptions should only be handled if they exceed a given severity.

   D. Errors and exceptions should be logged; handling is optional.

10. The best process to use for determining unexpected input validation problems is _____.

11. The _____ defines the proper configuration settings for an application.

12. The two elements of application hardening are _____ and _____.

13. Explain to your coworker the key difference between cross-site request forgery (XSRF) and cross-site scripting (XSS).

14. Input validation is especially well suited for the following vulnerabilities: _____, _____, and _____.

15. Your boss has asked you to identify two of the most dangerous software errors that your company should address as soon as possible. State where you can find the latest top 25 list of the most dangerous software errors and explain to your boss how you can address two of those top 25.

Answers

1. **C.** Fuzzing is the systematic application of malformed inputs to test how the program responds.

2. **A.** SQL injection is modifying a database query statement through false input to a function.

3. **A.** Cross-site scripting (XSS) is one of the most common web attack methodologies.

4. **C.** Website defacement is not normally performed via cross-site scripting attacks.

5. **B.** The client is not a suitable place to perform any critical value checks or security checks.

6. **D.** One way to defend against buffer overflow errors is to treat all input from outside a function as hostile.

7. **D.** Cross-site scripting (XSS) exploits the trust a user has for the site.

8. **A.** Cross-site request forgery (XSRF) is attacking a system by sending malicious input and relying upon the parsers and execution elements to perform the requested actions.

9. **B.** All errors/exceptions should be trapped and handled in the generating routine.

10. fuzzing

11. application configuration baseline

12. removing unneeded services/options; securing the remaining configuration

13. Cross-site request forgery (XSRF) exploits the trust a site has in the user's browser, while cross-site scripting (XSS) exploits the trust a user has for the site.

14. The answer should include any three of buffer overflow, reliance on untrusted inputs in a security decision, cross-site scripting (XSS), cross-site request forgery (XSRF), path traversal, and incorrect calculation of buffer size.

15. The Top 25 is maintained by MITRE, and is found at http://cwe.mitre.org/top25/.

CHAPTER 18

Mobile Device Security

In this chapter, you will

- Explore mobile security concepts
- Learn about mobile technologies
- Examine risk associated with mobile devices
- Examine risk associated with cloud environments

There has been an amazing convergence of business and individual usage of mobile devices. The convergence of cloud storage capabilities and Software as a Service (SaaS) is dramatically changing the landscape of mobile device usage. The ubiquitous presence of mobile devices and the need for continuous data access across multiple platforms have led to significant changes in the way mobile devices are being used for personal and business purposes. In the past, companies provided mobile devices to their employees for primarily business usage, but they were available for personal usage. With continuously emerging devices and constantly changing technologies, many companies are allowing employees to bring their own devices (BYOD: bring your own device) for both personal and business usage.

Device Security

Security principles similar to those applicable to laptop computers must be followed when using mobile devices such as smartphones and tablet computing devices. Data must be protected, devices must be properly configured, and good user habits must be encouraged. This chapter will review a large number of topics specific to mobile devices. You'll likely find that the security principles you've already learned apply and just need to be adapted to mobile technologies. This is one of the fastest-changing areas of computer security because mobile technology is likely the fastest-changing technology.

Full Device Encryption

Just as laptop computers should be protected with whole disk encryption to protect the laptop in case of loss or theft, you may need to consider encryption for mobile devices used by your company's employees. Mobile devices are much more likely to be lost or stolen, so you should consider encrypting data on your devices. More and more, mobile devices are used when accessing and storing business-critical data or other sensitive information. Protecting the information on mobile devices is becoming a business imperative. This is an emerging technology, so you'll need to complete some rigorous market analysis to determine what commercial product meets your needs.

Remote Wiping

Today's mobile devices are almost innumerable and are very susceptible to loss and theft. Further, it is unlikely that a lost or stolen device will be recovered, thus making even encrypted data stored on a device more vulnerable to decryption. If the thief can have your device for a long time, he can take all the time he wants to try to decrypt your data. Therefore, many companies prefer to just remotely wipe a lost or stolen device. *Wiping* a mobile device typically removes data stored on the device and resets the device to factory settings. There is a dilemma in the use of BYOD devices that store both personal and enterprise data. Wiping the device usually removes all data, both personal and enterprise. Therefore, if corporate policy requires wiping a lost device, that may mean the device's user loses personal photos and data. The software controls for separate data containers, one for business and one for personal, have been proposed but are not a mainstream option yet.

Lockout

A user likely will discover in a relatively short time that they've lost their device, so a quick way to protect their device is to remotely lock the device as soon as they recognize it has been lost or stolen. Several products are available on the market today to help enterprises manage their devices. Remote lockout is usually the first step taken in securing a mobile device.

Screen-locks

Most corporate policies regarding mobile devices require the use of the mobile device's screen-locking capability. This usually consists of entering a passcode or PIN to unlock the device. It is highly recommended that screen-locks be enforced for all mobile devices. Your policy regarding the quality of the passcode should be consistent with your corporate password policy. However, many companies merely enforce the use of screen-locking. Thus, users tend to use convenient or easy-to-remember passcodes. Some devices allow complex passcodes. As shown in Figure 18-1, the device screen on the left supports only a simple iOS passcode, limited to four numbers, while the device screen on the right supports a passcode of indeterminate length and can contain alphanumeric characters.

Some more advanced forms of screen-locks work in conjunction with device wiping. If the passcode is entered incorrectly a specified number of times, the device is automatically wiped. This is one of the security features of BlackBerry that has traditionally made it of interest to security-conscious users. Apple has made this an option on newer iOS devices. Apple also allows remote locking of a device from the user's iCloud account.

Figure 18-1 iOS lock screens

 EXAM TIP Mobile devices require basic security mechanisms of screen-locks, lockouts, device wiping, and encryption to protect sensitive information contained on them.

GPS

Most mobile devices are now capable of using the Global Positioning System (GPS) for tracking device location. Many apps rely heavily on GPS location, such as device-locating services, mapping applications, traffic monitoring apps, and apps that locate nearby businesses such as gas stations and restaurants. Such technology can be exploited to track movement location of the mobile device. This tracking can be used to assist in the recovery of lost devices.

Application Control

Most mobile device vendors provide some kind of application store for finding and purchasing applications for their mobile devices. The vendors do a reasonable job of making sure that offered applications are approved and don't create an overt security risk. Yet many applications request access to various information stores on the mobile device as part of their business model. Understanding what access is requested and approved upon installation of apps is an important security precaution. Your company may have to restrict the types of applications that can be downloaded and used on mobile devices. If you need very strong protection, your company can be very proactive and provide an enterprise application store where only company-approved applications are available, with a corresponding policy that apps cannot be obtained from any other source.

Storage Segmentation

On mobile devices, it can be very difficult to keep personal data separate from corporate data. Some companies have developed capabilities to create separate virtual containers to keep personal data separate from corporate data and applications. For devices that are used to handle highly sensitive corporate data, this form of protection is highly recommended.

Asset Control

Because each user can have multiple devices connecting to the corporate network, it is important to implement a viable asset tracking and inventory control mechanism. For security and liability reasons, the company needs to know what devices are connecting to its systems and what access has been granted. Just as in IT systems, maintaining a list of approved devices is a critical control.

Mobile Device Management

Mobile device management (MDM) is one of the hottest topics in device security today. MDM began as a marketing term for a collective set of commonly employed protection elements associated with mobile devices. When viewed as a comprehensive set of security options for mobile devices, every corporation should have and enforce an MDM policy. The policy should require

- Device locking with a strong password
- Encryption of data on the device
- Device locking automatically after a certain period of inactivity
- The capability to remotely lock the device if it is lost or stolen
- The capability to wipe the device automatically after a certain number of failed login attempts
- The capability to remotely wipe the device if it is lost or stolen

Password policies should extend to mobile devices, including lockout and, if possible, the automatic wiping of data. Corporate policy for data encryption on mobile devices should be consistent with the policy for data encryption on laptop computers.

In other words, if you don't require encryption of portable computers, then should you require it for mobile devices? There is not a uniform answer to this question; mobile devices are much more mobile in practice than laptops and are more prone to loss. This is ultimately a risk question that management must address: What is the risk and what are the costs of the options employed? This also raises a bigger question: Which devices should have encryption as a basic security protection mechanism? Is it by device type or by user based on what data would be exposed to risk? Fortunately, MDM solutions exist, making the choices manageable.

 EXAM TIP Mobile device management (MDM) is a marketing term for a collective set of commonly employed protection elements associated with mobile devices.

Device Access Control

The principles of access control for mobile devices need to be managed just like access control from wired or wireless desktops and laptops. This will become more critical as storage in the cloud and SaaS become more prevalent. Emerging tablet/mobile device sharing intends to provide the user with a seamless data access experience across many devices. Data access capabilities will continue to evolve to meet this need. Rigorous data access principles need to be applied, and they become even more important with the inclusion of mobile devices as fully functional computing devices. When reviewing possible solutions, it is important to consider seeking proof of security and procedures rather than relying on marketing brochures.

Removable Storage

Because removable devices can move data outside of the corporate-controlled environment, their security needs must be addressed. Removable devices can bring unprotected or corrupted data into the corporate environment. All removable devices should be scanned by antivirus software upon connection to the corporate environment. Corporate policies should address the copying of data to removable devices. Many mobile devices can be connected via USB to a system and used to store data—and in some cases, vast quantities of data. This capability can be used to avoid some implementations of data loss prevention mechanisms.

Disabling Unused Features

As with all computing devices, features that are not used or that present a security risk should be disabled. Bluetooth access is particularly problematic. It is best to make Bluetooth connections undiscoverable. But users will need to enable it to pair with a new headset or car connection, for example. Requiring Bluetooth connections to be undiscoverable is very hard to enforce, but should be encouraged as a best practice. Users should receive training as to the risks of Bluetooth—not so they avoid Bluetooth, but so they understand when they should turn it off. Having a mobile device with access to sensitive information carries with it a level of responsibility. Helping users understand this and act accordingly can go a long way toward securing mobile devices.

Mobile Application Security

Devices are not the only concern in the mobile world. Applications that run on the devices also represent security threats to the information that is stored on and processed by the device. Applications are the software elements that can be used to violate security, even when the user is not aware. Many games and utilities offer value to the user, but at the same time they scrape information stores on the device for information.

Key and Credential Management

The MDM marketplace is maturing quickly. Key and credential management services are being integrated into most MDM services to ensure that existing strong policies and procedures can be extended to mobile platforms securely. These services include protection of keys for digital signatures and S/MIME encryption and decryption. Keys and credentials are among the highest-value items that can be found on mobile devices, so ensuring protection for them is a key element in mobile device security. The keys and credentials stored on the device can be used by multiple applications. Providing protection of these keys while still maintaining usability of them is an essential element of modern mobile application security.

Authentication

When mobile devices are used to access business networks, authentication becomes an issue. There are several levels of authentication that can be an issue. Is the device allowed to access the network? Is the user of the device a network user? If so, how do you authenticate the user? Mobile devices have some advantages in that they can store certificates, which by their very nature are more secure than passwords. This moves the authentication problem to the endpoint, where it relies on passcodes, screen-locks, and other mobile device protections. These can be relatively weak unless structured together, including wiping after a limited number of failures. The risk in mobile authentication is that strong credentials stored in the device are protected by the less rigorous passcode and the end user. End users can share their mobile devices, and by proxy unwittingly share their strong corporate authentication codes.

Geo-tagging

Photos taken on mobile devices or with cameras that have GPS capabilities can have location information embedded in the digital photo. This is called *geo-tagging*. Posting photos with geo-tags embedded in them has its use, but it can also unexpectedly publish information that users may not want to share. For example, if you use your smartphone to take a photo of your car in the driveway and then post the photo on the

Internet in an attempt to sell your car, if geo-tagging was enabled on the smartphone, the location of where the photo was taken is embedded as metadata in the digital photo. Such a posting could inadvertently expose where your home is located. There has been much public discussion on this topic, and geo-tagging can be disabled on most mobile devices. It is recommended that it be disabled unless you have a specific reason for having the location information embedded in the photo.

Application Whitelisting

As discussed in the "Application Control" section earlier in the chapter, controlling what applications a device can access may be an important element of your company's mobile device policy. Application whitelisting and blacklisting enables you to control and block applications available on the mobile device. This is usually administered through some type of MDM capability. Application whitelisting can improve security by preventing unapproved applications from being installed and run on the device.

Encryption

Just as the device should be encrypted, thereby protecting all information on the device, applications should be encrypted as well. Just employing encryption for the data store is not sufficient. If the device is fully encrypted, then all apps would have to have access to the data, in essence bypassing the encryption from an app point of view. Apps with sensitive information should control access via their own set of protections. The only way to segregate data within the device is for apps to manage their own data stores through app-specific encryption. This will allow sensitive data to be protected from rogue applications that would leak data if uniform access was allowed.

Transitive Trust/Authentication

Security across multiple domains/platforms is provided through trust relationships. When trust relationships between domains or platforms exist, authentication for each domain trusts the authentication for all other trusted domains. Thus, when an application is authenticated, its authentication is accepted by all other domains/platforms that trust the authenticating domain or platform. Trust relationships can be very complex in mobile devices, and often security aspects aren't properly implemented. Mobile devices tend to be used across numerous systems, including business, personal, public, and private. This greatly expands the risk profile and opportunity for transitive trust–based attacks. As with all other applications, mobile applications should be carefully reviewed to ensure that trust relationships are secure.

BYOD Concerns

BYOD has many advantages in business, and not just from the perspective of device cost. Users tend to prefer having a single device rather than carrying multiple devices. Users have less of a learning curve on devices they already have an interest in learning.

Data Ownership

BYOD blurs the lines of data ownership because it blurs the lines of device management. If a company owns a smartphone issued to an employee, the company can repossess the phone upon employee termination. This practice may protect company data by keeping the company-issued devices in the hands of employees only. However, a company cannot rely on a simple factory reset before reissuing a device, because factory resetting may not remove all the data on the device. If a device is reissued, it is possible that some of the previous owner's personal information, such as private contacts, still remains on the device. On the other hand, if the employee's device is a personal device that has been used for business purposes, upon termination of the employee, it is likely that some company data remains on the phone despite the company's best efforts to remove its data from the device. If that device is resold or recycled, the company's data may remain on the device and be passed on to the subsequent owner. Keeping business data in separate MDM-managed containers is one method of dealing with this issue.

Support Ownership

Support costs for mobile devices are an important consideration for corporations. Each device has its own implementation of various functions. While those functions typically are implemented against a specification, software implementations may not fully or properly implement the specification. This may result in increased support calls to your help desk or support organization. It is very difficult for a corporate help desk to be knowledgeable on all aspects of all possible devices that access a corporate network. For example, your support organization must be able to troubleshoot iPhones, Android devices, tablets, and so forth. These devices are updated frequently, new devices are released, and new capabilities are added on a regular basis. Your support organization will need viable knowledge base articles and job aids in order to provide sufficient support for the wide variety of ever-changing devices.

Patch Management

Just as your corporate policy should enforce the prompt update of desktop and laptop computers to help eliminate security vulnerabilities on those platforms, it should also require mobile devices to be kept current with respect to patches. Having the latest applications, operating system, and so on is an important best defense against viruses, malware, and other threats. It is important to recognize that "jailbreaking" or "rooting" your device may remove the manufacturer's security mechanisms and protection against malware and other threats. These devices may also no longer be able to update their applications or OS against known issues. Jailbreaking or rooting is also a method used to bypass security measures associated with the device manufacturer control, and in some locations, this can be illegal. Mobile devices that are jailbroken or rooted should not be trusted on your enterprise network or allowed to access sensitive data.

Antivirus Management

Just like desktop and laptop computers, smartphones, tablets, and other mobile devices need protection against viruses and malware. It is important that corporate policy and personal usage keep operating systems and applications current. Antivirus and malware protection should be employed as widely as possible and kept up-to-date against current threats.

Forensics

Mobile device forensics is a rapidly evolving and fast-changing field. Because devices are evolving so quickly and changing so fast, it is difficult to stay current in this field. Solid forensics principles should always be followed. Devices should be properly handled by using RF-shielded bags or containers. Because of the rapid changes in this area, it's best to engage the help of trained forensics specialists to ensure data isn't contaminated and the device state and memory are unaltered. If forensics are needed on a device that has both personal and business data, then policies need to be in place to cover the appropriate privacy protections on the personal side of the device.

Privacy

When an employee uses his personal device to perform his work for the company, he may have strong expectations that privacy will be protected by the company. The company policy needs to consider this and address it explicitly. On company-owned devices, it's quite acceptable for the company to reserve the right to access and wipe any company data on the device. The company can thus state that the user can have no expectation of privacy when using a company device. But when the device is a personal device, the user may feel stronger ownership. Expectations of privacy and data access on personal devices should be included in your company policy.

On-boarding/Off-boarding

Most companies and individuals find it relatively easy to connect mobile devices to the corporate network. Often, there are no controls around connecting a device other than having a Microsoft Exchange account. When new employees join a company, the on-boarding processes need to include provisions for mobile device responsibilities. It is easy for new employees to bypass security measures if they are not part of the business process of on-boarding.

Employee termination needs to be modified to include termination of accounts on mobile devices. It's not uncommon to find terminated employees with accounts or even company devices still connecting to the corporate network months after being terminated. E-mail accounts should be removed promptly as part of the employee termination policy and process. Mobile devices supplied by the company should be collected upon termination. BYOD equipment should have its access to corporate resources terminated as part of the off-boarding process. Regular audits for old or unterminated accounts should be performed to ensure prompt deletion of accounts for terminated employees.

Adherence to Corporate Policies

Your corporate policies regarding BYOD devices should be consistent with your existing computer security policies. Your training programs should include instruction on mobile device security. Disciplinary actions should be consistent. Your monitoring programs should be enhanced to include monitoring and control of mobile devices.

User Acceptance

BYOD inherently creates a conflict between personal and corporate interests. An employee who uses her own device to conduct corporate business inherently feels strong ownership over the device and may resent corporate demands to control corporate information downloaded to the device. On the other hand, the corporation expects that corporate data will be properly controlled and protected and thus desires to impose remote wiping or lockout requirements in order to protect corporate data. An individual who loses her personal photos from a special event will likely harbor ill feelings toward the corporation if it wipes her device, including those irreplaceable photos. Your corporate BYOD policy needs to be well defined, approved by the corporate legal department, and clearly communicated to all employees through training.

Architecture/Infrastructure Considerations

Mobile devices consume connections to your corporate IT infrastructure. It is not unusual now for a single individual to be connected to the corporate infrastructure with one or more smartphones, tablets, and laptop or desktop computers. Some infrastructure implementations in the past have not been efficient in their design, sometimes consuming multiple connections for a single device. This can reduce the number of available connections for other end users. It is recommended that load testing be performed to ensure that your design or existing infrastructure can support the potentially large number of connections from multiple devices.

Multiple connections can also create security issues when the system tracks user accounts against multiple connections. Users will need to be aware of this so that they don't inadvertently create incident response situations or find themselves locked out by their own actions. This can be a tricky issue requiring a bit more intelligent design than the traditional philosophy of one userid equals one current connection.

Legal Concerns

It should be apparent from the various topics discussed in this chapter that there are many security challenges presented by mobile devices used for corporate business. Because the technology is rapidly changing, it's best to make sure you have a solid legal review of policies. There are both legal and public relation concerns when it comes to mobile devices. Employees that use both company-owned and personal devices have responsibilities when company data is involved. Policies and procedures should be reviewed on a regular basis to stay current with technology.

Acceptable Use Policy

Similar to your acceptable use policies for laptops and desktops, your mobile device policies should address acceptable use of mobile or BYOD devices. Authorized usage of corporate devices for personal purposes should be addressed. Disciplinary actions for violation of mobile device policies should be defined. BYOD offers both the company and the user advantages; ramifications should be specifically spelled out, along with the specific user responsibilities.

 EXAM TIP Mobile devices offer many usability advantages across the enterprise, and they can be managed securely with the help of security-conscious users. Security policies can go a long way toward assisting users in understanding their responsibilities associated with mobile devices and sensitive data.

On-board Camera/Video

As discussed in the "GPS" section, many mobile devices include on-board cameras, and the photos/videos they take can divulge information. This information can be associated with anything the camera can image, whiteboards, documents, even the location of the device when the photo/video was taken via geo-tagging. Another challenge presented by mobile devices is the possibility that they will be used for illegal purposes. This can create liability for the company if it is a company-owned device. Despite all the potential legal concerns, possibly the greatest concern of mobile device users is that their personal photos will be lost during a device wipe originated by the company.

Chapter Review

In this chapter, you became acquainted with the breadth and depth of security challenges posed by mobile devices. Most of the important security concerns already present in the corporate environment extend to mobile devices. BYOD presents a unique challenge, as the devices may no longer be owned by the company, requiring more deliberate security policies and procedures. Most of the security concerns related to mobile devices can be dealt with using approaches already well understood in the security arena. It is important to craft rigorous, comprehensive policies and procedures and to keep them current so they don't fall behind the technology advances in mobile devices.

Questions

To help you prepare further for the CompTIA Security+ exam, and to test your level of preparedness, answer the following questions and then check your answers against the correct answers at the end of the chapter.

PART IV

1. Why is it important to disable geo-tagging on your mobile device?

    A. Geo-tagging makes it so your friends can confirm you took the photos.

    B. Geo-tagging can inadvertently expose the location where photos were taken.

    C. Geo-tagging is a great hobby.

    D. Geo-tagging can enable correlation of photos and locations.

2. Why is it important to terminate employee access upon employee termination?

    A. It is well known that mobile devices/users often still have access months after termination.

    B. Terminated employees can be trusted to not access corporate applications.

    C. Terminated employees own their own devices in a BYOD environment.

    D. The corporation has control of all devices owned by terminated employees.

3. What is one reason that mobile devices can complicate support?

    A. Mobile devices are written to meet specifications and do so with reliability.

    B. All mobile devices implement required functions in the same way.

    C. The vendor can provide required support for mobile devices.

    D. The sheer variety of available devices can severely complicate the support training required.

4. Which of the following correctly describes application whitelisting?

    A. Denying access to all applications

    B. Allowing access to unapproved applications

    C. Allowing access only to specifically approved applications

    D. Denying access to specifically approved applications

5. What type of testing should be performed to ensure your network/systems can support mobile device connections?

    A. Load testing

    B. Disaster recovery testing

    C. Regression testing

    D. Both black-box and white-box testing

6. Why is it important to disable unused features on mobile devices?

    A. Disabling unused features reduces the avenues of attack.

    B. Enabling unused features reduces the avenues of attack.

    C. Disabling unused features increases user ease of use.

    D. Enabling unused features increases user ease of use.

7. What is the most important thing to remember regarding performing forensics on a mobile device?

   A. Mobile devices will retain state when powered off.

   B. The device will change state once the battery power is consumed.

   C. Mobile device forensics is very similar to standard workstation forensics.

   D. It is best to rely on specially trained personnel.

8. A coworker asks you to describe the principle of transitive trust. Write one sentence that describes transitive trust.

9. You enter the elevator to find the CEO standing next to you. She asks you to describe the key elements that should be considered regarding BYOD devices. List five essential elements of a BYOD strategy.

10. Your boss calls you to his office and asks you to explain the advantages and disadvantages of BYOD. List two challenges BYOD presents.

11. You have a mobile device that you use to access the corporate network. List three threats with respect to loss of sensitive data associated with the mobile device.

12. List five elements that should be explicitly detailed in an acceptable use policy for mobile devices on a network.

13. What elements does an MDM solution offer a business with respect to mobile device security?

14. List five protections that should be considered before allowing mobile devices to access critical data on the network.

15. List three significant issues associated with jailbroken or rooted mobile devices.

Answers

1. **B.** Geo-tagging can inadvertently expose the location where photos were taken.

2. **A.** Terminated employees often have access to use devices after termination, sometimes even months after termination.

3. **D.** The number and variety of mobile devices can significantly complicate support.

4. **C.** Whitelisting allows access only to specifically approved applications.

5. **A.** Load testing should be performed to ensure your network/systems can support mobile device connections.

6. **A.** Disabling unused devices significantly reduces the avenues of attack.

7. **D.** It is best to rely on specifically trained personnel.

8. Authentication for each domain/platform trusts the authentication for all other trusted domains/platforms.

9. A BYOD strategy should include device locking with a strong password, data encryption, automatic device locking after a certain period of inactivity, remote locking if a device is lost or stolen, automatic wiping after a certain number of failed login attempts, and remote wiping if a device is lost or stolen.

10. BYOD blurs the lines of device ownership and corporate data ownership. Another challenge is the shared location of company and personal data.

11. Apps that scrape contact/phone directory lists, malware that steals data, physical loss of the device, and shoulder surfing to view sensitive information onscreen.

12. Acceptance of company data and its restrictions on the device (remote wiping), responsibilities to have auto-lock engaged, physical protection of the device, use of only approved apps, duty to report stolen or lost devices, responsibility to keep the device up-to-date with respect to OS and applications, implications of a corporate MDM solution.

13. An MDM policy should require

- Device locking with a strong password
- Encryption of data on the device
- Device locking automatically after a certain period of inactivity
- The capability to remotely lock the device if it is lost or stolen
- The capability to wipe the device automatically after a certain number of failed login attempts
- The capability to remotely wipe the device if it is lost or stolen

14. Passwords, security of key store, device encryption, locking of device, remote wiping of device, failed login protections, antivirus/anti-malware protections, application security.

15. Failure to accept new updates, unknown state of internal protection mechanisms, legal issues with respect to licensing.

Host-based Security

In this chapter, you will

- Discover the appropriate solutions to establish host security
- Understand how to implement the appropriate controls to ensure data security
- Examine host-based security controls and applications
- Learn how to ensure data security across multiple environments

Host-based security takes a granular view of security by focusing on protecting each computer and device individually instead of addressing protection of the network as a whole. When host-based security is used, each computer is relied upon to protect itself. A wide array of options can be employed at the host level as part of an enterprise security solution.

Host Security

Most environments are filled with different operating systems (Windows, Linux, OS X), different versions of those operating systems, and different types of installed applications. Also, today, host-based security for mobile device operating systems is an important security issue, which expands the operating system list to include iOS, Android, and BlackBerry. Each operating system has security configurations that differ from other systems, and different versions of the same operating system may in fact have variations between them. Ensuring that every computer is "locked down" to the same degree as every other system in the environment can be overwhelming and often results in an unsuccessful and frustrating effort.

Host security is important and should always be addressed. Security, however, should not stop there, as host security is a complementary process to be combined with network security. If individual host computers have vulnerabilities embodied within them, then network security can provide another layer of protection that will, hopefully, stop any intruders who have gotten that far into the environment.

Operating System Security and Settings

Operating systems are complex programs designed to provide a platform for a wide variety of services to run. Some of these services are extensions of the OS itself, while others are stand-alone applications that use the OS as a mechanism to connect to other

341

programs and hardware resources. It is up to the OS to manage the security aspects of the hardware being utilized. Things such as access control mechanisms are great in theory, but it is the practical implementation of these security elements in the OS that provides the actual security profile of a machine.

Early versions of home operating systems did not have separate named accounts for separate users. This was seen as a convenience mechanism; after all, who wants the hassle of signing into the machine? This led to the simple problem that all users could then see and modify and delete everyone else's content. Content could be separated by using access control mechanisms, but that required configuration of the OS to manage every user's identity. Early versions of many OSs came with literally every option turned on. Again, this was a convenience factor, but it led to systems running processes and services that they never used, and increasing the attack surface of the host unnecessarily.

Determining the correct settings and implementing them correctly is an important step in securing a host system. This chapter explores the multitude of controls and options that need to be employed properly to achieve a reasonable level of security on a host system.

OS Hardening

Operating system developers and manufacturers all share a common problem: they cannot possibly anticipate the many different configurations and variations that the user community will require from their products. So rather than spending countless hours and funds attempting to meet every need, manufacturers provide a "default" installation for their products that usually contains the base OS and some more commonly desirable options, such as drivers, utilities, and enhancements. Because the OS could be used for any of a variety of purposes, and could be placed in any number of logical locations (LAN, DMZ, WAN, and so on), the manufacturer typically does little to nothing with regard to security. The manufacturer may provide some recommendations or simplified tools and settings to facilitate securing the system, but in general, end users are responsible for securing their own systems. Generally, this involves removing unnecessary applications and utilities, disabling unneeded services, setting appropriate permissions on files, and updating the OS and application code to the latest version.

This process of securing an OS is called *hardening*, and it is intended to make the system more resistant to attack, much like armor or steel is hardened to make it less susceptible to breakage or damage. Each OS has its own approach to security, and while the process of hardening is generally the same, different steps must be taken to secure each OS. The process of securing and preparing an OS for the production environment is not trivial; it requires preparation and planning. Unfortunately, many users don't understand the steps necessary to secure their systems effectively, resulting in hundreds of compromised systems every day.

 EXAM TIP   System hardening is the process of preparing and securing a system and involves the removal of all unnecessary software and services.

You must meet several key requirements to ensure that the system hardening processes described in this section achieve their security goals. These are OS independent and should be a normal part of all system maintenance operations:

- The base installation of all OS and application software comes from a trusted source, and is verified as correct by using hash values.

- Machines are connected only to a completely trusted network during the installation, hardening, and update processes.

- The base installation includes all current service packs and updates for both the OS and applications.

- Current backup images are taken after hardening and updates to facilitate system restoration to a known state.

These steps ensure that you know what is on the machine, can verify its authenticity, and have an established backup version.

Anti-malware

In the early days of PC use, threats were limited: most home users were not connected to the Internet 24/7 through broadband connections, and the most common threat was a virus passed from computer to computer via an infected floppy disk (much like the medical definition, a computer virus is something that can infect the host and replicate itself). But things have changed dramatically since those early days, and current threats pose a much greater risk than ever before. According to SANS Internet Storm Center, the average survival time of an unpatched Windows PC on the Internet is less than 60 minutes (http://isc.sans.org/survivaltime.html). This is the estimated time before an automated probe finds the system, penetrates it, and compromises it. Automated probes from botnets and worms are not the only threats roaming the Internet—viruses and malware spread by e-mail, phishing, infected websites that execute code on your system when you visit them, adware, spyware, and so on. Fortunately, as the threats increase in complexity and capability, so do the products designed to stop them.

Antivirus

Antivirus products attempt to identify, neutralize, or remove malicious programs, macros, and files. These products were initially designed to detect and remove computer viruses, though many of the antivirus products are now bundled with additional security products and features.

Although antivirus products have had nearly two decades to refine their capabilities, the purpose of the antivirus products remains the same: to detect and eliminate computer viruses and malware. Most antivirus products combine the following approaches when scanning for viruses:

- **Signature-based scanning** Much like an intrusion detection system (IDS), the antivirus products scan programs, files, macros, e-mails, and other data for known worms, viruses, and malware. The antivirus product contains a virus dictionary with thousands of known virus signatures that must be frequently updated, as new viruses are discovered daily. This approach will catch known viruses but is limited by the virus dictionary—what it does not know about, it cannot catch.

- **Heuristic scanning (or analysis)** Heuristic scanning does not rely on a virus dictionary. Instead, it looks for suspicious behavior—anything that does not fit into a "normal" pattern of behavior for the OS and applications running on the system being protected.

Because signature-based scanning is a familiar concept, let's examine heuristic scanning in more detail. *Heuristic scanning* typically looks for commands or instructions that are not normally found in application programs, such as attempts to access a reserved memory register. Most antivirus products use either a weight-based system or a rule-based system in their heuristic scanning (more effective products use a combination of both techniques). A *weight-based system* rates every suspicious behavior based on the degree of threat associated with that behavior. If the set threshold is passed based on a single behavior or a combination of behaviors, the antivirus product will treat the process, application, macro, and so on that is performing the behavior(s) as a threat to the system. A *rule-based system* compares activity to a set of rules meant to detect and identify malicious software. If part of the software matches a rule, or if a process, application, macro, and so on performs a behavior that matches a rule, the antivirus software will treat that as a threat to the local system.

Some heuristic products are very advanced and contain capabilities for examining memory usage and addressing, a parser for examining executable code, a logic flow analyzer, and a disassembler/emulator so they can "guess" what the code is designed to do and whether or not it is malicious.

As with IDS/IPS products, encryption and obfuscation pose a problem for antivirus products: anything that cannot be read cannot be matched against current virus dictionaries or activity patterns. To combat the use of encryption in malware and viruses, many heuristic scanners look for encryption and decryption loops. Because malware is usually designed to run alone and unattended, if it uses encryption, it must contain all the instructions to encrypt and decrypt itself as needed. Heuristic scanners look for instructions such as the initialization of a pointer with a valid memory address, manipulation of a counter, or a branch condition based on a counter value. While these actions don't always indicate the presence of an encryption/decryption loop, if the heuristic engine can find a loop, it might be able to decrypt the software in a protected memory space, such as an emulator, and evaluate the software in more detail. Many viruses share common encryption/decryption routines that help antivirus developers.

Current antivirus products are highly configurable and most offerings will have the following capabilities:

- **Automated updates** Perhaps the most important feature of a good antivirus solution is its ability to keep itself up to date by automatically downloading the latest virus signatures on a frequent basis. This usually requires that the system be connected to the Internet in some fashion and that updates be performed on a daily (or more frequent) basis.

- **Automated scanning** Most antivirus products allow for the scheduling of automated scans so that you can designate when the antivirus product will examine the local system for infected files. These automated scans can typically be scheduled for specific days and times, and the scanning parameters can be configured to specify what drives, directories, and types of files are scanned.

- **Media scanning** Removable media is still a common method for virus and malware propagation, and most antivirus products can be configured to automatically scan optical media, USB drives, memory sticks, or any other type of removable media as soon as they are connected to or accessed by the local system.

- **Manual scanning** Many antivirus products allow the user to scan drives, files, or directories (folders) "on demand."

- **E-mail scanning** E-mail is still a major method of virus and malware propagation. Many antivirus products give users the ability to scan both incoming and outgoing messages as well as any attachments.

- **Resolution** When the antivirus product detects an infected file or application, it can typically perform one of several actions. The antivirus product may quarantine the file, making it inaccessible; it may try to repair the file by removing the infection or offending code; or it may delete the infected file. Most antivirus products allow the user to specify the desired action, and some allow for an escalation in actions, such as cleaning the infected file if possible and quarantining the file if it cannot be cleaned.

Antivirus solutions are typically installed on individual systems (desktops, servers, and even mobile devices), but network-based antivirus capabilities are also available in many commercial gateway products. These gateway products often combine firewall, IDS/IPS, and antivirus capabilities into a single integrated platform. Most organizations will also employ antivirus solutions on e-mail servers, as that continues to be a very popular propagation method for viruses.

While the installation of a good antivirus product is still considered a necessary best practice, there is growing concern about the effectiveness of antivirus products against developing threats. Early viruses often exhibited destructive behaviors; were poorly written, modified files; and were less concerned with hiding their presence than they were with propagation. We are seeing an emergence of viruses and malware created by professionals, sometimes financed by criminal organizations or governments, that go to great lengths to hide their presence. These viruses and malware are often used to steal sensitive information or turn the infected PC into part of a larger botnet for use in spamming or attack operations.

 EXAM TIP Antivirus is an essential security application on all platforms.

PART IV

Anti-spam

The bane of users and system administrators everywhere, *spam* is essentially unsolicited or undesired bulk electronic messages. While typically applied to e-mail, spam can be transmitted via text message to phones and mobile devices, as postings to Internet forums, and by other means. If you've ever used an e-mail account, chances are you've received spam.

From a productivity and security standpoint, spam costs businesses and users billions of dollars each year, and it is such a widespread problem that the U.S. Congress passed the CAN-SPAM Act of 2003 to empower the Federal Trade Commission to enforce the act and the Department of Justice to enforce criminal sanctions against spammers. The act establishes requirements for those who send commercial e-mail, spells out penalties for spammers and companies whose products are advertised in spam if they violate the law, and gives consumers the right to ask e-mailers to stop spamming them. Despite all our best efforts, however, spam just keeps coming; as the technologies and techniques developed to stop the spam get more advanced and complex, so do the tools and techniques used to send out the unsolicited messages.

Here are a few of the more popular methods used to fight the spam epidemic; most of these techniques are used to filter e-mail, but could be applied to other mediums as well:

- **Blacklisting** Blacklisting is essentially noting which domains and source addresses have a reputation for sending spam and rejecting messages coming from those domains and source addresses. This is basically a permanent "ignore" or "call block" type capability. Several organizations and a few commercial companies provide lists of known spammers.

- **Content or keyword filtering** Similar to Internet content filtering, this method filters e-mail messages for undesirable content or indications of spam. Much like content filtering of web content, filtering e-mail based on something like keywords can cause unexpected results, as certain terms can be used in both legitimate and spam e-mail. Most content-filtering techniques use regular expression matching for keyword filtering.

- **Trusted servers** The opposite of blacklisting, a trusted server list includes SMTP servers that are being "trusted" not to forward spam.

- **Delay-based filtering** Some Simple Mail Transfer Protocol (SMTP) servers are configured to insert a deliberate pause between the opening of a connection and the sending of the SMTP server's welcome banner. Some spam-generating programs do not wait for that greeting banner, and any system that immediately starts sending data as soon as the connection is opened is treated as a spam generator and dropped by the SMTP server.

- **PTR and reverse DNS checks** Some e-mail filters check the origin domain of an e-mail sender. If the reverse checks show the mail is coming from a dial-up user, home-based broadband, or a dynamically assigned address, or has a generic or missing domain, then the filter rejects it, as these are common sources of spam messages.

- **Callback verification**   Because many spam messages use forged "from" addresses, some filters attempt to validate the "from" address of incoming e-mail. The receiving server can contact the sending server in an attempt to validate the sending address, but this is not always effective, as spoofed addresses are sometimes valid e-mail addresses that can be verified.

- **Statistical content filtering**   Statistical filtering is much like a document classification system. Users mark received messages as either spam or legitimate mail and the filtering system learns from the users' input. The more messages that are seen and classified as spam, the better the filtering software should get at intercepting incoming spam. Spammers counteract many filtering technologies by inserting random words and characters into the messages, making it difficult for content filters to identify patterns common to spam.

- **Rule-based filtering**   Rule-based filtering is a simple technique that merely looks for matches in certain fields or keywords. For example, a rule-based filtering system may look for any message with the words "get rich" in the subject line of the incoming message. Many popular e-mail clients have the ability to implement rule-based filtering.

- **Egress filtering**   Some organizations perform spam filtering on e-mail leaving their organization as well, and this is called egress filtering. The same types of anti-spam techniques can be used to validate and filter outgoing e-mail in an effort to combat spam.

- **Hybrid filtering**   Most commercial anti-spam methods use hybrid filtering, or a combination of several different techniques to fight spam. For example, a filtering solution may take each incoming message and match it against known spammers, then against a rule-based filter, then a content filter, and finally against a statistic-based filter. If the message passes all filtering stages, it will be treated as a legitimate message; otherwise, it is rejected as spam.

Much spam filtering is done at the network or SMTP server level. It's more efficient to scan all incoming and outgoing messages with a centralized solution than it is to deploy individual solutions on end-user machines throughout the organization. E-mail is essentially a proxied service by default: messages generally come into and go out of an organization's mail server. (Users don't typically connect to remote SMTP servers to send and receive messages, but they can.) Anti-spam solutions are available in the form of software that is loaded on the SMTP server itself or on a secondary server that processes messages either before they reach the SMTP server or after the messages are processed by the SMTP server. Anti-spam solutions are also available in appliance form, where the software and hardware are a single integrated solution. Many centralized anti-spam methods allow individual users to customize spam filtering for their specific inbox, specifying their own filter rules and criteria for evaluating inbound e-mail.

Anti-spyware

Most antivirus products will include anti-spyware capabilities as well. While antivirus programs were designed to watch for the writing of files to the file system, many current forms of malware avoid the file system to avoid this form of detection. Newer antivirus products are adapting and scanning memory as well as watching file system access in an attempt to detect advanced malware. *Spyware* is the term used to define malware that is designed to steal information from the system, such as keystrokes, passwords, PINs, and keys. Anti-spyware helps protect your systems from the ever-increasing flood of malware that seeks to watch your keystrokes, steal your passwords, and report sensitive information back to attackers. Many of these attack vectors work in system memory to avoid easy detection.

Pop-up Blockers

One of the most annoying nuisances associated with web browsing is the pop-up ad. Pop-up ads are online advertisements designed to attract web traffic to specific websites, capture e-mail addresses, advertise a product, and perform other tasks. If you've spent more than an hour surfing the Web, you've undoubtedly seen them. They're created when the website you are visiting opens a new web browser window for the sole purpose of displaying an advertisement. Pop-up ads typically appear in front of your current browser window to catch your attention (and disrupt your browsing). Pop-up ads can range from mildly annoying, generating one or two pop-ups, to system crippling if a malicious website attempts to open thousands of pop-up windows on your system.

Similar to the pop-up ad is the pop-under ad that opens up behind your current browser window. You won't see these ads until your current window is closed, and they are considered by some to be less annoying than pop-ups. Another form of pop-up is the hover ad that uses Dynamic HTML to appear as a floating window superimposed over your browser window. To some users, pop-up ads are as undesirable as spam, and many web browsers now allow users to restrict or prevent pop-ups with functionality either built into the web browser or available as an add-on. Internet Explorer contains a built-in Pop-up Blocker (shown in Figure 19-1 and available from the Tools menu in Internet Explorer 11).

Firefox also contains a built-in pop-up blocker (available by choosing Tools | Options and then selecting the Content tab). Popular add-ons such as the Google and Yahoo! toolbars also contain pop-up blockers. If these freely available options are not enough for your needs, many commercial security suites from McAfee, Symantec, and Check Point contain pop-up blocking capabilities as well. Users must be careful when selecting a pop-up blocker, as some unscrupulous developers have created adware products disguised as free pop-up blockers or other security tools.

 EXAM TIP Pop-up blockers are used to prevent websites from opening additional web browser windows or tabs without specific user consent.

Pop-ups ads can be generated in a number of ways, including JavaScript and Adobe Flash, and an effective pop-up blocker must be able to deal with the many methods used to create pop-ups. When a pop-up is created, users typically can click a close or cancel button inside the pop-up or close the new window using a method available through the OS, such as closing the window from the taskbar in Windows. With the advanced

PART IV

Figure 19-1
Pop-up Blocker in
IE 11

features available to them in a web development environment, some unscrupulous developers program the close or cancel button in their pop-ups to launch new pop-ups, redirect the user, run commands on the local system, or even load software.

Pop-ups should not be confused with adware. Pop-ups are ads that appear as you visit web pages. Adware is advertising-supported software. Adware automatically downloads and displays ads on your computer after the adware has been installed, and these ads are typically shown while the software is being used. Adware is often touted as "free" software, as the user pays nothing for the software but must agree to allow ads to be downloaded and displayed before using the software. This approach is very popular on smartphones and mobile devices.

Patch Management

Most computer programs are large and complex mixes of interrelated software modules written by dozens or even thousands of separate individuals. With the push toward GUI-based functionality and enhanced capabilities that has occurred over the past several years, operating systems have continued to grow and expand. Vendors typically follow a hierarchy for software updates:

- **Hotfix** This term refers to a (usually) small software update designed to address a specific problem, such as a buffer overflow in an application that exposes the system to attacks. Hotfixes are typically developed in reaction to a discovered problem and are produced and then released rather quickly. Hotfixes typically address critical security-related issues and should be applied to the affected application or OS as soon as possible.

- **Patch**   This term usually refers to a more formal, larger software update that may address several or many software problems. Patches often contain enhancements or additional capabilities as well as fixes for known bugs. Patches are usually developed over a longer period of time.

- **Service pack**   This term usually refers to a large collection of patches and hotfixes rolled into a single, rather large package. Service packs are designed to bring a system up to the latest known good level all at once, rather than requiring the user or system administrator to download dozens or hundreds of updates separately.

EXAM TIP   All software will require changes/patches over time. Managing patches is an essential element of a security program.

Operating System Patching

Windows 7 contains approximately 40 million lines of code, and although it may not be one of the largest, other modern operating systems are in the same range. As OSs continue to grow and introduce new functions, the potential for problems with the code grows as well. It is almost impossible for an OS vendor to test its product on every possible platform under every possible circumstance, so functionality and security issues do arise after an OS has been released. To the average user or system administrator, this means a fairly constant stream of updates designed to correct problems, replace sections of code, or even add new features to an installed OS.

Every OS, from Linux to Windows, requires software updates, and each OS has different methods of assisting users in keeping their systems up to date. Microsoft, for example, typically makes updates available for download from its website. While most administrators or technically proficient users may prefer to identify and download updates individually, Microsoft recognizes that nontechnical users prefer a simpler approach, which Microsoft has built into its operating systems. In Windows 7 and 8 and Windows Server 2012, Microsoft provides an automated update functionality that will, once configured, locate any required updates, download them to your system, and even install the updates if that is your preference. In Microsoft Windows, the Windows Update utility (see Figure 19-2) can perform an on-demand search for updates or be configured to scan for, download, and even install updates automatically—essentially the same functions as Automatic Updates with a new look. An especially nice feature of Windows Update is the ability to scan for and download patches for other Microsoft software, such as Office, as well as updates and patches for the OS itself.

How you patch a Linux system depends a great deal on the specific version in use and the patch being applied. In some cases, a patch will consist of a series of manual steps requiring the administrator to replace files, change permissions, and alter directories.

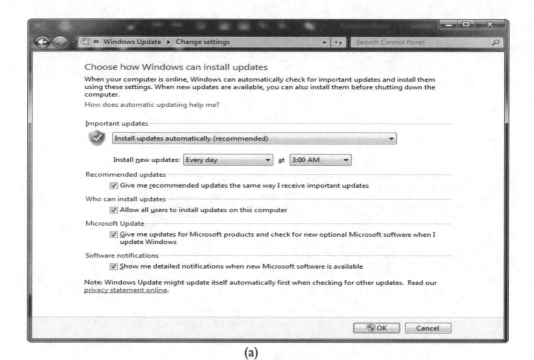

Figure 19-2 Windows Update utility screenshots (*continued*)

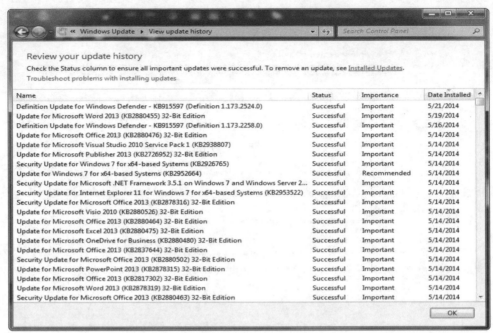

(c)

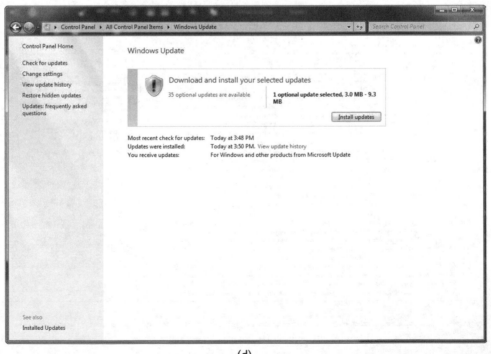

(d)

Figure 19-2 Windows Update utility screenshots

In other cases, the patches are executable scripts or utilities that perform the patch actions automatically. Some Linux versions, such as Red Hat, have built-in utilities that handle the patching process. In those cases, the administrator downloads a specifically formatted file that the patching utility then processes to perform any modifications or updates that need to be made.

Regardless of the method you use to update the OS, it is critically important to keep systems up to date. New security advisories come out every day, and while a buffer overflow may be a "potential" problem today, it will almost certainly become a "definite" problem in the near future. Much like the steps taken to baseline and initially secure an OS, keeping every system patched and up to date is critical to protecting the system and the information it contains.

Application Updates

Just as operating systems need patches, so do applications. Managing the wide variety of applications and the required updates from numerous different software vendors can be a daunting challenge. This has created a niche market for patch management software. In most enterprises, some form of automated patch management solution is used, both to reduce labor and to ensure updates are applied appropriately across the enterprise.

Whitelisting vs. Blacklisting Applications

Applications can be controlled at the OS at the time of start via blacklisting or whitelisting. *Blacklisting* is essentially noting which applications should not be allowed to run on the machine. This is basically a permanent "ignore" or "call block" type capability. Whitelisting is the exact opposite: it consists of a list of allowed applications. Each of these approaches has advantages and disadvantages. Blacklisting is difficult to use against dynamic threats, as the identification of a specific application can easily be avoided through minor changes. Whitelisting is easier to employ from the aspect of the identification of applications that are allowed to run—hash values can be used to ensure the executables are not corrupted. The challenge in whitelisting is the number of potential applications that are run on a typical machine. For a single-purpose machine, such as a database server, whitelisting can be relatively easy to employ. For multipurpose machines, it can be more complicated.

Microsoft has two mechanisms that are part of the OS to control which users can use which applications:

- **Software restrictive policies**   Employed via group policies and allow significant control over applications, scripts, and executable files. The primary mode is by machine and not by user account.

- **User account level control**   Enforced via AppLocker, a service that allows granular control over which users can execute which programs. Through the use of rules, an enterprise can exert significant control over who can access and use installed software.

On a Linux platform, similar capabilities are offered from third-party vendor applications.

Trusted OS

A *trusted OS* is one that is designed to allow multilevel security in its operation. This is further defined by its ability to meet a series of criteria required by the U.S. government. Trusted OSs are expensive to create and maintain because any change must typically undergo a recertification process. The most common criteria used to define a trusted OS is the Common Criteria for Information Technology Security Evaluation (abbreviated as Common Criteria, or CC), a harmonized security criteria recognized by many nations, including the United States, Canada, Great Britain, and most of the EU countries, as well as others. Versions of Windows, Linux, mainframe OSs, and specialty OSs have been qualified to various Common Criteria levels.

Host-based Firewalls

Personal firewalls are host-based protective mechanisms that monitor and control traffic passing into and out of a single system. Designed for the end user, software firewalls often have a configurable security policy that allows the user to determine which traffic is "good" and is allowed to pass and which traffic is "bad" and is blocked. Software firewalls are extremely commonplace—so much so that most modern OSs come with some type of personal firewall included.

Beginning with the Windows XP Professional operating system, Microsoft has included a host-based firewall solution in all modern Windows OSs. The Windows Firewall is fairly configurable; it can be set up to block all traffic, make exceptions for traffic you want to allow, and log rejected traffic for later analysis. With each OS since, Microsoft has expanded the capabilities and configurability of the firewall.

Linux-based OSs have had built-in software-based firewalls (see Figure 19-3) for a number of years, including TCP Wrappers, ipchains, and iptables.

TCP Wrappers is a simple program that limits inbound network connections based on port number, domain, or IP address and is managed with two text files called

Figure 19-3
Linux firewall

hosts.allow and hosts.deny. If the inbound connection is coming from a trusted IP address and destined for a port to which it is allowed to connect, then the connection is allowed.

Ipchains is a more advanced, rule-based software firewall that allows for traffic filtering, Network Address Translation (NAT), and redirection. Three configurable "chains" are used for handling network traffic: input, output, and forward. The input chain contains rules for traffic that is coming into the local system. The output chain contains rules for traffic that is leaving the local system. The forward chain contains rules for traffic that was received by the local system but is not destined for the local system. Iptables is the latest evolution of ipchains. Iptables uses the same three chains for policy rules and traffic handling as ipchains, but with iptables, each packet is processed only by the appropriate chain. Under ipchains, each packet passes through all three chains for processing. With iptables, incoming packets are processed only by the input chain, and packets leaving the system are processed only by the output chain. This allows for more granular control of network traffic and enhances performance.

In addition to the "free" firewalls that come bundled with OSs, many commercial personal firewall packages are available. Programs such as ZoneAlarm from Check Point Software Technologies provide or bundle additional capabilities not found in some bundled software firewalls. Many commercial software firewalls limit inbound and outbound network traffic, block pop-ups, detect adware, block cookies, block malicious processes, and scan instant messenger traffic. While you can still purchase or even download a free software-based personal firewall, most commercial vendors are bundling the firewall functionality with additional capabilities such as antivirus and anti-spyware.

PART IV

Host-based Intrusion Detection

The first IDSs were host-based and designed to examine activity only on a specific host. A host-based IDS (HIDS) examines log files, audit trails, and network traffic coming into or leaving a specific host. HIDSs can operate in real time, looking for activity as it occurs, or in batch mode, looking for activity on a periodic basis. Host-based systems are typically self-contained, but many of the newer commercial products have been designed to report to and be managed by a central system. Host-based systems also take local system resources to operate. In other words, an HIDS will use up some of the memory and CPU cycles of the system it is protecting. Early versions of HIDSs ran in batch mode, looking for suspicious activity on an hourly or daily basis, and typically looked only for specific events in a system's log files. As processor speeds increased, later versions of HIDSs looked through the log files in real time and even added the ability to examine the data traffic the host was generating and receiving.

Most HIDSs focus on the log files or audit trails generated by the local OS. On Linux systems, the examined logs usually include those created by syslog, such as messages, kernel logs, and error logs. On Windows systems, the examined logs are typically the three main Event logs: Application, System, and Security. Some HIDSs can cover specific applications, such as FTP or web services, by examining the logs produced by those specific applications or examining the traffic from the services themselves. Within the log files, the HIDS is looking for certain activities that typify hostile actions or misuse, such as the following:

- Logins at odd hours
- Login authentication failures
- Addition of new user accounts
- Modification or access of critical system files
- Modification or removal of binary files (executables)
- Starting or stopping processes
- Privilege escalation
- Use of certain programs

In general, most HIDSs will operate in a very similar fashion. Figure 19-4 shows the logical layout of a typical HIDS. By considering the function and activity of each component, you can gain some insight into how HIDSs operate.

As on any IDS, the *traffic collector* on an HIDS pulls in the information the other components, such as the analysis engine, need to examine. For most host-based systems, the traffic collector pulls data from information the local system has already generated, such as error messages, log files, and system files. The traffic collector is responsible for reading those files, selecting which items are of interest, and forwarding them to the analysis engine. On some host-based systems, the traffic collector will also examine specific attributes of critical files, such as file size, date modified, or checksum.

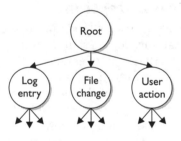

Figure 19-4
Host-based IDS
components

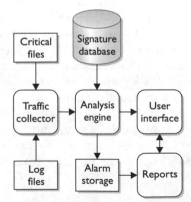

The *analysis engine* is perhaps the most important component of the IDS, as it must decide what activity is "okay" and what activity is "bad." The analysis engine is a sophisticated decision-making and pattern-matching mechanism—it looks at the information provided by the traffic collector and tries to match it against known patterns of activity stored in the signature database. If the activity matches a known pattern, the analysis engine can react, usually by issuing an alert or alarm. An analysis engine may also be capable of remembering how the activity it is looking at right now compares to traffic it has already seen or may see in the near future so that it can match more complicated, multistep malicious activity patterns. An analysis engine must also be capable of examining traffic patterns as quickly as possible, as the longer it takes to match a malicious pattern, the less time the IDS or human operator has to react to malicious traffic. Most IDS vendors build a "decision tree" into their analysis engines to expedite pattern matching.

In IDSs, a decision tree is used to help the analysis engine quickly examine traffic patterns. The decision tree helps the analysis engine eliminate signatures that don't apply to the particular traffic being examined so that the engine can make the fewest number of comparisons. For example, in the following illustration, the sample IDS decision tree shown may contain a section dividing the traffic into three sections based upon origin of the traffic (a log entry for events taken from the system logs, file changes for modifications to critical files, or user actions for something a user has done). When the analysis engine looks at the traffic pattern and starts down the decision tree, it must decide which path to follow. If it is a log entry, the analysis engine can then concentrate on only the signatures that apply to log entries; it does not need to worry about signatures that apply to file changes or user actions. This type of decision tree allows the analysis engine to function much faster, as it does not have to compare traffic to every signature in the database, just the signatures that apply to that particular type of traffic.

The *signature database* is a collection of predefined activity patterns that have already been identified and categorized—patterns that typically indicate suspicious or malicious activity. When the analysis engine has a traffic pattern to examine, it will compare that pattern to the appropriate signatures in the database. The signature database can contain anywhere from a few to a few thousand signatures, depending on the vendor, type of IDS, space available on the system to store signatures, and other factors.

The *user interface* is the visible component of the IDS—the part that humans interact with. The user interface varies widely depending on the product and vendor and could be anything from a detailed GUI to a simple command line. Regardless of the type and complexity, the interface is provided to allow the user to interact with the system: changing parameters, receiving alarms, tuning signatures and response patterns, and so on.

To better understand how an HIDS operates, take a look at examples from a Linux system and a Windows system.

On a Linux system, the HIDS is likely going to examine any of a number of system logs—basically large text files containing entries about what is happening on the

PART IV

system. For this example, consider the following lines from the "messages" log on a Red Hat system:

```
Jan 5 18:20:39 jeep su(pam_unix)[32478]: session opened for user bob by (uid=0)
Jan 5 18:20:47 jeep su(pam_unix)[32516]: authentication failure;
   logname= uid=502 euid=0 tty= ruser=bob rhost= user=root
Jan 5 18:20:53 jeep su(pam_unix)[32517]: authentication failure; logname= id=5
02 euid=0 tty= ruser=bob rhost= user=root
Jan 5 18:21:06 jeep su(pam_unix)[32519]: authentication failure; logname= uid=5
02 euid=0 tty= ruser=bob rhost= user=root
```

In the first line, you see a session being opened by a user named *bob*. This usually indicates that whoever owns the account bob has logged in to the system. On the next three lines, you see authentication failures as user bob tries to become *root*—the superuser account that can do anything on the system. In this case, user bob tries three times to become root and fails on each try. This pattern of activity could mean a number of different things—bob could be an admin who has forgotten the password for the root account, bob could be an admin and someone has changed the root password without telling him, bob could be a user attempting to guess the root password, or an attacker could have compromised user bob's account and is now trying to compromise the root account on the system. In any case, the HIDS will work through its decision tree to determine whether an authentication failure in the message log is something it needs to examine. In this instance, when the IDS examines these lines in the log, it will note the fact that three of the lines in the log match one of the patterns it has been told to look for (as determined by information from the decision tree and the signature database), and it will react accordingly, usually by generating an alarm or alert of some type that appears on the user interface or in an e-mail, page, or other form of message.

On a Windows system, the HIDS will likely examine the Application logs generated by the OS. The three main logs (Application, System, and Security) are similar to the logs on a LINUX system, though the Windows logs are not stored as text files and typically require a utility or application, such as Event Viewer, to read them.

```
Failure Audit  1/5/2013  6:47:29 PM  Security  Logon/Logoff        529  SYSTEM
Failure Audit  1/5/2013  6:47:27 PM  Security  Logon/Logoff        529  SYSTEM
Failure Audit  1/5/2013  6:47:26 PM  Security  Logon/Logoff        529  SYSTEM
Success Audit  1/5/2013  6:47:13 PM  Security  Privilege Use       578  Administrator
Success Audit  1/5/2013  6:47:12 PM  Security  Privilege Use       577  Administrator
Success Audit  1/5/2013  6:47:12 PM  Security  Privilege Use       577  Administrator
Success Audit  1/5/2013  6:47:06 PM  Security  Account Management  643  SYSTEM
Success Audit  1/5/2013  6:46:59 PM  Security  Account Management  643  SYSTEM
```

In the first three lines of the Security log, you see a Failure Audit entry for the Logon/Logoff process. This indicates someone has tried to log in to the system three times and has failed each time (much like our Linux example). You won't see the name of the account until you expand the log entry within the Windows Event Viewer tool, but for this example, assume it was the Administrator account—the Windows equivalent of the root account. Here again, you see three login failures—if the HIDS has been programmed to look for failed login attempts, it will generate alerts when it examines these log entries. Although the logs look different between Linux and Windows, the necessary information to make appropriate determinations is contained in both; the system just needs to extract it from the OS format.

 EXAM TIP Host-based intrusion detection systems and host-based firewalls can provide additional layers of security in a defense-in-depth strategy.

Advantages of HIDSs

HIDSs have certain advantages that make them a good choice for certain situations:

- *They can be very operating system specific and have more detailed signatures.* An HIDS can be very specifically designed to run on a certain OS or to protect certain applications. This narrow focus lets developers concentrate on the specific things that affect the specific environment they are trying to protect. With this type of focus, the developers can avoid generic alarms and develop much more specific, detailed signatures to identify malicious traffic more accurately.

- *They can reduce false positive rates.* When running on a specific system, the IDS process is much more likely to be able to determine whether the activity being examined is malicious. By more accurately identifying which activity is "bad," the IDS will generate fewer false positives (alarms generated when the traffic matches a pattern but is not actually malicious).

- *They can examine data after it has been decrypted.* With security concerns constantly on the rise, many developers are starting to encrypt their network communications. When designed and implemented in the right manner, an HIDS will be able to examine traffic that is unreadable to a network-based IDS. This particular ability is becoming more important each day as more and more websites start to encrypt all of their traffic.

- *They can be very application specific.* On a host level, the IDS can be designed, modified, or tuned to work very well on specific applications without having to analyze or even hold signatures for other applications that are not running on that particular system. Signatures can be built for specific versions of web server software, FTP servers, mail servers, or any other application housed on that host.

- *They can determine whether or not an alarm may impact that specific system.* The ability to determine whether or not a particular activity or pattern will really affect the system being protected assists greatly in reducing the number of generated alarms. Because the IDS resides on the system, it can verify things such as patch levels, presence of certain files, and system state when it analyzes traffic. By knowing what state the system is in, the IDS can more accurately determine whether an activity is potentially harmful to the system.

PART IV

Disadvantages of HIDSs

HIDSs also have certain disadvantages that must be weighed into the decision to deploy this type of technology:

- *The IDS must have a process on every system you want to watch.* You must have an IDS process or application installed on every host you want to watch. To watch 100 systems, then, you would need to deploy 100 HIDSs.

- *The IDS can have a high cost of ownership and maintenance.* Depending on the specific vendor and application, an HIDS can be fairly costly in terms of time and manpower to maintain. Unless the HIDS is some type of central console that allows administrators to maintain remote processes, administrators must maintain each IDS process individually. Even with a central console, with an HIDS, there will be a high number of processes to maintain, software to update, and parameters to tune.

- *The IDS uses local system resources.* To function, the HIDS must use CPU cycles and memory from the system it is trying to protect. Whatever resources the IDS uses are no longer available for the system to perform its other functions. This becomes extremely important on applications such as high-volume web servers where fewer resources usually means fewer visitors served and the need for more systems to handle expected traffic.

- *The IDS has a very focused view and cannot relate to activity around it.* The HIDS has a limited view of the world, as it can see activity only on the host it is protecting. It has little to no visibility into traffic around it on the network or events taking place on other hosts. Consequently, an HIDS can tell you only if the system it is running on is under attack.

- *The IDS, if logged locally, could be compromised or disabled.* When an IDS generates alarms, it will typically store the alarm information in a file or database of some sort. If the HIDS stores its generated alarm traffic on the local system, an attacker that is successful in breaking into the system may be able to modify or delete those alarms. This makes it difficult for security personnel to discover the intruder and conduct any type of post-incident investigation. A capable intruder may even be able to turn off the IDS process completely.

Active vs. Passive HIDSs

Most IDSs can be distinguished by how they examine the activity around them and whether or not they interact with that activity. This is certainly true for HIDSs. On a *passive* system, the IDS is exactly that—it simply watches the activity, analyzes it, and generates alarms. It does not interact with the activity itself in any way, and it does not modify the defensive posture of the system to react to the traffic. A passive IDS is similar to a simple motion sensor—it generates an alarm when it matches a pattern much as the motion sensor generates an alarm when it sees movement.

An *active* IDS contains all the same components and capabilities of the passive IDS with one critical exception—the active IDS can react to the activity it is analyzing. These reactions can range from something simple, such as running a script to turn a process on or off, to something as complex as modifying file permissions, terminating the offending processes, logging off specific users, and reconfiguring local capabilities to prevent specific users from logging in for the next 12 hours. The depth and breadth of response is limited only by the imagination of the implementer, as scripts can automate nearly anything.

Resurgence and Advancement of HIDSs

The past few years have seen a strong resurgence in the use of HIDSs. With the great advances in processer power, the introduction of multicore processors, and the increased capacity of hard drives and memory systems, some of the traditional barriers to running an HIDS have been overcome. Combine that with the widespread adoption of always-on broadband connections, a rise in the use of telecommuting, and a greater overall awareness of the need for computer security, and solutions such as an HIDS start to become an attractive and sometimes effective solution for business and home users alike.

The latest generation of HIDSs has introduced new capabilities designed to stop attacks by preventing them from ever executing or accessing protected files in the first place, rather than relying on a specific signature set that only matches known attacks. The more advanced host-based offerings, which most vendors refer to as host-based intrusion prevention systems (IPSs), combine the following elements into a single package:

- **Integrated system firewall**   The firewall component checks all network traffic passing into and out of the host. Users can set rules for what types of traffic they want to allow into or out of their system.

- **Behavioral- and signature-based IDS**   This hybrid approach uses signatures to match well-known attacks and generic patterns for catching "zero-day" or unknown attacks for which no signatures exist.

- **Application control**   This allows administrators to control how applications are used on the system and whether or not new applications can be installed. Controlling the addition, deletion, or modification of existing software can be a good way to control a system's baseline and prevent malware from being installed.

- **Enterprise management**   Some host-based products are installed with an "agent" that allows them to be managed by and report back to a central server. This type of integrated remote management capability is essential in any large-scale deployment of host-based IDS/IPS.

- **Malware detection and prevention**   Some HIDSs/HIPSs include scanning and prevention capabilities that address spyware, malware, rootkits, and other malicious software.

Hardware Security

Hardware, in the form of servers, workstations, and even mobile devices, can represent a weakness or vulnerability in the security system associated with an enterprise. While hardware can be easily replaced if lost or stolen, the information that is contained by the devices complicates the security picture. Data or information can be safeguarded from loss by backups, but this does little in the way of protecting it from disclosure to an unauthorized party. There are software measures that can assist in the form of encryption, but these also have drawbacks in the form of scalability and key distribution.

There are some hardware protection mechanisms that should be employed to safeguard information in servers, workstations, and mobile devices. Cable locks can be employed on mobile devices to prevent their theft. Locking cabinets and safes can be used to secure portable media, USB drives, and CDs/DVDs. Physical security is covered in more detail in Chapter 10.

 EXAM TIP Physical security is an essential element of a security plan. Unauthorized access to hardware and networking components can make many security controls ineffective.

Host Software Baselining

To secure the software on a system effectively and consistently, you must take a structured and logical approach. This starts with an examination of the system's intended functions and capabilities to determine what processes and applications will be housed on the system. As a best practice, anything that is not required for operations should be removed or disabled on the system; then, all the appropriate patches, hotfixes, and settings should be applied to protect and secure it.

This process of establishing software's base security state is called *baselining*, and the resulting product is a security baseline that allows the software to run safely and securely. Software and hardware can be tied intimately when it comes to security, so they must be considered together. Once the process has been completed for a particular hardware and software combination, any similar systems can be configured with the same baseline to achieve the same level and depth of security and protection. Uniform software baselines are critical in large-scale operations, because maintaining separate configurations and security levels for hundreds or thousands of systems is far too costly.

After administrators have finished patching, securing, and preparing a system, they often create an initial baseline configuration. This represents a secure state for the system or network device and a reference point of the software and its configuration. This information establishes a reference that can be used to help keep the system secure by establishing a known safe configuration. If this initial baseline can be replicated, it can also be used as a template when deploying similar systems and network devices.

Virtualization

Virtualization technology is used to allow a computer to have more than one OS present and, in many cases, operating at the same time. Virtualization is an abstraction of the OS layer, creating the ability to host multiple OSs on a single piece of hardware. One of the major advantages of virtualization is the separation of the software and the hardware, creating a barrier that can improve many system functions, including security. The underlying hardware is referred to as the host machine, and on it is a host OS. Either the host OS has built-in hypervisor capability or an application is needed to provide the hypervisor function to manage the virtual machines (VMs). The virtual machines are typically referred to as the guest OSs.

 EXAM TIP   A hypervisor is the interface between a virtual machine and the host machine hardware. Hypervisors are the layer that enables virtualization.

Newer OSs are designed to natively incorporate virtualization hooks, enabling virtual machines to be employed with greater ease. There are several common virtualization solutions, including Microsoft Hyper-V, VMware, Oracle VM VirtualBox, Parallels, and Citrix Xen. It is important to distinguish between virtualization and boot loaders that allow different OSs to boot on hardware. Apple's Boot Camp allows you to boot into Microsoft Windows on Apple hardware. This is different from Parallels, a product with complete virtualization capability for Apple hardware.

Virtualization offers much in host-based management of a system. From snapshots that allow easy rollback to previous states, faster system deployment via preconfigured images, ease of backup, and the ability to test systems, virtualization offers many advantages to system owners. The separation of the operational software layer from the hardware layer can offer many improvements in the management of systems.

Snapshots

A *snapshot* is a point-in-time saving of the state of a virtual machine. Snapshots have great utility because they are like a savepoint for an entire system. Snapshots can be used to roll a system back to a previous point in time, undo operations, or provide a quick means of recovery from a complex, system-altering change that has gone awry. Snapshots act as a form of backup and are typically much faster than normal system backup and recovery operations.

Patch Compatibility

Having an OS operate in a virtual environment does not change the need for security associated with the OS. Patches are still needed and should be applied, independent of the virtualization status. Because of the nature of a virtual environment, it should have no effect on the utility of patching, as the patch is for the guest OS.

Host Availability/Elasticity

When you set up a virtualization environment, protecting the host OS and hypervisor level is critical for system stability. The best practice is to avoid the installation of any

PART IV

applications on the host-level machine. All apps should be housed and run in a virtual environment. This aids in the stability by providing separation between the application and the host OS. The term *elasticity* refers to the ability of a system to expand/contract as system requirements dictate. One of the advantages of virtualization is that a virtual machine can be moved to larger or smaller environments based on needs. If a VM needs more processing power, then migrating the VM to a new hardware system with greater CPU capacity allows the system to expand without having to rebuild it.

Security Control Testing

When applying security controls to a system to manage security operations, it is important to test the controls to ensure that they are providing the desired results. Putting a system into a VM does not change this requirement. In fact, it may complicate it because of the nature of the guest OS–to–hypervisor relationship. It is essential to specifically test all security controls inside the virtual environment to ensure their behavior is still effective.

Sandboxing

Sandboxing refers to the quarantine or isolation of a system from its surroundings. Virtualization can be used as a form of sandboxing with respect to an entire system. You can build a VM, test something inside the VM, and, based on the results, make a decision with regard to stability or whatever concern was present.

Host-based Security Controls

Security controls can be implemented on a host machine for the express purpose of providing data protection on the host. This section explores methods to implement the appropriate controls to ensure data security.

Cloud Storage

Cloud computing is the use of online resources for storage, processing, or both. When storing data in the cloud, encryption can be used to protect the data, so that what is actually stored is encrypted data. This reduces the risk of data disclosure both in transit to the cloud and back, as well as while in storage.

SAN

A storage area network (SAN) is a means of storing data across a secondary dedicated network. SANs operate to connect data storage devices as if they were local storage, yet they are separate and can be collections of disks, tapes, and other storage devices. Because the dedicated network is separate from the normal IP network, accessing the SAN requires going through one of the attached machines. This makes SANs a bit more secure than other forms of storage, although loss through a compromised client machine is still a risk.

Handling Big Data

Big data is the industry buzzword for very large data sets being used in many enterprises. Data sets in the petabyte, exabyte, and even zettabyte range are now being explored in some applications. Data sets of these sizes require special hardware and software to handle them, but this does not alleviate the need for security. Planning for security on this scale requires enterprise-level thinking, but it is worth noting that eventually some subset of the information makes its way to a host machine for use. It is at this point that the data is vulnerable, because whatever protection scheme is in place on the large storage system, the data is outside that realm now. This means that local protection mechanisms, such as provided by Kerberos-based authentication, can be critical in managing this type of protection scheme.

Data Encryption

Data encryption continues to be the best solution for data security. Properly encrypted, the data is not readable by an unauthorized party. There are numerous ways to enact this level of protection on a host machine.

Full Disk

Full disk encryption refers to the act of encrypting an entire partition in one operation. Then as specific elements are needed, those particular sectors can be decrypted for use. This offers a simple convenience factor and ensures that all of the data is protected. It does come at a performance cost, as the act of decrypting and encrypting takes time. For some high-performance data stores, especially those with latency issues, this performance hit may be critical. Although better performance can be achieved with specialized hardware, as with all security controls, there needs to be an evaluation of the risk involved versus the costs.

Database

Major database engines have built-in encryption capabilities. The advantage to these encryption schemes is that they can be tailored to the data structure, protecting the essential columns while not impacting columns that are not sensitive. Properly employing database encryption requires that the data schema and its security requirements be designed into the database implementation. The advantage is in better protection against any database compromise, and the performance hit is typically negligible with respect to other alternatives.

Individual Files

Individual files can be encrypted as well in a system. This can be done either at the OS level or via a third-party application. Managing individual file encryption can be tricky, as the problem moves to an encryption key security problem. When using built-in encryption methods with an OS, the key issue is resolved by the OS itself, with a single key being employed and stored with the user credentials. One of the advantages of individual file encryption comes when transferring data to another user. Transporting a single file via an unprotected channel such as e-mail can be done securely with single-file encryption.

Removable Media

Removable media, by its very nature, can be moved to another location, making the securing of the data stored on the device essential. Again, encryption becomes the tool of choice, and a wide range of encryption methods and applications support the protection of removable media. Microsoft BitLocker, built in to current editions of its Enterprise, Ultimate, and Pro OSs, offers the ability to protect data stored on removable media.

Mobile Devices

Mobile device security, covered in detail in Chapter 18, is also essential when critical or sensitive data is transmitted to mobile devices. The protection of mobile devices goes beyond simple encryption of the data, as the device can act as an authorized endpoint for the system, opening up avenues of attack.

Hardware-based Encryption Devices

Hardware-based encryption devices are designed to assist in the encryption/decryption actions via hardware rather than software on a system. Integration of encryption functionality via hardware offers both performance and security advantages for these solutions.

TPM

The *Trusted Platform Module (TPM)* is a hardware solution on the motherboard, one that assists with key generation and storage as well as random number generation. When the encryption keys are stored in the TPM, they are not accessible via normal software channels and are physically separated from the hard drive or other encrypted data locations. This makes the TPM a more secure solution than storing the keys on the machine's normal storage.

HSM

A *hardware security module (HSM)* is a device used to manage or store encryption keys. It can also assist in cryptographic operations such as encryption, hashing, or the application of digital signatures. HSMs are typically peripheral devices, connected via USB or a network connection. HSMs have tamper protection mechanisms to prevent physical access to the secrets they protect. Because of their dedicated design, they can offer significant performance advantages over general-purpose computers when it comes to cryptographic operations. When an enterprise has significant levels of cryptographic operations, HSMs can provide throughput efficiencies.

 EXAM TIP Storing private keys anywhere on a networked system is a recipe for loss. HSMs are designed to allow the use of the key without exposing it to the wide range of host-based threats.

USB Encryption

Universal Serial Bus (USB) offers an easy connection mechanism to connect devices to a computer. This acts as the mechanism of transport between the computer and an external device. When data traverses the USB connection, it typically ends up on a portable device and thus requires an appropriate level of security. Many mechanisms exist, from encryption on the USB device itself, to OS-enabled encryption, to independent encryption before moving the data. Each of these mechanisms has advantages and disadvantages, and it is ultimately up to the user to choose the best method based on the sensitivity of the data.

Hard Drive

Because hard drives exist to store information, having the drive itself offer encryption services can provide flexibility in terms of performance and security. It is possible to buy hard drives today with integrated AES encryption, so that the drive content is secured and the keys can be stored separately in a TPM. This offers significant performance and security enhancements over other software-based solutions.

Data Security

Data or information is the most important element to protect in the enterprise. Equipment can be purchased, replaced, and shared without consequence; it is the information that is being processed that has the value. *Data security* refers to the actions taken in the enterprise to secure data, wherever it resides: in transit, at rest, or in use.

Data in Transit

Data has value in the enterprise, but for the enterprise to fully realize the value, data elements need to be shared and moved between systems. Whenever data is *in transit*, being moved from one system to another, it needs to be protected. The most common method of this protection is via encryption. What is important is to ensure that data is always protected in proportion to the degree of risk associated with a data security failure.

Data at Rest

Data at rest refers to data being stored. Data is stored in a variety of formats: in files, in databases, and as structured elements. Whether in ASCII, XML, JavaScript Object Notation (JSON), or a database, and regardless of on what media it is stored, data at rest still requires protection commensurate with its value. Again, as with data in transit, encryption is the best means of protection against unauthorized access or alteration.

Data in Use

Data is processed in applications, is used for various functions, and can be at risk when in system memory or even in the act of processing. Protecting data while in use is a much trickier proposition than protecting it in transit or in storage. While encryption can be used in these other situations, it is not practical to perform operations on encrypted data. This means that other means need to be taken to protect the data.

Protected memory schemes and address space layout randomization are two tools that can be used to prevent data security failures during processing. Secure coding principles, including the definitive wiping of critical data elements once they are no longer needed, can assist in protecting data in use.

 EXAM TIP Understanding the need to protect data in all three phases, in transit, at rest, and in use, is an important concept for the exam. The first step is to identify the phase the data is in, and the second is to identify the correct means of protection for that phase.

Permissions/ACL

Access control lists (ACLs) form one of the foundational bases for security on a machine. ACLs can be used by the operating system to make determinations as to whether or not a user can access a resource. This level of permission restriction offers significant protection of resources and transfers the management of the access control problem to the management of ACLs, a smaller and more manageable problem.

Data Policies

Data has a need for protection commensurate with the risk associated with its loss or alteration. A data security policy is the best way to determine the sensitivity level of the data and to manage the security structure for the data.. Central to a data security policy is the identification of risk, typically done through levels of data classification. Once this has been accomplished, then the tasks to secure the data can be addressed. There are several associated tasks worth examining.

Wiping

The act of deleting a file does not actually delete the data from a file system. To actually destroy the data itself requires a more intensive and invasive procedure known as *wiping*. Wiping works by going into a data structure and replacing the data to be destroyed with an alternative pattern. There are applications available that can perform levels of data wiping on a system, destroying the information. Wiping can also be used to clear other sections of the file space where the data may once have resided but is now gone. Clearing slack space and free space can be important elements in preventing data leakage after use. (One note of caution: modern journaling operating systems can keep track of all changes, including wiping, making it possible to undo various forms of wiping.) Although time consuming and tedious to do, these safeguards in the OS can prevent good data hygiene unless they are suspended during the wipe operation.

Disposing

Disposing of data seems simple—just delete the file. But as just discussed, file deletions do not work that way. In addition, how does one know where all the copies of a particular set of data reside? When addressing the disposal question from a data-centric point of view, problems arise such as, "Where do all of the copies exist?" When addressing it from a device perspective, the question shifts to, "Has the device been wiped before we dispose of the device?" Both of these aspects need to be addressed in the data security policy.

Retention

Data retention is the act of addressing how long you should keep your data. Although "forever" seems to be a simple answer, it isn't necessarily the correct one, depending on the data. Some data has no further purpose in the enterprise after a period of time, and retaining it only wastes resources. Other elements may have statutory or regulatory requirements dictating that data be preserved for some minimal period of time. The data retention policy should clearly address these elements so that data is kept for as long as it is needed and a mechanism is in place to determine when it can be disposed of safely.

Storage

The data protection policy should include details as to how the data should be secured in storage. These details should cover both electronic and physical storage (once printed, the papers may need to be secured physically). The policy should also address methods of protection for storage in terms of key management and levels of encryption.

Chapter Review

In this chapter, you became acquainted with the principles behind securing the host machine, including the data and applications that run on it. The chapter opened with an examination of operating systems, how to harden them, and the standard security precautions of security software and patching practices. It next covered the topics associated with physical access, followed by a presentation of security applications of firewalls and intrusion detection as well as whitelisting of applications. Virtualization and its implications were also covered in the first half of the chapter.

The latter half of the chapter covered the topic of data security, including encryption, policy, and the use of appropriate controls to ensure data security. You read about the use of hardware-specific devices, including TPM and HSMs, as well as how to manage data across the enterprise, from the cloud, to SAN, to removable media.

Questions

To help you prepare further for the CompTIA Security+ exam, and to test your level of preparedness, answer the following questions and then check your answers against the correct answers at the end of the chapter.

1. You've been asked to set up a temporary Internet café for a conference your company is hosting. You have ten laptops to use in your café and need to keep them from "wandering off" once you have them set up and running. What should you use to help physically secure these laptops?

   A. Locking cabinets

   B. Cable locks

   C. Locking USB ports

   D. Password-protected screensaver

2. On those laptops you're setting up for the Internet café, you want to make sure that no one downloads or installs anything to infect the systems. What type of protection should you install before allowing guests to use these laptops?

   A. Anti-spam software

   B. Pop-up blocking software

   C. Antivirus software

   D. Virtualization software

3. You also want to lock down which programs can be run by the guests visiting your Internet café. What's the best way to prevent users from running programs you don't want them to run?

   A. Application whitelisting

   B. Application blacklisting

   C. Trusted operating system

   D. Host-based firewall

4. The Internet café you are building will be directly connected to the Internet. You will need to protect each system from Internet-based scans, probes, and attacks. What kind of protective mechanism should you deploy to protect against Internet-based threats?

   A. Anti-spam software

   B. Host-based firewall

   C. Host-based sandboxing

   D. Anti-malware software

5. Your colleague who is helping you set up the Internet café just asked you if the laptops you're setting up are protected against a recently discovered vulnerability. You are quite sure they are protected because you employ which of the following to ensure security updates are installed on a regular basis?

   A. Quality assurance program

   B. Application blacklisting

   C. Patch management system

   D. Trusted operating system

6. Your boss wants you to create a "golden image" for all corporate workstations. You are in charge of ensuring that all of the right software and drivers are installed and that the configuration of the system is correct before you create the image. This process is known as:

   A. Host software baselining

   B. Host application whitelisting

   C. Host operating system hardening

   D. Host image configuration

7. If an operating system is certified for use in multilevel security environments, it might also be called which of the following?

   A. Secure operating system

   B. Resistant operating system

   C. Trusted operating system

   D. SELinux

8. Your colleague tells you about this great new technique for testing new applications and software that he downloads from the Internet. He uses a virtual machine to test the software and see if it does anything malicious. If it does, then he simply deletes the affected virtual machine. Your colleague is describing what security practice?

   A. Application whitelisting

   B. Security control testing

   C. Snapshot testing

   D. Sandboxing

9. Your boss wants you to order her a new laptop, one with a special chip that will allow her to store encryption keys using BitLocker to protect her drive. What special chip is your boss talking about?

   A. Trusted Platform Module

   B. PKI Module

   C. BitLocker Encryption Module

   D. FIPS 140 Chip

10. When data is stored on a hard drive and is not currently being accessed, this is referred to as:

    A. Data in transit

    B. Data at rest

    C. Data in use

    D. Data in storage

11. Your colleague is in the process of securing a Windows Server 2012 computer. He's removed all unnecessary software, turned off unnecessary services, turned on the firewall, patched it, and so on. What process is your colleague performing?

    A. Operating system hardening

    B. Production system preparation

    C. Security control testing

    D. Patch management

12. One of your SANs is reaching capacity. During your investigation, you notice a very large number of transaction logs and backups from the customer service database. When you ask why there are so many logs, you're told that no one knows how long they're supposed to keep those logs and when it's okay to delete them. What should your organization develop to help prevent runaway accumulation of log files?

   A. Data encryption policy

   B. HSM policy

   C. Data retention policy

   D. Customer service policy

13. Which of the following technologies is used to help secure access to "big data"?

   A. HSM encryption

   B. Kerberos-based authentication

   C. Account whitelisting

   D. Secure protocol methodology

14. Your manager is extremely worried about attacks occurring inside your network between systems. He's convinced that someone from Engineering is attacking his system just to "mess with him." You don't currently have any good way to monitor the traffic between your manager's system and the rest of the network. Which of the following capabilities could you recommend to help your manager see if his system is really under attack?

   A. Host-based vulnerability scanner

   B. Host-based intrusion detection system

   C. Host-based pop-up blocker

   D. Host-based anti-spyware

15. A developer wants you to set up a system she can run multiple tests on with the ability to return the system to its starting configuration over and over again as she tests out different versions of code. She thinks virtualization might be the way to go. What virtualization capability will help satisfy her testing and rollback requirement?

   A. Sandboxing

   B. Snapshots

   C. Host elasticity

   D. Baselining

Answers

1. **B.** Cable locks are a good way to secure laptops to a desk or table. They allow access to the laptop keyboard, USB ports, and optical drive and secure the laptop to whatever the cable is mounted to.

2. **C.** If you are looking for protection from things that "infect" your computer, you should install a good antivirus program, ensure it receives regular updates, and configure it to perform regular scans, including on removable media.

3. **A.** A good way to ensure that only programs you want to run are allowed to run is to use application whitelisting. An application whitelist is a list of programs that the administrator has granted permission to run on that system.

4. **B.** If a system is directly connected to the Internet and you need to protect it from Internet-based probes, scans, and attacks, you will definitely need a host-based firewall. A host-based firewall performs the same functions as a network-based firewall—it blocks traffic you don't want coming in and allows traffic going out that you want to go out. But a host-based firewall only works at the host level—it only protects the system it is running on.

5. **C.** A patch management system allows you to control and track the patch status of any system it is managing. With a patch management system, you can schedule updates, determine which updates are applied, and verify the patch status of any connected system.

6. **A.** Host software baselining is the establishment of all essential requirements of both the operating system and applications installed on a host system.

7. **C.** Trusted operating system is used to refer to an operating system that provides support for multilevel security and meets the specifications for use as a trusted operating system.

8. **D.** Your colleague is describing the process of sandboxing. A "sandbox" is a means for separating untrusted code and applications from trusted code and applications. When sandboxing is done correctly, anything that happens in the sandbox is controlled and is prevented from harming the host system.

9. **A.** Your boss wants a laptop with a Trusted Platform Module (TPM). A TPM is a specialized chip that stores encryption keys specific to the host system for hardware authentication. When BitLocker encrypts an entire drive, it stores the encryption keys within the TPM.

10. **B.** Data that is stored on a drive but is not currently being accessed is referred to as "data at rest."

11. **A.** Your colleague is performing operating system hardening—he's securing the system by reducing vulnerabilities and minimizing the potential attack surface. Removing unnecessary software and services, patching, and restricting the traffic that can go into or out of the system are all steps to help secure, or "harden," the system against potential attacks.

12. **C.** In this situation your organization could really use a good data retention policy. A data retention policy balances the legal, business, or operational need to keep records against the risk and cost of keeping those records. The policy should also clarify how long records should be kept and under what circumstances it's permissible to destroy those records.

13. **B.** Kerberos-based authentication is one of the methods used to help secure access to "big data." Kerberos is a network authentication protocol that uses "tickets" to allow systems to identify and authenticate each other even if the network they are operating on is insecure.

14. **B.** A host-based intrusion detection system (or HIDS) would help your manager determine whether or not his system is under attack. An HIDS works in the same fashion as a network-based IDS, but it operates at the host level. It examines traffic coming into and leaving the host for attack signatures and patterns. An HIDS can only really protect the system it is installed on.

15. **B.** The ability to work with snapshots inside a virtualization environment will satisfy the developer's requirements. Snapshots are copies of the state of a virtual machine at a specific point in time—the file system, memory contents, power state, and so forth are all captured and stored as part of the snapshot. Users have the ability to roll back or revert to snapshots that restore the virtual machine to the state captured by that snapshot, regardless of any changes that were made to the virtual machine.

CHAPTER 20

Securing Alternative Environments

In this chapter, you will

- Learn how to compare and contrast alternative methods to mitigate security risks in static environments
- Understand the role of security in alternative environments
- Examine risk associated with alternative environments

Traditionally, the term *computing* has been associated with mainframes, servers, workstations, and network components. Today, computing also plays a role in many other environments, from ATM machines and SCADA control systems to embedded systems, smartphones, and gaming consoles.

There are a wide variety of methods that can be employed to assist in securing of nontraditional systems. Some of these are direct copies of methods employed in traditional IT systems, while others are unique to these alternative environments.

Alternative Environments

Alternative environments are those that are not traditional computer systems in a common IT environment. This is not to say that these environments are rare; in fact, there are millions of systems, composed of hundreds of millions of devices, all across society. Computers exist in many systems where they perform critical functions specifically tied to a particular system. These alternative systems are frequently static in nature; that is, their software is unchanging over the course of its function. Updates and revisions are few and far between. While this may seem to be counter to current security practices, it isn't: because these alternative systems are constrained to a limited, defined set of functionality, the risk from vulnerabilities is limited. Examples of these alternative environments include embedded systems, SCADA systems, mobile devices, mainframes, game consoles, and in-vehicle computers.

SCADA

SCADA is an acronym for *supervisory control and data acquisition*, a system designed to control automated systems in cyber-physical environments. SCADA systems control manufacturing plants, traffic lights, refineries, energy networks, water plants, building automation and environmental controls, and a host of other systems. SCADA is also known by names such as distributed control systems (DCS) and industrial control systems (ICS), the variations depending on the industry and the configuration. Where computers control a physical process directly, a SCADA system likely is involved.

Most SCADA systems involve multiple components networked together to achieve a set of functional objectives. These systems frequently include a human machine interface (HMI), where an operator can exert a form of directive control over the operation of the system under control. SCADA systems historically have been isolated from other systems, but the isolation is decreasing as these systems are being connected across traditional networks to improve business functionality. Many older SCADA systems were air gapped from the corporate network; that is, they shared no direct network connections. This meant that data flows in and out were handled manually and took time to accomplish. Modern systems wished to remove this constraint and added direct network connections between the SCADA networks and the enterprise IT network. These connections increase the attack surface and the risk to the system, and the more they resemble an IT networked system, the greater the need for security functions.

SCADA systems have been drawn into the security spotlight with the Stuxnet attack on Iranian nuclear facilities, initially reported in 2010. Stuxnet is malware designed to specifically attack a specific SCADA system and cause failures resulting in plant equipment damage. This attack was complex and well designed, crippling nuclear fuel processing in Iran for a significant period of time. This attack raised awareness of the risks associated with SCADA systems, whether connected to the Internet or not (Stuxnet crossed an air gap to hit its target).

Embedded Systems

Embedded system is the name given to a computer that is included as an integral part of a larger system. From computer peripherals like printers, to household devices like smart TVs and thermostats, to the car you drive, embedded systems are everywhere. Embedded systems can be as simple as a microcontroller with fully integrated interfaces (a system on a chip) or as complex as the tens of interconnected embedded systems in a modern automobile. Embedded systems are designed with a single control purpose in mind and have virtually no additional functionality, but this does not mean that they are free of risk or security concerns. The vast majority of security exploits involve getting a device or system to do something it is capable of doing, and technically designed to do, even if the resulting functionality was never an intended use of the device or system.

The designers of embedded systems typically are focused on minimizing costs, with security seldom seriously considered as part of either the design or the implementation. Because most embedded systems operate as isolated systems, the risks have not been significant. However, as capabilities have increased, and these devices have become networked together, the risks have increased significantly. For example, smart printers have been hacked as a way into enterprises, and as a way to hide from defenders. And when next-generation automobiles begin to talk to each other, passing traffic and other information between them, and begin to have navigation and other inputs being beamed into systems, the risks will increase and security will become an issue. This has already been seen in the airline industry, where the separation of in-flight Wi-Fi, in-flight entertainment, and cockpit digital flight control networks has become a security issue.

 EXAM TIP Understand static environments, systems in which the hardware, OS, applications, and networks are configured for a specific function or purpose. These systems are designed to remain unaltered through their lifecycle, rarely requiring updates.

Building-automation systems, climate control systems, HVAC systems, elevator control systems, and alarm systems are just some of the examples of systems that are managed by embedded systems. Although these systems used to be independent and stand-alone systems, the rise of hyperconnectivity has shown value in integrating them. Having a "smart building" that reduces building resources in accordance with the number and distribution of people inside increases efficiency and reduces costs. Interconnecting these systems and adding in Internet-based central control mechanisms does increase the risk profile from outside attacks.

Phones and Mobile Devices

When mobile phones first appeared, they were analog devices intended merely to add portability to the ubiquitous phone system. Today, mobile phones and other mobile devices like tablets are portable computer systems with significant capabilities. A few decades ago, only supercomputers exceeded the processing power, memory, and graphics capability of a current mobile phone. With this power came new uses for these devices, and today mobile devices are a major endpoint in all sorts of enterprises.

Mobile devices may seem to be a static environment, one where the OS rarely changes or is rarely updated, but as these devices become more and more ubiquitous in capability, this is not turning out to be the case. Mobile devices have regular software updates to the OS, and users add applications, making most mobile devices a complete security challenge. Mobile devices frequently come with Bluetooth connectivity mechanisms. Protection of the devices from attacks against the Bluetooth connection, such as bluejacking and bluesnarfing, is an important mitigation. To protect against unauthorized connections, a Bluetooth device should always have discoverable mode turned off unless the user is deliberately pairing the device.

There are many different operating systems used in mobile devices, the most common of these by market share are Android and iOS from Apple. Android is by far the largest footprint, followed distantly by Apple's iOS. Microsoft and BlackBerry have their own OSs, but neither has major numbers of users.

Android

Android is a generic name associated with the mobile OS that is based on Linux. Google acquired the Android platform, made it open source, and began shipping devices in 2008. Android has undergone several updates since, and most systems have some degree of customization added for specific mobile carriers. Android has had numerous security issues over the years, ranging from vulnerabilities that allow attackers access to the OS, to malware-infected applications. The Android platform continues to evolve as the code is cleaned up and the number of vulnerabilities is reduced. The issue of malware-infected applications is much tougher to resolve, as the ability to create content and add it to the app store (Google Play) is considerably less regulated than in the Apple and Microsoft ecosystems.

The use of mobile device management (MDM) systems is advised in enterprise deployments, especially when BYOD occurs. This and other security aspects specific to mobile devices are covered in Chapter 18.

iOS

iOS is the name of Apple's proprietary operating system for its mobile platforms. Because Apple does not license the software for use other than on its own devices, Apple retains full and complete control over the OS and any specific capabilities. Apple has also exerted significant control over its application store, which has dramatically limited the incidence of malware in the Apple ecosystem.

Jailbreaking

A common hack associated with mobile devices is the jailbreak. *Jailbreaking* is a process by which the user escalates their privilege level, bypassing the operating system's controls and limitations. The user still has the complete functionality of the device, but also has additional capabilities, bypassing the OS-imposed user restrictions. There are several schools of thought concerning the utility of jailbreaking, but the important issue from a security point of view is that running any device with enhanced privileges can result in errors that cause more damage because normal security controls are typically bypassed.

Mainframe

Mainframes represent the history of computing, and although many people think they have disappeared, they are still very much alive in enterprise computing. Mainframes are high-performance machines that offer large quantities of memory, computing power, and storage. Mainframes have been used for decades for high-volume transaction systems as well as high-performance computing. The security associated with mainframe systems tends to be built into the operating system on specific-purpose mainframes. Mainframe environments tend to have very strong configuration control mechanisms and very high levels of stability.

Mainframes have become a cost-effective solution for many high-volume applications because many instances of virtual machines can run on the mainframe hardware. This opens the door for many new security vulnerabilities—not on the mainframe hardware per se, but rather through vulnerabilities in the guest OS in the virtual environment.

Game Consoles

Computer-based game consoles can be considered a type of embedded system designed for entertainment. The OS in a game console is not there for the user, but rather there to support the specific applications or game. There typically is no user interface to the OS on a game console for a user to interact with; rather, the OS is designed for a sole purpose. With the rise of multifunction entertainment consoles, the attack surface of a gaming console can be fairly large, but it is still constrained by the closed nature of the gaming ecosystem. Updates for the firmware and OS-level software are provided by the console manufacturer. This closed environment offers a reasonable level of risk associated with the security of the systems that are connected. As game consoles become more general in purpose and include features such as web browsing, the risks increase to levels commensurate with any other general computing platform.

In-vehicle Computing Systems

Motor vehicles have had embedded computers in them for years, regulating engine functions, environmental controls, and dashboard displays. Recently, the functionality has expanded to onscreen entertainment and navigation systems. As the functionality of the systems is expanding, with the addition of networking capability, the same security risks associated with other networked systems emerge. As the in-vehicle computing systems continue to integrate with mobile electronics, and with the coming vehicle-to-vehicle and vehicle-to-roadway communications, security risks will increase and become a pressing issue.

Methods

Many of the alternative environments can be considered static systems. Static systems are those that have a defined scope and purpose and do not regularly change in a dynamic manner, unlike most PC environments. Static systems tend to have closed ecosystems, with complete control over all functionality by a single vendor. A wide range of security techniques can be employed in the management of alternative systems. Network segmentation, security layers, wrappers, and firewalls assist in the securing of the network connections between these systems. Manual updates, firmware control, and control redundancy assist in the security of the device operation.

Network Segmentation

Network segmentation is the use of the network architecture to limit communication between devices. A variety of networking mechanisms can be used to limit access to devices at the network level. Logical network segmentation can be done via VLANs, MAC and IP address restrictions at routers and switches, firewall filtering, and access control mechanisms. One of the challenges with alternative systems is that the devices themselves may not have typical security controls such as access controls or encryption included in their function sets. This makes external controls such as network segmentation even more critical as part of a security solution.

Security Layers

The use of different layers to perform different functions has been a staple of computer science for decades. Employing layers to enforce security aspects has also been a long-standing concept. Not all layers have the same information or processing capability, and using each layer to achieve a part of the security solution leads to more robust security solutions. While a network can manage traffic based on networking information, this is not a complete security solution. Adding additional layers, such as application layer firewalls and authentication services, adds additional security functions that further reduce the risk associated with the system.

Application Firewalls

Application firewalls are policy-enforcement mechanisms that operate at the application layer to enforce a set of communication rules. While a network firewall examines network traffic and enforces rules based on addresses, an application firewall adds significantly greater ability to control an application's communications across the network.

Manual Updates

All systems eventually require updates to fix issues, patch vulnerabilities, and even change functionality. In alternative environments, these changes are in many cases done in a manual manner. Manual updates can be used to restrict the access to the system, preventing unauthorized changes to a system. In some cases, because of scale, an automated system may be used to push out the updates, but the principle of tightly controlling access to system update functionality needs to be preserved.

Firmware Version Control

Firmware is present in virtually every system, but in many embedded systems, it plays an even more critical role, as it may also contain the OS and application. Maintaining strict control measures over the changing of firmware is essential to ensuring the authenticity of the software on a system. Firmware updates require extreme quality measures to ensure that errors are not introduced as part of an update process. Updating firmware, although only occasionally necessary, is a very sensitive event, for failure can lead to system malfunction. If an unauthorized party is able to change the firmware of a system, as demonstrated in an attack against ATMs, an adversary can gain complete functional control over a system.

Wrappers

As discussed in Chapter 19, TCP wrappers are structures used to enclose or contain some other system. Wrappers have been used in a variety of ways, including to obscure or hide functionality. A Trojan horse is a form of wrapper. Wrappers also can be used to encapsulate information, such as in tunneling or VPN solutions. Wrappers can act as a form of channel control, including integrity and authentication information that a normal signal cannot carry. It is common to see wrappers used in alternative environments to prepare communications for IP transmission.

Control Redundancy and Diversity

Defense in depth is one of the underlying security fundamentals, and this is especially needed in alternative environments. Many alternative environments are not equipped with on-board encryption, access control, or authentication services. This makes the controls that surround the device even more critical in ensuring secure operation.

Designing overlapping controls such that each assists the others but does not duplicate them adds significant strength to a security solution. The objective is to raise barriers to entry, preventing unauthorized parties from reaching vulnerabilities, and to mitigate those vulnerabilities they can reach such that the attacker cannot proceed further. There is no such thing as perfect security, but a series of overlapping controls can make exploitation nearly impossible.

When the system is in an alternative environment, whether static or not, the principles of security still apply. In fact, in many cases, they are even more critical because the devices themselves have little to no security functionality and thus depend on the supporting environment to be secure. A diversity of controls in redundant, overlapping structures is the best method of providing this level of mitigation.

 EXAM TIP Understand static environment security methods. Static systems require security and techniques such as network segmentation, security layers, firewalls, wrappers, and other security controls.

Chapter Review

In this chapter, you became acquainted with securing alternative environments. Alternative environments include nonstandard IT systems, such as SCADA systems, embedded systems, mobile devices, mainframes, in-vehicle systems, and game consoles. The chapter also covered the application of security methods, such as network segregation, security layers, application firewalls, manual updates, secure firmware control, wrappers, and diverse control sets.

Questions

To help you prepare further for the CompTIA Security+ exam, and to test your level of preparedness, answer the following questions and then check your answers against the correct answers at the end of the chapter.

1. List five examples of alternative environments.

2. What is an issue associated with the jailbreaking of a mobile device?

   A. Vendor updates to the OS may no longer be properly applied.

   B. Applications will run more efficiently.

   C. Geolocation is more accurate.

   D. Encryption from the vendor will work more efficiently.

3. What is the purpose of mobile device management (MDM)?

   A. It is a malicious jailbreak tool.

   B. It provides the capability to secure, monitor, and support mobile devices.

   C. It is a virus found in the wild.

   D. It provides higher bandwidth.

4. Which of the following is an example of the unique risks associated with an alternative environment device?

   A. It allows data loss of corporate data.

   B. It permits access to the Internet.

   C. It manipulates network configurations.

   D. It allows total control of a physical system.

5. What is one of the most fundamental security practices that should be followed regarding the use of Bluetooth devices?

   A. Bluetooth devices should always be kept in discoverable mode.

   B. Bluetooth devices should be used in TCP mode.

   C. Bluetooth devices should be exempt from BYOD policies.

   D. Bluetooth should always have discoverable mode turned off unless the user is deliberately pairing a device.

6. Which of the following describes a characteristic of alternative systems?

   A. They have embedded security functionality that prevents hacking.

   B. They only run Windows.

   C. Using Linux makes them more secure.

   D. They are designed without typical security functionality as part of their structure.

7. Which of the following best defines static systems?

   A. They have no memory.

   B. They are designed for only one task.

   C. They are configured for specific functions and designed to run unaltered.

   D. They do not have a user interface.

8. What are three critical static environment security methods?

9. Name five methods through which network segregation can be accomplished.

10. Application firewalls operate at what layer?

   A. Application layer

   B. Firewall layer

   C. MAC address layer

   D. Network layer

11. What is unique about mainframes with respect to security?

   A. They are highly flexible systems.

   B. They run an OS that does not have vulnerabilities.

   C. They are isolated from the Internet.

   D. They have all been retired and are not a significant issue anymore.

12. Firmware updates in static systems:

   A. Should be made to run automated and unattended, as these systems may not have users to oversee updates

   B. Should be managed by a manual, tightly controlled process

   C. Are unnecessary because static systems by definition don't have firmware updates

   D. Are always done using a wrapper

13. A wrapper can be used to do which of the following?

   A. Decrease a packet size to a minimum size for transport

   B. Provide for network segregation in an alternative system

   C. Provide authentication services for data

   D. Provide application firewall functionality in a static system

14. What is a primary security issue associated with embedded systems?

   A. A reduced set of functionality

   B. A limited budget (cost)

   C. Lack of network connections

   D. Processing power

15. What issues should a security policy for alternative environments address?

Answers

1. Examples of alternative environments are SCADA and automation systems, mobile devices (including iOS and Android), game consoles, embedded systems, and mainframes.

2. A. Vendor updates to the OS may no longer be properly applied if you jailbreak your device.

3. **B.** MDM provides the capability to secure, monitor, and support mobile devices.

4. **D.** Alternative environments are typically methods of applying computer control to physical processes such as HVAC, elevators, alarms, and so forth. Malfunctions can have real-world physical consequences. Total control of a physical system can present unique risks.

5. **D.** Bluetooth devices should always have discoverable mode turned off unless the user is deliberately pairing a device.

6. **D.** Common basic security functionality such as encryption, authentication, and access control is not included in many alternative systems.

7. **C.** Static environments such as embedded systems, SCADA, and others are configured for specific functionality and are designed to run without updates or system alterations.

8. Possible answers include network segmentation, manual updates, wrappers, firmware control, control redundancy, and diversity.

9. MAC address filtering, IP address routing, VLANs, access control management, and application layer filtering.

10. **A.** Application layer firewalls enforce communication rules at the application layer.

11. **A.** Mainframes are highly flexible, capable of hosting multiple virtualized OSs and presenting a fairly complex security posture in a modern enterprise. Although the base OS may be very secure, the large number and variety of VM instances can pose an interesting challenge from a security standpoint.

12. **B.** Because firmware updates can completely change the functionality of a device and because of the lack of internal security controls, they should be tightly controlled and manually performed.

13. **C.** Wrappers can be used to provide integrity and authentication services for data streams, such as in tunneling and VPNs.

14. **B.** Cost is a driving concern in the design of many embedded systems, the result of which is reduced functionality to only those functions that are absolutely needed. Security is often viewed as not important enough to include in any significant fashion.

15. The security policy should address the same issues that are addressed in regular IT environments. Policies should be specific regarding what needs to be accomplished, not how it should be accomplished. Alternative environments need the same basic security functionality as regular IT systems. Data and systems should be protected to a level commensurate with the risk of failure.

Access Control and Identity Management

CHAPTER 21

Access Control and Authentication

In this chapter, you will

- Learn about the methods and protocols for remote access to networks
- Distinguish between identification, authentication, authorization, and accounting (AAA) protocols
- Be introduced to AAA methods and the security implications in their use
- Compare and contrast the function of authentication services
- Given a scenario, select the appropriate identification, authentication, authorization, or access control

Access control and authentication are important to control who has access to computer systems and resources. Principles of controlling access and properly authenticating apply to both internal access and remote access. Remote access requirements are more rigorous, but the same principles can be applied to internal access.

Remote access enables users outside a network to have network access and privileges as if they were inside the network. Being *outside* a network means that the user is working on a machine that is not physically connected to the network and must therefore establish a connection through a remote means, such as dialing in, connecting via the Internet, or connecting through a wireless connection. A user accessing resources from the Internet through an Internet service provider (ISP) is also connecting remotely to the resources via the Internet.

Authentication Services

Authentication is the process of establishing a user's identity to enable the granting of permissions. To establish network connections, a variety of methods are used, which depend on network type, the hardware and software employed, and any security requirements. Microsoft Windows has a specific server component called Remote Access Service (RAS) that provides remote access capabilities to client applications on computers running Windows. Cisco has implemented a variety of remote access methods through its networking hardware and software. UNIX systems also have built-in methods to enable remote access.

The process of connecting by remote access involves two elements: a temporary network connection and a series of protocols to negotiate privileges and commands. The temporary network connection can occur via the Internet, wireless access, or any other method of connecting to a network. Once the connection is made, the primary issue is authenticating the identity of the user and establishing proper privileges for that user. This is accomplished using a combination of protocols and the operating system on the host machine.

The three steps in the establishment of proper privileges are authentication, authorization, and accounting (AAA). *Authentication* is the matching of user-supplied credentials to previously stored credentials on a host machine, and it usually involves an account username and password. Once the user is authenticated, the authorization step takes place. *Authorization* is the granting of specific permissions based on the privileges held by the account. Does the user have permission to use the network at this time, or is her use restricted? Does the user have access to specific applications, such as mail and FTP, or are some of these restricted? These checks are carried out as part of authorization, and in many cases, this is a function of the operating system in conjunction with its established security policies. A last function, *accounting*, is the collection of billing and other detail records. Network access is often a billable function, and a log of how much time, bandwidth, file transfer space, or other resources were used needs to be maintained. Other accounting functions include keeping detailed security logs to maintain an audit trail of tasks being performed. All of these standard functions are part of normal and necessary overhead in maintaining a computer system, and the protocols used in remote access provide the necessary input for these functions.

By using encryption, remote access protocols can securely authenticate and authorize a user according to previously established privilege levels. The authorization phase can keep unauthorized users out, but after that, encryption of the communications channel becomes very important in preventing unauthorized users from breaking in on an authorized session and hijacking an authorized user's data or credentials. As more and more networks rely on the Internet for connecting remote users, the need for and importance of remote access protocols and secure communication channels will continue to grow.

When a user connects to the Internet through an ISP, the user is establishing a connection to the ISP's network, and the same security issues apply. The issue of authentication, the matching of user-supplied credentials to previously stored credentials on a host machine, is usually done via a user account name and password. Once the user is authenticated, the authorization step takes place.

Access controls define what actions a user can perform or what objects a user is allowed to access. Access controls are built upon the foundation of elements designed to facilitate the matching of a user to a process. These elements are identification, authentication, and authorization.

RADIUS

Remote Authentication Dial-In User Service (RADIUS) is a protocol that was developed originally by Livingston Enterprises (acquired by Lucent) as an AAA protocol. It was submitted to the Internet Engineering Task Force (IETF) as a series of RFCs: RFC 2058 (RADIUS specification), RFC 2059 (RADIUS accounting standard), and updated RFCs 2865–2869 are now standard protocols. The IETF AAA Working Group has proposed extensions to RADIUS (RFC 2882).

RADIUS is designed as a connectionless protocol utilizing User Datagram Protocol (UDP) as its transport-level protocol. Connection type issues, such as timeouts, are handled by the RADIUS application instead of the transport layer. RADIUS utilizes UDP ports 1812 for authentication and authorization and 1813 for accounting functions (see Table 21-2 in the "Common Remote Access Ports" section).

RADIUS is a client/server protocol. The RADIUS client is typically a network access server (NAS). The RADIUS server is a process or daemon running on a UNIX or Windows Server machine. Communications between a RADIUS client and RADIUS server are encrypted using a shared secret that is manually configured into each entity and not shared over a connection. Hence, communications between a RADIUS client (typically an NAS) and a RADIUS server are secure, but the communications between a user (typically a PC) and the RADIUS client are subject to compromise. This is important to note, for if the user's machine (the PC) is not the RADIUS client (the NAS), then communications between the PC and the NAS are typically not encrypted and are passed in the clear.

RADIUS Authentication

The RADIUS protocol is designed to allow a RADIUS server to support a wide variety of methods to authenticate a user. When the server is given a username and password, it can support Point-to-Point Protocol (PPP), Password Authentication Protocol (PAP), Challenge Handshake Authentication Protocol (CHAP), UNIX login, and other mechanisms, depending on what was established when the server was set up. A user login authentication consists of a query (Access-Request) from the RADIUS client and a corresponding response (Access-Accept or Access-Reject) from the RADIUS server, as you can see in Figure 21-1.

The Access-Request message contains the username, encrypted password, NAS IP address, and port. The message also contains information concerning the type of session the user wants to initiate. Once the RADIUS server receives this information, it searches its database for a match on the username. If a match is not found, either a default profile is loaded or an Access-Reject reply is sent. If the entry is found or the default profile is used, the next phase involves authorization, for in RADIUS, these steps are performed in sequence. Figure 21-1 shows the interaction between a user and the RADIUS client and RADIUS server and the steps taken to make a connection:

1. A user initiates PPP authentication to the NAS.

2. The NAS prompts for
   - username and password (if PAP), or
   - challenge (if CHAP).

3. User replies with credentials.

4. RADIUS client sends username and encrypted password to the RADIUS server.

5. RADIUS server responds with Accept, Reject, or Challenge.

6. The RADIUS client acts upon services requested by user.

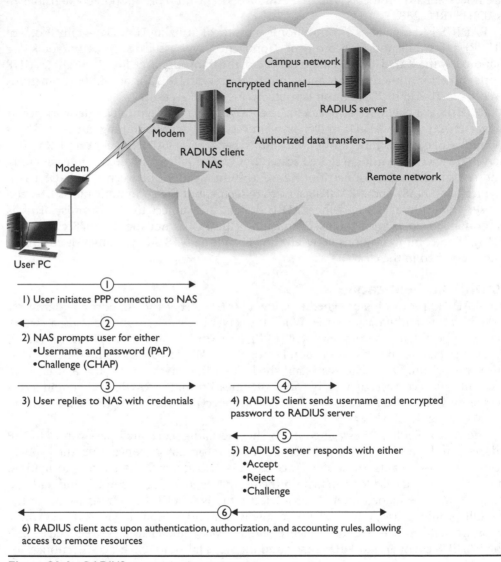

Figure 21-1 RADIUS communication sequence

RADIUS Authorization

In the RADIUS protocol, the authentication and authorization steps are performed together in response to a single Access-Request message, although they are sequential steps, as shown in Figure 21-1. Once an identity has been established, either known or default, the authorization process determines what parameters are returned to the client. Typical authorization parameters include the service type allowed (shell or framed), the protocols allowed, the IP address to assign to the user (static or dynamic), and the access list to apply or static route to place in the NAS routing table. These parameters are all defined in the configuration information on the RADIUS client and server during setup. Using this information, the RADIUS server returns an Access-Accept message with these parameters to the RADIUS client.

RADIUS Accounting

The RADIUS accounting function is performed independently of RADIUS authentication and authorization. The accounting function uses a separate UDP port, 1813 (see Table 21-2 in the "Common Remote Access Ports" section). The primary functionality of RADIUS accounting was established to support ISPs in their user accounting, and it supports typical accounting functions for time billing and security logging. The RADIUS accounting functions are designed to allow data to be transmitted at the beginning and end of a session, and it can indicate resource utilization, such as time, bandwidth, and so on.

When RADIUS was first designed in the mid-1990s, the role of ISP NASs was relatively simple. Allowing and denying access to a network and timing usage were the major concerns. Today, the Internet and its access methods have changed dramatically, and so have the AAA requirements.

TACACS+

The Terminal Access Controller Access Control System+ (TACACS+) protocol is the current generation of the TACACS family. TACACS+ has extended attribute control and accounting processes.

One of the fundamental design aspects is the separation of authentication, authorization, and accounting in this protocol. Although there is a straightforward lineage of these protocols from the original TACACS, TACACS+ is a major revision and is not backward-compatible with previous versions of the protocol series.

TACACS+ uses TCP as its transport protocol, typically operating over TCP port 49. This port is used for the login process, and is reserved in the assigned numbers database maintained by IANA (RFC 3232). In the IANA specification, both UDP and TCP port 49 are reserved for TACACS login host protocol (see Table 21-2 in the "Common Remote Access Ports" section).

TACACS+ is a client/server protocol, with the client typically being an NAS and the server being a daemon process on a UNIX, Linux, or Windows server. This is important to note, for if the user's machine (usually a PC) is not the client (usually an NAS), then communications between the PC and NAS are typically not encrypted and are passed in the clear. Communications between a TACACS+ client and TACACS+ server are encrypted using a shared secret that is manually configured into each entity and is not shared over a connection. Hence, communications between a TACACS+ client (typically an NAS) and a TACACS+ server are secure, but the communications between a user (typically a PC) and the TACACS+ client are subject to compromise.

PART V

TACACS+ Authentication

TACACS+ allows for arbitrary length and content in the authentication exchange sequence, enabling many different authentication mechanisms to be used with TACACS+ clients. Authentication is optional and is determined as a site-configurable option. When authentication is used, common forms include PPP PAP, PPP CHAP, PPP EAP, token cards, and Kerberos. The authentication process is performed using three different packet types: START, CONTINUE, and REPLY. START and CONTINUE packets originate from the client and are directed to the TACACS+ server. The REPLY packet is used to communicate from the TACACS+ server to the client.

The authentication process is illustrated in Figure 21-2, and it begins with a START message from the client to the server. This message may be in response to an initiation from a PC connected to the TACACS+ client. The START message describes the type of authentication being requested (simple plaintext password, PAP, CHAP, and so on). This START message may also contain additional authentication data, such as username and password. A START message is also sent as a response to a restart request from the server in a REPLY message. A START message always has its sequence number set to 1.

When a TACACS+ server receives a START message, it sends a REPLY message. This REPLY message will indicate whether the authentication is complete or needs to be continued. If the process needs to be continued, the REPLY message also specifies what additional information is needed. The response from a client to a REPLY message requesting additional data is a CONTINUE message. This process continues until the server has all the information needed, and the authentication process concludes with a success or failure.

TACACS+ Authorization

Authorization describes the actions associated with determining permission associated with a user action. This generally occurs after authentication, as shown in Figure 21-2, but this is not a firm requirement. A default state of "unknown user" exists before a user is authenticated, and permissions can be determined for an unknown user. As with authentication, authorization is an optional process and may or may not be part of a site-specific operation. When it is used in conjunction with authentication, the authorization process follows the authentication process and uses the confirmed user identity as input in the decision process.

The authorization process is performed using two message types: REQUEST and RESPONSE. The authorization process is performed using an authorization session consisting of a single pair of REQUEST and RESPONSE messages. The client issues an authorization REQUEST message containing a fixed set of fields that enumerate the authenticity of the user or process requesting permission and a variable set of fields enumerating the services or options for which authorization is being requested.

The RESPONSE message in TACACS+ is not a simple yes or no; it can also include qualifying information, such as a user time limit or IP restrictions. These limitations have important uses, such as enforcing time limits on shell access or IP access list restrictions for specific user accounts.

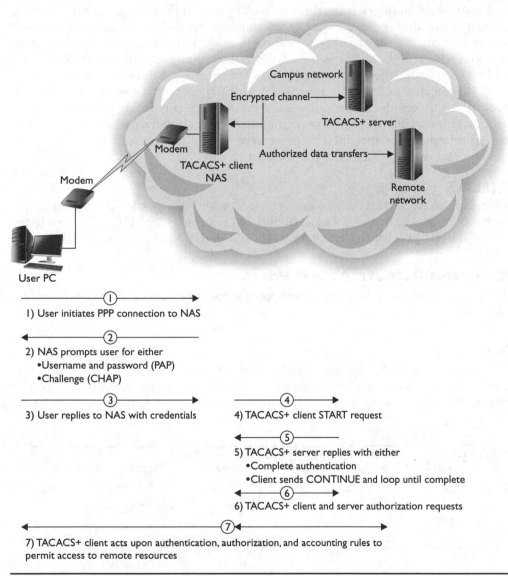

Campus network

Encrypted channel

TACACS+ server

Modem

TACACS+ client
NAS

Authorized data transfers

Remote
network

Modem

User PC

1) User initiates PPP connection to NAS

2) NAS prompts user for either
  •Username and password (PAP)
  •Challenge (CHAP)

3) User replies to NAS with credentials

4) TACACS+ client START request

5) TACACS+ server replies with either
  •Complete authentication
  •Client sends CONTINUE and loop until complete

6) TACACS+ client and server authorization requests

7) TACACS+ client acts upon authentication, authorization, and accounting rules to permit access to remote resources

Figure 21-2   TACACS+ communication sequence

TACACS+ Accounting

As with the two previous services, accounting is also an optional function of TACACS+. When utilized, it typically follows the other services. *Accounting* in TACACS+ is defined as the process of recording what a user or process has done. Accounting can serve two important purposes:

- It can be used to account for services being utilized, possibly for billing purposes.
- It can be used for generating security audit trails.

TACACS+ accounting records contain several pieces of information to support these tasks. The accounting process has the information revealed in the authorization and authentication processes, so it can record specific requests by user or process. To support this functionality, TACACS+ has three types of accounting records: START, STOP, and UPDATE. Note that these are record types, not message types as earlier discussed.

START records indicate the time and user or process that began an authorized process. STOP records enumerate the same information concerning the stop times for specific actions. UPDATE records act as intermediary notices that a particular task is still being performed. Together, these three message types allow the creation of records that delineate the activity of a user or process on a system.

XTACACS

Extended TACACS (XTACACS) is an extension of TACACS that separates the tasks of authentication, authorization and accounting. As with TACACS, XTACACS is considered end-of-life by Cisco, which promotes TACACS+, RADIUS, and Kerberos as replacements.

Common Remote Access Ports

Table 21-1 shows some remote access support solutions and should be memorized for the exam.

Kerberos

Developed as part of MIT's project Athena, Kerberos is a network authentication protocol designed for a client/server environment. The current version is Kerberos Version 5 release 1.12.1 and is supported by all major operating systems. Kerberos securely passes

Table 21-1 Common TCP/ UDP Remote Access Networking Port Assignments	TCP Port Number	UDP Port Number	Keyword	Protocol
	20		FTP-Data	File Transfer (Default Data)
	21		FTP	File Transfer Control
	22		SSH	Secure Shell Login
	22		SCP	SCP uses SSH
	22		SFTP	SFTP uses SSH
	23		TELNET	Telnet
	25		SMTP	Simple Mail Transfer
	53	53	DNS	Domain Name Server
	80		HTTP	Web
	110		POP3	E-mail
	139		NetBIOS	NetBIOS
	443		HTTPS	HTTPS
	3389	3389	RDP	Remote Desktop Protocol

a symmetric key over an insecure network using the Needham-Schroeder symmetric key protocol. Kerberos is built around the idea of a trusted third party, termed a *key distribution center (KDC)*, which consists of two logically separate parts: an authentication server (AS) and a ticket-granting server (TGS). Kerberos communicates via "tickets" that serve to prove the identity of users.

Taking its name from the three-headed dog of Greek mythology, Kerberos is designed to work across the Internet, an inherently insecure environment. Kerberos uses strong encryption so that a client can prove its identity to a server and the server can in turn authenticate itself to the client. A complete Kerberos environment is referred to as a Kerberos *realm*. The Kerberos server contains user IDs and hashed passwords for all users that will have authorizations to realm services. The Kerberos server also has shared secret keys with every server to which it will grant access tickets.

The basis for authentication in a Kerberos environment is the ticket. Tickets are used in a two-step process with the client. The first ticket is a ticket-granting ticket issued by the AS to a requesting client. The client can then present this ticket to the Kerberos server with a request for a ticket to access a specific server. This client-to-server ticket is used to gain access to a server's service in the realm. Since the entire session can be encrypted, this will eliminate the inherently insecure transmission of items such as a password that can be intercepted on the network. Tickets are timestamped and have a lifetime, so attempting to reuse a ticket will not be successful.

 EXAM TIP Kerberos is a third-party authentication service that uses a series of tickets as tokens for authenticating users. The steps involved are protected using strong cryptography.

The steps involved in Kerberos authentication are

1. The user presents credentials and requests a ticket from the Key Distribution Server (KDS).

2. The KDS verifies credentials and issues a ticket-granting ticket (TGT).

3. The user presents a TGT and request for service to the KDS.

4. The KDS verifies authorization and issues a client-to-server ticket.

5. The user presents a request and a client-to-server ticket to the desired service.

6. If the client-to-server ticket is valid, service is granted to the client.

To illustrate how the Kerberos authentication service works, think about the common driver's license. You have received a license that you can present to other entities to prove you are who you claim to be. Because other entities trust the state in which the license was issued, they will accept your license as proof of your identity. The state in which the license was issued is analogous to the Kerberos authentication service realm, and the license acts as a client-to-server ticket. It is the trusted entity both sides rely on to provide valid identifications. This analogy is not perfect, because we all probably have heard of individuals who obtained a phony driver's license, but it serves to illustrate the basic idea behind Kerberos.

LDAP

A *directory* is a data storage mechanism similar to a database, but it has several distinct differences designed to provide efficient data-retrieval services compared to standard database mechanisms. A directory is designed and optimized for reading data, offering very fast search and retrieval operations. The types of information stored in a directory tend to be descriptive attribute data. A directory offers a static view of data that can be changed without a complex update transaction. The data is hierarchically described in a treelike structure, and a network interface for reading is typical. Common uses of directories include e-mail address lists, domain server data, and resource maps of network resources.

To enable interoperability, the X.500 standard was created as a standard for directory services. The primary method for accessing an X.500 directory is through the Directory Access Protocol (DAP), a heavyweight protocol that is difficult to implement completely, especially on PCs and more constrained platforms. This led to the Lightweight Directory Access Protocol (LDAP), which contains the most commonly used functionality. LDAP can interface with X.500 services, and, most importantly, LDAP can be used over TCP with significantly less computing resources than a full X.500 implementation. LDAP offers all of the functionality most directories need and is easier and more economical to implement, hence LDAP has become the Internet standard for directory services. LDAP standards are governed by two separate entities depending upon use: The International Telecommunication Union (ITU) governs the X.500 standard, and LDAP is governed for Internet use by the IETF. Many RFCs apply to LDAP functionality, but some of the most important are RFCs 2251 through 2256 and RFCs 2829 and 2830.

Secure LDAP

Secure LDAP refers to LDAP over SSL/TLS. LDAP over TCP is a plaintext protocol, meaning data is passed in the clear and is susceptible to eavesdropping. Encryption can be used to remedy this problem, and the application of SSL/TLS-based service will protect directory queries and replies from eavesdroppers. SSL/TLS provides several important functions to LDAP services. It can establish the identity of a data source through the use of certificates, and it can also provide for the integrity and confidentiality of the data being presented from an LDAP source. Because LDAP and SSL/TLS are two separate, independent protocols, interoperability is more a function of correct setup than anything else. To achieve LDAP over SSL/TLS, the typical setup is to establish an SSL/TLS connection and then open an LDAP connection over the protected channel. To do this requires that both the client and the server be enabled for SSL/TLS. In the case of the client, most browsers are already enabled. In the case of an LDAP server, this specific function must be enabled by a system administrator. This setup initially is complicated, so it's definitely a task for a competent system administrator.

Once an LDAP server is set up to function over an SSL/TLS connection, it operates as it always has. The LDAP server responds to specific queries with the data returned from a node in the search. The SSL/TLS functionality operates to secure the channel of communication, and it is transparent to the data flow from the user's perspective. From the outside, SSL/TLS prevents observation of the data request and response, ensuring confidentiality.

SAML

Security Assertion Markup Language (SAML) is a single sign-on capability used for web applications to ensure user identities can be shared and are protected. It defines standards for exchanging authentication and authorization data between security domains. It is becoming increasingly important with cloud-based solutions and with Software-as-a-Service (SaaS) applications as it ensures interoperability across identity providers.

SAML is an XML-based protocol that uses security tokens and assertions to pass information about a "principal" (typically an end user) with an SAML authority (an "identity provider" or IdP) and the service provider (SP). The principal requests a service from the SP, which then requests and obtains an identity assertion from the IdP. The SP can then grant access or perform the requested service for the principal.

Authorization

Authorization is the process of permitting or denying access to a specific resource. Once identity is confirmed via authentication, specific actions can be authorized or denied. Many types of authorization schemes are used, but the purpose is the same: determine whether a given user who has been identified has permissions for a particular object or resource being requested. This functionality is frequently part of the operating system and is transparent to users.

The separation of tasks, from identification to authentication to authorization, has several advantages. Many methods can be used to perform each task, and on many systems, several methods are concurrently present for each task. Separation of these tasks into individual elements allows combinations of implementations to work together. Any system or resource, be it hardware (router or workstation) or a software component (database system), that requires authorization can use its own authorization method once authentication has occurred. This makes for efficient and consistent application of these principles.

Least Privilege

One of the most fundamental approaches to security is *least privilege*. This concept is applicable to many physical environments as well as network and host security. Least privilege means that an object (such as a user, application, or process) should have only the rights and privileges necessary to perform its task, with no additional permissions. Limiting an object's privileges limits the amount of harm that can be caused, thus limiting an organization's exposure to damage. Users may have access to the files on their workstations and a select set of files on a file server, but they have no access to critical data that is held within the database. This rule helps an organization protect its most sensitive resources and helps ensure that whoever is interacting with these resources has a valid reason to do so.

Different operating systems and applications have different ways of implementing rights, permissions, and privileges. Before operating systems are actually configured, an overall plan should be devised and standardized methods should be developed to ensure that a solid security baseline is implemented. For example, a company might want all of the accounting department employees, but no one else, to be able to access employee payroll and profit margin spreadsheets stored on a server. The easiest way to implement this is to develop an Accounting group, put all accounting employees in this group, and assign rights to the group instead of each individual user.

As another example, a company could require implementing a hierarchy of administrators that perform different functions and require specific types of rights. Two people could be tasked with performing backups of individual workstations and servers; thus, they do not need administrative permissions with full access to all resources. Three people could be in charge of setting up new user accounts and password management, which means they do not need full, or perhaps any, access to the company's routers and switches. Once these baselines are delineated, indicating what subjects require which rights and permissions, it is much easier to configure settings to provide the least privileges for different subjects.

The concept of least privilege applies to more network security issues than just providing users with specific rights and permissions. When trust relationships are created, they should not be implemented in such a way that everyone trusts each other simply because it is easier to set it up that way. One domain should trust another for very specific reasons, and the implementers should have a full understanding of what the trust relationship allows between two domains. If one domain trusts another, do all of the users automatically become trusted, and can they thus easily access any and all resources on the other domain? Is this a good idea? Can a more secure method provide the same functionality? If a trusted relationship is implemented such that users in one group can access a plotter or printer that is available on only one domain, for example, it might make sense to purchase another plotter so that other, more valuable or sensitive resources are not accessible by the entire group.

Another issue that falls under the least privilege concept is the security context in which an application runs. All applications, scripts, and batch files run in the security context of a specific user on an operating system. These objects will execute with specific permissions as if they were a user. The application could be Microsoft Word and be run in the space of a regular user, or it could be a diagnostic program that needs access to more sensitive system files and so must run under an administrative user account, or it could be a program that performs backups and so should operate within the security context of a backup operator. The crux of this issue is that programs should execute only in the security context that is needed for that program to perform its duties successfully. In many environments, people do not really understand how to make programs run under different security contexts, or it just seems easier to have them all run under the administrator account. If attackers can compromise a program or service running under the administrative account, they have effectively elevated their access level and have much more control over the system and many more possibilities to cause damage.

 EXAM TIP The concept of least privilege is fundamental to many aspects of security. Remember the basic idea is to give people access only to the data and programs that they need to do their job. Anything beyond that can lead to a potential security problem.

Separation of Duties

Another fundamental approach to security is separation of duties. This concept is applicable to physical environments as well as network and host security. Separation of duties ensures that for any given task, more than one individual needs to be involved. The task is broken into different duties, each of which is accomplished by a separate individual. By implementing a task in this manner, no single individual can abuse the system for his or her own gain. This principle has been implemented in the business world, especially financial institutions, for many years. A simple example is a system in which one individual is required to place an order and a separate person is needed to authorize the purchase.

While separation of duties provides a certain level of checks and balances, it is not without its own drawbacks. Chief among these is the cost required to accomplish the task. This cost is manifested in both time and money. More than one individual is required when a single person could accomplish the task, thus potentially increasing the cost of the task. In addition, with more than one individual involved, a certain delay can be expected as the task must proceed through its various steps.

Access Control

The term *access control* describes a variety of protection schemes. It sometimes refers to all security features used to prevent unauthorized access to a computer system or network. In this sense, it may be confused with *authentication*. More properly, *access* is the ability of a subject (such as an individual or a process running on a computer system) to interact with an object (such as a file or hardware device). Authentication, on the other hand, deals with verifying the identity of a subject.

To understand the difference, consider the example of an individual attempting to log in to a computer system or network. Authentication is the process used to verify to the computer system or network that the individual is who he claims to be. The most common method to do this is through the use of a user ID and password. Once the individual has verified his identity, access controls regulate what the individual can actually do on the system—just because a person is granted entry to the system does not mean that he should have access to all data the system contains.

Consider another example. When you go to your bank to make a withdrawal, the teller at the window will verify that you are indeed who you claim to be by asking you to provide some form of identification with your picture on it, such as your driver's license. You might also have to provide your bank account number. Once the teller verifies your identity, you will have proved that you are a valid (authorized) customer of this bank. This does not, however, mean that you have the ability to view all information that the bank protects—such as your neighbor's account balance. The teller will control what information, and funds, you can access and will grant you access only to the information that you are authorized to see. In this example, your identification and bank account number serve as your method of authentication and the teller serves as the access control mechanism.

	Process 1	Process 2	File 1	File 2	Printer
Process 1	Read, write, execute		Read, write	Read	Write
Process 2	Execute	Read, write, execute	Read, write	Read, write	Write

Table 21-2 An Access Control Matrix

In computer systems and networks, access controls can be implemented in several ways. An access control matrix provides the simplest framework for illustrating the process and is shown in Table 21-2. In this matrix, the system is keeping track of two processes, two files, and one hardware device. Process 1 can read both File 1 and File 2 but can write only to File 1. Process 1 cannot access Process 2, but Process 2 can execute Process 1. Both processes have the ability to write to the printer.

While simple to understand, the access control matrix is seldom used in computer systems because it is extremely costly in terms of storage space and processing. Imagine the size of an access control matrix for a large network with hundreds of users and thousands of files. The actual mechanics of how access controls are implemented in a system varies, though access control lists (ACLs) are common. An ACL is nothing more than a list that contains the subjects that have access rights to a particular object. The list identifies not only the subject but the specific access granted to the subject for the object. Typical types of access include read, write, and execute, as indicated in the example access control matrix.

No matter what specific mechanism is used to implement access controls in a computer system or network, the controls should be based on a specific *model* of access. Several different models are discussed in security literature, including discretionary access control (DAC), mandatory access control (MAC), role-based access control (RBAC), and rule-based access control (also RBAC).

Discretionary Access Control

Both *discretionary access control* and *mandatory access control* are terms originally used by the military to describe two different approaches to controlling an individual's access to a system. As defined by the "Orange Book," a Department of Defense document that at one time was the standard for describing what constituted a trusted computing system, DACs are "a means of restricting access to objects based on the identity of subjects and/or groups to which they belong. The controls are discretionary in the sense that a subject with a certain access permission is capable of passing that permission (perhaps indirectly) on to any other subject." While this might appear to be confusing "government-speak," the principle is rather simple. In systems that employ DACs, the owner of an object can decide which other subjects can have access to the object and what specific access they can have. One common method to accomplish this is the permission bits used in UNIX-based systems. The owner of a file can specify what permissions (read/write/execute) members in the same group can have and also what permissions all others can have. ACLs are also a common mechanism used to implement DAC.

Mandatory Access Control

A less frequently employed system for restricting access is mandatory access control. This system, generally used only in environments in which different levels of security classifications exist, is much more restrictive regarding what a user is allowed to do. Referring to the "Orange Book," a mandatory access control is "a means of restricting access to objects based on the sensitivity (as represented by a label) of the information contained in the objects and the formal authorization (i.e., clearance) of subjects to access information of such sensitivity." In this case, the owner or subject can't determine whether access is to be granted to another subject; it is the job of the operating system to decide.

 EXAM TIP   Common information classifications include High, Medium, Low, Confidential, Private, and Public.

In MAC, the security mechanism controls access to all objects, and individual subjects cannot change that access. The key here is the label attached to every subject and object. The label will identify the level of classification for that object and the level to which the subject is entitled. Think of military security classifications such as Secret and Top Secret. A file that has been identified as Top Secret (has a label indicating that it is Top Secret) may be viewed only by individuals with a Top Secret clearance. It is up to the access control mechanism to ensure that an individual with only a Secret clearance never gains access to a file labeled Top Secret. Similarly, a user cleared for Top Secret access will not be allowed by the access control mechanism to change the classification of a file labeled Top Secret to Secret or to send that Top Secret file to a user cleared only for Secret information. The complexity of such a mechanism can be further understood when you consider today's windowing environment. The access control mechanism will not allow a user to cut a portion of a Top Secret document and paste it into a window containing a document with only a Secret label. It is this separation of differing levels of classified information that results in this sort of mechanism being referred to as *multilevel security*.

Finally, just because a subject has the appropriate level of clearance to view a document does not mean that she will be allowed to do so. The concept of "need to know," which is a DAC concept, also exists in MAC mechanisms. "Need to know" means that a person is given access only to information that she needs in order to accomplish her job or mission.

 EXAM TIP   If you are trying to remember the difference between MAC and DAC, just remember that MAC is associated with multilevel security.

Role-Based Access Control

ACLs can be cumbersome and can take time to administer properly. Another access control mechanism that has been attracting increased attention is *role-based access control (RBAC)*. In this scheme, instead of each user being assigned specific access permissions for the objects associated with the computer system or network, each user is assigned a set of roles that he or she may perform. The roles are in turn assigned the access permissions necessary to perform the tasks associated with the role. Users will thus be granted permissions to objects in terms of the specific duties they must perform—not according to a security classification associated with individual objects.

Rule-Based Access Control

The first thing that you might notice is the ambiguity that is introduced with this access control method also using the acronym RBAC. *Rule-based access control* again uses objects such as ACLs to help determine whether access should be granted or not. In this case, a series of rules are contained in the ACL and the determination of whether to grant access will be made based on these rules. An example of such a rule is one that states that no employee may have access to the payroll file after hours or on weekends. As with MAC, users are not allowed to change the access rules, and administrators are relied on for this. Rule-based access control can actually be used in addition to or as a method of implementing other access control methods. For example, MAC methods can utilize a rule-based approach for implementation.

 EXAM TIP Do not become confused between rule-based and role-based access controls, even though they both have the same acronym. The name of each is descriptive of what it entails and will help you distinguish between them.

Job Rotation

An interesting approach to enhancing security that is gaining increasing attention is through job rotation. The benefits of rotating individuals through various jobs in an organization's IT department have been discussed for a while. By rotating through jobs, individuals gain a better perspective of how the various parts of IT can enhance (or hinder) the business. Since security is often a misunderstood aspect of IT, rotating individuals through security positions can result in a much wider understanding of the security problems throughout the organization. It also can have the side benefit of not relying on any one individual too heavily for security expertise. When all security tasks are the domain of one employee, if that individual were to leave suddenly, or if the individual were to become disgruntled and try to harm the organization, security could suffer. On the other hand, if security tasks were understood by many different individuals, the loss of any one individual would have less of an impact on the organization.

One significant drawback to job rotation is relying on it too heavily. The IT world is very technical and often expertise in any single aspect takes years to develop. This is especially true in the security environment. In addition, the rapidly changing threat environment, with new vulnerabilities and exploits routinely being discovered, requires a level of understanding that takes considerable time to acquire and maintain.

Time of Day Restrictions

Time of day restrictions are designed to allow access to systems or applications only during the hours they are expected to be used. Facility entry systems typically restrict access to a facility during certain times. For example, if a person has no need to ever work on weekends or outside of normal business hours, then the system will not let them enter the facility outside of normal business hours. This can also be applied to phone systems, especially fax lines or conference room phones where long-distance calls can be made. Time of day restrictions can prevent unauthorized personnel from placing toll phone calls for personal benefit at company expense.

Authentication

Authentication is the process of verifying an identity previously established in a computer system. There are a variety of methods of performing this function, each with its advantages and disadvantages. These are the subject of this section of the chapter.

Biometrics

Biometrics and their use in access control mechanisms is covered in detail in Chapter 10.

Username

A username is one authentication element that meets the "something you know" criteria. As described later in this chapter, it is best to not share your username, but a username is not a security method. Users should assume that their username is compromised.

Smart Card

A *smart card* (also known as an *integrated circuit card [ICC]* or *chip card*) is a pocket-sized card with embedded integrated circuits that is used to provide identification security authentication. The advent of smart cards has enabled strong cryptographic methods of authentication. Smart card technology has proven reliable enough that it is now part of a governmental standard for physical and logical authentication.

Common Access Card

The Common Access Card (CAC) is a smart card approximately the size of a standard credit card that satisfies two-factor authentication (something you know and something you have) for active-duty military personnel, Department of Defense (DoD) personnel, and contractors. As such, it is used as the primary card to obtain physical access to controlled spaces and access to defense computer systems and networks. The CAC provides for digital signatures and authentication, integrity, and non-repudiation.

PART V

Personal Identity Verification Card

The Personal Identity Verification (PIV) card is a smart card for U.S. federal employees and contractors. Similar to the DoD CAC, it contains the required information for the cardholder to access federal facilities and systems. Federal Information Processing Standard (FIPS) 201 documents the requirements for a common identification standard for all federal employees and contractors. This smart card includes a cryptographic chip and connector, as well as a contactless proximity card circuit. It also has standards for a printed photo and name on the front. Biometric data can be stored on the card, providing an additional authentication factor, and if the PIV standard is followed, several forms of identification are needed to be issued a card.

Multifactor Authentication

Multifactor authentication (or multiple-factor authentication) is simply the combination of two or more types of authentication. Three broad categories of authentication can be used: what you are (for example, biometrics), what you have (for instance, tokens), and what you know (passwords and other information). Two-factor authentication combines any two of these before granting access. An example would be a card reader that then turns on a fingerprint scanner—if your fingerprint matches the one on file for the card, you are granted access. Three-factor authentication would combine all three types, such as a smart card reader that asks for a PIN before enabling a retina scanner. If all three correspond to a valid user in the computer database, access is granted.

 EXAM TIP Two-factor authentication combines any two methods, matching items such as a token with a biometric. Three-factor authentication combines any three, such as a passcode, biometric, and a token.

Multifactor authentication methods greatly enhance security by making it very difficult for an attacker to obtain all the correct materials for authentication. They also protect against the risk of stolen tokens, as the attacker must have the correct biometric, password, or both. More important, multifactor authentication enhances the security of biometric systems by protecting against a stolen biometric. Changing the token makes the biometric useless unless the attacker can steal the new token. It also reduces false positives by trying to match the supplied biometric with the one that is associated with the supplied token. This prevents the computer from seeking a match using the entire database of biometrics. Using multiple factors is one of the best ways to ensure proper authentication and access control.

HOTP

HMAC-based One-Time Password (HOTP) is an algorithm that can be used to authenticate a user in a system by using an authentication server. (HMAC stands for Hash-based Message Authentication Code.) It is defined in RFC 4226, dated December 2005.

TOTP

The Time-based One-Time Password (TOTP) algorithm is a specific implementation of an HOTP that uses a secret key with a current timestamp to generate a one-time password. It is described in RFC 6238, dated May 2011.

CHAP

Challenge Handshake Authentication Protocol (CHAP) is used to provide authentication across a point-to-point link using PPP. In this protocol, authentication after the link has been established is not mandatory. CHAP is designed to provide authentication periodically through the use of a challenge/response system sometimes described as a *three-way handshake*, as illustrated in Figure 21-3. The initial challenge (a randomly generated number) is sent to the client. The client uses a one-way hashing function to calculate what the response should be and then sends this back. The server compares the response to what it calculated the response should be. If they match, communication continues. If the two values don't match, then the connection is terminated. This mechanism relies on a shared secret between the two entities so that the correct values can be calculated.

Microsoft has created two versions of CHAP, modified to increase its usability across their product line. MSCHAPv1, defined in RFC 2433, has been deprecated and dropped in Windows Vista. The current standard version 2, RFC 2759, was introduced with Windows 2000.

 EXAM TIP CHAP uses PPP, which supports three functions:
—Encapsulate datagrams across serial links
—Establish, configure, and test links using LCP
—Establish and configure different network protocols using NCP

PPP supports two authentication protocols:
—Password Authentication Protocol (PAP)
—Challenge Handshake Authentication Protocol (CHAP)

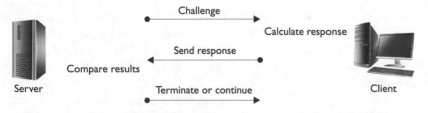

Figure 21-3 The CHAP challenge/response sequence

PART V

PAP

Password Authentication Protocol (PAP) authentication involves a two-way handshake in which the username and password are sent across the link in clear text. PAP authentication does not provide any protection against playback and line sniffing. PAP is now a deprecated standard.

 EXAM TIP PAP is a cleartext authentication protocol and hence is subject to interception. CHAP uses a challenge/response handshake protocol to secure the channel.

EAP

Extensible Authentication Protocol (EAP) is a universal authentication framework defined by RFC 3748 that is frequently used in wireless networks and point-to-point connections. Although EAP is not limited to wireless and can be used for wired authentication, it is most often used in wireless LANs.

Implicit Deny

What has become the Internet was originally designed as a friendly environment where everybody agreed to abide by the rules implemented in the various protocols. Today, the Internet is no longer the friendly playground of researchers that it once was. This has resulted in different approaches that might at first seem less than friendly but that are required for security purposes. One of these approaches is *implicit deny*.

Frequently in the network world, decisions concerning access must be made. Often, a series of rules will be used to determine whether or not to allow access. If a particular situation is not covered by any of the other rules, the implicit deny approach states that access should not be granted. In other words, if no rule would allow access, then access should not be granted. Implicit deny applies to situations involving both authorization and access.

The alternative to implicit deny is to allow access unless a specific rule forbids it. Another example of these two approaches is in programs that monitor and block access to certain websites. One approach is to provide a list of specific sites that a user is *not* allowed to access (blacklist). Access to any site not on the list would be implicitly allowed. The opposite approach (the implicit deny approach) would block all access to sites that are not specifically identified as authorized (whitelist). As you can imagine, depending on the specific application, one or the other approach would be appropriate. Which approach you should choose depends on the security objectives and policies of your organization.

 EXAM TIP Implicit deny is another fundamental principle of security, so make sure you understand this principle. Similar to least privilege, this principle states that if a user hasn't specifically been allowed access, then access should be denied.

Trusted OS

A *trusted OS* is an operating system that demonstrates the ability to provide for multilevel security and can meet a defined set of criteria (typically from a government agency). Due to the amount of effort and time involved in development, testing, and certification, only a few operating systems, such as Trusted Solaris and HP-UX 10.26, have undergone the process to become trusted operating systems.

Authentication Factors

Authentication is the process of binding a specific ID to a specific computer connection. Historically, three categories are used to authenticate the identity of a user. Originally published by the U.S. government in one of the Rainbow series manuals on computer security, these categories are

- Something you know (such as a password)
- Something you have (such as tokens)
- Something you are (static biometrics such as fingerprints or iris pattern)

Today, because of technological advances, a new category has emerged, patterned after subconscious behavior:

- Something you do (dynamic biometrics such as typing patterns or gait)

And because of GPS and other location-based technologies, a fifth category can be used:

- Somewhere you are

These methods can be used individually or in combination. These controls assume that the identification process has been completed and the identity of the user has been verified. It is the job of authentication mechanisms to ensure that only valid users are admitted. Described another way, authentication is using some mechanism to prove that you are who you claimed to be when the identification process was completed.

The most common method of authentication is the use of a password. For greater security, you can add an element from a separate group, such as a smart card token—something a user has in her possession. Passwords are common because they are one of the simplest forms and use memory as a prime component. Because of their simplicity, passwords have become ubiquitous across a wide range of systems.

Another method to provide authentication involves the use of something that only valid users should have in their possession. A physical-world example of this would be a simple lock and key. Only those individuals with the correct key will be able to open the lock and thus gain admittance to a house, car, office, or whatever the lock was protecting.

EXAM TIP The use of a token is a common method of using "something you have" for authentication. A token can hold a cryptographic key, or act as a one-time password (OTP) generator, or it can be a smart card that holds a cryptographic key. These devices can be safeguarded using a PIN and lockout mechanism to prevent use if stolen.

A similar method can be used to authenticate users for a computer system or network (though the key may be electronic and could reside on a smart card or similar device). The problem with this technology, however, is that people do lose their keys (or cards), which means they can't log in to the system, and somebody else who finds the key may then be able to access the system, even though they are not authorized. To address this problem, a combination of the something-you-know/something-you-have methods is often used so that the individual with the key can also be required to provide a password or passcode. The key is useless unless you know this code.

The third general method to provide authentication involves something that is unique about you. We are accustomed to this concept in our physical world, where our fingerprints or a sample of our DNA can be used to identify us. This same concept can be used to provide authentication in the computer world. The field of authentication that uses something about you or something that you are is known as *biometrics*. A number of different mechanisms can be used to accomplish this type of authentication, such as a fingerprint scan, iris scan, retinal scan, or hand geometry. All of these methods obviously require some additional hardware in order to operate. The inclusion of fingerprint readers on laptop computers is becoming common as the additional hardware is becoming cost effective.

Advances in the ability to do pattern recognition have led to the ability to identify users based on habits, such as how a person walks, types, or writes. These factors can be used to examine motor-specific skills that are virtually impossible to mimic, leading to the ability to determine identity by something one does or an action they perform.

Lastly, location can be used to assist in determination of identity. If a person is badged into the office, then a foreign IP address is probably not them. Likewise, if recent activity has come from a series of known IP addresses, then a new IP address that is located some distance away that is not within a reasonable travel radius is suspect.

While these five approaches to authentication appear to be easy to understand and in most cases easy to implement, authentication is not to be taken lightly, since it is such an important component of security. Potential attackers are constantly searching for ways to get past the system's authentication mechanism, and they have employed some fairly ingenious methods to do so. Consequently, security professionals are constantly devising new methods, building on these three basic approaches, to provide authentication mechanisms for computer systems and networks.

Identification

Identification is the process of ascribing a computer ID to a specific user, computer, network device, or computer process. The identification process is typically performed only once, when a user ID is issued to a particular user. User identification enables authentication and authorization to form the basis for accountability. For account-ability purposes, user IDs should not be shared, and for security purposes, user IDs should not be descriptive of job function. This practice enables you to trace activities to individual users or computer processes so that they can be held responsible for their actions. Identification usually takes the form of a logon ID or user ID. A required characteristic of such IDs is that they must be unique.

Certificates

Certificates are a method of establishing authenticity of specific objects, such as an individual's public key or downloaded software. A digital certificate is generally an attachment to a message and is used to verify that the message did indeed come from the entity it claims to have come from. The digital certificate can also contain a key that can be used to encrypt future communication.

Tokens

An access token is a physical object that identifies specific access rights, and in authentication, falls into the "something you have" factor. Your house key, for example, is a basic physical access token that allows you access into your home. Although keys have been used to unlock devices for centuries, they do have several limitations. Keys are paired exclusively with a lock or a set of locks, and they are not easily changed. It is easy to add an authorized user by giving the user a copy of the key, but it is far more difficult to give that user selective access unless that specified area is already set up as a separate key. It is also difficult to take access away from a single key or key holder, which usually requires a rekey of the whole system.

In many businesses, physical access authentication has moved to contactless radio frequency cards and proximity readers. When passed near a card reader, the card sends out a code using radio waves. The reader picks up this code and transmits it to the control panel. The control panel checks the code against the reader from which it is being read and the type of access the card has in its database. The advantages of this kind of token-based system include the fact that any card can be deleted from the system without affecting any other card or the rest of the system. In addition, all doors connected to the system can be segmented in any form or fashion to create multiple access areas, with different permissions for each one. The tokens themselves can also be grouped in multiple ways to provide different access levels to different groups of people. All of the access levels or segmentation of doors can be modified quickly and easily if building space is re-tasked. Newer technologies are adding capabilities to the standard token-based systems. Smart cards can also be used to carry identification tokens. The primary drawback of token-based authentication is that only the token is being authenticated. Therefore, the theft of the token could grant anyone who possessed the token access to what the system protects.

The risk of theft of the token can be offset by the use of multifactor authentication (defined in the next section). One of the ways that people have tried to achieve multifactor authentication is to add a biometric factor to the system. A less expensive alternative is to use hardware tokens in a challenge/response authentication process.

PART V

In this way, it functions as both a something-you-have and something-you-know authentication mechanism. Several variations on this type of device exist, but they all work on the same basic principles. The device has an LCD screen and may or may not have a numeric keypad. Devices without a keypad will display a password (often just a sequence of numbers) that changes at a constant interval, usually about every 60 seconds. When an individual attempts to log in to a system, he enters his own user ID number and then the number that is showing on the LCD. These two numbers are either entered separately or concatenated. The user's own ID number is secret, and this prevents someone from using a lost device. The system knows which device the user has and is synchronized with it so that it will know the number that should have been displayed. Since this number is constantly changing, a potential attacker who is able to see the sequence will not be able to use it later, since the code will have changed. Devices with a keypad work in a similar fashion (and may also be designed to function as a simple calculator). The individual who wants to log in to the system will first type his personal identification number into the calculator. He will then attempt to log in. The system will then provide a challenge; the user must enter that challenge into the calculator and press a special function key. The calculator will then determine the correct response and display it. The user provides the response to the system he is attempting to log in to, and the system verifies that this is the correct response. Since each user has a different PIN, two individuals receiving the same challenge will have different responses. The device can also use the date or time as a variable for the response calculation so that the same challenge at different times will yield different responses, even for the same individual.

Multifactor

Multifactor is a term that describes the use of more than one authentication mechanism at the same time. An example of this is the hardware token, which requires both a personal ID number (PIN) or password and the device itself to determine the correct response in order to authenticate to the system, as presented in the previous section. This means that both the something-you-have and something-you-know mechanisms are used as factors in verifying authenticity of the user. Biometrics are also often used in conjunction with a PIN so that they, too, can be used as part of a multifactor authentication scheme, in this case, something you are as well as something you know. The purpose of multifactor authentication is to increase the level of security, since more than one mechanism would have to be spoofed in order for an unauthorized individual to gain access to a computer system or network. The most common example of multifactor security is the common ATM card most of us carry in our wallets. The card is associated with a PIN that only the authorized cardholder should know. Knowing the PIN without having the card is useless, just as having the card without knowing the PIN will also not provide you access to your account.

 EXAM TIP The required use of more than one authentication system is known as multifactor authentication. The most common example is the combination of password with a hardware token. For high security, three factors can be used: password, token, and biometric.

Single Sign-on (SSO)

Single sign-on is a form of authentication that involves the transferring of credentials between systems. As more and more systems are combined in daily use, users are forced to have multiple sets of credentials. A user may have to log in to three, four, five, or even more systems every day just to do her job. Single sign-on allows a user to transfer her credentials, so that logging into one system acts to log her into all of them. This has an advantage of reducing login hassles for the user. It also has a disadvantage of combining the authentication systems in a way such that if one login is compromised, they all are for that user.

Mutual Authentication

Mutual authentication describes a process in which each side of an electronic communication verifies the authenticity of the other. We are accustomed to the idea of having to authenticate ourselves to our ISP before we access the Internet, generally through the use of a user ID/password pair, but how do we actually know that we are really communicating with our ISP and not some other system that has somehow inserted itself into our communication (a man-in-the-middle attack)? Mutual authentication provides a mechanism for each side of a client/server relationship to verify the authenticity of the other to address this issue.

Vulnerabilities

The primary vulnerability associated with all of these methods of remote access is the passing of critical data in the clear. Plaintext passing of passwords provides no security if the password is sniffed, and sniffers are easy to use on a network. Even plaintext passing of user IDs gives away information that can be correlated and possibly used by an attacker. Plaintext credential passing is one of the fundamental flaws with Telnet and is why SSH was developed. This is also one of the flaws with RADIUS and TACACS+, as they have a segment unprotected. There are methods for overcoming these limitations, although they require discipline and understanding in setting up a system.

The strength of the encryption algorithm is also a concern. Should a specific algorithm or method prove to be vulnerable, services that rely solely on it are also vulnerable. To get around this dependency, many of the protocols allow numerous encryption methods, so that should one prove vulnerable, a shift to another restores security.

As with any software implementation, there always exists the possibility that a bug could open the system to attack. Bugs have been corrected in most software packages to close holes that made systems vulnerable, and remote access functionality is no exception. This is not a Microsoft-only phenomenon, as one might believe from the popular press. Critical flaws have been found in almost every product, from open system implementations such as OpenSSH to proprietary systems such as Cisco's IOS. The important issue is not the presence of software bugs, for as software continues to become more complex, this is an unavoidable issue. The true key is vendor responsiveness to fixing the bugs once they are discovered, and the major players, such as Cisco and Microsoft, have been very responsive in this area.

PART V

Federation

Federation, or *identity federation*, defines policies, protocols, and practices to manage identities across systems and organizations. Its ultimate goal is to allow users to seamlessly access data or systems across domains. Federation is enabled through the use of industry standards such as SAML, discussed earlier in the chapter.

Transitive Trust/Authentication

Security across multiple domains is provided through trust relationships. When trust relationships between domains exist, authentication for each domain trusts the authentication for all other trusted domains. Thus, when an application is authenticated by a domain, its authentication is accepted by all other domains that trust the authenticating domain.

It is important to note that trust relationships apply only to authentication. They do not apply to resource usage, which is an access control issue. Trust relationships allow users to have their identity verified (authentication). The ability to use resources is defined by access control rules. Thus, even though a user is authenticated via the trust relationship, it does not provide access to actually use resources.

A transitive trust relationship means that the trust relationship extended to one domain will be extended to any other domain trusted by that domain. A two-way trust relationship means that two domains trust each other.

 EXAM TIP Transitive trust involves three parties: If A trusts B, and B trusts C, in a transitive trust relationship, then A will trust C.

Chapter Review

In this chapter, you became acquainted with many methods that can be used to achieve security under various access conditions, and the number is growing as new protocols are developed to meet the ever-increasing use of remote access. From the beginnings of Telnet, to advanced authentication mechanisms of RADIUS and Kerberos, the options are many, but the task is basically the same: perform the functions of identification, authentication, authorization, and accounting while protecting message and data security from outside intervention.

Your choice of an access solution will depend on several factors, including security requirements, the type of network, the type of clients, required access methods, scalability, existing authentication mechanisms, and cost. Each system has its strengths and weaknesses, and when properly employed, each can be used effectively within its own limitations. There is no best solution at the present time.

Questions

To help you prepare further for the CompTIA Security+ exam, and to test your level of preparedness, answer the following questions and then check your answers against the correct answers at the end of the chapter.

1. Which of the following UDP ports does RADIUS use?

   A. 22 and 23

   B. 49 and 65

   C. 512 and 513

   D. 1812 and 1813

2. Which protocol is designed to replace RADIUS?

   A. LDA

   B. TACACS

   C. TACACS+

   D. Diameter

3. Which of the following TCP ports does TACACS+ use?

   A. 22 and 23

   B. 49 and 65

   C. 989 and 990

   D. 512 and 513

4. Which of the following correctly describes "authentication" in the authentication, authorization, and accounting (AAA) protocols?

   A. Manage connection time and cost records

   B. The process of determining whether a user has permission

   C. A mechanism to remotely connect clients to networks

   D. Connects access to a previously approved user ID

5. Which of the following correctly describes communications between a TACACS+ client and server?

   A. Communication between a TACACS+ client (typically an NAS) and a TACACS+ server is subject to compromise, but the communication between a user (typically a PC) and the TACACS+ client is secure.

   B. Communication between a TACACS+ client (typically an NAS) and a TACACS+ server is secure, but the communication between a user (typically a PC) and the TACACS+ client is subject to compromise.

   C. Communication between a TACACS+ client (typically a PC) and a TACACS+ server is subject to compromise, but the communication between a user (typically an NAS) and the TACACS+ client is secure.

   D. Communication between a TACACS+ client (typically a PC) and a TACACS+ server is secure, but the communication between a user (typically an NAS) and the TACACS+ client is subject to compromise.

PART V

6. Which of the following is *not* a function supported by Point-to-Point Protocol (PPP)?

    A. Password Authentication Protocol (PAP)

    B. Establish, configure, and test links using link control protocols (LCP)

    C. Establish and configure different network protocols using network control protocols (NCP)

    D. Encapsulate datagrams across serial links

7. What is another way of describing Challenge Handshake Authentication Protocol (CHAP)?

    A. Tunnel endpoints

    B. Encapsulating one packet within another

    C. Three-way handshake

    D. Message encapsulation during transmission

8. Which port does Telnet use?

    A. UDP port 22

    B. TCP port 22

    C. UDP port 23

    D. TCP port 23

9. In multifactor authentication, which of the following is not a possession factor (something the user has)?

    A. One-time pad

    B. Magnetic card stripe

    C. PIN

    D. USB token

10. A fingerprint is an example of:

    A. Something you have

    B. Something you know

    C. Something you are

    D. A shared secret

11. In preparation for taking the CompTIA Security+ certification exam, you and one of your buddies are asking each other questions. Your buddy asks, "What are the six steps to establish a RADIUS connection?" How would you answer?

12. Your study partner next asks, "What are the seven steps to establish a TACACS+ connection?" How would you answer?

13. As a computer security professional, it is very important that you are able to describe to your superiors how Kerberos authentication works. List the six steps in Kerberos authentication.

14. List five different factors that can be used to establish identity, and give an example of each.

15. Match the port and the service:

A. 139	1. FTP
B. 80	2. DNS
C. 21	3. POP3
D. 3389	4. NetBIOS
E. 110	5. HTTP
F. 53	6. RDP

Answers

1. **D.** RADIUS uses UDP (and TCP) ports 1812 and 1813.

2. **D.** Diameter is designed to replace the RADIUS protocol.

3. **B.** TACACS+ uses UDP and TCP ports 49 and 65.

4. **D.** Authentication is a cornerstone element of security, connecting access to a previously approved user ID.

5. **B.** Communication between a TACACS+ client (typically an NAS) and a TACACS+ server is secure, but the communication between a user (typically a PC) and the TACACS+ client is subject to compromise.

6. **A.** Password Authentication Protocol (PAP) is not a function supported by Point-to-Point Protocol (PPP). PAP is a different protocol.

7. **C.** Another way to describe Challenge Handshake Authentication Protocol (CHAP) is a three-way handshake.

8. **D.** Telnet uses TCP port 23.

9. **C.** A PIN is a knowledge factor (something you know).

10. **C.** A fingerprint is a biometric and thus is something you are.

11. The steps to establish a RADIUS connection are 1) A user initiates PPP authentication to the NAS; 2) The NAS prompts for either a username and password (if PAP) or a challenge (if CHAP); 3) The user replies with credentials; 4) The RADIUS client sends the username and encrypted password to the RADIUS server; 5) The RADIUS server responds with Access-Accept, Access-Reject, or Access Challenge; 6) The RADIUS client acts upon services requested by the user.

PART V

12. The steps to establish a TACACS+ connection are 1) A user initiates PPP connection to the NAS; 2) The NAS prompts for either a username and password (if PAP) or a challenge (if CHAP); 3) The user replies with credentials; 4) The TACACS+ client sends a START request to the TACACS+ server; 5) The TACACS+ server responds with either authentication complete or the client sends CONTINUE until complete; 6) The TACACS+ client and server exchange authorization requests; 7) The TACACS+ client acts upon services requested by the user.

13. The six steps in Kerberos authentication are 1) User presents his credentials and requests a ticket from the key distribution center (KDC); 2) The KDC verifies credentials and issues a ticket-granting ticket (TGT); 3) The user presents a TGT and request for service to the KDC; 4) The KDC verifies authorization and issues a client-to-server ticket (or service ticket); 5) The user presents a request and a client-to-server ticket to the desired service; 6) If the client-to-server ticket is valid, service is granted to the client.

14. Something you know (password)
Something you have (token)
Something you are (biometric)
Something you do (walk/gait or typing pattern)
Somewhere you are (current location)

15. Match the port and the service:

A. 139	4. NetBIOS
B. 80	5. HTTP
C. 21	1. FTP
D. 3389	6. RDP
E. 110	3. POP3
F. 53	2. DNS

Account Management

In this chapter, you will

- Learn the differences between user, group, and role management
- Explore password policies
- Understand best practices for installing security controls for account management
- Understand best practices for configuring security controls for account management

As more users started sharing systems, it became obvious that some way of separating and restricting users was needed, which led to the concepts of users, groups, and privileges. These concepts continue to be developed and refined and are now part of what we call account management.

Account management is also frequently called privilege management. Privilege management is the process of restricting a user's ability to interact with the computer system. A user's interaction with a computer system covers a fairly broad area and includes viewing, modifying, and deleting data; running applications; stopping and starting processes; and controlling computer resources. Essentially, controlling everything a user can do to or with a computer system falls into the realm of account management.

User, Group, and Role Management

To manage the privileges of many different people effectively on the same system, a mechanism for separating people into distinct entities (users) is required, so you can control access on an individual level. It's convenient and efficient to be able to lump users together when granting many different people (groups) access to a resource at the same time. At other times, it's useful to be able to grant or restrict access based on a person's job or function within the organization (role). While you can manage privileges on the basis of users alone, managing user, group, and role assignments together is far more convenient and efficient.

User

The term *user* generally applies to any person accessing a computer system. In privilege management, a user is a single individual, such as "John Forthright" or "Sally Jenkins." This is generally the lowest level addressed by privilege management and the most common area for addressing access, rights, and capabilities. When accessing a computer system, each user is generally given a *user ID*—a unique alphanumeric identifier he or she will use to identify himself or herself when logging in or accessing the system. User IDs are often based on some combination of the user's first, middle, and last name and often include numbers as well. When developing a scheme for selecting user IDs, you should keep in mind that user IDs must be unique to each user, but they must also be fairly easy for the user to remember and use. Because the user ID is used to identify the person who performed specific actions, it is important to not have generic or shared credentials. Either of these situations makes traceability to an authorized user difficult if not impossible.

 EXAM TIP Unique, nonshared user IDs for all users of a system are important when it comes time to investigate access control issues.

With some notable exceptions, in general, a user wanting to access a computer system must first have a user ID created for him on the system he wishes to use. This is usually done by a system administrator, security administrator, or other privileged user, and this is the first step in privilege management—a user should not be allowed to create his own account.

Once the account is created and a user ID is selected, the administrator can assign specific permissions to that user. Permissions control what the user is allowed to do on the system—which files he may access, which programs he may execute, and so on. While PCs typically have only one or two user accounts, larger systems such as servers and mainframes can have hundreds of accounts on the same system.

Account policy enforcement is an important part of user credential systems. Managing credentials begins with policies that state the desired objectives. Key elements of the policy include elements such as prohibition against sharing accounts and against generic accounts not assigned to a user. For users that have multiple roles, multiple accounts may be necessary, but these need to be delineated by policy rather than on an ad hoc basis. Credential management rules, such as password policy, should be enacted, including lockout and recovery procedures. When users no longer are authorized, such as when they leave the firm or change jobs, the accounts should be disabled, not removed.

Groups

Under privilege management, a *group* is a collection of users with some common criteria, such as a need for access to a particular data set or group of applications. A group can consist of one user or hundreds of users, and each user can belong to one or more groups. Figure 22-1 shows a common approach to grouping users—building groups based on job function. Role-based access control (RBAC) is implemented via groups in a modern OS.

By assigning a user membership in a specific group, you make it much easier to control that user's access and privileges. For example, if every member of the engineering department needs access to product development documents, administrators can place

Figure 22-1

Logical represen-
tation of groups

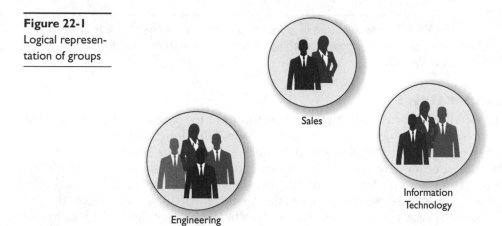

Sales

Engineering

Information
Technology

all the users in the engineering department in a single group and allow that group
to access the necessary documents. Once a group is assigned permissions to access a
particular resource, adding a new user to that group will automatically allow that user
to access that resource. In effect, the user "inherits" the permissions of the group as
soon as she is placed in that group. As Figure 22-2 shows, a computer system can have
many different groups, each with its own rights and privileges.

As you can see from the description for the Administrators group in Figure 22-2,
this group has complete and unrestricted access to the system. This includes access to
all files, applications, and data. Anyone who belongs to the Administrators group or is
placed in this group will have a great deal of access and control over the system.

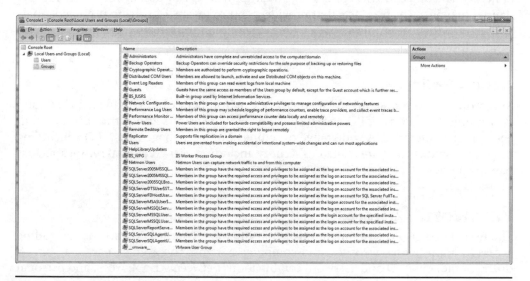

Figure 22-2   Group management screen in Windows

EXAM TIP   Placing users in groups and managing groups can reduce account management workload and complexity on large systems and domain environments.

Multiple Roles

A single individual often may have the business need for accounts with separate sets of permissions. Consider a small company, where a developer can also be the tester and move content into production. It is much safer to issue three accounts to the individual—one for development, one for test, and one for production—than to combine the permissions under one account. This allows the safety of account-based/role-based security, and although it increases the cognitive workload for the individual to remember three accounts, it prevents accidents where the user believes they are in one system and execute commands intended for a different one.

Account Policy Enforcement

The key method used to access most systems is still one based on passwords. Passwords need to be managed to provide appropriate levels of protection. They need to be strong enough to resist attack, and yet not too difficult for users to remember. A password policy can act to ensure that the necessary steps are taken to enact a secure password solution, both by users and by the password infrastructure system.

Credential Management

Credential management refers to the processes, services, and software used to store, manage, and log the use of user credentials. Credential management solutions are typically aimed at assisting end users to manage their growing set of passwords. There are credential management products that provide a secure means of storing user credentials and making them available across a wide range of platforms, from local stores to cloud storage locations.

Group Policy

Microsoft Windows systems in an enterprise environment can be managed via Group Policy objects (GPOs). GPOs act through a set of registry settings that can be managed via the enterprise. A wide range of settings can be managed via GPOs, including numerous settings that are related to security, including user credential settings such as password rules.

Password Policies

The user ID/password combination is by far the most common means of controlling access to applications, websites, and computer systems. The average user may have a dozen or more user ID and password combinations between school, work, and personal use. To help users select a good, difficult-to-guess password, most organizations implement and enforce a password policy, which typically has the following components:

- **Password construction** How many characters a password should have, the use of capitalization/numbers/special characters, not basing the password on a dictionary word, not basing the password on personal information, not making the password a slight modification of an existing password, and so on.

- **Reuse restrictions** Whether or not passwords can be reused, and, if so, with what frequency (how many different passwords must you use before you can use one you've used before).

- **Duration** The minimum and maximum number of days a password can be used before it can be changed or must be changed, also known as *password expiration period*. It is common to use 1 day as a minimum and 90 days as a maximum. The 90 days is a balance between sufficient changes considering both user convenience and security.

- **Protection of passwords** Not writing down passwords where others can find them, not saving passwords and not allowing automated logins, not sharing passwords with other users, and so on.

- **Consequences** Consequences associated with violation of or noncompliance with the policy.

Domain Password Policy

A *domain password policy* is a password policy for a specific domain. Because these policies are usually associated with the Windows operating system (see Figure 22-3), a domain password policy is implemented and enforced on an Active Directory domain controller. The domain password policy usually falls under a GPO and has the following elements:

- **Enforce password history** Tells the system how many passwords to remember and does not allow a user to reuse an old password.

- **Maximum password age** Specifies the maximum number of days a password may be used before it must be changed.

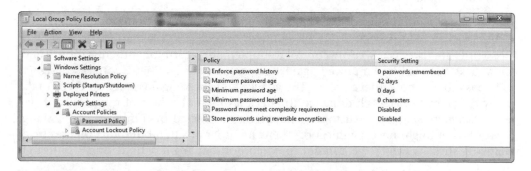

Figure 22-3 Password policy options in Windows Local Group Policy Editor

PART V

- **Minimum password age**   Specifies the minimum number of days a password must be used before it can be changed again.

- **Minimum password length**   Specifies the minimum number of characters that must be used in a password.

- **Password must meet complexity requirements**   Specifies that the password must meet the minimum length requirement and have characters from at least three of the following four groups: English uppercase characters (A through Z), English lowercase characters (a through z), numerals (0 through 9), and nonalphabetic characters (such as !, $, #, %).

- **Store passwords using reversible encryption**   Essentially the same as storing a plaintext version of the password; should be used only when applications use protocols that require the user's password for authentication (such as Challenge Handshake Authentication Protocol, or CHAP). Because this is reversible, it should be avoided if possible.

Passwords are nearly ubiquitous in their applications. They have several key advantages, such as they are always with the user. One challenge in the management of passwords is the password dilemma: "The more difficult we make it for attackers to guess our passwords, and the more frequently we force password changes, the more difficult the passwords are for users to remember and the more likely they are to write them down." The only solid solutions to the password dilemma involve compromises between pure security elements and usability elements.

 EXAM TIP   Key security controls associated with passwords include password complexity rules, lockout rules, and expiration timelines.

Sophisticated systems have been devised using lockouts after a limited number of failures. This prevents automated guessing programs from driving through all of the passwords until they find a correct one. Lockouts can be timed for automatic reset, say 5 minutes after every three failures. This reduces the help desk load for password resets. Password systems can have automated reset mechanisms built around knowledge systems. This can enable users to reset their own passwords, again without help desk interaction, making the system more efficient to operate.

Password Attacks

Passwords are used as a security control to implement a form of authentication. There are attacks that can be employed against password systems, that is, attacks designed to bypass them and achieve access. The attacks employed against passwords can take many different forms, each designed to attack a different aspect of the password system. *Dictionary attacks* use custom dictionaries constructed of common words, slang, or words that might have significance. There are programs that build dictionaries from elements such as web page content, or even content from a hard drive. Although these tools may generate millions of passwords or more, automated checkers can still go through a list such as this quickly. Users tend to create passwords from things they can remember, using sources available to or created by users, and this can provide a means of guessing them.

Brute-force attacks use the power of a computer to create a list of random passwords and use these to test the system. A *hybrid* attack is a combination of dictionary and brute-force attacks. A technique related to these attacks is the *birthday attack* scenario. The birthday attack scenario is named after the birthday problem in probability, a scenario where you use the power of combinations to achieve a match. Rather than attempting to match a specific password, you are attempting to match any password. This greatly reduces the number of attempts needed to achieve a specific level of probability. A birthday attack is not against a specific account, but rather any account that matches. This may seem awkward, but many attacks are not aimed at a specific account, but rather at any account that gets them access.

The strength of a password is related to its length and complexity. Any password that is easily guessed is by nature a bad password, as are sequences such as "12345678" or phrases such as "letmein." The ideal password is long and random and has upper- and lowercase letters, numbers, and symbols, making it impossible to guess and requiring a long time to brute force. More password details are covered in Chapter 15.

 EXAM TIP Different types of attacks are used against different vulnerabilities in a password system. It is important to understand the difference between brute-force, dictionary, hybrid, and birthday attacks.

Account Auditing

As with all security controls, an important aspect of security controls that are used to mitigate risk is a monitoring component. Logs are the most frequently used component, and with respect to privileged accounts, logging can be especially important. Reviewing access control logs for root-level accounts is an important element of securing access control methods. Because of the power and potential for misuse, administrative or root-level accounts should be closely monitored. One important element for continuous monitoring of production would be the use of an administrative-level account on a production system.

 EXAM TIP Logging and monitoring of failed login attempts provide valuable information during investigations of compromises.

A strong configuration management environment will include the control of access to production systems by users that can change the environment. Root-level changes in a system tend to be significant changes, and in production systems these changes would be approved in advance. A comparison of all root-level activity against approved changes will assist in the detection of activity that is unauthorized.

Chapter Review

In this chapter, you became acquainted with security aspects of account management. The chapter presented account policy issues, including multiple account/roles and/or shared accounts, credential management, group policies, and generic account prohibitions. It also presented password policy elements, such as complexity requirements, expiration, recovery, history, reuse, and length requirements. The chapter addressed the issues of user account elements, such as lockout, disablement, and logging.

Questions

To help you prepare further for the CompTIA Security+ exam, and to test your level of preparedness, answer the following questions and then check your answers against the correct answers at the end of the chapter.

1. What is the recommended timeframe to change passwords that balances password security with user convenience?

    A. 30 days

    B. 90 days

    C. 120 days

    D. 180 days

2. Which of the following password lengths gives the greatest password strength?

    A. 4 characters

    B. 8 characters

    C. 15 characters

    D. The use of a single-word passphrase

3. From a practical standpoint, how many times should password entry be allowed before locking the account?

    A. 1 time

    B. 3 times

    C. 10 times

    D. 24 times

4. Which of the following represents the strongest password policy provisions?

    A. Construction, reuse, duration, protection, consequences

    B. Never communicate a password by e-mail, never write a password down

    C. Length, expiration, complexity, account sharing, password sharing/recording

    D. Prohibition of dictionary words, inclusion of digits, never write a password down

5. What is the password dilemma?

   A. Good password policy defines password length, expiration, prohibition of dictionary words, and complexity.

   B. Password selection is an individual activity, and ensuring that individuals are making good selections is the realm of the organization's password policy.

   C. The use of a common word, phrase, or name.

   D. The more difficult we make it for attackers to guess our passwords, and the more frequently we force password changes, the more difficult the passwords are for users to remember and the more likely they are to write them down.

6. Why should passwords not be written down?

   A. Writing passwords down helps you remember the password better.

   B. If an attacker gains physical access to a work area, it is easier to find a password.

   C. Writing down passwords usually results in easier passwords being chosen.

   D. Writing down passwords makes it easier to use the same password for several accounts.

7. Which of the following provides valuable information during investigations of intrusions?

   A. Access logs for key files

   B. Number of root-level logins

   C. IP addresses of logins

   D. Number of failed login attempts

8. Which of the following correctly defines password policy?

   A. A set of rules, applicable to a specific domain, designed to enhance computer security by requiring users to employ and maintain strong passwords

   B. How many passwords one has to remember and prevents a user from reusing old passwords

   C. A set of rules designed to enhance computer security by requiring users to employ and maintain strong passwords

   D. The minimum number of characters that must be used in a password

9. Which of the following implements the strongest domain password policy?

   A. Enforce password history, maximum password age, minimum password age, minimum password length

   B. Password construction, reuse restrictions, duration, protection of passwords, consequences

   C. Length, expiration, complexity, account sharing, password sharing/recording

   D. Prohibition of dictionary words, inclusion of digits, never write a password down

PART V

10. List three types of password attacks.

11. List three important user account factors to mitigate account risks.

12. Your coworker tells you that he's devised a great way to remember his password. He started with a really strong password, and now he just changes the last two characters each time a password change is required. What is the weakness of what your friend is doing?

13. Your boss has asked you to prepare for the executive staff meeting a one-slide presentation that outlines the five components of a good password policy. List the five points you'd put on that slide.

14. Choose two elements of a good password policy and, within the context of the password dilemma, explain the problems those policy elements could present.

15. Match the password policy issue with the attack it mitigates:

    A. Password length   1. Dictionary attack
    B. Password file access   2. Birthday attack
    C. Password complexity   3. Brute-force attacks

Answers

1. **B.** Ninety days is a reasonable balance between security and user convenience.

2. **C.** Fifteen characters is the strongest of these choices, as a single word will not likely be longer than 15 characters.

3. **B.** Three retries is reasonable.

4. **A.** Provisions for construction, reuse, duration, protection, and consequences will create the strongest password policy.

5. **D.** The password dilemma is defined as, "The more difficult we make it for attackers to guess our passwords, and the more frequently we force password changes, the more difficult the passwords are for users to remember and the more likely they are to write them down."

6. **B.** Passwords should not be written down because if an attacker gains physical access to a work area, it is easier for the attacker to find a password.

7. **D.** Failed login attempts, especially large numbers of them, indicate an attempt to brute force access.

8. **C.** Password policy is a set of rules designed to enhance computer security by requiring users to employ and maintain strong passwords.

9. **A.** Enforce password history, maximum password age, minimum password age, and minimum password length are the elements of a domain password policy.

10. Dictionary, brute-force, hybrid, and birthday attacks are methods used to discover passwords.

11. Factors used to mitigate risk associated with user accounts include password complexity, account lockout, account disablement, shared accounts, and generic account prohibitions.

12. While your coworker's password is still strong, it really isn't changing significantly. If his account were compromised, it could be devised that he is just incrementally changing the password by only two characters.

13. The five key components of a password policy are password construction, reuse restrictions, duration, protection of passwords, and consequences.

14. Overly complex password construction could result in people writing down the password. Reuse restrictions could result in people reusing minor permutations of a password. Duration could result in people recording their passwords as they change too frequently or using minor permutations. Protection of passwords could result in people still hiding their passwords, just in more "creative" but still weak locations. Consequences could lead people to covering up actions relating to password policy.

15. A. Password length   3. Brute-force attacks
    B. Password file access   2. Birthday attack
    C. Password complexity   1. Dictionary attack

PART VI

Cryptography

Cryptographic Concepts

In this chapter, you will

- Identify the different types of cryptography
- Learn about current cryptographic methods
- Understand how cryptography is applied for security
- Given a scenario, utilize general cryptography concepts

Cryptography is the science of *encrypting*, or hiding, information—something people have sought to do since they began using language. Although language allowed them to communicate with one another, people in power attempted to hide information by controlling who was taught to read and write. Eventually, more complicated methods of concealing information by shifting letters around to make the text unreadable were developed. These complicated methods are cryptographic algorithms, also known as *ciphers*. The word "cipher" comes from the Arabic word *sifr*, meaning empty or zero.

General Cryptographic Concepts

Historical ciphers were simple to use and also simple to break. Because hiding information was still important, more advanced transposition and substitution ciphers were required. As systems and technology became more complex, ciphers were frequently automated by some mechanical or electromechanical device. A famous example of a modern encryption machine is the German Enigma machine from World War II. This machine used a complex series of substitutions to perform encryption, and interestingly enough, it gave rise to extensive research in computers.

When material, called *plaintext*, needs to be protected from unauthorized interception or alteration, it is encrypted into *ciphertext*. This is done using an algorithm and a key, and the rise of digital computers has provided a wide array of algorithms and increasingly complex keys. The choice of specific algorithm depends on several factors, and they will be examined in this chapter.

Cryptanalysis, the process of analyzing available information in an attempt to return the encrypted message to its original form, required advances in computer technology for complex encryption methods. The birth of the computer made it possible to easily execute the calculations required by more complex encryption algorithms. Today, the computer almost exclusively powers how encryption is performed. Computer technology has also aided cryptanalysis, allowing new methods to be developed, such as linear and differential cryptanalysis. Differential cryptanalysis is done by comparing the input plaintext to the output ciphertext to try to determine the key used to encrypt the information. Linear cryptanalysis is similar in that it uses both plaintext and ciphertext, but it puts the plaintext through a simplified cipher to try to deduce what the key is likely to be in the full version of the cipher.

Symmetric

Symmetric encryption is an older and simpler method of encrypting information. The basis of symmetric encryption is that both the sender and the receiver of the message have previously obtained the same key. This is, in fact, the basis for even the oldest ciphers—the Spartans needed the exact same size cylinder, making the cylinder the "key" to the message, and in shift ciphers, both parties need to know the direction and amount of shift being performed. All symmetric algorithms are based upon this *shared secret* principle, including the unbreakable one-time pad method.

Figure 23-1 is a simple diagram showing the process that a symmetric algorithm goes through to provide encryption from plaintext to ciphertext. This ciphertext message is, presumably, transmitted to the message recipient, who goes through the process to decrypt the message using the same key that was used to encrypt the message. Figure 23-1 shows the keys to the algorithm, which are the same value in the case of symmetric encryption.

Unlike with hash functions, a cryptographic key is involved in symmetric encryption, so there must be a mechanism for key management. Managing the cryptographic keys is critically important in symmetric algorithms because the key unlocks the data that is being protected. However, the key also needs to be known or transmitted in a secret way to the party with whom you wish to communicate. This key management applies to all things that could happen to a key: securing it on the local computer, securing it on the remote one, protecting it from data corruption, and protecting it from loss, as well as probably the most important step, protecting the key while it is transmitted between the two parties. Later in the chapter we will look at public key cryptography, which greatly eases the key management issue, but for symmetric algorithms, the most important lesson is to store and send the key only by known secure means.

 EXAM TIP   Common symmetric algorithms are 3DES, AES, Blowfish, Twofish, and RC4.

Figure 23-1
Layout of a symmetric algorithm

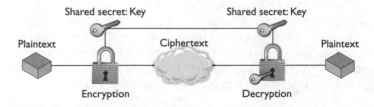

Symmetric algorithms are important because they are comparatively fast and have few computational requirements. Their main weakness is that two geographically distant parties both need to have a key that matches exactly. In the past, keys could be much simpler and still be secure, but with today's computational power, simple keys can be brute forced very quickly. This means that larger and more complex keys must be used and exchanged. This key exchange is difficult because the key cannot be simple, such as a word, but must be shared in a secure manner. It might be easy to exchange a 4-bit key such as *b* in hex, but exchanging the 128-bit key *4b36402c5727472d5571373d22675b4b* is far more difficult to do securely. This exchange of keys is greatly facilitated by our next subject, asymmetric, or public key, cryptography.

Public Key or Asymmetric

Asymmetric cryptography is more commonly known as public key cryptography. Asymmetric cryptography is in many ways completely different from symmetric cryptography. While both are used to keep data from being seen by unauthorized users, asymmetric cryptography uses two keys instead of one. It was invented by Whitfield Diffie and Martin Hellman in 1975. The system uses a pair of keys: a private key that is kept secret and a public key that can be sent to anyone. The system's security relies upon resistance to deducing one key, given the other, and thus retrieving the plaintext from the ciphertext.

Public key systems typically work by using complex math problems. One of the more common methods is through the difficulty of factoring large numbers. These functions are often called *trapdoor functions*, as they are difficult to process without the key, but easy to process when you have the key—the trapdoor through the function. For example, given a prime number, say 293, and another prime, such as 307, it is an easy function to multiply them together to get 89,951. Given 89,951, it is not simple to find the factors 293 and 307 unless you know one of them already. Computers can easily multiply very large primes with hundreds or thousands of digits, but cannot easily factor the product.

The strength of these functions is very important: because an attacker is likely to have access to the public key, he can run tests of known plaintext and produce ciphertext. This allows instant checking of guesses that are made about the keys of the algorithm. RSA, Diffie-Hellman, elliptic curve cryptography (ECC), and ElGamal are all popular asymmetric protocols.

Asymmetric encryption creates the possibility of digital signatures and also corrects the main weakness of symmetric cryptography. The ability to send messages securely without senders and receivers having had prior contact has become one of the basic concerns with secure communication. Digital signatures will enable faster and more efficient exchange of all kinds of documents, including legal documents. With strong algorithms and good key lengths, security can be assured.

Asymmetric cryptography involves two separate but mathematically related keys. The keys are used in an opposing fashion. One key undoes the actions of the other and vice versa. So, as shown in Figure 23-2, if you encrypt a message with one key, the other key is used to decrypt the message. In the top example, Alice wishes to send a private message to Bob. So, she uses Bob's public key to encrypt the message. Then, since only Bob's private key can decrypt the message, only Bob can read it. In the lower example, Bob wishes

Figure 23-2
Using an asymmetric algorithm

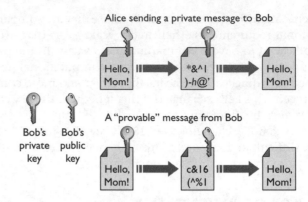

Alice sending a private message to Bob

Bob's private key   Bob's public key

A "provable" message from Bob

to send a message, with proof that it is from him. By encrypting it with his private key, anyone who decrypts it with his public key knows the message came from Bob.

EXAM TIP   Public key cryptography always involves two keys, a public key and a private key, which together are known as a *key pair*. The public key is made widely available to anyone who may need it, while the private key is closely safeguarded and shared with no one.

Asymmetric keys are distributed using certificates. A digital certificate contains information about the association of the public key to an entity, and additional information that can be used to verify the current validity of the certificate and the key. When keys are exchanged between machines, such as during an SSL/TLS handshake, the exchange is done by passing certificates.

Symmetric vs. Asymmetric

Both symmetric and asymmetric encryption methods have advantages and disadvantages. Symmetric encryption tends to be faster, is less computationally involved, and is better for bulk transfers. But it suffers from a key management problem in that keys must be protected from unauthorized parties. Asymmetric methods resolve the key secrecy issue with public keys, but add significant computational complexity that makes them less suited for bulk encryption.

Bulk encryption can be done using the best of both systems by using asymmetric encryption to pass a symmetric key. By adding in ephemeral key exchange, you can achieve perfect forward secrecy, discussed later in the chapter. Digital signatures, a highly useful tool, are not practical without asymmetric methods.

Session Keys

A *session key* is a symmetric key used for encrypting messages during a communication session. It is generated from random seeds and is used for the duration of a communication session. When correctly generated and propagated during session setup, a session key provides significant levels of protection during the communication session and also can afford perfect forward secrecy. Session keys offer the advantages of symmetric encryption, speed, strength and simplicity, and with key exchanges possible via digital methods, significant levels of automated security.

Key Exchange

Cryptographic mechanisms use both an algorithm and a key, with the key requiring communication between parties. In symmetric encryption, the secrecy depends upon the secrecy of the key, so insecure transport of the key can lead to failure to protect the information encrypted using the key. *Key exchange* is the central foundational element of a secure symmetric encryption system. Maintaining the secrecy of the symmetric key is the basis of secret communications. In asymmetric systems, the key exchange problem is one of key publication. Because public keys are designed to be shared, the problem is reversed from one of secrecy to one of publicity.

Early key exchanges were performed by trusted couriers. People carried the keys from senders to receivers. One could consider this form of key exchange to be the ultimate in *out-of-band* communication. With the advent of digital methods and some mathematical algorithms, it is possible to pass keys in a secure fashion. This can occur even when all packets are subject to interception. The Diffie-Hellman key exchange is one example of this type of secure key exchange. The Diffie-Hellman key exchange depends upon two random numbers, each chosen by one of the parties and kept secret. Diffie-Hellman key exchanges can be performed *in-band*, and even under external observation, as the secret random numbers are never exposed to outside parties.

Fundamental Methods

Modern cryptographic operations are performed using both an algorithm and a key. The choice of algorithm depends on the type of cryptographic operation that is desired. The subsequent choice of key is then tied to the specific algorithm. Cryptographic operations include encryption for the protection of confidentiality, hashing for the protection of integrity, digital signatures to manage non-repudiation, and a bevy of specialty operations such as key exchanges.

While the mathematical specifics of these operations can be very complex and are beyond the scope of this level of material, the knowledge to properly employ them is not complex and is subject to being tested on the CompTIA Security+ exam. Encryption operations are characterized by the quantity and type of data, as well as the level and type of protection sought. Integrity protection operations are characterized by the level of assurance desired. As described in Chapter 19, data is characterized by its usage: data in transit, data at rest, or data in use. It is also characterized in how it can be used, either in block form or stream form, as described next.

Block vs. Stream

When encryption operations are performed on data, there are two primary modes of operation, block and stream. Block operations are performed on blocks of data, enabling both transposition and substitution operations. This is possible when large pieces of data are present for the operations. Stream data has become more common

PART VI

Block Ciphers	Stream Ciphers
Require more memory to process	Faster than block in operation
Stronger	More difficult to implement correctly
High diffusion	Low diffusion
Resistant to insertions/modifications	Susceptible to insertions and/or modifications
Susceptible to error propagation	Low error propagation
Can provide for authentication and integrity verification	Cannot provide integrity or authentication protections
Common algorithms: 3DES, AES	Common algorithms: A5, RC4

Table 23-1 Comparison of Block and Stream Ciphers

with audio and video across the Web. The primary characteristic of stream data is that it is not available in large chunks, but either bit by bit or byte by byte, pieces too small for block operations. Stream ciphers operate using substitution only and therefore offer less robust protection than block ciphers. A table comparing and contrasting block and stream ciphers is presented in Table 23-1.

Elliptic Curve

Elliptic curve cryptography (ECC) works on the basis of elliptic curves. An *elliptic curve* is a simple function that is drawn as a gently looping curve on the X, Y plane. Elliptic curves are defined by this equation:

$$y^2 = x^3 + ax^2 + b$$

Elliptic curves work because they have a special property—you can add two points on the curve together and get a third point on the curve.

For cryptography, the elliptic curve works as a public key algorithm. Users agree on an elliptic curve and a fixed curve point. This information is not a shared secret, and these points can be made public without compromising the security of the system. User 1 then chooses a secret random number, K_1, and computes a public key based upon a point on the curve:

$$P_1 = K_1 \times F$$

User 2 performs the same function and generates P_2. Now user 1 can send user 2 a message by generating a shared secret:

$$S = K_1 \times P_2$$

User 2 can generate the same shared secret independently:

$$S = K_2 \times P_1$$

This is true because

$$K_1 \times P_2 = K_1 \times (K_2 \times F) = (K_1 \times K_2) \times F = K_2 \times (K_1 \times F) = K_2 \times P_1$$

The security of elliptic curve systems has been questioned, mostly because of lack of analysis. However, all public key systems rely on the difficulty of certain math problems. It would take a breakthrough in math for any of the mentioned systems to be weakened dramatically, but research has been done about the problems and has shown that the elliptic curve problem has been more resistant to incremental advances. Again, as with all cryptography algorithms, only time will tell how secure they really are. The big benefit of ECC systems is that they require less computing power for a given bit strength. This makes ECC ideal for use in low-power mobile devices. The surge in mobile connectivity has brought secure voice, e-mail, and text applications that use ECC and AES algorithms to protect a user's data.

Quantum Cryptography

Cryptography is traditionally a very conservative branch of information technology. It relies on proven technologies and does its best to resist change. A big new topic in recent years has been *quantum cryptography*, which is based on quantum mechanics, principally superposition and entanglement. A discussion of quantum mechanics is out of the scope of this text, but the principle we are most concerned with in regard to cryptography is that in quantum mechanics, the measuring of data disturbs the data. What this means to cryptographers is that it is easy to tell if a message has been eavesdropped on in transit. This allows people to exchange key data while knowing that the data was not intercepted in transit.

This use of quantum cryptography is called *quantum key distribution*. This is currently the only commercial use of quantum cryptography, and while there are several methods of sending the key, they all adhere to the same principle. Key bits are sent and then checked at the remote end for interception, and then more key bits are sent using the same process. Once an entire key is sent securely, symmetric encryption can then be used. The other field of research involving quantum mechanics and cryptography is quantum cryptanalysis. A quantum computer is capable of factoring large primes exponentially faster than a normal computer, potentially making the RSA algorithm, and any system based on factoring prime numbers, insecure. This has led to research in cryptosystems that are not vulnerable to quantum computations, known as post-quantum cryptography.

Hashing

Hashing functions are commonly used encryption methods. A *hashing function* is a special mathematical function that performs one-way encryption, which means that once the algorithm is processed, there is no feasible way to use the ciphertext to retrieve the plaintext that was used to generate it. Also, ideally, there is no feasible way to generate two different plaintexts that compute to the same hash value. Figure 23-3 shows a generic hashing process.

Common uses of hashing algorithms are to store computer passwords and to ensure message integrity. The idea is that hashing can produce a unique value that corresponds to the data entered, but the hash value is also reproducible by anyone else running the same algorithm against the data. So you could hash a message to get a message authentication code (MAC), and the computational number of the message would show

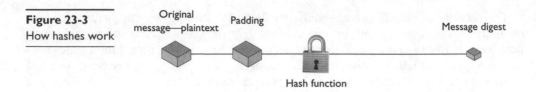

Figure 23-3
How hashes work

Original message—plaintext   Padding   Message digest

Hash function

that no intermediary has modified the message. This process works because hashing methods are typically public, and anyone can hash data using the specified method. It is computationally simple to generate the hash, so it is simple to check the validity or integrity of something by matching the given hash to one that is locally generated. HMAC, or Hash-based Message Authentication Code, is a special subset of hashing technology. It is a hash algorithm applied to a message to make a MAC, but it is done with a previously shared secret. So, the HMAC can provide integrity simultaneously with authentication.

A hash algorithm can be compromised with what is called a *collision attack*, in which an attacker finds two different messages that hash to the same value. This type of attack is very difficult and requires generating a separate algorithm that will attempt to find a text that will hash to the same value of a known hash. This must occur faster than simply editing characters until you hash to the same value, which is a brute-force type attack. The consequence of a hash function that suffers from collisions is that integrity is lost. If an attacker can make two different inputs purposefully hash to the same value, she might trick people into running malicious code and cause other problems. Popular hash algorithms are the Secure Hash Algorithm (SHA) series, the RIPEMD algorithms, and the Message Digest (MD) hash of varying versions (MD2, MD4, MD5).

 EXAM TIP   The hashing algorithms in common use are MD2, MD4, MD5, SHA-1, SHA-256, SHA-384, and SHA-512.

Hashing functions are very common, and they play an important role in the way information, such as passwords, is stored securely and the way in which messages can be signed. By computing a digest of the message, less data needs to be signed by the more complex asymmetric encryption, and this still maintains assurances about message integrity. This is the primary purpose for which the protocols were designed, and their success will allow greater trust in electronic protocols and digital signatures.

Ephemeral Keys

Ephemeral keys are cryptographic keys that are used only once after generation. When an ephemeral key is used as part of the Diffie-Hellman scheme, it forms an Ephemeral Diffie-Hellman (EDH) key exchange. An EDH generates a temporary key for each connection, never using the same key twice. This provides for perfect forward secrecy.

Cryptographic Objectives

Cryptographic methods exist for a purpose, to protect the integrity and confidentiality of data. There are many associated elements with this protection to enable a system-wide solution. Elements such as perfect forward secrecy, non-repudiation, key escrow, and others enable successful cryptographic implementations.

Perfect Forward Secrecy

Perfect forward secrecy is a property of a public key system in which a key derived from another key is not compromised even if the originating key is compromised in the future. This is especially important in session key generation, where the compromise of future communication sessions may become compromised; if perfect forward secrecy were not in place, then past messages that had been recorded could be decrypted.

Transport Encryption

Transport encryption is used to protect data that is in motion. When data is being transported across a network, it is at risk of interception. An examination of the OSI networking model shows a layer dedicated to transport, and this abstraction can be used to manage end-to-end cryptographic functions for a communication channel. When utilizing the TCP/IP protocol, TLS is one specific method of managing the security at the transport level. SSL is another example of transport layer security. Managing a secure layer of communications is an essential element in many forms of computer operations.

Non-repudiation

Non-repudiation is a property that deals with the ability to verify that a message has been sent and received so that the sender (or receiver) cannot refute sending (or receiving) the information. An example of this in action is seen with the private key holder relationship. It is assumed that the private key never leaves the possession of the private key holder. Should this occur, it is the responsibility of the holder to revoke the key. Thus, if the private key is used, as evidenced by the success of the public key, then it is assumed that the message was sent by the private key holder. Thus, actions that are signed cannot be repudiated by the holder.

Key Escrow

The impressive growth of the use of encryption technology has led to new methods for handling keys. *Key escrow* is a system by which your private key is kept both by you and by a third party. Encryption is adept at hiding secrets, and with computer technology being affordable to everyone, criminals and other ill-willed people began using encryption to conceal communications and business dealings from law enforcement agencies. Because they could not break the encryption, government agencies began asking for key escrow. Key escrow in this circumstance is a system by which your private key is kept both by you and by the government. This allows people with a court order to retrieve

PART VI

your private key to gain access to anything encrypted with your public key. The data is essentially encrypted by your key and the government key, giving the government access to your plaintext data.

Key escrow is also used by corporate enterprises, as it provides a method of obtaining a key in the event that the key holder is not available. There are also key recovery mechanisms to do this, and the corporate policies will determine the appropriate manner in which to safeguard keys across the enterprise.

Key escrow that involves an outside agency can negatively impact the security provided by encryption, because the government requires a huge, complex infrastructure of systems to hold every escrowed key, and the security of those systems is less efficient than the security of your memorizing the key. However, there are two sides to the key escrow coin. Without a practical way to recover a key if or when it is lost or the key holder dies, for example, some important information will be lost forever. Such issues will affect the design and security of encryption technologies for the foreseeable future.

 EXAM TIP Key escrow can solve many problems resulting from an inaccessible key, and the nature of cryptography makes the access of the data impossible without the key.

Steganography

Steganography, an offshoot of cryptography technology, gets its meaning from the Greek word *steganos*, meaning covered. Invisible ink placed on a document and hidden by innocuous text is an example of a steganographic message. Another example is a tattoo placed on the top of a person's head, visible only when the person's hair is shaved off.

Hidden writing in the computer age relies on a program to hide data inside other data. The most common application is the concealing of a text message in a picture file. The Internet contains multiple billions of image files, allowing a hidden message to be located almost anywhere without being discovered. The nature of the image files also makes a hidden message difficult to detect. While it is most common to hide messages inside images, they can also be hidden in video and audio files.

The advantage to steganography over cryptography is that the messages do not attract attention, and this difficulty in detecting the hidden message provides an additional barrier to analysis. The data that is hidden in a steganographic message is frequently also encrypted, so should it be discovered, the message will remain secure. Steganography has many uses, but the most publicized uses are to hide illegal material, often pornography, or allegedly for covert communication by terrorist networks. While there is no direct evidence to support that terrorists use steganography, the techniques have been documented in some of their training materials.

Steganographic encoding can be used in many ways and through many different media. Covering them all is beyond the scope of this book, but we will discuss one of the most common ways to encode into an image file, *LSB encoding*. LSB, Least Significant Bit, is a method of encoding information into an image while altering the actual visual image as little as possible. A computer image is made up of thousands or millions of pixels, all defined by 1s and 0s. If an image is composed of Red Green Blue

(RGB) values, each pixel has an RGB value represented numerically from 0 to 255. For example, 0,0,0 is black, and 255,255,255 is white, which can also be represented as 00000000, 00000000, 00000000 for black and 11111111, 11111111, 11111111 for white. Given a white pixel, editing the least significant bit of the pixel to 11111110, 11111110, 11111110 changes the color. The change in color is undetectable to the human eye, but in an image with a million pixels, this creates a 125KB area in which to store a message.

Digital Signatures

A *digital signature* is a cryptographic implementation designed to demonstrate authenticity and identity associated with a message. Using public key cryptography, a digital signature allows traceability to the person signing the message through the use of their private key. The addition of hash codes allows for the assurance of integrity of the message as well. The operation of a digital signature is a combination of cryptographic elements to achieve a desired outcome. The steps involved in digital signature generation and use are illustrated in Figure 23-4. The message to be signed is hashed, and the hash is encrypted using the sender's private key. Upon receipt, the recipient can decrypt the

Figure 23-4
Digital signature operation

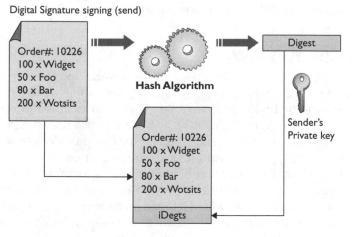

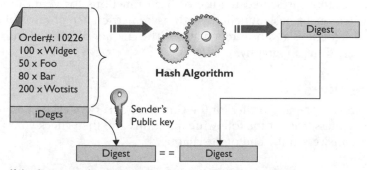

If the digests match, message authenticity and integrity are assured.

hash using the sender's public key. If a subsequent hashing of the message reveals an identical value, two things are known: First, the message has not been altered. Second, the sender possessed the private key of the named sender, so is presumably the sender him- or herself.

A digital signature does not by itself protect the contents of the message from interception. The message is still sent in the clear, so if confidentiality of the message is a requirement, additional steps must be taken to secure the message from eavesdropping. This can be done by encrypting the message itself, or by encrypting the channel over which it is transmitted.

Use of Proven Technologies

When setting up a cryptographic scheme, it is important to use proven technologies. Proven cryptographic libraries and proven cryptographically correct random number generators are the foundational elements associated with a solid program. Homegrown or custom elements in these areas can greatly increase risk associated with a broken system. Developing your own cryptographic algorithms is beyond the abilities of most groups. Algorithms are complex and difficult to create. Any algorithm that has not had public review can have weaknesses. Most good algorithms are approved for use only after a lengthy test and public review phase.

Chapter Review

In this chapter, you became acquainted with the principles of cryptography. The chapter opened with the concepts of cryptography, including the description of vocabulary elements associated with general cryptography. An examination of the fundamental methods of cryptography, encryption, and hashing was presented in terms of the types of algorithms and the types of data. Data can be in either block form, where many bytes are present at a time for encryption, or in stream form, where bytes are spaced temporally. Encryption algorithms are either symmetric or asymmetric in nature. The issue of key exchange, a challenge in the case of symmetric encryption, was presented, including methods such as ephemeral Diffie-Hellman exchanges that offer perfect forward secrecy. Newer methods, including elliptic curve and quantum-based cryptography, were also covered.

The chapter presented the use of hash functions for verification of integrity. The combination of hash functions with asymmetric encryption enables things such as digital signatures and non-repudiation. The chapter concluded with such topics as key escrow and steganography.

Questions

To help you prepare further for the CompTIA Security+ exam, and to test your level of preparedness, answer the following questions and then check your answers against the correct answers at the end of the chapter.

1. Why are session keys utilized?

   A. To protect each session individually.

   B. To get the benefits of both types of encryption ciphers.

   C. Session keys provide a higher bit strength.

   D. Session keys can be safely shared, similar to public keys.

2. Why is hashing a unique form of cryptography?

   A. Hashing uses ten times the bit strength of regular encryption.

   B. Hashing is a hidden encryption cipher that allows you to have encrypted text that appears the same as unencrypted text.

   C. Hashing is a one-way function, with no way to extract the plaintext from the ciphertext.

   D. Hashing allows you to share all details of the algorithm publicly, without a loss to security.

3. What factors are important to a digital signature? (Choose all that apply.)

   A. Confidentiality

   B. Integrity

   C. Availability

   D. Non-repudiation

4. What is a popular use of ECC?

   A. Cryptography on low-power mobile devices

   B. More efficient SSL key exchange for servers

   C. The enforcement of a larger keyspace

   D. Steganography

5. When would out-of-band key exchange be used?

   A. When using a stream cipher.

   B. When using varying length keys, such as a one-time pad.

   C. It is a key component of Diffie-Hellman.

   D. It is required as part of using the AES algorithm.

6. How does a block cipher handle plaintext input?

   A. It generates a key of the same length as the input and encrypts the text.

   B. It uses a hash algorithm to reduce the input to match the current key.

   C. It divides the input into predefined lengths, and pads the remainder to maintain a set length.

   D. It encrypts it only to the private key.

PART VI

7. When you get an SSL certificate from a web page, what kind of cipher is used?

    A. One-time pad

    B. Symmetric

    C. Asymmetric

    D. All of the above

8. Which of the following is a popular use of key escrow?

    A. Key sharing for groups

    B. Having keys prepared for future use

    C. Home use

    D. Enterprise environment

9. Which of the following describes a pitfall of new or proprietary algorithms?

    A. They could have an unknown weakness.

    B. They could have too low a key strength.

    C. They have deliberate weaknesses placed in them by the government.

    D. All of the above.

10. What makes steganography so hard to detect?

    A. There are many images on the Internet.

    B. It involves changes in the image that are too subtle to detect.

    C. The data can be encrypted and encoded in a proprietary manner.

    D. All of the above.

For questions 11–15, assume the following scenario: You have been asked to develop software specs for a new cloud-based file-sharing application that will primarily be used to store and share password information.

11. What are the advantages to using an asymmetric cipher as part of the design? (Choose all that apply.)

    A. Integrity

    B. Non-repudiation

    C. Authentication of users

    D. Secure key exchange

    E. Fast encryption

    F. Ability to add multiple users to the encryption

12. Where would you use a symmetric cipher as part of the design?

    A. For passphrase storage

    B. For authenticating users

  C. Multiuser collaboration

  D. File transfers to and from the cloud

13. In what situation would this application benefit from key escrow?

  A. User forgets their private key passphrase

  B. Government legal action

  C. Security audits

  D. Both A and B

  E. Both A and C

14. What key exchange method would be optimal for an online solution?

  A. In-band

  B. Out-of-band

  C. Both A and B

  D. Neither A nor B

15. When would non-repudiation be important to your application?

  A. An attacker breaks the encryption algorithm.

  B. One user adds a new user to the system.

  C. A collaborative user makes changes to a document that need to be securely tracked.

  D. Non-repudiation would not be important.

Answers

1. B. Session keys allow a communication to get the benefits of both types of encryption ciphers. Asymmetric is used for key exchange, and symmetric, the faster protocol, is used for data encryption.

2. C. Hashing is a one-way function that creates a digest of the message and cannot be reversed to extract the source plaintext.

3. B and D. Integrity and non-repudiation are the important factors of digital signatures. A document can be hashed to a value, and that value can be signed by the sender's key. If any change is made to the document, the hash will change, and because the hash is signed, the attacker cannot re-encrypt the changed hash with a key they don't possess. If the hash is correct, the sender signed it.

4. A. ECC requires less power for a given key strength, making ECC a good candidate for mobile devices.

5. **B.** Out-of-band key exchange can best be used if the length of the key must match the length of the message, as in a one-time pad cipher. Alternatively, it can be useful when a key exchange protocol cannot be used securely.

6. **C.** A block cipher divides the input into predefined lengths called blocks, and then pads any remainder to make a complete block.

7. **C.** SSL certificates are part of a public key infrastructure, using asymmetric keys.

8. **D.** Key escrow, or key recovery, is popular in an enterprise environment where systems exist that would lose large volumes of data if the primary passphrase were lost.

9. **A.** Any algorithm that has not had public review can have weaknesses in the algorithm. Most good algorithms are only approved for use after a lengthy public review phase.

10. **D.** All three answers are correct. There are so many images, sound files, and video files on the Internet that scanning all of them for hidden messages would be an unachievable task. Also, the changes are so minimal as to be very difficult to detect. The data can also be encrypted to make pattern analysis much more difficult, and the encoding can be proprietary to avoid leaving a known pattern in image pixels.

11. **C, D, and F.** The best answers are authentication of users, secure key exchange, and ability to add multiple users to the encryption. Asymmetric keys will allow each user to be authenticated, as they should be the only ones with access to the private keys. Asymmetric keys also allow secure exchange of any necessary session keys, and as asymmetric keys are user based, the removal of a single user can be accomplished without compromising the security of the data.

12. **D.** Symmetric ciphers are good at performing encryption quickly, allowing for good file transfer speeds.

13. **D.** Both a forgotten key passphrase and a court-ordered government action could be possible uses of key escrow.

14. **A.** In-band key exchange would be an optimal design for an online solution. The delays caused by out-of-band key exchange would greatly limit usability and slow adoption of the application.

15. **C.** Non-repudiation is important in a collaborative environment so that changes to documents can be securely tracked and the person who made the changes cannot deny having made the changes.

CHAPTER 24

Cryptographic Methods

In this chapter, you will

- Learn how to use appropriate cryptographic methods in any given scenario
- Learn the comparative strengths and performance of algorithms
- Learn how to use appropriate PKI methods in any given scenario
- Learn how to perform certificate management and associated component operations in any given scenario

The use of cryptographic algorithms grows every day. More and more information becomes digitally encoded and placed online, and all of this data needs to be secured. The best way to do that with current technology is to use encryption. This chapter considers some of the tasks cryptographic algorithms accomplish and those for which they are best suited. It presents the different cryptographic methods and their appropriate use.

Hashing

As introduced in Chapter 23, hashing functions are commonly used cryptographic methods. Common uses of hashing algorithms are to store computer passwords and to ensure message integrity. HMAC, or Hash-based Message Authentication Code, is a special subset of hashing technology. So, the HMAC can provide integrity simultaneously with authentication. Popular hash algorithms are Message Digest (MD5), the Secure Hash Algorithm (SHA) series, and the RIPEMD algorithms.

MD5

Message Digest (MD) is the generic version of one of several algorithms that are designed to create a message digest or hash from data input into the algorithm. MD algorithms work in the same manner as SHA in that they use a secure method to compress the file and generate a computed output of a specified number of bits. They were all developed by Ronald L. Rivest of MIT. The current version is MD5, while previous versions were MD2 and MD4. MD5 was developed in 1991 and is structured after MD4 but with additional security to overcome the problems in MD4. In November 2007, researchers published their findings on the ability to have two entirely different

Win32 executables with different functionality but the same MD5 hash. This discovery has obvious implications for the development of malware. The combination of these problems with MD5 has pushed people to adopt a strong SHA version for security reasons.

SHA

Secure Hash Algorithm (SHA) refers to a set of hash algorithms designed and published by the National Institute of Standards and Technology (NIST) and the National Security Agency (NSA). These algorithms are included in the SHA standard Federal Information Processing Standards (FIPS) 180-2 and 180-3. Individually, each standard is named SHA-1, SHA-224, SHA-256, SHA-384, and SHA-512. The latter four variants are occasionally referred to as SHA-2. Because of collision-based weaknesses in the SHA-1 and SHA-2 series, NIST conducted a search for a new version, the result of which is known as SHA-3.

SHA-1

SHA-1, developed in 1993, was designed as the algorithm to be used for secure hashing in the U.S. Digital Signature Standard (DSS). It is modeled on the MD4 algorithm and implements fixes in that algorithm discovered by the NSA. It creates a message digest 160 bits long that can be used by the Digital Signature Algorithm (DSA), which can then compute the signature of the message. This is computationally simpler, as the message digest is typically much smaller than the actual message—smaller message, less work. SHA-1 works, as do all hashing functions, by applying a compression function to the data input.

At one time, SHA-1 was one of the more secure hash functions, but it has been found vulnerable to a collision attack. Thus, most implementations of SHA-1 have been replaced with one of the other, more secure SHA versions. The added security and resistance to attack in SHA-1 does require more processing power to compute the hash. In spite of these improvements, SHA-1 is still vulnerable to collisions and is no longer approved for use by government agencies.

SHA-2

SHA-2 is a collective name for SHA-224, SHA-256, SHA-384, and SHA-512. SHA-2 is similar to SHA-1, in that it will also accept input of less than 2^{64} bits and reduces that input to a hash. The SHA-2 series algorithm produces a hash length equal to the number after SHA, so SHA-256 produces a digest of 256 bits. The SHA-2 series became more common after SHA-1 was shown to be potentially vulnerable to a collision attack.

SHA-3

SHA-3 is the name for the SHA-2 replacement. In 2012, the Keccak hash function won the NIST competition and was chosen as the basis for the SHA-3 method. Because the algorithm is completely different from the previous SHA series, it has proved to be more resistant to attacks that are successful against them. Because the SHA-3 series is relatively new, it has not been widely adopted in many cipher suites yet.

EXAM TIP The SHA-2 and SHA-3 series are currently approved for use. SHA-1 has been discontinued.

RIPEMD

RACE Integrity Primitives Evaluation Message Digest (RIPEMD) is a hashing function developed by the RACE Integrity Primitives Evaluation (RIPE) consortium. It originally provided a 128-bit hash and was later shown to have problems with collisions. RIPEMD was strengthened to a 160-bit hash known as RIPEMD-160 by Hans Dobbertin, Antoon Bosselaers, and Bart Preneel.

RIPEMD-160

RIPEMD-160 is an algorithm based on MD4, but it uses two parallel channels with five rounds. The output consists of five 32-bit words to make a 160-bit hash. There are also larger output extensions of the RIPEMD-160 algorithm. These extensions, RIPEMD-256 and RIPEMD-320, offer outputs of 256 bits and 320 bits, respectively. While these offer larger output sizes, this does not make the hash function inherently stronger.

Symmetric Encryption

Symmetric encryption algorithms are used for bulk encryption because they are comparatively fast and have few computational requirements. Common symmetric algorithms are DES, 3DES, AES, Blowfish, Twofish, RC2, RC4, RC5, and RC6.

 EXAM TIP Ensure you understand DES, 3DES, AES, Blowfish, Twofish, and RC4 symmetric algorithms for the exam.

DES

DES, the Data Encryption Standard, was developed in response to the National Bureau of Standards (NBS), now known as the National Institute of Standards and Technology (NIST), issuing a request for proposals for a standard cryptographic algorithm in 1973. NBS specified that the DES standard had to be recertified every five years. While DES passed without a hitch in 1983, the NSA said it would not recertify it in 1987. However, since no alternative was available for many businesses, many complaints ensued, and the NSA and NBS were forced to recertify it. The algorithm was then recertified in 1993. NIST has now certified the Advanced Encryption Standard (AES) to replace DES.

3DES

Triple DES (3DES) is a follow-on implementation of DES. Depending on the specific variant, it uses either two or three keys instead of the single key that DES uses. It also spins through the DES algorithm three times via what's called *multiple encryption*.

Multiple encryption can be performed in several different ways. The simplest method of multiple encryption is just to stack algorithms on top of each other—taking plaintext, encrypting it with DES, then encrypting the first ciphertext with a different key, and then encrypting the second ciphertext with a third key. In reality, this technique is less effective than the technique that 3DES uses, which is to encrypt with one key, then decrypt with a second, and then encrypt with a third.

This greatly increases the number of attempts needed to retrieve the key and is a significant enhancement of security. The additional security comes with a price, however. It can take up to three times longer to compute 3DES than to compute DES. However, the advances in memory and processing power in today's electronics make this problem irrelevant in all devices except for very small, low-power handhelds.

The only weaknesses of 3DES are those that already exist in DES. Because different keys are used with the same algorithm, the effective key length is longer than the DES keyspace and this results in greater resistance to brute-force attack, making 3DES stronger than DES to a wide range of attacks. While 3DES has continued to be popular and is still widely supported, AES has taken over as the symmetric encryption standard.

AES

Because of the advancement of technology and the progress being made in quickly retrieving DES keys, NIST put out a request for proposals for a new Advanced Encryption Standard (AES). It called for a block cipher using symmetric key cryptography and supporting key sizes of 128, 192, and 256 bits. After evaluation, NIST had five finalists:

- **MARS**   IBM
- **RC6**   RSA
- **Rijndael**   John Daemen and Vincent Rijmen
- **Serpent**   Ross Anderson, Eli Biham, and Lars Knudsen
- **Twofish**   Bruce Schneier, John Kelsey, Doug Whiting, David Wagner, Chris Hall, and Niels Ferguson

In the fall of 2000, NIST picked Rijndael to be the new AES. It was chosen for its overall security as well as its good performance on limited-capacity devices. AES has three different standard key sizes, 128, 192, and 256, designated AES-128, AES-192, and AES-256, respectively.

While no efficient attacks currently exist against AES, more time and analysis will tell if this standard can last as long as DES has.

EXAM TIP   In the world of symmetric cryptography, AES is the current gold standard of algorithms. It is considered secure and is computationally efficient.

RC4

RC is a general term for several ciphers all designed by Ron Rivest—RC officially stands for Rivest Cipher. RC1, RC2, RC3, RC4, RC5, and RC6 are all ciphers in the series. RC1 and RC3 never made it to release, but RC2, RC4, RC5, and RC6 are all working algorithms.

RC4 was created before RC5 and RC6, but it differs in operation. RC4 is a stream cipher, whereas all the symmetric ciphers we have looked at so far have been block-mode ciphers. A stream cipher works by enciphering the plaintext in a stream, usually bit by bit. This makes stream ciphers faster than block-mode ciphers. Stream ciphers accomplish this by performing a bitwise XOR with the plaintext stream and a generated key stream. RC4 can use a key length of 8 to 2048 bits, though the most common versions use 128-bit keys. The algorithm is fast, sometimes ten times faster than DES. The most vulnerable point of the encryption is the possibility of weak keys. One key in 256 can generate bytes closely correlated with key bytes. Proper implementations of RC4 need to include weak key detection.

EXAM TIP   RC4 is the most widely used stream cipher and is used in popular protocols such as Transport Layer Security (TLS) and WEP/WPA.

Blowfish

Blowfish was designed in 1994 by Bruce Schneier. It is a block-mode cipher using 64-bit blocks and a variable key length from 32 to 448 bits. It was designed to run quickly on 32-bit microprocessors and is optimized for situations with few key changes. The only successful cryptanalysis to date against Blowfish has been against variants that used reduced rounds. There does not seem to be a weakness in the full 16-round version.

Twofish

As mentioned previously, Twofish was one of the five finalists in the AES competition. Like other AES entrants, it is a block cipher utilizing 128-bit blocks with a variable-length key of up to 256 bits. This algorithm is available for public use, and has proven to be secure. Twofish is an improvement over Blowfish in that it is less vulnerable to certain classes of weak keys.

Asymmetric Encryption

Asymmetric cryptography is in many ways completely different from symmetric cryptography. Also known as *public key cryptography*, the algorithms are built around hard-to-reverse math problems. The strength of these functions is very important: because an attacker is likely to have access to the public key, he can run tests of known plaintext and produce ciphertext. This allows instant checking of guesses that are made about the keys of the algorithm. RSA, Diffie-Hellman, elliptic curve cryptography (ECC), and ElGamal are all popular asymmetric protocols. We will look at all of them and their suitability for different functions.

EXAM TIP Asymmetric methods are significantly slower than symmetric methods and thus are typically not suitable for bulk encryption.

RSA

RSA is one of the first public key cryptosystems ever invented. It can be used for both encryption and digital signatures. RSA is named after its inventors, Ron Rivest, Adi Shamir, and Leonard Adleman, and was first published in 1977. This algorithm uses the product of two very large prime numbers and works on the principle of difficulty in factoring such large numbers. It's best to choose large prime numbers from 100 to 200 digits in length that are equal in length.

This is a simple method, but its security has withstood the test of more than 30 years of analysis. Considering the effectiveness of RSA's security and the ability to have two keys, why are symmetric encryption algorithms needed at all? The answer is speed. RSA in software can be 100 times slower than DES, and in hardware, it can be even slower.

RSA can be used to perform both regular encryption and digital signatures. Digital signatures try to duplicate the functionality of a physical signature on a document using encryption. Typically, RSA and the other public key systems are used in conjunction with symmetric key cryptography. Public key, the slower protocol, is used to exchange the symmetric key (or shared secret), and then the communication uses the faster symmetric key protocol. This process is known as electronic *key exchange*.

Diffie-Hellman

Diffie-Hellman was created in 1976 by Whitfield Diffie and Martin Hellman. This protocol is one of the most common encryption protocols in use today. It plays a role in the electronic key exchange method of the Secure Sockets Layer (SSL) protocol. It is also used by the SSH and IPsec protocols. Diffie-Hellman is important because it enables the sharing of a secret key between two people who have not contacted each other before.

There are several variants of the Diffie-Hellman key exchange. Ephemeral Diffie-Hellman (EDH) is a variant where a temporary key is used in the key exchange rather than reusing the same key over and over. This is done to create perfect forward secrecy, a desirable property covered in Chapter 23. Elliptic Curve Diffie-Hellman (ECDH) is a variant of the Diffie-Hellman protocol that uses elliptic curve cryptography. ECDH can also be used with ephemeral keys, becoming Elliptic Curve Diffie-Hellman Ephemeral (ECDHE), to enable perfect forward security.

 EXAM TIP Diffie-Hellman is the gold standard for key exchange, and for the exam, you should understand the subtle differences between the forms DH, EDH, ECDH, and ECDHE.

ECC

Elliptic curve cryptography (ECC) was covered in detail in Chapter 23. What is important to note from a use perspective is that ECC is well suited for platforms with limited computing power, such as mobile devices.

The security of elliptic curve systems has been questioned, mostly because of lack of analysis. However, all public key systems rely on the difficulty of certain math problems. It would take a breakthrough in math for any of the mentioned systems to be weakened dramatically, but research has been done about the problems and has shown that the elliptic curve problem has been more resistant to incremental advances. Again, as with all cryptography algorithms, only time will tell how secure they really are. The big benefit of ECC systems is that they require less computing power for a given bit strength. This makes ECC ideal for use in low-power mobile devices. The surge in mobile connectivity has brought secure voice, e-mail, and text applications that use ECC and AES algorithms to protect a user's data.

 EXAM TIP Ensure you understand RSA, ECC, and Diffie-Hellman variants of asymmetric algorithms for the exam.

Cryptographic Applications

A few applications can be used to encrypt data conveniently on your personal computer. These programs are representative of a wide range of stand-alone cryptographic applications. One noted exception to the list is TrueCrypt, a popular cryptographic application that ceased distribution in 2014 to much mystery and speculation. Since it was apparently pulled by the development team, this program should no longer be relied upon for security.

PGP

Pretty Good Privacy (PGP), created by Philip Zimmermann in 1991, passed through several versions that were available for free under a noncommercial license. PGP is now a commercial enterprise encryption product. It can be applied to popular e-mail programs to handle the majority of day-to-day encryption tasks using a combination of symmetric and asymmetric encryption protocols. One of the unique features of PGP is its use of both symmetric and asymmetric encryption methods, accessing the strengths of each method and avoiding the weaknesses of each as well. Symmetric keys are used for bulk encryption, taking advantage of the speed and efficiency of symmetric encryption. The symmetric keys are passed using asymmetric methods, capitalizing on the flexibility of this method.

GnuPG/GPG

GnuPG (Gnu Privacy Guard, or simply GPG) is an open source implementation of the OpenPGP standard. This command-line–based tool is a public key encryption program designed to protect electronic communications such as e-mail. It operates similarly to PGP and includes a method for managing public/private keys.

PAP/CHAP

The Password Authentication Protocol (PAP) is a plaintext authentication mechanism. Because it is a plaintext protocol, it really isn't suited for authentication in today's environment. PAP has been replaced by Challenge Handshake Authentication Protocol (CHAP), which is designed to provide authentication periodically through the use of a challenge/response system sometimes described as a three-way handshake, providing a secure means of authentication.

NT LAN Manager

NT LAN Manager (NTLM) is an authentication protocol designed by Microsoft for use with the Server Message Block (SMB) protocol. SMB is an application-level network protocol primarily used for sharing files and printers on Windows-based networks. NTLM was designed as a replacement for the LANMAN protocol. The current version is NTLMv2, which was introduced with NT 4.0 SP4. Although Microsoft has adopted the Kerberos protocol for authentication, NTLMv2 is still used when

- Authenticating to a server using an IP address
- Authenticating to a server that belongs to a different Active Directory forest
- Authenticating to a server that doesn't belong to a domain
- No Active Directory domain exists ("workgroup" or "peer-to-peer" connection)

HMAC-MD5 is used in the NT LAN Manager version 2 challenge-response protocol.

Wireless

In the wireless realm, there are three commonly deployed security suites: Wired Equivalent Privacy (WEP), Wi-Fi Protected Access (WPA), and WPA2. WEP has been shown to have numerous weaknesses, primarily associated with the initiation of the RC4 cipher. WPA was developed to overcome these weaknesses, but it still suffers from deficiencies. WPA2 addresses all of these and uses AES for confidentiality. WPA2 offers a pre-shared key (PSK) option, where a shared secret is previously shared between parties and is used to establish the secure channel.

WPA2 comes in two variants, WPA2-PSK (Pre-Shared Key), which is primarily used by most home and small business users, and WPA2-Enterprise, used in the corporate world. WPA2-Enterprise has a much more complicated setup involving the use of a RADIUS authentication server and avoids the necessity to share a key in advance. Hackers have managed to crack WPA2-PSK, but WPA2-Enterprise has not yet been cracked. The best solution for WPA2-PSK is to use a long, random key (greater than 25 characters) and a random SSID that is also long, as the SSID is used in pre-computed rainbow tables during an attack.

 EXAM TIP WPA2 is the most secure method to secure wireless, with WPA2-Enterprise being best for business and WPA2-PSK for home/small business.

One-time Pads

One-time pads are an interesting form of encryption in that they theoretically are perfect and unbreakable. The key is the same size or larger than the material being encrypted. The plaintext is XOR'ed against the key producing the ciphertext. What makes the one-time pad "perfect" is the size of the key. If you use a keyspace full of keys, you will decrypt every possible message of the same length as the original, with no way to discriminate which one is correct. This makes a one-time pad unable to be broken by even brute-force methods, provided that the key is not reused. This makes a one-time pad less than practical for any mass use.

Comparative Strengths and Performance of Algorithms

There are several factors that play a role in determining the strength of a cryptographic algorithm. First and most obvious is the size of the key and the resulting keyspace. One method of attack is to simply try all of the possible keys in a brute-force attack. The other factor is referred to as *work factor*, which is a subjective measurement of the time and effort needed to perform operations. If the work factor is low, then the rate at which keys can be tested is high, meaning that larger keyspaces are needed. Work factor also plays a role in protecting systems such as password hashes, where having a higher work factor can be part of the security mechanism.

Use of Algorithms/Protocols with Transport Encryption

The movement of data across networks is referred to as *transport*. Encrypting transport mechanisms is one of the key elements in protecting data in motion. Data can be encrypted independent of the transport mechanism, and then passed over open channels, or the channel itself can be encrypted.

HTTPS

Most web activity occurs using the Hypertext Transfer Protocol (HTTP), but this plaintext protocol is prone to interception. HTTPS uses the Secure Sockets Layer (SSL) or Transport Layer Security (TLS) to secure the channel before the transfer of information. HTTPS uses the standard TCP port 443 for TCP/IP communications rather than the standard port 80 used for HTTP. Early HTTPS implementations made use of the 40-bit RC4 encryption algorithm, but with the relaxation of export restrictions, most implementations now use 128-bit encryption. The appropriate set of algorithms is chosen from cipher suites during the SSL/TLS protocol negotiation.

SSL

Secure Sockets Layer (SSL) was invented by Netscape as a solution to the lack of confidentiality associated with web traffic. SSL works by encrypting the communication channel, beginning with a Diffie-Hellman key exchange and negotiating a set of parameters that can include encryption and authentication methods. The most recent version is 3.0, but as of October 2014, all SSL versions have known exploitable flaws and should not be enabled.

PART VI

TLS

Transport Layer Security (TLS) is an IETF creation that is very similar to SSL. TLS was created as a replacement for SSL, and in many cases when TLS is being used, people incorrectly refer to it as SSL. There are several versions of TLS: 1.0, 1.1, and 1.2. As with SSL, during the channel setup, the choice of algorithms is performed by choosing one of the cipher suites that both sides of the connection have in common.

IPsec

IPsec is a collection of IP security features designed to introduce security at the network or packet-processing layer in network communication. Other approaches have attempted to incorporate security at higher levels of the TCP/IP suite, such as at the level where applications reside. IPsec is designed to be used to provide secure virtual private network (VPN) capability over the Internet. In essence, IPsec provides a secure version of the IP by introducing authentication and encryption to protect layer 4 protocols. IPsec is optional for IPv4 but is required for IPv6. Obviously, both ends of the communication need to use IPsec for the encryption/decryption process to occur. IPsec uses HMAC-SHA1 for integrity and authenticity and uses AES for confidentiality.

IPsec provides two types of security service to ensure authentication and confidentiality for either the data alone (referred to as IPsec *transport mode*) or for both the data and the header (referred to as *tunnel mode*). IPsec introduces several new protocols, including the Authentication Header (AH), which basically provides authentication of the sender, and the Encapsulating Security Payload (ESP), which adds encryption of the data to ensure confidentiality. IPsec also provides for payload compression before encryption using the IP Payload Compression Protocol (IPComp). Frequently, encryption negatively impacts the ability of compression algorithms to fully compress data for transmission. By providing the ability to compress the data before encryption, IPsec addresses this issue.

SSH

Secure Shell (SSH) is a secure replacement for Telnet, a plaintext transport protocol. OpenSSH is a popular SSH implementation, and the current version is 6.6. On the OpenSSH website (www.openssh.com/), a list of known vulnerabilities for past versions is presented. OpenSSH supports 3DES, Blowfish, and AES.

 EXAM TIP   For the exam, you should expect questions on transport encryption and HTTPS, SSL/TLS, IPsec, and SSH, all of which are CompTIA Security+ objectives. You should understand in which scenarios each is employed.

Cipher Suites

In many applications, the use of cryptography occurs as a collection of functions. Different algorithms can be used for authentication, encryption/decryption, digital signature, and hashing. The term *cipher suite* refers to an arranged group of algorithms. For instance, TLS has a published TLS Cipher Suite Registry at www.iana.org/assignments/tls-parameters/tls-parameters.xhtml.

Strong vs. Weak Ciphers

There is a wide range of ciphers, some old and some new, each with its own strengths and weaknesses. Over time, new methods and computational abilities change the viability of ciphers. The concept of strong versus weak ciphers is an acknowledgement that, over time, ciphers can become vulnerable to attacks. The application or selection of ciphers should take into consideration that not all ciphers are still strong. When selecting a cipher for use, it is important to make an appropriate choice. For example, if a server offers SSL v2 and v3, you should choose v3 only, as v2 has been shown to be vulnerable.

Key Stretching

Key stretching is a mechanism that takes what would be weak keys and "stretches" them to make the system more secure against brute-force attacks. A typical methodology used for key stretching involves increasing the computational complexity by adding iterative rounds of computations. To extend a password to a longer length of key, you can run it through multiple rounds of variable-length hashing, each increasing the output by bits over time. This may take hundreds or thousands of rounds, but for single-use computations, the time is not significant. When one wants to use a brute-force attack, the increase in computational workload becomes significant when done billions of times, making this form of attack much more expensive.

The common forms of key stretching employed in use today include Password-Based Key Derivation Function 2 and Bcrypt.

PBKDF2

Password-Based Key Derivation Function 2 (PBKDF2) is a key derivation function designed to produce a key derived from a password. This function uses a password or passphrase and a salt and applies an HMAC to the input thousands of times. The repetition makes brute-force attacks computationally unfeasible.

Bcrypt

Bcrypt is a key-stretching mechanism that uses the Blowfish cipher and salting, and adds an adaptive function to increase the number of iterations. The result is the same as other key-stretching mechanisms (single use is computationally feasible), but when attempting to brute force the function, the billions of attempts make it computationally unfeasible.

The Basics of Public Key Infrastructures

A public key infrastructure (PKI) provides all the components necessary for different types of users and entities to be able to communicate securely and in a predictable manner. A PKI is made up of hardware, applications, policies, services, programming interfaces, cryptographic algorithms, protocols, users, and utilities. These components work together to allow communication to manage asymmetric keys facilitating the use of public key cryptography for digital signatures, data encryption, and integrity. Refer to Chapter 23 if you need a refresher on these concepts. Although many different applications and protocols can provide the same type of functionality, constructing and implementing a PKI boils down to establishing a level of trust.

If, for example, John and Diane want to communicate securely, John can generate his own public/private key pair and send his public key to Diane, or he can place his public key in a directory that is available to everyone. If Diane receives John's public key, either from him or from a public directory, how does she know it really came from John? Maybe another individual is masquerading as John and has replaced John's public key with her own, as shown in Figure 24-1. If this took place, Diane would believe that her messages could be read only by John and that the replies were actually from him. However, she would actually be communicating with Katie. What is needed is a way to verify an individual's identity, to ensure that a person's public key is bound to their identity and thus ensure that the previous scenario (and others) cannot take place.

In PKI environments, entities called *registration authorities (RAs)* and *certificate authorities (CAs)* provide services similar to those of the Department of Motor Vehicles (DMV). When John goes to register for a driver's license, he has to prove his

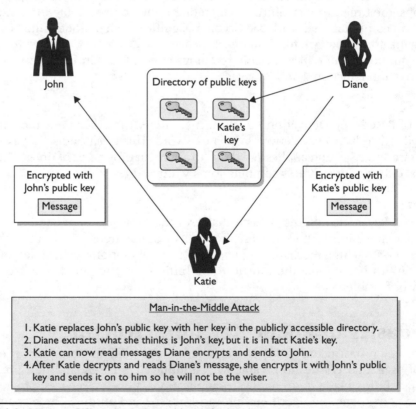

Figure 24-1 Without PKIs, individuals could spoof others' identities.

identity to the DMV by providing his passport, birth certificate, or other identification documentation. If the DMV is satisfied with the proof John provides (and John passes a driving test), the DMV will create a driver's license that can then be used by John to prove his identity. Whenever John needs to identify himself, he can show his driver's license. Although many people may not trust John to identify himself truthfully, they do trust the third party, the DMV.

In the PKI context, while some variations exist in specific products, the registration authority will require proof of identity from the individual requesting a certificate and will validate this information. The registration authority will then advise the CA to generate a certificate, which is analogous to a driver's license. The CA will digitally sign the certificate using its private key. The use of the private key assures the recipient that the certificate came from the CA. When Diane receives John's certificate and verifies that it was actually digitally signed by a CA that she trusts, she will believe that the certificate is actually John's—not because she trusts John, but because she trusts the entity that is vouching for his identity (the CA).

This is commonly referred to as a *third-party trust model*. Public keys are components of digital certificates, so when Diane verifies the CA's digital signature, this verifies that the certificate is truly John's and that the public key the certificate contains is also John's. This is how John's identity is bound to his public key.

This process allows John to authenticate himself to Diane and others. Using the third-party certificate, John can communicate with her, using public key encryption, without prior communication or a preexisting relationship. Once Diane is convinced of the legitimacy of John's public key, she can use it to encrypt and decrypt messages between herself and John, as illustrated in Figure 24-2.

Figure 24-2
Public keys are components of digital certificates.

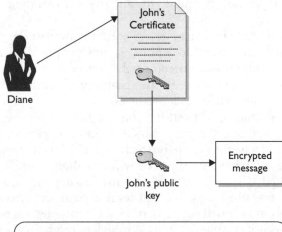

1. Diane validates the certificate.
2. Diane extracts John's public key.
3. Diane uses John's public key for encryption purposes.

PART VI

Numerous applications and protocols can generate public/private key pairs and provide functionality similar to what a PKI provides, but no trusted third party is available for both of the communicating parties. For each party to choose to communicate this way without a third party vouching for the other's identity, the two must choose to trust each other and the communication channel they are using. In many situations, it is impractical and dangerous to arbitrarily trust an individual you do not know, and this is when the components of a PKI must fall into place—to provide the necessary level of trust you cannot, or choose not to, provide on your own.

What does the "infrastructure" in "public key infrastructure" really mean? An infrastructure provides a sustaining groundwork upon which other things can be built. So an infrastructure works at a low level to provide a predictable and uniform environment that allows other, higher-level technologies to work together through uniform access points. The environment that the infrastructure provides allows these higher-level applications to communicate with each other and gives them the underlying tools to carry out their tasks.

 EXAM TIP Make sure you understand the role of PKI in managing certificates and trust associated with public keys.

Certificate Authorities

The CA is the trusted authority that certifies individuals' identities and creates electronic documents indicating that individuals are who they say they are. The electronic document is referred to as a *digital certificate*, and it establishes an association between the subject's identity and a public key. The private key that is paired with the public key in the certificate is stored separately. As noted in Chapter 23, it is important to safeguard the private key, and it typically never leaves the machine or device where it was created.

The CA is more than just a piece of software, however; it is actually made up of the software, hardware, procedures, policies, and people who are involved in validating individuals' identities and generating the certificates. This means that if one of these components is compromised, it can negatively affect the CA overall and can threaten the integrity of the certificates it produces.

Every CA should have a certification practices statement (CPS) that outlines how identities are verified; the steps the CA follows to generate, maintain, and transmit certificates; and why the CA can be trusted to fulfill its responsibilities. It describes how keys are secured, what data is placed within a digital certificate, and how revocations will be handled. If a company is going to use and depend on a public CA, the company's security officers, administrators, and legal department should review the CA's entire CPS to ensure that it will properly meet the company's needs, and to make sure that the level of security claimed by the CA is high enough for their use and environment. A critical aspect of a PKI is the trust between the users and the CA, so the CPS should be reviewed and understood to ensure that this level of trust is warranted.

The *certificate server* is the actual service that issues certificates based on the data provided during the initial registration process. The server constructs and populates the digital certificate with the necessary information and combines the user's public key with the resulting certificate. The certificate is then digitally signed with the CA's private key.

Registration Authorities

The registration authority (RA) is the component that accepts a request for a digital certificate and performs the necessary steps of registering and authenticating the person requesting the certificate. The authentication requirements differ depending on the type of certificate being requested.

The types of certificates available can vary between different CAs, but usually at least three different types are available, and they are referred to as *classes*:

- **Class 1** A Class 1 certificate is usually used to verify an individual's identity through e-mail. A person who receives a Class 1 certificate can use his public/private key pair to digitally sign e-mail and encrypt message contents.

- **Class 2** A Class 2 certificate can be used for software signing. A software vendor would register for this type of certificate so it could digitally sign its software. This provides integrity for the software after it is developed and released, and it allows the receiver of the software to verify from whom the software actually came.

- **Class 3** A Class 3 certificate can be used by a company to set up its own CA, which will allow it to carry out its own identification verification and generate certificates internally.

Each higher class of certificate can carry out more powerful and critical tasks than the one below it. This is why the different classes have different requirements for proof of identity. If you want to receive a Class 1 certificate, you may only be asked to provide your name, e-mail address, and physical address. For a Class 2 certification, you may need to provide the RA with more data, such as your driver's license, passport, and company information that can be verified. To obtain a Class 3 certificate, you will be asked to provide even more information and most likely will need to go to the RA's office for a face-to-face meeting. Each CA will outline the certification classes it provides and the identification requirements that must be met to acquire each type of certificate.

In most situations, when a user requests a Class 1 certificate, the registration process will require the user to enter specific information into a web-based form. The web page will have a section that accepts the user's public key, or it will step the user through creating a public/private key pair, which will allow the user to choose the size of the keys to be created. Once these steps have been completed, the public key is attached to the certificate registration form and both are forwarded to the RA for processing. The RA is responsible only for the registration process and cannot actually generate a certificate. Once the RA is finished processing the request and verifying the individual's identity, the RA will send the request to the CA. The CA will use the RA-provided information to generate a digital certificate, integrate the necessary data into the certificate fields (user identification information, public key, validity dates, proper use for the key and certificate, and so on), and send a copy of the certificate to the user. These steps are shown in Figure 24-3. The certificate may also be posted to a publicly accessible directory so that others can access it.

Note that a 1:1 correspondence does not necessarily exist between identities and certificates. An entity can have multiple key pairs, using separate public keys for separate purposes. Thus, an entity can have multiple certificates, each attesting to separate public key ownership. It is also possible to have different classes of certificates, again with different keys. This flexibility allows entities total discretion in how they manage their keys, and the PKI manages the complexity by using a unified process that allows key verification through a common interface.

 EXAM TIP The RA verifies the identity of the certificate requestor on behalf of the CA. The CA generates the certificate using information forwarded by the RA.

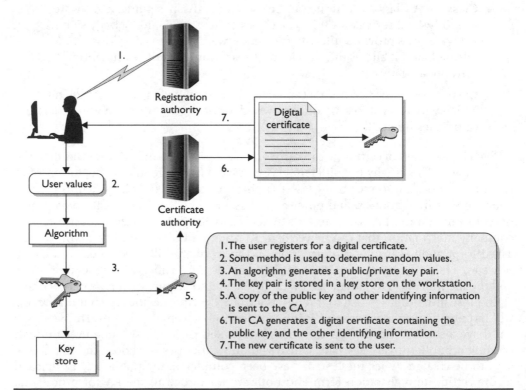

Figure 24-3 Steps for obtaining a digital certificate

If an application creates a key store that can be accessed by other applications, it will provide a standardized interface, called the *application programming interface (API)*. In Mozilla and Linux systems, this interface is usually PKCS #11, and in Microsoft applications, the interface is Cryptography API: Next Generation (CNG) for Microsoft Vista and later. As an example, Figure 24-4 shows that Application A went through the process of registering a certificate and generating a key pair. It created a key store that provides an interface to allow other applications to communicate with it and use the items held within the store.

The local key store is just one location where these items can be held. Often, the digital certificate and public key are also stored in a certificate repository so that they are available to a subset of individuals.

Trust and Certificate Verification

We need to use a PKI if we do not automatically trust individuals we do not know. Security is about being suspicious and being safe, so we need a third party that we *do* trust to vouch for the other individual before confidence can be instilled and sensitive communication can take place. But what does it mean that we trust a CA, and how can we use this to our advantage?

When a user chooses to trust a CA, she will download that CA's digital certificate and public key, which will be stored on her local computer. Most browsers have a list of CAs configured to be trusted by default, so when a user installs a new web browser, several of the most well-known and most trusted CAs will be trusted without any change of settings. An example of this listing is shown in Figure 24-5.

In the Microsoft CNG environment, the user can add and remove CAs from this list as needed. In production environments that require a higher degree of protection, this list will be pruned, and possibly the only CAs listed will be the company's *internal* CAs. This ensures that digitally signed software will be automatically installed only if it was

Figure 24-4
Some key stores can be shared by different applications.

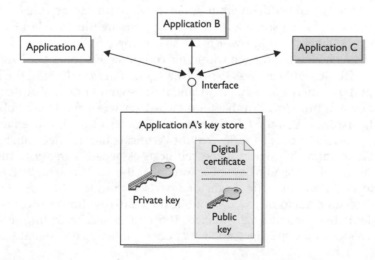

Figure 24-5
Browsers have a long list of CAs configured to be trusted by default.

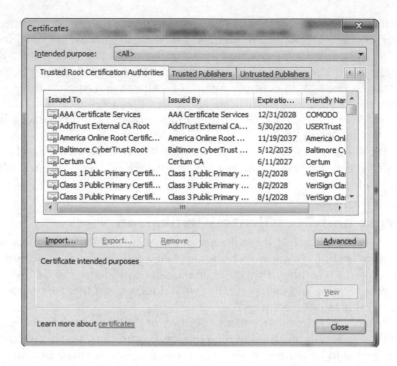

signed by the company's CA. Other products, such as Entrust, use centrally controlled policies to determine which CAs are to be trusted, instead of expecting the user to make these critical decisions.

A number of steps are involved in checking the validity of a message. Suppose, for example, that Maynard receives a digitally signed message from Joyce, who he does not know or trust. Joyce has also included her digital certificate with her message, which has her public key embedded within it. Before Maynard can be sure of the authenticity of this message, he has some work to do. The steps are illustrated in Figure 24-6.

First, Maynard will see which CA signed Joyce's certificate and compare it to the list of CAs he has configured within his computer. He trusts the CAs in his list and no others. (If the certificate was signed by a CA he does not have in the list, he would not accept the certificate as being valid, and thus he could not be sure that this message was actually sent from Joyce or that the attached key was actually her public key.)

Maynard sees that the CA that signed Joyce's certificate is indeed in his list of trusted CAs, so he now needs to verify that the certificate has not been altered. Using the CA's public key and the digest of the certificate, Maynard can verify the integrity of the certificate. Then Maynard can be assured that this CA did actually create the certificate, so he can now trust the origin of Joyce's certificate. The use of digital signatures allows certificates to be saved in public directories without the concern of them being accidentally or intentionally altered. If a user extracts a certificate from a repository and creates a message digest value that does not match the digital signature embedded

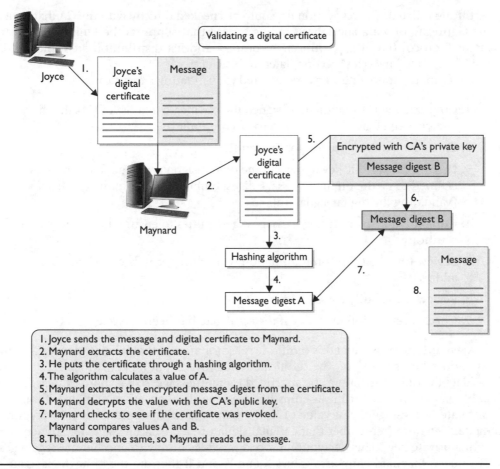

1. Joyce sends the message and digital certificate to Maynard.
2. Maynard extracts the certificate.
3. He puts the certificate through a hashing algorithm.
4. The algorithm calculates a value of A.
5. Maynard extracts the encrypted message digest from the certificate.
6. Maynard decrypts the value with the CA's public key.
7. Maynard checks to see if the certificate was revoked.
   Maynard compares values A and B.
8. The values are the same, so Maynard reads the message.

Figure 24-6 Steps for verifying the authenticity and integrity of a certificate

within the certificate itself, that user will know that the certificate has been modified by someone other than the CA, and he will know not to accept the validity of the corresponding public key. Similarly, an attacker could not create a new message digest, encrypt it, and embed it within the certificate because he would not have access to the CA's private key.

But Maynard is not done yet. He needs to be sure that the issuing CA has not revoked this certificate. The certificate also has start and stop dates, indicating a time during which the certificate is valid. If the start date hasn't happened yet, or the stop date has been passed, the certificate is not valid. Maynard reviews these dates to make sure the certificate is still deemed valid.

Another step Maynard may go through is to check whether this certificate has been revoked for any reason, so he will refer to a list of revoked certificates to see if Joyce's

PART VI

certificate is listed. The revocation list could be checked directly with the CA that issued the certificate or via a specialized online service that supports the Online Certificate Status Protocol (OCSP). (Certificate revocation and list distribution are explained in the "Certificate Lifecycles" section, later in this chapter.)

To recap, the following steps are required for validating a certificate:

1. Compare the CA that digitally signed the certificate to a list of CAs that have already been loaded into the receiver's computer.

2. Calculate a message digest for the certificate.

3. Use the CA's public key to decrypt the digital signature and recover what is claimed to be the original message digest embedded within the certificate (validating the digital signature).

4. Compare the two resulting message digest values to ensure the integrity of the certificate.

5. Review the identification information within the certificate, such as the e-mail address.

6. Review the validity dates.

7. Check a revocation list to see if the certificate has been revoked.

Maynard now trusts that this certificate is legitimate and that it belongs to Joyce. Now what does he need to do? The certificate holds Joyce's public key, which he needs to validate the digital signature she appended to her message, so Maynard extracts Joyce's public key from her certificate, runs her message through a hashing algorithm, and calculates a message digest value of X. He then uses Joyce's public key to decrypt her digital signature (remember that a digital signature is just a message digest encrypted with a private key). This decryption process provides him with another message digest of value Y. Maynard compares values X and Y, and if they are the same, he is assured that the message has not been modified during transmission. Thus, he has confidence in the integrity of the message. But how does Maynard know that the message actually came from Joyce? Because he can decrypt the digital signature using her public key, this indicates that only the associated private key could have been used. There is a miniscule risk that someone could create an identical key pair, but given the enormous keyspace for public keys, this is impractical. The public key can only decrypt something that was encrypted with the related private key, and only the owner of the private key is supposed to have access to it. Maynard can be sure that this message came from Joyce.

After all of this he reads her message, which says, "Hi. How are you?" All of that work just for this message? Maynard's blood pressure would surely go through the roof if he had to do all of this work only to end up with a short and not very useful message. Fortunately, all of this PKI work is performed without user intervention and happens behind the scenes. Maynard didn't have to exert any energy. He simply replies, "Fine. How are you?"

Digital Certificates

A digital certificate binds an individual's identity to a public key, and it contains all the information a receiver needs to be assured of the identity of the public key owner. After an RA verifies an individual's identity, the CA generates the digital certificate, but how does the CA know what type of data to insert into the certificate?

The certificates are created and formatted based on the X.509 standard, which outlines the necessary fields of a certificate and the possible values that can be inserted into the fields. As of this writing, X.509 version 3 is the most current version of the standard. X.509 is a standard of the International Telecommunication Union (www.itu.int). The IETF's Public-Key Infrastructure (X.509), or PKIX, working group has adapted the X.509 standard to the more flexible organization of the Internet, as specified in RFC 3280, and is commonly referred to as PKIX for Public Key Infrastructure (X.509).

The following fields are included within an X.509 digital certificate:

- **Version number**   Identifies the version of the X.509 standard that was followed to create the certificate; indicates the format and fields that can be used.

- **Subject**   Specifies the owner of the certificate.

- **Public key**   Identifies the public key being bound to the certified subject; also identifies the algorithm used to create the private/public key pair.

- **Issuer**   Identifies the CA that generated and digitally signed the certificate.

- **Serial number**   Provides a unique number identifying this one specific certificate issued by a particular CA.

- **Validity**   Specifies the dates through which the certificate is valid for use.

- **Certificate usage**   Specifies the approved use of the certificate, which dictates intended use of this public key.

- **Signature algorithm**   Specifies the hashing and digital signature algorithms used to digitally sign the certificate.

- **Extensions**   Allows additional data to be encoded into the certificate to expand the functionality of the certificate. Companies can customize the use of certificates within their environments by using these extensions. X.509 version 3 has extended the extension possibilities.

Figure 24-7 shows the actual values of these different certificate fields for a particular certificate in Internet Explorer. The version of this certificate is V3 (X.509 v3), and the serial number is also listed—this number is unique for each certificate that is created by a specific CA. The CA used the MD5 hashing algorithm to create the message digest value, and it then signed with its private key using the RSA algorithm. The actual CA that issued the certificate is Root SGC Authority, and the valid dates indicate how long this certificate is valid. The subject is MS SGC Authority, which is the entity that registered this certificate and is the entity that is bound to the embedded public key. The actual public key is shown in the lower window and is represented in hexadecimal.

Figure 24-7
Fields within a
digital certificate

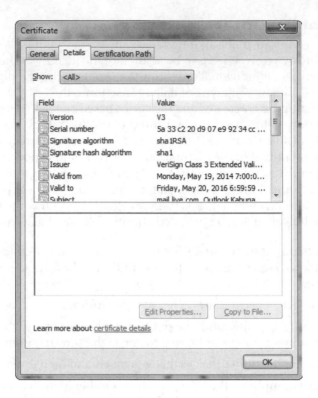

The subject of a certificate is commonly a person, but it does not have to be. The subject can be a network device (router, web server, firewall, and so on), an application, a department, a company, or a person. Each has its own identity that needs to be verified and proven to another entity before secure, trusted communication can be initiated. If a network device is using a certificate for authentication, the certificate may contain the network address of that device. This means that if the certificate has a network address of 10.0.0.1, the receiver will compare this to the address from which it received the certificate to make sure a man-in-the-middle attack is not being attempted.

Certificate Attributes

Four main types of certificates are used:

- End-entity certificates
- CA certificates
- Cross-certification certificates
- Policy certificates

End-entity certificates are issued by a CA to a specific subject, such as Joyce, the Accounting department, or a firewall, as illustrated in Figure 24-8. An end-entity certificate is the identity document provided by PKI implementations.

A *CA certificate* can be self-signed, in the case of a stand-alone or root CA, or it can be issued by a superior CA within a hierarchical model. In the model in Figure 24-8, the superior CA gives the authority and allows the subordinate CA to accept certificate requests and generate the individual certificates itself. This may be necessary when a company needs to have multiple internal CAs, and different departments within an organization need to have their own CAs servicing their specific end-entities (users, network devices, and applications) in their sections. In these situations, a representative from each department requiring a CA registers with the more highly trusted CA and requests a CA certificate.

Cross-certification certificates, or *cross-certificates*, are used when independent CAs establish peer-to-peer trust relationships. Simply put, they are a mechanism through which one CA can issue a certificate allowing its users to trust another CA.

Within sophisticated CAs used for high-security applications, a mechanism is required to provide centrally controlled policy information to PKI clients. This is often done by placing the policy information in a *policy certificate*.

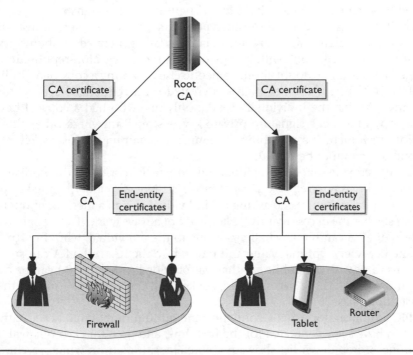

Figure 24-8 End-entity and CA certificates

PART VI

Certificate Lifecycles

Keys and certificates should have lifetime settings that will force the user to register for a new certificate after a certain amount of time. Determining the proper length of these lifetimes is a trade-off: shorter lifetimes limit the ability of attackers to crack them, but longer lifetimes lower system overhead. More sophisticated PKI implementations perform automated and often transparent key updates to avoid the time and expense of having users register for new certificates when old ones expire.

Certificate lifetimes means that the certificate and key pair has a lifecycle that must be managed. Certificate management involves administrating and managing each of these phases, including registration, certificate and key generation, renewal, and revocation.

Registration and Generation

A key pair (public and private keys) can be generated locally by an application and stored in a local key store on the user's workstation. The key pair can also be created by a central key-generation server, which will require secure transmission of the keys to the user. The key pair that is created on the centralized server can be stored on the user's workstation or on the user's smart card, which will allow for more flexibility and mobility.

In most modern PKI implementations, users have two key pairs. One key pair is often generated by a central server and used for encryption and key transfers. This allows the corporate PKI to retain a copy of the encryption key pair for recovery, if necessary. The second key pair, a digital signature key pair, is usually generated by the user to make sure that she is the only one with a copy of the private key. Non-repudiation can be challenged if there is any doubt about someone else obtaining a copy of an individual's signature private key. If the key pair was created on a centralized server, that could weaken the case that the individual was the only one who had a copy of her private key. If a copy of a user's signature private key is stored anywhere other than in her possession, or if there is a possibility of someone obtaining the user's key, then true non-repudiation cannot be provided.

The act of verifying that an individual indeed has the corresponding private key for a given public key is referred to as *proof of possession*. Not all public/private key pairs can be used for digital signatures, so asking the individual to sign a message and return it to prove that she has the necessary private key will not always work. If a key pair is used for encryption, the RA can send a challenge value to the individual, who, in turn, can use her private key to encrypt that value and return it to the RA. If the RA can successfully decrypt this value with the public key that was provided earlier, the RA can be confident that the individual has the necessary private key and can continue through the rest of the registration phase.

The PKI administrator usually configures the minimum required key size that users must use to have a key generated for the first time, and then for each renewal. In most applications, a drop-down list shows possible algorithms from which to choose, and possible key sizes. The key size should provide the necessary level of security for the current environment. The lifetime of the key should be long enough that continual renewal will not negatively affect productivity, but short enough to ensure that the key cannot be successfully compromised.

CSR

A *certificate signing request (CSR)* is the actual request to a CA containing a public key and the requisite information needed to generate a certificate. The CSR contains all of the identifying information that is to be bound to the key by the certificate generation process.

Renewal

The certificate itself has its own lifetime, which can be different than the key pair's lifetime. The certificate's lifetime is specified by the validity dates inserted into the digital certificate. These are beginning and ending dates indicating the time period during which the certificate is valid. The certificate cannot be used before the start date, and once the end date is met, the certificate is expired and a new certificate will need to be issued.

A renewal process is different from the registration phase in that the RA assumes that the individual has already successfully completed one registration round. If the certificate has not actually been revoked, the original keys and certificate can be used to provide the necessary authentication information and proof of identity for the renewal phase.

The certificate may or may not need to change during the renewal process; this usually depends on why the renewal is taking place. If the certificate just expired and the keys will still be used for the same purpose, a new certificate can be generated with new validity dates. If, however, the key pair functionality needs to be expanded or restricted, new attributes and extensions may need to be integrated into the new certificate. These new functionalities may require more information to be gathered from the individual renewing the certificate, especially if the class changes or the new key uses allow for more powerful abilities.

This renewal process is required when the certificate has fulfilled its lifetime and its end validity date has been met. This situation differs from that of a certificate revocation.

Revocation

A certificate can be revoked when its validity needs to be ended before its actual expiration date is met, and this can occur for many reasons: for example, a user may have lost a laptop or a smart card that stored a private key; an improper software implementation may have been uncovered that directly affected the security of a private key; a user may have fallen victim to a social engineering attack and inadvertently given up a private key; data held within the certificate may no longer apply to the specified individual; or perhaps an employee left a company and should not be identified as a member of an in-house PKI any longer. In the last instance, the certificate, which was bound to the user's key pair, identified the user as an employee of the company, and the administrator would want to ensure that the key pair could not be used in the future to validate this person's affiliation with the company. Revoking the certificate does this.

If any of the previously listed things happens, a user's private key has been compromised or should no longer be mapped to the owner's identity. A different individual may have access to that user's private key and could use it to impersonate and authenticate as the original user. If the impersonator used the key to digitally sign a message, the receiver would verify the authenticity of the sender by verifying the signature by using the original user's public key, and the verification would go through perfectly—the receiver would believe it came from the proper sender and not the impersonator. If receivers could look at a list of certificates that had been revoked before verifying the digital signature, however, they would know not to trust the digital signatures on the list. Because of issues associated with the private key being compromised, revocation is permanent and final—once revoked, a certificate cannot be reinstated. If this were allowed and a user revoked his certificate, the unauthorized holder of the private key could use it to restore the certificate validity.

For example, if Joe stole Mike's laptop, which held, among other things, Mike's private key, Joe might be able to use it to impersonate Mike. Suppose Joe writes a message, digitally signs it with Mike's private key, and sends it to Stacy. Stacy communicates with Mike periodically and has his public key, so she uses it to verify the digital signature. It computes properly, so Stacy is assured that this message came from Mike, but in truth it did not. If, before validating any certificate or digital signature, Stacy could check a list of revoked certificates, she might not fall victim to Joe's false message.

The CA provides this type of protection by maintaining a *Certificate Revocation List (CRL)*, a list of serial numbers of certificates that have been revoked. The CRL also contains a statement indicating why the individual certificates were revoked and a date when the revocation took place. The list usually contains all certificates that have been revoked within the lifetime of the CA. Certificates that have expired are not the same as those that have been revoked. If a certificate has expired, it means that its end validity date was reached.

The CA is the entity that is responsible for the status of the certificates it generates; it needs to be told of a revocation, and it must provide this information to others. The CA is responsible for maintaining the CRL and posting it in a publicly available directory.

 EXAM TIP The Certificate Revocation List is an essential item to ensure a certificate is still valid. CAs post CRLs in publicly available directories to permit automated checking of certificates against the list before certificate use by a client. A user should never trust a certificate that has not been checked against the appropriate CRL.

What if Stacy wants to get back at Joe for trying to trick her earlier, and she attempts to revoke Joe's certificate herself? If she is successful, Joe's participation in the PKI can be negatively affected because others will not trust his public key. Although we might think Joe may deserve this, we need to have some system in place to make sure people cannot arbitrarily have others' certificates revoked, whether for revenge or for malicious purposes.

When a revocation request is submitted, the individual submitting the request must be authenticated. Otherwise, this could permit a type of denial-of-service attack, in which someone has another person's certificate revoked. The authentication can involve an agreed-upon password that was created during the registration process, but authentication should not be based on the individual proving that he has the corresponding private key, because it may have been stolen, and the CA would be authenticating an imposter.

The CRL's integrity needs to be protected to ensure that attackers cannot modify data pertaining to a revoked certification from the list. If this were allowed to take place, anyone who stole a private key could just delete that key from the CRL and continue to use the private key fraudulently. The integrity of the list also needs to be protected to ensure that bogus data is not added to it. Otherwise, anyone could add another person's certificate to the list and effectively revoke that person's certificate. The only entity that should be able to modify any information on the CRL is the CA.

The mechanism used to protect the integrity of a CRL is a *digital signature*. The CA's revocation service creates a digital signature for the CRL. To validate a certificate, the user accesses the directory where the CRL is posted, downloads the list, and verifies the CA's digital signature to ensure that the proper authority signed the list and to ensure that the list was not modified in an unauthorized manner. The user then looks through the list to determine whether the serial number of the certificate that he is trying to validate is listed. If the serial number is on the list, the private key should no longer be trusted, and the public key should no longer be used. This can be a cumbersome process, so it has been automated in several ways that are described in the next section.

One concern is how up-to-date the CRL is—how often is it updated and does it actually reflect *all* the certificates currently revoked? The actual frequency with which the list is updated depends upon the CA and its certification practices statement (CPS). It is important that the list is updated in a timely manner so that anyone using the list has the most current information. CRL files can be requested by individuals who need to verify and validate a newly received certificate, or the files can be periodically pushed down (sent) to all users participating within a specific PKI. This means the CRL can be pulled (downloaded) by individual users when needed or pushed down to all users within the PKI on a timed interval.

The actual CRL file can grow substantially, and transmitting this file and requiring PKI client software on each workstation to save and maintain it can use a lot of resources, so the smaller the CRL is, the better. It is also possible to first push down the full CRL, and after that initial load, the following CRLs pushed down to the users are *delta* CRLs, meaning that they contain only the changes to the original or base CRL. This can greatly reduce the amount of bandwidth consumed when updating CRLs.

In implementations where the CRLs are not pushed down to individual systems, the users' PKI software needs to know where to look for the posted CRL that relates to the certificate it is trying to validate. The certificate might have an extension that points the validating user to the necessary *CRL distribution point*. The network administrator sets up the distribution points, and one or more points can exist for a particular PKI. The distribution point holds one or more lists containing the serial numbers of revoked certificates, and the user's PKI software scans the list(s) for the serial number of the certificate the user is attempting to validate. If the serial number is not present, the user is assured that it has not been revoked. This approach helps point users to the right resource and also reduces the amount of information that needs to be scanned when checking that a certificate has not been revoked.

One last option for checking distributed CRLs is an online service. When a client user needs to validate a certificate and ensure that it has not been revoked, he can communicate with an online service that will query the necessary CRLs available within the environment. This service can query the lists for the client instead of pushing down the full CRL to each and every system. So if Joe receives a certificate from Stacy, he can contact an online service and send it the serial number listed in the certificate Stacy sent. The online service would query the necessary CRLs and respond to Joe by indicating whether or not that serial number was listed as being revoked.

One of the protocols used for online revocation services is the previously mentioned Online Certificate Status Protocol (OCSP), a request and response protocol that obtains the serial number of the certificate that is being validated and reviews CRLs for the client. The protocol has a responder service that reports the status of the certificate back to the client, indicating whether it has been revoked, it is valid, or its status is unknown. This protocol and service saves the client from having to find, download, and process the right lists.

 EXAM TIP Certificate revocation checks are done either by examining the CRL or using OCSP to see if a certificate has been revoked.

Suspension

Instead of being revoked, a certificate can be *suspended*, meaning it is temporarily put on hold. If, for example, Bob is taking an extended vacation and wants to ensure that his certificate will not be used during that time, he can make a suspension request to the CA. The CRL would list this certificate and its serial number, and in the field that describes why the certificate is revoked, it would instead indicate a hold state. Once Bob returns to work, he can make a request to the CA to remove his certificate from the list.

Another reason to suspend a certificate is if an administrator is suspicious that a private key might have been compromised. While the issue is under investigation, the certificate can be suspended to ensure that it cannot be used.

Key Destruction

Key pairs and certificates have set *lifetimes*, meaning that they will expire at some specified time. It is important that the certificates and keys are properly destroyed when that time comes, wherever the keys are stored (on users' workstations, centralized key servers, USB token devices, smart cards, and so on).

The goal is to make sure that no one can gain access to a key after its lifetime has ended and use this key for malicious purposes. An attacker might use the key to digitally sign or encrypt a message with the hopes of tricking someone else about his identity (this would be an example of a man-in-the-middle attack). Also, if the attacker is performing some type of brute-force attack on your cryptosystem, trying to figure out specific keys that were used for encryption processes, obtaining an old key could give him more insight into how your cryptosystem generates keys. The less information you supply to potential hackers, the better.

Note that in modern PKIs, encryption key pairs usually must be retained long after they expire so that users can decrypt information that was encrypted with the old keys. For example, if Bob encrypts a document using his current key and the keys are updated three months later, Bob's software must maintain a copy of the old key so he can still decrypt the document. In the PKI world, this issue is referred to as *key history maintenance*.

Private Key Protection

Although a PKI implementation can be complex, with many different components and options, a critical concept common to all PKIs must be understood and enforced: the private key needs to stay private. A digital signature is created solely for the purpose of proving who sent a particular message by using a private key. This rests on the assumption that only one person has access to this private key. If an imposter obtains a user's private key, authenticity and non-repudiation can no longer be claimed or proven.

When a private key is generated for the first time, it must be stored somewhere for future use. This storage area is referred to as a *key store*, and it is usually created by the application registering for a certificate, such as a web browser, smart card software, or other application. In most implementations, the application will prompt the user for a password, which will be used to create an encryption key that protects the key store. So, for example, if Cheryl used her web browser to register for a certificate, her private key would be generated and stored in the key store. Cheryl would then be prompted for a password, which the software would use to create a key that will encrypt the key store. When Cheryl needs to access this private key later that day, she will be prompted for the same password, which will decrypt the key store and allow her access to her private key.

Unfortunately, many applications do not require that a strong password be created to protect the key store, and in some implementations, the user can choose not to provide a password at all. The user still has a private key available, and it is bound to the user's identity, so why is a password even necessary? If, for example, Cheryl decided not to use a password, and another person sat down at her computer, he could use her web browser and her private key and digitally sign a message that contained a nasty virus. If Cheryl's coworker Cliff received this message, he would think it came from Cheryl, open the message, and download the virus. The moral to this story is that users should be required to provide some type of authentication information (password, smart card, PIN, or the like) before being able to use private keys. Otherwise, the keys could be used by other individuals or imposters, and authentication and non-repudiation would be of no use.

Because a private key is a crucial component of any PKI implementation, the key itself should contain the necessary characteristics and be protected at each stage of its life. The following list sums up the characteristics and requirements of proper private key use:

- The key size should provide the necessary level of protection for the environment.
- The lifetime of the key should correspond with how often it is used and the sensitivity of the data it is protecting.
- The key should be changed and not used past its allowed lifetime.
- Where appropriate, the key should be properly destroyed at the end of its lifetime.
- The key should never be exposed in clear text.
- No copies of the private key should be made if it is being used for digital signatures.
- The key should not be shared.
- The key should be stored securely.
- Authentication should be required before the key can be used.
- The key should be transported securely.
- Software implementations that store and use the key should be evaluated to ensure they provide the necessary level of protection.

If digital signatures will be used for legal purposes, these points and others may need to be audited to ensure that true authenticity and nonrepudiation are provided.

CA Private Key

The most sensitive and critical public/private key pairs are those used by CAs to digitally sign certificates. These need to be highly protected because if they were compromised, the trust relationship between the CA and all of the end-entities would be threatened. In high-security environments, these keys are often kept in a tamper-proof hardware encryption store, only accessible to individuals with a need to access.

Key Recovery

One individual could have one, two, or many key pairs that are tied to his or her identity. That is because users can have different needs and requirements for public/private key pairs. As mentioned earlier, certificates can have specific attributes and usage requirements dictating how their corresponding keys can and cannot be used. For example, David can have one key pair he uses to encrypt and transmit symmetric keys. He can also have one key pair that allows him to encrypt data and another key pair to perform digital signatures. David can also have a digital signature key pair for his work-related activities and another pair for personal activities, such as e-mailing his friends. These key pairs need to be used only for their intended purposes, and this is enforced through certificate attributes and usage values.

If a company is going to perform and maintain a key recovery system, it will generally back up only the key pair used to encrypt data, not the key pairs that are used to generate digital signatures. The reason that a company archives keys is to ensure that if a person leaves the company, falls off a cliff, or for some reason is unavailable to decrypt important company information, the company can still get to its company-owned data. This is just a matter of the organization protecting itself. A company would not need to be able to recover a key pair that is used for digital signatures, since those keys are to be used only to prove the authenticity of the individual who sent a message. A company would not benefit from having access to those keys and really should not have access to them, since they are tied to one individual for a specific purpose.

Two systems are important for backing up and restoring cryptographic keys: key archiving and key recovery. The *key archiving system* is a way of backing up keys and securely storing them in a repository; *key recovery* is the process of restoring lost keys to the users or the company. *Recovery agent* is the term for an entity who is given a public key certificate for recovering user data that is encrypted. This is the most common type of recovery policy used in PKI, but adds the risk of the recovery agent having access to secured information.

If keys are backed up and stored in a centralized computer, this system must be tightly controlled, because if it were compromised, an attacker would have access to all keys for the entire infrastructure. Also, it is usually unwise to authorize a single person to be able to recover all the keys within the environment, because that person could use this power for evil purposes instead of just recovering keys when they are needed for legitimate purposes. In security systems, it is best not to fully trust anyone.

 EXAM TIP Key archiving is the process of storing a set of keys to be used as a backup should something happen to the original set. Key recovery is the process of using the backup keys.

Dual control can be used as part of a system to back up and archive data encryption keys. PKI systems can be configured to allow multiple individuals to be involved in any key recovery process. When a key recovery is required, at least two people can be required to authenticate by the key recovery software before the recovery procedure is performed. This enforces *separation of duties*, which means that one person cannot complete a critical task by himself. Requiring two individuals to recover a lost key together is called *dual control*, which simply means that two people have to be present to carry out a specific task.

This approach to key recovery is referred to as the *m of n authentication*, where *n* number of people can be involved in the key recovery process, but at least *m* (which is a smaller number than *n*) *must* be involved before the task can be completed. The goal is to minimize fraudulent or improper use of access and permissions. A company would not require all possible individuals to be involved in the recovery process, because getting all the people together at the same time could be impossible considering meetings, vacations, sick time, and travel. At least some of all possible individuals must be available to participate, and this is the subset *m* of the number *n*. This form of

PART VI

secret splitting can increase security by requiring multiple people to perform a specific function. Requiring too many people can increase issues associated with availability, while requiring too few increases the risk of a small number of people compromising a secret.

 EXAM TIP Secret splitting using *m* of *n* authentication schemes can improve security by requiring that multiple people perform critical functions, preventing a single party from compromising a secret.

All key recovery procedures should be highly audited. The audit logs should capture at least what keys were recovered, who was involved in the process, and the time and date. Keys are an integral piece of any encryption cryptosystem and are critical to a PKI environment, so you need to track who does what with them.

Key Escrow

Key recovery and *key escrow* are terms that are often used interchangeably, but they actually describe two different things. You should not use them interchangeably after you have read this section.

Key recovery is a process that allows for lost keys to be recovered. Key escrow is a process of giving keys to a third party so that they can decrypt and read sensitive information when this need arises. Key escrow almost always pertains to handing over encryption keys to the government, or to another higher authority, so that the keys can be used to collect evidence during investigations.

A key pair used in a person's place of work may be required to be escrowed by the employer, for obvious reasons. First, the keys are the property of the enterprise, issued to the employee for use. Second, the firm may have need for them after an employee leaves the firm. Key escrow by businesses can make total sense, provided that the escrowed keys are stored in a manner to prevent their unauthorized use.

 EXAM TIP Key escrow, allowing another trusted party to hold a copy of a key, has long been a controversial topic. This essential business process provides continuity should the authorized key-holding party leave an organization without disclosing keys. The security of the escrowed key is a concern, and it needs to be managed at the same security level as the original key.

Public Certificate Authorities

An individual or company may decide to rely on a CA that is already established and being used by many other individuals and companies—this would be a *public CA*. A company, on the other hand, may decide that it needs its own CA for internal use, which gives the company more control over the certificate registration and generation process and allows it to configure items specifically for its own needs. This second type of CA is referred to as a *private CA* (or *in-house CA*).

A public CA specializes in verifying individual identities and creating and maintaining their certificates. These companies issue certificates that are not bound to specific companies or intercompany departments. Instead, their services are to be used by a larger and more diversified group of people and organizations. If a company uses a public CA, the company will pay the CA organization for individual certificates and for the service of maintaining these certificates. Some examples of public CAs are VeriSign (including GeoTrust and Thawte), Entrust, and GoDaddy.

One advantage of using a public CA is that it is usually well known and easily accessible to many people. Most web browsers have a list of public CAs installed and configured by default, along with their corresponding root certificates. This means that if you install a web browser on your computer, it is already configured to trust certain CAs, even though you might have never heard of them before. So, if you receive a certificate from Bob, and his certificate was digitally signed by a CA listed in your browser, you can automatically trust the CA and can easily walk through the process of verifying Bob's certificate. This has raised some eyebrows among security professionals, however, since trust is installed by default, but the industry has deemed this is a necessary approach that provides users with transparency and increased functionality. Users can remove these CAs from their browser list if they want to have more control over who their system trusts and who it doesn't.

Earlier in the chapter, the different certificate classes and their uses were explained. No global standard defines these classes, the exact requirements for obtaining these different certificates, or their uses. Standards are in place, usually for a particular country or industry, but this means that public CAs can define their own certificate classifications. This is not necessarily a good thing for companies that depend on public CAs, because it does not provide enough control to the company over how it should interpret certificate classifications and how they should be used.

This means another component needs to be carefully developed for companies that use and depend on public CAs, and this component is referred to as the *certificate policy (CP)*. This policy allows the company to decide what certification classes are acceptable and how they will be used within the organization. This is different from the CPS, which explains how the CA verifies entities, generates certificates, and maintains these certificates. The CP is generated and owned by an individual company that uses an external CA, and it allows the company to enforce *its* security decisions and control how certificates are used with *its* applications.

Trust Models

A *trust domain* is a construct of systems, personnel, applications, protocols, technologies, and policies that work together to provide a certain level of protection. All of these components can work together seamlessly within the same trust domain because they are known to the other components within the domain and are trusted to some degree. Different trust domains are usually managed by different groups of administrators, have different security policies, and restrict outsiders from privileged access.

Most trust domains (whether individual companies or departments) are not usually islands cut off from the world—they need to communicate with other, less-trusted domains. The trick is to figure out how much two different domains should trust each other, and how to implement and configure an infrastructure that would allow these two domains to communicate in a way that will not allow security compromises or breaches. This can be more difficult than it sounds.

One example of trust considered earlier in the chapter is the driver's license issued by the DMV. Suppose, for example, that Bob is buying a lamp from Carol and he wants to pay by check. Since Carol does not know Bob, she does not know if she can trust him or have much faith in his check. But if Bob shows Carol his driver's license, she can compare the name to what appears on the check, and she can choose to accept it. The *trust anchor* (the agreed-upon trusted third party) in this scenario is the DMV, since both Carol and Bob trust it more than they trust each other. Since Bob had to provide documentation to prove his identity to the DMV, that organization trusted him enough to generate a license, and Carol trusts the DMV, so she decides to trust Bob's check.

Consider another example of a trust anchor. If Joe and Stacy need to communicate through e-mail and would like to use encryption and digital signatures, they will not trust each other's certificate alone. But when each receives the other's certificate and sees that they both have been digitally signed by an entity they both do trust—the CA—then they have a deeper level of trust in each other. The trust anchor here is the CA. This is easy enough, but when we need to establish trust anchors between different CAs and PKI environments, it gets a little more complicated.

When two companies need to communicate using their individual PKIs, or if two departments within the same company use different CAs, two separate trust domains are involved. The users and devices from these different trust domains will need to communicate with each other, and they will need to exchange certificates and public keys. This means that trust anchors need to be identified, and a communication channel must be constructed and maintained.

A trust relationship must be established between two issuing authorities (CAs). This happens when one or both of the CAs issue a certificate for the other CA's public key, as shown in Figure 24-9. This means that each CA registers for a certificate and public key from the other CA. Each CA validates the other CA's identification information and generates a certificate containing a public key for that CA to use. This establishes a trust path between the two entities that can then be used when users need to verify other users' certificates that fall within the different trust domains. The trust path can be unidirectional or bidirectional, so either the two CAs trust each other (bidirectional) or only one trusts the other (unidirectional).

As illustrated in Figure 24-9, all the users and devices in trust domain 1 trust their own CA 1, which is their trust anchor. All users and devices in trust domain 2 have their own trust anchor, CA 2. The two CAs have exchanged certificates and trust each other, but they do not have a common trust anchor between them.

The trust models describe and outline the trust relationships between the different CAs and different environments, which will indicate where the trust paths reside. The trust models and paths need to be thought out before implementation to restrict and control access properly and to ensure that as few trust paths as possible are used. Several different trust models can be used: the hierarchical, peer-to-peer, and hybrid models are discussed in the following sections.

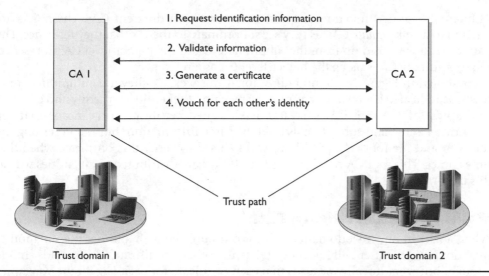

1. Request identification information

2. Validate information

3. Generate a certificate

4. Vouch for each other's identity

CA 1

CA 2

Trust path

Trust domain 1   Trust domain 2

Figure 24-9   A trust relationship can be built between two trust domains to set up a communication channel.

Hierarchical Trust Model

The first type of trust model we'll examine is a basic hierarchical structure that contains a root CA, an intermediate CA, leaf CAs, and end-entities. The configuration is that of an inverted tree, as shown in Figure 24-10. The root CA is the ultimate trust anchor for all other entities in this infrastructure, and it generates certificates for the intermediate CAs, which in turn generate certificates for the leaf CAs, and the leaf CAs generate certificates for the end-entities.

Figure 24-10
The hierarchical trust model outlines trust paths.

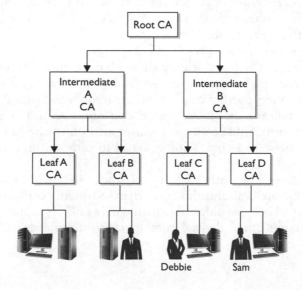

Root CA

Intermediate A CA

Intermediate B CA

Leaf A CA

Leaf B CA

Leaf C CA

Leaf D CA

Debbie

Sam

Intermediate CAs function to transfer trust between different CAs. These CAs are referred to as *subordinate CAs,* as they are subordinate to the CA that they reference. The path of trust is walked up from the subordinate CA to the higher-level CA; in essence, the subordinate CA is using the higher-level CA as a reference.

As shown in Figure 24-10, no bidirectional trusts exist—they are all unidirectional trusts, as indicated by the one-way arrows. Since no other entity can certify and generate certificates for the root CA, it creates a self-signed certificate. This means that the certificate's issuer and subject fields hold the same information, both representing the root CA, and the root CA's public key will be used to verify this certificate when that time comes. This root CA certificate and public key are distributed to all entities within this trust model.

Walking the Certificate Path

When a user in one trust domain needs to communicate with another user in another trust domain, one user will need to validate the other's certificate. This sounds simple enough, but what it really means is that each certificate for each CA, all the way up to a shared trusted anchor, also must be validated. If Debbie needs to validate Sam's certificate, as shown in Figure 24-10, she actually also needs to validate the Leaf D CA and Intermediate B CA certificates, as well as Sam's.

So in Figure 24-10, we have a user, Sam, who digitally signs a message and sends it and his certificate to Debbie. Debbie needs to validate this certificate before she can trust Sam's digital signature. Included in Sam's certificate is an issuer field, which indicates that the certificate was issued by Leaf D CA. Debbie has to obtain Leaf D CA's digital certificate and public key to validate Sam's certificate. Remember that Debbie validates the certificate by verifying its digital signature. The digital signature was created by the certificate issuer using its private key, so Debbie needs to verify the signature using the issuer's public key.

Debbie tracks down Leaf D CA's certificate and public key, but she now needs to verify this CA's certificate, so she looks at the issuer field, which indicates that Leaf D CA's certificate was issued by Intermediate B CA. Debbie now needs to get Intermediate B CA's certificate and public key.

Debbie's client software tracks this down and sees that the issuer for the Intermediate B CA is the root CA, for which she already has a certificate and public key. So Debbie's client software had to follow the *certificate path,* meaning it had to continue to track down and collect certificates until it came upon a self-signed certificate. A self-signed certificate indicates that it was signed by a root CA, and Debbie's software has been configured to trust this entity as her trust anchor, so she can stop there. Figure 24-11 illustrates the steps Debbie's software had to carry out just to be able to verify Sam's certificate.

This type of simplistic trust model works well within an enterprise that easily follows a hierarchical organizational chart, but many companies cannot use this type of trust model because different departments or offices require their own trust anchors. These demands can be derived from direct business needs or from interorganizational

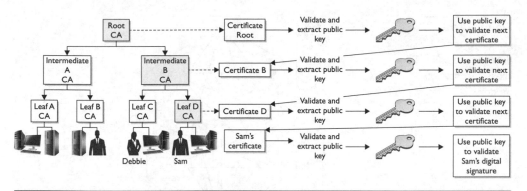

Figure 24-11 Verifying each certificate in a certificate path

politics. This hierarchical model might not be possible when two or more companies need to communicate with each other. Neither company will let the other's CA be the root CA, because each does not necessarily trust the other entity to that degree. In these situations, the CAs will need to work in a peer-to-peer relationship instead of in a hierarchical relationship.

Peer-to-Peer Model

In a *peer-to-peer trust model*, one CA is not subordinate to another CA, and no established trusted anchor between the CAs is involved. The end-entities will look to their issuing CA as their trusted anchor, but the different CAs will not have a common anchor.

Figure 24-12 illustrates this type of trust model. The two different CAs will certify the public key for each other, which creates a bidirectional trust. This is referred to as *cross-certification*, since the CAs are not receiving their certificates and public keys from a superior CA, but instead are creating them for each other.

Figure 24-12
Cross-certifica-
tion creates a
peer-to-peer PKI
model.

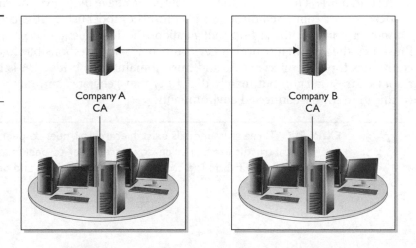

Figure 24-13
Scalability is a drawback in cross-certification models.

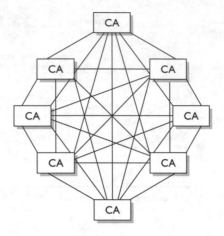

One of the main drawbacks to this model is scalability. Each CA must certify every other CA that is participating, and a bidirectional trust path must be implemented, as shown in Figure 24-13. If one root CA were certifying all the intermediate CAs, scalability would not be as much of an issue. Figure 24-13 represents a fully connected *mesh architecture*, meaning that each CA is directly connected to and has a bidirectional trust relationship with every other CA. As you can see in this illustration, the complexity of this setup can become overwhelming.

Hybrid Trust Model

A company can be complex within itself, and when the need arises to communicate properly with outside partners, suppliers, and customers in an authorized and secured manner, this complexity can make sticking to either the hierarchical or peer-to-peer trust model difficult, if not impossible. In many implementations, the different model types have to be combined to provide the necessary communication lines and levels of trust. In a *hybrid trust model*, the two companies have their own internal hierarchical models and are connected through a peer-to-peer model using cross-certification.

Another option in this hybrid configuration is to implement a *bridge CA*. Figure 24-14 illustrates the role that a bridge CA could play—it is responsible for issuing cross-certificates for all connected CAs and trust domains. The bridge CA is not considered a root or trust anchor, but merely the entity that generates and maintains the cross-certification for the connected environments.

 EXAM TIP Three trust models exist: hierarchical, peer-to-peer, and hybrid. Hierarchical trust is like an upside-down tree. Peer-to-peer is a lateral series of references, and hybrid is a combination of hierarchical and peer-to-peer trust.

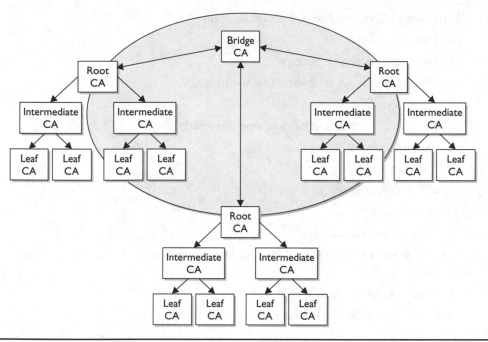

Figure 24-14 A bridge CA can control the cross-certification procedures.

Chapter Review

In this chapter, you became acquainted with the application of cryptographic algorithms. Hash values were the first type covered, followed by symmetric algorithms. Asymmetric algorithms followed, and then common cryptographic applications were presented. The chapter then presented public key infrastructure (PKI), the essential elements to manage public keys. Much of this chapter is a repeat from earlier material, but what is important to learn is which cryptographic algorithms are employed under which circumstances.

Questions

To help you prepare further for the CompTIA Security+ exam, and to test your level of preparedness, answer the following questions and then check your answers against the list of correct answers at the end of the chapter.

1. Why is DES no longer considered effective?

   A. It only works with public keys.

   B. Its keyspace is too small.

   C. It was replaced by the one-time pad method.

   D. It was replaced by AES.

2. What does SSL depend on for authentication?

   A. The SHA-1 hash

   B. The client's digital signature

   C. Hierarchy of trust established by the root CA

   D. The private key password

3. What are unique characteristics of one-time pads? (Choose all that apply.)

   A. Extremely difficult key sharing

   B. Integrity

   C. 4096-bit symmetric keys

   D. Unbreakable

   E. Vulnerable to weak keys

4. Which of the following would you use to authenticate users in a confidential fashion?

   A. Password Authentication Protocol

   B. Challenge Handshake Authentication Protocol

   C. Both A and B

   D. Neither A nor B

5. What would you use to create an HMAC?

   A. TLS

   B. MD5 or SHA

   C. AES

   D. Bcrypt

6. Which cipher depends on the difficulty in factoring primes?

   A. AES

   B. SHA

   C. RC4

   D. RSA

7. How is Twofish superior to its predecessor, Blowfish?

   A. Twofish is an asymmetric algorithm.

   B. Twofish uses more complex S-boxes to prevent dictionary attacks.

   C. Twofish has less of a vulnerability against certain classes of weak keys.

   D. All of the above.

8. SSH uses public keys for what purpose?

    A. Encryption

    B. Session key exchange

    C. Client authentication

    D. Both A and B

    E. Both B and C

    F. All of the above

9. Diffie-Hellman is representative of what branch of cryptography?

    A. Stream cipher

    B. Symmetric

    C. Asymmetric

    D. Hash function

10. When a CSR is generated, what is actually sent to the CA?

    A. An encrypted challenge to be decrypted by the CA

    B. The public key of the applicant and some identifying information

    C. The private and public keys of the applicant and X.509 information

    D. A PKCS #12 message

For questions 11–15, assume the following scenario: The CIO of your company read about public key infrastructure in a trade magazine and now feels that a new PKI system can solve all of the company's security problems. He asks you to design and implement the PKI system to support all the encryption processes used by your company and to manage and secure all the keys used.

11. What algorithms are you likely to need to support all of the goals the CIO has laid out for you?

    A. SSL

    B. SHA

    C. AES

    D. DES

    E. RSA

    F. CHAP

12. Which of the following is most likely to provide perfect forward secrecy?

    A. 3DES

    B. Blowfish

    C. EDH

    D. SHA-3

13. The desktop support team wants to add another authentication factor. What would be your recommendation?

A. Stand-alone biometrics

B. Smart cards with digital signatures

C. Rolling authentication codes

D. Contactless access cards

14. The CIO asks you to ensure that all e-mails have strict non-repudiation. How can a PKI system solve this issue?

A. Managing symmetric keys for e-mail encryption

B. Forcing all users to use two-factor authentication when accessing the e-mail server

C. Using PKI to support TLS on the SMTP delivery

D. Issuing a digital certificate to all users for signing e-mails

15. When a PKI system is used in conjunction with file and folder encryption, what is a potential risk?

A. A lost or damaged key can lock data away permanently.

B. Encryption prevents backups from being run.

C. Once the root key of the PKI is compromised, all the encrypted data can be read.

D. Encryption never has risks.

Answers

1. **B.** DES is no longer considered effective because its original 56-bit keyspace is much too small considering the speed of modern computers. Brute force can reveal the key in a matter of days or even hours.

2. **C.** SSL authentication is handled by the server's certificate being signed by a trusted authority, creating a hierarchy of trust—since you trust the root authority, you trust anything signed by the root, including the certificate signed by the root.

3. **A and D.** One-time pads rely on a key length matching or exceeding the input length of the plaintext. This makes it very difficult to securely share keys of the exact length you need, or you will need to share huge reams of key material. Additionally, the key material must be as close to random as possible. Once you can share the keys properly and they are sufficiently random, you do have a cipher that is for all practical purposes unbreakable, as it is not subject to known cryptanalysis.

4. **B.** Challenge Handshake Authentication Protocol (CHAP) is the correct choice because it protects the authentication information via a handshake and key exchange.

5. **B.** You could use MD5 or SHA to create a keyed Hash Message Authentication Code.

6. **D.** RSA is an asymmetric cipher, so it has both a public key and a private key. The public key is the product of two very large prime numbers, and the difficulty of returning to the original primes used to create the product ensures the security of the cipher.

7. **C.** Blowfish was susceptible to certain classes of weak keys. Twofish does not display this weakness.

8. **E.** SSH uses public keys to exchange the encryption session key at startup. It can also use public keys to authenticate the connected client if configured to do so.

9. **C.** Diffie-Hellman methods are asymmetric methods.

10. **B.** A CSR is primarily the applicant's public key with some additional information so that the signed certificate can be generated.

11. **B, C,** and **E.** RSA would be the public key cipher, with AES used as the symmetric cipher and SHA as the hashing algorithm.

12. **C.** Ephemeral Diffie-Hellman—the key part is *ephemeral*, which refers to the use of a temporary (and not reused) key; this provides for perfect forward secrecy.

13. **B.** Smart cards could leverage the new PKI implementation and provide an in-house solution to the two-factor authentication issue.

14. **D.** Issuing a digital certificate will allow all users to sign e-mails as they are sent, requiring their private key present at the time of sending and ensuring non-repudiation.

15. **A.** The loss of a key when key escrow is not included on the system could make data unrecoverable.

PART VI

PART VII

Appendixes and Glossary

OSI Model and Internet Protocols

In this appendix, you will

- Learn about the OSI model
- Review the network protocols associated with the Internet

Networks are interconnected groups of computers and specialty hardware designed to facilitate the transmission of data from one device to another. The basic function of the network is to allow machines and devices to communicate with each other in an orderly fashion.

Networking Frameworks and Protocols

Today's networks consist of a wide variety of types and sizes of equipment from multiple vendors. To ensure an effective and efficient transfer of information between devices, agreements as to how the transfer should proceed between vendors are required.

The term *protocol* refers to a standard set of rules developed to facilitate a specific level of functionality. In networking, a wide range of protocols have been developed, some proprietary and some public, to facilitate communication between machines. Just as speakers need a common language to communicate, or they must at least understand each other's language, computers and networks must agree on a common protocol.

Communication requires that all parties have a common understanding of the object under discussion. If the object is intangible or not present, each party needs some method of referencing items in such a way that the other party understands. A *model* is a tool used as a framework to give people common points of reference when discussing items. Mathematical models are common in science, because they give people the ability to compare answers and results. In much the same way, models are used in many disciplines to facilitate communication. Network models have been developed by many companies as ways to communicate among engineers what specific functionality is occurring when and where in a network.

As the Internet took shape, a series of protocols was needed to ensure interoperability across this universal network structure. The Transmission Control Protocol (TCP), User Datagram Protocol (UDP), and Internet Protocol (IP) are three of the commonly used protocols that enable data movement across the Internet. As these protocols work in concert with one another, you typically see TCP/IP or UDP/IP as pairs in use. A basic understanding of the terms and of the usage of protocols and models is essential to discuss networking functionality, for it provides the necessary points of reference to understand what is happening where and when in the complex stream of operations that are involved in networking.

OSI Model

To facilitate cross-vendor and multicompany communication, in 1984, the International Organization for Standardization (ISO) created the Open Systems Interconnection (OSI) model for networking. The OSI model is probably the most referenced and widely discussed model in networking. Although it never fully caught on in North America, portions of it have been adopted as reference points, even to the extent of being incorporated into company names. Layer 2, layer 3, network layer, level 3—these are all references to portions of the OSI model. These references allow people to communicate in a clear and unambiguous fashion when speaking of abstract and out-of-context issues. These references provide context to detail in the complex arena of networking. The terms *level* and *layer* have been used interchangeably to describe the sections of the OSI model, although *layer* is the more common term.

The OSI model is composed of seven layers stacked in a linear fashion. These layers are, from top to bottom, application, presentation, session, transport, network, data-link, and physical. You can use a mnemonic to remember them: All People Seem To Need Data Processing. Each layer has defined functionality and separation designed to allow multiple protocols to work together in a coordinated fashion.

Although the OSI model is probably the most referenced, standardized network model, a more common model, the Internet model, has risen to dominate the Internet. The OSI model enjoys the status of being a formal, defined international standard, while the Internet model has never been formally defined. The Internet model is basically the same as the OSI model, with the top three OSI layers combined into a single application layer, leaving a total of five layers in the Internet model. Both models are shown in Figure A-1.

One aspect of these models is that they allow specific levels of functionality to be broken apart and performed in sequence. This delineation also determines which layers can communicate with others. At each layer, specific data forms and protocols can exist, which makes them compatible with similar protocols and data forms on other machines at the same layer. This makes it seem as if each layer is communicating with its counterpart on the same layer in another computer, although this is just a virtual connection. The only real connection between boxes is at the physical layer of these models. All other connections are virtual—although they appear real to a user, they do not actually exist in reality.

The true communication between layers occurs vertically, up and down—each layer can communicate only with its immediate neighbor above and below. In Figure A-2, the direct communication path is shown as a bold line between the two physical layers. All data between the boxes traverses this line. The dotted lines between higher layers

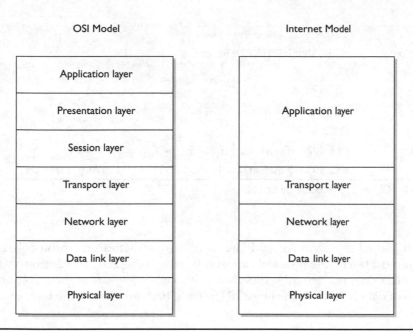

Figure A-1 OSI and Internet network models

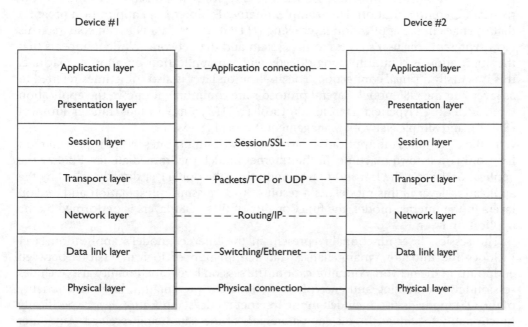

Figure A-2 Network model communication paths

Layer	Commonly Used Protocols
Application	HTTP, SNMP, SMTP, FTP, Telnet
Presentation	XDR
Session	SSL, TLS
Transport	TCP, UCP
Network	IP, ICMP
Data link	IEEE 802.3 (Ethernet), IEEE 802.5 (Token Ring), ARP, RARP
Physical	IEEE 802.3 (Ethernet) hardware, IEEE 802.5 (Token Ring) hardware

Table A-1　Common Protocols by OSI Layer

represent virtual connections, and the associated activities and protocols are also listed for most layers (the protocols are also listed in Table A-1). These dotted lines are virtual—data does not actually cross them, although it appears as though it does. The true path of data is down to the physical layer and back up to the same layer on another machine.

Application Layer

The application layer is the typical interface to the actual application being used. This is the layer of the communication stack that is typically responsible for initiating the request for communication. For example, Internet Explorer is an application program that operates in the application layer using HTTP to move data between systems. This layer represents the user's access to the system and the network. While it appears that the application is communicating directly with an application on another machine, this is actually a *virtual* connection. The application layer is also sometimes referred to as layer 7 in the OSI model. Several protocols are commonly found in the application layer, including Hypertext Transfer Protocol (HTTP), Simple Mail Transfer Protocol (SMTP), and Simple Network Management Protocol (SNMP).

In the OSI model, the application layer actually communicates with the presentation layer only on its own machine. In the Internet model, the immediate level below the application layer is the transport layer, and this is the only layer directly called by the application layer in this model. As a result of the "missing" presentation and session layers in the Internet model, the functionality of these OSI layers is performed by the application layer.

The session layer functionality present in the Internet model's application layer includes the initiation, maintenance, and termination of logical sessions between endpoints in the network communication. The session layer functionality also includes session-level accounting and encryption services. The presentation layer functionality of the OSI model is also included in the Internet model's application layer, specifically functionality to format the display parameters of the data being received. Any other functions not specifically included in the lower layers of the Internet model are specifically included in the application layer.

Presentation Layer

The presentation layer gets its name from its primary function: preparing for the presentation of data. It is responsible for preparing the data for different interfaces on different types of terminals or displays so the application does not have to deal with this task. Data compression, character set translation, and encryption are found in this layer.

The presentation layer communicates with only two layers—the application layer above it and the session layer below it. The presentation layer is also known as layer 6 of the OSI model.

Session Layer

The primary responsibility of the session layer is the managing of communication sessions between machines. The management functions include initiating, maintaining, and terminating sessions. Managing a session can be compared to making an ordinary phone call. When you dial, you initiate a session. The session must be maintained in an open state during the call. At the completion of the call, you hang up and the circuit must be terminated. As each session can have its own parameters, the session layer is responsible for setting them up, including security, encryption, and billing or accounting functions.

The session layer communicates exclusively with the presentation layer above it and the transport layer below it. The session layer is also known as layer 5 of the OSI model.

Transport Layer

The transport layer is responsible for dealing with the end-to-end transport of data across the network connection. To perform this task, the transport layer handles data entering and leaving the network through logical connections. It can add and use address-specific information, such as ports, to accomplish this task. A *port* is an address-specific extension that enables multiple simultaneous communications between machines. Should the data transmission be too large for a single-packet transport, the transport layer manages breaking up the data stream into chunks and reassembling it. It ensures that all packets are transmitted and received, and it can request lost packets and eliminate duplicate packets. Error checking can also be performed at this level, although this function is usually performed at the data link layer.

Protocols can be either connection oriented or connectionless. If the protocol is connection oriented, the transport layer manages the connection information. In the case of TCP, the transport layer manages missing packet retransmission requests via the sliding window algorithm.

The transport layer communicates exclusively with the session layer above it and the network layer below it. The transport layer is also known as layer 4 of the OSI model.

Network Layer

The network layer is responsible for routing packets across the network. Routing functions determine the next best destination for a packet and will determine the full address of the target computer if necessary. Common protocols at this level include IP and Internet Control Message Protocol (ICMP).

The network layer communicates exclusively with the transport layer above it and the data link layer below it. The network layer is also known as layer 3 of the OSI model.

Data Link Layer

The data link layer is responsible for the delivery and receipt of data from the hardware in layer 1, the physical layer. Layer 1 only manipulates a stream of bits, so the data link layer must convert the packets from the network layer into bit streams in a form that can be understood by the physical layer. To ensure accurate transmission, the data link layer adds end-of-message markers onto each packet and also manages error detection, correction, and retransmission functions. This layer also performs the media-access function, determining when to send and receive data based on network traffic. At this layer, the data packets are technically known as *frames*, although many practitioners use *packet* in a generic sense.

The data link layer communicates exclusively with the network layer above it and the physical layer below it. The data link layer is also known as layer 2 of the OSI model, and it is where LAN switching based on machine-address functionality occurs.

Physical Layer

The physical layer is the realm of communication hardware and software, where 1s and 0s become waves of light, voltage levels, phase shifts, and other physical entities as defined by the particular transmission standard. This layer defines the physical method of signal transmission between machines in terms of electrical and optical character-istics. The physical layer is the point of connection to the outside world via standard connectors, again determined by signal type and protocol.

The physical layer communicates with the physical layer on other machines via wire, fiber-optics, or radio waves. The physical layer also communicates with the data link layer above it. The physical layer is also referred to as OSI layer 1.

Internet Protocols

To facilitate cross-vendor product communication, protocols have been adopted to standardize methods. The Internet brought several new protocols into existence, a few of which are commonly used in the routing of information. Two protocols used at the transport layer are TCP and UDP, whereas IP is used at the network layer. In each session, one transport layer protocol and one network layer protocol is used, making the pairs TCP/IP and UDP/IP.

TCP

TCP is the primary transport protocol used on the Internet today, accounting for more than 80 percent of packets on the Internet.

TCP begins by establishing a virtual connection through a mechanism known as the TCP *handshake*. This handshake involves three signals: a SYN signal sent to the target, a SYN/ACK returned in response, and then an ACK sent back to the target to complete the circuit. This establishes a virtual connection between machines over which the data will be transported, and that is why TCP is referred to as being *connection oriented*.

TCP is classified as a reliable protocol and will ensure that packets are sent, received, and ordered using sequence numbers. Some overhead is associated with the sequencing of packets and maintaining this order, but for many communications, this is essential, such as in e-mail transmissions, HTTP, and the like.

TCP has facilities to perform all the required functions of the transport layer. TCP has congestion- and flow-control mechanisms to report congestion and other traffic-related information back to the sender to assist in traffic-level management. Multiple TCP connections can be established between machines through a mechanism known as *ports*. TCP ports are numbered from 0 to 65,535, although ports below 1024 are typically reserved for specific functions. TCP ports are separate entities from UDP ports and can be used at the same time.

UDP

UDP is a simpler form of transport protocol than TCP. UDP performs all of the required functionality of the transport layer, but it does not perform the maintenance and checking functions of TCP. UDP does not establish a connection and does not use sequence numbers. UDP packets are sent via the "best effort" method, often referred to as "fire and forget," because the packets either reach their destination or they are lost forever. It offers no retransmission mechanism, which is why UDP is called an unreliable protocol.

UDP does not have traffic-management or flow-control functions as TCP does. This results in much lower overhead and makes UDP ideal for streaming data sources, such as audio and video traffic, where latency between packets can be an issue. Essential services such as Dynamic Host Configuration Protocol (DHCP) and Domain Name Service (DNS) use UDP, primarily because of the low overhead. When packets do get lost, which is rare in modern networks, they can be resent.

Multiple UDP connections can be established between machines via ports. UDP ports are numbered from 0 to 65,535, although ports below 1024 are typically reserved for specific functionality. UDP ports are separate entities from TCP ports and can be used at the same time.

IP

IP is a connectionless protocol used for routing messages across the Internet. Its primary purpose is to address packets with IP addresses, both destination and source, and to use these addresses to determine the next hop to which the packet will be transmitted. As IP is *connectionless*, IP packets can take different routes at different times between the same hosts, depending on traffic conditions. IP also maintains some traffic-management information, such as time-to-live (a function to give packets a limited lifetime) and fragmentation control (a mechanism to split packets en route if necessary).

The current version of IP is version 4, referred to as IPv4, and it uses a 32-bit address space. The newer IPv6 protocol adds significant levels of functionality, such as security, improved address space, 128 bits, and a whole host of sophisticated traffic-management options. IPv4 addresses are written as four sets of numbers in the form v.x.y.z, with each of these values ranging from 0 to 255. Since this would be difficult to remember, a naming system for hosts was developed around domains, and DNS servers convert the host names, such as www.ietf.org, to IP addresses, such as 4.17.168.6.

Message Encapsulation

As a message traverses a network from one application on one host, down through the OSI model, out through the physical layer, and up another machine's OSI model, the data is encapsulated at each layer. This can be viewed as an envelope inside an envelope scheme. Since only specific envelopes are handled at each layer, only the necessary information for that layer is presented on the envelope. At each layer, the information inside the envelope is not relevant, and previous envelopes have been discarded—only the information on the current envelope is used. This offers efficient separation of functionality between layers. This concept is illustrated in Figure A-3.

As a message traverses the OSI model from the application layer to the physical layer, envelopes are placed inside bigger envelopes. This increases the packet size, but this increase is known and taken into account by the higher-level protocols. At each level, a header is added to the front end, and it acts to encapsulate the previous layer as data.

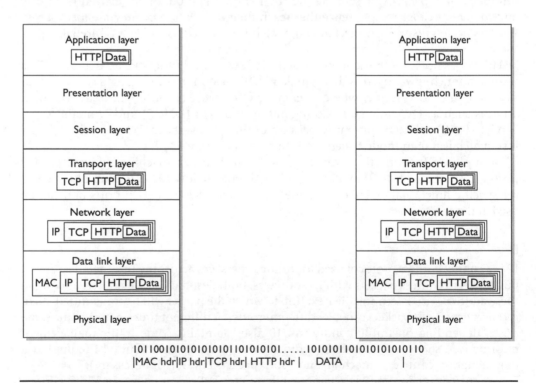

Figure A-3   OSI message encapsulation

At the physical level, the bits are turned into the physical signal and are transmitted to the next station.

At the receiving station, the bits are turned into one large packet, which represents the original envelope-within-envelope concept. Then each envelope is handled at the appropriate level. This encapsulation exists at the transport layer and lower, as this is the domain of a packet within a session.

Review

To help variable systems understand the functions performed in network communication, a common framework is necessary. This framework is provided by the OSI and Internet network models, which specify which functions occur, and in what order, in the transmission of data from one application to another across a network.

An understanding of the OSI model and thus the state in which the data exists as it transits a network enables a deeper understanding of issues related to security. Understanding that SSL occurs before TCP and IP allows you to understand how SSL protects TCP and IP from outside sniffing. Understanding the different protocols and what happens with data loss gives you a better understanding of how certain types of attacks are performed.

The essence of a framework is to allow enhanced understanding of relationships, and these network models perform this function for network professionals.

About the CD-ROM

The CD-ROM included with this book comes complete with Total Tester customizable practice exam software and a PDF copy of the book.

System Requirements

The software requires Windows XP or later and 30MB of hard disk space for full installation, in addition to a current or prior major release of Chrome, Firefox, Internet Explorer, or Safari. To run, the screen resolution must be set to 1024 × 768 or higher. The PDF copy of the book requires Adobe Acrobat, Adobe Reader, or Adobe Digital Editions.

Total Tester Premium Practice Exam Software

Total Tester provides you with a simulation of the live exam. You can also create custom exams from selected certification objectives or chapters. You can further customize the number of questions and time allowed.

The exams can be taken in either Practice Mode or Exam Mode. Practice Mode provides an assistance window with hints, references to the book, explanations of the correct and incorrect answers, and the option to check your answer as you take the test. Exam Mode provides a simulation of the actual exam. The number of questions, the types of questions, and the time allowed are intended to be a representation of the exam environment. Both Practice Mode and Exam Mode provide an overall grade and a grade broken down by certification objectives.

 NOTE Total Tester does not provide simulations of the exam's performance-based question type. For further discussion on this question type, please see the book's Introduction.

To take a test, launch the program and select the exam suite from the Installed Question Packs list. You can then select Practice Mode, Exam Mode, or Custom Mode. After making your selection, click Start Exam to begin.

Installing and Running Total Tester Premium Practice Exam Software

From the main screen, you may install the Total Tester software by clicking the Total Tester Practice Exams button. This will begin the installation process and place an icon on your desktop and in your Start menu. To run Total Tester, navigate to Start | (All) Programs | Total Seminars, or double-click the icon on your desktop.

To uninstall the Total Tester software, go to Start | Settings | Control Panel | Add/ Remove Programs (XP) or Programs And Features (Vista/7/8), and then select the Total Tester program. Select Remove, and Windows will completely uninstall the software.

PDF Copy of the Book

The entire contents of the book are provided as a PDF on the CD-ROM. This file is viewable on your computer and many portable devices.

- **To view the PDF on a computer**, Adobe Acrobat, Adobe Reader, or Adobe Digital Editions is required. A link to Adobe's website, where you can download and install Adobe Reader, has been included on the CD-ROM.

 NOTE   For more information on Adobe Reader and to check for the most recent version of the software, visit Adobe's web site at www.adobe.com and search for the free Adobe Reader or look for Adobe Reader on the product page. Adobe Digital Editions can also be downloaded from the Adobe web site.

- **To view the PDF on a portable device**, copy the PDF file to your computer from the CD-ROM, and then copy the file to your portable device using a USB or other connection. Adobe offers a mobile version of Adobe Reader, the Adobe Reader mobile app, which currently supports iOS and Android. For customers using Adobe Digital Editions and an iPad, you may have to download and install a separate reader program on your device. The Adobe website has a list of recommended applications, and McGraw-Hill Education recommends the Bluefire Reader.

Technical Support

Technical Support information is provided in the following sections by feature.

Total Seminars Technical Support

For questions regarding the Total Tester software or operation of the CD-ROM, visit **www.totalsem.com** or e-mail **support@totalsem.com**.

McGraw-Hill Education Content Support

For questions regarding the PDF copy of the book, visit **http://mhp.softwareassist.com** or e-mail **techsolutions@mhedu.com**.

For questions regarding book content, e-mail **customer.service@mheducation.com**. For customers outside the United States, e-mail **international_cs@mheducation.com**.

3DES   Triple DES encryption—three rounds of DES encryption used to improve security.

802.11   A family of standards that describe network protocols for wireless devices.

802.1X   An IEEE standard for performing authentication over networks.

AAA   *See* authentication, authorization, and accounting.

acceptable use policy (AUP)   A policy that communicates to users what specific uses of computer resources are permitted.

access   A subject's ability to perform specific operations on an object, such as a file. Typical access levels include read, write, execute, and delete.

access control   Mechanisms or methods used to determine what access permissions subjects (such as users) have for specific objects (such as files).

access control list (ACL)   A list associated with an object (such as a file) that identifies what level of access each subject (such as a user) has—what they can do to the object (such as read, write, or execute).

access point   Shorthand for wireless access point, the device that allows devices to connect to a wireless network.

Active Directory   The directory service portion of the Windows operating system that stores information about network-based entities (such as applications, files, printers, and people) and provides a structured, consistent way to name, describe, locate, access, and manage these resources.

ActiveX   A Microsoft technology that facilitates rich Internet applications, and therefore extends and enhances the functionality of Microsoft Internet Explorer. Like Java, ActiveX enables the development of interactive content. When an ActiveX-aware browser encounters a web page that includes an unsupported feature, it can automatically install the appropriate application so the feature can be used.

Address Resolution Protocol (ARP)   A protocol in the TCP/IP suite specification used to map an IP address to a Media Access Control (MAC) address.

Advanced Encryption Standard   The current U.S. government standard for symmetric encryption, widely used in all sectors.

Advanced Encryption Standard 256-bit   An implementation of AES using a 256-bit key.

adware   Advertising-supported software that automatically plays, displays, or downloads advertisements after the software is installed or while the application is being used.

AES   *See* Advanced Encryption Standard.

AES256   *See* Advanced Encryption Standard 256-bit.

air gap   The forced separation of networks, resulting in an air gap between systems. Communications across an air gap require a manual effort to move data from one network to another, as no network connection exists between the two networks.

algorithm   A step-by-step procedure—typically an established computation for solving a problem within a set number of steps.

annualized loss expectancy (ALE)   How much an event is expected to cost the business per year, given the dollar cost of the loss and how often it is likely to occur. ALE = single loss expectancy × annualized rate of occurrence.

annualized rate of occurrence (ARO)   The frequency with which an event is expected to occur on an annualized basis.

anomaly   Something that does not fit into an expected pattern.

application   A program or group of programs designed to provide specific user functions, such as a word processor or web server.

application programming interface (API)   A set of instructions as to how to interface with a computer program so that developers can access defined interfaces in a program.

application service provider (ASP)   A company that offers entities access over the Internet to applications and services.

ARP   *See* Address Resolution Protocol.

asset   Resources and information an organization needs to conduct its business.

asymmetric encryption   Also called public key cryptography, this is a system for encrypting data that uses two mathematically derived keys to encrypt and decrypt a message—a public key, available to everyone, and a private key, available only to the owner of the key.

audit trail   A set of records or events, generally organized chronologically, that records what activity has occurred on a system. These records (often computer files) are often used in an attempt to re-create what took place when a security incident occurred, and they can also be used to detect possible intruders.

auditing   Actions or processes used to verify the assigned privileges and rights of a user, or any capabilities used to create and maintain a record showing who accessed a particular system and what actions they performed.

authentication   The process by which a subject's (such as a user's) identity is verified.

authentication, authorization, and accounting (AAA)   Three common functions performed upon system login. Authentication and authorization almost always occur, with accounting being somewhat less common.

Authentication Header (AH)   A portion of the IPsec security protocol that provides authentication services and replay-detection ability. AH can be used either by itself or with Encapsulating Security Payload (ESP). Refer to RFC 2402.

availability   Part of the "CIA" of security. Availability applies to hardware, software, and data, specifically meaning that each of these should be present and accessible when the subject (the user) wants to access or use them.

backdoor   A hidden method used to gain access to a computer system, network, or application. Often used by software developers to ensure unrestricted access to the systems they create. Synonymous with *trapdoor*.

backup   Refers to copying and storing data in a secondary location, separate from the original, to preserve the data in the event that the original is lost, corrupted, or destroyed.

baseline   A system or software as it is built and functioning at a specific point in time. Serves as a foundation for comparison or measurement, providing the necessary visibility to control change.

Basic Input/Output System (BIOS)   A firmware element of a computer system that provides the interface between hardware and system software with respect to devices and peripherals. BIOS is being replaced by Extensible Firmware Interface (EFI), a more complex and capable system.

BGP   *See* Border Gateway Protocol.

biometrics   Used to verify an individual's identity to the system or network using something unique about the individual, such as a fingerprint, for the verification process. Examples include fingerprints, retinal scans, hand and facial geometry, and voice analysis.

BIOS   *See* Basic Input/Output System.

Blowfish   A free implementation of a symmetric block cipher developed by Bruce Schneier as a drop-in replacement for DES and IDEA. It has a variable-bit-length scheme from 32 to 448 bits, resulting in varying levels of security.

bluebugging   The use of a Bluetooth-enabled device to eavesdrop on another person's conversation using that person's Bluetooth phone as a transmitter. The blue-bug application silently causes a Bluetooth device to make a phone call to another device, causing the phone to act as a transmitter and allowing the listener to eavesdrop on the victim's conversation in real life.

bluejacking The sending of unsolicited messages over Bluetooth to Bluetooth-enabled devices such as mobile phones, tablets, or laptop computers.

bluesnarfing The unauthorized access of information from a Bluetooth-enabled device through a Bluetooth connection, often between mobile phones, desktops, laptops, and tablets.

Border Gateway Protocol (BGP) The interdomain routing protocol implemented in Internet Protocol (IP) networks to enable routing between autonomous systems.

botnet A term for a collection of software robots, or *bots*, that run autonomously and automatically and, commonly, invisibly in the background. The term is most often associated with malicious software, but it can also refer to the network of computers using distributed computing software.

bring your own device (BYOD) A term used to describe an environment where users bring their personally owned devices into the enterprise and integrate them into business systems.

buffer overflow A specific type of software coding error that enables user input to overflow the allocated storage area and corrupt a running program.

Bureau of Industry and Security (BIS) In the U.S. Department of Commerce, the department responsible for export administration regulations that cover encryption technology in the United States.

business continuity plan (BCP) The plan a business develops to continue critical operations in the event of a major disruption.

business impact analysis (BIA) An analysis of the impact to the business of a specific event.

business partnership agreement (BPA) A written agreement defining the terms and conditions of a business partnership.

BYOD *See* bring your own device.

cache The temporary storage of information before use, typically used to speed up systems. In an Internet context, refers to the storage of commonly accessed web pages, graphic files, and other content locally on a user's PC or a web server. The cache helps to minimize download time and preserve bandwidth for frequently accessed websites, and it helps reduce the load on a web server.

Capability Maturity Model (CMM) A structured methodology helping organizations improve the maturity of their software processes by providing an evolutionary path from ad hoc processes to disciplined software management processes. Developed at Carnegie Mellon University's Software Engineering Institute.

centralized management A type of privilege management that brings the authority and responsibility for managing and maintaining rights and privileges into a single group, location, or area.

CERT *See* Computer Emergency Response Team.

certificate A cryptographically signed object that contains an identity and a public key associated with this identity. The certificate can be used to establish identity, analogous to a notarized written document.

Certificate Enrollment Protocol (CEP) Originally developed by VeriSign for Cisco Systems to support certificate issuance, distribution, and revocation using existing technologies.

certificate revocation list (CRL) A digitally signed object that lists all of the current but revoked certificates issued by a given certification authority. This allows users to verify whether a certificate is currently valid even if it has not expired. A CRL is analogous to a list of stolen charge card numbers that allows stores to reject bad credit cards.

certification authority (CA) An entity responsible for issuing and revoking certificates. CAs are typically not associated with the company requiring the certificate, although they exist for internal company use as well (such as Microsoft). This term is also applied to server software that provides these services. The term *certificate authority* is used interchangeably with *certification authority*.

chain of custody Rules for documenting, handling, and safeguarding evidence to ensure no unanticipated changes are made to the evidence.

Challenge Handshake Authentication Protocol (CHAP) Used to provide authentication across point-to-point links using the Point-to-Point Protocol (PPP).

change (configuration) management A standard methodology for performing and recording changes during software development and operation.

change control board (CCB) A body that oversees the change management process and enables management to oversee and coordinate projects.

CHAP *See* Challenge Handshake Authentication Protocol.

CIA of security Refers to confidentiality, integrity, and availability, the basic functions of any security system.

cipher A cryptographic system that accepts plaintext input and then outputs ciphertext according to its internal algorithm and key.

ciphertext Used to denote the output of an encryption algorithm. Ciphertext is the encrypted data.

CIRT *See* Computer Emergency Response Team.

closed circuit television (CCTV) A private television system, usually hard-wired in security applications to record visual information.

cloud computing The automatic provisioning of computational resources on demand across a network.

cold site An inexpensive form of backup site that does not include a current set of data at all times. A cold site takes longer to get your operational system back up, but it is considerably less expensive than a warm or hot site.

collisions Used in the analysis of hashing cryptography, it is the property by which an algorithm will produce the same hash from two different sets of data.

Common Access Card (CAC) A smart card used to access federal computer systems, and to also act as an ID card.

Computer Emergency Response Team (CERT) Also known as a Computer Incident Response Team (CIRT), this group is responsible for investigating and responding to security breaches, viruses, and other potentially catastrophic incidents.

computer security In general terms, the methods, techniques, and tools used to ensure that a computer system is secure.

computer software configuration item *See* configuration item.

confidentiality Part of the CIA of security. Refers to the security principle that states that information should not be disclosed to unauthorized individuals.

configuration auditing The process of verifying that configuration items are built and maintained according to requirements, standards, or contractual agreements.

configuration control The process of controlling changes to items that have been baselined.

configuration identification The process of identifying which assets need to be managed and controlled.

configuration item Data and software (or other assets) that are identified and managed as part of the software change management process. Also known as *computer software configuration item*.

configuration status accounting Procedures for tracking and maintaining data relative to each configuration item in the baseline.

contingency planning (CP) The act of creating processes and procedures that are used under special conditions (contingencies).

Continuity of Operations Planning (COOP) The creation of plans related to continuing essential business operations.

Controller Area Network A bus standard for use in vehicles to connect micro-controllers.

cookie   Information stored on a user's computer by a web server to maintain the state of the connection to the web server. Used primarily so preferences or previously used information can be recalled on future requests to the server.

COOP   *See* Continuity of Operations Planning.

Counter Mode with Cipher Block Chaining Message Authentication Code Protocol (CCMP)   An enhanced data cryptographic encapsulation mechanism based upon the counter mode with CBC-MAC from AES, designed for use over wireless LANs.

countermeasure   *See* security control.

cracking   A term used by some to refer to malicious hacking, in which an individual attempts to gain unauthorized access to computer systems or networks. *See also* hacking.

CRC   *See* Cyclic Redundancy Check.

CRL   *See* Certificate Revocation List.

cross-site request forgery (CSRF or XSRF)   A method of attacking a system by sending malicious input to the system and relying upon the parsers and execution elements to perform the requested actions, thus instantiating the attack. XSRF exploits the trust a site has in the user's browser.

cross-site scripting (XSS)   A method of attacking a system by sending script commands to the system input and relying upon the parsers and execution elements to perform the requested scripted actions, thus instantiating the attack. XSS exploits the trust a user has for the site.

cryptanalysis   The process of attempting to break a cryptographic system.

cryptography   The art of secret writing that enables an individual to hide the contents of a message or file from all but the intended recipient.

Cyclic Redundancy Check (CRC)   An error detection technique that uses a series of two 8-bit block check characters to represent an entire block of data. These block check characters are incorporated into the transmission frame and then checked at the receiving end.

DAC   *See* Discretionary Access Control.

Data Encryption Standard (DES)   A private key encryption algorithm adopted by the government as a standard for the protection of sensitive but unclassified information. Commonly used in triple DES, where three rounds are applied to provide greater security.

Data Execution Prevention (DEP)   A security feature of an OS that can be driven by software, hardware, or both, designed to prevent the execution of code from blocks of data in memory.

Data Loss Prevention (DLP)   Technology, processes, and procedures designed to detect when unauthorized removal of data from a system occurs. DLP is typically active, preventing the loss, either by blocking the transfer or dropping the connection.

datagram   A packet of data that can be transmitted over a packet-switched system in a connectionless mode.

decision tree   A data structure in which each element is attached to one or more structures directly beneath it.

demilitarized zone (DMZ)   A network segment that exists in a semi-protected zone between the Internet and the inner, secure trusted network.

denial-of-service (DoS) attack   An attack in which actions are taken to deprive authorized individuals from accessing a system, its resources, the data it stores or processes, or the network to which it is connected.

DES   *See* Data Encryption Standard.

DHCP   *See* Dynamic Host Configuration Protocol.

Diffie-Hellman   A cryptographic method of establishing a shared key over an insecure medium in a secure fashion.

Diffie-Hellman Ephemeral (DHE)   A cryptographic method of establishing a shared key over an insecure medium in a secure fashion using a temporary key to enable perfect forward secrecy.

digital signature   A cryptography-based artifact that is a key component of a public key infrastructure (PKI) implementation. A digital signature can be used to prove identity because it is created with the private key portion of a public/private key pair. A recipient can decrypt the signature and, by doing so, receive the assurance that the data must have come from the sender and that the data has not changed.

digital signature algorithm (DSA)   A U.S. government standard for implementing digital signatures.

direct-sequence spread spectrum (DSSS)   A method of distributing a communication over multiple frequencies to avoid interference and detection.

disaster recovery plan (DRP)   A written plan developed to address how an organization will react to a natural or manmade disaster in order to ensure business continuity. Related to the concept of a business continuity plan (BCP).

discretionary access control (DAC)   An access control mechanism in which the owner of an object (such as a file) can decide which other subjects (such as other users) may have access to the object, and what access (read, write, execute) these objects can have.

distributed denial-of-service (DDoS) attack A special type of DoS attack in which the attacker elicits the generally unwilling support of other systems to launch a many-against-one attack.

diversity of defense The approach of creating dissimilar security layers so that an intruder who is able to breach one layer will be faced with an entirely different set of defenses at the next layer.

Domain Name Service (DNS) The service that translates an Internet domain name (such as www.mcgraw-hill.com) into IP addresses.

DRP *See* disaster recovery plan.

DSSS *See* direct-sequence spread spectrum.

dumpster diving The practice of searching through trash to discover material that has been thrown away that is sensitive, yet not destroyed or shredded.

Dynamic Host Configuration Protocol (DHCP) An Internet Engineering Task Force (IETF) Internet Protocol (IP) specification for automatically allocating IP addresses and other configuration information based on network adapter addresses. It enables address pooling and allocation and simplifies TCP/IP installation and administration.

dynamic link library (DLL) A shared library function used in the Microsoft Windows environment.

EAP *See* Extensible Authentication Protocol.

electromagnetic interference (EMI) The disruption or interference of electronics due to an electromagnetic field.

elliptic curve cryptography (ECC) A method of public key cryptography based on the algebraic structure of elliptic curves over finite fields.

elliptic curve Diffie-Hellman Ephemeral (ECDHE) A cryptographic method using ECC to establish a shared key over an insecure medium in a secure fashion using a temporary key to enable perfect forward secrecy.

Encapsulating Security Payload (ESP) A portion of the IPsec implementation that provides for data confidentiality with optional authentication and replay-detection services. ESP completely encapsulates user data in the datagram and can be used either by itself or in conjunction with Authentication Headers for varying degrees of IPsec services.

Encrypted File System (EFS) A security feature of Windows, from Windows 2000 onward, that enables the transparent encryption/decryption of files on the system.

escalation auditing The process of looking for an increase in privileges, such as when an ordinary user obtains administrator-level privileges.

evidence The documents, verbal statements, and material objects admissible in a court of law.

exposure factor A measure of the magnitude of loss of an asset. Used in the calculation of single loss expectancy (SLE).

Extensible Authentication Protocol (EAP) A universal authentication framework used in wireless networks and point-to-point connections. It is defined in RFC 3748 and has been updated by RFC 5247.

Extensible Markup Language (XML) A text-based, human-readable data markup language.

false positive Term used when a security system makes an error and incorrectly reports the existence of a searched-for object. Examples include an intrusion detection system that misidentifies benign traffic as hostile, an antivirus program that reports the existence of a virus in software that actually is not infected, or a biometric system that allows system access to an unauthorized individual.

FHSS *See* frequency-hopping spread spectrum.

file system access control list (FACL) The implementation of access controls as part of a file system.

File Transfer Protocol (FTP) An application layer protocol used to transfer files over a network connection.

File Transfer Protocol Secure (FTPS) An application layer protocol used to transfer files over a network connection, which uses FTP over an SSL or TLS connection.

firewall A network device used to segregate traffic based on rules.

flood guard A network device that blocks flooding-type DoS/DDoS attacks, frequently part of an IDS/IPS.

forensics (or computer forensics) The preservation, identification, documentation, and interpretation of computer data for use in legal proceedings.

free space Sectors on a storage medium that are available for the operating system to use.

frequency-hopping spread spectrum (FHSS) A method of distributing a communication over multiple frequencies over time to avoid interference and detection.

full disk encryption (FDE) The application of encryption to an entire disk, protecting all of the contents in one container.

Generic Routing Encapsulation (GRE) A tunneling protocol designed to encapsulate a wide variety of network layer packets inside IP tunneling packets.

Gnu Privacy Guard (GPG)   An application program that follows the OpenPGP standard for encryption.

GPG   *See* Gnu Privacy Guard.

GPO   *See* Group Policy object.

Group Policy object (GPO)   A method used by Windows for the application of OS settings enterprise-wide.

hacking   The term used by the media to refer to the process of gaining unauthorized access to computer systems and networks. The term has also been used to refer to the process of delving deep into the code and protocols used in computer systems and networks. *See also* cracking.

hard disk drive (HDD)   A mechanical device used for the storing of digital data in magnetic form.

hardware security module (HSM)   A physical device used to protect but still allow use of cryptographic keys. It is separate from the host machine.

hash   A form of encryption that creates a digest of the data put into the algorithm. These algorithms are referred to as one-way algorithms because there is no feasible way to decrypt what has been encrypted.

hash value   *See* message digest.

hashed message authentication code (HMAC)   The use of a cryptographic hash function and a message authentication code to ensure the integrity and authenticity of a message.

HDD   *See* hard disk drive.

heating, ventilation, air conditioning (HVAC)   The systems used to heat and cool air in a building or structure.

HIDS   *See* host-based intrusion detection system.

HIPS   *See* host-based intrusion prevention system.

honeypot   A computer system or portion of a network that has been set up to attract potential intruders, in the hope that they will leave the other systems alone. Since there are no legitimate users of this system, any attempt to access it is an indication of unauthorized activity and provides an easy mechanism to spot attacks.

host-based intrusion detection system (HIDS)   A system that looks for computer intrusions by monitoring activity on one or more individual PCs or servers.

host-based intrusion prevention system (HIPS)   A system that automatically responds to computer intrusions by monitoring activity on one or more individual PCs or servers and responding based on a rule set.

PART VII

hot site   A backup site that is fully configured with equipment and data and is ready to immediately accept transfer of operational processing in the event of failure on the operational system.

HSM   *See* hardware security module.

Hypertext Markup Language (HTML)   A protocol used to mark up text for use across HTTP.

Hypertext Transfer Protocol (HTTP)   A protocol for transfer of material across the Internet that contains links to additional material.

Hypertext Transfer Protocol over SSL/TLS (HTTPS)   A protocol for transfer of material across the Internet that contains links to additional material that is carried over a secure tunnel via SSL or TLS.

ICMP   *See* Internet Control Message Protocol.

identification (ID)   The first step in the authentication process where the user establishes a secret with the authentication system and is bound to a userid.

IEEE   *See* Institute for Electrical and Electronics Engineers.

IETF   *See* Internet Engineering Task Force.

impact   The result of a vulnerability being exploited by a threat, resulting in a loss.

incident response   The process of responding to, containing, analyzing, and recovering from a computer-related incident.

information security   Often used synonymously with computer security, but places the emphasis on the protection of the information that the system processes and stores, instead of on the hardware and software that constitute the system.

Infrastructure as a Service (IaaS)   The automatic, on-demand provisioning of infrastructure elements, operating as a service; a common element of cloud computing.

initialization vector (IV)   A data value used to seed a cryptographic algorithm, providing for a measure of randomness.

instant messaging (IM)   A text-based method of communicating over the Internet.

Institute for Electrical and Electronics Engineers (IEEE)   A nonprofit, technical, professional institute associated with computer research, standards, and conferences.

intangible asset   An asset for which a monetary equivalent is difficult or impossible to determine. Examples are brand recognition and goodwill.

integrity   Part of the CIA of security, the security principle that requires that information is not modified except by individuals authorized to do so.

interconnection security agreement (ISA) An agreement between parties to establish procedures for mutual cooperation and coordination between them with respect to security requirements associated with their joint project.

International Data Encryption Algorithm (IDEA) A symmetric encryption algorithm used in a variety of systems for bulk encryption services.

Internet Assigned Numbers Authority (IANA) The central coordinator for the assignment of unique parameter values for Internet protocols. The IANA is chartered by the Internet Society (ISOC) to act as the clearinghouse to assign and coordinate the use of numerous Internet protocol parameters.

Internet Control Message Protocol (ICMP) One of the core protocols of the TCP/IP protocol suite, used for error reporting and status messages.

Internet Engineering Task Force (IETF) A large international community of network designers, operators, vendors, and researchers, open to any interested individual concerned with the evolution of Internet architecture and the smooth operation of the Internet. The actual technical work of the IETF is done in its working groups, which are organized by topic into several areas (such as routing, transport, and security). Much of the work is handled via mailing lists, with meetings held three times per year.

Internet Message Access Protocol version 4 (IMAP4) One of two common Internet standard protocols for e-mail retrieval.

Internet Protocol (IP) The network layer protocol used by the Internet for routing packets across a network.

Internet Protocol Security (IPsec) A protocol used to secure IP packets during transmission across a network. IPsec offers authentication, integrity, and confidentiality services and uses Authentication Headers (AH) and Encapsulating Security Payload (ESP) to accomplish this functionality.

Internet Security Association and Key Management Protocol (ISAKMP) A protocol framework that defines the mechanics of implementing a key exchange protocol and negotiation of a security policy.

Internet service provider (ISP) A telecommunications firm that provides access to the Internet.

intrusion detection system (IDS) A system to identify suspicious, malicious, or undesirable activity that indicates a breach in computer security.

IPsec *See* Internet Protocol Security.

ISA *See* interconnection security agreement.

Kerberos A network authentication protocol designed by MIT for use in client/server environments.

PART VII

key   In cryptography, a sequence of characters or bits used by an algorithm to encrypt or decrypt a message.

key distribution center (KDC)   A component of the Kerberos system for authentication that manages the secure distribution of keys.

keyspace   The entire set of all possible keys for a specific encryption algorithm.

Layer 2 Tunneling Protocol (L2TP)   A Cisco switching protocol that operates at the data link layer.

LDAP   *See* Lightweight Directory Access Protocol.

least privilege   A security principle in which a user is provided with the minimum set of rights and privileges that he or she needs to perform required functions. The goal is to limit the potential damage that any user can cause.

Lightweight Directory Access Protocol (LDAP)   An application protocol used to access directory services across a TCP/IP network.

Lightweight Extensible Authentication Protocol (LEAP)   A version of EAP developed by Cisco prior to 802.11i to push 802.1X and WEP adoption.

load balancer   A network device that distributes computing across multiple computers.

local area network (LAN)   A grouping of computers in a network structure confined to a limited area and using specific protocols, such as Ethernet for OSI Layer 2 traffic addressing.

logic bomb   A form of malicious code or software that is triggered by a specific event or condition. *See also* time bomb.

loop protection   The requirement to prevent bridge loops at the Layer 2 level, which is typically resolved using the Spanning Tree algorithm on switch devices.

MAC   *See* mandatory access control, Media Access Control, or Message Authentication Code.

man-in-the-middle attack   Any attack that attempts to use a network node as the intermediary between two other nodes. Each of the endpoint nodes thinks it is talking directly to the other, but each is actually talking to the intermediary.

mandatory access control (MAC)   An access control mechanism in which the security mechanism controls access to all objects (files), and individual subjects (processes or users) cannot change that access.

master boot record (MBR)   A strip of data on a hard drive in Windows systems meant to result in specific initial functions or identification.

maximum transmission unit (MTU)   A measure of the largest payload that a particular protocol can carry in a single packet in a specific instance.

MD5   Message Digest 5, a hashing algorithm and a specific method of producing a message digest.

mean time between failure (MTBF)   The statistically determined period of time between failures of the system.

mean time to failure (MTTF)   The statistically determined time to the next failure.

mean time to repair (MTTR)   A common measure of how long it takes to repair a given failure. This is the average time, and may or may not include the time needed to obtain parts..

Media Access Control (MAC)   A protocol used in the data link layer for local network addressing.

memorandum of understanding (MOU)   A document executed between two parties that defines some form of agreement.

message authentication code (MAC)   A short piece of data used to authenticate a message. *See* hashed message authentication code.

message digest   The result of applying a hash function to data. Sometimes also called a hash value. *See* hash.

metropolitan area network (MAN)   A collection of networks interconnected in a metropolitan area and usually connected to the Internet.

Microsoft Challenge Handshake Authentication Protocol (MSCHAP)   A Microsoft-developed variant of the Challenge Handshake Authentication Protocol (CHAP).

mitigation   Action taken to reduce the likelihood of a threat occurring.

Monitoring as a Service (MaaS)   The use of a third party to provide security monitoring services.

MSCHAP   *See* Microsoft Challenge Handshake Authentication Protocol.

MTBF   *See* mean time between failure.

MTTF   *See* mean time to failure.

MTTR   *See* mean time to repair.

NAC   *See* Network Access Control.

NAP   *See* Network Access Protection.

PART VII

NAT *See* Network Address Translation.

National Institute of Standards and Technology (NIST) A U.S. government agency responsible for standards and technology.

NDA *See* non-disclosure agreement.

near field communication (NFC) A set of standards and protocols for establishing a communication link over very short distances. Used in mobile devices.

Network Access Control (NAC) An approach to endpoint security that involves monitoring and remediating endpoint security issues before allowing an object to connect to a network.

Network Access Protection (NAP) A Microsoft approach to Network Access Control.

Network Address Translation (NAT) A method of readdressing packets in a network at a gateway point to enable the use of local, nonroutable IP addresses over a public network such as the Internet.

network-based intrusion detection system (NIDS) A system for examining network traffic to identify suspicious, malicious, or undesirable behavior.

network-based intrusion prevention system (NIPS) A system that examines network traffic and automatically responds to computer intrusions.

Network Basic Input/Output System (NetBIOS) A system that provides communication services across a local area network.

network operating system (NOS) An operating system that includes additional functions and capabilities to assist in connecting computers and devices, such as printers, to a local area network.

Network Time Protocol (NTP) A protocol for the transmission of time synchronization packets over a network.

New Technology File System (NTFS) A proprietary file system developed by Microsoft, introduced in 1993, that supports a wide variety of file operations on servers, PCs, and media.

New Technology LANMAN (NTLM) A deprecated security suite from Microsoft that provides authentication, integrity, and confidentiality for users. Because it does not support current cryptographic methods, it is no longer recommended for use.

NFC *See* near field communication.

NIST *See* National Institute of Standards and Technology.

non-disclosure agreement (NDA)   A legal contract between parties detailing the restrictions and requirements borne by each party with respect to confidentiality issues pertaining to information to be shared.

non-repudiation   The ability to verify that an operation has been performed by a particular person or account. This is a system property that prevents the parties to a transaction from subsequently denying involvement in the transaction.

Oakley protocol   A key exchange protocol that defines how to acquire authenticated keying material based on the Diffie-Hellman key exchange algorithm.

object reuse   Assignment of a previously used medium to a subject. The security implication is that before it is provided to the subject, any data present from a previous user must be cleared.

one-time pad (OTP)   An unbreakable encryption scheme in which a series of nonrepeating, random bits are used once as a key to encrypt a message. Since each pad is used only once, no pattern can be established and traditional cryptanalysis techniques are not effective.

Online Certificate Status Protocol (OSCP)   A protocol used to request the revocation status of a digital certificate. This is an alternative to certificate revocation lists.

Open Vulnerability and Assessment Language (OVAL)   An XML-based standard for the communication of security information between tools and services.

operating system (OS)   The basic software that handles input, output, display, memory management, and all the other highly detailed tasks required to support the user environment and associated applications.

OVAL   *See* Open Vulnerability and Assessment Language.

PAC   *See* Proxy Auto Configuration.

Packet Capture (PCAP)   The methods and files associated with the capture of network traffic in the form of text files.

PAM   *See* Pluggable Authentication Modules.

pan-tilt-zoom (PTZ)   A term used to describe a video camera that supports remote directional and zoom control.

password   A string of characters used to prove an individual's identity to a system or object. Used in conjunction with a user ID, it is the most common method of authentication. The password should be kept secret by the individual who owns it.

Password Authentication Protocol (PAP)   A simple protocol used to authenticate a user to a network access server.

PART VII

Password-Based Key Derivation Function 2 (PBKDF2) A key derivation function that is part of the RSA Laboratories Public Key Cryptography Standards, published as IETF RFC 2898.

patch A replacement set of code designed to correct problems or vulnerabilities in existing software.

PBX *See* private branch exchange.

peer-to-peer (P2P) A network connection methodology involving direct connection from peer to peer.

penetration testing A security test in which an attempt is made to circumvent security controls in order to discover vulnerabilities and weaknesses. Also called a pen test.

permissions Authorized actions a subject can perform on an object. *See also* access controls.

personal electronic device (PED) A term used to describe an electronic device, owned by the user and brought into the enterprise, that uses enterprise data. This includes laptops, tablets, and mobile phones, to name a few.

Personal Identity Verification (PIV) Policies, procedures, hardware, and software used to securely identify federal workers.

personally identifiable information (PII) Information that can be used to identify a single person.

phreaking Used in the media to refer to the hacking of computer systems and networks associated with the phone company. *See also* cracking.

Plain Old Telephone Service (POTS) The term used to describe the old analog phone service and later the "land-line" digital phone service.

plaintext In cryptography, a piece of data that is not encrypted. It can also mean the data input into an encryption algorithm that would output ciphertext.

Pluggable Authentication Modules (PAM) A mechanism used in Linux systems to integrate low-level authentication methods into an API.

Point-to-Point Protocol (PPP) The Internet standard for transmission of IP packets over a serial line, as in a dial-up connection to an ISP.

Point-to-Point Protocol Extensible Authentication Protocol (PPP EAP) A PPP extension that provides support for additional authentication methods within PPP.

Point-to-Point Protocol Password Authentication Protocol (PPP PAP) A PPP extension that provides support for password authentication methods over PPP.

Point-to-Point Tunneling Protocol (PPTP)   The use of generic routing encapsulation over PPP to create a methodology used for virtual private networking.

Port Address Translation (PAT)   The manipulation of port information in an IP datagram at a point in the network to map ports in a fashion similar to Network Address Translation's change of network address.

pre-shared key (PSK)   A shared secret that has been previously shared between parties and is used to establish a secure channel.

Pretty Good Privacy (PGP)   A popular encryption program that has the ability to encrypt and digitally sign e-mail and files.

preventative intrusion detection   A system that detects hostile actions or network activity and prevents them from impacting information systems.

privacy   Protecting an individual's personal information from those not authorized to see it.

private branch exchange (PBX)   A telephone exchange that serves a specific business or entity.

privilege auditing   The process of checking the rights and privileges assigned to a specific account or group of accounts.

privilege management   The process of restricting a user's ability to interact with the computer system.

Protected Extensible Authentication Protocol (PEAP)   A protected version of EAP developed by Cisco, Microsoft, and RSA Security that functions by encapsulating the EAP frames in a TLS tunnel.

Proxy Auto Configuration (PAC)   A method of automating the connection of web browsers to appropriate proxy services to retrieve a specific URL.

PSK   *See* pre-shared key.

PTZ   *See* pan-tilt-zoom.

public key cryptography   *See* asymmetric encryption.

public key infrastructure (PKI)   Infrastructure for binding a public key to a known user through a trusted intermediary, typically a certificate authority.

qualitative risk assessment   The process of subjectively determining the impact of an event that affects a project, program, or business. It involves the use of expert judgment, experience, or group consensus to complete the assessment.

quantitative risk assessment   The process of objectively determining the impact of an event that affects a project, program, or business. It usually involves the use of metrics and models to complete the assessment.

RADIUS   Remote Authentication Dial-In User Service, a standard protocol for providing authentication services. It is commonly used in dial-up, wireless, and PPP environments.

RAID   *See* Redundant Array of Inexpensive Disks.

rapid application development (RAD)   A software development methodology that favors the use of rapid prototypes and changes as opposed to extensive advanced planning.

RAS   *See* Remote Access Service/Server.

RBAC   *See* rule-based access control or role-based access control.

RC4   A stream cipher used in TLS and WEP.

Real-time Transport Protocol (RTP)   A protocol for a standardized packet format used to carry audio and video traffic over IP networks.

Recovery Agent (RA)   In Microsoft Windows environments, the entity authorized by the system to use a public key recovery certificate to decrypt other users' files using a special private key function associated with the encrypting file system (EFS).

recovery point objective (RPO)   The amount of data that a business is willing to place at risk. It is determined by the amount of time a business has to restore a process before an unacceptable amount of data loss results from a disruption.

recovery time objective (RTO)   The amount of time a business has to restore a process before unacceptable outcomes result from a disruption.

Redundant Array of Inexpensive Disks (RAID)   The use of an array of disks arranged in a single unit of storage for increasing storage capacity, redundancy, and performance characteristics.

Remote Access Service/Server (RAS)   A combination of hardware and software used to enable remote access to a network.

repudiation   The act of denying that a message was either sent or received.

residual risk   Risks remaining after an iteration of risk management.

RIPEMD   A hash function developed in Belgium. The acronym expands to RACE Integrity Primitives Evaluation Message Digest, but this name is rarely used. The current version is RIPEMD-160.

risk   The possibility of suffering a loss.

risk assessment or risk analysis   The process of analyzing an environment to identify the threats, vulnerabilities, and mitigating actions to determine (either quantitatively or qualitatively) the impact of an event affecting a project, program, or business.

risk management   Overall decision-making process of identifying threats and vulnerabilities and their potential impacts, determining the costs to mitigate such events, and deciding what cost-effective actions can be taken to control these risks.

Rivest, Shamir, Adleman (RSA)   The names of the three men who developed a public key cryptographic system and the company they founded to commercialize the system.

role-based access control (RBAC)   An access control mechanism in which, instead of the users being assigned specific access permissions for the objects associated with the computer system or network, a set of roles that the user may perform is assigned to each user.

RTP   *See* Real-time Transport Protocol.

rule-based access control (RBAC)   An access control mechanism based on rules.

safeguard   *See* security controls.

SAN   *See* storage area network.

SCADA   *See* supervisory control and data acquisition.

SCEP   *See* Simple Certificate Enrollment Protocol.

Secure Copy Protocol (SCP)   A network protocol that supports secure file transfers.

Secure FTP   A method of secure file transfer that involves the tunneling of FTP through an SSH connection. This is different than SFTP, which is the Secure Shell File Transfer Protocol.

Secure Hash Algorithm (SHA)   A hash algorithm used to hash block data. The first version is SHA1, with subsequent versions detailing hash digest length: SHA256, SHA384, and SHA512.

Secure Hypertext Transfer Protocol (SHTTP)   An alternative to HTTPS, in which only the transmitted pages and POST fields are encrypted. Rendered moot, by and large, by widespread adoption of HTTPS.

Secure/Multipurpose Internet Mail Extensions (S/MIME)   An encrypted implementation of the MIME (Multipurpose Internet Mail Extensions) protocol specification.

Secure Shell (SSH)   A set of protocols for establishing a secure remote connection to a computer. This protocol requires a client on each end of the connection and can use a variety of encryption protocols.

Secure Shell File Transfer Protocol (SFTP)   A secure file transfer subsystem associated with Secure Shell protocol (SSH).

PART VII

Secure Sockets Layer (SSL) An encrypting layer between the session and transport layer of the OSI model designed to encrypt above the transport layer, enabling secure sessions between hosts.

Security Assertion Markup Language (SAML) An XML-based standard for exchanging authentication and authorization data.

security association (SA) An instance of security policy and keying material applied to a specific data flow. Both IKE and IPsec use SAs, although these SAs are independent of one another. IPsec SAs are unidirectional and are unique in each security protocol, whereas IKE SAs are bidirectional. A set of SAs is needed for a protected data pipe, one per direction per protocol. SAs are uniquely identified by destination (IPsec endpoint) address, security protocol (AH or ESP), and security parameter index (SPI).

security baseline The end result of the process of establishing an information system's security state. It is a known good configuration resistant to attacks and information theft.

security content automation protocol (SCAP) A method of using specific protocols and data exchanges to automate the determination of vulnerability management, measurement, and policy compliance across a system or set of systems.

security controls A group of technical, management, or operational policies and procedures designed to implement specific security functionality. Access controls are an example of a security control.

security information event management (SIEM) The name used for a broad range of technological solutions to the collection and analysis of security-related information across the enterprise.

segregation or separation of duties A basic control that prevents or detects errors and irregularities by assigning responsibilities to different individuals so that no single individual can commit fraudulent or malicious actions.

service level agreement (SLA) An agreement between parties concerning the expected or contracted up-time associated with a system.

service set identifier (SSID) Identifies a specific 802.11 wireless network. It transmits information about the access point to which the wireless client is connecting.

shielded twisted pair (STP) A physical network connection consisting of two wires twisted and covered with a shield to prevent interference.

Short Message Service (SMS) A form of text messaging over phone and mobile phone circuits that allows up to 160-character messages to be carried over signaling channels.

signature database A collection of activity patterns that have already been identified and categorized and that typically indicate suspicious or malicious activity.

Simple Certificate Enrollment Protocol (SCEP)   A protocol used in PKI for enrollment and other services.

Simple Mail Transfer Protocol (SMTP)   The standard Internet protocol used to transfer e-mail between hosts.

Simple Network Management Protocol (SNMP)   A standard protocol used to remotely manage network devices across a network.

Simple Object Access Protocol (SOAP)   An XML-based specification for exchanging information associated with web services.

single loss expectancy (SLE)   Monetary loss or impact of each occurrence of a threat. SLE = asset value × exposure factor.

single sign-on (SSO)   An authentication process by which the user can enter a single user ID and password and then move from application to application or resource to resource without having to supply further authentication information.

slack space   Unused space on a disk drive created when a file is smaller than the allocated unit of storage (such as a sector).

SMS   *See* Short Message Service.

sniffer   A software or hardware device used to observe network traffic as it passes through a network on a shared broadcast media.

social engineering   The art of deceiving another person so that he or she reveals confidential information. This is often accomplished by posing as an individual who should be entitled to have access to the information.

Software as a Service (SaaS)   The provisioning of software as a service, commonly known as on-demand software.

software development lifecycle methodology (SDLM)   The processes and procedures employed to develop software. Sometimes also called secure development lifecycle model when security is part of the development process.

solid-state drive (SSD)   A mass storage device, such as a hard drive, that is composed of electronic memory as opposed to a physical device of spinning platters.

SONET   *See* Synchronous Optical Network Technologies.

spam   E-mail that is not requested by the recipient and is typically of a commercial nature. Also known as unsolicited commercial e-mail (UCE).

spam filter   A security appliance designed to remove spam at the network layer before it enters e-mail servers.

spim   Spam sent over an instant messaging channel.

spoofing   Making data appear to have originated from another source so as to hide the true origin from the recipient.

SSD   *See* solid-state drive.

storage area network (SAN)   A dedicated network that provides access to data storage.

STP   *See* shielded twisted pair.

Structured Exception Handler (SEH)   The process used to handle exceptions in the Windows OS core functions.

Structured Query Language (SQL)   A language used in relational database queries.

Subscriber Identity Module (SIM)   An integrated circuit or hardware element that securely stores the International Mobile Subscriber Identity (IMSI) and the related key used to identify and authenticate subscribers on mobile telephones.

supervisory control and data acquisition (SCADA)   A generic term used to describe the industrial control system networks used to interconnect infrastructure elements (such as manufacturing plants, oil and gas pipelines, power generation and distribution systems, and so on) and computer systems.

symmetric encryption   Encryption that needs all parties to have a copy of the key, sometimes called a shared secret. The single key is used for both encryption and decryption.

Synchronous Optical Network Technologies (SONET)   A set of standards used for data transfers over optical networks.

tangible asset   An asset for which a monetary equivalent can be determined. Examples are inventory, buildings, cash, hardware, software, and so on.

Telnet   A network protocol used to provide cleartext bidirectional communication over TCP.

Temporal Key Integrity Protocol (TKIP)   A security protocol used in 802.11 wireless networks.

Terminal Access Controller Access Control System+ (TACACS+)   A remote authentication system that uses the TACACS+ protocol, defined in RFC 1492, and TCP port 49.

threat   Any circumstance or event with the potential to cause harm to an asset.

ticket-granting ticket (TGT)   A part of the Kerberos authentication system that is used to prove identity when requesting service tickets.

Time-based One-Time Password (TOTP)   A password that is used once and is only valid during a specific time period.

time bomb   A form of logic bomb in which the triggering event is a date or specific time. *See also* logic bomb.

TKIP   *See* Temporal Key Integrity Protocol.

token   A hardware device that can be used in a challenge-response authentication process.

Transaction Signature (TSIG)   A protocol used as a means of authenticating dynamic DNS records during DNS updates.

Transmission Control Protocol/Internet Protocol (TCP/IP)   A connection-oriented protocol for communication over IP networks.

Transport Layer Security (TLS)   A newer form of SSL being proposed as an Internet standard.

trapdoor   *See* backdoor.

Trivial File Transfer Protocol (TFTP)   A simplified version of FTP used for low-overhead file transfers using UDP port 69.

Trojan horse   A form of malicious code that appears to provide one service (and may indeed provide that service) but that also hides another purpose. This hidden purpose often has a malicious intent. This code may also be simply referred to as a *Trojan*.

Trusted Platform Module (TPM)   A hardware chip to enable trusted computing platform operations.

Unified Extensible Firmware Interface (UEFI)   A specification that defines the interface between an OS and the hardware firmware. This is a replacement to BIOS.

unified threat management (UTM)   The aggregation of multiple network security products into a single appliance for efficiency purposes.

Uniform Resource Identifier (URI)   A set of characters used to identify the name of a resource in a computer system. A URL is a form of URI.

uninterruptible power supply (UPS)   A source of power (generally a battery) designed to provide uninterrupted power to a computer system in the event of a temporary loss of power.

Universal Resource Locator (URL)   A specific character string used to point to a specific item across the Internet.

Universal Serial Bus (USB)   An industry-standard protocol for communication over a cable to peripherals via a standard set of connectors.

unshielded twisted pair (UTP)   A physical connection consisting of a pair of twisted wires forming a circuit.

usage auditing   The process of recording who did what and when on an information system.

user acceptance testing (UAT) The application of acceptance-testing criteria to determine fitness for use according to end-user requirements.

User Datagram Protocol (UDP) A protocol in the TCP/IP protocol suite for the transport layer that does not sequence packets—it is "fire and forget" in nature.

user ID A unique alphanumeric identifier that identifies individuals who are logging in or accessing a system.

vampire tap A tap that connects to a network line without cutting the connection.

video teleconferencing (VTC) A business process of using video signals to carry audio and visual signals between separate locations, thus allowing participants to meet via a virtual meeting instead of traveling to a physical location. Modern videoconferencing equipment can provide very realistic connectivity when lighting and backgrounds are controlled.

virtual local area network (VLAN) A broadcast domain inside a switched system.

virtual private network (VPN) An encrypted network connection across another network, offering a private communication channel across a public medium.

virtualization desktop infrastructure (VDI) The use of servers to host virtual desktops by moving the processing to the server and using the desktop machine as merely a display terminal. VDI offers operating efficiencies as well as cost and security benefits.

virus A form of malicious code or software that attaches itself to other pieces of code in order to replicate. Viruses may contain a payload, which is a portion of the code that is designed to execute when a certain condition is met (such as on a certain date). This payload is often malicious in nature.

Voice over IP (VoIP) The packetized transmission of voice signals (telephony) over Internet Protocol.

vulnerability A weakness in an asset that can be exploited by a threat to cause harm.

wireless access point (WAP) A network access device that facilitates the connection of wireless devices to a network.

war dialing An attacker's attempt to gain unauthorized access to a computer system or network by discovering unprotected connections to the system through the telephone system and modems.

war driving The attempt by an attacker to discover unprotected wireless networks by wandering (or driving) around with a wireless device, looking for available wireless access points.

web application firewall (WAF)   A firewall that operates at the application level, specifically designed to protect web applications by examining requests at the application stack level.

WEP   *See* Wired Equivalent Privacy.

wide area network (WAN)   A network that spans a large geographic region.

Wi-Fi Protected Access/Wi-Fi Protected Access 2 (WPA/WPA2)   A protocol to secure wireless communications using a subset of the 802.11i standard.

Wi-Fi Protected Setup (WPS)   A network security standard that allows easy setup of a wireless home network.

Wired Equivalent Privacy (WEP)   The encryption scheme used to attempt to provide confidentiality and data integrity on 802.11 networks.

Wireless Application Protocol (WAP)   A protocol for transmitting data to small handheld devices such as cellular phones.

wireless intrusion detection system (WIDS)   An intrusion detection system established to cover a wireless network.

wireless intrusion prevention system (WIPS)   An intrusion prevention system established to cover a wireless network.

Wireless Transport Layer Security (WTLS)   The encryption protocol used on WAP networks.

worm   An independent piece of malicious code or software that self-replicates. Unlike a virus, it does not need to be attached to another piece of code. A worm replicates by breaking into another system and making a copy of itself on this new system. A worm can contain a destructive payload but does not have to.

X.509   The standard format for digital certificates.

XML   *See* Extensible Markup Language.

XOR   Bitwise exclusive OR, an operation commonly used in cryptography.

XSRF   *See* cross-site request forgery.

XSS   *See* cross-site scripting.

INDEX

Symbols and Numbers

"/" sign, CIDR, 38
128-bit address notation, IPv6, 54–55
32-bit address notation, IPv4, 54
802.11. *See* wireless networking
802.1x
    mitigation techniques, 277–278
    secure network administration of, 28
    WPA2 using, 66

A

acceptable use. *See* AUP (acceptable use policy)
access control
    auditing user access, 269
    authentication factors, 407–411
    authentication methods, 403–407
    authentication services. *See* authentication
        services
    authorization. *See* authorization
    discretionary, 400
    job rotation for, 402
    locks for, 196
    logical network segmentation and, 379
    mandatory, 401
    matrix, 400
    mobile device, 331
    overview of, 399–402
    in physical security plan. *See* physical security
    PII Safe Harbor and, 156
    preventing shoulder surfing, 160–161
    preventing tailgating, 161, 237
    protecting confidentiality, 193
    review answers, 415–416
    review questions, 412–415
    role-based, 401–402
    rule-based, 402
    security policies, 84
    terminated employees and, 335
    time of day restrictions for, 403
    users habits enforcing, 158
    vulnerabilities, 411–412

access control lists. *See* ACLs (access control lists)
access lists
    overview of, 180
    RADIUS authorization, 391
    TACACS+ authorization, 392
access logs
    auditing, 268
    maintained by security guards, 181
access points. *See* APs (access points)
account management. *See* user account
    management
accounting function
    RADIUS, 391
    TACACS+, 393–394
ACLs (access control lists)
    attack surface of, 302–303
    confidentiality protected by, 193–194
    configuring, 7
    defined, 400
    host-based security using, 368
    network administration of, 27–28
    used by routers, 7
active HIDSs, 360
active tools, 297–298
ActiveX content, 261
Acunetix WVS (Web Vulnerability Scanner),
    293–294
add-ons, malicious, 261
Address Resolution Protocol (ARP) poisoning, 225
adherence to corporate duties, BYOD security, 336
administration. *See* network administration
administrator account, renaming, 270
Advanced Encryption Standard (AES), WPA2,
    66–67
Advanced Persistent Threat (APT), 162
advertisements
    adware, 205–206
    pop-up blockers against, 348
adware
    as malware, 205–206
    pop-ups vs., 349
agents, DDoS attacks, 214

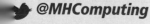